The
L/L Research
Channeling Archives

Transcripts of
the Meditation Sessions

Volume 17
October 3, 2004 to April 1, 2006

Don
Elkins

Jim
McCarty

Carla L.
Rueckert

ISBN: 978-0-945007-91-3

Published by L/L Research
Box 5195
Louisville, Kentucky 40255-0195

E-mail: contact@llresearch.org
www.llresearch.org

About the cover photo: *This photograph of Jim McCarty and Carla L. Rueckert was taken during an L/L Research channeling session on August 4, 2009, in the living room of their Louisville, Kentucky home. Jim always holds hands with Carla when she channels, following the Ra group's advice on how she can avoid any possibility of astral travel.*

DEDICATION

These archive volumes are dedicated to Hal and Jo Price, who faithfully and lovingly hosted this group's weekly meditation meetings from 1962 to 1975,

to Walt Rogers, whose work with the research group Man, Consciousness and Understanding of Detroit offered the information needed to begin this ongoing channeling experiment,

and to the Confederation of Angels and Planets in the Service of the Infinite Creator, for sharing their love and wisdom with us so generously through the years.

Table of Contents

INTRODUCTION

Welcome to this volume of the *L/L Research Channeling Archives*. This series of publications represents the collection of channeling sessions recorded by L/L Research during the period from the early seventies to the present day. The sessions are also available on the L/L Research website, www.llresearch.org.

Starting in the mid-1950s, Don Elkins, a professor of physics and engineering at Speed Scientific School, had begun researching the paranormal in general and UFOs in particular. Elkins was a pilot as well as a professor and he flew his small plane to meet with many of the UFO contactees of the period.

Hal Price had been a part of a UFO-contactee channeling circle in Detroit called "The Detroit Group." When Price was transferred from Detroit's Ford plant to its Louisville truck plant, mutual friends discovered that Price also was a UFO researcher and put the two men together. Hal introduced Elkins to material called *The Brown Notebook* which contained instructions on how to create a group and receive UFO contactee information. In January of 1962 they decided to put the instructions to use and began holding silent meditation meetings on Sunday nights just across the Ohio River in the southern Indiana home of Hal and his wife, Jo. This was the beginning of what was called the "Louisville Group."

I was an original member of that group, along with a dozen of Elkins' physics students. However, I did not learn to channel until 1974. Before that date, almost none of our weekly channeling sessions were recorded or transcribed. After I began improving as a channel, Elkins decided for the first time to record all the sessions and transcribe them.

During the first eighteen months or so of my studying channeling and producing material, we tended to reuse the tapes as soon as the transcriptions were finished. Since those were typewriter days, we had no record of the work that could be reopened and used again, as we do now with computers. And I used up the original and the carbon copy of my transcriptions putting together a manuscript, *Voices of the Gods*, which has not yet been published. It remains as almost the only record of Don Elkins' and my channeling of that period.

We learned from this experience to retain the original tapes of all of our sessions, and during the remainder of the seventies and through the eighties, our "Louisville Group" was prolific. The "Louisville Group" became "L/L Research" after Elkins and I published a book in 1976, *Secrets of the UFO*, using that publishing name. At first we met almost every night. In later years, we met gradually less often, and the number of sessions recorded by our group in a year accordingly went down. Eventually, the group began taking three months off from channeling during the summer. And after 2000, we began having channeling meditations only twice a month. The volume of sessions dropped to its present output of eighteen or so each year.

These sessions feature channeling from sources which call themselves members of the Confederation of Planets in the Service of the Infinite Creator. At first we enjoyed hearing from many different voices: Hatonn, Laitos, Oxal, L/Leema and Yadda being just a few of them. As I improved my tuning techniques, and became the sole senior channel in L/L Research, the number of contacts dwindled. When I began asking for "the highest and best contact which I can receive of Jesus the Christ's vibration of unconditional love in a conscious and stable manner," the entity offering its thoughts through our group was almost always Q'uo. This remains true as our group continues to channel on an ongoing basis.

The channelings are always about love and unity, enunciating "The Law of One" in one aspect or another. Seekers who are working with spiritual principles often find the material a good resource. We hope that you will as well. As time has gone on the questions have shifted somewhat, but in general the content of the channeling is metaphysical and focused on helping seekers find the love in the moment and the Creator in the love.

At first, I transcribed our channeling sessions. I got busier, as our little group became more widely known, and got hopelessly behind on transcribing. Two early transcribers who took that job off my hands were Kim

Howard and Judy Dunn, both of whom masterfully transcribed literally hundreds of sessions through the eighties and early nineties.

Then Ian Jaffray volunteered to create a web site for these transcriptions, and single-handedly unified the many different formats that the transcripts were in at that time and made them available online. This additional exposure prompted more volunteers to join the ranks of our transcribers, and now there are a dozen or so who help with this. Our thanks go out to all of these kind volunteers, early and late, who have made it possible for our webguy to make these archives available.

Around the turn of the millennium, I decided to commit to editing each session after it had been transcribed. So the later transcripts have fewer errata than the earlier ones, which are quite imperfect in places. One day, perhaps, those earlier sessions will be revisited and corrections will be made to the transcripts. It would be a large task, since there are well over 1500 channeling sessions as of this date, and counting. We apologize for the imperfections in those transcripts, and trust that you can ascertain the sense of them regardless of a mistake here and there.

Blessings, dear reader! Enjoy these "humble thoughts" from the Confederation of Planets. May they prove good companions to your spiritual seeking. ♣

For all of us at L/L Research,

Carla L. Rueckert

Louisville, Kentucky

July 16, 2009

YEAR 2004
OCTOBER 3, 2004 TO DECEMBER 12, 2004

L/L RESEARCH

L/L Research is a subsidiary of
Rock Creek Research &
Development Laboratories, Inc.

P.O. Box 5195
Louisville, KY 40255-0195

www.llresearch.org

Rock Creek is a non-profit
corporation dedicated to
discovering and sharing
information which may aid in
the spiritual evolution of
humankind.

SUNDAY MEDITATION
OCTOBER 3, 2004

Group question: The question this week has to do with the roots of the concept of what we call "terrorism," the attempts by a small group of people to gain that which they feel is their due and to gain it by violent means. We were referred back to the Biblical story of Sarah and Abraham where Abraham was unable to bear a child because Sarah was barren. He went in to Sarah's maid-servant, Hagar, who was Egyptian, and she bore him a son, Ishmael. Fourteen years later, when Abraham was 100, Sarah was blessed by the Lord God at that time to have a child who was named Isaac. These two were the children of Abraham but only Isaac achieved the inheritance. Ishmael was left to wander into the desert and to form the tribes of what we now call the Arabs. And it is the battle between the Arabs and the Jews that seems to be so violently apparent in our world today. So we were wondering if Q'uo could give us a philosophical background of this type of energy and how it can be resolved upon our planet Earth today.

(Carla channeling)

We are those of the principle known to you as Q'uo, and we greet you in the love and in the light of the one infinite Creator, in Whose service we come to you this day. It is a great privilege and pleasure to be with you and to share the beauty of your meditation and we offer you our gratitude for creating this moment and this experience of a circle of seeking that is expressing light and love as it sits together in query and in devotion.

It is our blessing to be called to this group for the purpose of sharing our thoughts on terrorism and we are happy to do so with the request—which is especially pointed as we talk concerning a somewhat hot issue, as this instrument would say—that you afford us the opportunity to offer you thoughts without our forcing you to believe them or take them in any way. Please allow us to share our thoughts with you while remaining in complete control over whether or not you wish to continue to think about these thoughts or in any way make them part of your process. For your integrity in doing so allows us to be assured of the freedom of your will. We would not in any way wish to be a stumbling block before your own process. And if you will allow us this freedom, it will allow us the freedom to speak freely. And this particular concern of ours is clearly about freedom. We thank you for that.

The query this day has to do with the philosophy behind terrorism. And as that query stands, we would find it very difficult to create a good answer, for we believe that philosophy as a branch of the circle of knowledge is not something that lends itself to the creation of a structure in which something like terrorism would be acceptable. When ethics is discussed as a philosophical system, it concerns not ways to take away freedom from entities but ways to safeguard their freedom. The Nietzschean superman[1]

---

[1] The theory that Nietzsche offered was that there was "a mode of psychologically healthier being beyond the common human condition. Nietzsche refers to this higher mode of being as

is perhaps the closest that respectable, shall we say, philosophy comes to offering a structure which justifies terrorism and its justification can be roughly shortened to the phrase that "might makes right." We would not wish to defend this philosophy in a group of ethical panelists; we would find it heavy going, indeed.

The aura of philosophy, therefore, cannot be said to lie over, or lend respectability to, terrorism and its sister acts, war and violence. The shorthand version of the most appropriate philosophical structure for terrorism is, "the squeaky wheel gets the grease." And this is, rather than proper philosophy, simply an explanation of why entities—whether they be individual or of a group nature—resort to and use the techniques of terror.

The Creator is not an organic entity, as far as we know. It does not have members, a mind, emotions or any of the other attributes of third-density humankind. Nor does it have the attributes of fourth-density humankind, or fifth-density, or sixth-density. The Creator, as we understand the one infinite Creator, is beyond all attempts to describe, limit or otherwise distinguish the Creator from some other entity. The Creator is in fact all that there is, seen and unseen, known and unknown, possible and impossible. The Creator is all states of mind, all ways of thinking, and is not exhausted by any such lists of attributes or descriptions. The attempt to get one's mind around the concept of the creative principle is always, in the end, an inutile attempt. It will not be useful.

On the other hand, attempting to delineate those characteristics of the Creator which entities within a certain density and of a certain culture can understand is very helpful. So we would not ask you to stop attempting to understand the Creator, we ask you only to realize that that which entities such as yourself have written concerning the Creator are words. They are not truths, they are words written down by entities attempting to understand that which cannot be understood.

'superhuman' (übermenschlich), and associates the doctrine of eternal recurrence—a doctrine for only the healthiest who can love life in its entirety—with this spiritual standpoint, in relation to which all-too-often downhearted, all-too-commonly-human attitudes stand as a mere bridge to be crossed and overcome." (From http://plato.stanford.edu/entries/nietzsche/.)

The query that you asked brought in the concept of a certain creative entity by the name of Yahweh, or Jehovah, whose orders, presumably, brought about the warlike actions of the one known as Joshua and all of those who did battle in order to achieve territory in the story which unfolds in the books of Moses within your Old Testament of the Holy Bible, so-called, within your literature. There have been unending numbers of attempts to understand the mind of this Old Testament figure, Yahweh, and this is why we began with the assertion that there is no figure known to literature which captures the essence of the creative principle. Certainly the one known as Yahweh falls far short of expressing what we understand to be some of the more obvious characteristics of the creative principle, those being its universality and its unity. How could a creative principle set one entity over another when, to the Creator, all things are one, all beings are children of the same parent, brothers and sister of one deity, one Creator?

However, the one known as Yahweh was a powerful force in acting through entities such as Moses, Joshua, and Abraham.

In the history of your people—not simply the religious history of your people but the political, economic and social history of your people—the story concerning Isaac and Ishmael is a story steeped in birth rights. And this is an interesting characteristic of the system used by the one known as Yahweh. We may describe Yahweh as an Earth guardian which entered into a plan to be of service to others without thinking through the ramifications of such a plan. When it chose to do work to create a new and better version of the Egyptian stock that was the genetic base of that region at that time, it chose one of two types of genetic beings that differed somewhat in their genetic heritage because of there being other genetic applications by other extraterrestrial entities in their past. They chose the entities that had the seemingly more appropriate basic characteristics of intelligence, culture and so forth. They separated out one group from another in a way which the creative principle would never have done, and created, therefore, a sub-race which these guardian entities considered new and better and therefore worthy of having the elbow room in which to bring forth the improvements in mind, body and spirit that those known as Yahweh felt were possible for such an assisted group.

Why it did not occur to these guardian entities that this would involve war-like actions such as the slaughter of many innocents, we cannot say. However it was so that your history and the psychic energies of these groups of peoples were altered forever by this interference. It created what is patently an unfair situation. And certainly, the sons and daughters of Isaac and Ishmael grieve as one people for this interference and for the many ramifications that it had.

When any situation enters the stream of history it also enters the stream of mythology. And through the passage of time and events, the history of the Israelites and the Ishmaelites has become very fuzzy and much, if not all, of the story as it happened in history has been lost. And what has remained are stories that catch the emotion, the energy, and the main points of the history, so that while you may attempt to trace the children of Ishmael and the tribes of Ishmael and so forth, such attempts will always be trammeled by the inevitable tendency of those who come after and who are in power to look at a situation which has gone before in a way that places events in the best possible light for those who have the laurels of winning upon their heads and are thus able to tell the story with the loudest voice. This telling of the story with the loudest voice is something that occurs at all times, in all phases of history and certainly within your cultures of this day. Yet, in looking at the history of warfare and terrorism, it may be seen that, generally, the issues have to do with groups of people who feel that it is their birthright to have certain perquisites[2] and rights. That feeling of entitlement is at the heart of violence, war and terrorism.

In terms of the creative principle, all lands are one, all people are one. The design of your particular third-density world was a design in which each of your genetic races was expected to express themselves dominantly for a certain period of time. It was never intended that one race dominate your planet for an extended period of time such as your white race has in many cases done. The energies of each race had a certain way of opening the heart and the quite variant ways of looking at the creative principle were expected to float and flow from one dominant culture to the next, to the next, in a rhythmic and natural manner. It was hoped at this point in your

development as a global group that there would be at this time among all of your cultures a tendency towards the feminine principle as the creative principle or the deity. For, in terms of the birthing of the fourth density of your planet, it is this creative, feminine energy that holds the light of service to others in the appropriate manner for assisting the one this instrument calls Gaia and many call the Earth or Terra in her very feminine and very profound labor. This has not occurred.

The energy placed by the group known as Yahweh into the entities which had come upon your sphere from the planet known as Mars created a stopping point, as if someone had put up a roadblock upon the energetic levels of the planet which held in place that energy which claims to be monotheistic, claiming to be one God; and yet which, by its very definition, can not be monotheistic in that it states it is a God of one nation. If there is a God of one nation and not of another, then, quite obviously, it is part of a multi-theistic system, or a system of more than one God.

And indeed, at the time of the [one] known as Moses, the world was poised upon the point of a pin, as it were, in attempting to move into true monotheism. Think of it, if you will, for we often have, as one of the members of our principle is the group of Ra which attempted to speak to the princes of Egypt in those times concerning the true creative principle which is One. The one known as Moses was well aware of this true monotheism and indeed, in his heart, was, shall we say, devoted to and trained up within this system. However, this entity and all of the entities involved in these times was a human being who was steeped in the culture of many gods and found it impossible to hold to a pure belief in one God in the attempt to be a leader of his people. Leader after leader among your peoples has faced this challenge. How does an entity who leads one group, and is responsible to and for one group, act in such a way that the group will feel that its rights are being preserved and those things to which it is entitled will be protected while simultaneously defending and maintaining the rights and the entitlements of all other groups? It is a tremendously subtle thing to attempt to unravel a specific situation in such a way that both of these values are maintained.

We would bring to your attention the one known as Mahatma Gandhi. We have spoken before of this

---

[2] perquisits: something claimed as an exclusive right.

entity. This was an entity who was very clever in ways which are, for the most part, reserved for those of service to self in their philosophy. Yet, this entity's vision was powerful in its unity and it refused to allow any thinking which closed the heart against any, even those which this entity perceived, with some justification, as suborning and limiting the rights of his own people. In all of Gandhi's dealings with the government of those who were British and who held the reins of rulership of his nation at that time, this entity refrained from, at any time, closing the heart against or lifting a weapon towards those entities which would be considered the enemy, that is the British. Using homely and easily understood physical metaphors, such as spinning the thread, this entity was able to put before his group the image of self-worth and independence. How can an entity see self-worth and independence in making thread out of cotton? Yet, the Indian people received the lesson that the one known as Gandhi offered.

In many, many ways, this entity made life very difficult for those of the British rulership of his nation. Yet, never was this entity less than cordial and civil. He could not have succeeded nor could his ideas have taken hold were he not coming from a place of genuine love. If he had hated his enemy, no matter had he done exactly the same things in his political posturing, he would not have succeeded. His integrity and purity of motive were such that those of India and those of Britain alike were able to see it, feel it, and in the end, respect it and respond to it. His working to aid his people, therefore, never took on the shades of violence or terrorism but retained the goodly hue of faith, love and hope.

When you see small groups or large unable to resist the techniques of terrorism, we would ask you to see groups which have become entangled with issues of entitlement and justice. In each situation, there is a path to peace. This path begins in the heart. It calls for men who are both clever and compassionate. It calls for those who are able to understand the techniques for service to self but whose purity of focus and whose open hearts are such as to avail them of the techniques of unconditional love. There is no justification for violence and yet it lies within the human heart to defend the group against those who are not a part of the group. This is part of the instinct with which each human being comes into incarnation. It is part of the heritage of the physical vehicle of the great ape of which you are a recent descendant. If you examine the customs of these great apes, as the one known as Desmond Morris has done, it becomes very clear, very quickly, that violence is something with which each human being must deal, not as a faraway thing, but as an intimate friend, as a part of the household of personality. One of the boarders of each of your bodies is violence.

The one known as G was saying that he did not believe he would be able to pull the trigger against another human being. This is a laudable and a noble sentiment. Yet is spoken by one who has never been in the position of defending those he loves from someone who would surely do them harm. The instinct of one who is being threatened is indeed to pull the trigger. When dealing with groups, that group instinct remains as lethal as that. No matter how many layers of civility and diplomacy are offered, beneath each situation and its endless rationales on both sides there lies a situation in which two groups—which are in truth, one—have accepted a model in which one group is over against another. Once this basic and existent situation is accepted, there can always be a rationale which leads to violence, whether it is violence offered by those who have the approval of other nations as belonging to a rightful group of nations or whether it does not have such approval and is therefore, without any choice for itself, considered an outlaw. When an outlaw attempts to achieve entitlement, it is considered terrorism. That is the only difference between terrorism and war. It is an artificial distinction based upon the underlying artificial distinction of groups defining themselves as separate.

Perhaps you have noticed in working with other entities that there is a tendency for entities to divide endlessly into groups and sub-groups and sub-sub-groups. There is a delight in finding a way in which one group has done the right thing and another group has been less successful. The feeling of being better than, stronger than, or more justified than another group is a feeling which is endlessly sought because it feels good. It feels good to belong. It feels good to be part of a virtuous, morally upright group. And so the posturing is endless, the facts and stories are told again and again and, in each telling, there is the twist put upon the tale to show the rightness of those who have been ascendant and the poverty of rightness in those who have been the losers. In our opinion, each story is distorted, each entitlement is questionable, and each rightful group is, at base, artificial and unhelpful. Yet, the whole object of third density is to face the individual entity, and the resultant groups that form from such individuals, with situation after situation which is enough of a puzzle to be worth the solving. And that solving gives each entity the opportunity to grow in terms of spiritual, mental, emotional and physical evolution.

So what we would leave you with in thinking about terrorism is how you, as an individual, can cease using the techniques of terror and war in how you work with yourself, in how you work with the most intimate of those about you: your spouses, your children, your parents, and your family; in how you work with those very intimate groups of employment, mutually shared goals of all kinds, in groups that come together to serve. How can you keep your heart open and stay devoted to the one infinite Creator? There will be many arguments that pull you endlessly off your center of gravity. And you will be off balance and out of your comfort zone again and again, for these are deeply profound difficulties your world faces at this time. Those who, as the one known as J mentioned, blew up Mars, are attempting now to blow up your Earth. They almost succeeded as a group in that land you know of as Atlantis. And energies mass once again for the attempt to achieve an Armageddon. It is an energy that is deeply entrenched in the genetic memory of this racial group which we would call the white race. Yet, because of the way that history has become stuck upon this monotheistic Yahweh and its resultant energies …

(Side one of tape ends.)

(Carla channeling)

It is a planetary experience once again.

What shall you do to grow your world into that loving, unified, peaceful world which each of you can envision? May we say that it begins with you, this day and this moment, not in a large way but in the most small way. What are your thoughts as you approach your next decision? Is there a desire to defend? Is there a desire to protect? Examine these desires. Is there the desire to embrace and to bring into One? Examine that desire. Examine your thoughts carefully to sift out those energies which have in them a lack of that focus and resonance which you can associate with the open heart.

We ask you as well to be clever, to work with the limitations and distortions of the culture about you rather than attempting to leave them behind. Attempt to work within them so that the very things that are designed to be limiting become those things that are freeing. This is the work of an immense amount of subtlety and cleverness and yet each of you has a good mind, a good power of reasoning and imagination, and a gift of creativity. We suggest that you add to those things humor, patience and an endless supply of thankfulness. How can you be joyful and peaceful within if your life is not grounded in the thankfulness that you are here, that you have this impossible task in front of you, and the time to address the purposes for which you entered incarnation? Keep that ground of thankfulness and that awareness of the self as just the beginning that opens to you the Creator that you are and see every door that is shut as a temporary thing, lifting away from anger, disappointment and hostility to embrace hope, faith and love.

This instrument informs us that we must move on and we would open the questioning now to specific queries that you may have at this time. Who would wish to ask a question at this time?

G: Q'uo, Iin the *Law of One* series, the questioner asked about which of the two paths was more positively polarizing, one path where you defend a positive entity from negative suppression or the second path where you allow the suppression by the negatively-oriented entities. Ra answered by using the example of Jesus' lack of desire to be defended as if that was the higher understanding or the higher way. Could you expand on why allowing suppression by the negatively-oriented entity seems or is the more polarizing of the two?

We are those of Q'uo, and are aware of your query, my brother. This question offers a chance to look at polarity in this particular sense of not defending the self, in that the one known as Jesus chose not to defend itself and was therefore given a quite ignominious death, a death reserved for those enemies of the state that were the worst. In doing so, this entity expressed the highest degree of a lack of defense of the self. The polarity involved in that choice was that which is gained by working against the whole impulse to defend the self. Laying down all choice of defending the self, therefore, expressed the one known as Jesus' absolute faith in the goodness of all entities, including his enemies.

Personally speaking, it was very successful in establishing [its own] polarity. If this entity had been more subtle and clever, it might have found ways to stay alive while expressing unconditional love and therefore gained for itself the opportunity to interact further through time as the agent of the creative principle. And, therefore, it can be seen that a choice which gains greatly in personal polarity may yet create a situation in which the gain in the polarity of the group was potentially less. It is difficult to grade, shall we say, the acts which a person may do or the thinking behind them and how that was. The best that this entity was able to achieve in its incarnation, at its time of choice, was the choice that it made.

May we answer you further?

G: I'll take a stab at it, Q'uo. Jesus was a martyr. He expressed to the fullest extent the fourth chakra, the open heart. Had he seated his experience in the blue ray and exercised the energies of wisdom, [had he] brought wisdom into his choice-making decisions and expressed that level of understanding, would wisdom then dictate to him, or inform him of, a choice in which he could have defended himself and polarized further?

We are those of Q'uo, and are aware of your query, my brother. Indeed, we were expressing that option as the road that was untraveled, as the one known as Robert Frost has spoken in his poem.[3] There is always a road that is untraveled whenever any choice is made. It is unknown because of the passage of time and circumstance whether that option would

---

[3] *The Road Not Taken*, by Robert Frost:

> Two roads diverged in a yellow wood
> and sorry I could not travel both
> And be one traveller, long I stood
> and looked down one as far as I could
> to where it bent in the undergrowth;
> Then took the other, as just as fair,
> and having perhaps the better claim
> because it was grassy and wanted wear;
> though as for that, the passing there
> had worn them really about the same,
> And both that morning equally lay
> in leaves no feet had trodden black.
> Oh, I kept the first for another day!
> Yet knowing how way leads on to way,
> I doubted if I should ever come back.
> I shall be telling this with a sigh
> Somewhere ages and ages hence:
> Two roads diverged in a wood, and I—
> I took the one less travelled by,
> and that has made all the difference.

have achieved for the one known as Jesus a result that would have been more in focus in terms of his vision. For this entity did not see that that road was better. And indeed, when each of you makes a choice, there is always the road that is not taken. That may from time to time come up in the mind, as the one known as V said in speaking of that object of great beauty which she passed up eight years ago. It must recur within the mind when choices have been made. Yet, the glory of such times is that they are times of true choice when that which you decide shall create a change in all that occurs from that point forward.

May we answer you further, my brother?

G: A follow up. I have a question about a different situation, involving the idea, the energy, of defense. Every situation is unique and in Jesus' case he had a vision which crystallized in his mind but, in general then, what choice would a blue-ray entity or an indigo-ray entity, in the situation where in order to defend you need to kill another to save your own life, make? Who's to say what choice an entity will make, for each situation is unique, but, in general, would a blue-ray entity see it within his understanding, within his parameters, to kill another to save his own life?

We are those of Q'uo, and are aware of your query, my brother. We believe you are asking if an entity whose blue-ray energy center is fully opened would be able in good conscience to take a life. And we may say that, in terms of that energy body, it is perfectly possible to do any action if that action is seen by that entity in a clear enough focus. The ability of the mind to create bias in situations is unending. And there are many entities who have gloriously expressed blue ray while killing others. That sense of entitlement is a strong thing. When an entity becomes absolutely convinced of the rightness of the need for violence, it becomes possible to have a fully functioning blue-ray energy, green-ray energy, and all other energies, and at the same time, to kill. This is why spiritual evolution is not a simple thing. For the mind within incarnation is constantly and inevitably blindsided by distortion. Consequently, it is a matter of picking your way, moment by moment, and thought by thought, coming back always to the fundamental basis of your own faith rather than depending upon an entity, a principle, or any other created structure.

May we answer you further, my brother?

G: That's very thought-provoking. That opens all other kinds of cans of worms in my mind, but, no thank you, Q'uo, and thank you for the answers you were able to give. Thank you, instrument.

We are those of Q'uo, and we thank you, my brother, as well.

Is there a final query at this time?

(No further queries.)

We are those of Q'uo, and as we do not hear any sound vibrations hitting this instrument's ears, we are assuming that we have run you out of questions this day. We just thank you with all of our hearts for bringing yourselves and your concerns to this circle of seeking. It is such a joy to share our thoughts with you and we hope we may encourage and find ways to support each of you as you go forward in your quest for truth and service and devotion to the one infinite Creator. We bless each of you and thank you and we leave you, as always, in the love and in the light of the one infinite Creator. We are those of Q'uo. Adonai. Adonai. ☥

L/L Research is a subsidiary of
Rock Creek Research &
Development Laboratories, Inc.

P.O. Box 5195
Louisville, KY 40255-0195

L/L RESEARCH

www.llresearch.org

Rock Creek is a non-profit
corporation dedicated to
discovering and sharing
information which may aid in
the spiritual evolution of
humankind.

SPECIAL MEDITATION
OCTOBER 10, 2004

Question from A: After a year of marriage I must admit my wife and I have a serious sexual problem. Without infringing upon the principles concerning free will, could Q'uo please comment on our current sexual difficulty? Could they confirm for me that my current situation has been planned by my higher self for guiding me in the positive direction? Aside from our personal problem, I wish to ask the difference between our spiritual evolution with and without sex. There are many monks or nuns who concentrate on their discipline in chastity. The Bible also has said, "For there are some eunuchs which were so born from their mother's womb, and there are some eunuchs which were made eunuchs of man, and there be eunuchs which have made themselves eunuchs for the kingdom of Heaven's sake." He said that is able to receive it, let him receive it, Matthew 9:12. On the other hand, Ra taught us that a healthy sexual intercourse strengthens our vital energy and emotional energy with each other.

Could Q'uo expand on these two concepts and describe their distinct advantages for our seeking journey?

(Carla channeling)

We are those of the principle known to you as Q'uo. We greet you in the love and in the light of the one infinite Creator, in Whose service we come to you this day. May we say what a privilege it is to experience your group energy. Its beauty is almost startling and we thank each of you for your great desire to seek the truth and your open hearts that reach out to each other with support and encouragement. We are most happy to offer our thoughts to the one known as A and would ask only that both he and all of those who hear or read these words be very diligent in taking responsibility for those things that you hear and guarding your own thought processes. For every thing that we say this day may not be an opinion that is helpful to you and we would not wish to be a stumbling block before any. So we would ask you please to consider carefully those thoughts that we share this day, realizing that we are not authorities over you in any way but only fellow travelers on the path. If something that we offer resonates to you, by all means use it. But if it does not resonate, please leave it behind without a second thought. In this way we may guard our own polarity and our observances of the free will of those to whom we speak this day. Thank you for that diligence, my friends.

The query of the one known as A is one which seems to be about sexuality. And certainly we shall share some of our thinking concerning sexuality with you. But we would begin by taking the discussion from a somewhat different level. The quest for happiness often seems to include that desire for a sexual partner that is appropriate and desirable and [who is] the one to whom the heart has been given. We have the greatest sympathy for each of you who exist in bodies that seem to be quite separate from the air and the ground and the chair that you're sitting on and certainly from the other bodies that inhabit this Earth with you. It is a feature of the third-density setup that there is the yearning built into the third-density human person for companionship. Certainly this yearning can become blunted or destroyed by abuse during the early years of incarnation and in many cases, this souring and embittering of the fellow feeling for companionship creates a situation in entities in which they honestly come to feel it is better to experience solitude than to risk the pain of abuse. In many cases, there honestly does not seem to be any way out of experiencing abuse when in relationship. This does not happen with all entities but it is an occurrence that happens to a significant number of those within your culture. Abuse is widespread.

There are all kinds of abuse. Much abuse does not register as abuse, unlike [the experiences of] those who are raped by family members or physically beaten. These entities experience other kinds of more subtle abuse which are just as punishing to the spirit within and which can alienate and separate and isolate that spirit within from the ability to trust others of their breed. If every human to whom you have given your heart seems to have abused you, it is understandable that, over time, there would come to be within you a determination not to be caught again in the snare and trap of love. And we would suggest to the one known as A and to the one known as B that this is a thread of thought that can be taken further in the privacy and the sanctity of the open heart. For with each of these entities there have been experiences in the young years of incarnation which have biased and soured those chords of natural trust and faith in one's fellow human that each child is born into the world experiencing as a steady state and as a normal way of life, unless, indeed, as some in this room have experienced, there have been abuses even from the womb.

However early in life these abuses begin to occur, they leave a mark. And while a scar is only that which is upon the surface, there are scars that go much deeper than physical scars. Healing from such memories—even unconscious memories of abuse— is greatly facilitated by the ability to talk through such experiences, such half-hidden memories as each may have, so that each can support each, each can comfort each, and each can forgive each. For there is a guilt implicit in the shutting off of human companionship even though it is necessary for the

experience of safety to be had. And this crux, this time, for the ones known as A and B, is a time for such examination, such discussion, and such healing. The one known as A asked if this indeed had been a situation planned by his higher self, by the guidance system that was co-planner of this incarnation with the one known as A before incarnation, and we may confirm this. It is not that the situation was set up in order that the one known as A and the one known as B may learn thus and so; rather, it was set up so that the one known as A and the one known as B may learn—and teach each other as they learn from each other. We may say that this is a situation in which both come to the relationship untrammeled by previous karma. There is balanced karma within this relationship. Each is completely free to love and serve the other without regard for previous lessons, previous incarnations, or previous hopes and fears. You may come to the situation knowing that you are fresh and new and hopeful with each other.

Sexuality seems to be a red-ray issue and yet a question such as this one is a sure indication that the entire energy body is involved in sexuality. It cannot be divided or split up into lower chakras and higher chakras; it must be gazed at from the viewpoint of the being as a whole. One is not a sexual being; one is a being that has sexuality as well as many, many other characteristics. Certainly the smooth and enjoyable expression of sexuality between mates has been intended by the creative principle to be a joy, a blessing, and a healing. The physical results of healthy expression of sexuality are well known to your culture and perhaps even overvalued. But there are tremendous benefits, as the one known as A has said, to a sexual companionship that stem from the ability of sexuality to bridge and close the gap between bodies. When one is inserting Tab A into Slot B—in the approved sexual manner—distance disappears and two become one. As bodies penetrate each other, so do hearts, minds, and emotions penetrate each other. The sadnesses are shared, the joys are shared, and there is no aloneness between the two who are truly exchanging energy. It was intended by the Creator to be a delight as well as a very efficient procreative act.

The intentions of the creative principle remain a mystery to us but it has been our observation, as gazing at third density from somewhat further along the path of evolution, that the sexual principle is a powerful and lasting one. It continues to be a unifying and celebratory event as the densities move on. We at sixth density, speaking as those of the group of Ra, still experience sexuality in the shape of fusion. We, speaking as Latwii of fifth density, still experience sexuality as we wish to experience it—choosing our form and our expression; yet our choices continue to be those of finding that one entity with whom we are most suited and enjoying a mated life together in the context of group living. And it is true of those who are of the Hatonn group in fourth density as well. We do not have as much choice, in terms of physical vehicles, yet we do have that continuing desire to be companioned and to share an intimate life with that companion. Sexuality is not going to go away because you leave this density; it is a continuing principle within what you may perhaps visualize, as we do, as a continuing series of illusions. So a query concerning sexuality is in no way a shallow one. Nor is it one that we can dispose of by discussing psychology or ways of encouraging various portions of the mind to alter their biases.

The Creator has more than one reason, however, for setting up sexuality in just such a way as it has within third density. For, within third density, there is a very specific, basic game plan, shall we say, for the school of life in third density and that game plan has to do with becoming able to open the heart and to love unconditionally. Now in this opening of the heart and becoming able to love unconditionally there is a choice to be made and that is the choice that the one known as G was speaking of earlier as between STO and STS—an abbreviation that many entities within this group use for service to self and service to others. It is a significant choice. It is a valid choice. Service to self is a way to evolve closer and closer to the one infinite Creator; service to others is a way also to evolve closer and closer to the one infinite Creator. We believe that the infinite One has a bias in favor of service to others and thusly has made that path somewhat easier. Nevertheless, the greatest difficulty for those who are awakening to their own spiritual destiny upon planet Earth is choosing the manner of evolution. Each within this circle has unconditionally chosen service to others and so have the one known as A and the one known as B. Consequently, we will lift up off of speaking of service to self and concentrate on the service-to-others path.

One of the greatest tools or resources of the service-to-others path is the attraction between sexually compatible people. This instrument has often thought that it was a kind of trick that the Creator played on us all, to make the attraction between the sexes so potent. It was as if the carrot, that carrot of attraction, were being dangled before the donkey's head; whereas, behind the donkey, the stick was being applied in terms of the results of that attraction. There is many an entity, both male and female, who, having entered the mated state, has quickly begun to feel that it is a terrible cheat for, instead of the continued bliss of the honeymoon, there has come quickly the realization that one is now responsible for that other entity, for paying the bills of that other entity and seeing that that other entity is fed and clothed and housed and, to some extent, happy. These are burdens which can be felt by many. We do not in any way deny the effort that is implied by such attraction. Once one has accepted a relationship, one is indeed in relationship and therefrom depends, if one chooses the mated state, a lifetime of service. And this is the trick that this instrument has noted: that the clever Creator has pulled people into a situation in which they almost cannot avoid being of service, for the society as a whole is quite judgmental concerning those who, in the married state, are not careful to provide for their spouses and mates, their children and other dependants. We look around the entities within this circle and see that several have experienced long, mated relationships, while others have experienced shorter and more ephemeral relationships. We are aware that those who have been mated for long periods of time are fully aware of the duties of the married state and yet at the same time, as we gaze within the minds of those involved, we see the joys and the gratitude that each feels for the benefits of that state. Within your culture, it has often seemed to break down, for the duties and the honors of service-to-others living are a challenge. Loving well is not done briefly. It is done persistently, patiently and with a tremendous amount of understanding and forgiveness required to keep the relationship from souring and becoming bitter.

In the case of the one known as A and the one known as B, the energies moving into the mated relationship were neatly divided betwixt lower chakras and higher chakras. It is unusual indeed for a marriage of choice between two entities to include only those higher chakras. Most often entities are drawn first by the shallow and superficial, the surface aspects of another human being. And those are those things which feed into sexual attraction—the appearance, the physical looks, and so forth. This was not the case with the ones known as A and B. Indeed, this relationship has much more of the energies of relationships within higher densities, where the attraction is that of a soul to another soul. And we do not believe that any love more deeply than the ones known as A and B and so we say to you that you have already achieved a great deal in your choice of each other. It took great courage for the one known as A to choose to marry an entity for whom he did not feel the requisite physical attraction expected of male entities within his culture. And yet, this was a conscious choice, a prayerful and thoughtful choice and we would not in any way suggest that it has been a mistake. Rather we would suggest that it is a unique situation and one in which there will not be a great deal of understanding from others within this society. And we, ourselves, are not those who are psychologists or therapists. We cannot solve the surface of the problem that presents itself, in terms of the lack of desire between these two entities. Yet, at the same time, we may offer some thoughts which may help as the ones known as A and B explore together the ramifications of the choices that they have made.

The one known as A asked concerning how evolution within third density would occur without sexuality as opposed to with sexuality. We've looked a little bit at the ways of a sexual mating. The sexually mated pair are set up, as it were, for a life of service to each other. The ones known as A and B have achieved this setup without the prod of sexuality, without the carrot of finding each other so attractive that they become bemused and foolish with each other and cannot think of what to say or how to say it.

Upon the other hand, there have been energies set in motion in the manner of coming together that can fruitfully be explored. The eunuch or monk who chooses to forego sexuality and sexual partners is not choosing to forego sexuality because it is an evil thing as much as they are choosing to place their energies and their service not to one person but to humankind as a whole or to the infinite Creator. We do not say that this is a mistake either; it is a valid choice. It is rather, however, like choosing not to use one of your legs or arms or stopping your ears so

that you cannot hear. It is a choice that places one a bit off balance as an entity dwelling in third density. For the body is as much a part of the entity as the mind or the spirit or the emotions. To ask the body to refrain from expressing its natural function is to ask the body to be a bit off balance. To the best of our ability, this would be our estimate of the difference between living without sexuality and living with sexuality. The entity which has expressed its sexuality, whether in the present or in the past, is a whole entity in a way that an entity which has foresworn sexuality cannot be. There is no loss of polarity if one chooses not to express sexuality but there is a greater likelihood of a healthy energy body which has the vitality to persist in seeking if all natural functions are seen as beautiful and holy.

The challenge, then, is to lift up from previous concepts of sexuality as being that which is involved with lower chakras only, so that sexuality may be seen as both natural and sacred. One of the archetypes with which this instrument is familiar is the archetype called The Lovers. In it, the central figure is a male and his hands are crossed so that his right hand is reaching over his left shoulder and his left hand is reaching over his right shoulder. In one hand he is holding the hand of a pure and pristine priestess figure; in the other hand he is holding the hand of a somewhat debased feminine figure which is seen to be prostituted and unclean. The virtuous female figure is veiled and almost hidden whereas the prostituted female figure is far less fully clothed and expresses great attraction. It is obvious that the central male figure is about to make a choice between two types of femininity. The one known as A has made his choice. Profoundly, absolutely, he has chosen the veiled and mysterious priestess for his mate.

And the question then becomes, "What does that archetypal figure do as he walks off into the archetypal sunset with his veiled bride?" And we would suggest to the ones known as A and B that the future lies open and free before them. Sacredness of virtue remains as one walks into that sunset. In a way, it would almost seem to be a debasing thing to introduce such a virtuous entity to sexuality and yet sexuality is not in and of itself that which is prostituted. Let us draw back from the physical—for the one known as A must always draw back from this in his own evolution, in his own habits of thinking, and in his own personality—and gaze at the true meaning, or, shall we say, a deeper meaning of this archetype. The feminine principle is the unconscious. It is that fertile volume in which all truth is written. The male principle is that entity which reaches to know the mystery, which wishes to plumb the depths of the volume of truth. The feminine principle represents the creative principle. When an entity approaches the feminine, an entity is approaching his own deepest self. Penetrating that mystery is the goal of the male principle. Being appreciated, courted, cherished and loved, the feminine principle can at last relax, release the veiling, and allow herself to bloom. And the truth comes bursting from every pore of such content. This is the deeper level of meaning of this archetypal figure.

We would encourage the ones known as A and B to allow whatever will occur to occur. If there comes to be desire between two such loving people, we rejoice with you. If there does not come to be desire between two such loving people, we do mourn with you for we do see the value and the beauty of the sexual relationship. But we ask each to know, beyond a shadow of a doubt, that you are doing the work that you came to do; and that as you explore this and other issues with each other, you are helping each other to bloom, you are helping each other to progress, and you are helping each other to heal.

We are aware that the one known as Carla has suggested to you a way in which you may learn all over again to touch each other with love. And we would commend this technique to you and suggest that if you find yourself comfortable in one phase of this four-phase progression, that you remain there as long as you are comfortable there. We would further suggest to you that when it is time to move ahead, then move onto the next phase. And if you spend the rest of your life in phase two or phase three, you will still have found more intimacy and have exchanged more good energy than many entities which have unsatisfactory, though technically perfectly functional, sexual lives. Happiness, the one known as T said earlier, is that which you begin with and then the world becomes a happy place. This is so true to us and we commend this thought to you. Allow yourselves first of all to be happy with each other.

(Side one of tape ends.)

(Carla channeling)

Allow yourselves to glory in the beauty of each other: the beauty of the mind, the beauty of the emotions, and the beauty of the soul within. This allows everything to settle into its right place and takes the emphasis off of that which is only a part of the whole. We encourage you to be with each other in meditation each day and to allow that unity in seeking to seed the garden of your lives. Who knows what plants shall grow? Know only that you shall grow those things that you both were placed here to grow and that you shall help each other to blossom.

We thank the one known as A for this excellent question and at this time would open this meeting to other queries if there are any. Is there a question at this time?

G: Q'uo, I have one. Recently in my life I've had opportunities for relationship and for sexual energy transfers and I've passed those by because, for one reason or another, I have felt that they would not work and therefore, out of consideration for the other person, I haven't engaged in anything physical that would lead to emotions being evolved or the commitments made of relationships, so I would like to ask you if that activity of waiting for a better opportunity, or for "Ms Right," is a wise activity? Or if I might wind up the person that has passed up opportunity that has knocked at the door in chasing an illusion, a fiction of my mind of something that is more to aligned to my dream of "her"?

We are those of Q'uo and are aware of your query, my brother. My brother, the density of choice is just that. There are no mistakes. There is as much virtue in one choice as another as long as each choice is made with a full and loving heart. The ways of love are a mystery. This instrument, for example, has memories of waiting for Mr. Right and feeling that she had indeed done precisely the right thing. This entity passed up many opportunities as well and it was her nineteenth year before she chose to offer herself to the entity to whom she had become engaged. It is also true that, in this entity's life, it was a very quick trip, shall we say, from the first ecstasy of waiting for Mr. Right and then choosing him and embracing him to being left at the altar by this entity. Was it a mistake to wait? This entity would not say so; for she developed, as a being, very naturally because she waited until her heart was completely engaged and her faith and trust were utter. And so her first experience of sexuality was utterly positive.

On the other hand, when an entity embraces thoughtlessly and becomes, as you have said, entangled with another entity without that benefit of utter faith and full choice, yet still, in many an instances, the carrot having been offered and the stick having been applied, the entity learns after the fact how to love because he has been forced into the situation of learning. This is why we cannot say that one way is better than another.

It is a matter of the personality shell of the entity and that nature which he was given at birth. Some entities are robust and relatively insensitive and take their pleasure where they find it. Others are more gentle and sensitive and must feel that they are loved and that they can love in return. They must be able to engage their faith and their trust before the picture comes right and it seems natural to move forward. We believe we speak to the latter type of entity and because of that we would say that you choose well to wait. There is no mistake in having the ideal of "the right person." We do not say that there is one right person for each entity. We do say, however, that it is well for a sensitive entity to wait very carefully and very thoughtfully and watchfully for the resonance and the depth that come when you make contact with a soul that is truly compatible with you and we encourage you to follow that way as long as it has resonance for you.

May we answer you further, my brother?

G: No, well done, Q'uo. Thank you very much.

We thank you, my brother. Is there a further query at this time?

J: Yes Q'uo, I'd like to pose a query. First I'd like to express my appreciation for your wisdom and consideration—how meaningful it is to me. And I would just like to ask about the discipline of the mind. You once suggested to me that the way that you go about setting up a ritual of the mind as used to its fullest potential is to take responsibility for every thought and you asked me to query further if I required more clarification and if you'd be so kind I'd love to hear more thoughts on this and how to discipline the mind.

We are those of Q'uo and are aware of your query, my brother. Indeed your question has many hidden aspects and we smile at the impossibility of

responding to all that you ask but we shall do our poor best to share a few thoughts with you, my brother.

What is it to take thought? For some the mind is a fairly easily managed tool. It runs along fairly predictable lines, easily influenced by such outside forces as family, friends, mass media, and the culture itself as it ticks along like an engine. For others, the choice of what to bring through into the personality shell has included the choice of a powerful intellect and, as this entity is well aware, a powerful intellect can hardly ever be shut down. So rather than the experience many have of taking thought, the experience is more of the mind racing along— sometimes in one gait, sometimes in another; sometimes on one level, sometimes on another but seldom, if ever, stopping and often thinking more than one thing at a time.

However, when such an entity chooses, it may slow that engine down by fastening upon one of the thoughts that is passing through. Often, there is a great help in terms of circumstance. The mind becomes focused because a circumstance arises in which there is a relationship that is being exercised and interaction is taking place or a subject has been raised and the mind is drawn to thinking concerning just that subject. We encourage the one known as J to take advantage of such times of natural focus. It is a good place to start to isolate the focus at that time and reflect upon it later. This helps the mind to move itself away from that reckless pony ride that it enjoys and to put the saddle on it, put the bridle on it, and start mastering this horse of a mind that is happily cavorting about the corral of your grey matter. Certainly, this instrument has much fellow feeling for you for this instrument's mind is such a run-away pony and does a good bit of cavorting. Yet this instrument has learned to take all of that activity very lightly. Its tendency is to wait for the focus in order to do the examination of thoughts and we would suggest this technique to you as well.

When you perceive an ethical situation or a point of consideration that is attractive to you, realize that this thought has been pointed out to you as a thought among thoughts that is worthy of special consideration. If there is a natural instinct to shy away from examining such a thought or such a focus, know then that you are truly on to something and pursue the consideration of that ethical question or that consideration, whatever it might be, with great passion.

Many thoughts that come before your mind and that you wish to examine are those with which you do not know what to do and in those cases where thought has become involved with emotion which has become involved with interaction with another human being or some other tangle like that, the best you can do in considering that particular thought is to sit with it. And this is a technique that is much underrated in your society. Some things are not there for you to solve. Some things are there for you to sit with. They are house guests and the mystery of that tangle is not going to be solved overnight. When it is solved it will be very simple but nature will take its good time allowing you to do the growing that you need to do in order to complete the pattern that is implicit in the tangle. All the tangles have very simple outcomes in terms of your ability, ultimately, to judge the value of thoughts. But there are many thoughts that are company, not to solve, but to sit with.

May we answer you further, my brother?

J: No, I appreciate your thoughts, thank you.

We thank you, my brother. Is there a final query at this time?

G: Real quick one for me, Quo. For over two years now I've been meditating every single day, or trying to at least, and though I've improved, I'm far from where I would like to be, and far from a single-pointed focus during my meditations, sometimes I am just thinking. Any tips, recommendations, suggestions, to improve my meditation? And thank you very much for your answer.

We are those of Q'uo, and are aware of your query, my brother. It is difficult to put into words the value of meditation. Certainly some entities are expert at achieving a one-pointed focus. The vast majority of entities, however, remain forever, to their own judgment, greatly imperfect and incompetent meditators whose thoughts arise again and again and again. And yet, the value [to an] entity of the meditative experience is undiminished by the self-perceived imperfection of the technique.

We would suggest that, without judgment or expectation, you simply seek the silence and listen for the Creator's footsteps. Wait for the Creator's arms to embrace you. Listen for the sound of the door to your heart opening wide. The gifts of silence cannot be expressed but the virtue of the attempt to enter the silence is absolute.

May we answer you further, my brother?

G: No. Gratitude once again. Thank you, Q'uo.

We thank each of you. It has been a wonderful experience for us to share our energy with you. We thank the ones known as A and B and we thank each of you in the circle today. Know that we are always with you if you request our presence. Our love and support are constant.

We leave you in all that there is: the love and the light of the one infinite Creator. We are those known to you as Q'uo. Adonai. Adonai. ❧

L/L Research is a subsidiary of
Rock Creek Research &
Development Laboratories, Inc.

P.O. Box 5195
Louisville, KY 40255-0195

L/L RESEARCH

www.llresearch.org

Rock Creek is a non-profit
corporation dedicated to
discovering and sharing
information which may aid in
the spiritual evolution of
humankind.

SPECIAL MEDITATION
OCTOBER 11, 2004

Question from A: "A comes to us with a question about guidance regarding her sacred contracts prior to this incarnation—what she might be guided to do with this incarnation, and also her divine purpose."

(Carla channeling)

We are those of the principle known to you as Q'uo, and we greet you in the love and in the light of the one infinite Creator. It is a great privilege to be with this group this day and we thank each of you for taking the time and the incredible effort and energy that it does take to satisfy the time for spiritual work. It creates a tremendous vortex of energy and we are most privileged to be called to your group to share thoughts with you in this vortex of purpose and circumstance. Thank you for this privilege. Thank you for the beauty of your vibrations as you sit in meditation and thank you for this circle of seeking.

We would ask each of you to protect us in our concern for not violating the principle of free will by listening very carefully to those things that we say and discriminating between those ideas which may resonate to you and those which do not. If they do resonate and feel familiar and useful to you, by all means run with them. Use them and work with them as you see fit. If there is no answering echo in your heart from thoughts that we offer, please, it would be the greatest favor to us if you would simply leave them behind, for we would not want to create a stumbling block before you. Truth is not an objective thing when it comes to metaphysical truth.

Truth is entirely subjective and your own powers of discrimination are more than adequate to knowing that which is for you and that which is not for you at this time. Thank you very much.

Your query concerns your sacred contract and your divine purpose and we would take those two separately, for the concept of a sacred contract is one which we find to be full of the pitfalls of the culture in which you live. You certainly have created contracts, and we say that in the plural rather than the singular, before this incarnation. These contracts have to do with relationships. In your considerations before this incarnation, you and the guidance system which is yours, sat down together and thoughtfully, carefully considered where you as a soul felt that you were with the issues of polarity and of balance. For it is desirable to [those] heavily polarized towards service-to-other and quite common and usual that there will be an issue of balance involved in choosing the relationships with which you set yourself up before incarnation. This is the balance between wisdom and love, for those who have come back into this incarnation from higher densities. It is easy to see the great benefit of unconditional love and it is easy to see the great benefit of true wisdom. It is sometimes difficult for an entity whose previous incarnational experiences have biased her in one or the other of those two qualities to be able to see how to correct a self-perceived imbalance between those two qualities. Therefore, the relationships that are set up have the function of offering repeated or theme-like cycles of catalyst in which, again and again, you will receive catalyst that brings up not only the service-to-others question of how to be of service, whether to be of service, and so forth; but also the question of using your open heart and your wisdom to address this catalyst, this situation, and this relationship. It is hoped that through these repeated, cyclical occurrences of catalyst in your life, you will slowly win through to a felt sense of where that balance point for you lies.

In this instrument, for instance, it was heavily overbalanced into love when it first began its incarnation and found it very easy to contemplate, for instance, the giving of the life for others or martyrdom short of giving the life, feeling that anything that could be done for others was worth any and all efforts from the instrument. The instrument has worked for decades to attempt to blend in the hard-won lessons of wisdom which she has recovered in this incarnation, thanks to the learn/teaching of entities such as the one known as Don and the one known Jim and many others with which she has had converse and communion.

For each entity, this balance is unique and the cues and clues and whispers for guidance are going to be unique and so we would not do this for you in any sense but simply say that this is a continuing issue that is very fruitful for you to consider as you find yourself in various situations with various of those with whom you have come in contact. The ones for whom you are attempting to do the body work and other sacred ministry of touch work are obviously those who have been given to you so that you may learn as well as offer your service. It is not sometimes so clear that the entity who cuts you off in traffic, the shopkeeper in the store who is attempting to assist you with your purchase, the postmistress at the post office, and the neighbor at the grocery store are contacts that are also equally helpful and equally on task and on target for your process. Yet this is so.

So we would recommend, in terms of your sacred contracts, that you realize that beneath the surface of errands and paperwork and the duties of the day, that those people that are in your life are each, very potentially, the owners with you of a sacred contract.

Now, when it comes to the work at hand for the life, the incarnational lessons, the incarnation service, there is not precisely a contract. It is as though you have envisioned setting up a business. This obviously is only a very rough analogy but this instrument has gone through the exercise of setting up a business and is aware of the things that you need to do and so that is what we are using from her mind, that technique that one has of setting out the basic purposes of that business and the assets that you have in starting the business and the challenges that you have and just looking one month down the road, one year down the road, five years down the road, and developing a game plan. Earlier in life, in the young years of childhood, it is difficult to find enough surety of focus to begin to realize, in any settled or mature sense, to what such large chunks of your time and talent and treasure will be given. However, as the years of incarnation pile up and experiences mount, there begins to be a more and more clear focus and we are aware that you would like to improve the clarity of this focus as you gaze about you at this business that you have started and wonder, "What is my next step? What is the true whole or the true character of this business of mine, this sacred business that I wish to be about?"

It is important to realize, however, that, in terms of a contract, your contract is simply to serve. You truly hoped before incarnation to serve and to learn. The learning is almost inevitable, for the accompaniment of service and the offshoots into learning that you receive from attempting to serve are numerous and countless. So we would ask you to lift up from attempting to nail down some sort of step-by-step contract and begin to realize that this is in your hands, not just now, but each day of the rest of your incarnation. Your service is malleable. It is not something like a puzzle of which you simply must fill in the blanks. This instrument is very fond of puzzles and she is used to taking the definitions and putting each letter into the square. You do not have that kind of puzzle in order to determine, with clarity, what your purpose is. Rather, it is as if you have been given a take-home test and it is an essay test. And you will be grading this test as well as taking it. And you may retake this test each day if you wish, or each year. You may reevaluate. You may reconsider. And we urge you to go back whenever there is a glitch, seemingly, in the process and do just that: review your parameters, review what you think you know about yourself, about your sense of where you are, your sense of what you want for your immediate future and so forth, so that you can have the feeling, at all times, that you are fresh, you are new, you are not plodding through a preconceived pattern at all. This is your growth, your blooming, and you have the watering can, the fertilizer, and the will to grow. Indeed, you play all the parts in this little garden of growth that is your sacred purpose.

The divine plan for each entity who takes breath upon planet Earth is greatly unified. The divine plan for each entity is for that entity to discover herself and to manifest the being that lies within so that, at the end of your incarnation, you are an energy field radiating in self-knowledge and truth.

Now let us look at that model a bit, for it sounds simple and yet it is sufficiently counter to the ways of thinking of your culture that our thoughts really bear some discussion in order to be at all really understood. When an entity in your culture starts to talk about herself, it is not in terms of being but in terms of doing: "This is what I do for a living, this is what I do for pleasure, and this is what I do to serve." Yet your divine purpose is to be. You came into incarnation as an energy field. You pulled through, from your total self, certain characteristics, as what this instrument would call a personality shell: your intelligence, your personality, the way you express yourself, the things that you are good at, the things that you do not seem to be good at, and so forth. These are as the very surface of a very deep body of water; the waves upon the surface only are these markers for what lies beneath the waves of personality. You have an infinite depth to your true self and you have connections between your waking consciousness that is so involved in the personality shell and your total self. Those threads of connection are slender and fragile but very, very strong in the sense that they cannot be broken. They can be disturbed and many times we find that the very silver chord itself has been roughly used, shall we say, so that it is difficult, at first, for entities to do the dream work, the visualization work, and the meditative work that help strengthen those inner connections between the surface self and the true self. However, we do not find, in this particular case, that that is what has happened; indeed, the connections between the conscious self and the subconscious self seem to be very vital and used very well and so we would simply encourage the one known as A to continue in those processes in which she is already involved, working with the dreams, the intuitions, and the silence itself.

The essence of self is a living thing. The name that entities have within incarnation is often felt to be inadequate and so other names are sought that seem to have a vibration that is more in accord with your inner sense of who you are, from the standpoint of higher densities or from the inner planes of your own density where your own metaphysical work takes place. However, no name is necessary. Your energy field itself is your name. Your vibration is your identity. We have no doubt as to who each is within this group, not because we know your name but because we see you as you are, vibrating away, coruscating[4] with light, color and texture. And each entity has her own inner structure, her own relationships and balances between the chakras and so forth.

So how can one penetrate illusion after illusion about the self and come more and more into a sense of who she is? That remains to us, as well as to you, a mystery in terms of being able to spell out how this works. It is an entirely intuitive process and the more that you can pay attention to the energies of your emotions, the more resources that you will have.

Now, in this regard, let us look at two different levels of emotion, for working with the instant, easy surface emotions is one thing, working with the deeper emotions is another. First of all, let us gaze at the easy and surface emotions. Immediately coming into this instrument's mind when we speak of surface emotions are those irritations that she experiences, for instance, in her car when she is in traffic. It is very easy to feel upset when one is cut off in traffic. This is a good emotion to look at and it teaches, but what it teaches is significantly different from what the deeper emotions may teach. For a surface reaction, that which comes instantly and dives away quickly, is as a newspaper. It speaks of what is occurring at this particular moment. It does not speak of the deeper processes that are taking place within incarnation within your being. It is simply the momentary disturbance of the surface of the water. Yet, each disturbance is worth looking at. For in each disturbance there is a separation of self from other self and in each occurrence this separation can fruitfully be examined to determine

---

[4] coruscating: "1. To give forth flashes of light; sparkle and glitter: *diamonds coruscating in the candlelight*. 2. To exhibit sparkling virtuosity: *a flutist whose music coruscated throughout the concert hall.*"

that which pulled you apart from your fellow being and then to find ways to heal that separation; to find unity once again with that stranger or friend which has pulled you off balance.

Even when a momentary occurrence delights one, yet still, again, it is important to examine that to see if the light has an undercurrent of separation in it and, if so, what that was. What you are trying to do in examining these very surface events is to improve your point of view. The exercise of going deeper, looking for the love, looking for the unity beneath the separation or disharmony is cumulative in its effect upon widening and deepening one's instinctual default point of view. And the point of view is crucial, for at that point of view from which you look at the world you will see certain patterns in a certain way. As your point of view widens, broadens and strengthens in its uncompromisingly metaphysical orientation, you will begin to see a different world. And as that world becomes stronger in its metaphysical point of view, so your lessons will come to you on rounder wheels and with more grease in them, smoother, easier, more understandable. So the little irritations of the day are not simply dross to be swept away like dirt in the spume of the froth of a wave. This is good material to scoop up with the hand. Take a good look at it before you toss it out.

Working with the deeper emotions is a slower and more subtle process and is entirely intuitive. It demands that you begin to realize when your deeper emotional bodies have been penetrated. You need to begin to see that time where you have felt an essential, true emotion, whether it is joy or grief or irritation. These deeper emotions are as notes and it is important for you to be able to play your instrument, to know it well, and to be able to tune it, as this instrument was earlier talking about tuning her physical, her mental, her emotional, and her spiritual bodies for the receiving of this contact which is presently ongoing. You are an instrument, you are a crystal instrument. Your energies express themselves in color rather than sound, in light rather than music, yet they are most substantially there and are your deeper expression of being. They are those things which will not disappear when your physical vehicle has gone again into the dust from which it was formed. As a citizen of eternity, then, you are not just working upon what is evident and obvious—your physical being, your momentary

thoughts and so forth—you are working on the permanent part of yourself, insofar as you are able.

What you are attempting to do, as we said earlier, is to become more truly yourself, to sing your crystal song ever more beautifully, ever more truly on pitch, ever more deeply, honestly, the essence that is you. This is the whole of your divine purpose. You came to stand, as this instrument would say, as the lamp upon the hill,[5] as the lighthouse before all, not to push them around, not to reach out to them with some great message, but simply to be there, shining your light in your way. For in that light's influence, you shall be of the service for which you came into this world. That lighthouse shall bring you the sailors who need your particular energy. That lighthouse shall warn off the rocks those who need to be warned off the rocks in your vicinity. You have no need to reach out. You have no need to look forward or even to look back. Your need, in terms of your divine purpose, is to be who you are, proudly, with self-confidence, with quietness, and with great persistence.

We are aware, from your discussion before this reading, that there are many things upon the plate of the one known as A right now, many directions that she can go: the energy work, the Flower of Life work, the sacred geometry, and various other aspects of her studies and so forth. Do not drown in the details This is what we would say in this regard. Take them lightly to a certain extent. Laugh with yourself. Draw cartoons joking with yourself concerning your great purpose, for you do have a great purpose! It is a wonderful purpose. Yet it is not a purpose in that sense where you tie action to circumstance and say, "This is what I must do." You need more to come to a continuing series of what this instrument would call epiphanies or realizations about who you are and why you are here, the nature of your essence, the nature of your big business at which you are looking.

We would speak briefly of the query concerning the sword-bearing and we would guide the one known as A simply to examine the archetype of the Archangel Michael. This entity is part of what this instrument would call a mythological system which this entity uses herself in her own spiritual work. She

---

[5] *Holy Bible*, Luke 11:33: "No one after lighting a lamp puts it in a cellar or under a bushel, but on a stand, that those who enter may see the light."

uses all four of the Archangels as she tunes herself for contact. The one known as Michael is that energy which is of the East. It is of fire and it, as a figure, has a sword. Sometimes when this instrument visualizes the four archetypical Archangels and the four elements, she finds the figure of Michael standing. His sword may be drawn but pointed down at the Earth, or his sword may be drawn and held upwards, or his sword may be in his scabbard. He may be kneeling or he may be standing. There is not simply one wooden or archetypal figure of the element of fire. Rather, it is a living, breathing entity that has been moved into by countless entities in the process of their spiritual work through millennia. And, therefore, this thought-form has a tremendous amount of power which it is very, very oriented to share with you. So the question for you as a sword-bearer is, "What is the truth that that sword is protecting?" And, in any particular case, in any particular situation, "Does the sword need to be drawn? Does the sword need to be bated? And if the sword is drawn, does it need to be in a non-challenging or in a challenging mode?" Thusly, it may be fruitful for you before moving into situations in which you sense that truth will be an issue, to sense into how that figure is standing. Go into the silence and ask it to be visual to you. Ask it to show you how its posture and the position of the sword can give you clues as to your own part, your own role, in this particular encounter.

Those who protect the truth are light beings and light bearers. And each of those within this circle is certainly a companion with you, the one known as A, in this regard, as all are light bearers, all being, to some extent, way-showers. Remember though, that you are not showing a road or a direction. Everything you have to show is implicit in the light of your being. So allow these situations to come to you and then allow the deepest truth within you to address itself to the situation. You spoke earlier concerning when someone comes to you for body work, not knowing what that work will be until the time is there and you ask within. So is that energy of the sword. Do not ask ahead but only on the occasion, "What is my role? How shall I shine?" And trust your being above all.

We do recommend to all who are attempting to deepen their spiritual aspects that you partake of the silence in your own way. There is a common prejudice for silent meditation and against other forms of silence but we would encourage the one known as A to explore all forms of silence: the silence of walking in nature, for instance, the silence of visualization or contemplation, the silence involved in reading from spiritual material and then sitting and allowing the ideas just to roll around and form their own patterns. There are hidden connections within all of the various studies and those which you do not think of as studies but which do indeed blend into the studies because they are called by the studies as confirmations or additions. Observe the signs and the symbols, as the one known as A was saying that she does. And try to keep a daily energy available, if only for five minutes during that day, for working within the silence.

Silence is as the tabernacle. When one enters the silence it is like entering a building of a certain type. It is a sacred building. Within the silence lies the Creator that is the heart of you. And, indeed, that silence finds its home within your heart. Take the time to enter your own heart and to sit and listen. For it is spoken truth that the still, small voice of silence offers the truth of your being.

We thank the one known as A for this opening question and would at this time ask if there are any questions that she might have to follow up this main question. We are those of Q'uo.

A: That's a lot to think of. Somehow all the questions I have don't seem to be very important!

What is this quantum learning or quantum something I've been told I'm going to be experiencing or going through? Quantum, "quantumming," what does that mean?

We are those of Q'uo and are aware of your query, my sister. The concept of a quantum, is a concept of, say, a semester in school, or a unit of something that, once that is done, it is done and one goes on to what one must go on to another quantum in order to continue. In quantum physics, the quantum is as the universe and it can be filled with just so many items and then that is the complete amount that can fit into that quantum. In your terms we would probably move more through the meaning of a semester that has been completed. The amount of learning which you have gone through, up to this point, has given you more and more and more detail. And as you move into your next field of study, there will be much more detail. We would suggest that what happens is that, as detail after detail after detail is added, there comes a crucial time when, just as in a super-saturated solution, more and more is added to the water. Suddenly, the solution goes away and a crystal appears and this is what you are in the process of achieving in terms of your study. The result of this study will be not that you will lose the detail, precisely, but that it will have a certain pattern. It will have a certain crystalline arrangement where it all makes sense, to a certain degree. It is another way of saying that you are not filling in the blanks in a puzzle, you are putting in your information to make a crystal, and that crystal will be a simplified, central structure of awareness. Notice we did not say knowledge, we said awareness, where, when you hear from someone who has come to you for help, in this and this and this and this detail, you will see it not in terms of a tally of one plus two plus three plus four, "Oh, that's four details," you will see that in terms of, "Ah, I believe I am beginning to see the shape of this entity's bias, this entity's distortion." And from that simplified point of view, you have a much clearer idea, a sense of how to help that person, of how to serve that person, of what is possible, what is not possible, what you are able to say without infringing on her learning process, what you are not able to say without infringement upon her learning process. It is as if …

(Side one of tape ends.)

(Carla channeling)

… you are cramming in more and more detail, not to achieve complexity but to get to the point where the crystal of awareness forms for you. You cannot force this to occur. You cannot hurry the process.

A: Am I almost there?

We are those of Q'uo, and we may confirm that most of the detail that you need for this crystal to form is indeed there. But it is not known to us nor can it be known to you ahead of time when that crystal shall form or what details still need to come in order for you to go, "Oh, I see it now." Yet, this time will come and we can only encourage you not to hurry it, not to look for it, but to do the work day by day and detail by detail, of receiving the information, seating the information, and using the information.

May we answer you further, my sister?

A: I have been doing some work with a teacher by the name of S who involves herself with work regarding the removal of crystals and, in aligning with the crystalline grid, is this work beneficial? Is this beneficial to me?

We are those of Q'uo, and we find that to answer this query in any way would infringe upon your learning process and therefore we respectfully would request that we just pass this question up and simply encourage you to follow your heart, to sense into this relationship and this learning, and to see how it feels to go further into those interests that she has.

May we answer you further in any other way, my sister?

A: Well, speaking of infringement, in the work that I'm involved at, I am in the process of learning more about removing heavy dust or objects in one's auric fields. Of course, my intention is always to ask for permission to remove it but I have had concerns to know if this is in any way an infringement upon others' growth process, the removal of objects in the auric layers?

We are those of Q'uo, and are aware of your query, my sister. Let us look at this question carefully, for there is a good lesson to be learned here. When you are attempting to be of service, it is important to investigate the parameters of which you do not have any idea beforehand. These parameters have to do not with your person or structure but with the person or structure of the entity who has come to you for help.

You need to find a way to address the question with the entity whom you are attempting to help. This instrument has done such work before with a pendulum, asking for a yes or no answer and putting the questions very carefully: "Does the guidance system of the one whom I am trying to help feel that this entity is ready for the removal of this distortion from the energy body?" Form a way, whether it is be penduling or other techniques which may be known to you and feel more convenient or comfortable, of getting in contact with the inner guidance system of the entity whom you are attempting to help and being absolutely sure that the guidance system is giving permission for this entity to be healed. This will clear the way for the healing to be done and it will enlist the help of that entity's higher self so that you are not alone in attempting to aid but you are simply part of the divine creative principle at work in response to one who has asked and has been given the potential for an answer. It is well written, "Knock, and it shall be opened to you. Ask and you shall receive."

You may trust that an entity who comes to you is consciously asking for help and that it is well to explore the subconscious processes involved in this person and to be sure that you are not indeed using your power and your ability to remove from a person that speck of dirt which that person needs removed at that particular time. Better, indeed, to tell such a person, "I can do this much but I can not go further," than to place that person in an unprotected and unguarded situation in which she somehow does not feel safe and secure.

Is there a final query at this time?

A: Out of curiosity, could you tell me anything about my home planet or the solar system that I am from, and will this be my last incarnation here?

We are those of Q'uo and, my sister, we would prefer not to explore the question of your antecedents for they are closely guarded by your higher self and we would not be those who placed you in a position of knowledge before your higher self offered its own way of giving permission. Know that these details will come to you in dreams, or in casual converse with those who are psychic who happen to communicate with you at the time in which you are ready for them. Up until that time, realize that for each person who has taken incarnation upon planet Earth, planet Earth is the native planet. You are truly one who lives here, one who breathes the air, and is part of the planet itself. This is your native land at this time and shall be until such time as you do not any longer draw breath.

As to it being your final incarnation, my sister, you have the potential for this to be your final incarnation. As this instrument would say with a big smile, "Don't screw up."

With that, and the encouragement at all times to use humor, for it is truly a divine gift, we would leave you in the love and in the light of the one infinite Creator. Please know that at any time that you would appreciate our vibration underlining your own and our love embracing you, you have only to mention our name mentally and we will be with you. You never need to be alone.

We are those of Q'uo. Adonai. Adonai.

L/L Research is a subsidiary of
Rock Creek Research &
Development Laboratories, Inc.

P.O. Box 5195
Louisville, KY 40255-0195

L/L Research

www.llresearch.org

Rock Creek is a non-profit
corporation dedicated to
discovering and sharing
information which may aid in
the spiritual evolution of
humankind.

© 2009 L/L Research

Sunday Meditation
November 14, 2004

Group question: The question today has to do with breaking our forms and our rituals when it seems appropriate in order to let in the light better, shall I say. We are wondering if Q'uo could give us some guidance as to how to recognize when this is appropriate or how to, shall we say, roll with the punch when it seems inevitable. We are aware that, even when times and things don't look like they're working out the way they should and they seem to be totally askew, that all is well and all is perfect. How can we see that and how can we find a path that isn't so deleterious to our own journey, sabotaging ourselves? Somewhere in there, Q'uo, I'm sure you could find something to talk about!

(Carla channeling)

We are those known to you as the principle of Q'uo and we greet you in the love and in the light of the one infinite Creator, Whom we serve. It is a great blessing to be called to your group this day to speak concerning forms and rituals and breaking them and making them and understanding how form works with the entity that you are. And we look forward to sharing our opinions with you. But we would ask you before we begin, as always, to use your discrimination very carefully in listening to what we have to say. We are not authority figures or teachers in the traditional sense of feeling that we know more than you do. Rather, we are those with perhaps a more varied palette of experiences from which to draw than you. However, we are brothers and sisters, walking with you on one path, the path which we all share. And it will allow us to speak freely if you will take complete responsibility for whether or not you use any of the thoughts that we share at this time. If you will promise to let all thoughts that do not resonate with you to fall away, then we will feel much more free to speak without being concerned that we may infringe upon someone's free will or invade someone's rightful process of evolution.

First of all, let us speak a bit about how we see you and ourselves, for both you and we have form—not the same kind of form, but we do have that which could be recognized as an ego or an identity, as do you. You experience bodies. You experience a characteristic shape to the way you think and the way you process catalyst and create memory. And yet the essence of each of us is without form, in that traditional sense of a shape to be described or something to be seen, known and identified. Each of you, each of us, is an essence. If we were to be mechanical, we might describe each of us as a system of energy fields within the greater energy field of the universe or the Creator. Yet, this does not catch the magic of the soul, for each of you is indescribably unique. There has only ever been one of you and in all of the heartbeats of the infinite Creator, in all the creations stretching into infinity, there will never be another you. You are precious beyond telling to the infinite One because you have come through eons of form and experience to reach the richness and the variety of the mystery of you that you now experience; not precisely as your identity but as that upon which your identity within this incarnation stands. For you are so much more than this local experience, this lifetime, this personhood.

We see you as glowing crystals, instruments through which the Creator moves, playing Its tunes, Its joyful songs, Its mournful hymns and all of the thousand, thousand songs of being. And we hear you. We hear the wind of spirit move through you. We hear the song you sing, and we stand in awe of the beauty of that song and the poignancy of the heart that sings that song. We see you glow with the colors of energy touched by the myriad momentary experiences which are shaping you at this time. And we rest in that light and we drink of the richness of the beauty that you represent. You are a face of the Creator that has never been seen before and will never be seen again. You have a reality beyond any expression, beyond any response. You are beyond our laughter and our tears; beyond our appreciation or our admiration. You escape us. Each entity that is part of the Creator overflows any way we might have of grasping or understanding you. You are too much. Any limit we might think to put on your identities is folly, for you will exceed it—carelessly, casually or earnestly and intentionally. You cannot help being more than you could ever imagine and know. This is the essence of you, as we understand souls. There is no holding you, there is no limiting you, there is truly no instructing you or guiding you. There is only appreciating the face of the Creator as you express the beingness of your nature.

Each of you moved into the pattern in which you are now dancing for very good reasons. Each of you entered this particular incarnation with fairly coherent plans for service and for learning. Each of you stood as on the brink of a great abyss and planned. You packed, shall we say, a personality; you packed the baggage that you needed. Some of you packed with immense generosity and no concern whatsoever in the fate of redcaps in your wake, towing valise upon valise of personality traits and quirks. Others of you chose to pack just a bag or a backpack: a simple, stable, structure of life seeing as being needed, a straightforward personality—not too much baggage, not too much to burden the soul as it takes on this experience. But whatever you packed, in the way of a personality shell, you put those things in your suitcases because you felt that they were what you would need in order to mine the

riches that you had prepared for yourself. And you did see yourself as a miner as you came into this lifetime. You buried your luggage within yourself, within the form of body, of face, name, history, parents, upbringing. You chose that carefully. And so you leapt into the abyss of incarnation, the archetypical fool, walking by faith and not by sight, jumping into the mystery.

What did you hope but that you would be ultimately and egregiously confused? Some of you packed more of that confusion than others. For some of you it took years and years of incarnation just to discover that you were not who you thought you were. Others of you came through from the word go, from the birth, knowing that you were not what those about you were attempting to tell you that you were. Whatever your beginnings, each of you in this circle of seeking has reached a point of incarnation where the ground has become level and the playing field is seen. Each acknowledges the mystery of selfhood. Each sees the self as a player of a certain kind of game. It is not a game of gain, but it is a gamble. Hands are dealt in this game and you play the cards which you were dealt. And you get to choose how you shall play those cards. You cannot choose the cards, yet you may shape the game by the way you play. The object of the game is an increase in awareness and the question with which you come to us this day regards how you can evaluate the kind of game that you are playing—to know whether that game is the appropriate one for you at this time; appropriate in terms of learning and in terms of service. For these were your twin goals upon taking life and breath and body.

How you burned to learn more about your true nature! You came into incarnation with certain prejudices concerning yourself. In your biased opinion you felt a better balance might be needed in one or another sense, in one or another phase of life and all that it has to offer. In your energy body you carried those biases and those hopes. This instrument is familiar with a seven-chakra body system so we may say that your incarnational lessons are scattered among those seven chakras and those seven ways of seeing energy. How do you deal with survival? That's the red ray. How do you deal with personal relationships? Orange ray. How do you deal with legal groups and responsibilities such as jobs, marriages, families? That's yellow ray. How do you work within your heart to open it and to become more fully the loving entity that you are by your very nature? That's green ray. How can you communicate and relate in terms of soul to soul? That's blue ray. How can you relate to the infinite Creator within yourself, within all of creation, and within the Creator itself? That is indigo ray. And who are you, really? That is violet ray. Each of you has unique incarnational lessons that you have asked yourself by the very way that you are built; by the very way that you tend to think. Each of you has biases you encounter again and again, biases which are unique to you. Again, these are gifts of the self to the self, gifts to be unwrapped at leisure and pondered through the years and the decades of an incarnation. This is the raw material[6] of your particular mystery. And that is the self before it meets the world that spins within your mind and before your eyes.

The one known as Julian of Norwich said it very simply. She is recalled by this instrument to have said, "All things are well. All things are well. All manner of things shall be well." And this is your matrix. You live in a creation in which you cannot put a step wrong. You cannot make a mistake. On the level of souls, you are immune to error. For there is nowhere to step that is outside of the creation. There are no choices to make that place you outside the ken of your guidance. You cannot choose wrongly, however. In a universe of infinite possibilities each choice that you make redefines your universe. Consequently, it is not a simple thing to determine right action and right choices for the self.

Let us look at the concept of forms. A pottery bowl is a form. Its function is to be empty. That which you take in fills that bowl in a certain way. Each of you may think of the self, the physical body, as a form. And, indeed, there is value in expressing yourself at the very basic level of physical form. How you express yourself involves the way you cut your hair, the decorations that you might wear, the clothes that you place upon your body, the garments that you choose, the colors, and the fabrics. All of these things enter into creating yourself as a picture or an image. You have spoken somewhat of mirrors and the way that entities around you are showing you aspects of yourself that you either like or of which you disapprove. Yet you realize that all of those images are you. It is very instructive sometimes

simply to look at oneself closely in the mirror, not at the image but into the image. And if you look closely, for instance, you might begin to see different faces move across your face as all of the forms that you have taken as a soul in various lifetimes begin to roll past your mind's eye. Or you might look into the eyes that are looking at you in the mirror and begin to see the infinity that lies within that form of physical body.

Habits and ways of life are also forms, bowls into which you are able to put your catalyst and brew your experience. Are you a shallow, wide bowl that picks up a great deal but at not a great deal of depth? Or are you a narrow, deep vase that can be filled with a great deal of water and go very, very deep but not terribly wide? Or has your eye for beauty caused you to become an amphora or some form of ewer in which there is shape and flow and pattern? What is the characteristic shape of your thoughts as you process from the inception of a thought about your day, your nature, or your choices? What is the shape, what is the form that that process takes within you? Are you satisfied with it? Do you have a sense of that deep content of which the one known as J was speaking, where the form of the life, the thoughts, the process are such good, stout helpers and are serving so well that there is no need sensed by the self to institute the breakage of the old form or the creation of a new one? Or are you in a situation where, as the one known as T said, there is a real question as to whether some parts of this form need to be broken and a new shape of thought and choice selected? Wherever you are, you are, as many have said within this circle, in the perfect position for this particular moment in your incarnation. Things are going well, however it may feel on the outside, that surface that the world knows as consensus reality.

We are aware that it is not helpful to the conscious mind that so much remains a mystery. It is often desired that the whole be known, that the pattern be clear, that the choices be laid out, analyzable, gettable, sensible, rational, and yet, you are not those things, for that would limit you far too much. And so those hopes of a simple solution, a clear and obvious answer to whatever questions you have, are thoughts that are not going to be rewarded by manifestation. You do remain a mystery and your choices do remain choices made by faith and not by sight. You cannot see to the end of your path You cannot figure out even one day in the future, much

---

[6] Carla: Ra Material!

less the burden of the remainder of your incarnation and all of its hopes for learning and for service.

And so you are thrown back upon your own senses, those senses that elude rationalization. This instrument often uses the term "resonance," and we find that it is a useful term because it expresses that for which we would wish you to search when you are asking yourself about the choices before you. The world says, do what is right. And yet, what is right for one entity at one moment will not be right for that entity [at another,] and will never be right for another entity even if it is [at] the same moment. Truth, reality and essence are endlessly subjective.

It is very helpful for you to begin to trust yourself, not because you know anything but because you are who you are. This is your material. This is your gift. What you make of yourself within this lifetime will only show a little bit on the surface of consensus reality. Your work, your interactions with others on the conscious level, all of those things that create fame and fortune and give a sense of power and validity, are but hair growing from the head of someone whose mind and heart are infinite. What you can express of yourself is a tiny portion of what you are actually doing here and what you are actually giving to yourself, to those around you, and to the infinite Creator as you live your life. It is hard for us to express just how little of your essence ever comes through into those things that the world values, those things you do—your career, your reputation, your doings—and how incredibly much of your essence escapes any such shallow manifestation and remains part of the dance of creation, part of the pattern of the Creator that is being woven and rewoven in an endless creation of tapestry as moments march on in consensus reality and your very short, very action-packed incarnation ticks away. You have all the time in the world, quite literally, and yet your time is very short. You are a paradox and you live a paradox.

How to value the forms, the things with which you shape your life, is as subjective and personal and intimate as what scent you prefer, what color you choose to wear, how you choose to express yourself. When you come to look upon an issue, then, your safest route is in trusting the self and looking for resonance. This instrument was saying earlier, apropos of a question about when one's limit has been reached, that, in her experience, the limits that she had reached and overstepped were not those that

she decided upon but those times when she realized that her nature had already made that choice for her and she was just getting the results of that election. It is not enough to feel that one is doing the right thing. It must also be, as one gazes at that thing, that one senses into it with a sense of resonance, a sense that this is alive for me.

For you see, forms can die while the life within the form still exists. Form in the sense of a ritual, for instance, is something that those entities who choose to play the card of religion will experience changing time and again. For within a religion, the forms do not change, but the way that an entity relates to those forms can change completely, so that in one moment, a form of expression of devotion to the one infinite Creator may be a source of tremendous comfort whereas in another moment, it may seem to be hollow and dead. And it is very important to listen to the self as it reacts to the form, not asking the self, "How can I relate to this wonderful form?" but rather asking the self, "How can this wonderful entity that I am find resonance in this form?" And if that form has no resonance, than it needs to be let go and another one chosen. Or, in some cases, it is a matter of waiting for another kind of form, another kind of ritual of living to form itself to you as you simply exist within the mystery of your own, often contradictory, feelings.

The one known as V was teasing earlier by saying that our answer is always meditation when it comes to [your asking us,] "How do I contact that part of myself that says this is resonant and that is not?" And we completely acknowledge the justness of her teasing. It is true that so often we simply ask you to meditate. And we would talk about that a minute because there is a substantive point to be made here. We are not going for a form of meditation when we suggest that you meditate. What we are attempting to do is lift you from form. Silence is an absence of form. Entities can create form for the silence by saying, "Well, I meet the silence in this and this way." And that may be Zen meditation, walking meditation, contemplation, visualization and so forth. We are attempting to help you lift away from the prisons that you create when you lean on form to the exclusion of observing the contents that that form is holding. In so many ways, you are seduced time and again by the more subtle forms of non-physical formation, ritual and habit.

How to lift entities away from that? In many cultures, instead of entering silence the practice of mystics is to enter rhythm by chanting, whirling and dancing. Repetitive movements, repetitive sounds, repetitive tones are things that will batter and finally break the habit of thought. Whether you are drawn to entering the formless by simply sitting down and stopping talking, by designing a particular kind of silence, or by entering into the chanting or other ritual which takes one out of oneself by out-talking the talker, is completely a matter of your own discernment. But the job that you face when you attempt to disconnect yourself from form is to get past the lions at the gate of your temple, that is, your heart. Those guardians do not want you inside if you are still of the world. They do not want you inside your precious heart still grumbling, worried, bargaining, rationalizing, justifying or worried about being right. There are many teachings …

(Side one of tape ends.)

(Carla channeling)

… of bringing oneself to one's own knees outside the door of the heart and laying it all down: every idea, every concept of self, every vestige of, "I did this," and, "I thought that," and, "I'm right"— emptying the self and becoming truly able to receive. However you get there, get there before you enter the sacred space of your own heart. For there the Creator awaits you, full of love, full of Its own nature, which is your nature as well, waiting to enfold you in the embrace of absolute and unconditional adoration and devotion.

The one known as D often says at the end of a reading, "You are loved more than you can ever possibly imagine." And this is true. Can you feel, as we speak about it, the quality and the abundance of that love? Can you sense into how justified and how completely approved of you are? You have no faults that are not forgiven, no perceived imperfections that the Creator does not see as balanced. Whatever your suffering, whatever the quandaries before you at this time, whatever those dreams are that you have not yet come into the experience of receiving, they are as nothing to the one infinite Creator. We hope that it is against that backdrop that you may stand and observe the issues before you in consensus reality. If you can gain a sense of the depth of the stability of your essence, you will know that your feet are in rich and substantial ground, ground that

will not move beneath your feet regardless of how many times everything disappears from beneath your feet within that shallow, manifested world of consensus reality. You will know that disasters and troubles and woes are indeed real in that shallow sense but they are backed up by a part of yourself that is larger and more substantial than that thin stream of event of catalyst and experience.

As you meet these woes, troubles and issues, do your best to continue seeing yourself as that crystalline entity that we described to you and know that all things are well, all things are well, and all manner of things shall be well.

We would at this time open the questioning to any further queries that you may have at this time.

J: Yes, Q'uo, this is J, and it's great to be in your energy. I was wondering if there was anything that I or anyone else in this room can do to help make this instrument more comfortable?

We are those of Q'uo, and are aware of your query, my sister. Indeed, each within this group has the capacity to aid this instrument in one way or another, as this instrument has the capacity to aid each within this group. May you enjoy the process of finding ways to serve each other and know that in all things there is reciprocity and balance. We thank the one known as J for this generous query and would encourage each within this circle to be aware of the many ways in which you are uniquely oriented to help and support those around you. What is your nature? What are your gifts? As you interact with those loving presences that are in your midst, you will find ever new ways to enhance the experience of the group of which you are a part.

May we answer you further, my sister?

J: I believe that each of us comes in on a different ray, one through seven, and I was wondering if you could tell me which ray it is that I came in on?

We are those of Q'uo, and are aware of your query, my sister. We find that responding to this query would be to infringe upon your free will and we apologize for giving that answer.

Is there another query at this time?

J: No, not at this time, thank you, Q'uo.

Is there another query at this time?

R: I have a question, Q'uo, from someone who can't be here but asks the following question which is somewhat specific, so I ask for forbearance if you cannot answer, but comments would be appreciated on this topic. Are migraine headaches connected to psychic greetings in any way?

We are those of Q'uo, and are aware of your query, my brother. As it happens we are able to respond to that query because of the way it was asked. Everything that one experiences can have a relationship to psychic greeting. Psychic greeting, as we understand this term, is a way of describing the experience of receiving resistance and the experience is often understood by an entity as being a kind of attack by another entity that is unseen. In actuality, greetings occur all the time because of the distortions which pull various parts of the energy body away from complete balance. For instance, with this instrument, it frequently receives physical discomfort because of its many physical distortions over decades of experiencing the process of a disease called rheumatoid arthritis. Because of the fact that various bones and joints and so forth have become distorted, they can be energized to ache more than they did before. The question that we would put to the one known as G, who, indeed, this instrument knows asked that question, would be, "Is it more helpful to think of a negative, unseen entity energizing a physical distortion within the vascular system which would cause the headaches? Or is it more helpful to realize that there is resistance because of distortions within the being?" If one projects to an outside entity the role of persecutor or attacker, then one, in a way, cheats oneself of the chance to come face to face with the shadow self. Is it more helpful to see oneself as a being which is meeting resistance from an enemy? Or is it more helpful to see the self as a being which is experiencing resistance from its shadow self? We would encourage any who experience the seeming energizing of a previous distortion [to perceive it] as a signal that suggests you take a good look at what is going on in the process of evolution, as you understand yourself and your situation and your process. This never departs entirely from mystery. The mists may clear, briefly, and one may have realizations and epiphanies concerning the self and the process, but the process is ongoing and the mists will again surround one. And those shadows will come out of that mist and impinge upon one. The question hopefully remains, "What is the message that such shadows bring? And, how may I respond well to that message?"

Is there another query at this time?

G: Q'uo, I have one. In the Law of One series, Ra is speaking of kundalini and cautions that, to attempt to raise the locus, which is defined as the meeting place between the inner and cosmic forces, to attempt to raise that locus without an understanding or awareness of the metaphysical principles of magnetism is to invite great imbalance. I was wondering if you could define more clearly what those metaphysical principles of magnetism are?

We are those of Q'uo, and are aware of your query, my brother. We look for a way to discuss this with you without impinging upon your process and do not find one and for that we do apologize. We would like to speak with you further. We would ask if you would perhaps move back into your studies, contemplate a bit more, and see what you could do to ask the question a different way. More help than that we cannot be and do again apologize.

Is there a final query at this time?

R: You are invited to stay for tea and cookies afterwards, Q'uo.

We are those of Q'uo, and are aware of your invitation, my brother, and we assure that we always stay for tea and cookies. And, indeed, into the night and into the next morning. You can get rid of us if you ask us to leave! We are devoted to this group and to each within it and you have only to request our presence for us to be with you.

Since we seem to have exhausted the questions at this time, we leave each of you as we found you, in the unity of the house of the Creator, the love and the light, the spirit and the form that is all that there is. We are those of Q'uo. Adonai. ❧

L/L Research is a subsidiary of
Rock Creek Research &
Development Laboratories, Inc.

P.O. Box 5195
Louisville, KY 40255-0195

L/L Research

www.llresearch.org

Rock Creek is a non-profit
corporation dedicated to
discovering and sharing
information which may aid in
the spiritual evolution of
humankind.

Sunday Meditation
November 28, 2004

Group question: The question today has to do with the relationship between love and fear. We are told that there is a relationship and that if we can learn how to [find the] balance in this relationship, that we can help love to overcome fear. Could Q'uo tell us the relationship between love and fear?

(Carla channeling)

We are those of the principle known to you as Q'uo, and we greet you in the love and in the light of the one infinite Creator, in Whose service we come to you this day. It is a privilege and a blessing for us to be called to your circle of seeking to offer our thoughts on the relationship between love and fear. We thank you for this privilege and would ask of you that you use your discrimination in listening to our thoughts, being sure not to take up any thought of ours with which you do not completely resonate. For not all of our thoughts will hit the mark. We ask you to be very careful to leave behind any thoughts that you do not particularly care for. This will enable us to share our thoughts freely without being concerned that we are infringing on your free will or disturbing the rhythm and rightness of your own process. We thank you for this consideration.

The query that you ask this day is at the heart of the movement from your present third-density world and experience to the fourth-density world of love. You dwell at this time in a density that is attempting to learn what it is to love unconditionally. In the next density, the density of love and understanding,

the atmosphere is one of unconditional love. It may seem to be paradise, standing in third density and thinking about living in unconditional love. And certainly, relatively speaking, it is paradise to dwell consciously in the atmosphere of total acceptance. However, the interplay betwixt love and fear continues in fourth density as the shadows, those shadows that you now experience in third density, are penetrated. That dynamic continues because, as light is brought into the darkness, it reveals more subtle patterns of shadow and light, so that the dynamic continues and deepens. As you move forward in the process of spiritual evolution, you will find yourself continuing to uncover areas that were previously unknown to you within the very complex pattern of your total personality. So this is not a question that will go away as you learn more. It is a question that will deepen and intensify, for there is no end to the mystery of this dynamic between love and fear.

In the world of ideas, qualities like love and fear are entities. To put a face and a body to love is perhaps to imagine a feminine figure, loving and maternal, with open arms and an open heart and a willingness to embrace. To put a face and a body to fear is perhaps to imagine a male figure clad in an enveloping cloak in which are gathered all of the treasures that this figure is attempting to hold tightly to himself. We describe them in this way for two reasons: firstly we wish to spark your own imagination, for it is instructive to think upon what love looks like to you and what fear looks like. But also we describe them in this fashion because there is a natural dynamic betwixt the feminine and the male principles and in the yin, or feminine, aspect, there is the expansiveness, the generosity, and that quality of unconditional love that is personified, say, in the image of Mother Mary, the Madonna, or Quan Yin, or Mother Earth, or mother nature. In the yang or male aspect of creation as a whole, there is the flexing of muscle and the contracting around ideals and ideas and those ideologies that give rise to action. We have said before that your culture, as a whole, is overbalanced towards the male principle and has, as this instrument would put it, gotten stuck in a repetitive cycle of male energy that is aggressive and, in many ways, based upon fear and the determination to respond to that fear by acquiring and controlling resources and power. Those who are in power within your various nation-states have many good reasons for these aggressions, these acquisitions, and this use of power, saying that is for the benefit of all. And yet, if one examines the heart of such concepts, the energy is wrapped up in fear and in contraction. So the surface of your culture is caught in that contracted state where there is a constant concern for safety and security and a constant quest for having sufficient resources to meet the future.

(The telephone answering machine is heard.)

(Carla channeling)

We are those of Q'uo, and are again with this instrument. We apologize for this delay; however, this instrument was distracted by the telephone message.

The ways of fear are insidious and they have become established within your culture to the point that the natural responses of most entities to the needs of the individual or the society are almost instinctively contracted and fear-based. There is little or no precedent within your leaders or within your role models for gazing at a situation in terms of trust, faith or love but rather an almost inevitable bias towards gazing at a situation from the standpoint of concern, worry, projection into the future, and contraction around these concerns and worries and projections. It is a time for your peoples which expresses the energy of that stuck, male domination. And we do not mean this in terms of sexuality, for many are the men among your peoples who are very

able to express feminine energy in their thinking and their actions and many are the female entities at this time who are experiencing their incarnations from the standpoint of fear and contraction. We speak instead of the dynamic betwixt yin and yang. The question then becomes how to free both men and women from the strictures and the limitations of the masculine viewpoint.

When you think about how it feels to be fearful, perhaps you may see that, involved in most experiences of fear-based thought, there is the habit of projection into the future. The one known as T2 and the one known as Jim were both speaking earlier of thinking ahead to jobs that need to be done or conversations that need to be held or situations that may arise. And the one known as Jim was speaking of the difference between positive projecting and negative projecting. In the sense of positive projection into the future, there is no projecting beyond what could be called architectural or structural projection. And we would offer the example that the one known as Jim has often given of how this entity would prepare for a pole vault during the field games of his school days by imagining and visualizing, with great integrity of detail, every step of running with the pole to the point where the pole was planted and the body weight was levered and lifted and the pole was allowed to lift the body up over the bar and then the rotation would be imagined and the successful dismount. And this entity would repeat this visualization, say, before going to bed and upon awakening, those times when he was most able to be in a very magical and focused frame of mind, so that by the time the one known as Jim came to the actual games and was ready to make his pole vault, he was relaxed and confident, having done this pole vault many times in his imagination. This is positive projection.

Negative projection, on the other hand, is far easier to describe because each of those in this circle of seeking has had the conversations in the mind that will be difficult or are expected to be difficult, and has experienced that repetition of thought where one begins to think, "Well, what if something happens, then what shall I say?" And then [one continues] thinking in a circular way again, "Well, what if this happens, then what shall I do?" simply riding that cycle around a circular course, again and again. In truth, such imaginings do not improve the way that such a conversation will actually go, because there is not simply the self involved in the equation but also the other self. And no matter how many imaginings one has done about what people will say, in the actual conversation, there is always a new and unique twist to how things turn out. And all of the vain imaginings fall away before the actual person and the actual conversation. Perhaps the most tragic outcome of such vain, circular imaginings would be that one renders oneself incapable of hearing the actual conversation because one has been deafened by one's expectations.

We would not discourage entities from looking into the future when it seems appropriate. What we would encourage, however, is the choice of positive projection, of imaging the graceful and efficient way to do something that needs to be done, imagining only your own actions and seeing them as completely successful. This is an excellent way to create positive expectation and a sense of confidence within yourself. The one known as Carla, who is the instrument at this session, was speaking earlier of how she could not see a way to complete her tasks in the situation in which she finds herself. This is because she is not able to use positive visualization, since she does not know what she can expect from herself. When there is a vacuum in a positive situation, it is very tempting to substitute negative projection and simply worry and be concerned about how the future will pan out.

We would simply suggest that, unless the concern is turned from worry into a dispassionate and calm review of possibilities for solutions, innovations that may improve the picture and so forth, there is no positive or constructive use for the worry. It is difficult simply to take one's worry and concern and lay it down. Yet, indeed, that would be our suggestion. Realize that fear has come to visit and has offered you a gift. Whether it is wrapped up in a plain brown paper bag or whether it is gift-wrapped and has a pretty ribbon, as concern sometimes has, it is, nevertheless, a package of fear. Such packages do not need to be opened. They can be laid aside and neglected while you, having rejected the fear, simply move onto other thoughts and concerns.

The one known as R was saying earlier that it is difficult to see how love and fear are two sides of the same coin. We began speaking of love and fear as entities, qualities in the Platonic sense, the world of

ideas.[7] And this is a very valid and real world where love and fear do indeed have infinite and ever-ongoing lives, as long as they are reflected in the hearts and the minds of those moving through the illusion of incarnation. However, it is easier to see the relationship between love and fear if we move from contemplating love and fear as pure entities and look at them as applied in the lives of each of you, so that they are not entities upon their own but they are rather a dynamic of choices between which you may choose as you encounter catalyst and find yourself making a choice. When you come to a cusp and are looking at an issue that is yours to look at, whether it is the right use of time, the right use of resources such as money, or any other issue, you come to the issue in some state of imbalance or bias. This instrument was speaking of her own fears earlier when she said that she had, consciously, to choose to substitute faith for fear. She had, consciously, to realize that all is well and perfect and when she did that, she made a new reality in which fear had no part.

The coin itself, with love on one side and fear on the other, is you yourself and what you think is important. You are the treasure here. You are the coin of the realm, shall we say. You are a thing of infinite value and when you have a concern, if you reach, with hope and trust and faith, you are reaching into the qualities of love. If instead you approach your issue by contracting into worry and projection, then your choice is fear. Shall you expand around an issue or shall you contract around an issue? That is your choice. Note that the energies of expansion are locked into the present moment. They do not drift into projections of the future or memories of the past. In the world of love, one begins with the knowledge that all is well. And this pulls one into focus in the center of the present moment. In truth, as we said earlier, it almost seems negligent or criminal within the society in which you find yourself to approach issues from a standpoint of love. It does not seem to be prudent or sensible to stay in the present moment and yet anything but the present moment is an illusion of mind. All that is truly yours to do with, to exert control over, or to make choices within is this present moment.

---

[7] Plato, a Greek philosopher writing about 400 BCE, suggested that there is a world of ideas which exists as a reality apart from our "shadow world" of consensus reality, and from which our consensus reality depends, though imperfectly realized.

So if you take that image of the self in the present moment as the coin and look to see what the heads and tails of that coin are, archetypically speaking it is very clear and shining in its simplicity. On one side is love, on the other side is fear. On the one side is expansion into an infinite present with infinite possibilities; on the other side is contraction into a knot and the determination that stems from that contraction to control, to be aggressive, and to make things safe. And this involves one in endless projections into the future and endless projections into the past in order to justify the projections into the future.

When one visits in a hospital, one may well be able to sense the presence of a kind of dark energy that seems somehow to be a part of the atmosphere of this place of supposed healing. This is because there are unseen entities from your inner planes that are negative in nature and that feed upon fear and pain. In any place where there is suffering, these entities will cluster and eat that energy that is coming off of the people that are suffering. When you yourself enter into the contraction around fear concerning an issue, you are, yourself, producing food that is very tasty for these unseen entities. And if your habit solidifies and deepens, so that you are constantly running fear-based thoughts and dwelling in the lands of worry and projection into an unsightly and worrisome future, you are solidifying a habit that will increasingly limit your ability to relax and enjoy the present moment.

To move away from these habits of contraction is to move from shadow into sunlight. We do not say that this journey from shadow to sunlight is going to be an easy one. It flies in the face of your cultural training to rely on trust and faith. There are many, many times in each day when you have the opportunity to move into worry. We can only encourage you to do as the known as T2 said, to remain somewhat centered and focused, more so than your everyday state; to be somewhat in a meditative state as you move through the moments of your day. For it is just in these tiny moments that the opportunities to make the choice between love and fear appear. The challenge is to be aware, when those moments arrive, so that you can stop yourself from being triggered into fear and the contraction around fear.

We are not encouraging you to lose all fear in dangerous situations. We are not encouraging you to stop steering your car away from an oncoming vehicle simply because you are not afraid. We would encourage you to avoid the oncoming vehicle, certainly. It is at the level of being concerned the next time you get in your vehicle that this will happen again, that we encourage you to choose to trust the moment and not to project into an uncertain future. At this moment all is well and if you must look into the future then look with hope. Think to yourself, I might be surprised at how well this will go. Visualize positively, if you must go into the future and whenever possible we encourage you to remain at peace and at rest and very alert and watchful for the universe is speaking to you.

One concept we would share with you in this regard is wrapped up in a phrase that this instrument knows from her study of the Holy Bible. It is a quote, "Be not afraid, for help is near." Help is always very near. The spirit is with you at all times and in all places, nearer to you than your breathing, closer to you than your eyes or your hands.[8] You are truly cherished and loved …

(Side one of tape ends.)

(Carla channeling)

… not because you have done something good, but because you are you and you are precious to the Creator.

Agents of spirit are in your heart and speaking within your mind but, more than that, all of creation is abuzz with awareness of you and your needs. Watch and see what images come to you; what animals, birds and tiny creatures cross your path that may have meaning to you and may have a message for you. Begin asking the creation around you for hints and clues. Begin expecting them and the creation will speak to you in ever-increasing ways.

This instrument is informing us that we must leave this topic and ask for other queries at this time and we shall leave you with just one more thought on this subject. The answer to this question is a part of your nature. The answer to what love is lies within you, now. For your nature is love. Love created you and you are a spark of that infinite love. In many ways, spiritual evolution is a process of allowing the

---

[8] Credit for this image may well be given to Joel Goldsmith, who used it many times, and with whose work the instrument is deeply familiar.

real you to come out of all the wrappings and cultural training and old habit. How you have been beaten down by what others have told you, how others have seen you, and so forth! Casting aside assumed wisdom is sometimes a very difficult and lengthy process. But the truth is speaking within you now; love is powerful within you now. So turn your ears inward to the silence of that heart within and listen for the footsteps of the One Who comes in love.

At this time we would open this meeting to further queries, if there are any. Is there a further question at this time?

T1: I have a question. May I speak?

We are those of Q'uo, and we encourage you to speak, my brother.

T1: We know that Q'uo is composed of three entities in the Confederation and I would like to know if there is a major speaker, speaking. Thank you.

We are those of Q'uo, and are aware of your query, my brother. We are composed, as you said, of three groups, one of fourth density, one of fifth density, and one of sixth density, in this instrument's and our way of describing our relative position and experience. This particular principle was created because this particular instrument has a certain way of tuning and preparing for contact with the Confederation entities. She prays for contact with the highest and best contact that she may handle in a stable and conscious manner. It is a very precise request. The entity whom she tended to receive upon making this prayer, prior to her contact with those of the Ra group, was the Latwii group and she had received those of Latwii fairly consistently for several years before experiencing the trance contact with those of the Ra group.

As each within this circle is aware, the contact with those of Ra was a very narrow-band contact which was only possible during that window of opportunity when the ones known as Don, Jim and Carla were all in the circle and when the one known as Don passed from this third-density experience, the possibility of further contact with this particular entity was ended. However, this instrument continued to tune and pray in the same manner and those of Latwii and others within the Confederation, including those of Hatonn and those of Ra, felt that

perhaps the creation of a principle would best respond to this instrument's very real desire for the highest and best contact of which she was capable. Since those of Ra could not speak with this instrument in a conscious and stable manner, there was no possibility for that social memory complex being the speaker. However, both those of Hatonn and those of Latwii had previously enjoyed sharing the thoughts of those of Ra in a teach/learning circle and the three groups decided that they would blend into one principle, with the ones known as Hatonn being responsible simply for projecting a vibration of love, of which I feel sure that each of you is aware as we speak. The ones known as Latwii took the responsibility for speaking to this instrument and the ones known as Ra were part of the process of defining just how to respond to the question that was presented to the principle of Q'uo. So, as those of Q'uo speak, it is those of Latwii who are creating the concepts which this instrument receives and translates into words.

May we answer you further, my brother?

T1: Thank you. A very detailed answer.

We thank you, my brother. Is there a question at this time?

T2: Yes, I had a question. Just before the other question I had again started to think as to this evening, dealing with folks that I have to deal with this evening, and immediately it popped into my head, "Please, don't focus on negative, fearful aspects of anything involved with this situation. Strictly attempt to think of the other people and what I can do to make them more comfortable with the situation." And I think my question to you is, does this thought come from you at that moment or is this a thought of my all-mind or is it some combination of both?

We are those of Q'uo, and are aware of your query, my brother. We see no difficulty or infringement in stating that the impulse of that thought came from your personal guidance but was enabled and assisted by your very recent interaction with us in that you truly entered into that which we were offering and were truly working with these ideas so that you softened the ground and enabled your ears to hear your own guidance.

May we answer you further, my brother?

T2: No, thank you very much.

We thank you, my brother. May we ask if there is a final query at this time?

T1: May I speak?

Yes.

T1: In the *Law of One* books I remember Ra told us that there is a complete transition into the fourth density in 2012. When I think of the current, chaotic war situation I wonder if this stage is delayed. I know you cannot give us the detailed dates but could you focus a little about the current situation? Thank you.

We are those of Q'uo, and we thank you, my brother, and are glad to attempt to speak to your query.

Firstly, the dating of the transition into full fourth-density energy for your planet is fixed. It is a matter of your time moving forward. Just as summer gives way to fall and fall gives way to winter, so one age gives way to another and one period of time is succeeded by another. For your particular planet and your particular solar system, there is a turning of energy, a rotation into new space/time as well as new time/space. That is inevitable and is as the ticking of the clock. This will have been accomplished just as it has been foreseen by many at the approximate date of late in the twelfth month of 2011.

So, roughly speaking, 2012 shall see the full realization, in terms of the inner planes of your planet and the time/space aspects of your planet. Fourth density, in 2012, will be your system of energy. Now, my brother, as you can well imagine, there is much energy upon your planet at this time embodied in the persons of the individuals living upon it and the societal groups and structures and governments that these people have created that will be quite inappropriately geared for welcoming fourth-density energy. As we have said, there is a habit of contraction and fear and attempt to control among your people which may well end in entities doing great damage to each other and to the planet because, faced with energies they cannot control, they may well contract themselves into the Armageddon that they so fear. We are very hopeful, however, that this will not occur. There is a growing groundswell among your peoples at the soul level of honest and deep revulsion and distaste for the energies of control and destruction.

There is a true hope among your peoples that is growing daily for the energies of love and trust and peace to come swelling up like buds opening into flowers in spring. When each of you chooses love over fear, you start something happening in the unseen worlds. You create an energy that is compatible with fourth density. Each time you choose to trust, to love, to have forbearance and compassion, to see the other person's point of view and truly walk in his shoes instead of your own, you are expanding the kingdom of fourth density right where you are. And the more people that begin consciously to do this, the faster this kingdom will expand. We say to you plainly, fourth density is all but complete. As you walk about in third density, the fourth density energy is stronger every day upon your planet. The Earth itself is vibrating largely in fourth density now. That is why so many entities are sensing the need to become closer in contact to the Earth itself, touching the ground, working with the Earth, working with plants and animals and those things that abide in the creation of the Father and have nothing to do with the world of the mind of man.

Health is abundant in the Earth itself. Its labor is ongoing but the birth is going well. Perhaps you have noticed many significant catastrophes occurring upon the Earth plane. This is the labor of Earth. It is attempting to move into fourth density without having to express, all at once, the incompatibility between third-density thought, as it exists upon the Earth at this time, and the fourth-density vibration that has been coming. It is attempting to vent the fear and the anger and the narrow-mindedness of humankind in little bits, in a volcano erupting but not so as to split the Earth, or a tsunami or a hurricane that destroys a good deal but does not destroy the globe, or an earthquake which expresses the distress of mother Earth but not in such a way as to destroy the planet as a whole.

We feel very hopeful that this grass roots upswelling from the soul level, of yearning for a world of love and peace, is powerful enough to continue to create the atmosphere in which the Earth may continue its final process of labor by venting these incompatible energies. Meanwhile you may well have noticed that there is an almost runaway experience of many within your plane at this time, of conditions such as cancer which seem to take people from their lives before their time. In many cases, these are situations in which entities have become hardened and set in their habits of thinking these habits being habitual and repetitive in terms of there being anger, fear and aggression. These entities are predisposing their physical vehicles to end the incarnation because the difficulties of dealing with such a mismatch in vibration between the third-density thought and the fourth-density incoming, unseen reality, is simply too great. You will find that there are many who depart their incarnations within the next few years because of their inability to welcome the expansive and healing vibrations of fourth density.

Contrarily, those coming into incarnation at this time are often very able to vibrate fourth-density values and ways of thinking so that as your children are growing up, they are representing individual cases where they have been more and more able to welcome fourth-density energies. They are seen by their own parents often as amazing beings and much has been spoken of these young entities, which are sometimes called Indigo Children or Crystal beings. There are many terms for them but their difference is that they have come into incarnation with some features of their fourth-density inner bodies activated as well as being activated in third density.

We would encourage you to see yourself as a secret agent of fourth density at this time. Have you heard the phrase, "Perform random acts of kindness"? This is the very essence of being a secret agent for love. The ones known as Ra long ago channeled through this instrument, "When faced with a situation, ask yourself the question, "Where is the love in this moment?" And we say to you, be an agent of that love, and be an instrument of peace. In all situations, there is at least a tiny peephole, a tiny window that lets in the light and the love of the one infinite Creator. Do what you can to find it. Make this transition into fourth density personal.

If you think in terms of world powers and world wars, you have no control and you can do no useful thing. However, that is a mental projection. You are the center of your universe and you have power. You are a magical being and you are the face of the Creator in the little place that you occupy in this vast creation. Be an agent. Be proud and happy to be an agent of the Creator and part of the creative principle. And let your light shine, let your love embrace.

May we answer you further, my brother?

T1: No, thank you. I am grateful.

We also are grateful for your heart and your question, my brother. And we thank this group as a whole for its energy and its beauty and its gift to us. We thank you for being able to share our humble thoughts with you and again we remind you to leave all thoughts behind that do not seem right to you, for we would not be a stumbling block in front of you. We are always with you if you ask for us and we leave you as we found you, in the love and in the light of the one infinite Creator. Adonai. Adonai. ☙

L/L RESEARCH

L/L Research is a subsidiary of
Rock Creek Research &
Development Laboratories, Inc.

P.O. Box 5195
Louisville, KY 40255-0195

www.llresearch.org

Rock Creek is a non-profit
corporation dedicated to
discovering and sharing
information which may aid in
the spiritual evolution of
humankind.

SUNDAY MEDITATION
DECEMBER 12, 2004

Group question: The question today has to do with the topic of psychic greetings. Many people look at just about anything that happens to them which is of what they would call a negative nature as a psychic greeting or a way of negative entities interfering in their spiritual growth. We are wondering if Q'uo could give us some information about how to determine whether or not our experience is of a psychic greeting nature. Does it matter if it is, in our overall spiritual growth? And is there anything, a ritual, a procedure, that we could use to balance the psychic greeting?

(Carla channeling)

We are those known to you as the principle of Q'uo. Greetings in the love and in the light of the one infinite Creator, in Whose service we come to you this day. We thank each of you for finding the time to form a circle of seeking and to call us to share our thoughts with you. It is a great privilege that you offer to us and we are most happy to respond with a full and grateful heart. But we would ask, as always, that each of you guard your thinking well and do not allow our thoughts to creep into your own mind and be used by you unless you honestly feel a resonance with them. If you do not feel a resonance with things that we might say, please leave them behind without a second thought. This will enable us to speak our thoughts freely without worrying about infringing upon your own free will and the sacredness of your own process of spiritual evolution.

The question that you ask this day concerning what psychic greeting is is a query that is, in a way, quite difficult to answer because the parameters of psychic greetings are, as several in the group have noted, subjective and varied. The essence of a psychic greeting is the intentionality of the greeter. Thusly, not all experienced resistance or experienced catalyst is of a psychic greeting nature. For the term to be properly used, the greeting needs to be one that is coming from a presence, whether it is an individual or a group entity. Further, this greeting has as its focus an encroachment into the energetic body rather than the physical body, in terms of its origin. So, one way of looking at psychic greeting would be a somewhat narrow and carefully delineated way in which psychic greetings are only those greetings which have been sent by an entity, most usually of the inner planes, with the intention of disrupting the process of spiritual evolution and causing an entity to stop its forward progress and to become lost in the side roads of inner questioning and suffering.

Under this definition, you may see that psychic greeting is a term that is much overused and often misused among your peoples. However, if one pulls one's focus back into looking at what your energetic bodies are and how they experience you and your thinking processes, the concept of psychic greeting may be perhaps redefined as psychic resistance and may be widened to include a wide variety of ways in which your energetic body can experience resistance, not necessarily only from entities but from the mechanism or, shall we say, the works or the machinery of the connection between space/time and time/space, as those two impinge upon the present moment and create the present moment itself, into which you come with your energetic body.

Let us look at your energetic body, for this bears some looking at in terms of working with this concept of psychic resistance. You have an energetic body that is composed, in the terms that this instrument is familiar with, of seven chakras in-body and one chakra directly above the body. And these chakras are in a coherent system. The system as a whole works only as well as the least balanced chakra, in general or large terms. In more specific applications, chakra by chakra and looking at relationships betwixt two or more chakras in a system, part of the chakra body may be working beautifully for you and may be well-balanced for you and yet, at the same time, because of over-activation or under-activation of other chakras, that particular balance may not be working for the overall best balance of the system as a whole. It is especially interesting we find, looking, for instance, as we have been invited to do, at this particular instrument's chakra system, that you do not find one chakra that is weak and the other ones strong; rather, you generally find correspondences betwixt two or even three chakras where there is an imbalance that is made up not simply of one chakra being a bit off-kilter but that chakra's imbalance shadowing or pulling at the balance of one or two other chakras. And in this instrument, we find that there are some weaknesses in both the red and the orange rays of the instrument which echo or reflect into the indigo ray and the way this works for this instrument is that there are areas of childhood pain, as this instrument was speaking of earlier, having to do with issues of survival and of the person's relationship with herself which can trigger emotions and processes which directly impinge upon and pull into deep imbalance, at least momentarily, the areas of indigo which have to do with self-worth.

For each entity, there are system-wide balances at which it is very helpful to look daily and then there are ongoing specific imbalances in specific chakras or combinations of chakras that benefit greatly from conscious contemplation and times of inner asking and challenging of the self, by the self. This is work best done by the self in solitude unless an entity has been able to create a metaphysical partnership with someone with whom there has been formed a bond of trust, so that in some cases it may be possible for two entities together to work on both chakra systems, each entity being a reflector and a mentor for the other, in finding creative ways to address the areas of suffering that have not been healed, that have come through the years within incarnation, carried as a treasure within the self, protected and cradled within the self as if these old areas of suffering were treasures too good to drop, too good to leave behind. It is worth asking the self how the self values these embedded crystals of pain and suffering. There is a great challenge involved in coming to grips with these crystalline, embedded areas of pain. The question to the self is always, "Are you ready to lay down and abandon this crystal? Is this a burden that you feel completely safe in letting go?" It may seem like a backwards question and yet this instrument is well aware of her ability to cradle and protect those pet areas of pain. How important is it to this instrument to say, "I am familiar with this area of pain. I am familiar with this kind of suffering"? There is a real difficulty in letting go of old pain. It has glueyness to it. It wants to adhere to you. Something that has repeated again and again, throughout an incarnation, takes on a life and an energy of its own. It ceases being a simple memory and instead becomes a living entity, a thought-form. Most so-called psychic greeting and also what we would call psychic resistance is generated within the individual's energy body by the entity itself at a subconscious level. Because each of these areas of embedded pain has a life of its own and an attractive ability of its own, these areas then generate signals that move into that present moment as it is breaking forth from space/time and time/space, angling for a target of opportunity. There are many layers to the present moment. There are many ways in which embedded pain can find an echo, a reflection, or a voice within the present moment. And so, some of the voices speaking to the energetic body will be those of a negative tone of voice. And that negativity will be cunningly and specifically crafted to fit into the present moment and to cause the experience of distraction or resistance.

For those who are experiencing a true psychic greeting, the entity with whom one is dancing is an outer entity whose existence does not depend upon you. For the general majority of psychic resistance that is experienced, the entity generating the resistance is the self. Does it make a difference? To the best of our ability to answer this question, the answer is no, it does not make a difference. One can call a psychic greeting the fault of an entity and respond to that entity or one can assume that, in the larger picture, all entities are the self and therefore it does not matter from where the greeting is coming but only that it is experienced as an offering to which a response is required. In the former way of looking at it, there may be a few cases, especially cases in which the identity of the psychic greeter is known, in which case it is efficient and skillful to name the greeting and say to whom it is perceived that the responsibility is due and therefore come into a time/space meeting with this individual or this group entity and, standing before the Creator, it is possible then to move into conversation with that entity and to effect a resolution. This resolution is in the form of expressions of love and gratitude for the greeting and the greeter. We note that this way of dealing with psychic greeting does not balance the greeting for the one who has originated the greeting. It however balances the greeting for you. For the most part, however, we feel that the most helpful way to look at a psychic resistance experience is to assume that stance before the Creator that we described before, where you have moved to the judgment seat, you have moved to the Creator's space, to that place where you have witnessed in spirit and where all of those who help you on unseen levels are acknowledged and thanked as witnesses. In this very metaphysical setting, you do precisely what you would do if indeed there was an entity involved: you open your heart and you invite in this area of resistance, however you are experiencing it. You acknowledge it, you look at it very carefully, not shirking or shying away from any detail but trying to plumb the depths of this greeting, of this resistance. How does it feel? What is happening to you? What energies of the chakra body does it seem to be concentrating on? What is the area that it is greeting? Where does the rubber meet the road? What is the nature of this experience? Do not rush through this part of the process because, as we said, there are many layers to experience. There are many parts of yourself and there are many vantage points from which to look at the various parts of yourself. What does red-ray resistance look like from the green-ray energy? From the blue-ray energy? What does indigo-ray and its dimming look like from green ray, from blue ray? And we focus on green ray

and blue ray because, in doing energetic work, the green ray is that great hall that is a totally sacred space. It is that house wherein you dwell, energetically. It is the doorway through which the Creator moves on an everyday, continuing basis, because it is the seat of unconditional love. This is the energy that created you. You are green-ray entities in terms of your basic nature. The stem of the flower that you are is green ray.

So, moving into this sacred space is moving into a safety zone. It is moving into a place where you are loved and where you love. You have the courage and the stamina that may be lacking in the chakra system as a whole at the moment. Moving into green ray is moving into a solid and secure place, a "gated" community, shall we say. You do have to get through your own gate! There are lions at the door of green ray. So lay aside your pride, your arrogance, and your pretensions of all kinds. Metaphysically speaking, drop to your knees, empty yourself and lay down your burdens. We wish to draw attention to this point once again because, in terms of psychic resistance it is all-important: the bravest and the hardest thing you will ever do is lay down your cross. Put it down, drop it! We do not know how to express to you the power of this decision. It is easy to make that decision in your head and say, "Yes, once and for all I lay down this burden. I will no longer be pulled off balance by this particular memory that has become an entity of childhood pain." But let an hour or a day go by and that decision made with the head alone is shuffled off into metaphysical Gehenna and a reset button is pushed somewhere deep within and that area of childhood pain is alive and well once again and angling for your next present moment.

There is a way to know when you have finally accessed a point of childhood pain in the green ray, energetically speaking. Because when you have been able to access it, to see it in all of its detail, and to lay it down, you will find yourself laughing. You will find yourself full of laughter and seeing the incredible humor of this effort. We cannot tell you in great detail how to come to that moment but we can tell you where to start: opening to your own pain, coming to know it—its heft, its shape, its density, its color, and most of all its texture within your life.

We suggest working with these energies from the blue-ray standpoint as well because calling upon the energies of blue ray is calling upon clear and honest communication. How do you communicate with yourself? Do you feel that you do a good job of communicating? Is there an edge to your communication with yourself? There usually are many edges to the way entities communicate with themselves; many ways in which the point of view is not straight-ahead but has a slant, an angle, or an edge to it so that perhaps you are not seeing a good picture. The power of blue ray, when called upon and asked in deep humility to come into your experience, is that power to throw light on a situation in such a way that you can see where you have an edge, where you have an angle, so that you are, perhaps, cheating yourself of a full and clear view of what your situation is.

When you have laid down your burden and said, "Yes, I give this back to the infinite," then there is that moment of embrace, of acceptance of the self as it was, as it is, and as you have every high hope that it will be. This is a heartbreak to do in terms of an entity feeling that he has made progress. It is very difficult to feel that one has indeed made progress [when] working with psychic resistance, because there is nothing that is "out there." It is all going on within the inner processes of the self. So there is no way to check against some objective standard and say, "Well, I have achieved Point 1 and Point 2; I am now on Point 3, and I am progressing through this process and at the end of it I will have succeeded." As most entities upon your surface experience, and as certainly those within this circle experience, the greeting is dealt with for the moment and then, at the next opportunity, it simply resurfaces and the work is there to do all over again.

We would encourage each of you not to be discouraged at the apparently cyclical nature of psychic resistance. Try to understand about yourself the multi-level nature of your being. You can find those pockets of pain and empty them and not realize that there is yet a deeper level from which that pocket of pain is being filled so that one pocket full of pain is found and emptied but that hollow remains within the energetic web, functioning as a kind of attractant hole into which more content is poured from those dark places that have not yet been found deep within the self. Some places of pain there are within the energetic body which cannot even be found doing work consciously because they were never experienced consciously. These include areas

of pain that were deliberately brought into the incarnation from previously unbalanced incarnations, and pain to which the unborn child was subjected prior to physical incarnation but not prior to metaphysical incarnation. Of such pain there is no actual memory because those processes of memory do not properly begin until the entity is breathing the air and has formally embarked upon the incarnation.

So it is as though there are springs of pain within you that come from so deep underground within your nature that you cannot root them out. And, for most entities, in one or two cases at least, these springs can be expected to function throughout the incarnation. It is to be noted that in these cases there is a purpose and a use for the work that must be done in response to these experiences of the pain springing forth from these deep fountains within. About suffering in general we may say that it is a part of the "refining fire" that this instrument is used to calling the incarnation. An incarnation for one who is attempting to learn does partake of the pain of that learning. Before incarnation this was understood by you and accepted. The reason for this careless and seemingly casual acceptance of future pain was that from before incarnation or from after incarnation, gazing into incarnation and knowing the full spectrum of the Creator and the nature of creation and of the process that one is embracing in coming into incarnation, it seemed like child's play. It seemed so obvious that there would be these moments of challenge and certainly there would be discomfort but there would always be this knowledge of the way things really are.

It is very difficult from beyond incarnation to believe it possible to forget the true nature of the self and the creation. And yet, memory is the first thing that goes at the beginning of an incarnation. Your incarnation is protected from your own knowledge so that it can be very real to you and it can have the effect that it is supposed to have and that you are hoping that it will have. However, from within incarnation, this is not a comforting thought. From within incarnation, you simply want the pain to go away and yet the pain of living is part and parcel of the experience of drawing breath.

There is a road. This instrument is steeped in the Christian traditions and so she thinks of this road as the King's Highway. Others might think of it as the Great Way or the Tao. The one know as R was saying earlier that there is protection for those working on spiritual process. This is true. However, the protection must be claimed and the work that we have been describing is done before that claiming can take place. The price of admittance to that road is the laying down of all burdens and the taking on of your own truth. In taking on your own truth, you are taking on a self that is perfect, not in the sense of doing nothing wrong, but in the sense of being one with the infinite Creator. The act of laying down and leaving behind the worldly self is key. Once you have lain down your burdens, once you have let your personality go, your sense of justification and rightness and all of those details of self, you come into a consciousness that is real, a consciousness that is yours now and tomorrow and forever. And once you have that self as your significant self, you cannot be moved from the road. It truly is the "royal road"[9] and when you are on it, you are one with all; all that you may perceive as those whom you wish to help, all that you may perceive of as those from whom you wish to learn, all entities, qualities and aspects of the Creator whatsoever. And you are all on this road together. You are in harmony; you are dancing, you are singing, and the movement is rhythmic and right. And you are part of the entire creation, wheeling in joy and opening up the infinite night to the light of stars.

(Side one of tape ends.)

(Carla channeling)

And on this royal road, one foot moving in front of the other is as the thunder of a mighty stallion or the beat of wings of a mighty eagle that is soaring high above the Earth and gazing with power and knowledge upon all that he sees. There is that feeling of being able to make strides upon that road and you are truly, as you dance with spirit, creating an ever more indelible impression of yourself that functions as a memory, so that you are more able to move into this space within yourself, where you feel your essence, the next time. It even begins to become a relief to drop the worldly details and to lay down

those burdens. But this is something that only occurs with a great deal of practice. This entity is thinking to herself how poorly she accomplishes this as she attempts to balance herself and to dance within her own experience, and yet, we say that each of you is doing excellent work. One cannot judge the self. That is not useful in terms of working with the energetic body.

If you look at this question from the intellectual or mindful level, it will be a party game for you, something that is enjoyable to think about, but there will be no solution. It is from the level of the heart and that alone that this psychic resistance may be dealt with in a useful and skillful way.

Part of your query that we would like to touch upon before we open the meeting to questions is whether there is some ritual that one may go through in order to halt the advance of psychic greeting or psychic resistance. And as we have suggested before, there is value to images and icons. What is your image of unconditional love? What image has power for you? This instrument has a tendency to say a one-word prayer, that word being, "Jesus." She does this with intention. The intention is to move into the mind and the heart of Jesus, to move into unconditional love itself. So, in seeing the name of this icon, this instrument pulls a vibration from memory into use and that vibration is every experience that she has had wherein she was able to rest in unconditional love, having prayed that prayer.

Prayer is an intensely intimate, personal activity and we cannot suggest to you what your icon for unconditional love should be. We can only suggest that you develop one, if you do not have one, and then that you use it with intention, being willing, when you start with that icon and that image, to sit with it until it has done its work in you so that when you open your eyes, you are seeing with the eyes of that icon. This is deep work and not to be undertaken lightly. But we believe that, in terms of instantaneous change, the use of icons and images in the mind is a good way to create changes in consciousness at will, this being the definition of one who does magic. Be a magical person. Call upon the magician within yourself and create for yourself the world in which you choose to live.

As always, spirit, in many ways, is there to help you. And we ourselves, if you wish to call upon our energies, will be there if you but think of us and ask

---

[9] This phrase has reflections back into the Christian work of Thomas à Kempis, who wrote material entitled The Royal Road, about the phrase, "Take up your cross and follow Me," and also into the study of the archetypical mind through the Tarot. The court cards of the Tarot can be considered a "royal road." Therefore, the implication of the use of this phrase is that working with this type of resistance is working with the archetypical mind.

us for your help. We thank you for this question and at this time would move into opening the meeting to further queries. Is there a question at this time?

(Pause)

We are those of Q'uo, and we find that the energy is indeed low and that the queries are, for the present, at an end. And so we thank each of you again and leave you, as we found you, in the love and in the light of the one infinite Creator. We are known to you as those of Q'uo. Adonai, my friends. Adonai. ❧

YEAR 2005

JANUARY 1, 2005 TO DECEMBER 19, 2005

L/L Research

L/L Research is a subsidiary of
Rock Creek Research &
Development Laboratories, Inc.

P.O. Box 5195
Louisville, KY 40255-0195

www.llresearch.org

Rock Creek is a non-profit
corporation dedicated to
discovering and sharing
information which may aid in
the spiritual evolution of
humankind.

SUNDAY MEDITATION
JANUARY 2, 2005

Group question: The question today has to do with the catastrophe that occurred a week ago this morning in south Asia. Ra has mentioned that during the transition into the fourth density, the Earth would be releasing heat, the pent-up heat of the anger, war and disharmony that has been so prevalent on this planet for most of its recorded history, human history. We're wondering if this earthquake and tsunami in south Asia is simply a part of that releasing of the heat? Is it a significant event that might signal a certain portion of this releasing of heat is completed? Could Q'uo give us an idea of what the real causes of such a catastrophe might be and what we might expect from our future in relation to further such catastrophes?

(Carla channeling)

We are those known to you as the principle of Q'uo, and we greet you in the love and in the light of the one infinite Creator, in Whose service we come to you this day. It is a great privilege to be called to your group once again and we thank you, each one of you, for reserving this time to be part of a circle of seeking. It is our privilege to reserve this time also and to share our thoughts with you on the question of the tsunami and earthquakes which you have experienced.

As always, we would ask for a favor of you as we speak with you today. We would ask you to guard well your discrimination and listen carefully to those things that we say, being sure to discard any thoughts of ours that you do not particularly like. We do not share thoughts in order to challenge you or to be a stumbling block but only to offer what aid we can to your own good and worthy process. If you are able to exercise discrimination, then we shall be able to share our thoughts without being concerned that we might infringe upon your free will. This is an ongoing concern of ours and we appreciate your consideration in this regard.

The query that you offer this day is most understandable in its focus of concern. Many among your people have recently entered the inner planes through the gateway of death because of the actions of the earthquakes and the tsunami that followed them. When such a large number of souls moves through the gateway of larger life, as this instrument calls the gateway of death, at one time, it has a profound effect upon the energy of the entire global sphere. The planet itself is aware of the change upon its surface and the energy field of the Earth itself does indeed change somewhat when the energy fields of so many souls have transitioned at the same time. In its way, it is indeed a profound experience for those upon the planet. And, as several in your group have noted, it was hoped by many upon your plane of existence, and upon other, more metaphysical planes of existence having to do with your planet, that the tragedy, as it mounted force upon force, would take the attention of large groups of your social complexes and remold them from the patterns of hostility and aggression into patterns of compassion, kindness and concern. It is a measure of the bewilderment and bemusement of a supposedly and so-called free people that the effect of the tragedy has not been more dislocating and more upsetting to the general patterns of thought amongst your societal complex.

Nevertheless, from the political or social point of view, or as this instrument would say, from the top down, among your societal groupings, there is almost the reaction of a marionette or a puppet to the etiolated and thinned-out discussion of an abstracted tragedy. There is the expected and almost knee-jerk type reaction of sending emissaries to be sure that the right kind of gesture is made. But the heart of the culture of your peoples has not been awakened, enlivened or enabled with the zeal and the passion to help that might have been possible in a more fortunate world, [a more] fertile period, among your peoples.

Indeed, there seems to have been, from the top down, shall we say, that feeling of hopelessness or even helplessness that seemed to descend upon the entity you call America when it became clear that, for the second time in a row, the seemingly free election of your peoples was compromised. Consequently, we cannot say to you that the energy we are experiencing on a societal level from your people is particularly hopeful concerning the structure of the, shall we say, chakra system of your people. We would not speak for the entire globe. We are aware that we include in the number to whom we speak this day, one from the continent of Australia. We do not presume to express here our impression of the energy of the Australian continent. We are at this time expressing the energy of the North American continent and it is, from the standpoint of large political or social groupings, a lackluster energetic picture where the heart has not been able to open completely and embrace the tragedy or even to imagine fully of what the tragedy consists. It is as though your peoples have been stunned, repeatedly, by a blunt instrument which we could only call, in general, fear, until the responses of your peoples have become less sharp and less full of life than would be the hope of any member of such a society.

We have said to you repeatedly that there is a groundswell of unconditional love that is struggling to come through, not from the top down or from the societal level down, but from the grass-roots

individual upwards. And it is this energy which we would encourage. You as individuals sitting as members of this circle have full sway and complete power over your own fundamental inner energies. Whatever the signals that each of you receives from the surrounding culture, it is still a matter of your own discrimination as to what you pick up and use and what you toss away and reject. And where you encounter that dimmed, blocked energy of the society, we encourage you to reject it. Where you are picking up from the society the narrowness of judgment and the pricklings of fear, we encourage you to reject that. Whatever signals you feel that you may be picking up from the society that speak to you of cynicism and of letting the suffering and the pain of others' tragedies go, we encourage you to reject those energies completely and instead to say, "No, I do not choose to be a part of an uncaring society. I choose rather to lift myself away from the old and stale habits of a tired and weary people and to stand on new ground in a new world, a world that I, myself, envision, a world about which I, myself, can be compassionate and can come to honor and love."

You have asked, concerning this particular disaster, whether it presages a series of such disasters or whether it completes the energy expenditure that is necessary in order to heal the Earth to a certain extent. And in this instance we may say it is a little of both. There are energies that this particular disaster is completing. However, this instance is one of what we may expect to be many such disturbances around this so-called ring of fire, and in each other ring of instability where your planetary skin needs to shift. [10]

We have discussed before this basic concept of the Earth needing to correct its magnetic energies. And slowly, very slowly, through storm after storm upon your planet, through hurricane and earthquake and fire, these energies are being shifted and in such a way as to retain the majority of life patterns on Earth in an intact and healthy form. This pattern of disaster followed by subsequent disaster and so forth

---

[10] According to http://pubs.usgs.gov/publications/text/fire.html, which has a good map of this, "Volcanic arcs and oceanic trenches partly encircling the Pacific Basin form the so-called Ring of Fire, a zone of frequent earthquakes and volcanic eruptions." This site also has resources for those wishing to know more about plate movements in general around the earth.

will continue until the adjustments that are necessary to complete the labor of Earth in its delivery of fourth-density Earth is done. These difficulties may be expected to be ongoing for several of your years. We cannot be more specific because, as this history of your peoples unfolds, it unfolds as it does because of how each of you lives.

It is difficult to explain how each of you is important here but it is so that it matters how each one of you thinks, not simply how you act but how you think. Because it is thought by thought that the energies of the fourth-density Earth shall be able to take their rightful place. And it is your thoughts where fourth density either does or does not have a home. This instrument was saying to the one known as M last week that, even though the goals of L/L Research are humble, there must be something to them because of the tremendous resistance that each member of L/L Research was experiencing and indeed continues to experience at this time. And we feel that this is an accurate observation in that it is in very simple goals such as L/L Research's stated goal of attempting to live by fourth-density values that things change, not just for those in this circle but for those upon your planetary sphere. We cannot erase tragedy or remove the dark colors of agony and suffering from the palette of experience that is available to humankind. We would not wish to. It is not that we wish for any to suffer but that it is as though life itself were a wound that must be healed by the living of that life. In the acting out and the completing of the patterns of an incarnation, there will almost certainly be fell and dire suffering for each entity somewhere between the cradle and the grave. For those who met their death in water with the tsunami, that suffering was brief and very harsh. For many others, the suffering simply continues: hungry people, homeless people, people who do not even have a city, people walking away from the destruction of their homes. And yet, as each of you sits in a snug and warm living room listening to these words, how can you connect? How can you respond? Let the scales fall from your eyes, let the muffling fall from your ears and you will hear the agony of Earth. You will see and feel the crushing blows of suffering. Let it overwhelm you for just a while. Let it take you up and drown you with the extremity so that you really know that death has walked your way and has made inroads in the family of humankind. Let the pain of that awareness recede just enough that you again remember that you are an individual and that you

are not completely swamped by the family from which you spring. Retain enough of that sensation of being drowned in a tragedy to give you keen awareness of the real tragedy of person after person after person being removed so suddenly from the Earth plane.

And be aware that the one place that you can be where you are with each of these souls is in what this instrument would call the "house of prayer." You cannot physically fly to those lands that were so washed by this terrible tsunami but you can be with each of those whose life was lost, cheering them on through the gate of death and into paradise. And you can be with those who remain and who are in need of help, sharing, in your prayerful thoughts, the energy of your consciousness as it mingles with theirs, for in the metaphysical realm, there is no distance, and all places are one.

Perhaps more than any other response, we would hope that each of you [might] create, out of your knowledge that this kind of transitory difficulty will continue among your peoples on a global basis, a daily time of remembrance for those who are suffering. For the suffering of your planet continues day by day. It is not limited to dire, sudden tragedy. There is ample tragedy, day by day, to touch your heart, to awaken you to the needs of a suffering people and to engage your passion for being part of a loving energy that stands without fear, ready to reach hand and voice in the cause of love.

At this point we would ask if there are any queries to follow up the main question?

T1: Yes, I have a question. We were speaking earlier about how it seems that most of these tragedies occur in poor, third-world countries who are not as able to take care of themselves as a lot of western nations. Are these people here to try to teach us, to show us which way to go? Or are they just unfortunate?

We are those of Q'uo, and are aware of your query, my brother. It may perhaps seem that the majority of difficulties are laid upon those who are already without any substance in terms of resources with which to take care of themselves. And yet, we would not say that such entities chose incarnations where they could live a certain way to demonstrate any lessons. Rather, it is a matter of entities moving into incarnation, fulfilling patterns that are indeed part of the energies of groups of entities which have incarnated into the Earth plane from elsewhere. And it could be argued, to some extent, that some of these global groups have unique characteristics in their archetypal makeup that would encourage the living of an incarnation in a place where they would experience a shortened life because of a natural disaster. This is especially true of those entities from Deneb. However, for the most part, it is an individual, person-by-person situation, where it is not so much a matter of good or bad fortune as of there being a pattern for incarnation laid out that includes such an experience. The antecedents or economic makeup of such entities is not nearly as important as, simply, their destiny. It is to be remembered in this regard that your own peoples received severe and repeated tragedies during your last hurricane season, especially in the state you know of as Florida, so that tragedy is certainly no respecter of economic status or any other individual detail.

May we answer you further, my brother?

T1: No, thank you, that's fine.

We thank you, my brother. Is there another query at this time?

T2: Q'uo?

Yes.

T2: I have a query. I'm trying to find the inspiration but I have the feeling sometimes that I have lost my way. I think I'm heading down the right path but then I have periods where I doubt. Are you able to talk about that and help me to think it through?

We are those of Q'uo, and are aware of your query, my brother. It is extremely common and normal for any entity who is attempting to seek along the path of faith to have moments of complete doubt. It would not be a path of faith were faith easy. Faith is not an easy thing. It seems easy at certain seasons. On a sunny day, for instance, it seems quite delightful to enjoy the breeze and to feel the sun on one's face. When the sun is clouded over and covered with rain and the rain is falling, it is not at all easy to retain a lightness of spirit and a joy within the heart. Indeed, when the sun disappears it could almost seem that it would never come out again with its saving light and its joyful rays. And yet, always, when the weather clears and the raindrops stop falling, the sun is still there and apparently always has been, shining up above the raindrops.

And so it is with each entity: the inner sun is always glowing, shining, its rays true until tomorrow and true until forever. Yet the inner landscape clouds up and the sun disappears, and suddenly the path of faith seems very cold and winding and beset with many thorns and thistles and no good places to stop and rest. And somehow, when the sun is gone and there does not seem to be any rest it becomes very difficult to think and to feel that unity with all that there is that was so obvious just a little while ago when it was sunny and warm. And yet, to be on the path of faith is a matter of identity. Is it not who you are? Is it not the adventure that you have set for yourself? And would you ever want to be anywhere else but on the adventure that you have set out upon with such hope?

So the key in times of inner rain and bad weather is memory. The key is to remember who you are and why you're here. Part of a path of faith is to retain faith in yourself. The world will take the view of what you think you are and make fun of you, and the world will be right for the world. But you are not on the world's path, you are on a path that you have chosen for yourself. And because you have determined that path for yourself, no one can tell you that you are wrong. Nor can they tell you …

(Side one of tape ends.)

(Carla channeling)

… that you are unequal to the challenge of remaining on task. Sometimes, to be a person of faith is simply to stand firm and to remember that you are a person of faith. And to a person of faith, all is well. Right now, in the midst of seeming imperfection, all is well.

In the fullness of time, and it could be five minutes or half an hour, your inner weather will part, and your faith will naturally reestablish itself. But that will not be the triumph for you. The triumph for you is to stand on your faith at that moment when all seems rainy and cold and uncomfortable and decidedly not a matter of faith. That is the moment of your triumph and it is simply to remember that, for a person of faith, simply saying the word "faith" is enough to bring you back to the center of that wonderful grace.

What is faith? It is not faith in anything, it is simply faith, a kind of knowing that all is well. The one known as St. Paul described it as the hope in things unseen.[11] In that moment where you wonder where your faith is, reach inward and touch your own living heart because it beats. In the sense of the world it beats, moving blood through the body and giving life to that organism. In the energetic sense, it beats the beats of eternity and it says, "All is well. All is well and all is love."

May we answer you further, my brother?

T2: No, thank you, Q'uo.

Is there a final query at this time?

(No further queries.)

As we seem to have exhausted the queries in this group for the night, we will take our leave of you, leaving you, as always, in the love and in the light of the one infinite Creator. We are known to you as the principle of Q'uo. Adonai, my friends. ❧

---

[11] *Holy Bible*, Hebrews 11:1: "Now faith is the assurance of things hoped for, the conviction in things not seen."

L/L Research is a subsidiary of
Rock Creek Research &
Development Laboratories, Inc.

P.O. Box 5195
Louisville, KY 40255-0195

L/L RESEARCH

www.llresearch.org

Rock Creek is a non-profit
corporation dedicated to
discovering and sharing
information which may aid in
the spiritual evolution of
humankind.

SUNDAY MEDITATION
JANUARY 16, 2005

Group question: This week, Q'uo, we would like to ask you if you could elaborate upon the pitfalls or distractions that the seeker of truth might run into when the seeking is new and if there is any other type of distraction or pitfall that occurs later on in the path of the seeker. Please give us a general rundown of what to be aware of as one is seeking what is loosely called the truth.

(Carla channeling)

We are those of the principle known to you as Q'uo, and we greet you in the love and in the light of the one infinite Creator, in Whose service we come to you this day. It is a great privilege to be called to your group and we are most happy to speak to you about the pitfalls and distractions of the spiritual path. But we would first, as always, like specifically to request of each of you that you retain the ability to discriminate very carefully as you listen to our thoughts, choosing only those thoughts that really seem good to you, with which you wish to work further and discarding the rest immediately. In this way we will feel much more confident that we will not interfere with your free will or disturb the sacredness of your own process.

In asking concerning the pitfalls and the distractions to which one who is attempting to follow a path of spirituality is prey, you ask a fairly broad question. The spiritual path in itself is an amazingly broad thoroughfare carrying, as it does, every being of third density as it attempts to walk between two worlds, the world of third-density consensus reality and the inner world that sometimes completely overtakes the outer world for its importance and clarity.

For the most part, entities who are not consciously walking a spiritual path stay comfortably within third density and enjoy the various images and illusions that pass before the eye, as the one known as G was saying earlier. It is a comfortable and a familiar thing to pass from image to image as one rises and goes through the day; following the employment, following the need for the body for meals and refreshment and for sleep. It is a less comfortable and sometimes frighteningly less familiar thing to follow a spiritual path. And each entity steps onto this path from a misty somewhere before the thought crossed the mind that there was an actual spiritual path. So this broad, spiritual path is home to all of you. Each foot in this room has kicked the dust of that path and that dust has similarly been kicked by every human being on the planet at one time or another. So there is a vast variety of attitudes from those who enter the path of spirit. Consequently, there are various kinds of pitfalls.

Let us approach this question from the standpoint of a model to use to see if you indeed are on the spiritual path. The model of the self on the spiritual path is a model in which you are focusing upon the "I" that you are. There are many uses of the first-person singular. When you think of yourself, you always think of yourself as the same self. When you are thinking of yourself as a spiritual entity on a path, who are you? Who is the "I" that speaks for you when you are on the spiritual path? How would that voice, that identity, that person be different from the "I" that speaks for you in less thoughtful roles?

Hopefully, as you begin to sense yourself as a spiritual entity, the "I" that speaks for you begins to come out of the mist of the surface "I," the surface personality. The model that this instrument carries in her mind of the entity on the spiritual path is a model in which she is following in the steps of Jesus the Christ. She does not have a model of herself as worshipping but as following after the example of a teacher who seemed to know precisely who he was. He identified himself as an agent of the Creator. This instrument, then, has a model of the self on the spiritual path in which she has an objective referent to who she is because she is following an entity who was of a certain personality. This entity identified himself strictly as the Son of the Father who was about his Father's business. And it is notable that this entity, in all of his preaching, has never been quoted as asking for worship but only as asking for being followed.

So we would ask entities who are looking at themselves upon the spiritual path quite simply, "Who are you?" Because this is the essential center of that which draws entities to the path of seeking. They become aware that all of the wisdom that has been acquired since their cradle experiences is not enough to satisfy the craving for identity and meaning. They realize that they are going to have to set off on a journey. It is not a journey in the physical world at all but it is very definitely a journey and it very definitely is upon a path that is common to all seekers.

Please realize that on this path you are not gathering as much as allowing things to fall away. The deep and true tones of your identity and your right process come clearly, plangently, sometimes plaintively and sometimes triumphantly, but unmistakably, from time to time there will come a moment—this instrument loves to call them "crystalline moments"—that ping like a bell with a very clear indication of meaning and resonance and in that moment, whatever the realization is, it is easy, it is effortless; and you realize that you have reaped the harvest that has been in process for a long

time. You finally hear and feel and see the work that you have done but you never know when that moment will come. Such is the progress of one upon the spiritual path.

Pitfalls, for the new entity to the path, can involve impatience and that reaching and grasping that are the indication of impatience. These are not difficulties that will end or sideline the spiritual seeking for an entity but such impatience does get in the way of a creation that is set to respond to your needs but in a timely fashion. This means sometimes that one must wait. It is very difficult to wrap one's mind around the necessity for simple waiting.

The one known as Jim was speaking earlier of his delight at finding the time during the off-season of his work to sit and soak in the silence, allowing the creation to speak as it would to him. This willingness to let oneself drift in the flow of the moment is a great resource for all seekers. The entity, Jim, spoke of sitting at sundown and allowing the light slowly, gradually, to fade away, listening to the sounds of the creatures of the day as they quieted down and listening to the creatures of the night begin to sing their night song and just allowing all of this creation to roll past his eyes and his ears and, walking into his abode at the end of that time, feeling curiously invigorated and refreshed. This model of patience is a great one to carry.

Realize that when a spiritually-oriented question is asked within, the answer may come in the next fifteen seconds but it also may come two weeks or two months later. Energies have been set in motion that now must be trusted. Moving from the question to the trusting and the waiting is a great skill to learn. When you sense impatience within yourself, gently remind yourself that in spiritual seeking there is no time.

As the seeker becomes more sophisticated, as learning builds upon learning, the pitfalls of the path can change. If you are one of those who feels that she has had some experience walking this path, realize that your pitfall may well be knowing too much or feeling that you understand. There is truly no end to the evolving self. As things fall away from you and you become more able to penetrate deeper within your consciousness, you will repeatedly find that you need to release concepts from their stricture. You need to be able to allow new insight to change your carefully built-up intelligence about yourself and the world around you. Do not hold on to your identity or your knowledge in the face of new information. Rather, place aside that which you feel that you know and enter fully into the investigation of that which resonates for you. Do not see it as something that challenges your information, but rather, see it as something that may well help you evolve and put into a whole new pattern the information that is still good for you. When experience mounts up, it is as though some entities were carrying around their entire history of experience and attempting to add everything new in on top of this large pile of acquired information from childhood and previous years. It is a good idea to keep that cup of selfhood tipped out and emptied so that it may receive new wine, new information.

There is a certain amount of pride that entities take sometimes in how many things that they have learned, how many books they have read or philosophies that they have studied or religious systems that they have penetrated and can speak about. This kind of pride is often a very deadening influence and we would encourage entities, always, to relate as simply and as directly as possible to ideas, to patterns of thought, and above all to entities around one who may be attempting to enter into conversation concerning spiritual matters. In a world that rushes continuously on so many levels, we would encourage a truly relaxed and lighthearted attitude towards the very serious business of seeking.

This instrument is typical of many upon the spiritual path in that she has a built-in yearning and hunger for devotion. She must be devoted, she must be serving, she has this sense of almost being driven to be as the one known as Jesus, the agent of the Creator. It is good to have that back-pressure; it is not a good thing to allow that pressure to make you hurry or hasten or become anxious. Allow that back-pressure to continue to motivate you but if it motivates you beyond the point at which you are patient and have a sense of proportion and humor concerning your path, then you have entered into that particular pitfall of eagerness and hurriedness.

What that will do to you, if you allow it to drive you, is to do more and more, to try more disciplines, to add a meditation if you haven't been doing a daily one, then add another one, and then make that one longer, and so forth. The end of such pressured seeking is that you burn out as a seeker and must sit by the side of that spiritual path for a while,

mopping your brow and breathing. It sometimes take years for a burnt-out seeker to recover his balance completely and to be able to get back into a real process that feels yeasty and good.

Walking the path is not a difficult thing, it is more a matter of its being a journey for the one who is ready for a long trek. In most paths available in third density there is a beginning, a middle, and an end. There is the learning process, there is the point in the middle in which you are working very hard and you are becoming better and that culminates with a job well done, a degree of education earned, a promotion at work, and so forth.

In the spiritual path, death is only the beginning. There are no endings, there are many, many beginnings, and there is no end of the middle. You are always in the middle of the spiritual path.

Perhaps the greatest gift is to know that you know nothing and that you will indeed fall into many a pitfall and yet it will not take you off the path. You cannot get lost beyond finding and if you do need to rest, even there at the side of the road you have company.

As to the distractions that are possible on the spiritual path, there is no end of distraction. But [this is true] only if you are of the mind to see things as either spiritual or worldly. If you make a demarcation between those two parts of Earthly existence, everything that is not specifically dedicated study will be seen as, in some way, a distraction.

However, we would suggest to you that all things that a spiritually-oriented entity does are spiritual. Going to the bathroom, doing the dishes, taking out the garbage, feeding the cat: these commonplace and everyday chores are necessary and cannot be construed to have any obvious spiritual characteristics. And yet this instrument, for example, finds ways to invest each of those activities with an awareness that is spiritual in its character.

What part of your day do you honestly feel is a distraction and only that? What thing that you do can you say has no spiritual value? If you can identify some of those items that can be seen as distractions, perhaps you could sit down and contemplate whether there is a way you might invest these chores with the sacred character that comes from service, from love, and from an awareness of who the self is in the spiritual sense. In our opinion, there is no true distraction to an entity whose heart is set upon the Creator because each and every action available to an entity for choice has the potential for being seen in a spiritual light.

One aspect of the spiritual path that we would mention before we would open the meeting to questions would be the simple aspect of silence versus sound, emptiness versus content, for those upon the spiritual path within your culture are coming to that path from a culture very rich in content. It is interesting to note that, within all of this content, critics of the culture often comment on the emptiness of that content, the illusion that it creates and the illusory nature of the image-after-image-after-image that creates the content, whether the medium of such images in the television, the radio, the newspaper or the computer.

A very great portion of the world has cultural influences that lead it more to the appreciation of silence, which seems to lack content, and yet which contains infinite meaning. In your content-rich culture, meaning itself is often lost. Consequently, if you are of the nature that appreciates content, we suggest that you choose your content, for truly, there are many pitfalls, if you would speak of it in that way, for those who are attempting to derive meaning from the surface aspects of your culture, as seen on the television or read in the newspaper. Do not fall into the pitfall of assigning too much meaning to those things that are on the surface. Allow meaning to be a mystery and silence to be your teacher.

We thank you for this question and feel that we perhaps have spoken long enough upon it. At this time we would open the meeting to further questions, if there are any. Is there a further query at this time?

G: Q'uo, I have a lengthy one and I apologize for its length but, hopefully, its answer should be simple. And it's easier to read straight from the paper.

(Reading) Q'uo, as I move forward in my path I am experiencing a phenomenon that can be described as the light growing lighter and the dark growing darker. I feel I am experiencing the extremes of what can conveniently be described as a spectrum of feeling. On one hand, I feel strength, vitality and the spiritual perception increase in moments where, basically, all the spiritual literature that points to the truth not only makes sense to me but becomes alive,

a living and flowing reality. And subsequently I feel more empowered through self-knowledge to call upon and invoke the higher forces to transform the lower self of me.

On the other hand, I feel ever more acutely the shadow side of myself: one with seemingly more venomous reactions to situations that create a souring and bittering within me. What I don't know is whether a shadow is growing more strongly in me as I reach for the light because I am neglecting to be conscious of certain aspects of my patterns or whether it is a case of simply becoming more aware of a shadow that is already within me and has been with me, alive and functioning without my conscious awareness to transform its ways. Can you help me to understand whether it is awareness of what is already there or the further creation of distorted thinking within my mind?

We are those of Q'uo, and are aware of your query, my brother. The concept of the shadow self is very helpful in attempting to walk into your own shoes as a being. It is difficult to wrap oneself around this idea of a shadow self. Perhaps if we called it a full-circle self it might be easier to see the construction of the being here, because each of us, we and you, are beings that replicate all aspects of the creation and the Creator. By the time that you have reached third density you have done a tremendous amount of amalgamation of experience. You have been elemental, you have been plant, you have been animal; now you are an animal with a conscience, basically, and you strive to go further. And we have become even more refined by experience, yet we carry the full-circle self, just as do you.

What is there in creation? Whatever you see, that's you. Any murderer on the block is you. Any thief on the dock is you. Any hero who has just saved the world is you. You are the soldier, you are the bread-winner, you are the mother bearing a child, you are everything. And you don't get to choose whether you have good in you or bad in you, so-called. You have it all. The strictures and disciplines of the parent for the child attempt to train the child up so that he will behave well and you have learned to behave well. Loving good, seeking the light, you have more and more been able to place yourself in situations and in environments where you were able to live in the sunny side of self, enjoying service and learning and devotion. And these things about you and about all entities are true. However, equally true is that self that does not get encouragement from virtue.

You still have that; you will always have that. It is part of the strength of who you are that you have that. You would not be able to be a full person and to move forward without the full-circle self. Nothing is left behind as you evolve. It becomes arranged in a more and more helpful way as you learn to balance yourself, chakra by chakra, issue by issue, and moment by moment. You are always in flux, so these moments where you become aware of that so-called evil part of yourself come and go. And it is sometimes quite disconcerting to become aware of particularly articulate and eloquent, angry or irritated thoughts. You feel yourself thinking a hateful thought which isn't fair at all and certainly would never be said aloud and you wonder where that came from and if the evil within you is somehow growing. We assure you it is not growing. It was always there. It chose this particular moment to reveal itself and this is a gift to you of self to self. Take it seriously, look at it carefully, and see, if you can, where the trigger lay that brought forward this particular part of yourself.

May we answer you further, my brother?

G: No, thank you, Q'uo. That was excellent.

We thank you, my brother. Is there a further query at this time?

S: I've had a question that I've been thinking about for some time. If I wanted to recover all the knowledge and wisdom of all the lifetimes that I had, how would I do that?

We are those of Q'uo, and are aware of your query, my brother. You are asking this query within third-density incarnation and our shortest answer would be to say that you would be able to recover that information …

(Side one of tape ends.)

(Carla channeling)

… immediately following your crossing of the gateway of death. Once through that gateway, reunited with full consciousness and full communication with your higher self, you would have the unimpaired memory of all that you have been and, indeed, all that you would be in the future. Within third density, it is not considered a helpful thing to have that full range of information

available. It is considered, as you know, much more helpful for a discreet curtain to be drawn over all previous experiences so that you may hit the particular incarnation in which you are involved running, and give it the serious consideration that it deserves, all on its own.

The ways of penetrating the veil of forgetting are limited within incarnation. There is the dreaming process and those who work with dreams are often able to recover memory of past lives as they gradually find themselves in dream landscapes which constitute a different environment that begins to have a reality of its own.

The most common way that entities are able to recover past life information is the contacting of the deep mind by the conscious mind which is done in sessions of regressive hypnosis in which, with the help of a hypnotist, the self is taken back before birth to previous lives and questions are asked which enable the person to recover some of those memories.

May we answer you further, my brother?

S: That gives me plenty to think about. I have nothing else at this time. Thanks.

We thank you, my brother. Is there another query at this time?

T: Q'uo, I don't know whether you are able to respond to this question. The image that I've received upon waking this morning, is that a symbol of my need for purification and cleansing?

We are those of Q'uo, and are aware of your query, my brother. We find ourselves up against the full stop of free will in this matter, my brother, and are not able to offer information except to encourage you to follow the line of thought upon which you have been moving because we feel that you are in a place which has a great deal of material and we encourage you to explore it.

May we answer you further?

T: No, thank you, Q'uo. I understand.

We appreciate your understanding, my brother. Sometimes we are able to offer little real information and we apologize for that.

Is there a final query at this time?

G: Q'uo. I have another one. Just a few paragraphs long this time. I'm sorry, I just need context for my questions.

(Reading) For years now I've been experiencing moments and time periods of a fuzziness of perception which slightly blurs the boundaries between dream and reality. As I've heard many others speak of this same experience, it feels as if the solidity of what was formerly a well-defined reality dissolves and all of a sudden everything in waking consciousness feels literally like a dream. There have been a few incidents of late in which I was seriously not sure if I actually said or did something in the "real world" or whether that same memory was the property of a nightly dream. Is this type of fuzziness the result of the incoming fourth-density energies and the resultant change in consciousness that they bring? Or perhaps, as was cautioned against in the *Law of One* series, these are symptoms of an over-hasty polarization and the twilight state that accompanies such an impatient drive for progress?

We are those of Q'uo, and are aware of your query, my brother. We cannot give you one single answer, yes or no, because, as we gaze into your pattern, we would say that perhaps two-thirds of those experiences are an artifact of your personality type. You, in common with this instrument, have a certain absent-minded quality that can create this feeling without there being any resonance or meaning to the happenstance. It simply is a time when you are scattered. There are other times, my brother, when there has been a significant shift in your perceptive web because of the intensity of your devotion. In the first instance, two-thirds of the experience, that is, there is no meaning involved, it is simply an artifact of personality. In the remainder of the cases there is great material that is there and it can usefully be mined. So we would suggest that you look for the kind of peculiar resonance that does attend such a shift in consciousness due to devotion.

The third possibility, which you suggested, was that you were experiencing basically a mistake, that you had rushed too much and so forth. And we would ease your mind in that regard, for it is not in either case an artifact of rushing or of trying too hard. Rather, it is a matter of the way that your particular personality has shaped up and the way it handles experiences that it cannot quite encompass with rational thought.

G: Cool beans! Thank you, Q'uo.

We thank you, my brother. You truly are a cool bean. This instrument is asking us why in the world we offered that bit of inanity and we do apologize to the instrument and to everyone else.

(Laughter)

And on that note we will leave you in the love and in the light of the one infinite Creator. It has been such a pleasure to be with you and to share your vibrations. Thank you for asking us. We are those of Q'uo. We leave you in the love and in the light of the one infinite Creator. Adonai. Adonai vasu. ✺

L/L RESEARCH

L/L Research is a subsidiary of
Rock Creek Research &
Development Laboratories, Inc.

P.O. Box 5195
Louisville, KY 40255-0195

www.llresearch.org

Rock Creek is a non-profit
corporation dedicated to
discovering and sharing
information which may aid in
the spiritual evolution of
humankind.

SPECIAL MEDITATION
JANUARY 20, 2005

(Carla channeling)

We are those of the principle known to you as Q'uo. Greetings in the love and in the light of the one infinite Creator, in Whose service we come to you this day. It is a great privilege to be called to your group and we thank each of you for doing so. Thank you indeed for taking the time out of your busy lives for this carefully delineated session of seeking. It is a privilege to be asked to give our opinion and we are glad to do so. But in order to be able to speak freely we would ask as a favor that each of you employ the most stringent discrimination, listening carefully to those things that we say and discarding any idea that does not resonate to you as if it were a newly recovered memory. In that way we will feel free to speak without worrying about the sacredness of your process being disturbed or your free will being abridged.

We greet the one known as J, and we ask this entity for his first query at this time.

J: Which avenue of application would this ARV technology[12] be encouraged to flourish in?

We are those of Q'uo, and are aware of your query, my brother. Your ARV process is that type of process which, by its very nature, as the one known as B noted, has a tendency to abridge free will. The challenge facing a practitioner of this process is to find information concerning the future, the knowledge of which does not abridge free will.

Let us talk a bit about this. The typical successful, inadvertent use of this technology is that of the entity who prays that something be changed. As an example, we would use this instrument's daily practice of intercessory prayer in which she prays that the health of those who have asked for her prayers be amended for the better. A good example, of which the one known as J may be aware, [is] that in the recent tsunami disaster, there was a man who placed his several young charges in a small boat and went out to sea to avoid the disaster. This entity told the wind and the waves, in the name of Jesus the Christ, to be calm and the sea became calm enough that this gentleman and his young charges survived the storm undamaged. It is these small miracles that entities have reliably been able to petition the universe, or the creative principle, if you will, to alter what this instrument would call a probability/possibility vortex.

The one known as B spoke concerning the intention behind the doing of the ARV process. And we would agree with this entity in that that which will tend to improve the reliability of this process is that intention which is single-minded and which has a purity of motive. The one known as J spoke earlier of hoping to create supply, money and success from using the technology of the ARV. We cannot speak

---

[12] ARV stands for Associative Remote Viewing. Here is a link to a website which discusses this technique: www.remote-viewing.com.

directly to this matter but we may suggest that such intentions are not blessed by spirit. The one known as B further noted that it is difficult for the forces of spirit even to understand the concept of supply or money, and this is also accurate.

The efforts, therefore, as they stand, offer a paucity of value which is recognizable to the forces of spirit. In order to create a better flow of energy for the one known as J, therefore, it is well to re-imagine or reconfigure those forces within the one known as J which are gathered together in order to do this work. The entity sees itself in a certain way, let us say, and re-imagining or reconfiguring the way the one known as J sees itself will be the most fundamentally helpful change in terms of improving the reliability of this process when it is used.

May we answer you further, my brother, on this point?

J: No, I think that's adequate. Would you please describe the proper ritual for entrance/exit for this process?

We are those of Q'uo, and we are aware of your query, my brother. We thank you for having the creativity and the imagination to ask this question. It is not a question that we can speak to specifically. However, we can talk about how the one known as J may configure his environment by speaking in terms of that which this instrument has done to create for herself a satisfactory environment in which to do sacred work.

First of all, note that this instrument intends a very simple and single-minded thing when she comes to the channeling process. She is placing herself in service to the one infinite Creator and she is defining carefully the way in which she will enter her workspace to do this service. She gathers about herself the artifacts of her faith. The artifacts which were about her during the contact with those of Ra lie within the room in which each of you is sitting at this time and these artifacts are familiar and dear to her, have been handled by her, and have meaning to her beyond the occasion of this particular session. The chalice, the incense, and the Bible open to the phrase, "In the beginning was the Word," all have a deep heart connection for this instrument. And they constitute to her, in a metaphysical rather than a physical way, a symbolic but very real safety. She rests her spirit amongst the artifacts of her faith. It is a reassurance on a subconscious level, and, in the context of her work, there is an implicit acceptance of her values by those who sit in circle with her. All of these aspects of the artifacts around her, therefore, act as a safety net so that she is able to feel quite free to let go and respond with very pure focus to the process of the channeling.

For the one known as J, these artifacts would not create any sort of safety net. And the challenge, therefore, for the one known as J is to identify within himself the very heart of faith for him. Faith is not a belief in anything and the artifacts that comfort the one known as J need not be religious at all. They need to create an ambience of emotional safety.

When one identifies one's faith, it can be done in many, many ways. The thinking along the lines of what to surround the self with needs, however, to be done with the heart, rather than the mind. For what you are looking for here is that which resonates within your deep mind. This is not necessarily a mind that resonates like any other; it is not necessarily going to resonate to spiritual or religious artifacts. Consequently, we would encourage the one known as J to spend some time thinking not about artifacts but about where the center of faith is for you. Where is that place within you that knows beyond any doubt that all is well and [is] that which is right and good and appropriate?

The whole question of doing this spiritual work does revolve around what the work is. Is it spiritual work? To this instrument, all things are sacred and all work is spiritual. What is your take on this reality? The more that you are able to penetrate the surface of your personality and move into the sacred space of your own heart, the better able you will be to consider this question. It would be our observation that there has been a lack of awareness on the part of the one known as J that there is an issue of whether or not this work is spiritual, whether or not this work is sacred. The forces of the Creator open to those who have realized the shape of their own sacredness and who have envisioned what it is they wish to do in terms of spiritual learning and spiritual service. Attempting to do this kind of work while personally unpolarized or weakly polarized is as one attempting to use electricity but finding a tremendous amount of resistance on the system that keeps the power from functioning well.

We would like to address the techniques for entry and exit of the sessions to some extent at this time.

This instrument was used to doing a ritual called the banishing ritual of the lesser pentagram[13] in order to prepare the place of working when this instrument and the group of which she was a part were doing trance channeling sessions. For conscious channeling, this instrument tunes itself by singing, praying and doing mental exercises designed to deepen the state of focus and to call the forces of spirit which she wishes to accompany her as she does her work.[14]

We can reliably recommend any form of tuning that the one known as J finds helpful and comfortable. It may not be the banishing ritual of the lesser pentagram. It might not be praying, as such. However, it is well to think of the self as a crystal that transmits and receives energy much as a radio. You are, shall we say, not a power source but that through which power passes. You may tune the field of your consciousness just as you would tune a radio to get the station that you want. This instrument tunes asking for the highest and best contact that she can carry in a conscious, stable manner of the energy of Jesus the Christ. It is a very specific request and therefore she is able to tune fairly accurately although she has no technical or specific knowledge of what she is doing. This tuning process is very helpful and we think that the one known as J may benefit from considering well what the tuning would be to reach the source that this entity wishes to reach.

At the end of a session of working, we would describe the conditions as being that you have gathered energy of a certain kind. It is light, but what is the color, what is the nature, what is the texture, of this light? We would encourage thinking upon this. In the model that this entity has of her own sessions, she sees the people in the group creating a force field or an energy field by their commingled energies and she sees light being pulled into that temple that has been created by the arching energies of the circle. At the end of each session she verbally requests that everyone release that light back to the Creator. This, in a metaphysical fashion,

cleanses the physical and metaphysical local area of the work that has just been done and returns the energy of the place to its neutral, worldly vibration.

It is well, whatever the ritual developed be, that it be seen as a cleansing and closing that is specifically sacred or spiritual in nature. Indeed, all of our recommendations have to do with investing this process with polarity or with the energy of love, so that the entity J, doing this work, is engaged and fixed into the process in a specifically spiritual or sacred way.

May we answer you further, my brother?

J: No, that is adequate. The next one is: Can you please help me in setting my overall intent for working with the ARV process?

We are those of Q'uo, and are aware of your query, my brother. We were speaking just now of setting an intention that was framed in spirituality. May we say that the concept of spirituality or sacredness is generally far too limited by peoples' concept of spirituality. Spirituality is not necessarily religiosity at all. It does not necessarily have any of the trappings of place or ritual. The heart of spirituality is caught up in an entity's definition of self.

When an entity begins to look into the nature of the self, worlds begin to open to him. We would encourage the one known as J to spend time daily asking the question, "Who am I?" And then allowing a lack of thinking or unnecessary motion. This could be in meditation, so called; this could be very fruitfully done in a natural setting. But whether it is formal meditation or walking in nature, the goal here is to free the mind from content and to allow it to be empty. Into this environment, just as into an empty cup, may come content that is immeasurable by words, and the nature of the self is something that is beyond words. This is why silence is the best environment in which to receive some of the deeper answers that you seek at this time.

Framing your intention sounds as though it is a matter of identifying your goal. And the one known as J has explained that there is no specific goal to this process: it is a process that can be used for many different goals. However, the one known as J has said repeatedly that he wishes to be helpful, to be of service using this technology, using this ARV. And this is the direction in which we would suggest that the one known as J move in his thinking. It is

---

[13] As found in William E. Butler's book, *The Magician, His Training and His Work.*

[14] Carla calls on the Holy Spirit, the Creator, Jesus the Christ and the Archangels while tuning for each session.

helpful to realize that the goals that are blessed by the forces of spiritual guidance are those goals in which the intention has been carefully crafted and focused towards helpfulness, compassion, kindness and other ways of describing the attributes of unconditional love.

A magician, so-called, is one who attempts to create changes in consciousness by his will. And, in a literal sense, the ARV protocols are a type of magic, in that sense. The question is, is it positive, neutral or negative in its intention? Examining an intention such as creating money, it may be seen that the polarity of that intention is mixed. There are positive aspects to wishing to have money in order to do good. Yet, there is the subtext of service to self. And this instrument has often said, in terms of attempting to make money from service, that she would prefer to remain poor in order that she is able to donate her work and keep the forces of money from it. This instrument has moved forward from that absolute goal of taking no money in that she is now doing sessions such as this one in which she does indeed accept funds although these funds are passed directly into the L/L Research coffers so that she is not personally gaining in any way, shape or form from doing spiritual work.

This is a worthy attitude in that it frees this instrument from any mixed polarity as she approaches the channeling. It is difficult, if not impossible, to conceive of an absolutely pure intention, as human entities are forever mixed in that their nature is 360 degrees of all that the Creator created. Consequently, each entity has a shadow side that is just as powerful and just as articulated as the positive or sunny side. As you ask yourself, "Who am I?" you shall more and more begin to see that you are everything and every quality. And then the question becomes, "What configuration or arrangement of these energies lies within your being?"

It is the goal of each entity throughout incarnation to penetrate more and more the surface teachings that have created a false self. The self as brought up by parents and teachers and other authority figures contains a great deal of material that is imagistic and it is as though you hold to yourself old images of self that are not current. As you learn more about yourself, you will find some of these false images or parts of self falling away and this will help you to clarify your nature and therefore your basic intention.

May we answer you further on this point, my brother?

J: No, that's adequate. You may have already touched on some of this but I'll ask the question anyway. Is there a proper physical alignment in compass degrees that the viewer must position himself to gain a better signal of the target he is trying to describe?

We are those of Q'uo. We are aware of your query. Thank you, my brother, for that question. We gaze at that which we can share without abridging free will. We are able to share the suggestion that a north/south alignment is helpful as is an east/west alignment. Lining up with north and south orients you to the dynamic betwixt air and water. Lining up east and west orients you to the dynamic between earth and fire. Either orientation is generally helpful and it may occur to the one known as J that in various applications one or the other alignment might be preferable. But we would suggest that using the cardinal directions is a good idea.

Further, we give this instrument the vision of the body being off of any ground and somewhat reclined as if this instrument were to lie back in the reclining chair so that there is a comfort level that is quite high. We might suggest that it is perhaps more helpful to cleanse the area in some metaphysical way than to be concerned with position or placement.

There are two other elements we would suggest as being helpful. And that would be to choose times of working in which there is what this instrument would call the full moon or near the full moon, as those energies involved at that time that are strong are those energies that are helpful for this work. We might also suggest that this entity find the necessary information concerning the eighteen-day spiritual cycle and determine the nature of his own eighteen-day cycle so as to avoid those times in which …

(Side one of tape ends.)

(Carla channeling)

… the energies are moving from low to high or high to low and are in a critical, unstable condition.

May we answer you further on that point, my brother?

J: No, that is fine. Thank you. Could you describe a few characteristics of a suitable coworker for me, please?

We are those of Q'uo, and are aware of your query, my brother. We are certainly able to describe to you some characteristics that would be helpful for you to consider in a coworker. But we would say first of all that there are times when an entity is creating roadblocks for himself and in this wise the one known as J has inadvertently created a block to finding that perfect partner in that the one known as J has not surrendered to his own deeper nature. It is difficult for us to give this instrument words that can reveal what we mean but it is as though the one known as J has locked a door against himself. The key to that door is a question or a hunger and we cannot give the one known as J this question or develop within him this hunger, yet it is within him and it is strong within him at this time and thusly we would suggest to the one known as J the value of love.

This is a key word and it is almost meaningless when said because it has been so abused. But the very nature of each entity in creation is love. The very nature of the Creator is love. All the energy, no matter what it looks like in creation, is some form of love. When the one known as J has found this hunger and has asked this question, rather than being a being standing outside his own heart he will be in that sacred space of his own heart. And it is from that place that life and love open up. We do not mean to be cryptic but if one's nature is love and if the question has to do with love and if the place inside the heart is described as unconditional love than perhaps we have offered you the help that we can offer you here.

Characteristics of a helpful coworker are: intelligence, self-awareness, humor and most of all, faith. If you can find someone who is faithful, gullible and open, then you will have done very well. However, we would suggest to the one known as J that, just as the one known as B has said, that entity will be drawn to you when the time of waiting is over. There will not be any need to find or seek out such an entity. Rather, the two of you will come together naturally just as has happened with each of those who has gathered at L/L Research. Each connection was the result of a process of like attracting like and as this instrument said earlier, the group was brought together by the Law of One.

Place your energies in self-disclosure and deep honesty as you peer within a self that is cunningly made to deceive as well as reveal. The process of getting to know the self takes all of the persistence that the one known as J has in abundance. It is an incarnationally long task. However, we feel that the one known as J will be surprised at how quickly things change once he is involved in the process of self-knowledge on a conscious basis. The universe is geared to respond to the questioner of self.

May we answer you further on that point, my brother?

J: No, that is fine, thank you. Next question: Will I be allowed to be successful with the ARV?

We are those of Q'uo, and are aware of your query, my brother. We do not find that this is a question that we are able to address and therefore we will simply pass. We apologize for the lack of information here.

J: Okay, another question that I have: Will A play a role in my future?

We are those of Q'uo, and are aware of your query, my brother. And once again we find that this is not an area in which we feel we can be useful to you. Is there a further query, at this time?

J: No, there is not.

B: Q'uo, when you referred to the directions, north, south, east and west, are you referring to the magnetic compass points or the rotational poles.

We are those of Q'uo, and are aware of your query, my brother. We were referring to magnetic rather than rotational values.

B: Thank you. *(To J.)* Anything else?

J: I have one further question, if you'll take a shot at it. There were blue lights, dim rectangles, on my ceiling two weeks ago when I woke up. Could you tell me what they were?

We are those of Q'uo, and are aware of your query, my brother. We find that in the work that you are doing you have opened for yourself gateways into various points within what this instrument would call the chakra system. And there are various ways of seeing elements of space and time within those systems that are symbolic. They consist of geometry and color. You were aware of and seeing into an inner-planes place which did not make sense to your conscious intelligence and therefore you were only able to see the color and geometry rather than being able to see into that world, as it were.

May we answer you further, my brother?

J: No, I am finished. Thank you.

We are those of Q'uo and, my brother, if you are finished, we are finished as well. We thank you for the tremendous effort that it took for you to be with us and to ask these questions. And we leave you as we found you, in the love and in the light of the one infinite Creator. We are known to you as those of Q'uo. Adonai. Adonai. ☥

L/L Research is a subsidiary of Rock Creek Research & Development Laboratories, Inc.

P.O. Box 5195
Louisville, KY 40255-0195

L/L RESEARCH

www.llresearch.org

Rock Creek is a non-profit corporation dedicated to discovering and sharing information which may aid in the spiritual evolution of humankind.

SUNDAY MEDITATION
FEBRUARY 6, 2005

Group question: The question today has to do with what it is to be a member of a group. We would like Q'uo to give us an indication of, is it something more physical, is it more metaphysical? Has it to do with commitment to ideals? Is it work effort offered, working for the general welfare of the group? What is it to be a member of a group? Especially a group in a spiritual community.

And also, as a second part of that, what is the most loving way to deal with any member of a group which is seen to fall short of the group ideals?

(Carla channeling)

We are known to you as the principle of Q'uo, and we greet you in the love and in the light of the one infinite Creator, in Whose service we come to you this day. It is a great privilege to be called to your group to talk about groups and, as always, we would ask for a favor from you and that is that each of you guards your discriminatory abilities well. Listen to those things that we share with you asking yourself if these thoughts are helpful to you or not. If they do not seem helpful to you or to resonate, then we ask you please to leave them aside without a second thought, for we would not interfere with your process or be a stumbling block. Do not respect authority, but question it. Always put everything to the test before you allow it strength or power within your own mind. For you know that which is yours. It will resonate and re-echo within you as if it were something that you just remembered, even though

you might not have heard the thought before. When thoughts are not resonant it is much better to leave them behind. With that understood, it will allow us to speak freely and have no fear that we will be infringing upon your free will, and we thank you for this consideration.

You ask us what it is to be a part of a group and since we are a part of several groups, let us begin there. We, speaking to you as the principle of Q'uo, are a group made up of three social memory complexes. We have, as complexes, chosen to serve in a unified way by sharing thoughts with those who are actively seeking, who are actively questioning, and who have the ability to listen to channels such as this one. We also speak directly within entities' dreams and meditations, not with words but with a basic vibrational energy which is as a carrier wave for your own vibrational nexus so that it is as though we were strengthening your basic signal and making it easier for you to hear yourself and to be aware of the reality of yourself.

Thus, we have come together as social memory complexes to serve in this way; and we have come together as a principle to serve together in this way with regard to this one instrument who requests the highest and best contact that she may receive. It is our way of responding to that request to form a three-party principle so that together we may maximize the nuances available to this instrument from spiritual sources. To be a part of this particular group, then, has been a very conscious and deliberate choice on our part. It has been a choice of all three of us social memory complexes to come together to serve and it has been a choice of these three complexes to serve together in this one instance.

We have the advantage of knowing where our center is. We have the advantage of having an awareness of our—we give this instrument a word she can not translate into English; it is not leadership, it suggests centrality but focuses beyond any physical entity or person and is wrapped up in the concept of the Creator Itself. But to us, that concept is very real, obvious and natural within the illusion of the Earth plane.

A Creator-centered group cannot function as though that Creator were obvious, clear and full of meaning. Within your density, the systems of illusion are paramount. That which you call consensus reality is illusory. And to seek for a center, or a Creator that has meaning within that consensus reality is to seek that which is not existent at that level in that reality. Consequently, that which we find natural, comfortable and obvious is not something we can explain to you and say, "Here is the rule for a group. Here is how you know you belong together in a group."

Within your consensus reality, however, within third density as you know it, the question of groups is central. This is due to the fact that within third density the progress of each individual is impossible without group interaction to some extent. An entity left entirely to himself cannot thrive. This is the way of third density. It was designed to be a density in which entities would learn more and more about who they were by interacting with other entities who were doing the same thing. It was an environment designed to deceive as much as to reveal, to confuse as much as to explicate. It was designed this way in order to advance the energies of growth, which are also the energies of confusion. And therefore, within third density the individuals who are seeking to advance spiritually, mentally, emotionally and physically have, more than anything else, their feelings and instincts to guide them. Those instincts naturally lead them into groups.

The most obvious kind of group within third density is the family. In the family, the center is physical: the progenitor has sired children and those children have sired children and so forth. And there is a family tree

from which one descends and of which one is a part. One cannot opt out of a family group. One's mother and father and so forth remain who they are and, indeed, were specifically chosen by each of you before entry into the incarnation that you enjoy at this present time.

The energies of entities within third density are also instinctively and naturally that which we would call political. There is the desire to organize the structure and tenor of one's existence for the perceived group and through time this has developed into the rise and fall of many different kinds of civilizations and cultures. Again, in such groups, the center is obvious. There is a perceived authority; that is, the leader of the state, the city, the nation, or whatever group is perceived to be the government, shall we say. Your people have created many different kinds of structures from which government depends. And at this time your experiences of political structures are for the most part happy in that, while there is often disagreement with the leaders of your structures within the Western civilizations or cultures, there is a perceived degree of freedom which is that which feels proper and appropriate. So that, while entities may feel disappointed or discomfited by specific leaders, there is that underlying trust in the processes that guard freedom and keep government from coming oppressive and a type of slavery.

Another obvious kind of group that you experience within your culture is the nuclear family; that is, the family made up of two who decide to marry. In this group, the center is obvious also and it is physical. There is a kind of family corporation which has been set up and it is a partnership. In all of these groups, there is no need to plumb the mysteries of the human spirit [and] more particularly, of your own spirit and your own nature.

When one attempts to begin a group which has as its focus the Creator, one begins to create a group which is based and founded in mystery. There is no obvious center, physically speaking, to such a group. Within this instrument's experience, the religious aspect of spiritual seeking has been emphasized and she has appreciated the physical centrality of group worship along the lines of her distortion, which is the Christian worship. Within the church atmosphere or group, again, there is a physical center. There is a place where entities gather to worship. There is a perceived leader of the worship, that being the rector or priest, and there is liturgy into which entities may enter. The means of joining such a group are ritually set out, those being baptism and confirmation.

For the purposes of this particular entity's seeking, however, belonging to a physical, religious group did not at all satisfy this entity's desire to serve the Creator. And in conjunction with others of like mind, this entity long ago began to make agreements, first with the one known as Don, to form a partnership of seeking service and giving. Then, after many years of serving at this level, there was a further agreement made with a third entity, the one known as Jim, and this agreement reached between three entities was manifested into the physical by the three entities sitting down together and making a group agreement. The external shape of this agreement was a document in which entities simply held their lives in common, their goods, their talent, and their time, offering all to the Creator: all for one and one for all.

When these three entities came together in this focus, the outward manifestations of grace which rained upon this group in abundance and plenty included channeled material which those within this group know as the Law of One information. And in general, throughout the years up until this threesome was expanded by many of those within this present circle, the peace, unity and harmony of this group and its focus were notable. As the time flew and the century turned, more abundance began to befall this group, more souls were called to this vicinity with that feeling that there was something here, some opportunity to serve, some possibility that was worth pursuing. And so, in idealistic hope, in the desire to serve, and in great positive harmony, entities began to come to create a spiritually-oriented family. Where before there had been a group of three and then two because of the loss through death of the one known as Don, there came to be six and seven and even eight within the household which had gathered in hopes to serve the infinite One.

Perhaps it may be seen, as you look at this developing pattern, that, at this point, this particular group that is L/L Research, or the family that has gathered around the ideas and ideals of L/L Research, has gone for quite some time without sitting down in counsel and agreeing upon a group focus, a group identity, and so forth.

Now, what is it to be a group? May we say that it is what you wish it to be. Do you wish your group to have a physical focus? Do you crave that state of agreed-upon contractual support? Or rather, do you crave a sense of independence in your seeking, in your service, and in your learning? For there can be confederations of like-minded entities which do not have specific agreements within the physical plane.

Now let us look at what each of you brings to the circle of seeking in terms of group potential. Each of you has a certain energy, that with which you came into the world, that which is your unique and wonderful gift to give. There is no energy that is like yours. The way you relate to each of the others within this circle is unique. The colors of each of you blending, aurally, energetically, chakra by chakra, are marvelous and complex. You each bring your level of awareness, your gifts, your time, your energy, and your being. Most of all, you bring that essential beingness. You also bring unseen friends. Each of you has spiritual guidance and in some cases this guidance is extremely well developed. And it is as though your family history is with you, not in the sense of your physicality but in the sense of your stream of soul energy: where you have been, with whom you have worked in other lives, in other densities, on other projects. So you bring to a group your own energy and the energy of your guidance system. You also bring with you that which you hope, that which you dream, that which you intend.

When speaking of group energy it is good to see in the members not simply that body which fills the chair or sits upon the floor, but to realize that entity as an energy, a power, and an extended structure that walks back through time and space, connecting as it goes with other levels on the inner planes and on the outer planes as well. There is a very rich embranchment of energies that each of you brings. And as you sit in a circle as you are now, you may see yourself as the circle of stones at Stonehenge or a circle of trees in a magic circle and especially may we use the simile of the trees because in the trees there are those branches and those branches reach out so that you are not simply the trunk of a tree here, you have unseen ramifications that blend within the unseen ramifications of others within your group.

When you choose to come together as the kind of outer group where there is a perceived center of authority, it is much easier to move forward in ways that everyone can understand than it is to do so when the group is as yours: stubbornly dedicated to a center that is unseen, hoping just as stubbornly to serve in ways that remain mysterious. This entity, for instance, has hopes of developing a sacred growth center in the country, a place where a community was designed to be set down to live. This entity, therefore, is attempting to sense into what it is to create a community. "What will be needed for that kind of community?" this instrument has asked many times. The sense that this instrument has had is that the main need is to keep the focus pure, to keep the love unconditional, and we could not argue with such simple intentions. But how difficult it is to keep all things loving and all things pure when one is dealing with entities within third density who are necessarily imperfect and unaware of many of the ramifications of the things that they do and say! This is where the question that the one known as V had becomes very important and that is, what is the best way within such a group to communicate? The luxury of full communication is not one that is offered to third-density entities. It is a luxury within third density for even two entities to be able to communicate fully. It is extremely rare for non-telepathic communication to be entirely successful.

What needs to be remembered is that unseen energy of the open heart. When one is dealing from the open heart there is a feeling that accompanies the words and it is that feeling which must carry the gaps made by the imperfections of the beings involved and fill those gaps.

You also asked what is the appropriate way, when one entity in the group has failed to meet the criteria of the group, to deal lovingly with that entity. And, indeed, this is a question that is close enough to the surface of consciousness of this instrument that we find it impossible to move very close to discussion of this aspect of the question. For, indeed, as this entity was saying earlier, it has attempted to be impeccable in open-heartedness, in the loving quality of communication, and yet it realizes that it has failed to serve, in a pure and full way, the forces of love in this moment. For there have been hard feelings, disappointments and other emotions that tend to pull groups apart and to tear down the very work that the entity known as Carla was attempting to do.

When a question is this close to the consciousness of a channel, we feel it is inappropriate to attempt to move through that interference and so we will simply say that, to all of those within this circle of seeking and to any who attempt to serve the one infinite Creator, it is well to realize that each is dealing with imperfectly realized human beings who have, nevertheless, legitimate hopes, dreams and intentions. The group that comes out of such a circle of seeking needs to be that group which is the real, the essential heart of each of those within the group. When you have no dogma upon which to lean, when you have no perceived authority figure upon which to depend, when it is a true circle of seeking, and when the center of that circle is that unseen yet deeply felt truth of the Creator, when it is the One that calls all towards it, then each must become a priest, each must become an authority, each must choose for itself how and in what way it wishes to create a group. You have the opportunity to accept that which the one known as Carla and the one known as Jim have created thus far and attempt to help that perceived, physical group which is Jim, Carla and L/L Research.

Yet, both the one known as Carla and the one known as Jim have stepped back from the position of centrality and perceived authority to request that a group be created with its unique focus created within the entire group.

There is no right or wrong way to create a group. Either the group of L/L Research, as it was before each of you came, or the group that L/L Research might become if all entered into the creation of a further flowering of this group, would be not only an acceptable group but a wonderful group. There is no downside to creating a group, as far as we know. There is only your sense of how you would wish to enter into the creation of the group. Is the group as it is that which is comfortable? Then let it be so and let authority stem from the ones known as Jim and Carla and their perceived desires. If there is a further focus that can be gathered, and we feel that there is that which has potential to grow that is more than simply the hopes of the ones known as Jim and Carla, then that too would be a wonderful and a more complex pattern. We cannot encourage you one way or the other. Indeed, we can only marvel at the energy that has pulled you this far, that has lifted you off and tossed you into the pattern in which you are now scrambling for all you are worth, attempting to perceive the pattern within the chaos, that pattern which is forming.

We cannot say to you that spirit has the answer for you. We cannot say to you that there is one right outcome. All the outcomes possible are equally right. It is in your hearts, in your hands, and in your speaking. We feel the tremendous love each of you has for yourself, for each other, for the one infinite Creator, and for your planet. We sense the depth and the richness of your intention to serve and we gaze at the beauty of your being. And we know that you shall create light and life and new things. We are glad to be a tiny part of the energy that you have together.

We encourage you always to look to the unseen center, to look to the mystery that has called you here, and that calls you forward now. What is your group? What shall you do? It is in your hands. It is in your hearts.

At this time we would open the meeting to further queries. Is there another question at this time?

G: Q'uo, who or what are the "lions at the gate of green ray"?

We are those of Q'uo, and are aware of your query, my brother. The figure of the lions at the gate of the temple is an ancient means of expressing a truth concerning spiritual gifts. The New York Public Library, that this instrument has seen, has just such lions sitting couchant upon the two sides of the steps leading up to its main entrance.

The mythical concept of lions at the gate goes back for many thousands …

(Side one of tape ends.)

(Carla channeling)

… of years in your cultures and has to do with that sense of safety that entities wish to feel when they go to bed at night and blow out their candle and lie in the darkness waiting for sleep. There is that desire to know that you are protected. The reality of your inner energy system is that you are indeed protected at each level so that unwise use of energy cannot actually destroy the energy body.

When one is attempting to move into the heart, one is attempting to enter a sacred space. Even more than the gates of a city or the gates of a library which are supposed to protect knowledge and wisdom, the gates of the heart protect you, your essential self. If you barge into that sacred space drinking and wenching and swearing and making a great deal of rude noise, you have entered a sacred space inappropriately and the heart chakra does not wish

to be entered inappropriately. Consequently, if you attempt to move into your heart chakra, to come through that door into that sacred space, when you are not appropriately tuned, you shall, in one way or another, be kicked out by the lions at the gate. That is the meaning of that figure.

May we answer you further, my brother?

G: Not right now Q'uo, thank you.

We thank you, my brother. Perhaps as you work with this figure there will come a series of queries that we may follow with you.

Is there another question at this time?

V: Q'uo, you talk about the guardian at the gate as a metaphor also for the guardian between levels so that we are protected and can not advance too swiftly. There is a theme in mythology of the guardian on the bridge and I would think that would also be a metaphor for the same protection but is there something further there—not just the protection between levels of spiritual advancement but is there something else there that causes that figure of the guardian on the bridge to show up in so many different cultures in mythology?

We are those of Q'uo. and are aware of your query, my sister. It is an interesting query for, as the one known as V so often does, she picks up the nuances that cover hidden meaning. And yes, my sister, the reason that the figure comes up so often is that it is built into the fabric of spirituality or metaphysics or the time/space play of creation, [so] that only the honest and single-minded entity will be able to thread through that narrow place, that eye of the needle. Whether it is an emotion or a learning or a realization or an astonishing epiphany, [with] each piece of yourself, as you are able to retrieve it, it is as though you are retrieving it through a very narrow space, over a very narrow bridge, through the eye of a needle or in another figure of that kind.

It is not that the forces of spirit are attempting to imprison or limit. It is rather that the way of time/space is that things are allowed to bloom when they have been fully felt. And the quality of that fullness has to do with being willing to surrender everything that is not that thing. There is a tremendous amount of releasing and letting go in the process of crossing that bridge, passing the lions, and so forth.

May we answer you further, my sister?

V: Yes. Can you can say whether in fact there is an entity that is the guardian on the bridge or if it is simply the conscious nature of reality?

We are those of Q'uo, and appreciate your query greatly, my sister. It is not that we refuse to say, it is that we are unable to encompass the actual nature of the reality of the metaphysical world. There are, in fact, many such guardians and they are entities and essences. They are archetypal in nature. However, for each entity, for you, for the one known as Carla, for each within this circle and each within the creation, the nature of the self helps to create those archetypes. That is a very difficult concept to wrap one's mind around, that, you are not only the seeker but you have a very powerful part in creating the world into which you are seeking. The truth, so called, is beyond all efforts to seek it. And you yourself, as creator of your world, create, in part, the truth that you are attempting to seek.

The study of myth and archetype, therefore, is an interactive walk through the house of mirrors. For in many ways the archetypes are given and are as they are. In other ways, the entities that you meet are entities that you have helped to create. But they are indeed specific entities. However, as well, the fabric of time/space does have built into it the intelligence to recognize, respect and create openings for mature, ripened or fully formed awareness, consciousness or realization.

In each entity there is an ongoing process which is somewhat complex having to do with learning, initiation, the follow-up to initiation, the beginning of new learning, and the cycle beginning over. Further, there is not simply one initiatory cycle going on for most entities. Within this circle, certainly, [this is so] because they are not only learning from third density onward; they are learning from fourth density, fifth density, or sixth density backwards. Consequently, there are several initiatory cycles going on in most of your lives at this time. Not all of the critical portions of these cycles will hit at the same time. Occasionally, more than one cycle will hit, in a critical sense, at the same time, thus creating more than usual feelings of confusion and chaos. And certainly, this instrument has experienced this concatenation of more than one cycle moving at one time.

Thus, the purpose of the lions at the gate is one which is in an infinite process of shifting in order to respond to where the gates are in that particular entity on that particular day on that particular level; and there may be more than one level, more than one gate, and more than one lion.

May we answer you further, my sister?

V: Is it then a true statement to say that the archetypes are, on one level, certainly independent and separate entities or outflowings of the universe, but how they manifest and when and under what circumstances is determined by the seeker.

We are those of Q'uo, and are aware of your query, my sister. Within limits, my sister, this is a fair statement. May we answer you further?

V: Not on that topic, thank you. We do have a separate question from our friend, B. He asks, "If a wanderer kills another during his third-density incarnation but also spiritually awakens to be of service to others and strives to love all from the heart, will he still be able to make the harvest?"

We are those of Q'uo, and are aware of your query, my brother. The energy of manslaughter is certainly an energy that carries with it that which this instrument knows to call karma. You may see such an action as placing one upon a wheel of sorts. The wheel carries with it the self, the other self, all of the feelings which were involved in creating this relationship between the two, and so forth. In the classic sense of karma and cause and effect, the action has as its consequence a loss of unity with other self and stopping that wheel of karma has to do with balancing the energies that were disturbed by this transaction.

In any action in which another's free will is abridged there is the necessity to seek the forgiveness of the one whose free will was abridged. In a deeper sense, the transaction has also harmed the self and perhaps more than the other self, it is the self that has been harmed. Consequently, stopping the wheel of karma involves forgiving the self as well as asking the forgiveness of the other self.

It is not for us to promise paradise, for we do not hang upon a cross. We do not gaze upon other crosses and say, "This day, you shall be with me in Paradise." We can tell the one known as B that the forces of unconditional love would indeed speak from the cross of suffering and redemption and say,

"Yes, you shall be with me in Paradise." And we can offer that hope and that truth to the one known as B. From the standpoint, however, of one who is upon the ground, gazing at that cross, there is the self and the life that is left to live and the realization that each and every day of that life there is a choice to live in self-forgiveness, in service, in faith, and in hope.

We would urge the one known as B to work on the depths of forgiving the self, for, indeed, it is, we would say, impossible to plumb the depths of human judgment. Release those forces of judgment and know that you have come into the present moment and in that present moment lives a new life, a new hope, and a new being that is you. In this present moment, choose and dedicate that moment to the service of the one infinite Creator, and we do not feel that there is a single force in this universe that could be denying to you the love and the light of the one infinite Creator.

Is there another query at this time?

T: Q'uo, I've had a challenge for many years avoiding distractions during meditation. And I feel that recently it is greater or maybe I've noticed it more. Do you have any advice that might help my self and others in this situation?

We are those of Q'uo, and are aware of your query, my brother. We would indeed suggest to the one known as T that he find the music within the noise. The excesses of twentieth century classical music notwithstanding, there have been many successful attempts to frame, in some way, the art behind the nature of modern noise. This instrument, when away at school, also found herself within a very noisy atmosphere, for this instrument's school was on a truck route and there was a red light at the bottom of a hill upon which this instrument slept. So during the night there would be the screeching of air brakes as large trucks on their route approached the red light at the bottom of this hill which was paved with brick. It created a sound not easily described but easily imagined and certainly loud. This instrument found that if she created a song in which she used the melody and the tones of these otherwise obnoxious sounds in the creating of the melody so that she was able to acknowledge it and even hum along with it, she was much more able to take it with a light heart and see it as part of the music of life.

We realize that it is more difficult to do this with the careless and thoughtless noise of those around one who do not have to come to a stop at a red light while making their living. It is much more difficult to forgive entities who are not busy about their business for making unnecessary noise. But if it may be seen, or heard, shall we say, as a part of the melody of life, then it may be easier to acknowledge it, take it in, and even to have fun with it.

May we answer you further, my brother?

T: Thank you Q'uo. I have mental thought and distractions during meditation where the mind wanders and it wanders off into myself. Do you have any thoughts on how to manage that within meditation?

We are those of Q'uo, and are aware of your query, my brother. Our feeling about distracting thoughts during meditation is that these are acceptable. Our way of dealing with them would simply be to watch them, to sit with them and be with them, not either to resist them or to enter into them but to be with them and watch them. Let them arise and let them fall away.

May we answer you further, my brother.

T: No, thank you and thank you for your presence during meditation.

We are those of Q'uo, and, my brother, you lift our hearts! We thank you for being aware of us.

Is there a final query at this time?

G: Q'uo, I have a friend who's experienced a repetition in circumstance that appears to have created in her life a very striking patterns, this time around with slightly different circumstances, a slightly different cast of characters but a pattern nonetheless. Do you have anything to share with her that might shed some light into the meaning of this particular pattern or what she might look at so that she can discern what the meaning, what the pattern might be telling her?

We are those of Q'uo, and are having difficulty making out a query.

G: I can try to rephrase, I'm sorry.

We would appreciate that, my brother. We are those of Q'uo.

G: She is interested in knowing the meaning behind this particular pattern, the why's, what the message is, what it's telling her. Would you have any information that might shed some light on to that meaning for her or give her some clues as to how she might go about discerning the meaning?

We are those of Q'uo, and we believe we are aware of your query, my brother. When there is a repetitive pattern, then it is well simply to write it down, to treat it as a research project, to list those things about the pattern that seem obvious, to journal about those things that do not seem obvious and simply to start attempting to come into possession of a feeling that you have full knowledge of everything about this pattern that you could possibly know on a conscious level. Then I think, my brother, that we may say that it is a matter of taking that pattern and gazing at it without mind; taking it into the silence; taking it into that place that does not have boundaries and does not have rules of logic. For often, when there is a repetitive pattern, that which is attempting to be said to the self by the self is not all of a piece but is rather part on one level and part on another and so forth, so that there needs to be some time and some silence to surround the thoughts of this so that a new pattern in which the jumbled pieces are reshuffled and found to form a new and more sensible pattern emerges.

May we answer you further, my brother?

G: No, thank you very much, instrument, and thank you, Q'uo.

We thank this group from our hearts for taking the time and the energy to come together as a circle of seeking. It is a beautiful thing for us to share and we just feel very privileged to have been called to you. Thank you for asking for our thoughts. It is a true blessing.

We leave you, as we found you, in all that there is, in the love, in the light, in the unity, the power, and in the peace of the one infinite Creator. We are known to you as those of Q'uo. Adonai. Adonai. ❧

L/L Research is a subsidiary of
Rock Creek Research &
Development Laboratories, Inc.

P.O. Box 5195
Louisville, KY 40255-0195

L/L RESEARCH

www.llresearch.org

Rock Creek is a non-profit
corporation dedicated to
discovering and sharing
information which may aid in
the spiritual evolution of
humankind.

SPECIAL MEDITATION
FEBRUARY 24, 2005

Question from A: How can I see beyond this very compelling physical density? I've had experiences that were Christ Consciousness. When in the midst of such a blessing there is no doubt that the true reality overlays this one. My dilemma is how to access that state of consciousness more often, to the point of living in this world. I'm very aware of the massive shifts and changes on the planet and feel them quite intensely, like earthquakes. I'm also experiencing miraculous cellular healing that's happening to the people with whom I'm working. I'm eager to position my consciousness in that place of receptivity in order to radiate as much as I can. I want to understand more about how the biological interfaces with the higher dimensions.

(Carla channeling)

We are those of the principle known to you as Q'uo, and we greet you in the love and in the light of the one infinite Creator, in Whose service we come to you this day. May we say what a privilege and a pleasure it is to be called to such a group, to be asked such questions in a circle of seeking. It is more of a blessing than we can say. It is in order to offer just such communication that we remain within your planet's inner planes at this time. The opportunity to work with the one known as A is a great blessing. And to be able to work with each of those within this circle is a great blessing also.

In order for us to protect the communication and to enable us to feel completely free to share our

opinion, we would ask one thing of each of you within this circle and that is to employ to the greatest extent your own discriminatory powers, for only you can know what the thoughts are within those things we have to say that may be helpful. If there is that within our discussion that does not resonate to you, we ask you please to drop it and let it go without a second thought. For we would wish not to be a stumbling block before you but only a resource as you, in great independence and integrity, work with your own spiritual evolution. We thank you for accommodating us in this way.

We would say to the one known as A that, my sister, your questions have touched us deeply. It is most heart-opening to us to experience the energy that you bring to this session. It is encouraging to us to feel the certainty and the wholeness of your true and authentic self and to find that you have collected so much of your authentic self into the personality shell that must at times tremble to receive such authenticity. May we say that the essential nature of consciousness is such that the physical body and to some extent the energy body must be worked with patiently and over time, again and again, to accommodate the growth of self-perception. And as the authentic, essential self becomes a clearer voice within the crowded consciousness, it is especially well for the entity to increase its stock of patience with itself. For, you see, the more work that has been done in consciousness, the more clear it becomes to the seeker that there is precious little done and much left to do. And as work advances in this area, that consciousness of lacking the entirety of self becomes sharper rather than less sharp in its delineation.

As service is rendered to the one infinite Creator, there begins to be established a rhythm of synchronicity and questions asked and answered, whether by bird or beast or wind or rain or the Earth or the fire or by a street sign or by a passing conversation or by a song heard on the radio. Information begins to burst out of every hedge and sound and event. And again, as this rhythm intensifies, one must ask the self to be more patient, more tolerant, and more compassionate towards the self. Please understand that what is asked of a physical body in incarnation is that it carry the consciousness. To most entities working within your third-density illusion, the burden of this consciousness is relatively light. There has not been the level or degree of work done that is sufficient in its intensity to threaten the structure of the physical or the emotional bodies. When, over a period of time, again and again, there have been realizations so that the consciousness that is collected into conscious mind grows in its integrity and in its fullness of being, this physical structure can be pressed. And more than that, the mental and emotional energies connected with the chakra body or the energy body, as this instrument often calls it, increases accordingly. This is not to say that you are in any danger of being overburdened by the fullness of your awareness. It is rather to say that it becomes ever more important to do the work that you have come to do and that you are doing, slowly, with infinite patience and with a great deal of lightness of spirit and a sense of humor concerning the garments of human roles that you play, of peoples' perceptions of you, of your perception of your self, and of the multi-layered tangle that you pass through as a conscious being in the everyday world of consensus reality.

When you are preparing yourself for meditation, find the light in the tiny details of entering into that door and through that door.

(Inaudible)

What you are doing when you become aware, as you have said, of the overlay of a greater reality, is moving through a portal which is guarded by lions, as they say in the figures of religion and myth. These guardians are there to protect you in going into that sacred space and they are there to protect the sacred space from your premature entry. You have had no trouble with these guardians of the gate but we wish you to grasp that our encouraging you always to take the time and to enjoy the preparation for work in consciousness is in order that you may, at all times, be in complete accord with these guardians so that they not only allow you into the sacred space of your own open heart, but shall indeed, as this instrument would say, watch your back and offer you their love, their light, and their protection so that no mortal error may set its foot across that sacred doorsill into the temple of your heart

(Inaudible)

What is it to move into the open heart? In the outer world of consensus reality, when a person says "I," it is understood that that person is referring to its personality, the "I" that seems to move about and speak through the body that you inhabit. The one known as A is very well aware that this is a surface and incomplete version of the "I" that she is. And indeed, my sister, your query has a great deal to do with becoming more and more comfortable with the "I" that consciousness is within you. For consciousness is a portion of the Godhead principle. It is not a [personal] "I." It necessarily has a great deal of the details of your personality shell involved and this is something that we may perhaps share with you in helping you to understand what is occurring within you. For you are dropping away and letting go of more than you are aware, perhaps, within the surface consciousness. Again, this is not only an excellent process for you personally, this is a process that, in its very proceeding with you, aids the planetary energies and the planet itself in coming into a new awareness of itself, its evolving consciousness. For you are not an island of self in the temple of the open heart. You are more and more a part of the ocean that in its illimitable and infinite way, expresses and contains all that there is.

You have within you and surrounding you many helpers. Some of these helpers are internal to your own guidance system. Some of these helpers have been drawn to you because of the work that you are doing in consciousness and because of the service that you offer to those about you as you do you work in energy for others and with others. And again, although all of these entities, energies and essences are fully aware of your thoughts, yet still, in order to smooth and make more flowing the relationships involved in this web of love that surrounds you and helps you, it is well within yourself to be clear as to your intention as you enter into your tuning process, as you enter into what challenging that you may do in the process of your work and as you, in brief, attend to the various details of your inner processes. These need to be intimate to you and private and we would only encourage you to respect and honor your feelings, your hunches, every tingle of sensing that you have regardless of how incorrect and seemingly ungrounded these feelings are. Know within yourself and trust that each of these feelings is given to you in order that you may attend to every nuance and clean every speck of impurity from any edge that you may vaguely suspect may be there.

You see, my sister, the work that you are doing attracts entities that are not lovely and that hunger not to enjoy or support your light but rather to remove you from the light, or, if that is found impossible to do, to dim that light by the forces of doubt and fear. It is not necessary to guard against such energies. When such energies seem to enter into a transaction that you experience within consciousness it is enough simply to say, "You may listen but you may not join the circle; you may hear, but you may not cross the line and enter into this sacred space." It is enough to bless and to send love and to release any fear. It is not necessary to storm into self-defensive action or to call upon names of power. For you are, in your integrity, one who has those names and those powers in a certain, very appropriate, configuration around you. This has been done not by your design but by the design of what this instrument calls spirit. Much is prepared for one who has done the kind of work that you have done. And this is not true simply for you, for as you have experienced in your incarnation, there are many entities who walk the planetary surface at this time who have done tremendous work in consciousness, who have found their essential self. And you are not dismayed by the size and the power that that essential self carries but wish only to find the right use of that power, and right way of service, and to this you offer every iota of energy that has been gathered from the temple of the larger self.

Your query as to how to bring more of that greater "I" into the ordinary life is that with which this instrument is enormously focused upon in her own process, so we find a very rich ground for speaking

to you. And yet, at the same time, because of issues with this instrument's own free will, we must walk a careful line in order that we not interfere with this instrument's own process.

Let us talk a bit about how we see this situation that you describe, of attempting to bring into the ordinary life the expanded thoughts (inaudible). This instrument often speaks of the self as a crystal being and of the energy field of the self as a crystalline energy, the kind of crystal that is used in radio transmission (inaudible). The energy body interpenetrates the physical body. It is inseparable from the physical body within incarnation and it is carefully designed to be so. The silver cord, as this instrument has learned to call it, is that time/space or metaphysical link that nevertheless has its tendrils within the connection between the yellow-ray chakra and the green-ray chakra, or the energy level upon which the ordinary life is lived and the energy of the open heart. There is in this crystalline [chakra-body] energy form a very specific, shall we say, spine upon which the chakras wrap the self and within which they are in dynamic association, one with another. The first triangle of energies is the red-ray chakra, the orange-ray chakra, and the yellow-ray chakra. In this instrument's system those energies have to do with survival, with personal relationships, and then with the groups with which one works in the physical incarnation. The fourth chakra, the green-ray chakra, is known to her as the heart chakra and we would say, in this instance, that it is important to realize that there is between the yellow-ray chakra and the green-ray chakra what we are showing to this instrument as a right angle turn. But it is a right angle into time/space from space/time. It is impossible to describe or to draw in any physical form that this instrument is aware of or that we can give through this instrument.

Nevertheless, call it a jog, if you will, in the path. In order to turn the corner into the open heart, there is this matter of the lions that guard the gate to the temple. There is the path to be envisioned, whether it is a set of steps, or any other figure that helps you personally to move through this process. There is a genuine turning to the One and it cannot be done lightly or casually. Further, it is as if you were announcing to the inner planes through which this time/space portal passes that you have become a magical being. You take on the greater identity, the "I" that is all that there is or, in this instrument's way of saying it, the Christ Consciousness. You take on the energies of unconditional love and in this configuration you represent a point which spreads to enclose your self and, if you are working with another, the entity with whom you are doing energy work. This other entity also then dwells within the sacred space that you have created and in this environment, that entity has the opportunity to make choices. It is as though you were the point within a pyramid at which health can be preserved or things can be transformed, that point at which healing takes place, at which growth may take place if chosen.

In the usual form of magical work, such a personality change is taken quite consciously and at the end of a magical work, that personality is put away with equal care and equally in a conscious manner. Some entities actually use a physical object to remind themselves of the change in their consciousness. Some use a crystal which they place upon their breast before work and which they take from their breast after work. Some use a ring and place the ring which has been dedicated from its origins to this work on their finger before a magical working, removing it after the working.

Now what you are talking about doing in bringing more and more of this greater "I" into the ordinary life is maintaining a magical personality and we, while having no trouble saying that you are capable of this at times and on some levels, would like to engage your own creative process so that you yourself are more and more capable of assessing your abilities to maintain within the ordinary bicker and baffle of life lived in the ordinary, everyday way, a magical personality. There are times when you are perfectly capable of doing this, my sister. There are times when it is wisest of you to leave the magical personality aside, very consciously and very deliberately, knowing that there are stresses and biases within your pattern at this time that would suggest that it would not be appropriate to take that job into time/space, or to ask the lions at the gate to allow you through into the heart of your being.

It is a matter of judgment. It is in some ways exactly the opposite of what you would prefer to do to be assessing, in a rational and linear manner, your situation, your energies, and the true state of your heart at a particular time. And yet we would ask you to do this in order to protect your soul's health and the integrity of your energy body as well as, in a

more gross and physical way, protecting your physical body from the stresses that might come from disregarding graininess in the texture of your own spirit at a particular time so that you are asking your heart to stay open and asking that Christ Consciousness, or that awareness of all that is, to attempt to penetrate through the cracks and crevices of an ordinary life that is perhaps off-kilter.

There is a good deal of imperfection that is perfectly allowable, for are not all entities within third density, by the very definition of such beings, imperfect? It is not the imperfections that can harm you, but rather the carelessness with yourself that could come around again and bite you for as you are too eager to move ahead, then so that eagerness has that side-effect that you may see in gazing at an immature entity who tries to do too much. There is the possibility of burn-out. There is the possibility of banging the knees and thumping the thumbs and the elbows and the head against various crags and rocks and stones along the path in ways that we cannot describe through this instrument.

What we are saying to you is that, to the extent that you are able, allow a sense of your own situation to form up before you experiment with bringing the magical personality into everyday life. And when you sense, in the process of doing that, that that magical self is in any strain or stress, then we would ask of you that you remove the crystal from your breast, that you take the ring from your hand, that you do, in other words, whatever it is that you have agreed with yourself to do to signal to yourself and to the lions at the gate that you are now leaving the building.

My sister, this instrument is smiling because she is aware that we were using one of her favorite phrases, "Elvis has now left the building." In a way, that is what we are asking you to do: to see the Christ Consciousness that is within you as what it is. It is your true self but it is a stranger in strange land within ordinary life and to bring it through it is necessary for you to have a foot firmly planted in both worlds. That kind of balance comes and goes in the best as well as the worst of seekers.

This instrument has a habit when she is tuning of consulting the archangels which she associates with the elements of earth, air, wind and fire, calling forth before her, Raphael and the gifts of air; behind her, Gabriel and the gifts of water; on her right hand,

Michael and the gifts of fire; and on her left hand, Auriel, and the gifts of earth. We might suggest to you that your experiment with calling these entities before you begin an experiment in toggling between the magical personality and everyday life and attempting to join them. Attempt, shall we say, to sense into what expression is on their faces, how their robes may catch the wind and what their hands are doing. See how they are relating to you. What is their posture? Are they sitting? Are they at rest? Are they excited? What do they hold in their hands to warn, to encourage, or to support?

Such figures as this, through repetition of use, can begin to yield to you a wealth of information which is coded to you personally. This forms up over time, as many things do in spiritual work. It may be that there are repetitions that you must go through where you receive absolutely nothing. But we might suggest that you work with this figure over a period of at least a month, once a day, to develop it as a resource for you if it is indeed going to work out to be one for you, as it has for this instrument. If it does not resonate to you to bring this very specific and encircling elemental energy about you in this way, then we would suggest doing some reading for yourself in the general subject matter of western ritual magic or as this instrument calls it, white magic, looking at the figure of the tree of life, looking at the figures of those energies such as the archangels that have been used by many faithful servants of the light for many centuries. The point is not to get into another person's system. The point is to access systems that have been worked upon by pure and loving spirits over long periods of time so that in working with these figures or tropes or structures, you are allying yourself with or following in the path of those who have done work in consciousness before you, smoothing the way, moving stones out of your way, and creating a sustaining and underlying energy that helps you keep your balance in finding your own very personal way.

It is a rightful and appropriate thing for you to do, to live more and more in expanded consciousness. And indeed, part of what this instrument has been attempting to do for many years has been exactly this: to stand, not just in the dust of the ordinary, but to know that dust for the sparkling, glorious, crystalline energy world that it also is. All things are sacred. All motes of matter are alive and full of spirit.

And why should you not, in your consciousness, unite the densities and harmonize the sacred and the seemingly non-sacred so that the ordinary is illuminated from within and all things become a temple? We salute you for the attempt and we wish you to understand fully that you have succeeded by desiring to do this thing.

Earlier this instrument was listening to an album of music that had been created by an enthusiast of the *Law of One* material. And the one known as Carla and the one known as Jim we were reading together the liner notes for this album. In it, the author, the one known as L, was writing a memory that she had of her grandmother. Her grandmother's advice, she said, was never to be discouraged if you were a political activist, no matter how impossible your goals seemed, or how much of a failure you were at achieving them within the world. For the sheer effort of standing for the truth, for justice, and for the light, was the absolute success of activism. By desiring to bring together the temple that lies within the open heart and the outside world, you have succeeded already in combining them. What we are asking you to do is take a care for your own self in its surface aspects, in its shallower nature …

(Side one of tape ends.)

(Carla channeling)

… so that you bring along the mundane, not as a free-loader hitching a ride on the back of the wagon, but as an honored and respected passenger. The tendency can be, for spiritually powerful entities, to think less of the physical and the mundane and to think more of that greater consciousness within. And yet the glory of third density is the combination of the two.

Each within this circle at this time is a crystal. It is receiving the infinite love and light of the one infinite Creator and it is transmitting that signal onward. Does it transmit it with its full integrity? Does it transmit it with an added blessing? These are questions each must ask the self. You cannot help transmitting the love and the light of the one Creator. But how it is colored is entirely the result of the configuration of energies in that energy body and the connections between the energy body and the physical body. Consequently, each seeker is as a unique kind of flower: the colors, the shapes of its opening, the bloom, the way that it reacts and responds to the sunlight and the rain of spirit, are unique to each. No two selves have the same beauty. Each is a perfect and unique treasure. And we wish for you to see yourself in just that way and to embrace all of these parts of self, not only in those moments when you can see perfectly well that all is one and all is perfect, but also in those times when you are most fragmented and least aware of the truth of the wholeness and perfection of your being. Value the self in those times of seeming chaos with precisely the same energy and enthusiasm that you have when you feel and know that all is well and all is one.

The truth, my sister, is very simple. You are already, in terms of time/space, combining the greater "I" and the mundane "I." However, as we said before, the challenge involved in living this truth is in evaluating your energies so that when you are weary, you rest; when you are ragged emotionally, you lay down the burden of your knowledge of who you are, and you allow yourself to crawl into the lap of the one infinite Creator, to curl up in that lap, and to go to sleep being rocked by one who loves you more than you could ever know. Let comfort wash over you and let yourself take when you need to take. It is extremely well that you find those times when you have hunger and you have thirst and you have need and to ask for that food, for that drink, for that answer, knowing, beyond a shadow of a doubt, that you are worthy and that all is being attended to.

At this time, although we have not addressed many of the nuances in your excellent series of question you began with, we feel that we have used that initial energy and in sufficient measure that we would stop and ask if there are additional questions or if you would like to take other directions in what remains of this session of working. We are those of Q'uo.

A: Okay, if I've read what you said correctly, you are saying that I need to relax into the process that is ongoing rather than worry about the process. Is that correct?

We are those of Q'uo, and are aware of your query, my sister. We believe that you have it quite well in hand. That is exactly what we are encouraging within you. It is a relaxation into the process that is ongoing. You have sharpened your will and you have made it single-pointed. This is something that is very often a difficulty for entities but this is that which you have done. This has made it possible for you to penetrate. You have also focused your faith and

again, this has allowed you to broaden and to deepen your work. Consequently, with faith and will in hand, and with a dedication that is complete, the work of outer things may rest. What remains is an incarnation bursting with possibilities The shape of the rest of your incarnation is not known to us. It is not known to us how those things trembling into being shall form themselves. It is only known to us that this process goes well for you and that you may indeed relax into it and enjoy it.

May we answer you further, my sister?

A: Yes. I feel a caution, not to be like one of those who are not wanting to move forward. I want to be maybe more discerning as to whether there is within my personality complex that which doesn't get enough consideration, that which we might call a shadow?

We are those of Q'uo, and are aware of your query, my sister. Let us look at this query, for it is an interesting one. What is an entity that doesn't "get it" but a mirroring or projection of the part of the self that doesn't get it? What is any entity out there that seems to represent those who cannot come forward into the light but a portion of the self? So, indeed, it could be said in a surface way that indeed there is a portion of the self that does not give enough respect to the shadow. However, we would not choose to frame it in that structure for the simple reason, yet not so simple, that we sense within you a full awareness of and respect for the shadow, however it may be described or however it may be perceived. We do not sense within you an uneasy relationship with the wolf within, with that which can bite or kill or steal or be in any way the shadow self. Rather, we sense within you a love that is human and that wishes to embrace and heal.

However, in many portions of those selves that present themselves to you, not for healing but simply as selves, there is within them the unreadiness to accept healing, the unwillingness to sustain growth. And consequently, that great love and embrace that you feel is that which is unwelcome on levels beyond the possibility of others to address. For they know not that they have any resistance to healing and growth. Consequently, it is a matter of being able to respect and make allowances for entities that are other than ready to embrace their own light. Let them be as they are and know that for them that which they are projecting into your consciousness, as biased as it seems, is the best they can do, and is all that they can do. They are at the limit of their abilities at this time. So the reaction towards them at this time is still love and is still an embrace but it is an embrace that allows them to be as they are and with no judgment or thoughts of the future but with the awareness that they are precisely *(inaudible)* [as they need to be.]

May we answer you further, my sister?

A: No, I think I understand that. I would ask about my upcoming trip to Egypt with David Wilcock … Is there anything that I could do to further my receptivity in that time?

We are those of Q'uo, and are aware of your query, my sister. We would simply say to you that we would encourage you to move serenely, to listen well, and to know that these energies too are those that are guarded by those who love you and who wish to help you to serve humankind and the Creator. Again, the secret in service is not to reach, not to withhold, but to move in serenity, in peace, and within your own integrity at all times.

May we answer you further, my sister?

(No further queries.)

We find that the energy for this session is beginning to wane and if you have one last question we would be glad to entertain it at this time before we leave this group and this instrument.

A: I think my last question would be, is there any specific protocol on crystalline notes that would help me further my work?

We are those of Q'uo, and are aware of your query my sister. We offer to this instrument the suggestion that she share with you that she herself has found comfort in using a tuning fork that is tuned to the "F" above middle "C," that she chose because it is, in some systems, the sound of the open heart. We would not wish to move any further than this into discussions of tonal work for the reason that we would be interfering with your own process. Nor do we feel that this is any more than a beginning for you, that perhaps if you launch yourself in some way in chanting or simply intoning that energy and, if you have such a tuning fork, balancing it actually on the heart chakra as you are doing the work, that perhaps it will lead you to your own discoveries and open your creative springs.

My sister, we cannot tell you how much pleasure we have found in working with your energies and the energies with each of those within this circle. We thank each and we leave each in the love and in the light of the one infinite Creator. Adonai. We are known to you as Q'uo. ❦

L/L RESEARCH

L/L Research is a subsidiary of Rock Creek Research & Development Laboratories, Inc.

P.O. Box 5195
Louisville, KY 40255-0195

www.llresearch.org

Rock Creek is a non-profit corporation dedicated to discovering and sharing information which may aid in the spiritual evolution of humankind.

SPECIAL MEDITATION
MARCH 4, 2005

Jim: *(Reading S's question.)* First of all, Q'uo, S would like to thank you for your service to her and to all of us on planet Earth at this time, a time when we are all in great need of assistance.

She would like some direction in her own path of seeking. She would like to polarize more positively and she would like some direction as to how she could do this more effectively. She would like you to speak to any blockages that you may have noticed within her mind/body/spirit complex and please give her direction on what she can do to unblock these blockages. She would also like some information on how she could balance love and wisdom in her own life. That is a big lesson for all of us and she would appreciate whatever you have to say in that regard.

(Carla channeling)

We are those known to you as the principle of the Q'uo, and we greet you in the love and in the light of the one infinite Creator, in Whose service we are. We thank the one known as S this day for calling us to this circle of seeking. We feel most privileged and honored to be allowed to share our thoughts with you and with this circle of seeking. And we would ask of you that which we always ask with any circle to which we offer thoughts, and that, my sister, is that you use your discrimination in listening to what we have to say. We may be right on target with some of our thoughts and with other thoughts we may miss completely. We need for you to know your own heart and your own needs to the point where, if

something does not make sense to you or if it grates in any way, you lay it aside without a second thought. This discrimination will enable us to speak freely without abridging the free will of yourself or in any way encroaching upon the sanctity of your process. With this understood, we are satisfied that we are in a good position to be able to speak with you and we thank you for your consideration.

You have asked this day about how to advance and refine your polarization so as to achieve a vibration that is consistent with the fourth density rather than the third density of existence as you know it and about how you can better balance yourself in each chakra of your energy body in order better to create the proper environment for this polarizing work in consciousness. You also asked about the relationship between love and wisdom and how that dynamic works and how it can be balanced, which we feel will probably take care of itself as we address the first two questions, but we shall revisit that before we open the meeting to further questions. We thank you for these questions. They are excellent and we simply hope that we may have some material that will serve as a resource for you on this great seeking that you express at this time.

Polarization is a matter of choice and of repeated choice and we find in gazing at your energy that you grasp this basic fact very well and that you have been working on the basic choice of service to others or service to self and not for a short length of time but for some time within your incarnation. The subtleties of choice, especially the repetitions of choice, are sometimes more of a challenge than others. Some choices seem very obvious: whether to respond in anger to anger or whether to respond in love. That is an obvious choice. Yet let us examine this example for subtlety and nuance. When someone speaks with you in a way that feels angry or hostile or jangling to you, certainly your first impulse is to, as this instrument would say, clean up your act as far as the response is concerned. And may we say that we feel that you do a fairly good job for the most part in your responses. Of course, one could find ways to criticize the self. But 95% of the time, shall we say, your basic work in this area is sound and we congratulate you on the kind of full-body effort that you are making to be a gentle spirit, one who does return love, who does not ask to be loved but rather seeks to love. This is the heart of the polarization for fourth-density graduation.

When someone does express negative emotion to you, however, there is more information there than the simple hostility. There is truth. It is the kind of truth that you see in a hall of mirrors at the midway of a carnival. There are no mirrors that show you a true image in such a hall of mirrors. Every mirror is crazed. Some create a tall and slender S, others create a short and fat S. Some warp you to the right and some warp you to the left. Some make wavy lines throughout your entire image so that your eyes and your nose and your mouth do not match up and your neck is at one side and your torso at another and your leg off on the other side again. How can these images be helpful? That is the question that we ask you. How can the crazed and incorrect images of negative emotion directed towards you be helpful?

It is a brave and a stalwart soul who is willing to look into that question; to look into the nuances and the subtleties of other entities with whom you have crossed paths and whose reaction to you is, in fact, a projection of their own process. And may we say that in every situation, no matter how much distortion that there is in that entity's reaction to you and in that hostility that is unfair and unjust, nevertheless there lies material to be mined in the quiet of one's own thoughts all the time. For each and every image of you that appears to you is pregnant with information. Perhaps some of this information drags you where you would rather not go, into the shadow side of self that brings before you material that is painful. The injustice and unfairness of such images of the self that they project, from another whose reactions to you are negative, is seemingly completely incorrect. Yet in that moment of interpenetration of the two energy bodies there is sacredness if you are willing to accept the challenge of sitting in sacred space with such unhappy and unjust colors, shapes and images.

There is an honor to be done to those who are unjust to you, who do not understand you and who cannot see who you really are. To honor and to mine this information that you have been given is often a challenge which you need to meet only through a process of time, revisiting the thoughts that were shared, the feelings that you felt upon receiving these unjustly offered thoughts and so forth. The process is not bound by your awareness of consensus-reality time. You can revisit this moment a year from now and it will still be as fresh and real as it was when it occurred. So if you do not do this immediately, feeling the pain, being unable to go further with this material at the present time, that is perfectly and wholly acceptable. There is no time limit on work in consciousness.

Sometimes it may help in this regard for you to keep a little journal and to write down those things you feel you cannot process at a certain moment. You may find that there is a pattern to this, that certain relationships are almost entirely beyond your ability to process in the present tense, as we think of those things, shall we say, in your consensus reality, in space/time. Nevertheless it helps sometimes to note down what you can about this material, to write down how you felt, note simply what was said, or how unjust or just it might be. This is not necessary for you to do. What is helpful is simply to mark the moment and to note especially everything you can remember about your initial reaction.

What is this initial reaction? Let us say that it is an entry into an underground river or stream of emotion, for you never feel emotion alone. It is not your emotion. Rather, it is a part of the color and brilliance of a system of subconscious, shall we say, waterways that begin with streams of emotion that are very small, that perhaps few people experience. They are highly colored and highly biased and may have to do only with you and another person and perhaps three or four dozen other entities on the face of your planet who have experienced just exactly that combination of emotions that creates this crystalline moment with its biases, distortions, color and beauty.

You are a crystal being and everything you feel has its truth. You are always worthy to feel what you feel. There is never such a thing as an unworthy emotion. Everything, from seemingly black to seemingly blatant white in polarity, is acceptable to the one infinite Creator. Your job is to see and know the truth of yourself. When you feel these emotions you may feel they are unworthy but they are not. They are your truth and in feeling this emotion you have entered into what this instrument calls the archetypal mind.

Within the archetypal mind there is a very rich, detailed and broad spectrum of waterways, shall we say, emotionally coming from the most biased and the most colored and the most unique to you, moving slowly down into larger waterways which you come into as you purify these emotions, as you find distortion and bias and see into that distortion and bias. Over time, through realization and other work in consciousness which is more deliberate and less spontaneous, you begin to purify and refine the sensing system of your energy body so that when you feel the next emotion, even if it is exactly that emotion that was yours the last time that you felt it in connection with this relationship that is ongoing, say, yet you begin to enter into a larger waterway [than that] in which you are in the company only of those few entities who have your biases and have run into an entity and interacted and that entity has reacted in the same way.

You begin, as you refine your own system of energy and the corresponding emotional capacity of that crystalline being that you are, to enter into the system of archetypal mind in such a way that you are in a larger company, with more people who have done more work, just as you have done more work. What you are aiming for here is not to remove emotions but to refine and purify emotions. You are looking for a deeper and deeper truth about yourself. Now, just as all water systems do, when the stream becomes a creek and the creek becomes a river, the river widens and develops energy and power and finally it reaches the ocean. The ocean of the archetypal consciousness is unconditional love. You cannot rush or hurry the sail that you are on. You can mend your sails on your boat; you can correct and re-correct your readings of the stars; you can check your rudder for strength, but you must sail as

the truth of your being is ready to sail. Penetrating too quickly into the water system and especially into the ocean of the archetypal mind is dangerous for you. It may swamp your boat. And it will certainly land you in a world of confusion that you cannot sort out by yourself. So as you do this work of attempting to increase your polarization, we encourage you to respect and honor every truth that each emotion offers to you, noting it down. And if you cannot handle working with it at this time, yet still honor and respect your truth, your color, and your brilliance.

Now let us look further at the way in which one polarizes. Let us step back from the question of polarization and look at the energy body with which you are working. For simplification and convenience, that energy body may be thought to consist of the various chakras. And this instrument is aware of a system in which the chakras are as the colors of the rainbow: red, orange, yellow, blue, green, indigo and violet, with the white chakra, shall we say, hovering just at the top of that energy body as a crown. The first three chakras—red, orange and yellow—are the chakras which we would suggest it is helpful to visit every day, asking yourself in meditation, "What are my issues with survival? What are my issues with personal relationships with myself and with those about me? And what are my issues with the groups which I have decided to join as a human being in consensus reality?" These three categories are the categories of the red, orange and yellow energies.

Every human being living through incarnation upon planet Earth has biases and distortions in those three chakras that need to be gazed at in peace, serenity and lack of judgment each day, not with a view to kicking out the unwanted emotions or the unwanted distortions, but with a humble and open-handed prayer to be given guidance. Ask for balance. Ask for your guidance system to find ways to show you how to better balance your fears about survival, your concerns regarding relationships, and your puzzlement concerning the feelings, requests and requirements of the various groups into which you have chosen to come. They may be those relationships of the birth family or the marriage family. They may be work-related. But each group has its own biases and its own distortions and these are not necessarily a part of your own process. Yet they can pull you and push you and affect the way you perceive yourself and your process.

We encourage you to do this work patiently and with a sense of humor, and, most of all, completely without self-judgment. The object here is not to judge the self or to decide how to better the self. The object is to come into an awareness of where you are today.

The reason that we so strenuously encourage this work is that where you want to go in the next chakra requires that these three chakras, the basic chakras, be in sufficient balance that the infinite supply of unconditional love and energy for life coming into your energy system from the root chakra or red-ray chakra can move upwards without significant blockage. We do not say without distortion but without significant blockage into the heart. If you cannot clear the lower chakras enough that you are getting a good supply of the infinite love and light of the one Creator into the heart chakra, then this is where you need to stop for the moment It is important for you to be able to rest in the sacred space of your own open heart and to know yourself there before you can really do work in consciousness with any confidence that you will not harm yourself or confuse yourself more than you clarify things for yourself. As we have said many times through this instrument, there are what this instrument calls "lions at the gate" guarding your entry into your own heart. Listen to those lions and find the patience with yourself to do the work that it takes to make entry into your heart in such a way that the lions not only allow you to pass, but give you the feeling that they are now guarding your back.

Then take a few moments to rest in the consciousness of yourself in its larger sense. For you have, when you pass the first three chakras and move into the heart, moved from the outer personality into the inner truth, from space/time into time/space and from judgment into redemption or forgiveness. For you have become a larger you. The "I" that is the first person singular of you is significantly changed in the atmosphere and the sanctity of the open heart. When you feel that you are beginning to vibrate with unconditional love, you have then achieved that expanded awareness of the truth of who you are. Resting, then, in this truth, it is now safe for you to do your work in consciousness.

Your first work in consciousness is to come into open communication with yourself. You have put judgment away. That is not part of your personality any more. You have put doubt away. You are dwelling as a citizen of eternity. Your possibilities have become infinite. The world has dropped away in terms of consensus reality and you are living at this moment, doing this work in time/space and in the company of all who have gone before you, living a life in faith, dwelling in the sacred temple of the open heart. Here you are never alone. The Creator Itself holds you in an embrace that is nearer to you than your breathing, closer to you than your body. If you need to—and it is sometimes necessary to realize that this is all you need and all you can bear—crawl into the lap of that great entity that is the Creator, however you may see this entity—mother, father, great principle. Crawl into this loving lap and rest. Do no more than that if this is what you need. Let angels surround you. Let the love that is completely unconditional, that created you and sustains you, now rock you and sing to you and sleep the sleep of one who is loved as a child is loved by its mother.

If, on the other hand, you dwell in that temple and are ready for more, then by all means move into those energies you wish to explore. If you feel that you have explored the blue-ray energy of open communication thoroughly and you are ready to move into work in consciousness, then you may work at visualization, meditation, contemplation or any other roads that you seem called at that one moment of work to begin to walk along. There are many paths. They do all lead to the Creator. You cannot take an incorrect path in thought or in meditation or in practice. And you need to move by feelings, by that resonance that tells you when you are on the right track. The blockages that you have spoken of are those within your energy body that would narrow the inrush area of the incoming energy of the one infinite Creator.

Now picture with us, if you will, the image of this metaphysical body that is interpenetrating your physical body. There are two sources of the love and the light of the one infinite Creator. One is universal. It moves from the base chakra upwards. The other source is much more focused and pointed. It is the result of the work in consciousness that you have previously done and that exact point at which you are now entering, doing this work at this moment. And this is experienced as coming down through the crown chakra into the violet ray. It moves from the violet ray according to the ways of your energy body. It will not harm you, and if it cannot move further than the violet ray, it will remain there and it will not pull the energy upward. However, when you have achieved an entrance into the open heart and are seated, shall we say, that is, physically speaking, in the green ray, in that temple of the heart, then your hands are empty and you are seeking. Then that universal energy may be pulled upward to where the intelligent direction of your guidance system would cause it to go and your guidance system's energy, coming down from above, will meet your universal energy at that point. This is work that cannot be thought out or done on purpose. Rather it is a matter of trusting your process and offering your prayer with empty hands, not saying "Lord, I need this; Lord, I need that," but saying, "I come to you seeking the truth of myself. Show me that which you have to offer me this day. Help me to be a part of the creative or godhead system. Give me my daily bread. Give me that which I may work with and learn from just for today." And then allow silence and faith to rest with you as you sit in the temple of your own heart.

Many things may come to you as you sit and rest. Again, take them in without judgment; without reservation. Repeat the process as often as you can, daily if possible, and over time you will begin to see why it is called a spiritual process.

My sister, you are asking for the hardest work imaginable within third density. It is work which the physical body literally cannot bear without help. That is why we so greatly encourage the clearing of the first three chakras before doing work in consciousness. You do not want to sublimate these basic red-yellow-orange issues in order to get at work in consciousness. No matter how boring or less than exciting it may seem to do the clearing work necessary before opening the heart, this is what protects your physical body and maintains it for you so that work in consciousness will not create a serious mismatch between third-density issues and fourth-density learning. You need, therefore, gently and patiently to bring that physical body into balance and bring the three chakras having to do with the physical body into more and more clarity. It is a matter of knowing who you are on so many levels.

And you shall not come to a place where you will know everything there is to know about your physical body or your physical energy body. New information will come to you every day. New situations will change your tuning in red ray or yellow ray or orange ray every day. So you cannot simply do the work and then move on. It is repetitive, daily work.

You already have an absolute and overwhelming love for how it feels to be in the open heart. And a great deal of your service in this incarnation has been done from an open heart. Yet we ask you, my sister, "What have you left behind in your rush to open the heart, and what do you need to collect lovingly and patiently so that when you move into your heart you bring all of yourself?"

Let us look at the figure of the redemptive Jesus, for the one known as Jesus, as you have told this instrument previously, is very dear to you. Therefore, we will use this particular teacher and what this teacher has to say about the open heart in looking at your situation.

The Creator requests of you that you take up your cross and follow the one known as Jesus. We are not speaking literally or dogmatically here, but we are using an image and a figure or a structure, if you will, which many people of faith have been able to use well. What is it to take up one's cross but to honor your suffering, to know it and not to turn away from it or to avoid it but take it upon yourself. It is said, "For his yoke is easy and his burden is light."[15] What makes this yoke easy? What makes this burden light?

The one known as Jesus said, "When you see me you do not see me but you see the Father who sent me."[16] Can you see how that illuminates the challenge to

---

[15] *Holy Bible*, Matthew 11:28-30: "Come to me, all you who labor and are heavy-laden, and I will give you rest. Take my yoke upon you, and learn from me; for I am gentle and lowly in heart, and you will find rest for your souls. For my yoke is easy and my burden is light."

[16] This saying is in several forms throughout the Gospels. Here is one version from John 10:25-29: "The works that I do in my Father's name, they bear witness to me; but you do not believe, because you do not belong to my sheep. My sheep hear my voice, and I know them, and they follow me; and I give them eternal life, and they shall never perish, and no one shall snatch them out of my hand. My Father, who has given them to me, is greater than all, and no one is able to snatch them out of the Father's hand. I and the Father are one."

take up your cross and follow? You are not following an entity known as Jesus. You are following the one the Father sent to do His will. You are following an entity that was described by the one known as Jesus over and over again in ways that would indicate that this entity wished, when you said the name "Jesus," not to think of a personal consciousness but to think of unconditional love. And this entity put itself on a cross to express what unconditional love is. This entity expressed it literally as the giving without expectation of return. And in that unconditional giving lies the key to the entry into fourth density.

So the one known as Jesus as a teacher was saying to you, "Love is the way; love is the truth and love is the life."[17] Thusly we say to you, as you focus yourself into work in consciousness, "Know who you are."

And in a way you are your pain. If you may see that you need to carry that cross into the sacred space of your own heart, you do not need to get rid of that pain. You need to honor that pain. And as you collect it into yourself, you are collecting all the darkness within you so that no shadow remains of which you would say, "That is not part of me." You wish to collect all of yourself into the sacred space and then you wish to follow the ways of unconditional love in that sacred space.

And how do you follow love but to trust it and to know that it is the truth of you? It is your larger consciousness and if you cannot yet feel every iota of that unconditional love then you should be patient and you should ask and you should await, in utter faith, the realization that is to come.

This instrument is instructing us that we must wind up our main question, and so we would simply once again touch upon your question concerning the balance between love and wisdom. And here, my sister, we would say to you that you have challenged yourself within this incarnation with this balance between love and wisdom. And why would you

challenge yourself? It is not because you do not have enough of either, but because you may have an overbalance towards love. And in that regard we would ask you, when doing work in consciousness, to visit the blockages within those first three chakras, asking yourself the question, "Am I worthy?"

The open heart knows the answer to that question, but when you are doing work in consciousness you are the Creator and so you have a great deal of capacity both to learn and to delude yourself. Therefore, examine the love you have for yourself and the redemption that you know that you possess. And wherever you find yourself unredeemed by your own self, wherever you find yourself judged by yourself, we ask you to move to the foot of the cross and look up into the eyes of the one known as Jesus. We remind you of the stress of this entity upon the cross as he hung between two thieves and murderers. We remind you that one thief asked the one known as Jesus, "Master, when you get to Paradise, will you think of me?" The one known as Jesus said, "This day you are with me in Paradise."

Your redemption is absolute. It is not time-bound. It is not local. It has nothing to do with how imperfect you are. It has to do with the fact that you too are part of the Creator.

We thank you, my sister, for these beautiful questions and for the delight it has been for us to share our thoughts with you on them and would ask at this time if there are follow-up questions that you would like to ask? We are those of Q'uo.

S: No. There is a great deal here for me to ponder, digest and work upon and use. And until I do that, I won't have any further questions. I need to think a great deal and work with it. And I thank you so, so very much for all that you are doing for us. This is a difficult time right now and I cannot express how much it means, the love and the care and the help that you give us.

(Carla channeling)

We are those of Q'uo, and, my sister, we thank you too and would express our humility in the face of the beauty that you offer to us. We thank each of those within this circle for the beauty of their being and for their willingness to stop and yield moments of their precious time in order that they may come to the circle of seeking and seek that truth. We seek it with you, my sister, and we simply leave you and

---

[17] *Holy Bible*, John 14:1-6: "' Let not your hearts be troubled; believe in God, believe also in me. In my Father's house are many rooms; if it were not so, would I have told you that I go to prepare a place for you? And, when I go and prepare a place for you, I will come again and will take you to myself, that where I am you may be also. And you know the way where I am going.' Thomas said to him, 'Lord, we do not know where you are going; how can we know the way?' Jesus said to him, 'I am the way, and the truth, and the life; no one comes to the Father but by me.'"

this circle in the love and in the light of the one infinite Creator. We rejoice. We are at peace and we rest in all that there is. We are those known to you as the principle of the Q'uo. Adonai. Adonai. ☙

Sunday Meditation
March 6, 2005

Group question: The question today has to do with guidance and how people can perceive guidance, how they can become aware of their guidance, and along a more specific line, we're wondering just exactly how guidance can be perceived by people who do what we would consider to be quite evil things like killing, controlling and torturing other people? Is it the case that guidance goes bad or is it the person, in the way they perceive the guidance? Could you give us some information on guidance, please?

(Carla channeling)

We are those of the principle known to you as Q'uo. We greet you in the love and in the light of the one infinite Creator, in Whose service we are. May we express our thanks to each of you for creating this circle of seeking and express what a privilege and a joy it is to be able to have the opportunity to share our thoughts through this instrument on the subject of guidance, both the positive and negative aspects of it. It is a large subject and we can but hope to make a beginning in this session of working. But we are most grateful to you for providing the energy and the question to create a sharing of energy amongst all of us and you. We offer this up to the Creator and would ask of you only that you continue throughout this session and when you think of this session to use absolute honesty in examining your feelings about the thoughts that we share. Your discrimination is priceless. No one else can know what is right for you

but you. You are the authority; we are not. We are only those who share thoughts. Please, if there are thoughts that we share this day that trouble you or in any way do not resonate for you, drop them. Put them down and leave them behind, for they are not a part of your process. If you will do us this favor it will help us to feel reassured that we can share our thoughts without in any way damaging your own free will or the sacredness of that process within you which is your spiritual evolution.

You ask this day concerning guidance and we find that without a certain amount of discussion before we begin talking about guidance itself, we have nothing on which to hang it: no structure which will hold us and hold the concepts about which we would like to speak. And so we would step back from that question long enough to share a few thoughts about the way we see you as beings.

We see you as entities with, as this instrument has said recently, feet firmly planted in two worlds. You are soundly and firmly entrenched from your birth onwards throughout incarnation in a world of illusion that this instrument calls third density. It is consensus reality, as it were. It is the world in which you meet people, make relationships, create a living for yourself and for your family, and find value, meaning and direction in a life that is full of choices. Upon entry into incarnation you receive a formative bath of cultural orientation. Your parents teach you what to think about the reality that meets your eyes.

You form biases based on incorrect information given to you by parents and teachers and other authority figures. You create biases within yourself by the pain you experience when you are too helpless to defend yourself from such pain. And when it becomes too much to bear, you create pockets of pain deep within yourself and you bury them over with good times and school assignments and the growing-up process. By the time you have reached what your culture would call adulthood, you have a set of biases within yourself which have created a somewhat colored and distorted view of this consensus reality. And this is the beginning that each of you has. This is your start towards the grand adventure of moving from consensus reality and its extremely limited choices and thoughts into a greater world, a world that is non-local, that this instrument would call the metaphysical world or the world of time/space. It is this world from which you came upon entering incarnation. It is this world that you agreed to forget upon birth so that you could, with absolute freedom of choice, find your way, through desire alone, into what is loosely called the truth.

Now let us look at this situation. The help that you have for this journey is your larger self. Here is a larger self that includes the Creator and all that there is. Through many, many experiences of all the densities of experience up until now in your space/time travels, you have explored the energies of the elements: the plant kingdom, the animal kingdom. You have come at last into the world of animals which bear consciousnesses that are non-local. This is the animal that you now are in third density or in your consensus-reality beingness. It is not that you are divided or split against yourself. It is that the surface of yourself is created by the experiences of a bio-computer that is strictly your brain dealing with every experience that has touched you, and especially hurt you, in such a way as to survive that experience. You remember the good times, you remember the difficult times, you remember the choices that you have made and those things that seemed to have worked for you. You have found ways to protect yourself, to defend yourself, to help yourself be comfortable and happy. And you have done all of this with that consciousness that this instrument would describe as a great ape's. Many instinctual behaviors have helped you to focus your energies in order to experience life as a comfortable thing.

At the same time, as you have become competent in working with your third-density body, making those choices and living your life, you have, whether early or late, whether suddenly or gradually, become aware of the larger universe that interpenetrates and surrounds consensus reality.

There are many attempts by authority figures in one's childhood, usually, to interest a growing being in the interests of religion. And often the first forays that a seeker has into that larger reality of the spirit is offered through the offices of religion. Sometimes, as in the case of this instrument, the orientation of the seeker is such that such entries into spirit actually work, and there is given to one such as this instrument the opportunity to live a life in faith; never leaving the comfortable confines of a parish church and yet glorying in the company of angels and archangels. And so it has been for this instrument. She did not reach far for her guidance system, for it was the [guidance system set up by the] one known as Jesus, whom she knew as a childhood friend. [This guidance system] is the one known as the Holy Spirit. [This is only] words to most people, but to this instrument [it is] a living being whom she has come to call Holly and with whom she talks every day.

For most entities who truly and deeply seek and will not be satisfied with the commonplaces that do not fill the empty places in the heart, none of this works. And so the seeker begins a journey; whereto he does not know. All he knows is that he is seeking to fill the empty place within. It is not given to the seeker to know that he is already in that larger universe that he so craves to know. To the seeker, it somehow is all out there and to be reached for. And yet, that is not the model that we would give you nor the model with which we would ask you to work in attempting to clarify and refine your contact with your own guidance. We would offer you rather the picture of yourself as a being that rests already in the sacred space within, so that the process of learning is actually a process of recovering or remembering who you are.

Now, before incarnation, you created things for yourself that will stand you in good stead. You created relationships that would try you, test you and teach you how to serve without any expectation of return. You created ways in which you could in some outer way be of some service to those around you. And it is a wonderful exploration to undergo in faith to look at each day with the question, "How can I help? How can I serve? Whom can I love? And what shall I learn?"

You do not ask these questions in a void. You ask them within the sacred space of your own heart.

That which we offer this instrument is offered in a very careful way. This instrument tunes for this contact as if she were a radio station, tuning to her highest and best self. And when she is there, knowing she is unworthy, but asking to be of service regardless, she offers herself with a whole and utter completeness to the highest and best energy that she knows. And in this instrument's case, this instrument asks for the energy of Jesus the Christ, or what many would call Christ Consciousness, and what this instrument prefers at times to call unconditional love. She asks for the highest and best contact that she can carry in a stable manner of unconditional love. Then she gathers around herself a group so that she does not bear this upon her own shoulders, at all, but rather is simply the group's focus and the translator of energy from one density, shall we say, or level, to another. It is a fairly complex practice and is geared towards the collection of information which has polarity and which therefore has power. She selects that target to which she attaches herself or with which she connects in order that she and this energy, this source that she has sought, may come together and create a body of words with the hope that such words may inform and inspire. There is risk involved in this work. It is the risk of receiving information that is not helpful, that is not positive, and that creates fear and anxiety rather than harmony, hope and community.

When an entity by itself seeks guidance, there is no such risk. The instructions from many sources within your consensus reality on this are very clear. The suggestion in general is to go within. Go into that inner room of prayer, closet oneself and listen to the silence. You see, guidance does not actually come in words. This instrument is not receiving direct guidance from us. This instrument is translating concepts that may have some power to heal or to help growth in your process. And in inner guidance, it is the same [conceptual] truth. So often, entities who feel that they have received guidance express it not in terms of words but in terms of epiphany, or realization. It is much larger than words can hold, this content of truth. The going into the silence is, first of all, to stop the self from talking; to divorce the self from the busy mind or what this instrument would call the monkey mind of third-density thought.

Now, many times, each of you within this circle has experienced that wonderful movement from local and linear thought into imagination. Connections become looser and they slide across disciplines and ways of thinking, finding friendly structures in unlikely places. And one begins to create castles in the air and have wonderful towers of thought that have come to one somehow sideways. This is guidance at its most elementary. When you have finally been able to begin to disconnect the relentlessly logical, linear mind and have lifted away from ratiocination to imagination, then you have become ready to behold your larger self. As you sit in the silence of no-thought, as you relax into that sacred space that silence builds within you, your body is able to relax and let go of its incredibly tenacious hold on your deeper consciousness. Physical changes occur to one who is simply sitting and resting. The blood pressure drops, the pulse slows, the brainwaves actually change and chemical changes occur throughout the body systems. You can breath more deeply at last and begin to release yourself into your fundamental seeking. You can begin at last to ask the questions that are too deep for words.

For most entities, the first thing that occurs when you move into the silence is that all of the things at which you have not wanted to look or which you have put aside because there was no time come up and are viewed by you. Do not resist these forays into seeming thoughts, for they are the material about which the very highest part of your subconscious being has been concerned. Welcome each of them as a guest without any attachment to how long that guest will stay. Sit with that guest. Listen and observe. This is something that has been stuck in your energy body. Let it get unstuck, but do not follow it. Allow it to express, allow it to rise, and allow it to fall again. This process may be all you can do for months if you are simply a beginner to silent meditation, and that is fully acceptable. That is progress of the greatest kind. Gradually you will become able to move deeper because you have begun clearing your energy body and those blockages and distortions that were most troubling you, that were most constricting the energy on its way to your open heart, will have been released, balanced, loved and accepted by you.

Have you any idea how unaccepted you are by yourself? You have only to go into meditation to discover that. Let the ghosts that haunt you visit you. They cannot hurt you. You are safe. Allow them to rise, and begin to look at those ghosts and the shadows that they represent as worthy, honored, loved, accepted and embraced. This is a powerful process and may we say that, in our opinion, it cannot be rushed. It can not be hurried. It has its own rhythm in your life in spirit. And once again, as you persist day by day in the discipline of allowing yourself to get to know yourself, you are clearing the way for an ever deeper understanding of who you are.

Each of you came here very focused on learning and service. And yet you walk through the veil of incarnation and you forget that focus so that as you live your life, you are learning not by rote, not by memorizing lessons that some teacher or authority figure has given you, but by every thought that you have, every desire that you are able to identify. The refinery of Earth is one in which you decide what to refine, what to pursue, what to bring up from the treasury of your own subconscious material and how to mine that material for the jewels that it contains. And it is in this model that we would talk to you about guidance.

You came into incarnation supported and bolstered, without any possibility of being abandoned or isolated, with a very solid, sturdy guidance system. It is up to you to create the structure with which you feel comfortable as a person for receiving this guidance. To some extent, you may do reading into religions, philosophies, myth and archetype, for each culture has ways of describing and structuring guidance. For the Native Americans, for instance, every animal has a role to play in guiding. Each animal that you meet, therefore, is a messenger. There are systems of guidance which employ inspired human beings who act as gurus; and these gurus are able to focus spirit in such a way that realizations come to the student who is devoted to the guru. There are those religious systems which ask of one that one follow a certain master such as the one known as Jesus, the one known as Buddha, or the one known as Allah and his prophet. There is an almost infinite array of ways to approach beginning to become aware of guidance.

In general, we would say that you must follow the path of greatest resonance. If there is a master who resonates to you so much that you wish to follow in the footsteps of that master, then you will take a certain path towards guidance. If you find that you are more comfortable following the chain of coincidences, of those things that speak to you from day-to-day, then life itself becomes the messenger of guidance. And, in many cases, by the simple discipline of beginning to record one's dreams or one's thoughts after meditation, one is able to gain access to that web of love and support that is all around you and waiting with the greatest of eagerness and joy for the opportunity to be heard. We describe this and characterize this as guidance of a positive or service-to-others nature.

You have also asked about guidance of a service-to-self nature, or a negative nature, such as the [guidance system of the] one known as Hitler and other obviously service-to-self entities who are not interested in helping others but in controlling them. Within the time/space densities from which guidance comes, the positive and the negative paths are separated. One within fourth or fifth density has chosen either to serve others or to serve the self. You as a positive spirit are receiving guidance from your own greater self at a density that is further on in space/time than your own. You are receiving back the information that you have won by earning it through lesson after lesson, service after service, and density upon density. When you receive guidance of a negative nature, it has not been arranged beforehand. It has not been planned before incarnation. Rather, it has the character of a predator and its prey. For the service-to-self entity that wishes to be a negatively-oriented guide for a third-density entity is actually looking to control the source of power and to be sure that that power does not turn towards the light but towards the darkness.

These entities are what this instrument would describe as vampiric in nature. They are looking to feed upon your love and to turn it into fear. The path of their ingress into your system of awareness has to do with those deeply buried spaces of pain, which are usually embedded during childhood but may have been embedded more recently, in the adulthood, as well. Usually the deepest pockets of pain and suffering within an entity's psyche are those that have been buried since childhood and have been well covered over. If you have distortions involving anger, for instance, such an entity can find a roost deep within you. And if you become interesting to such an entity because you have begun to seek the light and have therefore polarized and begun to accrue power to your being within incarnation, you will attract such entities' attention. And they will look throughout your armor of light, shall we say, throughout your energy body, to see where there is a hidden pocket of pain that is unknown or unaccepted by the conscious mind and unloved by the conscious heart. And into this pocket they will come and perch and wait for the opportunity to create fear, pain, division and so forth.

Each entity is vulnerable in her own way to such greeting. It is like a Chinese puzzle, in that the more such greeting is resisted, the stronger it can become. Had the one known as Hitler been able to turn and face the pain within him, this entity would not have been able to delude himself as he did; for indeed this entity believed that he was aiding not only himself but his entire race, with which he identified strongly, by excluding those who were not perfect, as was his race. To build up such prejudice is to move ever deeper into fear and exclusion. When in your life you see divisive energies, energies that judge and exclude and create a feeling of elitism and a sense that one is better than another entity or another group, you can easily finger the culprit. You have been beguiled by vampire energy into turning to a part of yourself in which the light is not developed.

There is always the choice, when this is perceived, as to how to deal with the situation. If you reject yourself and judge yourself for having come into this configuration of thought, then you are increasing those divisive energies and moving further from the love that you understand is positive. You are still engaged in loving but that love has been distorted into fear and into those negative emotions which attack, defend and create barriers.

Moving back into a gaze of the self, you may see that it comes down, ever and always, to this moment. Here is the moment of choice; here is the arena of so-called light and so-called darkness. Shall you love what you see or shall you reject it? All of polarity and all of your access to guidance rests on your decision, in this moment, to embrace, include and love; or to reject, exclude and fear. Here is where words like faith, grace and hope are seen to be entities of great beauty, power and truth. At the moment that you realize that you must ask for help, you have already begun to receive that help. It is as reflexive as breathing out and breathing in. Know that you are never alone when you seek the truth. Know that you are in the company of those that love you and wish only to support you.

How to access your guidance? There are as many ways as there are people. And we will be glad to explore any of those ways about which you wish to ask. Simply knowing yourself to be the being that you are is the beginning of a great adventure. And may we say that at any time that you wish us to aid in your meditation, we are glad to join you if you will but mentally request our presence. It is not that we have anything to add but our love. That love is as a carrier wave that enables you to meditate a little more smoothly and deeply. We gladly offer that and are most grateful to serve and we thank each of you who has asked us and who has been able to feel that underlying and undergirding steadiness that comes with meditating as part of a larger group. Be assured that you have an extended family of what this instrument would call angels and beings that have worked with you before that rest around you continuously and that bolster you on every side: before and behind, above and beneath. You rest in a web of love.

We would ask at this time if there are any queries before we leave this instrument and we thank each of you for enabling us to respond to such an excellent question. We are those of Q'uo.

Jim: I have a question, Q'uo, from K in Finland. She asks, "Did the planet Earth have an unusually great amount of extraterrestrial visitors from near and far after mid-September this past year, in 2004? Was there anything special happening around our planet that may have prompted this keen interest in us?"

We are those of Q'uo, and are aware of your query, my sister. We would not answer this query specifically. However, we would like to comment in general that as your planetary sphere and, indeed, the solar system in which it rests and dances, reaches this particular end-date of what this instrument calls third density upon planet Earth, there have been and will continue to be repeated waves of incredible energy that are rolling across your planetary sphere and the inner planes that are connected with this planet. They are waves of things leaving and things coming. It is as though night were falling and dawn was breaking and in between, as this instrument would say, "Katy, bar the door."

Again, it is a crowded universe.

Now let us focus briefly upon the linkage between third density and fourth density. In attempting to graduate from third density to fourth, this planetary sphere has so often repeated a singular error that it has been unable to achieve a complete planetary graduation in a long time, much longer than has been experienced by most planetary spheres. It is an extreme enough and unusual enough occurrence that it has created what this instrument would call a time lateral, or a shunt. The train of planet Earth's people has sort of gone off on a side track until it can bring itself together in love. Instead, repeatedly, it has brought itself together in fear. And this is not unusual considering that we see upon your planetary sphere those who have, as those of Mars did, destroyed their planetary surface by war; and as those of Atlantis did, destroyed their continent by misdirected crystal energy. The tendency, therefore, of this planet's people is to become wrapped in fear and cause an explosion of negative energy that is usually seen as war. This pattern has repeated itself through empire upon empire and now those who have, in the past, been a part of this pattern have almost finished what they can do to gather together what this instrument would call Armageddon or *Gotterdammerung*.

They have failed. We believe that we now see that this is so. Nevertheless, the thrashing of what this instrument would call the dragon's tail is yet mighty. Up until approximately—we give this instrument a figure of five years ago—the probability/possibility vortices were that this pattern would repeat itself. However, enough positive energy has begun to be gathered in the hearts of the planetary population of humankind upon planet Earth that the very likely polar shift that was expected before the end of your twentieth century was averted. What is occurring now on your planet as it goes through the labor of planet Earth into fourth density is that delicate task of releasing the negative energy collected by this planet in ways that do not destroy the planet. And so, as we have said before, you can see the tsunamis, the earthquakes, the catastrophes that are terrible but not Earth-shattering, and we mean that literally. Love has transformed your possibilities and now you gaze at the genuine possibility of bringing the planetary sphere together in a web of true love.

My friends, how much you have to balance! It is a staggering challenge. But the hearts of the people of planet Earth are beginning to come alive with a great desire to love each other; and this is your calling at this time. It is for this reason that you came to this incarnation. And we say to you, love one another. Waves of energy both positive and negative will continue to impact your planet. Every ghost that you did not ever want to see again will come directly face-to-face with you and if you are very lucky that ghost will be shown to you in an honest and loving mirror. That is the most for which you can hope. For in order for you to become a truly loving person, you shall need to embrace these energies, accept these ghosts as part of yourself, and integrate your personality more and more into that part of yourself that is the consciousness of living Godhead.

May you fare well with these birthing energies and become pioneers of fourth density.

Is there another query at this time?

(Pause)

We are those of Q'uo, and find that we have exhausted the questions in this circle of seeking for the moment. We say again to you what a privilege and a pleasure it is to be with you and to share our humble thoughts. And may we ask you again to discard them without a second thought if they trouble you. The beauty of your beings and your seeking humbles us and opens our hearts. Thank you, each of you. We are those of Q'uo, and we leave you as we found you, in the love and in the light of the one infinite Creator. Adonai. Adonai. ☥

L/L Research is a subsidiary of
Rock Creek Research &
Development Laboratories, Inc.

P.O. Box 5195
Louisville, KY 40255-0195

L/L RESEARCH

www.llresearch.org

Rock Creek is a non-profit
corporation dedicated to
discovering and sharing
information which may aid in
the spiritual evolution of
humankind.

SUNDAY MEDITATION
MARCH 20, 2005

Question from B: The question this week is as follows: We of this world have a tendency to form groups whose collective voice is iconified and represented by a name and a graphic symbol, such as [the company name of] "L/L Research" and its image of Don Quixote. Can you, Q'uo, expand on the nature and construction of a group name and symbol for a group based on the principles of the Law of One, and, if such a construct is advantageous, make some suggestions on effective ways to select an appropriate name and symbol for a group seeking service to others, based in fourth-density concepts?

(Carla channeling)

We are those known to you as the principle of Q'uo. Greetings in the love and in the light of the one infinite Creator, in Whose service we are. We are so gratified to be able to join your circle of seeking and to view the delicacy and beauty of your blooming souls as you sit seeking that which is so carelessly called the truth, that which is all that there is.

We are most happy to share our thoughts with you on symbols and how they are created and would ask of you one thing that will make it much easier for us to be able to speak freely and that is that each of you take full responsibility for how you take in that which we offer you. We are not always right. We are not a voice of unquestionable authority. We are just those, as are you, [who are] seeking the truth. So please, as you hear these thoughts, evaluate them for how they feel to you. And if they do not feel right; if they do not feel resonant to you, please, let them go. They will come again at a time in which you are ready to consider them. For now, they are not for you and you need not to pay attention. Choose carefully the object of your attention! If you will do that for us, then we will feel much more able to speak without worrying that we will be infringing upon your free will or your process of spiritual evolution.

You ask us this day concerning the creation of symbols and ways to typify, or create icons for, deep and precious thoughts within you, thoughts which are held in common by a group. We are most gratified to receive this question for it is a marvelously mind and heart-opening question for us to consider. It reaches deeply into your very nature and therefore it is with eagerness that we consider how to attack this question.

Perhaps we would, as we usually do, back up a bit from the question itself and consider the nature of those who are asking the question. Each of you has a structure as clear and lucid and in some ways linear as geography in terms of the nature of your self. We do not speak at this time in terms of your surface consciousness but rather in terms of that which you carry as a citizen of eternity, as a spirit or a soul.

Consciousness is something that you share with each other crystal being that walks your planet as a third-density, so-called human, entity. You share an infinitely deep nature that is mostly hidden from you. And that area which creates the symbols that endure is called the subconscious mind or the roots of consciousness or, as this instrument often calls it, the archetypical mind.

Myths are stories in which characters represent parts of the deep self. The stories that are told in myth relate the various parts of this deeper self in such a way that there is transformative power in the relationships and in the complexes of concepts that are held [within] the various points of the story and the symbols of character and plot within myth and archetype.

Each of you has a certain unique way of being able to see into the archetypical mind. so for each of you, even if you are working in a very established system of archetypal or mythical truth such as the Christian faith, the way that you are able to enter into these complexes of concepts, these characters and stories, is unique. Just as unique as are you. When you join a group, you hold most of your archetypical material in common. But each person within the group will inevitably and rightfully enter into a group-created archetype or story in a unique way. The more established mythical systems have gained power not only [because of] the accuracy of the descriptive power held within story and character but also because, through time, the people that have followed this path, this story and these characters have created an ineffable richness of subtlety and nuance that perhaps has never been written down and is not available for those who are simply trying to learn myth and archetype from reading.

Indeed, those who read and study archetypes are forever caught within the mind and are kept by their very mindfulness and scholarship from entering deeply into and becoming the archetypes that they study. However, those who release the archetypes at last from the stricture of mind and enter into them through the heart have entered into a path that has been followed by many. And as they walk the path that this story configures and suggests, they enrich that path by every thought that they think and every desire that arises in relation to this story and these characters, this myth and the archetypes that [the myth] pulls out of the geography of your deep mind.

Growing from the roots of these relatively fixed parts of the archetypal mind [is] a living plant, a living tree, shall we say, of knowledge, of understanding.

This is the advantage of entering into an established archetypical system such as a religious faith, a philosophy, or a mythical system indigenous to a culture, whether it be a primitive culture or a more seemingly civilized culture or, in the case of those who wish to create a group that has [not] been created before, a new culture, a new philosophy, or a new religious system. Therefore, there is an infinitely broad and rich panoply of choices when it comes to how to create the iconography and the notational system of a symbol for a group such as the name and the icon which was chosen by the ones known as Don and Carla in creating the name of L/L Research or Love and Light Research and the icon which was a symbol painted by the artist known as Pablo of the mythical character from literary culture known as Don Quixote.[18] This entity, Don Quixote, tilted at windmills and the ones known as Don and Carla were attracted to this dreaming of the impossible dream and seeking the highest and best in a world which seemed not to be capable of the highest and best but only capable of a landscape of tattered windmills swinging in the sun.

By choosing to localize their hopes and their dreams of enlarging and serving love and light and by choosing a symbol that was meaningful to both of the entities in this group, they were able to focus for themselves a certain stream of energy that helped both of them to become the dreamers of the impossible dream. As well, their focus was contagious and some 35 years after this symbol was chosen,[19] hundreds of thousands of entities have become acquainted with this particular stream of archetypal energy, have resonated with it to some degree, and have, to that degree, thought more

---

[18] From orwell.ru/library/articles/As_I_Please/Don_Quixote-ld: "Pablo Picasso's drawing of Don Quixote is one of the most popular graphic representations known of Cervantes's wondrous character. The drawing was made in 1955 for issue 581 of *Les Lettres Françaises*."

[19] Picasso's drawing of Don Quixote had been above Carla's desk since 1964. When Don and Carla formed a formal partnership in 1970, naming it L/L Research, they used the Don Quixote image. They first published under that name in 1976, with *Secrets of the UFO*. When Jim McCarty, Don Elkins and Carla combined Jim's non-profit foundation of Rock Creek Research and Development Labs, Inc., which Jim had formed in 1977, with their partnership to form a public foundation in 1980, the publishing name of L/L Research was chosen as a "dba" name for the group and the organization, formally called Rock Creek R & D Labs, has always done business as L/L Research.

about it, gained from it, and walked that path, enriching in ways ever unseen the path that now awaits an ever broader and easier ingress for others who come after them.

It is to be noted that, as the instrument said earlier, the beginning of the choosing of symbols was modest. This instrument had had a picture of Don Quixote over her desk since she was in college. And when the symbol was chosen at a later date, by about six years, from the time it was originally chosen by her, the one known as Don had simply run into that symbol for the first time because he knew the instrument. He had become used to that symbol and had thought about it and it resonated to him as well as to the instrument. And so when they talked about what to call their partnership, for indeed this was this beginning of L/L Research, they decided to call it that name because of the nature of their understanding of why they were here and who they were. To this day this instrument often asks people to consider who they are and why they are here. It is from these honest and humble beginning that symbols can be created and it is only from a knowledge of the self and the ability that is ever refined and purified to reach deeply into the heart of the self and come to the day's answer to those questions that the ability to enter into one's own archetypal mind is nourished.

Now, this instrument is aware that the group which has inspired the one known as B to ask this question is a group called "The Rangers." The Rangers is a name that is part of another literary composition, in this case a television play which was developed as a five-year story which was very consciously undertaken by its creators as that which would delve into the deeper aspects of groups and why they come together and what their goals are. In this television play, which is called *Babylon 5*, the Anla'shok or the Rangers are those who come from many different traditions, drawn together as a group by the desire to be of service to others. It is a kind of knighthood whose values are concerned with service to others, love for others, love of honor and duty and faithfulness to the cause that they choose to undertake.

Consequently, this instrument is aware that in no way, shape or form could such a group enter into an old or established mythical system, for the concepts of many different societies or kinds of people allying themselves to one another as a knighthood or a

group of honorable persons is not precisely configured in the myths of any one religion or culture. It is rather a construct based on understanding that is relatively novel, and that is the understanding that the variety of entities upon your planet at this time reaches across every culture, every religion, and every philosophy and yet has one underlying, infinite and eternal unity. We would therefore suggest that such a name and symbol might well be chosen based on relatively novel concepts. In other words, we are suggesting that it may in this case be fruitful to lift away from perceived mythical systems and to create a story and characters that resonate to this group.

We are not suggesting that new myths must be disassociated from the older mythical systems. It is very possible to use elements of perceived other systems of archetype in creating the name and the icon of a new group. However, we do suggest that any one story shall not satisfy the needs of such a far-ranging group.

What we would like to do is use this instrument's own awareness and offer some ideas which we can pluck from her somewhat broad stream of consciousness in attempting to offer different ways to think about, not so much the name as the symbolic system underlying the name, or the icon that would support the name, of such a group. It is possible, for instance, that the name, Rangers, is perfectly satisfactory. The reason we suggest that the name you have chosen so far may not be adequate is not so much the name as it is in the meaning that underlies the name and [this] is that that name was created by an entity whose desire was to put forth a concept in a certain colored and biased way that may not satisfy that need of the group to create a unique name which has layers of meaning that can be discussed and strengthened as the group develops.

We would not presume to make suggestions for such a name, nor would we presume to make finite or literal suggestions for a symbol. What we would like to do then, if you will give us permission mentally to do so, is to take a walk through this instrument's symbolic systems using various things about which she has thought in order to indicate to you the kind of thinking that might be helpful for this group to consider in creating its own authentic and unique notational system.[20]

We begin by noting that we would choose first to discuss a kind of symbol or notational system that has no spiritual or religious bias. And then we would like to work with this instrument's own religious system and its knowledge of that Confederation-type of philosophy with which she is most familiar and which she has often called the Law of One, to a certain extent. So we will be starting in one place and ending in another but we believe that both avenues are helpful and therefore we would include both for your consideration.

Firstly, we would like to talk about sacred geometry, as this instrument calls it. Now we find that this instrument is very little schooled or knowledgeable in the subject of sacred geometry. She has very little real information which we may use and so we will use very simple things which may be helpful in indicating the kind of thinking that you might consider.

This instrument sees the world of nature as a circle. That would be not just the second density but, in a foreshadowing or reflective way, the circle of all densities and their inner planes. For what the natural world and the extended natural world, leaving out third density, have in common is a full knowledge of the love and the light of the one infinite Creator. This creates within the natural world, as well as within the creation as a whole, an infinite array of possibilities. The circle of knowledge is ever expansive and this circle has no beginning and no end. And in it all things are in constant and unremitting balance.

Interestingly enough, in third density, there is what might be called a dead zone as far as the circle of knowledge is concerned. The circle is squared. Space and time become finite, measured. There is a beginning and an end to life, to knowledge, to civilizations, and to the world as any one generation of entities can know it.

This squareness or deadness is not without its possibilities, for the circle is contained within the square in the form of the consciousness that you carry. The spirit lies within you in its circularity and its infinity, waiting to be invoked by your desire.

You must reach as a spirit and ask for the opening of the door to infinity. You must ask within this square and within this deadness. There must come to each entity the birth of hope, the awakening of the faculties of faith and the beginning of a sense of self which is rounded into eternity. In this apparently barren field of Earth lies the fecund field that will grow any seed that you plant. What shall you choose to plant? What shall you choose to desire? How shall you break away from the corners that trap you into thinking that you are limited?

If this symbol of third density is a square, then perhaps we might say that the symbol of entry into a larger point of view or, in another context, entry into fourth density, is a delta, or a pyramid. This is a three-sided construct. Now, this instrument is aware of work which has been done researching the energies of this triangle-shaped figure in its three-dimensional form as a pyramid and is aware of the spiraling energy that has been found to be collected by the shape. This is the geometry of change. This is the shape of transformation. There is healing in such a shape, but, more importantly for this particular group and this particular question, there is growth.

The spiral from the top of the pyramid is that which is able to move into the fourth density or [into] that space between the densities where there is resistance through which this energy helps to push. Consequently, one has the circle, one has the square, and one has the delta, or the triangle.

Now, we do not give this instrument further information concerning any fourth-density construct, although we certainly encourage each to consider such constructs. Realize that the group is a group of third-density entities who wish to affect change and transformation within themselves and within the planet working within this square.

We would move then from the seemingly emotionally and spiritually neutral images of shapes to this instrument's religious or spiritual system because we would wish not to leave the square as a square but rather to reconfigure this four-sidedness or four-direction-ness into this instrument's religious system, which is that of the cross. There is great power in seeing the square in this rather inside-out configuration. So let us look a bit into this instrument's deeper musings concerning this symbol, for it has been used by this instrument to transfigure the deadness of physical incarnation; it

---

[20] A notational system is defined as a technical system of symbols used to represent special things.

has been used to awaken her circularity, her infinity within. And how has this been?

There are two aspects to this symbol of the cross. There is the vertical axis and there is the horizontal axis. The cross can be seen to be that upon which hangs a Redeemer which dies on this cross in order to purify and refine the consciousness of the world as it, Itself, as the Christ, was refined and purified by the sacrifice of self for love of other-self. However, we find that this instrument does not allow the one known as Jesus the Christ to lie supine[21] upon a cross. Rather, this instrument has never been able to configure this entity as being trapped by such a construct. But, rather, it has been seen by this instrument as a launching pad for an idea. And that is the idea that there is a larger life and that it is here today, alive, and promised in the greatest of love and the absolute certainty of the one known as Jesus the Christ's knowledge that such a thing as sacrifice, such a thing as utter, unconditional love, was that engine which would launch not only himself but all of creation and create a flowing stream that would reconfigure and free humankind from those corners of limitation that are suggested by every aspect of your human experience. Every attempt that humans make to be worthy, to be perfect, is hopeless. Every attempt to become worthy of the love and the light of the infinite Creator has failed before it has begun. There is no way to earn heaven. Rather, it must be fallen into, leapt into, embraced without knowing or seeing anything; embraced only because the resonance of this truth is irresistible.

And so this instrument does not see the cross as a symbol of suffering but rather as that which is the very springboard to infinity and eternity, and not in another world but in this world, in this day, and in this time. This symbol has created for her a way of looking up, looking down, and looking to each side. The square has become that which has opened up. There is the vertical member which is rooted in the earth and which reaches to the sky. And there is the horizontal member which this instrument has often thought of as symbolizing the everyday life. Certainly, each is nailed to an everyday existence that is inevitable. One gets up in the morning from one's rest and one has activity while one is conscious. One has many duties and responsibilities, many

thoughts and many desires as one goes about one's daily life. One feeds on food in order to survive and one gives food to others, whether it be physical supply or ideas or good counsel or poor counsel or any kind of intentional evil. And then one at last loses consciousness once again and after resting wakes again to do it over.

Yet one never repeats any instant of any day. It is always a new world. Yet it is a world that moves along the roads of ordinariness and it is within that ordinariness that all of the truth, all of the revelation, all of the realization, and all of the epiphany of transformation lies. It is upon this horizontal member that the refining fire continually burns. Just as each entity is rooted in earth and is reaching towards a larger awareness, so is it horizontal in its everyday-ness and its feeling of being ordinary.

There is great craving in entities who are seeking to become non-ordinary. Yet, the point of this entrance into non-ordinariness is at the point at which the vertical member and the horizontal member meet. There is a circle that describes you as a person upon the cross of life or within the square of life. Whether the corners are outer, as in a square, or whether the corners are of those members and seemingly moving into center, nevertheless, the circle is within the square, the circle is at the center of the cross. You are that focus of the infinite into the everyday. And the way you suffer configures your spiritual evolution. The way you circularize your square creates for you your path towards spiritual evolution.

Now we would also in this regard suggest two more things having to do with shapes and yet also moving back into the religious or spiritual, and, in some cases, cultural as well. Firstly, we would suggest that the horizontal member of such a cross may be seen to be, rather than that wood upon which stretches out the arms of the Christ, the symbol of infinity, which this instrument would describe as a lazy eight.[22] Infinity lies within the ordinary.

The other thing that we would suggest is the symbol from your Egyptian culture and from the spiritual or religious system of the Egyptians in your history, of

---

[21] supine: "lying on the back or having the face upward," with a secondary meaning of "marked by or showing lethargy, passivity, or blameworthy indifference.

[22]

the ankh or the Crux Ansata.[23] It is a kind of cross which is very descriptive of the possibilities of infinity and eternity because it forms in its upper member, the top part of the vertical member of the cross, a stylized circle. This circle is not round but rather is shaped very much like the half-spiral that shoots up from the top of the pyramid.

The discussion of this instrument's various symbolic representations and so forth need not go further for we do not intend to suggest in any way that the symbol for the group known as the Rangers contains any of these ideas. We wish only to suggest that, beginning with the bare essences of things that this group finds remarkable or interesting, [there] lies a richness that can be trusted. And we wish further to suggest that the mythical representations such as [are found within] this instrument's deeply felt and beloved Christianity are fruitful ground for digging into and uncovering relationships that may enrich and enliven and create resonances for the basic ideas that create the icon.

If one chose, for instance, the basic symbol of a triangle, then one would have to ask, what would the three sides represent? In terms of the Law of One, this instrument's mind would develop a simple answer: that the three sides would be basically love, wisdom, and power. This is very simple but very evocative. What is love? What does it evoke within one to think of love?

We use this example because, within the Law of One material, at one point the three of the research group at that time—the one known as Carla, the one known as Don, and the one known as Jim—were described by the one known as Ra as being well-balanced because the one known as Carla had a great deal of unconditional love in her makeup, enough to spill over and inspire others, whereas the one known as Don had a tremendous connection with wisdom, and the one known as Jim had an overwhelming degree of power. The differences [of the persons within the group] were harmonized in such a way as to create a sacred space. So the question that the Ra put to the group then sitting was, "How could this balance be helpful to the group and, in extension, to the creation?"

Again, with four sides, there would be the possibility of describing four ways of expressing the Creator. Obvious examples of four-ness are the four directions, the four archangels, and the four elements.

What is circularity or roundness?

And lastly, we suggest that because of the nature of the Rangers, there may need to be an overreaching or surrounding image that contains the symbol of angelic aid or wings, because of the fact that this group has as part of its value system the awareness that all things are conscious and alive and that those energies that surround one, whether in first density, second density, or so forth, are sentient and helpful, each element helping each. It is this energy which suggests to us the basic personification of, say, an angel or any winged figure from mythical systems that are seemingly helpful, as discussion mounts concerning such a design.

Certainly elements of design can be superimposed and designs can be created, each element of which means something to the members of the group. It may be that the symbol of the tree would be better for this group, say, than the symbol of an angel. But what we wish to suggest is the personification, just as the figure of Don Quixote, with his mad ideas and his tattered windmills becoming a wonderful world in which hope is possible, focused energy for the ones known as Don and Carla. It helps to have a personified figure or essence which is part of such an icon or symbol. It is helpful, shall we say, to have the cast of characters as well as the basic story.

This instrument has been saying to us for some time that we have talked for too long and it is time to open the meeting for further questions, [and so] we apologize. But we wished to produce this body of material through this instrument in one session in order to do what we could to share our awareness of the way concept complexes work and the way that ordinary people can create myth and archetype from within themselves. Let your ideas flower; let them bloom. We wish you the joy of this exploration. And we are, as always, with you to strengthen and undergird your basic meditative energies as you sink into the silence and ask.

23

We would at this time open this meeting to further queries. Is there another query at this time? We are those of Q'uo.

V: Q'uo, we have a question from D. He asks, "Could you please comment on the sources for the psychic messages leading to the formation of Swedenborgism and the Mormon religion?"

We are those of Q'uo, and are aware of your query, my brother. We may comment to a certain extent and we apologize for not commenting further than this but we move to the edge of the Law of Confusion and there we stop. This is for your protection as well as ours. And yet we realize that we may frustrate you and so we do apologize.

We may say, concerning inspired and inspiring charismatic figures such as these two entities, that there are two basic ways in which inspiration enters into the energy system and the body system of a so-called channel, prophet or charismatic figure.

The first is from phenomena such as the one known as Joseph[24] experienced. What did this entity experience? Of what he literally said, [and] the experience we cannot comment. But we can comment on a general tendency of entities to experience such things as UFOs or extraterrestrial contact in a way that agrees with their basic expectations. What an entity sees in a contact with a UFO or an extraterrestrial entity is, in the case of positive contact, never what it seems. It is a thought construct. And the thought construct is that which holds new thought which could not be engaged without using the reference points of an entity's previous belief system and its expectations of such a divine meeting.

The other way of charismatic or prophetic entities receiving inspiration is from sheer hard work: work in consciousness, work in meditation, prayer, doubt, despair and all of the rich emotional resources of the refining fire of human experience. In the case of the one known as Swedenborg, this was the path to opening the founts of inspiration. The work done by this entity over long periods of time was not that which predisposed this entity to receive a symbol and, in entering into this symbol, then to open up a mythical or archetypal system to this one entity. The entry was into its own heart and therefore there was a cleaner and less biased or colored body of material [produced] by this entity. This entity simply drew upon its vast and encyclopedic knowledge of the world in which it lived which it had gained through decades of scholarship and service to others.

There are those who are far more resonant with the working of the mythical system created by the one known as Joseph. There are others who dip into the inspirational writings of the one known as Swedenborg and find fuel that lights the fire of spirit within them. Each system of any kind created by inspired human beings has its points. This includes positive and so-called negative information. What is done with this information by the seeker is what creates its goodness or its poorness as a fulcrum of realization.

As always, we encourage the one known as D to read into the written work of such a group created by such an inspired figure, and sense into it for its resonance. If it has resonance for the one known as D, then it has virtue for the one known as D. If, in reading into this body of writing and sensing into its ramifications within his own reactions, there is no real connection, then we would suggest [that] the one known as D put it down.

Our other point is simply to remind the one known as D that the group that forms around an inspired figure is not the same thing as the original work of that inspired figure. To discover whether a system is worth investigating, investigate not the group but the heart of that which the inspired figure offered to the Creator and the creation as his unique service.

Is there a further query at this time? We are those of Q'uo.

G: Q'uo, what you described of as the "meal" of catalyst and growth and self-understanding has indeed been as you said it would be: lengthy, and, as I feel it to be, endlessly abundant and maybe even a little tasty. Being that it feels as if it's been such a long time that I've been working diligently on ingesting and digesting this meal, I can't help but anticipate and long for the course of dessert and I was wondering if you had any information on its whereabouts?

We are those of Q'uo, and are aware of your query, my brother. We say to the one known as G that we

---

[24] Joseph Smith was the channel or author of writings that became the *Book of Mormon*. It is on his story, which involved a kind of ET contact, and these received writings that the Mormon religion was founded.

are surprised that this entity has missed the desserts that he has had.

May we answer you further, my brother?

G: Q'uo, could you define, "missed," please?

We are those of Q'uo. My brother, when we said that you had missed dessert we simply meant that you had had it but had not been aware of the richness and sweetness of it. We assure the one known as G that there are sweets at every stop along the way. My brother, the sun comes up and the sun goes down and just as the ones who follow Allah have a Ramadan and a fast during the day, when the sun sets the feast begins. And so there have been delicious and wonderful repasts, filled with sweets, in your experience.

The awareness of this sweetness is sometimes lost in the overstimulation of the feast itself. There are many times when so much occurs that is meaningful to one [as well as] troubling and disconcerting [that it] takes ones attention so fully that those sweet meats tucked in round the edges are missed. We encourage the one known as G to contemplate this fast and feast of life lived in the fast lane of attempting to accelerate the pace of spiritual growth. As this instrument would say, the pace can blow you away, and the tears can seem to drown the joy. We encourage the one known as G to reflect upon what is as opposed to what is perceived.

There is within the open heart an everlasting dessert.

May we answer you further, my brother?

G: I'm sorry to belabor the point and I apologize to everybody for the time but I'm going to try this from one more angle. Dessert to me in that particular metaphor is embodied in a girl. I understand the dessert of that union with the Creator and all the rewards that come from spiritual seeking and knowing and accepting the self. Could you get prophetic at all or tell me anything about that particular dessert which my mind was set on? I'll drop it at that and thank you very much, Q'uo.

We are those of Q'uo, and are aware of your query, my brother. We cannot be prophetic for you, my brother, but we can note this: for those who are easy to please, the embodiment of dessert in the form of companionship comes very easily. But it is like a Chinese dessert: it does not last very long and in an hour you are hungry again! You seek for a dessert

that is profound and lifelong. How easy do you think that is to choose, my brother? And how shall you prepare to walk side-by-side with an entity that speaks to your deepest heart and that satisfies you, not for a day or for a week but for all of eternity?

May we ask if there is a final query at this time?

T: Q'uo, I'd like to ask about the Ark of the Covenant. Is it purely a myth or, if this object actually exists, what was its function?

We are those of Q'uo, and we may say very little about your query, my brother. For in part it is a myth and in part it was an actual relic. It was designed to be that which contained power and as a transformational apport,[25] shall we say, is that which came into the possession of an entity which called it forth by his spiritual nature, namely the one known as Moses. It was a literal, bodily, earthly object which was carried about and placed in temples and buried. Its reality, however, is mythical. As a relic, it is simply dust. In its time and in its place, it had a certain meaning to a certain people. Just as the pyramid, it is a shape that is no longer helpful, in our opinion. And so we would ask you to lift this symbol from its stricture and see that when one receives one's law, rule of life, or, as the Rangers have done recently, developed a code of ethics, and one places them in a certain structure, then that structure can be imaged out forth into the world, but is a valuable focus for one time, one place, and one group.

May we answer you further, my brother?

T: No, thank you Q'uo. As always, you help me to see the larger picture.

We thank you too, my brother, and we thank each who has queried this day and who has shared in the energy of this circle. It is such a blessing to us to be able to share this energy with you, to share the sacred space of your open hearts, and to speak to those who have asked.

We leave each of you in the love and in the light of the one infinite Creator. Adonai. Adonai. ♣

---

[25] apport: an object produced at a spiritualist's seance, supposedly by paranormal means.

L/L Research is a subsidiary of
Rock Creek Research &
Development Laboratories, Inc.

P.O. Box 5195
Louisville, KY 40255-0195

L/L RESEARCH

www.llresearch.org

Rock Creek is a non-profit
corporation dedicated to
discovering and sharing
information which may aid in
the spiritual evolution of
humankind.

SPECIAL MEDITATION
MARCH 30, 2005

Question from L: As a necessary part of my spiritual journey towards understanding the oneness of all in all, I long ago abandoned the practice of Christianity. This experience has taught me a lot, but now I feel that the time has come to reintegrate my path with my beloved Christian faith and walk again in Christ, but on a different level. Could Q'uo suggest some way or some path to follow which would permit me to do the transformative work I need to do, with the help of a religious faith or a Christ relationship?

(Carla channeling)

We are those of the principle known to you as the Q'uo. Greetings in the love and in the light of the one infinite Creator, in Whose service we come to you this day. We thank the one known as L greatly for this opportunity to speak upon the subject of the transformative path which winds in the spiral fashion to that place wherein her journey may once again include the walk with Jesus the Christ for which she has so yearned and for which she has now prepared herself.

We would ask of those within this circle this day that which we always do ask before we share our thoughts, and that is that each allow each thought to enter the mind without any expectation that it will be a good or a bad thought, and simply evaluate each thought on its own merits. If a thought seems resonant to you, then by all means use it and work with it, but if for any reason whatsoever your powers

of discrimination suggest that you should lay that thought aside, then please do so without a second thought. If you will each use your discrimination carefully and protect your own processes and your own paths of seeking then we are much more able to feel relaxed and confident that we are not infringing upon your free will by sharing our thoughts with you at this time. We thank you for this consideration.

My sister, we are aware of your question and we offer ourselves to you as those who would bring forth a series of thoughts. Perhaps our first thought is simply to say that when this instrument challenges spirits she does so in the name of Jesus the Christ and we come to her on that vibration. It is a vibration of unconditional love, and further it is an unconditional love that is willing to lift away from all concerns of self or the cost to the self of service to others, with the only goal being that of sharing in a wholehearted and complete way, insofar as we are able, the love and the light of the one infinite Creator as expressed through the unconditional love of Jesus the Christ. This is clearly a vibration which is other than that vibration which is spoken of in the body of work which you know of as the New Testament.

Moreover, it is not that vibration of the teachings of Jesus the Christ which has traditionally and up to the present time come through the offices of organized religion. Indeed, this instrument has done the work to integrate that which she receives from the readings from her Bible and the preachings that she hears at her parish church. There is always distortion in any word that is spoken in the languages of your planet. We also have distortions. Our basic energy is that of unconditional love but we, any preacher to whom you would speak, and, indeed, this instrument as counselor, all have significant biases and distortions. Each attempts to be the voice of unconditional love, and yet that unconditional love is as something that is more than and deeper than any words can say. And so we do not pretend to offer you authoritative information, but only to share thoughts with you that may serve to be resources for you as you move forward in your inner seeking.

To us it is important to make the distinction between words and truth, especially as we speak to one who wishes to follow the one known as Jesus the Christ. There have been layers upon layers of distortion, even before the writings attributed to the one known as Jesus the Christ were collected in the Gospels and written about, largely by the one known as Paul, but also by the one known as John, in the Letters and prophetic writings of the New Testament. The attempt to place a literal value on words that have been written down is an attempt that in our humble opinion is bound to fail. Just as the one known as Jesus the Christ could not be bound to an earthly cross but instead leapt up into the heavens, just so can the truth which this entity embodied and which this entity continues to embody not be bound to any cross or structure of words or sayings. It makes the one known as Jesus a more elusive-seeming figure, for it is so helpful seemingly to cling to the words that are so comfortable and so familiar.

We shall attempt to examine some of these words with you, but before we do that we would like to suggest one concept that may be helpful to you at this time. You may perhaps remember the story in the Gospels of that Easter morning when the one known as Jesus was visited by the ones known as Mary, Mary Magdalene and Peter. They had come to view the grave of the one known as Jesus. When they came they found not a grave with a stone at the door stopping it, but rather the stone rolled away. The linen wrappings which had been around the body of the one known as Jesus were folded and placed aside. And an entity, which Mary took to be

the gardener, was waiting for her and her companions in the opened tomb. Mary wept, for she was distraught, thinking that someone had stolen the body of her beloved Jesus. Then that entity, waiting for her, called her by name and when he said, "Mary," she knew him for the first time. And her tears turned to rejoicing, for she saw that indeed he had risen. She rushed to cling to him, but he stopped her, saying that he had not yet ascended and so he must be about his Father's business. And he departed from her to go into Galilee and to greet those other faithful disciples, and to let them know the good news of his rising from the tomb.

My sister, the one known as Jesus has now finished that personal business of greeting those that knew him in life. He has indeed completed his journey within your planetary third-density life, and he has, for all time and for all space, given himself to practicing the presence of unconditional love. It was necessary for this entity to move onward and to complete the more esoteric and what this instrument could call its inner-planes aspects of his journey within the incarnation, where he was known as Jesus the Christ, in order to come again as those who follow him call to him.

He cast a great portion of his consciousness upon the winds of Spirit, creating for all entities that call upon his name that energy which is of the Christ, and yet which is cast in such a way that this consciousness can come down into the energy system of each who calls upon his name. Many, including this instrument, have called this energy the Holy Spirit. We would make the distinction between the one known as Jesus the Christ and the Holy Sprit by saying that as you call upon Jesus, you call upon pure consciousness. No longer can you receive a personality, for this entity has indeed ascended. The pure gift of unconditional love, however, which he embodied remains as a perfect jewel, just as it is, and there is tremendous power in simply praying, "Jesus." There need be no content to that call. The bare word configures the presence of the Christ.

In contrast, the energy known as the Holy Spirit speaks in the colors and biases of your inner configuration of mind, body and spirit. When called upon, this energy combines itself with your higher self to create a kind of principle or group consciousness. This group consciousness combines that self which you have created in the fullness of your journey through what this instrument would call mid-sixth density with the pure consciousness of unconditional love. Thusly, there lies within you a home in which the spirit of Christ and the highest and best of yourself have combined. This is an intensely personal aspect of the Creator, and is that with which you may have actual conversation, as does this instrument.

Certainly it is not necessarily an easy thing to achieve. Such conversations may indeed take time to configure within yourself. Yet we assure you that this room is prepared for you. Your sacred space within is ready for you to enter at all times and in all places. You cannot be separated either from Jesus the Christ or from the Holy Spirit. By your love you have prepared and made ready this place within yourself. We say this in order to encourage you to rest from any concern that you can be separated from the love of the one known as Jesus the Christ and to reassure you that there is no need to reach for the counsel and wisdom of the Holy Spirit. The tongue of flame has touched your head; living fire has touched your lips, and you shall never be the same. And, indeed, in all the years of your wandering in exile, this has continued to be true.

We would say further that we would agree with the one known as L that it was necessary to walk away from that configuration within which she had received Jesus the Christ within the confines of organized religion, as this instrument would call it. We often find this to be true as we have worked with various entities who ask us questions of this nature through this instrument. It is as though the teaching concerning the one known as Jesus the Christ creates a kind of box in which the Christ cannot be contained. As a realization of the larger picture of creation, the Creator and the path of each entity through incarnation and towards a fuller understanding of the Creator come into being, the smaller picture will not endure. The smaller idea of unconditional love cannot be sustained. And so one must abandon that empty tomb of old belief and allow deadness to be rolled away, just as the one known as Jesus had to ascend in order to continue that good work which he had begun. Just so, at least once in most entities' search for a true understanding of unconditional love, must the comfortable old ways become a tomb and the entity who is seeking release those old ideas and move according to the true call of the Christ within, which is "Follow me."

In many ways, the path of those who leave organized religion is a path from belief to faith. Belief is a word which describes that which has an objective referent. There is belief in something. Creeds are statements of such belief systems. Catechisms are more detailed descriptions of that which one must believe in order to be saved, and for every preacher who preaches from a dogmatic point of view comes a stream of directives of how to believe in order to be saved.

There is nothing dogmatic about unconditional love. It is an energy that rests in faith. To the faithful heart, all is well. That which is, is enough and that which seems to be needed is simply expected. There is no knowing. There is no listing of principles. There is only an underlying and surrounding feeling that all is well, that one is full of what one needs and that which one has is ample. The faithful heart rests in gratitude, quietness and surety.

As you seek this transformative path that spirals into the energies of unconditional love ever more fully, we hope that you are able more and more to release any fears that you might be making a wrong step, thinking an incorrect thought, or exploring in areas that may not be appropriate. For the energy of unconditional love is a part of your nature.

Let us examine how this might be so, and how you might come into a deeper awareness of that gift of the Christ which is already within you.

The one known as Jesus the Christ said, "I am the vine; you are the branches."[26] When you consider the growing of a vineyard, you realize that many vine keepers will graft onto the parent vine other stock which will make a hybrid vine. So your first concern in being a branch of the true vine is not to take onto that vine anything that is not the true vine. This is why we began by saying that the consciousness of unconditional love cannot be bound by concepts and words. Those who attempt to teach how Jesus thought tend to attempt to bind words onto the true vine of unconditional love, as though explanation

---

[26] *Holy Bible*, John 15:4-5: "Abide in Me, and I in you. As the branch cannot bear fruit by itself, unless it abides in the vine, neither can you, unless you abide in Me. I am the vine; you are the branches. He who abides in Me, and I in him, he it is that bears much fruit, for apart from Me you can do nothing."

and explication will somehow create a better Jesus. Yet in truth, the true vine[27] is a mystery.

Certainly the one known as Jesus was rooted in the earth, had an incarnation, had a story to tell, and completed an earthly journey. But as this entity attempted to express his understanding of who he was, ever and again he would describe himself not in personal terms, but in terms of a relationship. This entity saw himself as one who was called to speak as his Father gave him wisdom to speak. He would say, "When you hear me, you do not hear **me**, you hear the one who sent me."[28] And again he would say, "I am the Son of man."[29] He saw himself as a human, but as a human who had laid down all that his personality shell said of him as an offering, so that he could be as much as possible an exemplar of all human beings. He looked upon the distortions within himself just as he looked upon the distortions he saw in all of those around him, not with judgment but with an incredible willingness to dissociate them from his true nature. He emptied himself, in other words, of personality in order more and more truly to be the person he truly was. He actively desired for his consciousness to become that consciousness that is caught up in unconditional love. When he used the word "I," he was not speaking of himself as a man with a personality. He had penetrated to the truth of himself, and when he found his true nature he found that it was caught up entirely in the "I" that is unconditional love itself.

When this instrument speaks to those that are not Christians, she often uses the term, Christ-consciousness. She is attempting to move entities past the concept of Christ as a person and to penetrate those walls that defend personhood, so that entities may feel that there is the possibility of perceiving a self that is free of those bounds of personality. The one known as Jesus said, "I am the

way, I am the truth, I am the life."[30] Please remember that the Creator had a name to the one known as Jesus, and that name was "I AM THAT I AM." Within incarnation this entity had opened up his personality shell, allowed it to fall away, and what was left was the pure consciousness of the Creator as this entity perceived it, and to this entity was given a perception of the Creator that was pure love.

Wisdom has no part in the consciousness of Jesus the Christ. There is considerably more wisdom and certainly more consolation in the energy of the Christ that is known as the Holy Spirit. The consciousness of Jesus the Christ is pure love. This is a good distinction to remember, for that which is facing each entity at this time within incarnation is the challenge of learning enough about unconditional love to begin to follow the ways of love and thusly to walk through the transformation from third density to fourth density; from the struggles of good and evil into the sunshine of pure love.

The one known as Jesus faces the struggle between good and evil in a very simple way. This entity simply said, "Get thee behind me, temptation, for I will serve my Father."[31] It is not a complicated path and it is often a path which involves suffering. The choice of love over fear can be seen to be quite brutal at times. Turning the other cheek, loving when one is reviled, bowing the head to those who would harm, and remaining meek in situations where those without the awareness of unconditional love would spring to defend themselves is harsh. We can only say that the rewards of keeping it simple and hewing

---

[27] *Holy Bible*, John 15:1-2: "I am the true vine, and My Father is the vine dresser. Every branch of mine that bears no fruit, He takes away, and every branch that does bear fruit He prunes."

[28] *Holy Bible*, John 14:9-10: "He who has seen me has seen the Father; how can you say, 'Show us the Father?' Do you not believe that I am in the Father and the Father in me?"

[29] *Holy Bible*, John 3:12-15: "If I have told you earthly things and you do not believe, how can you believe if I tell you heavenly things? No one has ascended into heaven but he who descended from heaven, the Son of man. And as Moses lifted up the serpent in the wilderness, so must the Son of man be lifted up, that whoever believes in him may have eternal life."

[30] *Holy Bible*, John 14:5-7: "Thomas said to him, 'Lord, we do not know where you are going. How can we know the way?' Jesus said to him, 'I am the way, and the truth, and the life; no one comes to the Father but by me. If you had known me, you would have known my Father also; henceforth you know Him and have seen Him.'"

[31] *Holy Bible*, Matthew 16:21-25 "From that time Jesus began to show his disciples that he must go to Jerusalem and suffer many things from the elders and chief priests and scribes, and be killed, and on the third day, be raised. And Peter took him and began to rebuke him, saying, 'God forbid, Lord! This shall never happen to you!' But he turned and said to Peter, 'Get behind me, Satan. You are a hindrance to me, for you are not on the side of God, but of men.' Then Jesus told his disciples, 'If any man would come after me, let him deny himself and take up his cross and follow me. For whoever would save his life will lose it, and whoever loses his life for my sake will find it.'"

to the ways of love are infinite. It is love and not cleverness that will clear the sight of those who feel that they may be blind on the inner planes. It is knowing that one is part of the true vine that will give the soul rest through difficult periods when all seems confused and help does not seem to be near.

We ask you to rest within your energy body at this time, to breathe in deeply, and to exhale deeply, knowing that you are breathing in the consciousness of Jesus the Christ and that you are breathing out that same consciousness. It is nearer to you than your thoughts or your hands or your feet. Indeed, your very heart pumps love … love … love … Your essence is true. It has been expressing and continues to express, through a physical body, a mental, and [an] emotional body that often seem very biased and distorted. And these bodies will fail, go down to the dust, and end. That portion of yourself that came into incarnation that is of the spirit is infinite and eternal. What is the glory of following one such as Jesus the Christ? That glory is in the focus of that one being, and how that lens of the infinite Creator can sharpen and delineate your path, so that you have a blazingly clear view of who you are and Whose you are. By all means welcome back into your consciousness the teacher known to you as Jesus. Insofar as it is necessary for you to do, love him as a human being, but remember always that he wished to express the truth of the Father. He wished to be the lens that would indeed focus you to become as he, the servant of the Father, an active, living portion of the Creator. His words are wrapped in silence. His truth is wrapped in mystery. But that Word of love, which is the consciousness of the Christ, is all in all.

At this time we would welcome any further questions that you may have. We are those of Q'uo. Is there a question?

L: I can't think of one. But I thank you very, very much.

My sister, it is such a joy to be able to share this time and, as this instrument is fond of saying, this energy with you. We truly are One and Jesus is Lord of all. For all time, and for all space, unconditional love is the essence of the Creator, and our path as well as yours winds ever closer to an awareness of that unity. Together may we serve, my sister. Together may we be that love. We leave you in the love and in the light of the one infinite Creator. Adonai. Adonai. ❧

L/L Research

L/L Research is a subsidiary of Rock Creek Research & Development Laboratories, Inc.

P.O. Box 5195
Louisville, KY 40255-0195

www.llresearch.org

Rock Creek is a non-profit corporation dedicated to discovering and sharing information which may aid in the spiritual evolution of humankind.

Sunday Meditation
April 3, 2005

Group question: The question today has to do with the concept of how inspiration works in our group as we come together, share our week with each other around the circle, look for a question, determine a question, and then Q'uo speaks upon this topic. In one way or another, the information moves into different levels of our consciousness and as we come out of meditation and speak with each other afterwards, it seems to get seated in our consciousness in some way. We were wondering if Q'uo could give us some information about how this quality or principle of inspiration works in a group and for each of us as individuals?

(Carla channeling)

We are those known to you as the principle of Q'uo. Greetings in the love and in the light of the one infinite Creator, in Whose service we come to you this day. We thank each of you for the beauty of your vibrations, the pleasure of your company in this circle of seeking and for the question that you offer as a group. As always, we would ask for your cooperation in listening to those things that we have to say with a careful ear, ready to forget any thought of ours that does not seem helpful to you. We would greatly appreciate this as it will give us the opportunity to speak freely, knowing that we are not infringing on your free will or looming over you as some sort of perceived authority. With this freedom, we are much more able to feel free to speak our

thoughts, person to person, shall we say, Creator to Creator.

The song that the one known as Jim chose for the tuning song that opens this meditation was most apt to the query which concerns inspiration and the group process.[32] It is interesting to us that two words in your English language are pronounced the same and have related meanings. In terms of your springtime, which you are now enjoying the very beginnings of in your area, it is the sun, s-u-n, that is shining ever more brightly and ever more immediately upon your faces. In terms of this instrument's distortion of religious seeking, she has entered the season of Easter which is the season of the son, s-o-n, and his seeming loss to the world and immediate reappearance within it as the risen Lord.

In a group such as yours, my friends, each of you is the sun/son. You cannot see yourself shining; you cannot see your risen aspect; you cannot see the radiance of your being for, from within your system of awareness, many things are upon your minds, many sorrows are upon your heart, many burdens are upon your shoulders. Your thinking processes are devious and multiple. Your emotional life, as this instrument was saying earlier, ebbs and flows. And there are many times of the most solemn and serious contemplation of the nature of the self, of the worth of the self, of the value of self-perceived processes. Is

---

[32] The tuning song was the Beatles' "Here Comes the Sun."

the attempt to accelerate the advent of spiritual evolution within the self efficient? Is it moving forward? Is the refining process ongoing? How difficult it is to answer any of these questions from within the system of the self. And when one bumps up against other-selves in the everyday and ordinary life, how clearly can we either perceive other-selves or perceive their reflections of ourselves as we interrelate?

The value of coming together, knowing ahead of time that there is a sacred space that has been prepared by intention, is great. For it allows the self in the midst of its everyday aspects to enter into a transformational space, a potentiated time, a dedicated nexus of opportunity. How humbly each of you brings yourself to this time, this space, and this nexus! Each of you knows the self to be unworthy. A glory of the decision to enter this opportunity is that you have come anyway. You have chosen freely and firmly to give yourself the opportunity for transformation. You have not judged yourself and found yourself unworthy. Faith lives within you: faith in your own self, bare of any pretension, faith in the value of sacred spaces and times, and faith in the group.

How the heart opens, given such an opportunity! And when you have formed the intention of becoming part of a circle of seeking, something happens to the way in which you listen to each other. It is as if, like a shaggy dog, you have shaken yourself off and all of the thoughts and feelings that have been clogging the system have been released. Your energy system clears. Your mind sharpens. And your heart feels at home at last within you. Light begins to gather. It is not light from without you, it is light from within you. The power within you, that has been slumbering, awakens, and you minister to each other. Love that is beyond words flows from every fiber of your being as you listen to each other. Even if you cannot say one word, your heart is radiating the infinite love and light that lies within you. Tongues of fire, as this instrument would describe the action of spirit, pour down upon you as your heart goes out, literally, to each other's spoken and unspoken feelings and thoughts. And within this potentiated space and time, peace descends, that peace which, indeed, passeth all understanding, and power flows and sparkles and dances as each cares for each.

What is the nature of spirit? It can certainly be seen as a rain that falls, as a blessing. In another way, it can be seen as that force not only from above but [also] from below that connects the infinite Creator in its undifferentiated and universal expression as infinite energy with the very articulated and very specific tongues of flame that are drawn into your body system and that subtle body system that this instrument would call the energy system or the chakra system by the nature, the color, the brilliance, and the balance within your very distorted and biased and yet innerly-balanced energy system.

As this process occurs, a focus develops within you. It is not only unique to you, but it is unique to you in this moment. And so each of you becomes a focused flame of spirit. You have been transfigured. The highest and best within you has found a point of eloquence within the silence of this nexus and your mirroring capabilities and capacities organize and become lucid. You become more and more helpful to each other and you spark each other so that each becomes more skillful and more inspired and more inspiring. And again, this may or may not have anything to do with what is said. It has to do with your essence, with that which is far beyond words or expression of any kind. Each of you is an energy. This energy has taken all of the infinite reaches of your every experience to come into manifestation at this moment. And this moment becomes a gift that you give to each other, freely, unthinkingly, for you have been renewed and therefore your creation has been renewed.

It is not that one person cannot do this alone, for one person can. But one person is a small group: there is you, and there is spirit. The mirroring process is lacking. You are, as it were, upon the stormy sea but without lighthouses, or, to put it another way, you are upon that stormy sea but without the buoys that ring that peculiar ring to let you know where the shore is, where home is, where the reefs and the perils may be that may keep you from that shore and from that home. Each of you becomes the lighthouse for each other person. When we say to you that there is tremendous value in the very distortions that you so bemoan when you speak of your failings, we realize that it is difficult for you to understand this. And yet if you think of the wind chime that makes beautiful music in the wind and then you think of the effect of the sounds of the buoys that float upon the ocean and warn of peril and sing of home, perhaps you can begin to see how much of a blessing it is to create the harmony of all of each of your very personal and unique sounds coming together in the harmony of the expressions of love in one sacred space. Can there ever be a disharmony in such a choir of individual and authentic bells ringing because of the rocking of the waters of manifestation and the wind of spirit?

The word, "inspiration," is a word that is literally talking about breath, wind—and when one speaks of breath or wind, one is speaking of the spirit. It is said in your holy work, the *Bible*, the wind blows where it will, and no one can bid it.[33] When the breath goes out of the body and does not return, the spirit has left the physical vehicle and what is left is dust. You have been raised into manifestation from the dust and the spirit has breathed into you and as you breathe in, you breath in the one infinite Creator, and as you breath out, you breath out that which you have made of that creative inspiration. In and out: this is the rhythm of your living. You are never still. You do not arrive at some sort of stasis in which all has been accomplished. If each breath is a question and each out-breath an answer, then the process may be seen never to end. You know not what you breathe in and you know not what you breath out. You can never know the extent to which your answer is useful to yourself or others. What you can know is that the supply of inward and outward motion is infinite.

That is why we say to you again and again, my friends, how precious is this moment, how dear is this breath. Feel, in this moment, how beautiful, how profound, is the quality of your love. Feel the devotion that lies beneath the roiled and stormy surface of the everyday. Feel at this moment the truth of the essential self. Feel the beauty of it trembling within you, too precious to express. And then breathe out and know the power of your every intention, thought and expression.

Each of you comes to this moment as a point of flame, that flame of spirit that shall renew the face of the Earth. Know your adequacy. Know yourself, and rest between each breath. Rest in the essence of the self.

What shall you do with this moment? Do not be self-conscious. Do not begin to analyze the process. It is impossible to unplait the braids of spirit and self and dust and interrelationship. It is enough to know that all of you and we are one. And in the combination of essences lies discovery, healing and growth.

We would at this time open this session to further questions. Are there further queries at this time?

V: Q'uo, we have some questions from the group we call the Rangers. One of them is: "Could you comment on this question: 'If one cannot be a monk of just one thing, can one be a monk of all things?' This question is really about how to deal with the desire to live in a spiritually potent manner without leaving society."

We are those of Q'uo, and are aware of your query, my brother. We believe that we understand this question and would begin the answer by defining, in some general way, the term, monk.[34] The monk is an entity which has dedicated its life to a discipline which has as its purpose the simplifying and the deepening of the course of a life so that, like a creek that has been brought into one channel, it may be more powerful to express devotion and service. It is entirely possible to be such a dedicated entity with or without the group which has formed itself around one religious system. It means, however, that such an entity must choose the rule of its life for itself, without the aid and, shall we say, the crutch of an established practice, a carefully articulated rule of life.

In light of the preceding discussion of the nature of such a group as this present circle of seeking, it becomes obvious that any rule of life is easier to think about, articulate and explore when there is a group of like-minded entities which creates that sacred space where each is helping each to bring each other home. A group such as the Rangers has indeed the potential for creating such a group without the necessity for being in one place at one time; for the communication system of your internet and e-mail creates another kind of immediacy in which questions common to all can be explored.

---

[33] *Holy Bible*, John 3:8: "The wind blows where it wills, and you hear the sound of it, but you do not know whence it comes or whither it goes; so it is with everyone who is born of the Spirit."

[34] monk: "a man who is a member of a brotherhood living in a monastery and devoted to a discipline prescribed by his order. Its derivation is from the Greek, 'monos' meaning 'single.'"

The key to being such a dedicated entity, however, lies in the continuing devotion to the development of and the living out of a rule of life.[35] This transforms the everyday into the sacred. In the life of a monk, devotion is expressed by every action, not just those times which are sacred in definition according to some practice, like the gathering for religious services or observances. Every aspect of the life of a monk is offered sacredness by the dedication of the entity to the rule of life of that particular monastic order. In such an entity's life, cleaning the house is equivalent to cleansing the spirit of imperfections. Washing the clothing, the body, and the dishes becomes equivalent to dipping one's seemingly soiled self, in aum and essence, into the transforming water that creates healing and cleanliness within. The preparation of the food necessary to feed the body becomes equivalent to the preparation of the sacrificed and dedicated self to the service of the one infinite Creator. Each thing that is done with the intention of expressing devotion to the one infinite Creator becomes sacred. Thusly, there is nothing in the everyday and ordinary life that is not sacred.

We welcome further questions upon these points from those known as the Rangers, but shall not attempt to anticipate them.

Is there another query at this time?

V: There are two further queries from the Rangers. One of them asks if Q'uo would comment on any connections between counter-culture movements of various decades such as the 50's beat generation, the 60's flower children and the 80's techno-rave movement?

We are those of Q'uo, and are aware of your query, my brother.[36] We would suggest two points of connection among many. The first connection is the one of the spirit and flesh. In each generation, the yearning for that which is beneath the surface expresses itself in ways both negative and positive in terms of what this instrument would describe as negative or critical expression and positive or radiant expression. The connection between these generational terms and their expressions, both critical and radiant, is the connection of the spirit within the boundaries of flesh yearning to express that "something more" that is felt, yet often cannot be found, in the everyday.

That quality that is so blessed within the young within incarnation is the quality that sees clearly the hypocrisy and the tomb-like structure of indifference that has been created by those whose hope has fled. And whether it is the critical and dark energy of the beat generation, the transcendent joy of the flower children, or the very mixed darkness and lightness of the techno-rave sorrow and joy, all expressed together, the energy is that of transformation, and this is that which wrenches spirit into flesh.

Those who are outside of the energy of these movements within the young are distracted, oftentimes, by the collateral images, icons and accessories, if you will, of such movements. Those who have experienced, from the inside out, these energies, know beyond any doubting the validity and the rightness of the spirit. And if it must be pulled or tugged or wrenched to appear within flesh then these energies are accepted and even welcomed.

It seems as though there is violence involved in such movements. And perhaps we would say that insofar as this may be so, it is due to the violent nature of the wind of spirit when it is called into a space that has not been prepared as a sacred space. However impure that energy seems, it is a true blessing not only to those who feel it and express it, but to the world which has been changed by its inclusion.

The other aspect that we would point out, in terms of the commonality of these movements, is that they have in common being much more native to and obvious to the nature of those who are awakening as wanderers or as those who are ready to be wanderers; that is, who are ready to graduate from third density into fourth; who are ready to drop the flesh and live in love. In a sense, this is about the release of fear. Love and fear cannot co-exist and the expression of love is the release of fear. It is the movement from death to larger life.

Is there another query at this time?

V: The last Ranger question is whether you would comment on the architect, LeCorbusier? I suspect he

---

[35] The "rule of life" for many religious orders begins with the principles of poverty, chastity and obedience. Included in a rule of life are such choices as how to observe a daily worship of the Creator, how to serve the Creator, and how to praise and thank the Creator. In some monastic orders the rule of life is quite long and complex, covering virtually every aspect and natural function of living.

[36] V was reading questions sent in by B.

is of wanderer origins and would like to know if it is possible to share why his work manifested through architecture?

We are those of Q'uo, and are aware of your query, my brother. In terms of specifics, it is not possible for us to discuss one entity such as LeCorbusier. However, it is interesting to look into the nature of how creativity works within a life experience. The same creative wind blows for all and on that wind lie melodies, themes, motifs and other avenues of intelligent expression of the fire of spirit. The energies of suffering and learning catch the facets of personality uniquely for each unique entity. And as an entity awakens within incarnation to the truth and beauty of its own being, possibilities open up in this and that way, unique to each entity. One entity may express creativity by growing a family and helping the young souls within that family to flower. Another entity may hear the call of a certain kind of expression of devotion and become a guardian of truth, an upholder of justice, or an agent of the healing power of human love. All professions call with the song of the muse to those entities whose personalities are shaped so that those structures hold their passion and give them avenues of expression. Every artist catches the wind of spirit and finds ways to draw images that catch the light and share the vision. Every musician hears those melodies that are drifting from angelic essences embedded within the inner planes and responsive to the winds of the times and the energies of the generation now alive. And so it is with those who see the value of shape and ratio and wish to create places for the heart and the spirit to thrive.

Is there another query at this time?

(Pause)

We are those of Q'uo, and since we seem to have exhausted the queries within the circle this day, we would leave you, as we found you, in the love and the light, the peace and the power, of the one infinite Creator. Adonai. Adonai. ✤

L/L Research is a subsidiary of
Rock Creek Research &
Development Laboratories, Inc.

P.O. Box 5195
Louisville, KY 40255-0195

L/L RESEARCH

www.llresearch.org

Rock Creek is a non-profit
corporation dedicated to
discovering and sharing
information which may aid in
the spiritual evolution of
humankind.

SUNDAY MEDITATION
APRIL 17, 2005

Group question: Today we are going to take potluck.

(Carla channeling)

We are those known to you as the principle of Q'uo. Greetings in the love and in the light of the one infinite Creator, in Whose service we come to you this day. May we say what a privilege and a blessing it is for us to join your circle of seeking. We thank each of you for taking that precious commodity of time and using it to form this circle, to make use of the sacred space of this place and this time and the combined energies of all of you, where you have created a temple of light. And into this temple we pray that all of our thoughts may combine to form an offering and an honestation to the one infinite Creator.

It is a privilege to respond to your question and, as we always do, we would ask that each of you be very careful in listening to what we have to say, being very ready to reject anything that does not ring true to you, for we would not be a stumbling block before you or interfere with your process in any way. Your free will is very precious to us and if you will take responsibility for discriminating between those things that ring true to you and resonate to you and those things which do not, we will feel much more free to express ourselves without worrying that we have infringed upon your free will. For we are no authority, but only seekers such as are you.

(Pause)

We paused so that this instrument could rearrange her microphone system. We felt that it would be on her mind throughout the session if she did not do that and so we appreciate your pausing with us.

We have little to say but we would say a bit before we ask for the first query. First of all, this instrument was concerned earlier because the one known as Hatonn, which is part of our group, had expressed itself in that she had caught the quality of the word, "Hatonn" [when challenging], and we would express that there is within this group the calling for unconditional love in its purity and that is the service which the one known as Hatonn so joyfully provides. We would at this time pause that the one known as Hatonn may express its nature in the silence between all of you and ourselves.

(Pause)

We are those of Q'uo, and are again with this instrument. May we say that the one known as Hatonn expresses that which is truly unconditional. It is pure presence. This instrument often prays, "Be present, be present." And yet, love is always present. It is your minds which are distracted from that presence. That presence is the heart of who you are and we hope that you will stoke up on those energies as you rest in unconditional love. For truly the days are here for each of you to experience incredible waves of energy. Some of the energy is what this instrument would call the highest and best and it enlivens and energizes you. Others of the waves of energy are those which are shrinking from the light and the love of the one infinite Creator, energies that are fleeing from the lucidity and the clarity of these times that are among you now. The new heaven and the new earth lives upon the planet Earth. It is being born, more and more. And so there are retroactive energies that are shrinking away from this clearer and brighter light, shall we say, not very accurately.

When these waves of energy hit you it will feel to you as if all things are resisting and are failing. We ask you to know that this is baffled and confused energy that does not tell you the truth, for you are succeeding. You are thriving. You are growing. And in that growth, things must fall away so that new things can emerge. We can only say to you: let it flow through you, let it fall away as it will; cling not and do not reach, but be. And allow the energies that are yours to come to you. Your desire is honed, your focus is becoming more and more clear. Trust yourself. Trust the system of guidance that surrounds you. Trust the Earth beneath your feet which is learning little by little to trust you. You are becoming creatures of love involved in a loving environment, and from the earth to the sky, from the East to the West, and the North to the South, your planet is coming alive with love. Can you hear it in the politics of the day? Only if you listen carefully and with selective ears.

Know then that this which is unseen has a power and that you are part of the web of love. Open yourself, therefore, to those energies of love that are awakening within you, more and more.

We would at this time ask if there is a query?

V: Thank you, Q'uo. We do have three queries from the Rangers. The first of them is: "What is the nature of that pairing between two beings who find in each other that love and wisdom that connects them 'not for a day, a week, or even a year, but for all eternity'?"[37]

We are those of Q'uo, and are aware of your query, my brother. May we say that the nature of the

energy betwixt two entities which have penetrated the veil of forgetting and have become able to experience each other as true beings, shall we say, as souls, is that energy which we would call selfhood. It is an awareness of unity. It normally comes wrapped in some clothing and that clothing tends to be partially that of sexuality and partially that of personality. The heart of a connection between two entities that have been able to form a bond that is eternal, however, is one of unity.

It is interesting to view the ways in which entities within third-density consensus reality are able to penetrate the masks or the costumes, shall we say, of appearance, personality and sexuality. Very often, it is the trigger of a sexual attraction or the attraction of intellect for intellect, or goodness for goodness, shall we say, heart for heart, that will trigger the opening of the space in which two entities may begin to create a unity between them.

When entities attempt to move from sexuality, shall we say, from the red-ray attraction, into a soul-to-soul relationship, there are boundaries which appear impossible to cross. For sexual relationships are based upon a self and an other-self and the connection between. When that dynamic remains as a central motif in a relationship, in its own way it delimits and describes the circumference of that particular relationship. And many are the couples that have been drawn together sexually and that express the chemical attraction of the polarity between those two entities for some time before finally discovering the country that lies beyond polarity.

Similarly, many triggered bondings have to do with the nature of the orange-ray chakra, shall we say, the chakra that has to do with subtler aspects of interpersonal relationships. And again, until the dynamics betwixt the personalities have to some extent been explored and released, the very thing that brought two entities together becomes that which limits that relationship.

And so it is as entities move upwards through the dimensions of relationship, exploring the aspects of relationship which have to do with becoming a family and then exploring the aspects of relationship which have to do with opening the heart to each other's humanness. There is almost always a delimiting factor involved in this opening of the heart. It would seem, once an entity has climbed up

---

[37] This phrase is a quote from an answer to a previous question to Q'uo in the March 20, 2005 session about finding a loving companion. The complete thought was, "And how shall you prepare to walk side-by-side with an entity that speaks to your deepest heart and that satisfies you, not for a day or for a week but for all of eternity?"

through the first three concerns of relationship into the open heart, that the way would be free and clear. And yet this is not so. When one at last enters that sacred precinct of the open heart and one rests together in that place of clear light, one views in the other the beginnings of great knowledge. And with this great knowledge comes a great price. That price is the shadow of all that is true about one. When one is heart to heart, when at last [one] is exposed and the humanness of the self is undefended, not simply from the other self, for the other self is ready to love unconditionally, that other self becomes a mirror which then reflects back to you for the first time, so that you can see it yourself, the picture of your own shadow.

It is a great knowledge and you are as naked as Adam and Eve in the Garden of Eden, standing before the tree of the knowledge of good and evil. Are you good? Are you evil? No. You are human: you are all that is. This is a great crux in the development of an eternal friendship, shall we say. If you shrink from the mirror of your shadow in the open heart, you then are forced back, past the lions at the gate, out into those lesser fields, plains and meadows of the one infinite Creator in which play the dynamics of personality.

Once you have faced yourself squarely in the mirror of the other, sitting together in the lap of the Creator, surrounded with arms of love, tickled by the beard of the Almighty, blessed upon the breast of the Mother, loved at last for all that you are, then at last you are free to begin what is sometimes a lengthy process but a joyful one. And that is the moving on from the open heart to the articulated heart. That is what this entity would describe as the energy of the blue ray or the throat chakra. Once you have begun the process of open communication with another, you find that miraculously that which used to divide you now begins to unite you. You find that the truth which seemed before to beat you down and to make you feel less now blesses and redeems and heals and clears the way for you to be.

Let us take a moment and look at that verb, to be. It is so underappreciated among your peoples! And yet this is what you came to do. You came to do something that has no doing to it, for being is more than anything else a matter of allowing yourself not to act but to express as an essence beyond thought, beyond deeds. What is the scent of a flower? What value can you say it has? It is beyond words. Can you see that? And can you see that the bouquet of your being is the most precious gift that you will ever have to give? It is your gift to the other, to the creation, and to the Creator. And what but the forces of great love can give you permission within third-density beingness to explore that essence of self?

So we would say that the nature of the quality of companionship that lasts not for a day or for a month or for a year but for eternity is that quality which has been formed in the fire of moving through tremendous amounts of dynamics: sexual, sensual, physical, emotional, mental, intellectual and finally into the area of the spiritual, into the area where two hearts can touch and become one, not because they are the same but because they are sparks of the same fire that are sharing with each other the incredible gift of their unique essence so that each is teaching each, each is healing each, and each fulfills the larger desire of each to become a flame of spirit.

Is there another query at this time?

V: Thank you Q'uo. The Rangers' next query asks, "In the higher densities, how does sexual attraction and companionship play out?"

We are those of Q'uo, and are aware of your query, my brother. There are some limits to that which we may say about this question but in general we would say that the sexuality which is so much a part of third-density entities has all of the aspects which higher densities' sexual energy transfers contain. However, within third density, as we have said, there is the beginning of sexual attraction that rests within the second-density physical vehicle within which you enjoy moving about the Earth at this time. The expression of sexual energy within this animalistic body is simple. It is a natural function which is uncomplicated and which calls body to body, depending upon the dynamics of sexual polarity. This instrument has often described the basic sexual attraction as chemical, and we would agree that it is a matter of the chemistry between two entities. Within third-density acculturation, the simple chemical attraction between two entities within red ray becomes overlaid with expectations and culturally-oriented standards of attraction which work not according to the ways of the body but according to the ways of the mind. And you must realize that within third density, the body is the creature of the mind. So very often there is a substantial amount of fairly shallow and inauthentic attraction concerned with sexual expression within third density.

Now, within fourth density these layers of acculturation fall away. Fourth-density entities, as well as fifth and sixth-density entities, have physical vehicles of a type. Each higher density's physical vehicle is, shall we say, more refined in type yet there is a physicality to it. Consequently, the nature of the physical vehicle determines the entry level of sexual attraction. It is difficult for you, perhaps, to imagine a sexual attraction that is based on the truth of each entity as seen by each other entity. And yet we would ask you to imagine a creation in which all entities are attracted to all other entities based on the truth of their beings. Higher-density bodies are attracted to truth in the harmonics of the truth within themselves to which they have the most commonality and from which they have the most to learn. So there is still a bi-polar aspect to higher-density sex within fourth density, but it is the near pole of commonality and the far pole of a mutual desire to learn from each other the mysteries of the essence, the fragrance of the being of each other. It is sexuality and teach/learning.

Within fourth density, the casual sexual expression is not simply common but is as much a part of courtesy as shaking hands is within your density. It is as if when entities meet, they have sex. That is the way that you would describe it within your density. The potential difference between the two entities is expressed naturally and without any shame, removal of clothing, or the exchange of bodily fluids. It is an energy exchange. The children produced of this energy exchange are those opportunities for souls who wish to learn from the two entities which exchanged energy in such a way as to make an opportunity. The bodies are more refined. Sexuality does not have those physicalities of third density. And yet there is the possibility for enormous love. And when it is seen between two entities that there is this unique potential for teaching and learning together, a mating is formed.

So you see the processes of the energy body continue to be red, orange, yellow, green, blue and indigo. And relationships continue to be refined through the interactions of two entities who have joined together. Yet, the work is subtler and deeper and, in its own way, narrower. We who speak are those of

fifth density and we carry the energies and the information of those within fourth density and within sixth density. In each density of those three, the physical bodies become more refined and in sixth density the bodies are what you would call photons. You are moving from heavy chemical bodies to lighter energy bodies to bodies of a certain type of light to bodies of limitless light, shall we say. This is very inexact and while we apologize for the inexactness, we can only express that there is information that would infringe upon your free will involved in attempting to explain to a more precise degree the evolution of mind, body and spirit.

We would ask in general that you simply consider the direction to be that of the refinement of the energy exchange between two entities. Your entity-ness shall not change. You shall continue to be you. As you form relationships within higher densities, your opportunities for learning and service shall be lifted and refined. This is not a difference in kind, but only a difference in quality. You are on the track which you shall continue upon.

Of seventh density, we cannot speak, for we have not yet experienced the density that is drawn directly back into the Creator to create the next octave of experience. We stay within this heartbeat of the one infinite Creator.[38]

Is there another query at this time?

V: Yes, the Rangers' third query reads, "Of the worlds Q'uo evolved from, how did they typically enter into fourth-density service? Namely, what cultures and sociological constructions did they move through on their way towards living in love?"

We are those of Q'uo, and are aware of your query, my sister. We find that we are up against the full stop of the Law of Free Will when it comes to describing experiences that are common to us, experiences which would pull you into a false place where you were hoping to be like us.

We would instead say a few words about the opportunities that lie before you at this time. For you are those with third-density bodies and fourth-density hearts—yearning with every fiber of your beings to live a fourth-density life, by fourth-density values, and with fourth-density qualities. The Earth

---

[38] This source has often spoken of the entire octave of densities in which we are now experiencing third density as one heartbeat of the Creator.

does not hold you back, for the Earth is vibrating fourth density. Your own inner nature does not hold you back, for you hold within you the energies of the universe. All of nature is willing for you to grow.

Then what holds you within the density of your choice? Certainly, you incarnated in a third-density body, but your very DNA, in every cell of your body, is waiting for you to remember who you are. And in the quality of your remembrance comes the opportunity to form new strands of fourth-density DNA. And this is happening among your peoples at this time. It is possible for you as well.

What shall you have to do to avail yourself of this remembrance? My friends, you shall have to allow the pain and the sorrow that you hold so dearly within you at this time to die; not simply to forgive it, but to allow it to fall away. Are you ready to die to this hard-won suffering that has soaked up a portion of your identity? Are you ready to be a creature of joy?

This instrument has talked about letting the sorrows and the sufferings of herself and others flow through her, but she does not do it. Oh, she is in love with suffering; she is ready to give up her life! Yet, when she can do that, then she is free within incarnation. And to some extent, little by little, she has let portions of herself fall away. She is ready not to hold on to difficult energies; here and there, now and again. And so we say to each of you, "Awake to love and joy and allow the dead self to bury itself, dust to dust, and ashes to ashes." We speak now not of the dust of the body, which is easily seen, but the dust and the ashes of old emotion held in their imbalance as if they were treasures.

What is the crucible and the refining fire all about but the taking of dead ash and dust and the compression of it into jewels? You carry coal within you: let it become a diamond. And if the pressure is fierce, embrace it and do not be afraid of the transforming and refining.

(Side one of tape ends.)

(Carla channeling)

It is a condign and just process.

Is there another query at this time?

V: Q'uo, that's all from the Rangers.

(Pause)

We are those of Q'uo, and because of the energies within the room, we would ask one more time, is there another query at this time?

(Pause)

We are those of Q'uo, and we do feel the strength of unasked questions within this group and that is perfectly acceptable to us. We are happy to let them be and to express to those with issues upon their hearts at this time our absolute and unwavering love for you and our gladness at any time to respond to any questions that you do have. We are always with you if you request our presence, that we may underline and underscore the stability of your own silence. We thank you so much for the great privilege of being allowed to speak with you and to share what humble information we may have. At this time we would leave you as we found you, in the love, the light, and the unity of the one infinite Creator. We are known to you as the principle of Q'uo. Adonai. Adonai. ♣

L/L RESEARCH

L/L Research is a subsidiary of Rock Creek Research & Development Laboratories, Inc.

P.O. Box 5195
Louisville, KY 40255-0195

www.llresearch.org

Rock Creek is a non-profit corporation dedicated to discovering and sharing information which may aid in the spiritual evolution of humankind.

SUNDAY MEDITATION
MAY 1, 2005

Group question: The question this week concerns the process by which we can release our suffering, get to the bottom of the suffering, find the causes for it, and make our way towards that quality which we might call joy. We're wondering if Q'uo can give us some idea about the process through which we go to release the suffering and what role joy has, and also, is there a discipline that we can utilize or a process through which we can discipline ourselves to release ourselves?

(Carla channeling)

We are the principle known to you as Q'uo, and we greet you in the love and the light of the one infinite Creator, in Whose service we come to you this day. My friends, the circle of seeking that you have created is a dazzling display of light and color. The combined field of your energies is perfectly beautiful and we thank you, as flowers of the field of Earth, for coming together and setting aside this time as sacred.

We search for the truth as well as you and we are fallible, so we would ask, as always, that each of you guard your hearing and your taking in of information carefully. Only you are the authority for yourself. Only you can discriminate for yourself as to what you feel is right for you to work with as an idea and what simply leaves you cold. If anything we say resonates to you, then by all means work with it. If something we say does not resonate for you, we ask you to toss it aside, carelessly, thoughtlessly, without

looking back. It is not for you, not now. With each of you doing that, we will feel much more free to speak our minds and to share with you in these clumsy things called words. We thank this instrument for the service she provides, but she is translating concept into words and there is always something lost in the translation. So what we can share we shall. And above all, that which we share is beyond the words, as you know. It is the essence of our and your energy together and for that shared energy we are profoundly grateful.

You have asked this day concerning our thoughts on how to release and let go of the suffering that you have experienced and that has become embedded not only in your surface memory but in those parts of the self that lie in a geography that is beneath the surface of self. You have asked us, basically, how to become miners and how to find and process suffering. There is indeed a process involved and yet it is not necessarily a process which takes time because it exists in time/space rather than space/time. It exists in a part of the memory that is not of your physical body or your physical mind but rather is a part of your consciousness. In life, as you experience an incarnation, the space/time and time/space components of memory and mind play back and forth. Dreams and thoughts and daydreams and imagination and the processes of internal review make a kaleidoscope that is constantly shifting between two worlds.

You, to some extent, have facility in shifting back and forth betwixt mind and consciousness, but the differences are subtle and it is well to realize those times when the nature of your personal reality shifts from the third-density concerns of mind to the multi-density concerns of time/space, which we would describe as that of consciousness.

We cannot promise you solutions for suffering but we can talk about some of the things involved in finding, in processing, and in releasing catalyst that has been, shall we say, undigested and buried in order to preserve the goodness of catalyst until it has been thoroughly used up.

The work of the one known as Ron, creator of the materials for Scientology, and the work of the one known as Silva, in creating the techniques of Silva Mind Control, both speak of embedded pain and its nature as being that which is underground in the unconscious part of the self so that one really must go after it. The hints that there is embedded suffering that one can go after are part of the everyday surface experience of life. You are taken out of your normal, peaceful mentality by something someone says or some act that you observe that creates in you a response. And you note, if you are clever and are watching yourself—which is always a good idea—that that reaction was out of proportion to the event that caused the reaction. That is your prime clue that something is going on within you that is in need of exploration.

As we have said to this group before, most embedded pain has been buried long ago when you were young in incarnational age and small in body. In childhood, you are undefended and those things which hit you hit you hard. You have listened to a lot of opinion from people that you perceive as God-like: parents, teachers and other authority figures. And you try to accept the things that they say and make sense of them, and judge and evaluate experience using those guidelines.

A couple of things happen. First of all, those very God-like entities that seemingly are the source of nurture and care create pain in their dealings with you, and you do not know what to do with the pain. It is not as though you can leave these people and choose to live somewhere else. In order to deal with living with someone you have come to fear as well as trust, you create within yourself a place to go in which you are safe. This asylum that you create for yourself is displaced from all others but yourself. The cost of creating such a place is the removal of your full self from the interface between yourself and your most intimate family life. Whereas in some mythical early babyhood perhaps all was well and there was no feeling of fear or distrust of the environment that was your home, fairly early you developed a sense of caution. And this has affected your ability to meet life with a full, frontal embrace.

For some entities, like this one whom we use as channel at this time, there has been a reintegration of a great deal of self with the immediate environment and, indeed, it was a process that was years in the making; a process wherein this instrument deliberately and consciously returned to the family environment and interacted with each of those entities from which she had come to feel displaced until she was satisfied within herself that she had again achieved a complete integration of herself into this original home so that there was no more fear in that place.

It is a rare entity that is able to do this work fully. Perhaps the parents have disappeared because of death, divorce or some other means of removal of those people from the environment. Perhaps there was such damage done that there is not the possibility of being able safely to go through the process of reintegration with the childhood environment. Whatever the reasons for an inability to fully come back into the original home within the memory, within the consciousness, and accept it fully with trust and love, the lack of that original goodness of home bears on the rest of the incarnation in terms of creating an environment in which the personality shell carries those original wounds from early childhood without being able to process them.

Certainly, there are opportunities later on in life, when one has grown up in terms of physical body adulthood, that are painful enough and displacing enough to create further pockets of pain that are then again buried because one is not able to deal with them fully at the time. The one known as Ron calls these pockets of pain engrams, and we feel that this is a handy word and we will use that word. We are simply speaking of crystallized memory that carries with it an emotional charge. We do not need to define suffering because each of you has suffered and knows the nature of human suffering. You know the many colors and textures of pain; you know how it can hit you full-face or from the side or from behind, and how each of these ways of being hurt has its own presence. You know how your emotional and nervous systems respond to these assaults and you know how just thinking about certain things that have happened to you can create the whole environment in which the suffering occurred for you as if it were yesterday instead of thirty years ago.

That is the situation for each of you as far as what this instrument might call baggage that you carry and do not even know that you are carrying. But as the one known as C said, when she gripped the courage fully to face herself and ask to be shown by her guidance system the suffering that she was carrying, she was overwhelmed with the richness of her load. Each of you has a suitcase full, shall we say, of real gems of pain and suffering that are neatly packed away, waiting for you to return to them, and, with love, to lift them to the light and to work with them.

Now let us talk about joy. The one known as R1 said that he wondered if joy and discipline were somehow incompatible, that perhaps if one were joyful one did not have discipline or somehow discipline might not seem to be that which would produce joy. And yet he sensed that discipline may be involved in discovering joy. As it happens, this instrument is more familiar with the landscape and the environment of joy than most because of what she would describe as brain damage. There is a much stronger link in her energy system between mind and consciousness than is usual among your people, and this entity toggles up into consciousness more often than not. When one is within that part of the mind which we would call consciousness, the default setting is joy. The nature of the one infinite Creator is joy. We might move beyond that word to the word ecstasy. We might even move into the word called orgasm, for the default setting of the creation and the Creator is absolute and infinite joy. In terms of your experience of it within a third-density body, it is orgasmic. In terms of consciousness—which is that which you carry within you at a deep level in incarnation and out of incarnation—it is simply that constant radiation of unconditional love which is like an infinitely rich experience of the most joyful and light-filled sense of self that can be imagined.

Each of you has a core self that has nothing to do with the way you express yourself, what you do for a living, how you speak, what your educational

experience is, or any of those details. That essential self is a self that you share with every living thing in the creation. And that essence rests in joy. For this instrument there are many times when she simply moves into that place of light and is lost to the consensus reality around her. Among your peoples, this state of mind is called mysticism and the gift that this state of mind offers to the one who slips into that ecstatic state from time to time is not a gift that can be shared, except in essence. Each of you can perhaps recall moments seeing something beautiful in the natural world or in the world of art or music, dance or just a moment in time when everything seemed right, that you got a whiff, a scent, of the perfection of all that is. My friends, this is a true perception.

You do live, regardless of the appearances around you, in a perfect creation where all things are evolving at the rate at which they can evolve. You brush up against an endless stream of other selves in your everyday life and they all have their perfection already within them. And so each of them is to you as a reflection, as a mirror, and you see yourself, again and again, in everyone you meet. Different people show you different sides of yourself. Certainly, many of the mirrors are crazed, as in a funhouse at a carnival and you are too tall or too wide or bent in the reflection. And yet it is you. What is that reflection attempting to show you? The questions, the process, are endless. And you are like a detective in a way, or one who puts together a very complex and three-dimensional puzzle. You create the world, again and again, new each day by the way you put the pieces together, by the way that you read the mirrors in your environment.

Consensus reality has a strong tendency to pull you away from consciousness into mind, away from joy into the concerns of the everyday, away from the unity and the peace and the power of your natural essence into the endless stream of detail and the constant rearrangement of detail to make structures with which you can live, within which you can work, and from which you can learn.

Where does discipline, then, come into this process of mining your engrams, bringing them to light, and working with them? There is a tremendous discipline involved simply in keeping your mind on track, in, as several have said in various ways, remembering who you are and why you are here. It is not a discipline that is rigid. Certainly, one with a sense of a discipline may create a rule of life in which there are certain things to be done each day in order to create the most favorable environment for spiritual evolution. There are those such as the one known as R1, the one known as T, and the one known as Carla who strive each day to set aside time for meditation. They do this because they have found that it is helpful. There is a fruit to this discipline of silence. But we are not speaking here of that rigid kind of management of time. Rather, we are speaking of the discipline, of the management, of mind, of thought, shall we say.

What have you thought about today? What of those thoughts have you taken seriously enough to listen to? Do you listen to your thoughts and do you follow them? We recommend it. The clues for where pain lies are embedded in your everyday thoughts. Certainly, it is helpful to use dreams, because dreams are the conversation that your consciousness has with you when it finally gets a chance for the floor. Your mind has been filibustering all day in endless conversations about how to do this and why to do that and you become mired in details. During your dream time, all of the things that you shoved aside because you really did not have time to think about that now have a chance to spring up and up they come. Listen to those things in your dreams that do come up, that you can remember. But more than that, listen to the seemingly trivial thoughts that pass through your mind during your day, in the midst of the hustle and bustle of life. And when you begin to see a pattern, think about it, follow it, pursue it as if you were a lover and that pattern of remembered pain was your sweetheart. What alleys and doorways you go through in pursuing that pain are out of time and out of place, existing in that closet, shall we say, within that haven that you created as a child. Your safe place has these treasures stashed away, safely stored until you get back to them and take them and look at them fully and lovingly.

You will predictably feel a good deal of resistance around doing this work. These things were put away because there was enough intensity and fear surrounding them that you felt unable to deal with them at the time that you experienced the catalyst that was the original wound. Taking it out again, you will experience all of those feelings. This instrument was speaking with the one known as Vara not too long ago about the nature of puncture wounds. [Vara and Carla] had both experienced puncture wounds and were talking about the fact that they cannot heal from the surface down. They can only heal by being exposed and healing from the bottom of the puncture upwards to the surface. Digging at an engram is much like this [in that] you are finally opening that place where there was infection, if you will. You must let the sunshine of your love and the rain of your faith cleanse that wound.

Interestingly enough, once you set yourself to do this work, the process can happen so quickly that your reaction to finding the source of that particular pain finally is joyful laughter. You look at that pain and experience the deep humorousness of that moment. For pain, once exposed, once seen for what it is, is not at all the monster that you hid away and the relief is palpable, the joy is intense, and the reaction is laughter. We hope that as you find these engrams, as you love them and look at them straight and embrace them as the wolf that bites, you will find that deep humor and that reaction of laughter coming to you.

Sometimes the process is not so speedy. Sometimes that is not the bottom. Even though you find that engram, it is attached to other engrams. You have created a network, a spider web, if you will, of connected pain. And you have connected pains that you have had later on in life to an even deeper pain. So sometimes the search for the true bottom of that particular pain is a search that must go on for a while. Be patient with yourself if this is so. Keep digging, keep mining. Realize that, just as in underground lodes of minerals that create gems, your pain has been under tremendous pressure for a long time. The common coal, shall we say, that was the original pain has gradually become diamond-like. It is not sitting there with the original blood and sweat on it but rather it has been recreated within you as a gift, as a treasure. Within you, in the nodes of pain, lie beautiful colors that you have earned and are a part of you that you would not wish to do without. Perhaps they are dark colors, certainly. But as part of your palette of creation, they give to your expression an incredible amount of depth and richness as you lift them from their storage into the light of your open heart, appreciate and give thanks for these gifts and these treasures.

The one known as R1 said earlier that he was finding in his spiritual search that the direction is from complexity to simplicity, and that he rather liked that direction. And we say to you as well, when your life has become truly yours, when you have found the freedom to be yourself, you will find that life has become very simple. Certainly, in terms of the details of the day, life is seldom simple. But in terms of knowing who you are and choosing what you wish to put your energy and time in on thinking about, each time that you are able to shed a layer of falsity from your own pattern you will find that you have simplified the life because you have been able to simplify your thoughts. The one known as Ra said many years ago that it was helpful to think this thought, to ask oneself this question, "Where is the love in this moment?" When you ask that question, you open your heart

(Side one of tape ends.)

(Carla channeling)

When you open your heart, the Creator embraces you and shares Its heart with you and when you and the Creator are one and abide in each other [then] all things are one and filled with love. May you come often into that open heart, into that consciousness of that one Creator. And when you leave those precincts to attend to the details of the day, may you go forth carrying that essence with you. The radiation of that open heart blesses all whose lives you touch and is your gift to the creation, the Creator, and all those whom you meet. There is no better gift, my friends, than your beauty and radiance. May you trust and have faith in yourself and may you come to know more and more deeply that you carry within you the truth and the freedom that that truth brings.

This instrument is telling us that it is time for us to open the meeting to further questions and so we allow this to be the response to that wonderful question. We just thank you for asking such a great question for us to work with. It has been a real pleasure and we have not done it justice, we know, but perhaps we shall have another go at it at a future time.

Is there another query at this time?

T: Yes, I have a question that I spoke of earlier to the group about meditating when one is feeling down, depressed, just bad about things in general. It should be the time when you go to meditate but I find it very difficult to do that. Could you comment on any ideas about how to help yourself make the situation more conducive at that moment to meditate when you are in a bad frame of mind?

We are those of Q'uo, and are aware of your query, my brother. The tendency of an entity who is distressed or depressed is to wish to seek a numbness, a lessening of the jangling of the nerves or the awareness of the pain involved in whatever has caused that kind of discomfort. And certainly, when one moves into meditation, the opposite effect occurs: the sense of reality becomes sharper and the landscape clarifies. Therefore, it is natural, my brother, that you would find it difficult to move into the silence, for that silence speaks and those still, small voices that speak in the silence tell uncomfortable truths and bring up material that simply intensifies and sharpens the original discomfort.

In one sense we would say to you it is a good discipline to go ahead and move into that silence, despite the resistance. However, we might suggest that it would be helpful to you, if you decide to go that way, to create a routine that is in the creation of the Father, as this instrument would call it. The meditative walk through the natural environment gives the process of meditation the boost of the support of the first and second-density creatures: the earth, the air, the fire, and water are around you in the creation, as are second-density entities such as trees and plants and those entities such as birds and animals with which you share the creation. Their nature is not trammeled with third-density concerns and so they are instinctively supportive of you, my brother. It is very grounding to be in touch with the earth. This instrument, for instance, finds it helpful simply to pull a few weeds at the end of the day, not because she is making such a huge difference in her garden, but mostly because the contact is so soothing and so beneficial to her.

Sometimes it helps to change from an indoor environment or a working environment to the natural environment. It is not that it softens the blow of silence. Silence can be very confrontive. Meditation can be uncomfortable when one is dealing with things one does not understand. Yet we encourage you to continue the discipline of meditation and simply change the venue, moving from the civilized and domestic environment of house and chair and so forth to the stillness of motion as you walk and take your meditation, with motion being a part of it.

We would also comment on that which the one known as R1 said at the time that you originally had spoken of asking this query. The one known as Ron said that he had found it helpful, when one was mired in terms of one's own process, to get out of that box of self, to focus on doing something for someone else. We would agree with this assessment, and say that it is a tremendous help to the process of understanding the self to get out of the small circle that one has worn in the carpet by going around and around the same thought, lifting oneself into another environment, looking at another problem, looking at how to serve another entity. All of these are very helpful in terms of freeing the self up from a bondage which has not been perceived but is very real. For one ties oneself into a pattern by habit and it helps to pull oneself out of it.

We would say, however, that it is also helpful to realize that doing this is a technique which bypasses the inner work in any direct manner. So it is well, say, at the end of the day to come back to that concern in a contemplative setting and to ask yourself at the end of the day, "What do I still see here? What is catching me? Where are the triggers involved in this situation and how does my highest and best self see into this situation, given that love and that wisdom that have come to me in this day?" For you truly have grown today. So it is helpful, shall we say, in the evening or before you go to bed or as you are going to sleep to move in a peaceful and contemplative way into your own thoughts once again, asking yourself what the harvest of the day is. What have you gained, what have you released, what has caught you, and why?

The one known as R2 said that he distinctly remembered reading many times that we have said it is the questions that you ask that are truly valuable rather than the answers which you receive. Let yourself be curious. Let yourself ask. Be bold. For you see, what you are trying to burn through is the numbness and the resistance that you have learned to defend yourself by using in your daily life. You want to get to that place where you are in the default setting and yet you are kept from it by the cotton wool that you have battened in order to protect yourself. Wonderful is that moment when you blow it all away with the true wine of unconditional love and acceptance so that you are in full body contact with yourself, your essence, and who you really are.

These are times to be prized, remembered and found again and again.

May we answer you further, my brother?

T: I had another thought. I hate to take so much time but it occurred to me, while you were speaking there, of course, a very good way to get beyond those bad feelings would be to develop a true sense of appreciation for the catalyst that was coming your way and causing this depression or whatever it may be. But it also occurred to me that deep down, maybe a person harbors anger about the incarnation that they've come into in this life and if one is able to forgive one's true self for the cards that were dealt in a particular incarnation, to truly forgive, this would help the entire situation. Could you comment briefly on that?

We are glad to comment on this observation for it is excellent and profound. Again we have trouble dealing with this in words because it would be handy to think of this sort of process as having a beginning, a middle, and an ending. But in actuality, in consciousness you are swimming in states of awareness. And because you have come into a state of awareness once does not mean that you have finished a process. It means that you have found yourself in a certain state of consciousness. Once you have found it, at least if you trust in yourself, you can believe it and you know it is there and is something that you can seek once again. But spiritual evolution is not a straight line, it is a spiral. It is like you are walking up stairs that move around the hub of self in terms of your experiences so that, as you come to that same place again, you can say to yourself, "I recognize this place, this state of mind, I know this, I've been here before," but you actually are in a different place, because you have spiraled into that place and you are now, shall we say, at a different rung on the ladder, a different level of awareness. You learn from everything and you carry everything in whatever state of learning has processed through you.

It is most true that a great incarnational lesson that is common to all those who take incarnation is simply forgiving oneself for the choices made in coming into incarnation. Before incarnation, everything looks pretty easy. Standing outside the incarnational miasma of what this instrument would call the world of maya or illusion, your memory is intact. You understand who you are. You understand the goals and the missions that you have set for yourself for this particular incarnation. You understand the use of pain and suffering and the necessity for it, the gift of it, indeed. For it is this very displacing pain that alerts one to some situation that needs to be worked out, some patterns that needs to be resolved. You see it all very clearly and as a whole. Then you plunge into the womb and the parents' arms, and everything clouds over and nothing is simple. Until you enter through the gates of death into larger life and again regain your complete memory and are able to see your life as a whole, the incarnation itself is spent with at least a substantial portion of your time being given over to trying to figure out what the situation really is, what is really going on, what you are really seeing, what you are really hearing, what is really coming into your perceptive web.

Here is where faith enters in. By faith, you can simply affirm that all is well, that what you need is coming to you, and that what you have to give is something for which there is an audience. By faith, you can know that you are useful, even if you are stuck in bed, sick as a dog, and unable to do anything. By faith, even if you are stuck in a job where you do not see how you are truly helping, you can know that you are helping [because] you are you and the love with which you do that job is the greatest gift in the world and one worthy to be given. We ask you, then, to explore that resource of faith and to ask for help because there is a strong support system available, designed specifically for you and involving quite a few entities who have been drawn to you because of the beauty of your soul and the fervor of your seeking. They must be asked before they can help. Once you ask for this support, you will find it everywhere.

May we answer you further, my brother?

T: No, thank you very much.

We thank you, my brother. Is there a further query at this time?

S: Here it is, another year I've been given the opportunity to learn. Derby's coming up next week and Wilko and Afleet look pretty good. Can I put five bucks on a horse for ya? Can you give us a little inside scoop here?

We are those of Q'uo, and are aware of your query, my brother. It is good to feel your humor and your energy and may we say that we would never bet on a sure thing. We will leave that to you.

Is there another query at this time?

S: Well, not from me.

(Pause)

S: Well, I lied! I got another one. Stepdaughter is soon to give birth and we've gotten some information on this new baby, this new entity coming in, and I'd be curious to get your perspective and your thoughts and your impressions on this new soul.

We are those of Q'uo, and are aware of your query, my brother, which actually is not a query at all but a request for observation on the miracle of the infinite moving into illusion. May we say that each soul that enters into incarnation at this time is a pioneer of fourth density. This entity, like so many entities being born at this time, shall have a specific set of difficulties which are the result of that dual activation of third and fourth-density bodies. The challenge for such entities is to find those about them which are aware of their uniqueness and are able to work with them as equals from a very young age. We congratulate you on this miracle and encourage all within the family to rally around this soul. As the one known as Wordsworth said, there are streams of glory around any birth.[39] The radiance around any soul fresh from the Creator is a wonderful thing to see. May you see yourself in this new child's face. May you feel yourself to be as new as this child. May you give yourself the opportunity to live a new life.

May we answer you further, my brother?

S: No, thank you.

Is there a final query at this time?

(Pause)

---

[39] This is a misquote. Here is the original quotation, from the long poem, "Intimations of Immortality from the Recollections of Early Childhood," by William Wordsworth:

Our birth is but a sleep and a forgetting:
The soul that rises with us, our life's Star,
Hath had elsewhere its setting,
And cometh from afar:
Not in entire forgetfulness,
And not in utter nakedness,
But trailing clouds of glory do we come
From God, Who is our home."

We are those of Q'uo, and find that we have once again exhausted the supply of questions in the group. May we say what a pleasure and a privilege it has been to share energy with each of you. Thank you for this opportunity. We leave you as we found you, in the love and in the light of the one infinite Creator. Adonai. Adonai. ♣

L/L Research is a subsidiary of
Rock Creek Research &
Development Laboratories, Inc.

P.O. Box 5195
Louisville, KY 40255-0195

L/L Research

www.llresearch.org

Rock Creek is a non-profit
corporation dedicated to
discovering and sharing
information which may aid in
the spiritual evolution of
humankind.

Sunday Meditation
May 15, 2005

Group question: The question this week has to do with change and renewal and the circumstances of such within each of us who seeks. We are wondering if there has been an influx of this energy that allows changes, if it's available to everybody or if the changes that the people in this group have been going through recently are a product of people who seek. Could you give us some information on what allows changes, renewal, rebirth and transformation with seekers of truth? Is it more the qualities that are set up within the person or qualities that are within the environment about the person?

(Carla channeling)

We are those known to you as the principle of Q'uo. We are going to pause immediately in order that this instrument may adjust her microphones in order that we may go on with this communication.

(Pause)

We are those of Q'uo, and are once again with this instrument. We thank each of you for allowing us to make these adjustments for the recording. It is helpful for those in the larger group of L/L Research, as it is so called in your planetary way of speaking, that we are able to impress the magnetic tape with our words so that it can be used as a resource for more people than those who are sitting in this circle of seeking at this time.

We would thank each of you who has come here this day for the dedication of your time and your focus at this moment in your life. It is a great blessing to us to be able to address such questions as you have put to us this day and we thank you for your seeking for the truth and also, and separately, for the real beauty of each of you as you join in the circle and blend your vibrations to be amalgamated or amassed as a group consciousness in this sacred place. The beauty of you assembled here is stunning and we are humbled and feel very privileged to be called to your group.

As always, we would ask you to take exquisite care in discriminating between those thoughts of ours which seem to be helpful to you and those which do not. If you will discard without a second thought any of our opinions that do not ring true to you, it will enable us to speak freely. We are not people of authority. We are those who have perhaps walked a few steps further on the path of evolution of mind, body and spirit than have you, but we still seek and we are still learning. We thank you for observing this fastidiousness in your discrimination of thoughts, for that will enable us to speak without being concerned that we will interfere with your process or infringe upon your free will.

You ask us this day concerning the process of letting go of that which we perceive within ourselves to be used up or old or dead and how to embrace the process of transformation, transfiguration and rebirth. We are most glad to address this mélange of subjects with you. The challenge for us is where to start.

Perhaps we would start with the comment made by the one known as Jim in laying out this question for us concerning the emerging of a new wave of energy. As this instrument said earlier in conversation and as we have said several times in the past little while to this group, there have been repeated waves of energy that have been global in their scope and indeed have affected your entire solar system in some cases. Some of these energetic bursts are coming from within the inner processes of your planetary sphere as it, as this instrument said earlier, undergoes a continuation of a fairly lengthy and not particularly easy labor as it births the fourth-density Gaia, that planetary being which is fully sentient and is evolving in her own right.

The other bursts of energy which have hit this planet, and indeed your entire solar system, are those coming from what this instrument has sometimes called the great central Sun and are informed by the combined love and concern of various of the larger groups of entities who wish this planet and indeed this solar system well. For it is a time in this planetary cycle when there is a great deal of attention focused upon this planet from all over what you would call your major galaxy. The birth of fourth-density planet Earth goes well; the baby is very much alive. The resistance set up by fourth-density energies striking a very divided group of those who dwell upon the surface of planet Earth has set up waves of interference which could be seen to be as a planet-wide system of psychic greeting, if you will, in that all of those who are attempting at this time to embrace fourth-density values and live in a way that is compatible with graduation into fourth density can reliably expect at this time and in the near future to be visited by those entities and situations which offer the clearest possible catalyst having to do with all third-density energies that are still embraced that mitigate against the acceptance of fourth-density energies.

We give this instrument the phrase, "the ghost in the machine." *The Ghost in the Machine* was a literary work which purported to deal with the effects of mechanization upon Western culture. And there was this concept of the machine age as taking the soul from entities so that they were witnesses more to the machine than to their own beings. The culture in which you are bathed and in which you dance at this

time has given you gifts. As the one known as A earlier, there are biases and distortions built into the developing spirit within incarnation upon planet Earth by entities such as parents, teachers and other authority figures which, for weal or for woe, create bias, create within each of you opinions as to what is good, what is painful, and what is trustworthy in your environment. These gifts include, as we have said before, nuggets of the most precious pain and suffering which you have taken into yourselves, often at times when you were too young and too defenseless to do anything with this pain. Consequently, it has gone down into the earth of your subconscious as a little nugget or engram of crystallized pain.

And so as you come through your own experiences as an adult entity and as one which has chosen to accelerate the pace of your spiritual evolution within incarnation, you have cast yourselves in the role of miners going after this buried treasure and lifting it to the light of the present moment within your own open heart so that you can realize the gifts that you have given yourself and finally open them and do something with them.

We build to some extent upon past information in this session and so would encourage any who become confused by anything that we have to say to seek those two previous times of asking in which this group worked together on how to clear old suffering from the mind/body/spirit complex that is each of you.[40] Our basic concept is that of, as this instrument said earlier, helping each of you to come into a celebration of yourself. We do not encourage this celebration on the level of third density. It is not our orientation to encourage the energies within you of personality. We do not object at all to your personalities! However, as this instrument said earlier, the personality shell that each of you brought into incarnation was brought in order that you might have the tools and resources that you needed in order to follow the agenda that you had set out for yourself prior to incarnation. The resources that you gave yourself included people such as your parents and many people within your life with whom you had made agreements before incarnation. They were not necessarily agreements to work together for the service of the one infinite Creator.

---

[40] The two previous sessions in which this subject was discussed are those L/L Research Sunday Meditation sessions dated April 17, 2005 and May 1, 2005.

In some cases, they were agreements to clear up or balance adhering catalyst that sometimes is called karma by your peoples. Some of these people showed up in your life as people with whom you seemed to have nothing but a continuing argument or for whom you could not feel as you "ought,"—and we use that word in quotes—especially people in your family whose object, in this incarnation, seems to be to create interference and resistance in your own pattern.

In many cases, this person was chosen specifically so that you could work on loving yourself. It is often very difficult to approach in a direct way the central challenge of loving the self and so you are given mirrors. Sometimes the mirrors are loving and honest and you get a pretty fair image of yourself, one that you can look upon with some feelings of stability and trust in that image that you are seeing.

When you look at yourself through the mirror of other entities, such as those about whom we spoke, those that give you the catalyst, the interference and resistance, you are a looking at a very skewed and distorted mirror of yourself and yet it is a mirror of those parts of yourself with which you have had arguments in the past, perhaps not even in this lifetime but in between incarnations or in other incarnations. Perhaps you do not have adhering catalyst with this entity. Perhaps you put that entity in your life simply to learn to love without expectation of return. However, as you forgive that entity for its skewed picture of you, you begin to see that you have only to forgive yourself in order to create room within that portion of yourself that we would call the heart.

Now, we have spoken of the heart chakra and about how that, although it seems that it is a wonderful place, always open, always loving and so forth, actually the heart chakra is a real challenge to negotiate. As you move through clearing the red, orange and yellow-ray chakras, as you move through issues of survival, personal relationships, and group or legal relationships, you are able to become clear because you have done the work associated with those energies. They do not include the energies of loving. They include, rather, work done in balancing, accepting and understanding the nature of those energies of red, orange, and yellow ray.

When one reaches the heart chakra, one enters an outer courtyard in which, in this instrument's system of images, is seen the sellers of sacrificial doves and other temple accoutrements, postcards and tourist items. You see crowds of entities associated with all the work that you have done in the lower three chakras, entities and situations which you have not entirely digested, entities and situations which are unloved by you, unforgiven, unaccepted and not seen as a worthy part of the self. Do not fear that you shall be offenders in entering the sacred space of your own heart with all this baggage, for there are lions at the gate of the inner temple.

Fortunately, at any time that you wish to circumnavigate the detailing and processing of all these entities, the lions at the gate are satisfied if you can simply accept that, as this instrument said earlier, you are a flawed human entity whose nature is to some extent to be distorted and in error. If you can let that suffice, you may put down the baggage of the crowds. You do not have to chase the moneylenders out of the temple today. You do not have to forgive all that you have brought into the outer courtyard of the heart today. It is enough that you love and accept yourself as you are. For such a one, the temple lions bow and welcome you in.

You are immediately and without any more hesitation in that place within the heart that is sacred and in which the Creator sits waiting for you with infinite patience and love. There you have a place of rest and renewal. We do encourage each of you who seeks to let go of old pain to meet the lions at that gate squarely, daily, to walk in and sit down and let yourself be loved, understood and totally accepted. The part of you that is the Creator can only come into its own when it is nourished by companionship with the divine. Silence within this sacred space is a powerful resource that will offer you much clarity through time, whether or not you have any awareness of work done or things understood or any sort of mystical satori.

And let us take a look at the suggestion of the one known as A that there are these crystallized nuggets of pain about which one can do nothing. We would agree that the energy of inertia is such that, left untended, left unrecognized, shall we say, these nuggets are there for life. They do not float to the surface and go through the process of refinement and acceptance by themselves. Your will is all-important. Your choices are all that create the opportunity for you to accelerate the pace of your spiritual growth.

We have talked to some extent about the efficacy of identifying the entrances to these underground points of pain. The adits to this particular kind of pain can be seen well as triggers. And you know that a trigger has been pulled when you begin having reactions or responses of an emotional or mental type that are in excess of the reaction that would be considered appropriate by your wisest, highest and best self. As the one known as C said, the tip-off is when you begin to experience being pulled away from your center of self.

When you feel this occurring, you have two choices. The choice of most entities who are not focused on analyzing their thoughts and pursuing a course of the discipline of the personality is to allow the tape that has been triggered to roll. And it will roll, just as it has rolled ever since the first instance of this type of experience, probably in your childhood, until it has come to its end, at which time you will be free again to live a normal and centered life. Until that tape is done you are temporarily listening to or acting out the contents of that tape, whatever that is.

Your other choice is to take the moment of recognition that you have been triggered and make the choice to stop and say to yourself, "I am being triggered." Then ask yourself what the triggering event was, how it happened, how it can be analyzed and so forth, using your mind until you have satisfactorily, to yourself, analyzed the trigger. And then move that very difficult fourteen inches from head to heart and ask from the heart, "What is my best self's response to this trigger?"[41] When you ask the question, it might be helpful, if you have not done this as this instrument has for years, to have a pen and paper at hand or be sitting at a typewriter or a keyboard, because you will get information concerning what your highest and best self would do.

Asking what your highest and best self would do is asking for your guidance system to kick in. You have a great guidance system. The problem entities have with their guidance system is that it must be activated. It is an entity that is yourself at a future time, in terms of your third-density physics. It is yourself in the midst of sixth density. This instrument calls her guidance system the Holy Spirit, or Holly. Other entities call their guidance system a guidance system, or their guru, or any of a number of other constructions in which guidance is explained, one way or another. But it is actually quite a complex web of entities. Certainly, chief among them is the Creator-driven version of yourself, moving back to you from sixth density. But you have picked up many entities from the inner planes, as this instrument would call them, who have been attracted to you because of the beauty of your hope and faith, or because of the kind of mission that you came into incarnation to pursue, or for any of a number of other reasons, resulting in the opinion of inner-planes entities that you are a person that they would like to help. They range from tiny children who simply want to help you find lost things to the most wonderful and complex personalities, masters, gurus or entities of that type from various of the inner planes that have been drawn to you because they feel they might be able to prove to be a resource in your own process. Some of these entities have names, some of them are simply energies or essences. Some of them speak in ways such as we do, in concepts which come up through the subconscious mind. Some of them speak through coincidence, birds, animals or street signs, using your environment to find ways to communicate a word or a concept or a feeling with you. Some of them speak to you in sleep and some, such as we, are there during meditation if you ask us to join you so that we may deepen the stability of your basic meditative state.

It is a tremendous resource to ask yourself what your best self would do in a triggered situation. You may not be able to use that information at the present time; it takes some repetition to learn how to stop the tape before it has finished its roll. You may have to listen to that tape all the way through once again, but, when you have been through this process, you are at least listening to the tape consciously, aware that you are no longer in consensus reality: you are playing a tape. That is all it is. It is a piece of information frozen in its original distorted form for you to play again and again until you finally get what is on that tape.

In a way, it is as if pain were a joke and when you finally get the joke, the laughter clears the pain. It is not that you are a joke or that suffering is a joke. It is that you are dwelling in a thoroughgoing illusion.

---

[41] This question is part of a system of teaching created by Marianne Weidlein, whose web site is www.empoweringvision.com/site/70-Coaching.html. Carla has studied with Ms. Weidlein.

The things that occur to you are in the nature of a parable or story. You think, if you do not look closely, that you are simply experiencing the surface of life and yet life has innumerable levels. And depending upon the clarity of your consciousness and your comfort level within yourself, you are very capable of moving quickly through many layers of reality, moving from surface illusion into any number of levels that are more real than the surface illusion. You can at one time be in a cartoon, a carnival, a school, and a temple. All of these environments are layered within you and all are equally valid. In fact, you have an infinite array of valid points of view.

Where is the key, then, on where to stand to look at your experience and to deal with it in ways that clear old suffering and that welcome and invite transformation and rebirth? In one sense, the key is to stop thinking and to be. We have said innumerable times to this group that your job here is to be. We have said that your basic mission is to be yourself. And if you look at our previous discussion you may perhaps begin to see into just how complex a thing it is to clear away the debris of stray thoughts and old habits and achieve that which is simply "to be."

The one known as Réne said, "I think, therefore I am."[42] And we would say to the one known as Réne, "We are, therefore we think." The mind has been given a great deal of respect in late centuries. From the 18th century onward, the mind has gained ascendancy over the faculties of the heart. The world has become a skeptic. It does not live by faith, but by what it can prove and see and hear. In some ways, this is an asset. For when one lives only by faith, that faith can degenerate rapidly into superstition and irrationality takes one on many a fanciful journey that is no more valid than being a ghost in the machine.

But to be yourself is somewhat of a challenge, simply because there are overlays upon overlays upon overlays of things you think about yourself, things other people think about you that you have taken on as if they were your own and so forth. Your culture is relentless in its insistence that you think of yourself in narrowly channeled slots of identity. And we encourage you to cast off each and every attempt

of the culture to limit you for you are, and each of us in the creation is, an infinite and illimitable being. We cannot express to you how many experiences you have had that have brought you here today, even within this incarnation. Yet you came into this incarnation as part of the stream of one soul, one cell, shall we say, of the body of creation. You are unique and yet you are not limited by that sum that is you. You cannot be summed up by your experiences to this point because you are alive in the way that the Creator is alive: eternally and infinitely. You are, in fact, a part of the Creator and you take part in the reality of that identity in a way that is so deep that you cannot remove it from yourself. No matter how much you yearn to be able to say, "I am me," you shall never understand the totality of who you are because so much of it is lost up in the part of you that is not of this density and not of this world but is rather of all densities …

(Side one of tape one ends.)

(Carla channeling)

… and all worlds. Stretching out the self and shaking off the clothing of an incarnation is a wonderful exercise. You cannot shake away your core identity. For it is from this identity that you have the focus to draw breath. Your identity is far deeper than what you came in with at birth and far deeper than what you will leave with when you enter the gates of larger life. Your identity at heart is that of the Creator. You asked, "How can we make room in ourselves for transformation? How can we make use of these rolling waves of renewal energy that are flowing into the planet at this time?" And we would say open yourself to the limitless possibilities of yourself and stop believing the publicity about yourself, from yourself, and from those around you. Release yourself from the seemingly helpful mooring of those anchors of selfhood that you have thrown down to hold the boat against the current. For there is a system of currents in that sea of becoming of which entities upon the inner planes have so much more awareness than do you. Allow yourself at last to float free, without an anchor overboard that holds you in some perceived safe harbor. You may consider yourself then as a vehicle, moorless upon the surface of this inner ocean, as the physical vehicle of a boat, a ship, shall we say. You have a rudder. That rudder is your desire. Set your desire by that which is the deepest-felt hope of your heart. And sense into the oncoming winds and play with those winds and sail

---

[42] Réne Descartes said it in Latin first: "Cogito ergo sum." Translated, that is, "I think, therefore I am."

before that wind and for the first time experience that feeling of, "I am who I am."

We ask you to think about this as we leave this subject, for this instrument is telling us that we must go on.

Endemic to your culture—and we specifically speak of the Western culture—is a concept of self that is ruthlessly independent of others. Now this works for third-density work. One is almost forced to think of oneself as over against "them," the others that are in your world. In terms, however, of spiritual evolution at this time for each of you, it is helpful to realize that you are not simply evolving yourself. You are evolving your race, and by that we mean humankind. As the Creator is in you, so you are a co-Creator that is involved in humankind. And it is specifically helpful to think of the larger self at this time when the planet under your feet, as an entity, is moving into new birth. It needs that so-called "hundredth monkey effect"[43] of which the ones known as S1 and S2 were speaking, to be realized and known for the truth. You are not simply evolving for yourself; you are evolving for humankind. As you forgive yourself, the world becomes that much more able to consider forgiving itself. Any work that you do is shared out amongst the developing social complex of your planetary mind.

You are not alone and you are not "part of the group." You are a cell in the body of the Creator which is manifested at this time upon the surface of your planet. You have very special gifts. You are a specialized cell. Some of you are healers, some of you are communicators, and some of you are those who love. There are as many specializations as there are parts of the body and it is a very complex body. But you are doing what you are doing as part of that body and you do not know what effect you may have outside of your own sphere of awareness. Yet we assure you that no loving acceptance that you are able to achieve of yourself stops with yourself. It

echoes, as the pebble into the pond, to the very edges of that pond.

The Archangel known as Michael is that entity which expresses the gifts and powers of fire and that entity at this time is at attention on the behalf of planet Earth. Be aware of the power that you wield at this time. Know that the sword of truth was never sharper and never more ready to sever you from old pain. We encourage you to embrace every seeming obstacle, resistance and difficulty, asking it what its gift is for you, embracing it, accepting it, and loving it.

We thank each of you for developing this group question and at this time would open the meeting to follow-up questions and any other queries that you may have at this time. Is there a question at this time?

S2: I have one. I have a crystal which has come into my mind in the last few days. And as we were talking about this crystal and getting some information, we couldn't quite translate or couldn't quite get the words. I was wondering if you could tell us what the message or the word was or where the entities were from or whatever comes to your mind?

We are those of Q'uo, and are aware of your query, my brother. As you know, we draw back from questions of the nature that you put forward now, simply because these questions are very leading and involved intimately and specifically with the process that is developing for what the one known as C [has called] your "group of four." We would simply say that there is indeed, as you have already expressed, no error or chance involved in this transmitter, receiver and transducer coming into your group, or as this instrument has said, into your pocket.[44]

As many physical objects, such as the jewelry this instrument wears and the doll it has on its lap, function, your crystal functions as a collector and transmitter of information and energy. Without such collecting devices, you would still receive the same information. The devices come to you because you, on an inner level, have committed yourself to taking on the substantially enhanced work of getting the information at a faster rate. The way to work with such energy collectors as these is to lean into

---

[43] Ken Keyes, Jr., wrote a little book called *The Hundredth Monkey*. This book is on the web at www.testament.org/testament/100thmonkey.html. The basic theme of this book is described by the author as "the Hundredth Monkey Phenomenon, which I learned about in talks by Marilyn Ferguson and Carl Rogers. This phenomenon shows that when enough of us are aware of something, all of us become aware of it."

[44] The crystal S2 was asking about was a globular crystal that S2 had been carrying in his trousers' pocket.

them; in other words, to "clap for Tinkerbell,"[45] to believe that they are efficacious and therefore to preset your mind to receive information. This instrument earlier suggested that you retain a pen and paper when you have this crystal with you in order that you might jot down thoughts that come to you that do not seemingly come from your surface mind. This is one good way of coming into an enhanced awareness of the nature of this collector. What is it collecting? On what level is it working with you? What kind of information does it have? Do you find it helpful? This kind of process is what we would encourage you to pursue. The difference between [one who is so working and] one who is working with a mind but not a full heart or a focused desire is that interesting things keep occurring to them which they do not particularly note down. Therefore, interesting things simply keep occurring. When one begins to focus in on the type of interesting thing that might be occurring at a particular time and one begins to look deeper, that focus stands you in good stead and separates you from the casual observer. The deeper you are willing to go with such a collecting device, the more information you are able to collect.

We offer you the simple caution of awareness. Be aware that what you learn, you are then tested upon. What you ask for, you will be given. When you knock, the door is opened and you step into a reality of which you are then responsible for being aware. To those to whom much is given, there lies, as a result, a responsibility. What shall you do with all of that which this device gives you? That would be our caution to you. It is exhilarating to move quickly, but in the ways of metaphysical development, as you move you collect spiritual gravity and things can weigh heavily into your process.

Therefore, when you do sense that you are, shall we say, being tested on what you have learned recently, do not panic. You have studied; you have learned; now here is a test. Meet that test with your heart open and your guidance system notified that you need help and right quickly. You will be fine; there is no failing grade in these tests. Nevertheless, if you are not able to participate in a test so that you have

seen the pattern of that test, then you will simply receive that test in another way at another time.

Therefore, we would say to you that it is well to take a good rest when you see such a test coming up. Focus not on more study, but on getting the metaphysical equivalent of a good night's rest. Consult your guidance system, root down into your earth, your environment, your relationships, and especially your relationship with yourself, and then sail on, fearless and full of love for the moment, for the test, for the Creator, and for your part in it all as a cell of the creative principle.

May we answer you further, my brother?

S2: A lot to think about, quite helpful though, unlike your answer on the Derby! It was a 50-1 shot and not a sure thing, but that's okay. But I'm always very grateful for your time, your efforts, and your valuable wisdom.

We are those of Q'uo and we thank you, my brother. You are valuable to us, too. Is there another query at this time?

A: Yes, I have a question. I'm hoping this is appropriate tonight and if you can't answer it I can quite understand. It's with regard to the American military bases that are being closed all over the country. Does this have something to do with moving through a natural progression to the fourth density or does it have more to do with the possibility of creating internment camps within the United States in order to reduce the population of the Earth?

We are those of Q'uo, my sister, and are aware of your query. We would content ourselves with saying that, to the best of our knowledge, the energies having to do with the closing of these bases does not fit in at all with the energies of fourth density. Rather, they fit in with third-density energies which are reacting quite violently and negatively to the incoming fourth-density positive energies of planet Earth, as it shall be very soon. The reasons for these closures are very involved in third-density political and economic agendas which do not, shall we say, have that stamp of unconditional love at all. Further than that, my sister, we would prefer not to explore for we do not feel that it is our place to discuss the machinations of the world of illusion of your peoples. We can simply say that your natural tendency to distrust and suspect less than pure

---

[45] In Barrie's classic children's book, *Peter Pan*, Tinkerbell is a fairy-like creature who can only thrive if humans believe in her and clap for her. As they applaud her, her light shines brighter and brighter.

motives for such fairly substantial and massive changes is fairly accurate. We do not say that there are internment camps in your politicians' minds but simply that there are wheels within wheels and machinations within machinations among those who hold power among your people.

We would also offer our humble suggestion that, in terms of metaphysical progress among your people, the goal of understanding such machinations may helpfully be described as knowing what [it] is in order to love it and forgive it unconditionally. Recall the plight of the thief and the murderer upon the cross next to the one known as Jesus. When this entity asked the one known as Jesus if Jesus would remember him when he came into his glory, the one known as Jesus replied, allegedly, "This day you shall be with me in Paradise."[46] As we said earlier, you are not moving into Paradise by yourself. Your culture and all of the people of the tribe of humankind hope to come with you. Love them.

May we answer you further, my sister?

A: No thank you, I understand and totally accept the answer. Thank you.

We thank you, my sister. We are those of Q'uo and would ask if there is another query at this time?

V: Q'uo, I wonder if you would speak to the mechanism by which mineral communicates with an organic entity such as a human.

We are those of Q'uo, and are aware of your query, my sister. This is a subtle question, my sister, but we will attempt through this instrument, which has no scientific background whatsoever, to give you some coherent answer.

Minerals are full of first-density energy. That energy is fully conversant with the one infinite Creator and is alive. There is no part of your environment that is not fully alive with the exception of, as this instrument would say, the distance between your ears, which, in terms of third density, is truly a dark

zone, not nearly as alive with the infinite Creator as are all densities but the third. Thusly, the energies of mineral are very vulnerable to impression by thought.

For one who grasps the interrelatedness of all things, the space defined by the angles and spaces within those angles of a crystal are especially vulnerable [to] impression by thought, especially when it is a thought connected with emotional energy such as a heartfelt thought, shall we say. Unfortunately, in many cases, those wishing to impress crystals with thought are those which impress them with negative thoughts. In fact, there are entities who have created cultures in which negative thoughts are ritually impressed upon, say, a rock or a crystal and then buried in order to do something with that negativity. However, crystals can also be impressed with positive thoughts or with a personality.

May we answer you further, my sister?

V: Sure go ahead. *(Laughter)* I was happily listening!

We are those of Q'uo, and are aware that although you have not asked a question, you wish us to reexamine the one that you asked in the first place. We shall do so.

Each substance, beginning with air, fire, earth and water, has a nature. And within that nature there lie avenues of expression, communication and relationship. You can come into relationship with an element, an animal, a location, a word, a letter—any substance that has been created by the Creator or by you. These relationships are real. They are natural. The creation was designed to connect each part with each part.

Within third density there is this inevitable sense of being separate which is born of the fact that, as we said, the dark space between the ears, the mind of the physical vehicle which you enjoy as your body, is simply not aware of the connectedness of itself with all things. You are not aware that you have a force field that ends as you sit upon the chair upon which you are sitting. Yet it is simply a field. You do not stop and the chair begin; rather, you and the chair are sharing space. And the fields of force that are the chair and that are you have agreed to rest upon each other according to the laws of physics within third density. It creates a very tidy world where chair does not become person, person does not become chair, and chair does not sink into floor, and so forth. It

---

[46] From the *Holy Bible*, Luke: 23:39-43: "One of the criminals who were hanged railed at him, saying, 'Are you not the Christ? Save yourself and us!' But the other rebuked him, saying, 'Do you not fear God, since you are under the same sentence of condemnation? And we, indeed, justly; for we are receiving the due reward of our deeds, but this man has done nothing wrong.' And he said, 'Jesus, remember me when you come in your kingly power.' And he said to him, 'Truly, I say to you, today you will be with me in Paradise.'"

creates a system of illusion in which you can have a sense of time and process and within this illusion you have this sense of time passing and one thing leading to another and things flowing forward. Yet in truth, they flow in all directions at once, and you are part of the chair, the chair is part of the floor, and all are part of your planet.

To encourage communication with any substance, whether it is an element such as air, an item you can hold in your hand such as the global crystal which you looked at this day, or anything else, the mindset that is most helpful is simply to know that such communication is already taking place so that you become the one that is responsible for this communication going forward; you are the one that brings yourself to that entity with which you wish to communicate and say, "All right, I'm listening, what have you to tell me?" Then be prepared, because you will receive impressions. You have the ability to receive them directly if you can believe in the goodness of your perceptions. There are various good processes by which entities are helped to become more aware of what they know and of how to stand on that knowing in such a way that your hearing is freed up and you are open-minded. However, the communication between the universe, all parts of it, and yourself is ongoing. It is a matter of how much of it you want to tune into and how you structure for yourself the experience of collecting that information.

May we answer you further, my sister?

V: Thank you. On the subject of our tidy laws of physics, then, with respect to my experience off the shore of South Africa,[47] could we say that was as simple as an agreement between my field and that of the water to break those laws?

We are those of Q'uo, and are aware of your query, my sister. We certainly could say that, my sister, and we believe that you are correct, in essence, in thinking so.

May we answer you further?

V: I would be delighted if you would answer further because I don't think it was quite that simple.

My sister, we are those of Q'uo, and are aware of your query. We are also aware that this question is a question which we would need to explore with you at some length. May we suggest, if you are interested in pursuing this question, that you either ask it as the main question at another public meeting or that you and this instrument and a third person agree at another time to hold a personal session in which we might be able to move into this subject with the fastidiousness which such a fairly complex subject would need.

V: Thank you, Q'uo, I suspected that would be the case.

We are those of Q'uo, my sister, and we thank you for your understanding. It is not that the laws of free will inhibit us at this time, for you have that understanding which enables us to speak. We would simply be fleshing out concepts that are already within your own learning process and well-crystallized. Nevertheless, it is too many words for this particular session, as the energy begins to wane.

We would, in fact, at this time ask if there is a final query?

(No further queries.)

We are those of Q'uo, and we thank this group for its wonderful questions and its great beauty. We are always with you if you ask for us to deepen your meditation and to love you. We leave you as we found you, in the love, the light, the power, and the peace of the one infinite Creator. We rejoice at this opportunity to serve and thank you profoundly. We are those known to you as the principle of Q'uo. Adonai. Adonai. ❧

---

[47] V was underwater when she was a teenager working with a Christian service group in the Transkei for some twenty minutes according to the records of the camp of which she was a part and yet she did not drown!

L/L Research is a subsidiary of
Rock Creek Research &
Development Laboratories, Inc.

P.O. Box 5195
Louisville, KY 40255-0195

L/L Research

www.llresearch.org

Rock Creek is a non-profit
corporation dedicated to
discovering and sharing
information which may aid in
the spiritual evolution of
humankind.

Special Meditation
May 17, 2005

Vara: Our question [from D] today is in two parts: "I am feeling that a big focus of my process right now is in letting go of parts of my identity which have to do with prior conditioning within this incarnation. Could you offer me any comments you might feel appropriate and helpful on what is this identity and what does [the] letting go of in this context?

"I seek transformation at this time. I see myself as a server. As I transform, what is my service? What kind of service am I looking for? And who is the entity that is of service as I let go of my previous identity?"

(Carla channeling)

We are those known to you as the principle of Q'uo. Greetings in the love and in the light of the one infinite Creator in Whose service we come here this day. We wish to thank the one known as D for setting aside this time in order to seek what is loosely called the truth. We hope that we are able to aid you and those in this group, as well as any who may read these words at a later time, by those opinions that we share. But, as always, we would protect this service by our request that each of you be completely responsible for the way that you listen to those things which we say. Please realize that we are not authorities over you in any way but rather those who would share thoughts with you as those somewhat more experienced than you on some aspects of walking the path of the seeker. It would enable us to speak freely without being concerned for possible infringement on your free will if you will listen carefully to each thought and then accept it for further work as a resource or reject it as not having resonance within your own subjective search at this time, according to your own inner discrimination. We thank you for this service, it will enable us to offer ours.

My brother, the odor of bread that is being created permeates the air that this instrument breathes and enables us a good opening to the subject of identity and transformation. The question that you ask is tied up with those two concepts of transformation and of identity. What is it that is transformed when an entity goes through transformation and what is the definition of identity? How does that identity change when one is dropping away bits and pieces of one's cultural conditioning?

The loaf of bread that is being created at this time in this house's bread machine was at one time a mixture of unrelated components: flower, water, butter, salt and yeast. Prior to their incarnation as a nascent loaf of bread, their only identity was of the pool of wheat-ness or water-ness or salt-ness that such elements and green and growing things possess. Now, as heat is applied to them and pressure in the baking process, they are shortly to become a new and living entity: a loaf of freshly baked bread. And they will carry that identity until each crumb of that loaf is ingested by the humans of this household, or, too stale to eat, given to the squirrels and the chipmunks and the birds outside this household in the yard. It will then become food to nourish and nurture the living things that dine upon it.

Where shall its identity go? Shall it cease to be? May that never be so. Each loaf of bread, indeed each grain of salt and speck of wheat, never ceases once it has found existence in the illusion that you know as third-density Earth. The energy that was created out of nothing in the wheat, the water, and the salt, is transformed into bread. It is then transformed into energy for those who eat the bread. And the energy of those who eat the bread is eternal, and in its turn, that energy is a gift given to the one infinite Creator which, in Its way, eats it and is nourished by it. All that you are, all that you have been, and all that you will be is of one piece. As you drop away things that seem to be you, we ask you to realize that you are not dropping away the identity of that unique being that is yourself. You are refining that identity in the refining fire of the furnace of third-density Earth.

It is fairly said that your Earth is as the athanor and you are as the magician that places base elements into the athanor in order to make gold. It is not that you are altering beyond recognition your identity in refining yourself, but rather that you are burning away those things which you perceive as being no longer necessary to bolster or support your identity. Transformation, then, can be seen not so much as a dropping away of one whole identity and the picking up of another, as it can be seen to be a process of simplification where you are cleaning away the crumbs of self that have been used up, brushing the garment of self to remove these crumbs from your invisible and shining self so that the clothing which you wear before the one infinite Creator is ever more truly a representative of your heart and your soul.

Let us look for a bit at this question of identity. It is certainly true that the entities around you and around almost all entities who are brought up in traditional western culture are taught that their identity is a matter of who their parents are, what their religion is, where they live, and where they go to school. Depending upon the nature of the culture, various children will be given other information concerning who they are and why they are on planet Earth. However, in almost all cases the details are circumstantial, having to do not with what one feels oneself to be from the inside out, but rather of what one's circumstances of birth and circumstance are, the estate into which one was born in terms of class, race, location, belief system and so forth.

We do not deny that these details remain important to any entity within third density for the duration of their incarnation. Many of these primary relationships represent agreements for what this instrument might call lessons that one has agreed with another entity to undertake because of that relationship. In this instrument's case, for example, this instrument agreed with both parents to come into an environment which required that one of her incarnational lessons, that is, one of those lessons that would loom large for the entire incarnation, would be given a good start by them in that they would require her to love them without any expectation of return. This instrument's parents have passed through the gates into larger life over a decade ago in this instrument's life and yet she does not find any lack of those who would help her to practice this incarnational lesson of loving without expectation of return.

In this kind of way, the details of birth and circumstance remain important. They have set you up for those points of focus upon which you wished to center your attention during this time of living and blooming. However, to lean too heavily upon such circumstantial details in forming an idea of one's identity is to embrace the superficial and to distract oneself from the deeper issues involved in incarnation and in transformation within that incarnation. These details are as the bread and the salt and the water—they are not the yeast.

The yeast, or growing agent for incarnation, lies within you and is part of you. It could be called love. Love is that word which is so overused by your culture that it virtually means nothing and so we would ask you to take a fresh look at what loves is and how it acts to grow the elements of your personality into a cohesive, rich and fragrant offering to the one infinite Creator.

In your *Bible* are the words, "In the beginning was the Word." That creative Word is love. And we use that word as we would use the word, "Logos," and as the one known as John used the word Logos in writing that opening phrase to the gospel of John, "In the beginning was the Logos." You came here to incarnation upon planet Earth as a certain kind of creature. You are a creature of love, you are a child of the Father Whose name is love. You are an agent of the creative principle and you have dropped into awareness within this very skewed and delimited version of awareness that is life on planet Earth in order, basically, to bloom.

It is very difficult to think of the main and centrally constituent service to the one infinite Creator as that of being and yet that is what you came to Earth to do; you came here to be yourself, to breath the air, to participate in the illusion of planet Earth, to go through each and every detail of receiving catalyst, responding to catalyst, moving through the periods of joy and suffering that this catalyst offers you, and always your chief responsibility is to be yourself, to feel truly, to examine yourself as fully as you can and to know yourself to the very limit of your ability. You wish to know yourself not to judge yourself or condemn yourself or to pat yourself on the back but simply to become aware of who you are.

This process of becoming aware takes you down many a street. Some of the streets of self down which you walk are broad and have a good deal of traffic. Others of the by-lanes and byways that you explore are far off the beaten track and do not have a great many other entities walking them. Every avenue, street, and lane which calls to you has information to share with you and is worthy of your exploration. However, you have undoubtedly found already that many streets both wide and narrow have not been profitable or useful for you to explore beyond a certain point, and so you move on.

In a sense, your life as you have experienced it up until this point could be looked back upon in the eyes of one who keeps a journal of one's life on the road. And yet the places that you have been and the relationships into which you have entered do not in any way define or limit your identity—for much has been going on within that consciousness that you carry as part of your being.

Now what is it that you are? That is a question about which we could speak for a long time but, to give a shorter answer and one more useful for this conversation, we would say that you are a very organic mixture of mind and consciousness. The mind portion of yourself encompasses your physical body, the bio-computer that you inherited with the physical body at birth and that you call your mind, or brain, and the emotions that you possess that are of an instinctual nature. These are all a part of the

dust from which you came as a body and to which you shall return as a body. As you return to the dust, so shall your personality shell and the untutored, untaught emotions connected with instinctual behavior as inherited with the body that you now experience life within.

Your consciousness is the part of yourself that flowed into manifestation not only in this incarnation but in all incarnations in which you were embodied from what we may loosely call a soul stream that is infinite and eternal. Before the world was created you were who you are. Your identity is now as it was then and that same identity shall be taken with you when that portion of your soul that is embodied now within incarnation moves back into the full soul stream that is your cosmic identity.

When you speak of dropping from yourself those things that would keep you from being a more refined and real version of yourself, you are not actually speaking of dropping anything that is intrinsic to your identity; you're speaking of dropping aspects of your personality shell for which you no longer feel that there is any use.

This is a subtle process and cannot be said, in most cases, to be one which has clear-cut steps. Perhaps you have cut into an onion and then attempted to peel the onion. As you cut into the onion, you may see layers of onion skin and then matter, and then another layer of onion skin and softer matter and so forth. The only portion of the onion that is taken away before the food itself is used is that outer skin which was as the field surface that protected the vulnerable fruit within from spoiling until it could be used.

So it is with your personality shell. Various details of the ego, as this instrument would call it, with which you came into incarnation, you may well have found increasingly inutile to you. And you have decided that since they are no longer useful, they may be peeled away and dropped into the recycle bin. And we congratulate you upon this. There are, however, many, many layers to go. There is much of your selfhood that is quite stubborn in adhering itself to you as part of your identity. As you drop away items of personality such as the station into which you were born, the skills with which you were given credit for having as a young person, the facets of personality which were particularly praised or for which you were given particularly blame, [they] can be found in the maturing process to be less and less useful and so, eventually, more and more, such details are found to be mere crumbs of matter that are no longer useful or efficient at describing the self or defining the characteristics of who you are. And so they are refined away, healed away, or burned away by the decision of your consciousness to do so, by the natural processes of loss within incarnation, by circumstance, or by sudden or gradual realizations of the self, by the self, that create a new point of view, a new place to stand from which you view the world with new eyes. And suddenly, great chunks of what you thought was yourself are no longer useful.

It is not that you are trying to cleanse yourself of secret faults, or clean house by pulling away anything that you still feel akin to, or a kinship to, within you. It is a much more organic and natural process. You are not asked to drop things away from the self before their time. All of the distortions which you possess are useful to you until you consciously perceive that they have lost their kick, they have lost their usefulness to you and are no longer necessary. And so they fall away from you, whether or not you intend for them to. Like old habit, you may reach for one of these old points of identity and find that it simply is no longer there. This is, perhaps, the most benign and natural way to evolve.

What is identity? It begins with the letter "I," and that letter sums up identity: "I." What is the "I" of you? As you become more and more interesting to yourself, we believe that you will find that the "I" of yourself has more and more to do with consciousness and less and less to do with mind. As you circle ever closer to the center of your onion and see layer after layer of false self fall away, we believe that you shall find the "I" of you to be ever more involved with the soul stream from which you came, which is, in its essence, a spark of the one infinite Creator.

Now let us look at the concept of transformation. If we view transformation from the standpoint of space/time, we shall be looking from the past to the present to the future. We would specifically rather not take that point of view in looking at transformation, for we are not suggesting to you that transformation has to do with changing a past self in the present to a future self. We would rather give you a model that makes little sense in terms of looking at time as a stream with past, present and future. We would give you a circular model of time

and space in which, at the beginning of an evolutionary process, you are experiencing yourself on the surface of a ball of selfhood, and you are roaming around on the surface of that ball in search of who you are, much as you wander around on the surface of the globe, wandering from place to place, seeing affinities of self with various places and in relationship with various people in those various places, always restless and always wandering, and never able to penetrate into any depth of awareness of what it is to be yourself and what it is to know the self and therefore to know what you were thinking when you decided to enter incarnation on planet Earth.

At the center of that selfhood lies the center of that precious word, "I." The heart of who you are lies at the center of that onion of self and you have been hungry to penetrate the layers and to go to the heart and to serve from that center. We congratulate you, my brother, on aiming your focus at such a profound depth and we would like to do all that we can to provide resources for you to use in achieving your goal. We can assure you that the process of transformation does take place within the illusion of space and time but we can also assure you that everything that you need will be provided to you seemingly from the surface of that onion, seemingly from one present moment after another in which you receive the harvest of much guidance that is all around you at all times so that you are always being given hints and inklings of what the creation would like for you to consider on any given day at any particular moment. Sometimes you will notice your thoughts echoing back to you in a particularly resonant way and we encourage you to take a good look at what you're thinking at those times, using your intellect as well as your heart, to look as deeply as you can into the processes of thinking and the burden of those thoughts.

This instrument has a good friend who once said to her that she felt as though she were an entity whose center was nothingness. She said that she was capable of dazzling people with her wit and so people expected her to be interesting and humorous and she produced the fodder that they expected, they munched upon it and were happy and felt that they knew her, but she said that she felt she knew better because she had been inside that [which] created that fodder of wit, intelligence and humor, and in her own judgment there was nothing at the center that was herself.

We would ask for you to look at that figure once again of the onion. Indeed, if one peels away layer after layer after layer of the onion, at the last layer one is left with the material in one's hand of nothing at all, and that is where consciousness begins. You stand now at that point of awareness where you see that the center of your earthly personality is nothing at all. And we ask you to stand right there and feel how firm that footing really is. What have you lost when you have lost your earthly identity? My brother, you have lost the details of a life, you have not lost its essence, you have not lost your identity. You have lost space and time and you have come into a new world. It is a world of essences and concepts. Words and details have been left behind but essences and purified emotions fill this new world with richness beyond all imagining. You are, in fact, a far richer and more complex entity, once you have shed the everyday, than you could ever create using the dull crayons and waxy colors of space/time and the locality of the illusion which you experience on planet Earth.

That unimaginable richness that is you has, however, a good use for the relatively meaningless details that go into creating the personality shell with which you can meet the faces that you meet within incarnation. Your physical vehicle and the details of your Earthly pilgrimage are very useful to you. Without a body you would have no way to interact with those other entities that are so unimaginably rich and so incredibly unaware of who they are, with whom you come into contact each and every day. Celebrate your humanity, therefore, and do not look down upon it simply because it is very minor in terms of its importance within your identity.

(Side one of tape ends.)

(Carla channeling)

Rather, take hold of that error-prone, distorted and heavily flawed creature that is you within incarnation, that creature that is aging and that has many false ideas that are continually being updated and the old ideas dropped. Know how much more than that you are and yet celebrate the rags and tags of personality that are you as you are today, because without them you could not go on this pilgrimage, you could not give yourself as a living gift to the one

infinite Creator and you could not have the time and the space to bloom and to be.

My brother, in all truth, you came here to give yourself to the Creator, to the world in which you live, and to yourself. The giving of yourself to the one infinite Creator is easier and easier as you go through the maturation process, for you are irresistibly drawn to that Creator out of simple devotion and the need to be ever closer to the source and ending of your identity. To be a servant of the world in which you live becomes ever easier as you grow more and more aware of who you truly are and become aware at an ever deeper level of what that means. Once you begin to have some idea of the richness of who you are, once you come into that open heart of self and feel your kinship with and eventual identity with the one infinite Creator, that very realization draws to you with increasingly simplicity and accuracy and rapidity those situations in which you can be of help, those relationships within which you can be of service, and those moments when your open heart shines its truth and its light as a lighthouse shines its beacons over a stormy sea, helping others find their safe places and alerting them to the rocks and the reefs of error that are stumbling blocks before them.

Much of what you came here to do as service lies before you, you do not have to reach out to it. Being who you are is the magnet that will draw all things that are needed to you, day by day.

Before we leave this main subject, we would simply encourage you, my brother, to find for yourself a daily round of centering activity that brings you into the silence of your inner room. We encourage you to use some of that silence passively, sinking into the space created by not speaking and not following the unbidden thoughts that arise. We encourage you to dedicate part of that time of self-discovery to contemplation. What you contemplate depends very much on what is of interest to you on that particular day. You may wish simply to move through an analysis of the thoughts that you have thought that day, the feelings that you have felt, looking for points of resonance and patterns of repetition, looking fairly mechanically to begin to grasp the nature of your walk, the nature of your own path of seeking. Many entities lose the chance to follow their own thoughts simply by shrugging them off as being less than clear or less than advanced. And yet we assure you, my brother, that all of those things that have moved you are grist for your mill and the harvest of understanding that is potentially available simply from observing the self, are many. And lastly, we encourage you, in your times of inner seeking, to remember to ask for help, for you have a very generous and capable guidance system that is always eager to communicate with you. Whether you wish to do this through journaling, analyzing your dreams, or simply by contemplation, is unimportant to your guidance system. It will work with whatever structure you create in order to hear it.

Giving this time to yourself is not selfish, it is the act of one who knows that in order to be of service, the self must be known to the self. The phrase that this instrument learned as being indicative of the motto of a white, ceremonial magician is, "I desire to know in order to serve." And this is the motto that we recommend for you in terms of taking the time for yourself in order to avail yourself of the riches, the unimaginable riches that lie within you.

We would at this time ask if there is a further question from the one known as D.

D: No further question.

Is there another query in this group at this time?

Vara: Not from me, Q'uo.

We are those of Q'uo, and since we have exhausted the present questions in this group, we leave you as we found you, in the love and light of the one infinite Creator. It has been our pleasure and our privilege to speak with you this day and we thank you once again for creating this moment and this circle of seeking within this sacred place.

We are known to you as the principle of Q'uo. Adonai. Adonai. ❧

L/L RESEARCH

L/L Research is a subsidiary of Rock Creek Research & Development Laboratories, Inc.

P.O. Box 5195
Louisville, KY 40255-0195

www.llresearch.org

Rock Creek is a non-profit corporation dedicated to discovering and sharing information which may aid in the spiritual evolution of humankind.

SPECIAL MEDITATION
MAY 18, 2005

Question from T: Please offer me any information you feel might be helpful regarding the journey I have taken, where I am in it right now, and what would be appropriate for me to consider in terms of spiritual principles in looking forward.

We are those known to you as the principle of Q'uo. Greetings, in the love and in the light of the one infinite Creator. It is our privilege to be called to this circle of seeking and we thank the one known as T for asking us to speak with him concerning the query that he has posed for us concerning his journey. We greet each in this circle: the one known as C, the one known as G, the one known as T, and the one known as Carla, thanking each for having put aside their time for this opportunity to seek the truth. As always, we would ask that each listen carefully to those things which we have to offer, using your discrimination to take hold of those ideas that you feel may be good resources for you, and to cast aside any and all ideas that do not resonate as being helpful to you at this time, for we would not be a stumbling block before you or interfere in any way with the process of your spiritual evolution. If you can do this for us, then we shall feel free to speak our mind. We would not wish to infringe upon your free will and it is for that reason that we especially ask you to use your powers of discrimination and trust only yourself as the authority over what is true for you. Truth is essentially a very subjective matter. What is true for us may not be so for you. We thank you for being

able to do that for us so that we may speak freely. In no way are we to be considered as authorities.

You have asked about the journey that you are on, where you are in it, and what spiritual principles might be helpful as you proceed on the journey, and we thank you for this question. Indeed, we are walking with you on that journey, which is one common to all of us. We each have our personal and individual identities and yet the journey itself is a common one, common to all who are parts of the one infinite Creator who have been spun out of the heart of the Creator to gather experiences and offer the blooming of the self back to the one infinite Creator as a gift. In that sense, it is a common journey and we walk always in company with each other and never alone.

Let us talk a bit, my brother, concerning this concept of being on a journey within incarnation. It is indeed a long and winding road upon which this journey takes place upon. It begins before incarnation with you and your guidance system coming together to choose carefully the resources with which you would choose to garb or clothe yourself for this incarnational experience. Indeed, you chose your gifts as well as those things which you might consider your frailties or your faults. You chose people in your life which you felt would make excellent companions for you and you chose those people within your life which you hoped would serve as catalyst for you, giving you what in incarnation you call pain and suffering. For, although your main reason for incarnating was that which you wished to offer and give, you also chose certain balances on which to work, most notably the balance between love and wisdom. Like many entities, you chose lessons such as learning to love without expectation of return, and learning to listen with compassion to those entities who do not think as do you and whose logic does not run as does yours. The choice to focus on compassion, patience and tolerance was part of the reason that you chose some of those entities within your life with which it is less than comfortable and convenient for you to deal with.

You gave yourself gifts of personality and character and as well you gave yourself those things which you now perceive within incarnation as faults. You did this with exquisite care, feeling that this assortment of details of personality were those choices that would best serve you as you attempt to mature, to balance the gifts that are within you, and to seek your true self.

The journey of incarnation is a journey to the center of the self. It seems as though it were a long and ever-expanding trek. As the years go by and as the Earth upon which you enjoy life revolves around your sun body, it seems as though it is a long trail which you are walking, and yet, my brother, we would suggest that the actual journey is from the outside, or the surface of this ball or sphere of life experience towards its very center. From the skin, the eyes, and the awareness inwards towards the very center of your heart. Consequently, if we do not seem to speak in terms of linear achievements, the past, the present, and the future, it is because we are gazing at your journey from a different standpoint. The standpoint from which we gaze at your experience is that standpoint of the soul which is in time/space. We rest within your consciousness to look at those hopes that you had for incarnation before your entry into it.

My brother, you have indeed penetrated the outer surface of your incarnation to a substantial extent. You have begun to see into who you are. We would say that, in terms of those hopes that you had before incarnation, you have more successfully achieved things in the outer layers of living, such as right livelihood and excellent companionship for the journey of incarnation than you have achieved substantial success, according to your hopes before

incarnation, in penetrating to the very heart of who you are. We say this not to chastise you, but in order to motivate you to continue the exploration of who you are in an ever deeper and more profound sense. The very center of your hope for incarnation, in terms of achievement, was that achievement which we would call "blooming." You are, as any living entity, a being which first comes into bud, and then, through the application of much sunlight and water and the right environment for growth, into bloom. Your hope was to blossom and to yield the harvest of that blossoming to the one infinite Creator, to the planet into which you incarnated in order to serve, and to all of those upon the planet, that race of humankind which you love so dearly and wish so keenly to help.

Your sojourn has brought you much awareness and your compassion for others has greatly deepened. We would say the chief stumbling block in your way at this time is a lack of compassion for yourself and we would encourage you to pursue that hardness of heart within yourself, towards yourself, with singleness of heart and with great stores of compassion and self-forgiveness.

It is a common mis-emphasis among your peoples to emphasize the doing over the being and to value things accomplished in the outer world over a growing realization of yourself as an essence. Many things have changed within your life in the most recent past few of your years. Things have dropped away from your personality shell and your identity has correspondingly shifted.

We would encourage you to continue this process of releasing things about yourself that you thought to be true as you discover new truth and new being within yourself. It is in coming into a present moment awareness of who you are that you more and more free yourself from the limitations imposed upon you by your self-concept. Your hope, before incarnation, was that you would come into a more and more full awareness of that essential nature of yourself that is not bound up in the personality shell or in the emotions connected with instinctual behavior as inherited from your physical body, but to be able more and more to avail yourself of that larger personality that you would call the soul or the spirit. And again, the more that you enter into this essential and deeper personality, the less entirely personal your selfhood becomes. For as you get closer to the heart of who you are, you take on those aspects of the self that are wrapped up in the larger self—or as this instrument would call it, the Creator-self.

When an entity thoughtlessly uses the word, "I," that entity is referring to the personality shell. Certainly, that entity is one-of-a-kind and very idiosyncratic and unique. However, as you cast off items of your personality shell and enter more and more into your spirit-self, you do not in any way remove or limit your identity as "I." Rather, you retain the uniqueness of yourself as a spark of the one infinite Creator, yet you become more and more aware that this Creator-self has its roots in the Creator Itself so that you have more and more of an awareness of the solidity at the center of your true identity.

My brother, you have made excellent progress in achieving the goals set for yourself, by yourself, before incarnation. And we would say that at this time, and for your foreseeable future within incarnation, we would see your chief goal yet to be realized as coming into a fuller and fuller awareness of who you are and Whose you are.

We shall be glad to come back to this query, but because there are several questions that we have to cover, we would like to hold our request for follow-up questions until all of your questions as written down have been responded to. Is there a second query at this time?

T: I feel as though I'm doing the right job but question whether I am in the right place. Please comment in any way you feel appropriate, pointing me in the direction of service to others that most fully fulfills my purpose in being.

We are those of Q'uo, and are aware of your query, my brother. We would indeed agree with you that you have found the most creative and satisfactory outlet for your considerable gifts as a healer, my brother. While we cannot comment directly on the question of your location, we could offer some thoughts upon this question that might perhaps serve as resources as you consider the question of right location.

It has often been said to and by this instrument that the one thing that remains constant, no matter where one travels, is that at the end of one's journey one shall still find oneself. Therefore, we would

suggest that location and the choice of location involve consideration of two things.

The first is whether or not the location at which you now reside has a resonance for you. If the place where you live does not feel like home to you, we would encourage you to search by whatever means that you have at your disposal until you find a location which seems to you to have the resonance and the familiarity of home. It is a comfort to any entity to feel that they are nestled in a place that is safe and comfortable to them. Certainly, this is a luxury that is not always attained, and many are those upon your planet who are not at all comfortable, nor do they feel safe. Nevertheless, as an ideal situation, it seems to us to be incontrovertibly so that it is far easier to focus on your service to others when your basic needs are being met and you feel a sense of rightness about where you are.

The second consideration in right location, we would suggest, is that of resonant service. There are times when the location itself is resonant to you but you have found that there is some kind of tangle concerning personalities that dwell within this location, or situations that seem to crop up within the location in which you find yourself. And you wonder within yourself whether or not making a new start in a new location would, shall we say, comb these personalities or circumstances out of your hair and enable you to make a fresh start. If this is indeed the case in your situation, then we would suggest that it is well to consider the question of how these entities and circumstances form a pattern. We would encourage you to take a slow, thoughtful and careful look at any difficulties and entanglements that you may feel at this time. The likelihood is that in moving to another location without grasping, understanding, accepting, balancing and forgiving the entities and circumstances that now trouble you, you will continue to be generating through the magnetism of that which you are, shall we say, putting out into your atmosphere around you the same patterns in other places that you have created where you are now.

If this is indeed the case, that is, that your location itself is resonant but there are things about the situation within that location that seem troubling, then we would encourage you, before even thinking of moving, to enter into these situations looking for the pattern underlying the situation.

(Carla coughs.)

We apologize on behalf of this instrument for the coughing.

You are not looking at the situation in order to assign blame. Rather, we would suggest that you are looking into a hall of mirrors. The people around you and the situations which come from interaction with these people are giving you a somewhat distorted and skewed image or series of images of yourself. Even when these images are highly distorted, they yet have valuable information for you concerning, perhaps, things about yourself which are in what this instrument would describe as the shadow side of self, that part of the self that is not developed and is not often visited because it is that side of the self which is the thief, the murderer, the liar, and other negative images that you have undoubtedly carefully kept away from developing and being shown to the world.

Nevertheless, these facets of self exist, not only in yourself but in all people. Nor are they to be ignored, abandoned or denied. Rather, they are to be understood as parts of the 360 degrees of self that make you up. You are a spark of the one infinite Creator and within that Creator lies all that there is, both of the light and of the so-called darkness. We do not encourage you to develop that darkness by loving the darkness and encouraging within yourself the energies of selfishness and service to self. Rather, we ask you to realize that these darker energies within you are a part of you that you can redeem and balance by your loving of them within you.

It is these darker energies that, when beguiled and charmed by you in the fullness of your soul personality, become within incarnation those deeper elements of your will and your focus which serve to stiffen and make strong your spine and create within you a real edge to that determination to use your will and your focus in order to refine your personality. Loving and accepting these darker images of self does not mean encouraging illicit or immoral behavior. Rather, it encourages you to integrate the darkness into your whole self, to accept the wolf within, as this instrument would call it, to embrace those things about yourself that are the least attractive so that you can cuddle them, lull them into sleep when necessary, and create a structure for them within yourself in which they are given useful work to do for the light, realizing that you have only

to love those portions of self in order to place them where they belong in the balance of your energies. You are then freed to know yourself in a more complete way.

Therefore, when these images of self are shown to you again you are much more able to look those images directly in the eye and say, "Yes, that too, am I. And I give that aspect of myself to my higher self because it knows just how this part of myself needs to fit into my whole self in order to create a perfect balance so that I may be free to do the will of my highest and best self."

May we ask for the third question at this time?

T: I believe I am a wanderer from the sixth density. Can you confirm this for me? Please comment on penetrating the veil of forgetting.

We are those of Q'uo, and are aware of your query, my brother. We can indeed confirm that you are a wanderer from the sixth density. As to the veil of forgetting, we realize that there are many entities who upon awakening wish to penetrate the veil of forgetting and to discover more about the journey that they have taken up until this incarnation.

For our part, my brother, we are reluctant to encourage you to penetrate this veil. We believe that in many cases there is a permeability to the veil that comes by stages and we feel that it is helpful and healthy for this to occur as long as it occurs naturally, that is, within the context of your process of seeking and discerning what you would call your way forward at this time.

We have found that in many cases when entities penetrate the veil of forgetting and discover one or more of their past incarnations, these entities then pull themselves back into the patterns of those incarnations to some extent, and that they tend to explain things about their present incarnation in terms of the dynamics of past incarnations. We find this to be somewhat deleterious to the progression of evolvement of your spirit because you move into the pattern that has already been explored in the past life rather than staying carefully within the present moment and the present incarnational experience.

We may share with you our opinion that you do not have adhering catalyst, or what this instrument would call karma, coming into this incarnational experience. The people with whom you have agreements in this life are not entities with whom the agreements are concerned with past-life balance. Your agreements all have to do with serving together or learning from each other within this present incarnation.

If you begin to receive bleed-through memories, especially within the dreaming, then you will know that your higher self has seen fit to begin informing you concerning experiences that you have had in past experiences of incarnation. And you can then ask yourself how this information might be helpful in grasping a current situation or in observing a certain pattern of thought that you have observed about yourself and are attempting to penetrate so that you may evolve as a spirit.

The spiritual principles involved in any wanderer's entry into incarnation are those principles involved with service to others. It is for that reason that wanderers seek incarnation within planet Earth at this time. You have had the distinct and clear perception that you can make a difference in this lifetime. After the incarnation begins, it is much more difficult to have that clear vision that you had before incarnation concerning the nature of your service. As we said earlier, it is very easy for it to seem, to one within incarnation, that service has to do with what one does. And indeed, the outer services are wonderful and create a substantial gift to the one infinite Creator. Yet, my brother, the heart of your service is in the nature of your beingness.

We ask you to consider penetrating to the very center of who you are within incarnation as that goal to which you may bend every effort and serve with the greatest of joy and the feeling of peace that comes with knowing that you are on the right track. Let the being that you are being be your main concern, for as you refine and simplify your concept of who you are, as you breathe in the air and breath it back out and focus on essence, you will find that all of those things that you need in order to express a doingness will come to you very naturally, as if drawn to you magnetically.

May we ask for the next query, my brother?

T: Please comment in any way you are able concerning health issues for me. I have trouble swallowing as food gets stuck in my throat. My mother's side of the family donated this tendency to me.

We are those of Q'uo, and are aware of your query, my brother. We can to some extent comment on this question and would agree that, to some extent, the difficulty that you have in the region of the throat chakra is purely mechanical and has to do with your genetic heritage. However, in asking that question, we are also agreeing with your inference that there may be more to that particular difficulty than the physical aspects of its manifestation and we would like to look at the way …

(Side one of tape ends.)

(Carla channeling)

… the blue-ray energy center or the blue-ray chakra manifests its distress within the everyday life.

Let us look first at the opening of the heart chakra and all that it entails. Basically, the opening up of the green-ray chakra or the heart chakra is a tremendous job. It involves much more than simply the opening of the heart, for there is a two-fold opening of that heart. The first opening is simply the lifting of all concerns into the heart. There are many issues concerning survival and personal relationships, as well as group relationships such as marriage and the workplace, within which many people get stuck. And [so they] never bring these issues up into the heart. You, my brother, long ago began to do so and through the years you have penetrated the first heart, that outer temple, shall we say, and moved into the inner temple of unconditional love. You have brought more and more of your whole self into that inner temple. However, my brother, we would say that you have not brought all of your self into that inner temple as of yet. It is the parts of yourself that are as yet unredeemed by your love, your compassion, and your full acceptance, that are creating for you at once an under-energizing and an over-activation of the blue-ray chakra. These are two separate concerns and so we would look at them one at a time.

The under-activation of the blue-ray chakra is due to a lack of a feeling of self-worth which is because of the fact that you have not yet concluded the process of self-forgiveness and self-acceptance that you have begun in opening your heart. The over-activation is a matter of your very active and strong will, which is encouraging you onward to communicate ever more openly and to move ever more fully into those energies of full sharing, fully open communication, and that self which wishes to move on into work in consciousness, or into indigo-ray work.

So there is at once a certain amount of under-activation of blue ray because of work left undone in moving fully into the open heart and an unwise application of the will that is in advance of your true situation, where you are very much wishing to move onward into more advanced work. And yet, at the same time, you cannot bring to bear the full amount of energy of the one infinite Creator that is flowing through your energy body. This also is a portion of the reason that you are experiencing some difficulty in the blue-ray chakra region of your body.

As you know, my brother, there are various techniques, dealing strictly with the physical body, for enabling the actions of swallowing to improve. And we would encourage you to look into those techniques. But we would also encourage you to go on a hunt for your lost little dogies, as this instrument would call those stray parts of the self that are still wandering in the pastureland of your unredeemed and unforgiven self. Find the lamb that is not yet in the fold of your forgiveness. Go and get it, bring it home, and love it, forgive it, accept it, and know yourself to be fully there and fully worthy.

May we ask for the final query?

T: Our dog, Y, acts in such a way that I feel she is harvestable to third density. Can you confirm this?

We are those of Q'uo, and yes, my brother, we can confirm the harvestability of your mind/body/spirit complex known as Y.

We would at this time ask if there are any follow-up questions from the one known as T?

T: I had a channeled reading ten or twelve years ago when there was a reference made to myself and an aspect of Neptune and I was just wondering if Q'uo has any comment about that?

We are those of Q'uo, and are aware of your query, my brother. The question had to do with whether there are aspects of Neptune that might be fruitfully considered in the process of the one known as T at this time.

We would encourage you, my brother, to examine fully the so-called astrological chart of your natal birth, looking for the placement of that energy, and of all energies having to do with water, within that chart. The energies of Neptune are certainly those

which have a bearing upon the incarnation of any wanderer and we feel that there is productive ground there for exploration. However, we would also encourage you to examine less traditional ways of viewing the birth chart, such as that given in the book known to this instrument as *The Invisible Garment*[48] in which these energies are gazed at in a non-traditional way.

This and all ways of looking at the energies involved at the moment of birth are ways of looking into the archetypal influences which you have chosen to ring about yourself as companions and allies. These are all energies that anyone may access within the deeper self, and yet, in each lifetime, the entity chose just that particular arrangement of energies and so we would encourage your investigation of these energies, especially, as you said, that energy known to be of Neptune.

May we answer you further, my brother?

T: If we are sixth density, and we die to third, from a harvestability standpoint, where do we go: sixth, third or fourth? I'm not sure how to ask the question.

We are those of Q'uo, and are aware of your query, my brother. You asked us, since you came from sixth density to third, upon being harvested, where do you go? Do you go to fourth density or back to sixth? We believe we understand your query, my brother, and we would say that it is unknown to us at this time as to what your decisions shall be once you have graduated. The challenge for each entity that goes through the veil of forgetting and takes incarnation in third density is so to recapitulate the lessons of third density that you are able to clear third density and walk the steps of light into fourth density. For all of those who are able to graduate, that is the first destination, that being the larger life of unconditional love. Once you have cleared the barriers that keep you from moving again to the place of your choosing beyond third density, you shall then undergo a period of reflection and a discussion with your higher self such as you had before incarnation, discussing the possibilities as you see them at that time and where the resonance for you, the place of service for you next seems to lie. It shall not be known or decided until that moment.

---

[48] Connie Kaplan, *The Invisible Garment: 30 Spiritual Principles That Weave the Fabric of Human Life*: San Diego, CA, Jodere Group, [c2004], ISBN 1-58872-089-6.

We would encourage you in the context of being still within third density to focus upon living from the open heart so that you are already living in unconditional love and are harvestable. You remember much as soon as you clear the process of death, but it is your state of being before the death process that determines whether you are free to move back into higher densities or whether you have been caught by the third-density energies of light and dark, good and evil, and so forth so that you must again take third-density existence. We do realize that you, like many wanderers, have no great affection for the environment of third density and so we would greatly encourage you to look to the wholeness and integrity of your heart energy and attempt more and more to live very genuinely and naturally in those sacred precincts of unconditional love which are so dear to you.

May we answer you further, my brother?

T: I don't have any more questions. I do have a comment. Carla and Jim are supposed to send me some information that either came through you or Ra on healing. I'm a chiropractor and I want to do some different stuff. If you might have any comments on that I would appreciate it.

We are those of Q'uo, and are aware of your query, my brother. The one known as Carla has endeavored to find this information for you, and interestingly enough, neither she nor the one known as Jim has been able to locate this information. It is not a problem that is infinite for there are other locations in which this information can be found. However, that has been the reason that you have not yet received this information. The instrument is aware of the need to find these lost documents and has been working towards locating them.

What we would say concerning the information is that, like all information, it has a certain amount of power but its power in and of itself is infinitesimal compared to the power that it grows to possess when in the hands of one who uses gifts that are given with a full and open heart. We know that with or without this information, the broader and deeper avenues that you seek will come to you. We have not investigated the deeper reasons of the misplacement of this information but would simply offer our opinion that your path is one which is open before you. When this information is found, it shall be sent to you and we encourage you to seize upon it and to absorb it, realizing that you enliven these simple exercises that the ones known as Ra have offered. It is you that create the living gift rather than any pieces of information.

Our reflections upon leaving you, my brother, are simply to thank you with all of our heart for the beauty of your spirit and the richness of your blooming. We cannot tell you how much we admire and love you and at any time you would wish us to be a part of your meditations, you have only to ask for our presence. We do not offer words or images but if you ask for our presence what we will do is to enter into your meditation with you in such a way as to deepen and help to stabilize your basic level of focus within meditation.

We thank you so much for giving us the opportunity to share our thoughts. And we honor you. We leave you as we found you, in the love and in the light of the one infinite Creator. We are known to you as the principle of Q'uo. Adonai. Adonai. ☙

L/L RESEARCH

L/L Research is a subsidiary of
Rock Creek Research &
Development Laboratories, Inc.

P.O. Box 5195
Louisville, KY 40255-0195

www.llresearch.org

Rock Creek is a non-profit
corporation dedicated to
discovering and sharing
information which may aid in
the spiritual evolution of
humankind.

SPECIAL MEDITATION
MAY 20, 2005

Jim: *(Reading C's question.)* "I believe I'm a sixth-density wanderer. Q'uo, can you confirm this and would you please offer any comments on being a wanderer that you feel might be helpful for me to consider?"

(Carla channeling)

We are those known to you as the principle of Q'uo. Greetings in the love and in the light of the one infinite Creator, in Whose service we come to you this day. We thank this instrument, the one known as C, and all who join this group for setting aside the time, the effort, and the presence in order to create a circle of seeking. We find it a great privilege to join you and to respond to your request for conversation on the question you have vibrated and we are glad to answer this and all questions from the one known as C.

However, before we begin, we would, as always, like to request very carefully that the one known as C and any who might see these words please use the utmost care and discrimination in listening to them. We are not authorities and in sharing our observations and opinions we are not expecting you to believe us. Indeed, it would be alarming to us were you to swallow everything that we said as if it were true. We ask you to realize that you, yourself, are the only person capable of grasping whether or not thoughts and opinions are useful to you at this time in your process of seeking. Thoughts that are helpful to you have a resonance and when you hear them it is almost as if you were not hearing them for the first time but were being gently reminded of something that you already knew and had temporarily forgotten. If our thoughts do not have this kind of resonance for you we would ask that you set them aside without a second thought, for we would not be a stumbling block before you. If you will take care to listen carefully and to discriminate between our thoughts, choosing only those that are good for you, then we will feel comfortable in sharing our thoughts freely. Above all things, we wish not to infringe upon your free will or interfere with the process of your spiritual evolution.

My sister, we can confirm that you are a wanderer and that you come from the so-called sixth density, or the density of unity. We would offer a few observations and comments upon the condition of being a wanderer and are pleased that you have requested our opinions on this matter.

The wanderer is as one who has sacrificed a great deal in order to risk the forgetting process and enter into incarnation for service to others. It is a courageous decision to make and we congratulate the one known as C on having plunged into incarnation in third density for such a loving and service-to-others reason.

The nature of service to others is often greatly misunderstood among your peoples because the emphasis, as we said recently to the one known as T, is so often construed to be that of doing in outer service to others that mounts up or amounts to something in the eyes of the world. Certainly, you have already in this incarnation offered service to others of a substantial kind that has indeed come to the notice of the world. However, we ask you to think of yourself as a crystalline being whose nature is basically to share your beauty with the world, with yourself, and with the infinite Creator. If you can think of yourself as a gem or a crystal, then you shall be able perhaps to come close to understanding what we are talking about when we say that the heart of service to others is in the essence of your being rather than in the details of your outer service.

When you observe a crystal or a gem, you are content simply to gaze upon its beauty. You can see the way the facets of the gem catch the light and you can see the beauty radiating from those points of light and from the true colors evident in the gem or the crystal. You do not demand of the crystal that it do something but rather you behold its beauty and it, in its own way, changes you for having beheld it. This is the nature of your own being as well. You have come among the people of Earth to be, to breath the air, to open your heart, and to gaze with love and compassion upon the world that you see before you in this moment. All that you are is gathered together in your heart and is radiating from you as the light within the lighthouse radiates out into the air, into the atmosphere, to greet all who come near it and enjoy the beauty of its radiance. The one known as Jesus the Christ said that it was a good thing for entities to allow their light to shine before humankind and not to hide it under a shade. Above all, my sister, we would encourage you to do just that: to let your light and your truth shine before all of those with whom you come in contact.

We are not encouraging you to share ideas or other items of belief, for we would not be encouraging you then to be but to do. We simply encourage you to find your way into your open heart and to do the work that is necessary in order to keep that heart open. Your essence is locked up in this very sacred space. When you awaken in the morning, before you even rise from your bed, we would encourage you to center into that heart, that sacred space within you where the Creator Itself dwells; to touch into the very center of your being and, at each point during the day when you feel yourself being pulled away from that center, when you can and when it is convenient, take a moment, gently and firmly, to move your consciousness back to its center, and let it shine.

All that you are is in that radiant energy and we assure you, my sister, that those things that you and the Creator have prepared together for you to do as outer service will be magnetized to you and will come to you as you are ready to pick them up and do them. Awaken each day, my sister, knowing that this will be a productive day. This day shall be your gift to the one infinite Creator.

My brother, would you please vibrate the second question?

Jim: *(Reading C's question.)* "I've received memories of past lives that relate directly to people currently in my life. This leads me to believe that I am trapped in karma. Can you confirm? And if the answer is "Yes," can you advise me as to what ways I can balance these karmic debts? If you are unable to confirm that I am karmically trapped, can you comment on this concept in any way helpful to me at this time?"

We are those of Q'uo, and are aware of your query, my sister. My sister, we cannot confirm that you are trapped in what you and this instrument both call "karma." There are entities who are trapped in adhering karma and who have come to this incarnation in order to find balance and forgiveness of a pattern into which not only you but another entity are caught together. However, my sister, this is not your situation. In fact, you entered into your present incarnation free of any adhering karma and, with regard to the one known as T, in a situation of balanced karma wherein you both have worked before as a team. This teamwork extends beyond you and the one known as T into unseen realms, for there are those of your social memory complex within unseen realms both inner and outer, that is, both native to this planet and beyond this planetary orb, that are also involved in helping you and the one known as T move forward in those goals to which you both have dedicated yourself towards accomplishing within this incarnational experience. In this way, you are set up very solidly in terms of being surrounded by many unseen friends and with a very strong system of guidance that is available to you.

We are, however, aware that your query involves the reason for your awareness of other entities' patterns and we would at this time offer a few comments on the kind of service for which you provided yourself with this information as a part of, shall we say, your personality shell. Before incarnation, you and your guidance system together spoke in many different ways concerning the hopes that you personally had for your service to the people of planet Earth. You responded greatly to the concept of helping all of humankind and yet there is a portion of your soul stream that wished to bring service down to the small details and to the individual entities that you would meet within this incarnation. It was your hope that, by giving yourself these awarenesses of the subconscious material involved in the entities with whom you came in contact, you would be able to see into these patterns in a way that was filled with compassion and unconditional love.

You have, in past incarnations and between incarnations, done a good deal of work in loving entities and whole cultures and societies. This is an activity which involves a great deal of concentration and focus for in doing this work you are not accomplishing anything but the radiation of absolute love as a coherent stream, rather like what this instrument would call the stream of a laser, so that the entity or civilization upon which you bent your loving gaze would feel there was absolutely no doubt that they were loved. This stream of love, through time, regardless of all obstacles, is an activity at which you have in the past been extremely good. It was your hope that during this incarnation as well and in spite of every obstacle thrown up by the many distractions offered by the physical body and the stray emotions of the personality shell of that body, you would, when prompted by being around entities which were in need of this kind of reassurance, be able to love, not simply in general but very specifically, according to the subtleties and nuances of the patterns of personality and the dynamics of that personality's interaction with what you could call the forces of polarity; [that you would] be able to envelop and embrace them in the light of your living and consciously sent love. Many are the entities which are not vulnerable to love offered in open communication because of damage that is done to them in their past within [this] incarnation. The gift that you are able to give to these entities, without any obstacle or resistance on their part, is this unspoken, unannounced, silent radiation of unconditional love.

We are not suggesting that you have nothing to offer such entities. We are simply suggesting that the service which you created for yourself before incarnation having to do with this ability to perceive patterns within other entities was simply to be there for them as a loving presence. It would not be surprising to us if entities which had found their icy hearts thawing in the presence of your loving heart began to find it possible to enter into communication with you. And certainly, my sister, you are free to offer any information and inspiration that comes to you if such communication is undertaken by the other self whom you are loving. Nevertheless, we ask you to realize that this is as, what this instrument would call, the icing on the cake. It is wonderful if you are able to share helpful thoughts and opinions with such entities but your true service is accomplished when that entity is loved by you.

We would at this time ask the one known as Jim if there is another query.

Jim: *(Reading C's question.)* The third question is: "In observing a recurrent pattern in my life, I believe that one of my incarnational lessons is overcoming the illusion of abandonment. I believe I've mastered this illusion after encountering it on all sides. Can you confirm? Can you speak in any way helpful to me on this concept?"

We are those of Q'uo, and are aware of your query, my sister. To the one known as C we would say that, indeed, she has done a great deal of useful and helpful work in perceiving that incarnational lesson of loving through perceived negative responses such as abandonment, rejection and betrayal. We would not say that the one known as C has mastered this catalyst. Indeed, when one chooses an incarnational lesson, one is working not to master the lesson or to pass some perceived outer test. One is choosing a theme or a motif that will last for the duration of the incarnation. When such a lesson is chosen, it is chosen, at least by those wanderers who are from sixth density, almost surely with the intention of striking a finer or more refined balance between the energies of love and wisdom. The energies of love, by themselves, do not have the balance, nor do the energies of wisdom by themselves have the balance. They are as the dynamics of your soul stream after it has chosen its polarity and while it yet retains the shape of an individuated soul. In other words, my sister, you chose this theme of the apparent perception of being abandoned or betrayed in order to give yourself experience in responding to this perceived catalyst not simply with love and not simply with wisdom but with an ever increasing awareness of the balance between those two energies.

If you are abandoned and you respond completely with love, you have very successfully balanced the negative emotion that was handed to you with a responsive, positive answer. And yet, you yourself are responding from the position of being flattened by the emotional impact of the experience as it has worked its way through your chakra system or, as this instrument would call it, your energy body. If you respond to the experience of being abandoned with wisdom that is unalloyed or pure, you do not have that experience of being emotionally flattened or crushed by the experience. You simply move on, choosing not to react at all. However, this action does not embrace, envelop and accept in fullness the worthiness of the entity who has abandoned you. Consequently, you have designed for yourself this theme or motif, this incarnational lesson, as it were, so that you may work on striking the balance in your response that is, in this instrument's terms, the most musical, the most crystalline.

Think of yourself as a wind instrument, say, a wind chime that responds to the wind. As the elements of the wind chime are blown and tossed about by the wind, they strike each other and create sound. Your hope in this practice is not simply to love, embrace and accept the entity who has seemingly offered you negative catalyst and not simply to remain uncrushed and unflattened by the experience, but so to combine these elements that you are lifted up and free of the flattening effect and at the same time your continued and abiding love of the one who has seemingly wronged you has lifted up that person also. In this way, your hope, then, is to have balanced the forces of love and wisdom within you while remaining highly positively polarized in service to others. In this way, the suffering that is inevitable when catalyst strikes the seeker is honored and then the experience is raised up as an offering to the one infinite Creator. And there is the experience, in a very small way, as the one known as Jesus the Christ [had], of the suffering having been redeemed by great and unconditional love, so that you have the experience of the cross and the experience of resurrection as well.

In general, we may say that within the incarnational lessons that each wanderer chooses for herself, the goal is not simply to learn a lesson. The goal is to practice a kind of lesson in such a way that the soul stream that is practicing this lesson is, little by little, purified and refined in the fire of planet Earth and the incarnation that you are now experiencing, so that that soul's essence becomes ever more beautiful and is ever more completely dedicated to serving the one infinite Creator. Thusly, it is not so much that you are learning lessons but that you are learning how to give yourself as a gift in every thought and in every action to the Creator whom you love so unconditionally and who loves you so unconditionally.

My brother, is there another query that is on the paper at this time?

Jim: *(Reading C's question.)* There is one more: "In the dream state, for over twelve years, I've been nurturing babies during sleep. I offer them physical care, they offer me telepathic teaching and seem more conscious than I. I've cared for these babies in normal Earth-type nurseries and also in underwater nurseries. Some are not of Earth and possess a center of gravity that makes them unstable on our surface. I deliver these children to ships where I assume that their proper star families will continue their caregiving. Can you confirm that I'm giving an actual service in these actions?"

We are those of Q'uo, and are aware of your query, my sister. My sister, you are not the first entity to ask us concerning service to these infants and we may assure you that you are being a very real and genuine service to them by the love with which you nurse and embrace them and the care which you take of them. May we say that indeed these entities are not of your race, yet they have intimate ties with your planetary sphere and with humankind and are, in their own way, wanderers in your so-called inner planes where they have come to serve. Your service to them is very real and we thank you for the fastidiousness with which you approach this highly unorthodox service.

They are indeed cared for by others as well as yourself and by realms other than that which you experience in the dreaming state. The theme of your service within incarnation at this time, as you can see, is little understood among the people of Earth, for you have come here to love. And we thank you, my sister, for the great care that you have taken in every way that you may find to dedicate yourself to this service and to this incarnation with a whole heart and an untroubled mind.

May we say that at any time that you would wish to call on us to deepen your meditation or to be with you in the dream time you have only to ask mentally for us to be with you and we are glad to lend our vibrations to yours.

At this time, we would ask the one known as C if there are any questions that she has, either as a follow-up to what we have said so far or in addition to what we have said?

C: Are children that are of the negative polarity and have tried to *(inaudible)* and I've been able to sway at least one of them into discarding the other … Am I participating in bringing light into a darker element of this group of children?

We are those of Q'uo, and are aware of your query, my sister. We believe that you have stated the situation fairly. You are as the lighthouse and you shine over stormy waters, giving your love and your light that is as a beacon. Your fidelity to unconditional love, by its very nature, is able to create [awareness] within entities which may be being tempted to join what you would call the darker side of the left-hand path of service to self in such a way that such entities cannot deny the truth of that light which they see before them. Naturally, their will is free and they may choose that darker path …

(Side one of tape ends.)

(Carla channeling)

… but they choose it in [a] full awareness that only your loving presence can give them of what their situation actually is. Please be aware that many things within this particular construct of your dreaming time are archetypal in nature rather than literal so that the infants are not truly infants, the spaceships that seemingly are going to other planets are actually within the inner planes of this planet, and so forth. Yet the situation itself and the entities that are moving within this particular pattern and hope in their own way to be of service at this time are extremely grateful for that energy which you bring to their situation. It is yet one more example of the incredible oneness of the infinite Creator so that each becomes a teacher to each and this stretches across bands of race and star location and all of the infinite sub-planes of your inner realms.

May we answer you further, my sister?

(Pause)

We are those of Q'uo, and we would ask before we close the session if there is a final query.

C: I would appreciate information about a blue star that I see all the time. I see it with my outer eyes and my inner eye.

We are those of Q'uo, and are aware of your query, my sister. We find that we are not able to share with you on this point because this is a feature of a pattern which you are currently working on within your own process. We may comment to you that the color of this star and the crystalline nature of the star are both keys that you may use in working with the energies of this shape and color. These shape and color details have their echoes within the archetypal system of your own thoughts and also, in a literal sense, within the constellation of your energy body. That is, the blue-ray chakra is suggested by the blue color and the crystalline nature of the star or its fusion nature, shall we say, is also an element that is likely to be helpful in pursuing this image. As you work with it, realize that you do not have to interpret it or decipher it all at once, for it may be seen not simply as information but also as companionship.

We would at this time leave this group as we found it, in the love and in the light of the one infinite Creator. We thank each of those present for their beauty and for their service to us in asking us to share our opinion. It has been a true privilege to be able to do so. We leave you in the love and in the light of the one infinite Creator. We are known to you as Q'uo. Adonai. Adonai. ❧

L/L RESEARCH

L/L Research is a subsidiary of
Rock Creek Research &
Development Laboratories, Inc.

P.O. Box 5195
Louisville, KY 40255-0195

www.llresearch.org

Rock Creek is a non-profit
corporation dedicated to
discovering and sharing
information which may aid in
the spiritual evolution of
humankind.

© 2009 L/L RESEARCH

SPECIAL MEDITATION
JUNE 14, 2005

Forest Row, East Sussex, Britain

(Carla channeling)

We are those known to you as the principle of Q'uo. Greetings in the love and in the light of the one infinite Creator. We are most happy to entertain the questions of the ones known as J and A. We would ask for the one known as J's first question after we share a few thoughts.

Firstly, may we say that it is a privilege and a pleasure to share your vibrations at this time. Your dedication of this time to create a sacred space is a blessing to us, for it enables us the opportunity to be of service and this we greatly appreciate.

We would request, as always, that each, not only the ones known as J and A, but any who hear or read these thoughts, be completely and profoundly responsible for discriminating between those thoughts of ours which will be helpful and those thoughts of ours which miss the mark and have no resonance in your particular process. We need for you to discard those thoughts that are not useful and to move on without a second thought. We wish greatly not to be perceived as entities of any authority, but only as fellow seekers. Your strict observation of our request will enable us to speak freely, without being concerned that we may trespass upon the freedom of your will, for the process of spiritual evolution is heavily dependent upon your

refusal to accept any authority but your own. We thank you for this kindness.

At this time we would request the one known as J's first question.

J: I will describe an event and then ask some questions, if that's OK.

In 1992, I was at a rave and had taken too many drugs. I had what I believe was a heart attack and whilst recovering an hour or so later, I had the following experience. It seemed as though I was bathed in a beam of light from above and had what appeared to be a telepathic deal being struck and then had the following visions.

I was on stage at an outside concert and then saw two golden-colored, roughly humanoid light beings descend from the sky. Each grabbed one of my hands and then pulled my soul out of my body and we flew off into space.

I feel that at that point when my heart had its attack, a sixth-density entity and I agreed that I would give way so that it could take over my own incarnational agenda and in return I would allow the use of my own body so that it could also complete its agenda. In other words, I feel I became a walk-in.

Can you please confirm this?

We are those of Q'uo, and we are aware of your query, my brother. Before we respond to this query, we would ask your patience while we readjust the position of this instrument.

(Pause)

We are those of Q'uo, and are again with this instrument. We thank you for your patience. We believe this configuration will support this instrument's physical vehicle in a more appropriate manner than her previous position.

My brother, we can confirm that you are a walk-in and that the events which you have described are approximately accurate. We feel that you are still working with this experience and so what we can say concerning this particular experience is limited. However, there are spiritual principles involved in the phenomenon of the conscious taking on of a spiritual agenda. In the case of walk-ins, there are actually two entities who have chosen to give over their lives to that spiritual agenda.

Now, what does this signify? How does this play out, shall we say, in the ordinary life of an entity, who like any other is frail, human and error prone? Certainly a wanderer or a walk-in is not a privileged being. In fact, there is a great deal of suffering involved in choosing an incarnation upon a density of experience that is, shall we say, heavier and rarer in light. There is a sacrifice involved, the taking upon oneself of the cross, in such an experience. You would not have chosen this experience except that you had a great desire to serve not only the one infinite Creator but also this particular tribe which you may call humankind. Your heart was broken by the sorrow and the suffering of the entities of planet Earth, and you felt that you could make a difference.

When we address a walk-in, we are speaking to both personality shells, the one that has been suppressed and the one that has chosen to become ascendant. Now, let us be clear that this suppression is not a matter of being blanked out or being removed. Rather, the ascendant personality shell has agreed to carry out both agendas and to attempt to balance both personalities so that the maximum amount of bloom may occur for each flower of the Creator. For this is what you are. You are a living plant in the fields of the Earth. You have grown as one flower, yet you have two blooms. Your system is complex. You do not have what you night call a simple way to grow. Yet understand this: you are a true species of your own. You are not grafted, one upon the other. Rather, both are grafted upon the one infinite Creator. You have become an entity which, in addition to living one life, has agreed to live one compound life. That does not create for you a difficulty. However, you may notice from time to time that there is more confusion in, shall we say, the subconscious thought-patterns of your so-called mind than would be normal for most entities.

We would recommend, therefore, that as a walk-in you allow yourself one period of meditation for the suppressed personality and one period of meditation for the ascendant personality, not necessarily separating the meditations but offering more time to silence in the day than you might otherwise dedicate, because there is the constant intertwining of these agendas of which we have spoken.

We would also encourage you to rest in the arms of what this instrument would call the creation of the Father to a degree that may seem excessive to some. This is due to your being both a sixth-density wanderer and a sixth-density walk-in. You have difficulty remaining grounded. This is entirely understandable and it can be quite sufficiently balanced by contact, and we mean this literally, with the earth. We might even encourage the one known as J or, should we say, the ones known as J to interact proactively with the more highly developed intelligences among the second-density animals and especially your trees. Know and depend upon the strength, the power, the love and the dedication of such entities as these trees to sustain and to encourage the balance of your power and your peace within you, for trees act as a kind of sieve, straining away the useless, the transitory, and the incorrect.

There are many ways in which those who remember better times can become distracted from the main agenda of their incarnation. My brother, your main agenda is to learn to be yourself. You had complete confidence in yourself when you chose to enter into incarnation. As all humans and as all entities of which we know do, you have made errors in judgment. Do not be distracted by the process of learning. You have striven to be yourself by removing yourself from environments which did not feel to you like the real world. We would encourage you instead to ask each day to remember that faith that you had in yourself, in your power and in your peace, for all entities of whatever density of origin are magical, crystalline beings of tremendous power and at the very heart of that beingness lies the utter simplicity and peace of unconditional love.

The one known as J had asked earlier about what the Logos is, and we say to you, my brother, in potential you are the Logos, the living Word. You have bought at a dear price this precious flesh that is often seemingly so inconvenient. You have purchased the opportunity of your lifetime because you wished to become the light upon the hill that radiates the love and the light of the one infinite Creator. How can you radiate that light? By becoming more and more aware of who you are, and being that entity that you truly feel yourself to be.

This instrument recently heard the words, "Lift up your heads, ye gates, and be ye lifted up, ye everlasting doors, for the King of glory shall come in."[49] Say to the world each day, "Lift up your heads, oh ye gates, for I carry in my heart the identity of unconditional love and that unconditional love lives in me, unworthy and error-prone as I am, and the King of glory shall come into this world only through the likes of myself." Then pray, my brother, for transparency. Do not be brought down into concern by your frailty but allow all concern and worry to flee away before the light that flows through you and flows through all who choose to become transparent to that which they carry. What a precious task, my brother! And it is one that is new each day, as new as the dawning.

We apologize to you for not responding in fuller detail to your query concerning the specifics of your experience. But until you have finished your process of mining this treasure trove of insight into your situation, we must bow to the Law of Confusion.[50] We need, for our own polarity, to leave such things that are beyond the bounds of discussion to your free will so that you and you alone can make the choices that will increase your polarity and ground you in such a way that you stand as sturdy as an oak upon the land, rooted in the love and in the light of the one infinite Creator.

May we have your next question, my brother?

J: Thank you very much, Q'uo, I appreciate it.

In 2001 I took a lot of magnesium and phosphorous. I found myself in what felt like an extremely powerful drug effect and started to become delusional. I then had the following visions.

I did not see something in the room I was in, but rather I believed I was experiencing a conscious awareness of a reality I can only describe as being out in space, but without the burning stars. There were thousands, possibly millions or billions of glowing spheres of light all swirling round each other in one spherical group.

I perceived a conscious connection to all these entities, who wanted to laugh, cry, etc. Then I saw a place where there was my physical self next to a glowing, golden-colored light-being in a very strange, golden environment that I cannot describe properly in words. I feel that at that point I had a fully conscious connection with my higher self. Can you confirm this please, or not?

We are those of Q'uo, and are aware of your query, my brother. We are in the peculiar position of both confirming and not confirming that you were in complete contact with your higher self at that moment. In terms of your precise experience at that time we believe that the closest we can come through this instrument to describing your situation is that you had what this instrument would call a blow-through into the precise point where the indigo-ray center meets intelligent infinity. That is not to say you had moved through into intelligent infinity. It is rather to say that you were experiencing a state wherein you were one with the atomic structure of a particular part of a fairly liquid environment, much like the point at the top of the pyramid at Giza where energy is collected and when it bursts forth, it spirals into intelligent infinity. What you were seeing was atomic structure. It looks much like a night sky would to your physical eyes.

The more important point that we would like to make is that at all times and in all places you are in complete contact with your higher self. It is not dependent upon the self-perceived state of being that you are experiencing. Complete contact with one's higher self may or may not be ecstatic. It may or may not be joyful. There are many, many ways to access the higher self. However, as this instrument said earlier in conversation, the higher self is in the innermost part of your heart, to use a much overused and misunderstood term. It is the innermost part of that essence of yourself which does not experience much change within incarnation. It is

---

[49] The Psalm of which this verse is a part had been read as part of Carla's morning offering that morning.

[50] For Confederation entities such as the Ra group, the Law of Confusion is synonymous with the Law of Free Will or Non-Infringement.

the innermost part of the heart of your true self, which as you have said this day is a citizen of eternity, and to capitulate further things that were said earlier in a non-sacred environment, we would say within this sacred space that you live and move and have your being in the unity and in the love of your open heart.

The "I" that is you lives within you, not within a place to which you must reach, yet that entity that is your higher self must respect and abide by the laws of free will and timing. In terms both of free will and of right action, it must be called forth. Yet realize this, when you knock upon the door and ask, that door is opened before you can complete the thought. When you cry for help, for guidance, that help has arrived before you can complete your cry. There is no pause, no hesitation, no earning, and no buying to guidance. It is not to be deserved. It is not to be bought. It is free. It is part of you and it is intrinsic to you. What keeps you from the awareness of your higher self is your concept that there is a separation between that part of you that lives in consensus reality and that part of you that is divine. There is no separation. You are the Creator in flesh.

You are a very young Creator. You are a toddler. You are in third density and you cannot remember the things that you have already learned. Why did you do this to yourself? You did it because you wished to serve. How inconvenient it is sometimes to serve! How maddening! How frustrating! And yet it is for this that you took flesh. And you did not take flesh alone. You brought with you all that you need but you must ask for it, not once, but every day and every moment. This instrument prays each morning at her morning offering, "Help me to remember and focus on who I am and why I am here." We cannot promise you an easy life, my brother. We cannot promise you the sense of things accomplished for there is always more. Many have said to this entity, "You seem so driven." It is very simple. This entity remembers why she is here and she is greedy: she wants to fill her life, every moment and every breath, with love. Her problem is to remember to allow herself to be loved, and, my brother, we would ask you to remember also that being of service to others is at least as much a matter of allowing people to love you as it is remembering to love people. Energy moves circularly and in a spiral, always upward, always seeking, but it must not stop and it must not simply go one way. Think

of the way the spiral in DNA rises. It does not rise in one spiral, it rises in two and this in the fairly primitive DNA of your third density. One spiral is the loving, the giving. The other spiral is the accepting of love and the receiving. Let yourself become that entity who does not know if it is loving or being loved, but only knows that is a creature of love.

Is there a further question my brother?

J: Can you speak to whether or not I should share this experience with other people or whether or not I should keep it to myself to honor the Law of Confusion?

We are those of Q'uo, and are aware of your query, my brother. We may indeed speak to this query, for it is indeed very simple. Service can only be performed when it is requested. One cannot serve proactively by reaching out and collaring someone with information. One may serve at all times by radiating the love and the light of the one infinite Creator. Unless asked concerning either your experience or that type of experience of which your experience is an example, we would suggest that you serve by loving, by resting as an instrument rests in the hands of the musician that plays it. Let the Creator play you. You are an instrument. The Creator knows the song. And when the moment comes for you to sing, you shall have the notes that the Creator has given you. When asked concerning such experiences, share freely. When not asked concerning such experiences, relate from the level of the self meeting the self, that is to say, the Creator meeting the Creator.

Is there a further query at this time?

J: No, thank you, Q'uo, that's wonderful. Thank you very much

We thank you, my brother, and may we say what a pleasure it is to share energy with you at this time.

We believe that there are queries from the one known as A, and we would ask the one known as Vara to read the first query from this entity.

Vara: (Reading A's question.)[51] "Thank you, Q'uo. I'd like to greet those of Q'uo with this statement: You are a pure blessing to us in this moment, I thank you

---

[51] The request for this session came in from a person in Portugal who wrote the request by snail-mail letter. J kindly agreed to sit for A's questions as well as his own.

so much for such integrity of spirit and love. I would ask if you could give any account on the meaning of this tide of light service, as it is being carried in such amount and quantity as yours."

My brother, we are aware of your query, and we thank you for your kind words.

We and all of those of the Confederation who serve at this time serve because we have been called to your people. We have been called to your group. We have been called to the service of planet Earth. We are called because it is time for your planet to be born. There is a tremendous focusing of love and light from all of those who respond to this calling from your peoples. It is our privilege and our blessing to be so called. There are also those with darker energies, which this instrument calls the service-to-self polarity, and to some extent they have also been called to your planet by those desiring to move ahead on the path of service to others. A wide range of information is available. Those who wish to receive messages of hope and truth along the path of service to others have called to us, and to you, children of Earth, the brothers and sisters of sorrow have come. We are your kindred and we feel your sorrow. We cannot take your suffering upon us. We cannot participate in your choices.

A clear choice lies before you. Shall you move with your planet into fourth density to create a new heaven and a new Earth as this instrument would say, quoting from her *Bible*? Or shall you play in the fields of third density for a while longer? It is your choice. It is very doubtful if any of those who listen to our voice will ever turn to service to self but it is very possible for those of you who respond at this moment to our vibrations and to our words to lose enthusiasm and to refrain from making the choice to serve.

If you are tired, if you are weary, we encourage you to rest. We do not encourage you to press forward when you are too tired. We ask you, please, to take time to sit and give yourself a rest, to demand nothing of yourself at all. This entity often, watching the television in what she considers a semi-vegetative state or reading one of her romances or science fiction or mystery novels, feels guilty at least to some extent because she has stopped trying, and she is resting by the side of the road. May we say that there is wisdom in the resting, for you do not wish to burn out like a flame that has burnt too hot. Let yourself

cool off; let yourself become grounded; let yourself move down into your heaviest body. And then gently, after you have rested, take a deep breath, let it out, and say to yourself, "Shall we dance again? Shall we hit the road? Shall we have some fun?"

Is there a further query at this time?

Vara: Yes, thank you. *(Reading A's question.)* "I feel somewhere other that we have been helped by assistance unknown, and rather that the phenomenon of channeling has got many sides, that which you are, think or do is in a way or other a by-product of other influences, not always identical, but in this context, responsible for our progression. Would you comment on this?"

We are those of Q'uo, and are aware of your query, my brother. It is true that all entities are channels, just as we spoke earlier of being an instrument which the Creator plays. You as well as we are channels. We can say that to the best of our intention and ability, we do not tamper or meddle with any entity. We do not influence you more than we are asked to influence you. We are happy to share our thoughts, but we do not have the power to make you different than you are. In sharing energy with you, we both change to some extent, for we have shared the uniqueness of each other's being, for each of us is a spark of the one infinite Creator. Each of us is unique, each of us has grown through millions of choices, and has recorded amazing and varied experiences through many lifetimes. And certainly we are intercommunicative and there are special relationships between inner-planes densities or unseen planes, shall we say, to be more precise, and those who dwell upon the Earth plane. But we would say that to see the phenomenon of channeling and to see the effect of channeling clearly, it is well to imagine that you are standing in a great garden with all of the entities of all of the densities of Earth, and they are all singing their song, and as they sing the Creator is conducting. There are millions of notes and yet the harmony is complete. If you take part you will disturb that harmony, so allow yourself to be an instrument in the hands of the one Creator and go forth in faith that the Creator knows His music.

Is there a further query, my brother?

Vara: There is. *(Reading A's question.)* "Would you comment on the correlations between the various higher bodies and my experience, which is this:

"I was near the old venerable Zen master and he was repeating his mantra about the child. I saw a living flame of pure ecstasy without stint, then suddenly I rose up in a great enlightenment and said to him, 'Behold, that is the child.' I would like to know anything you feel is appropriate to share on this matter?"

We are those of Q'uo, and are aware of your query, my brother. We cannot share with you concerning this incident in any detail for you are still developing your understanding of this gift. Please be aware that when you see images and visions such as this one you are heavily influenced by your culture and your religious upbringing. You see in coded ways because you have distorted or colored your subconscious mind in its higher or closer sub-conscious aspects, using the archetypal material that you have studied, both in the Christian and in the Indian ways. This can create a confusing landscape. The East and the West do not speak in the same archetypal ways. What is of one meaning to Christianity is of another meaning to an Indian archetypal system. There is confusion in the resulting salad. We do not feel, however, that there is any mistake whatsoever in the paths that you have taken or in the somewhat complex imagery that has resulted from your very deep and devoted studies in both of these areas. See what you can do to penetrate the details of cultural imagery in this vision, moving to the heart and the essence. What does the child represent? Not to someone else, not to an authority figure especially, but to you. And how is that meaningful to you? What pattern in your incarnation does this touch upon, and in what light? We welcome your use of your mind. The intellect and the powers of analysis have their points. See how many different organisations you can place upon this image and this story that you have told yourself. Then lift up off analysis and thought and let the feeling of this experience enter your heart. It is within the sacred space of the open heart that you are fed from the springs of truth that lies beyond words, and, my brother, this is what you crave and this is where you are going, beyond the words to the essence.

Is there a further query, my brother?

Vara: (*Reading A's question.*) "On a related note, I would ask what relationship is between this entity and the legendary Seneca Lucius Anaius, the Roman."

We are those of Q'uo, and are aware of your query, my brother. And we must laugh because this instrument has answered this query for us already, for she said that she felt that probably we would say that the work on this question was not yet done in your own process. It is sometimes difficult to be patient and wait for yourself to do the work. How much easier to have an authority figure give you the information that you crave! Yet to do so would be to steal a precious gift from you. Take your time to investigate this question. When you have come to a settled opinion about this particular pattern and this particular interest, then perhaps we could confirm your opinion, but that is far as we can go in helping you with your teach/learning process, as this instrument would call it. For you are your teacher. We are only those who help when asked.

We thank you for this query and would ask if there is another query at this time?

Vara: Thank you Q'uo. On a personal note, I as Vara would like to ask if you could offer any insight into the rectal bleeding that the instrument and her husband are experiencing at this time.

We are those of Q'uo, and are aware of your query, my sister, and we can speak to this, for the one known as Carla has come to a fairly settled opinion concerning this experience. To an extent she is precisely correct: the bleeding has to do with the separation of several thousand miles between herself and her husband. The one known as Jim, that she calls Mick, has experienced this and more as a result of being separated from the one known as Carla. And as she has said it is so that when two have become truly one, the bodies of those two entities are aware of that bond and a separation of the magnitude of three weeks on two continents is enough to create a concern within the physical bodies of both entities for their very survival.

However, there is more depth to the symbolism of the bleeding, for both of them consciously chose the separation in order to be of service. And as is the case in a substantial number of sacrifices, blood is, shall we say, the physical expression of sacrifice. It is in its way holy or sacred and it serves as a representative emblem of the depth of dedication and of the cost of this service. It is in fact the chalice offered up to the one infinite Creator. If concern enters either the one known as Jim or the one known as Carla's minds, there could be toxic repercussions. If it is taken to be an offering and offered freely, it shall pass. There is in many cases the concept that suffering must be costly, and we say to you, suffering does not have to be costly. Suffering does not have to be blood in the chalice. Yet if there is the necessity for that emblem, let us remember with you, for we too admire and follow unconditional love and its servants, the teaching of the one known as Jesus the Christ, who said, "This is my body; this is my blood; it is given for you: take this in remembrance of me." Take your own blood, symbolically speaking. Know that you are a body to be broken in service. And therefore give yourself, bless your sacrifice, break that body, offer it up and rejoice, for you are not your body. None is body, all are the result of the sacrifice. Move beyond the emblem of sacrifice and what do you see? Remembrance of the one infinite Creator; knowledge and understanding of the power and the peace that lies beyond; all giving and all receiving. And that lives and rests in joy. Nothing is lost, no matter what occurs, for all is one. May you then rejoice, lift the self from the cross and choose the ascension into bliss, for that too is an aspect of service.

May we answer you further, my sister?

Vara: No, thank you.

Is there a further query at this time?

Vara: Yes, actually. I would ask if there is further insight you might offer into how we might make the instrument more comfortable for the remaining duration of this journey.

We are those of Q'uo, and are aware of your query my sister. We thank you for the concern which you offer. There are those techniques of which you know: the tending to the body with massage for sore muscles, with heat when the entity is cold, with rest when the entity is tired. And we are aware that you often see this entity cranky as a small child who will not go down for her nap. Encourage her to nap, my sister, but do it with lightness.

And remember that you have entered into this service and you, as well, must be tended. You must tend to yourself, for this instrument is frail. Therefore, we would ask that you, after you tend to this instrument, with equal love and appreciation tend to the one known as Vara.

May we answer you further, my sister?

Vara: No, thank you, Q'uo.

We thank you, my sister. Is there a final query at this time?

Vara: No, Q'uo, thank you very much.

We thank you and we smile with you, my sister. It is good to be with this group and we have enjoyed it. It has been a great blessing and a privilege. We leave you, reminding you, each and every one, that you are perfect, that you have arrived, that you have nowhere to go. You have only to become aware of who and where you are. Do not be deceived by the details of the illusion of the outer world. Hew only unto your inner sense of rightness and truth, and remember the light touch in the midst of all your proper actions, your meditations, your service, and so forth. Remember the great healing effect of laughter. Laugh easily and laugh long and let yourself be healed.

We leave you, as we found you, in the love and in the light of the one infinite Creator. We are those known to you as the principle of Q'uo. Adonai. Adonai. ✢

L/L RESEARCH

L/L Research is a subsidiary of
Rock Creek Research &
Development Laboratories, Inc.

P.O. Box 5195
Louisville, KY 40255-0195

www.llresearch.org

Rock Creek is a non-profit
corporation dedicated to
discovering and sharing
information which may aid in
the spiritual evolution of
humankind.

SPECIAL MEDITATION
JUNE 17, 2005

Question from D: Since 1997 I have suffered depression and anxiety as my awakening occurred. My previous view of reality changed completely. In 2000 I broke down completely. I've had the feeling that psychic greeting is involved in this illness and breakdown. I sensed I had inadvertently invited thought forms into my life which were not friendly. Can you confirm this?

(Carla channeling)

We are those known to you as the principle of Q'uo, and we greet you, my brother, in the love and in the light of the one infinite Creator, in Whose service we come to you this day. May we thank you for setting aside this time for sacred seeking and for offering to us the beauty of your vibrations. We share in them with the light and return our infinite love to you. It is our privilege and our pleasure to share with you upon any subject which you would have the pleasure in asking.

As always, we would ask a gift of you and that is that you listen to those things which we have to say with a jaundiced and judgmental mind. Be ready to ignore us if anything that we say does not ring true to you. We are not infallible beings nor are we authorities; we are your fellow seekers. If you will take responsibility for responding only to those thoughts that resonate to you as if they were memories that we helped you to recover, and to lay aside all other thoughts that do not ring true, then that will free us up to be able to speak with you without being concerned that we would interfere with your free will or be a stumbling block to your progress. We greatly thank you, my brother, for this consideration.

To respond to your question concerning psychic greeting and the experiences through which you have gone, we would begin by saying that we can indeed confirm that that which you would call psychic greeting has occurred and indeed there are two separate types of psychic greeting that have occurred. We are able to share this information with you because we feel that you have a somewhat crystallized concept of what is actually occurring and we are simply deepening your understanding.

Firstly, in considering the question of greeting, we would say that there is a type of psychic greeting, as it is generally known among your people, although some call it psychic attack, that is indeed from an entity that is not of your density. This is relatively rare and occurs when an entity, for some reason, has attracted the attention of a service-to-self entity of the unseen or inner planes. You attracted the interest of such an entity by the purity and the focus of your seeking of the light of truth. You were ruthless in this seeking. This is, my brother, what is needed. You cannot have pity upon the personality shell which you enjoy at this time if you wish to uncover a deeper portion of the reality or essence of yourself. You must simply ask and, after asking, not look away. And this you have done.

There is a quality to this kind of courage which is what this instrument would call ethical or moral. Those who seek with such intent stand close to the light that they seek. For you see, my brother, that which you seek is already with you and in asking, you have received it. In receiving truth, you receive very pure light and this is what caused the attention of what we would call a mischievous service-to-self entity who wished to distract you from your journey of seeking to come to you.

In the process of the suffering which ensued, you burned away the opportunity for this entity to disturb your life. It is not that this entity wished to go away, nor does it still, it is that you have achieved the ability to love it, to accept it, to embrace it, and to know it as part of yourself. It is very frustrating to this entity to be so loved. And so this entity, most of the time, is forced to retire from propinquity to your spirit, mind or emotions. From time to time you may feel that you are being greeted once again. This is an old friend, is it not, and you may say to it once again, "Old friend, you are part of me. I love you, I accept you, and I embrace you." And it shall react as it will. You, however, shall be unharmed. It cannot touch you in any substantive way.

We would then, secondly, speak to that other time of psychic greeting, as this instrument would call it, which is far more common among your peoples. We were speaking earlier in talking with the one known as I concerning the crystalline nature of all entities. You are as a crystal, receiving, transmitting and transducing energy. There are some kinds of light that come into your being which you dearly love. You develop those aspects of self. You turn the crystal of self to the station that receives that light and you work with it, patiently and endlessly, with joy. And so those portions of yourself develop, become refined, and strengthen their connections to the one infinite Creator.

There are other facets of this gem that you are at which you have not enjoyed looking. Therefore, you turn them away from the source of light and choose not to develop them. Could we ever blame an entity for not wishing to work with the murderer within, with the thief, with the liar, or any of those roles or facets of self that do create valid and worthy parts of the circle of being that you represent? You are all things. You are not simply the good part, as it is known among your people or in your culture. You are everything. You contain every emotion. You have every thought.

The psychic greeting that is common among your people is the greeting of self to self. [It is the] greeting of the self by the projections of that self, seen in the mirror of the self's thoughts or the thoughts or the actions of another self that resonate to you and call forth from you the necessity to look at and to experience to some degree that portion of yourself which this facet represents that has been evoked. The facets of the shadow self have not been developed by you. You have not yet appreciated the poignancy and the profundity of these energies. What lies behind the eyes and thoughts of one who wishes another harm? What lies behind the door of fear? What lies behind the capacity of an entity to fend for itself when it feels that its survival is threatened?

How difficult these things are to examine. And yet this is the work that you came here to do. You came to develop the undeveloped portions of the self and so to integrate into your circle of being, that they too may become able to catch the light, to focus the power and the peace of the one infinite Creator, and to integrate themselves as the deep underside of your being that gives to you your grit, your determination, and your persistence. These are wonderful parts of yourself. When developed, they constitute the best of you, just as every facet of your being constitutes the best of you. And as you integrate them and begin to see the commonalities throughout the circle of being, for the first time in your incarnation you become able to love yourself.

Why is this important when the whole point of a service-to-others incarnation is to love and serve others? My brother, we say to you, the point is that you cannot love another beyond your capacity to love yourself. When you have ceased to judge yourself and have forgiven yourself for being error prone and human, for having undeveloped light that you didn't find yet, then you are able to understand and forgive the frailties of those about you. You become, in your very being, a nurturer and a lover of souls, and this you have craved and sought.

And so these harsh and unremitting periods of suffering came upon you, not to punish you and not to distort you in any way that you chose not to turn but rather to allow you the time and the space to behold yourself; not simply the pleasant bits, the parts you could trot out and show to family and friends, but, more importantly, those parts of yourself with which you had hard work to do. What a nightmare it is the first time you see a part of yourself that has simply gone neglected and lies like a rubbish heap at the depths of your soul! How you would wish that it were not you! But all things are you and you are all things.

You have come through this fire. Yet this is a fire that shall never burn down within incarnation, for this is your opportunity to refine your being. Therefore, these patterns of seeing the undeveloped parts of the self will continue. Think of it as if you were on a spiral, moving ever upward towards the light. As your incarnational themes come around again like the leitmotif in the opera, you hear the tune. "Ah," you say, "Parsifal has arrived." Or, "Ah, it's Peter," or "the Wolf." Such are the experiences within your orchestral works for recognizing characters that are part of yourself that have come around again, singing their song and telling their story to you. Do not be dismayed. You came here to meet these parts of yourself, to go on a journey with them, to listen to their music, and to hear their story. Each time that this theme repeats, the motif shall lead you into a different level of work. You do not repeat the work. You are at a different place in the spiral each time the repetition of them occurs. So do not assume that you know that story yet. You have not heard this version! But rejoice in the occurrence of this work. And as you take it up with joy, rather than reluctantly, the motif shall come to greet you and shall be generous with its truth.

This instrument has often talked, in the context of her life in community in the last several months and years, of the experiencing of community as a hall of mirrors and she has often said, "The most you can hope from the hall of mirrors is that the mirrors speak to you gently, lovingly and honestly." Everyone that you meet is a mirror to you. My brother, most of them are not kind and they are certainly not capable of being honest. Therefore, you feel as though you are in a carnival, in the house of crazy mirrors that show you to be too tall or too short or too fat or too thin to represent your true image. Let this be so. Let the distortions be as they are and then say, "What do I see in this mirror that can help me to grow?"

You will come to appreciate the mirrors that give you a true image and, indeed, they are priceless.

May we ask if there is another query at this time?

D: Is such a so-called greeting, of a seemingly unfriendly nature, a bad thing? Or is it just part of the process of awakening? Please comment in any way you might find helpful.

We are those of Q'uo, and are aware of your query, my brother. We would certainly feel, beyond a shadow of a doubt, that this process, while harsh, is extremely helpful and indeed is a necessary part of your particular path. You have not chosen an easy path. You have chosen to hew to a very precise upward-spiraling line of light. You want the truth.

We would say to you at this time, my brother, to keep that focus but to release the harshness of your determination and accept instead the knowledge that that determination has matured. You will not deviate from your seeking. You do not have to put guards upon yourself at this time. We would give you one word and that is, "Remember." Whenever you have doubts as to the benefits of this process of refining the self in the fire of experience, ask yourself to remember and that will bring back to you the entire flood of knowledge of self and of all through which you have been. We hope that you can begin to respect the suffering that you have endured for what it is: a service to your own seeking.

For some, the choice of focus is one which does not take on this laser-like quality. There is a softness to the focus. You would even perhaps see it as fluffy or marshmallowy or sweet. That does not mean that they are not doing their work. It means that [what] they are suffering will be of a different quality. It would be, shall we say, of a quality that you might call messy or vague. Yet they are suffering and their process will go on much longer than your own in terms of getting to the point where they can begin to relax into their own truth. You wished for a steeper path on hard rock and so you have been climbing a mountain. And now, we must say to you, here is another challenge. Have you heard the saying, "First there is a mountain; then there is no mountain; then there is."? This instrument knows these words by the song by the one known as Donovan. It is time for you to see no mountain but only the love and the light of the mystery of the one infinite Creator.

There will come a time for the laser view. When it comes, put on your hiking gear, grab your pitons, and go forth to scale the mountain. But know that you are in a world of illusion, when you so climb, that is somewhat different than the world of illusion in the stage when there is no mountain.

Now, the world where there is no mountain is a mystery too. A laser-like view has no value for it can bore through infinity forever and still there is no mountain. There is only a state of being in which the truth expresses itself in essence rather than in light. To say this another way, at a certain point you enter that nexus of self between the balance of love and the balance of light and you move from light to love, from wisdom to love, from articulated understanding to essential understanding. The adjustment to accept a mystery you cannot plumb and you cannot express is substantial. Give yourself the time to make these deep settling-in motions that you would feel when you settled into a new chair or when you first took the controls of a new car. It's a little different to drive the car of essence than it is to drive the laser beam of seeking the truth. Know that you have not stopped seeking the truth but that you must balance such precise work with periods of allowing all that there is to be the ocean in which you swim, the air in which you breath, the earth upon which you walk, and the fire which warms you. You cannot get hold of things in this period to talk about them or to penetrate them. In a way, you are in mid-air. You have walked off the precipice. Shall you fall or shall your faith that all is well keep you comfortable and safe?

We believe that this entire process is precisely along the lines that your higher self and you chose when first you considered entering incarnation upon planet Earth and that all is indeed well. This is our perception. We hope that you too may find some truth to this perception and that you may give yourself that release from worry or concern that you may have missed a step or suffered in vain. We believe your pattern is unfolding in absolute perfection and we are with you, my brother, as are many entities and essences of spirit as you move forth in courage, confidence and peace.

Is there another query at this time, my brother?

D: Could you talk about the spiritual principles involved in the kind of extremity of suffering which I feel I've sort of had, through which I went, the kind of extremity of suffering through which I went?

We are those of Q'uo, and are aware of your query, my brother. The spiritual principle involved in the suffering which you have undergone is the principle of balance. Let us say that a great desire to serve can pull you away from the point of balance which is most helpful for your body, mind and spirit within incarnation, rendering you less useful than you were as an instrument for singing the song of your soul. You have a very individual, unique song to sing for you are a one-of-a-kind singer, as are all instruments of the one infinite Creator.

When such imbalance has occurred, through distortions created and enhanced during childhood especially, the inner self must choose its method of coming into balance again and becoming once again a more true, tuned instrument. The Creator wishes to play you most sweetly. The decision that you made was to pierce through the gloom of confusion, and so you did. This was a costly decision in terms of the suffering involved. It was also highly efficient. You burned a great deal of accumulated confusion. You polished the facets of your gem with great vigor and nerve. And we salute you, my brother, as a man of fire and principle, as a slayer of the dragon, shall we say. You have created for yourself a very friendly dragon who still loves the fire but will make you toast. You have come more and more into balance.

Where shall this search take you? We do not know, this is entirely your decision. But by such extremity of suffering, you not only climbed upon the cross of your perceived incorrectness, you have also freed yourself from that cross and ascended to your next paradise. There you shall also find ways to suffer, ways to learn, and ways, above all, to be kind and compassionate to yourself. As you rest in the mid-air of faith, know that you are a creature of unconditional love and that as you achieved the cross of suffering, so now you have achieved the redemption, the understanding of yourself.

This point of balance is always moving and your work shall never be done, any more than anyone's work is ever done. The road, as it is said in this instrument's [memory] of songs sung, goes on forever. The group is known as the Allman Brothers and this instrument greatly loves that song. The road, my brother, indeed, goes on forever. Nothing is finished, it merely spirals upward, ever seeking the love and the light that lies not without you, for you call it down into yourself by your seeking and seat it in the depths of your heart. Therefore, in that mid-air of faith, know that you rest in your own open heart.

May we answer you in any further way, my brother?

D: No, thank you, that's fine. Thank you very much.

We thank you, my brother, and we would ask this group who has come together in sacred seeking if there is a final query at this time?

(No further queries.)

In that case, we leave you in the love and in the light of the one infinite Creator. Thank you for giving to us this precious gift of time and space and such beauty as we cannot express. We are those known to you as the principle of Q'uo. We leave you, as we found you, in the love and in the light of the one infinite Creator. Adonai. Adonai. ☙

L/L RESEARCH

L/L Research is a subsidiary of
Rock Creek Research &
Development Laboratories, Inc.

P.O. Box 5195
Louisville, KY 40255-0195

www.llresearch.org

Rock Creek is a non-profit
corporation dedicated to
discovering and sharing
information which may aid in
the spiritual evolution of
humankind.

SPECIAL MEDITATION
JUNE 18, 2005

St Albans Spiritualist Church, St Albans, Hertfordshire, England

(The first half of this meeting was an introductory speech given by Carla earlier on this same day.)

Carla: If you are interested in seeing information on the internet from our group, we have two websites. Our group is called L and L [L/L] Research so [our web address] is www.llresearch.org. The other one is more of a café of ideas, shall we say, and lots of different ideas are on that site, not just our own. The first one is the archive of all my channeling and speeches and so forth and it's all for free. There's no subscription to it. There's no subscription to either one. The other one is www.bring4th.org. You're welcome to check us out. [There is] information that I brought with me [about] the first book of five books of the channeling of the *Law of One*, by Ra, and I brought lots of brochures so if you wanted to get the rest [of the series] you could send the brochure back to us and order it yourself later.

I wrote an owner's manual for people, actually. I finally decided we need one! We have spark plugs; we need to know how to change them! So that's called *A Wanderer's Handbook*. There are a few copies back there. And there are some tapes of my beloved companion and research partner, Don Elkins, called *The Spiritual Significance of UFOs*. I wasn't too careful about recording him in his many, many times of speaking about his research, but this one time that I did record him we got a good speech from him and if you'd like to listen to what he had to say, there are tapes back there.

There's also a tape I made in the 80's. I just wrote lots of people around the world that speak English and said, "Would you like to send a sample of your channeling?" And I made a tape of different channels who have different things to say but interestingly enough, if you're a positive channel, the information all harmonizes, so that no matter whether it's Buddhist or Christian or whatever, if you're keying into the spiritual rather than the strictly religious, you'll find that the information harmonizes nicely. And some of them are UFO entities; some of them aren't. But there's that tape.

There are coloring books. If you have children and you're looking for something that's spiritual, there's a coloring book called, *What is Love?* that your kid can color.

And I wrote a book for people that already have a psychic aspect that they are trying to develop. It doesn't teach you how to channel! It's called *A Channeling Handbook* and perhaps some of the principles I talk about in that book might help. I think that's what we brought with us.

And, of course, we brought lots of brochures so that you can just take our brochure home and maybe order something later.

So, you have all been talking with each other. What's your thought? Would you like just to ask questions in the group, here, just me and you? Or would you rather experience a channeling?

Group: *(General agreement on choosing to have a channeling.)*

Okay, well, could you come up with a group question? The gentlemen in the red shirt was asking a very interesting question about desire. He said that he had been finding more and more that the key to his process at this time was desire but that perhaps he hadn't gone deep enough in his desire; that he'd been thinking about what he desired rather than asking his heart what his heart's desire was and could he know a little bit more about how that worked. If we wanted to, we could take one question after another or we could, as a group, create a question. It doesn't matter to me.

Questioner: Is it possible to take one question after another?

It is. Now we'll need to have Vara next to me because I tend to go out of my body and I don't want to do that, I want to stay conscious. It's healthier for me as a person. So, if you want to do that then …

(Vara moves to sit beside Carla and the microphone is adjusted.)

The next thing is we need to find a way to tune the group. We're a little bit scattered. Is there a song that you all love to sing that we could sing together or would you like to do the Lord's Prayer? I'd like to find some way of bringing our voices together because the breath is the spirit and we are wind instruments, so as we speak those words … would the Lord's Prayer be all right?

Group: *(General agreement.)*

Then as we speak that prayer then I would ask you to think about what you're saying. They are very simple thoughts in the prayer but it's an interesting prayer, especially, you know, some of those phrases like, "Let it be on Earth as it is in Heaven." When you finally become able to accept the fact that you do contain heaven within and that you can know the thoughts of heaven then you begin to internalize that prayer. So as we say the prayer together, let's do that. And if you would, ask the question of P. *(Carla indicates P, sitting beside Vara.)* And then P will ask

me because I have a hearing problem and I won't get it sometimes but P will speak directly to me and re-ask the question so that I can [hear better.]

And if it's all right, then, since we're going to take a series of questions, we'll try to keep the answers short, I will mentally request that we not go on too long about any one but we'll try to get some answers here that would be resources for all of you.

Vara: Are you comfortable? Can I get you another cushion?

I'm just fine. And let me put my hand on yours here. Okay. All right, let us pray together.

Group: "Our Father who are in Heaven, hallowed be Thy name. Thy kingdom come, Thy will be done on Earth as it is in Heaven. Give us this day our daily bread and forgive us our trespasses as we forgive those who trespass against us. And lead us not into temptation but deliver us from evil. For Thine is the kingdom and the power and the glory, forever and ever. Amen."

(Carla channeling)

We are those known to you as the principle of Q'uo. We greet you in the love and in the light of the one infinite Creator in Whose service we come to you. May we thank you for giving us the opportunity of viewing the beauty of your souls. We [also] thank you for setting aside time and space to create a sacred circle of seeking and for inviting us to share our thoughts with you.

We would ask of you one thing before we begin and that is that you listen to us with a very careful sense of discrimination, listening for those thoughts that resonate to you as if we had reminded you of a truth that you already know. Please do not accept us as authority figures. If any thought that we share with you does not ring true, we would ask you to leave it behind without a second thought. For truth is a deeply subjective thing. Your personal truth is living and evolving within you and what is true for you yesterday may not be true for you tomorrow. Therefore, in order for us to know that we are not infringing on your free will, we would ask you to be careful discriminators, using only those thoughts of ours which seem to you to be helpful as a resource for your own growth. If you can do that for us then we will feel free to share our thoughts with you without being concerned that we would constitute a stumbling block before you. We thank you for this kind consideration and would now ask if there is a question at this time? We would ask the one known as P to offer us a question after he has heard it and refined it so that he may ask it of us. We will pause while the first question is received. We are those of Q'uo.

P: The question is: "Should desire come from the heart or should it come from the mind? Why is desire such an important thing in life and where does it come from?"

We are those known to you as Q'uo, and are aware of your query, my brother. This instrument has been speaking about the self as a crystal. Everything that you have experienced throughout all of your incarnations up until this point and within this incarnation, everything that has gone into your process has created of you a unique crystalline nature. This crystalline nature has the kind of power that a radio station, shall we say, has. You have the ability to receive energy, you have the ability to transmit or send forth energy, and you have the ability to change energy that you receive and send it out in a different way. This is called transducing energy.

As a crystal, one of your desires, shall we say, is to regularize and harmonize the aspects of this crystal and thusly to be able to become single-pointed and focused. The key to this is something this instrument would call the will. Working to sharpen and hone the will is the work of many lifetimes and, my brother, at the point in your process during this incarnation where you are at this time, you have matured your understanding of your own power. This has freed your energy to conceive of the possibility of gathering that power and of focusing it.

In order to focus the will, the various and several desires that you may have experienced as aspects or portions of your desire to serve the one infinite Creator have begun to seem to you to be less than focused, less than satisfactory, and you realize that to express your truth, you have the need to integrate, harmonize and unify these several virtuous desires into a one-pointed focus. The focus for you at this moment is what you now seek. It is as if, having accepted your own power, your own magical nature as a crystalline being and as an aspect of the divine principle, you now wish to become one thing and to allow that unified desire of the will to shine forth. There are many aspects of this desire that we cannot speak to for it is the very active part of your process and we can not learn for you.

What we would suggest to you as you work (*inaudible*) extremely positive and accurate perception (*inaudible*) is that you focus upon your being rather than upon that which you are doing. This is a very difficult concept to understand amongst the people of your culture, for the people of your culture are bent upon doing and accomplishing in the outer world. What is not understood is that it is the being that informs the doing. It is the essence within you that creates, shall we say, a magnet, a kind of magnetizing effect, that brings to you those things that you need in order to continue to develop and bloom as a crystalline being and to continue to be able to breath deeper, to radiate more simply and more purely, and to allow the refining process to harmonize all things so that in your very being you draw to you those thing which you would wish to do to be of service.

We realize that your query and each query that we speak to has a tremendous amount more that we could explore but we hope that these few words give you some seed thoughts which you may develop at your leisure.

May we ask the one known as P if there is a second query at this time?

P: (*Reading*) "Could you please tell us how we may connect more with spirit and our guardians?"

We are those of Q'uo, and are aware of your query, my sister. This instrument has said earlier that that which you seek lies within you. Your guidance lies within the deepest part of your being. We would say to you that it is as if your highest and best self, that has already gone through the lessons of love and the lessons of wisdom and the lessons of the balance between love and wisdom, was available to you from the future. This instrument calls her guidance the Holy Spirit. Others call guidance many different names. Some relate to guidance through a guru, others move into the world of nature and find their guidance in the stillness of the pond and the whispering of the leaves in the wind. However you like to conceive of your guidance system, what we would encourage you to consider is that you may trust that you have it. It is as much a part of you as your breathing and indeed is closer to you than that process.

When you ask for guidance, it is already answering you. So your challenge is to remember to ask and then, when you have asked, to realize that you are being answered. It may not be obvious to you immediately. Sometimes it takes a while for those expectations that you have for how guidance really works to lift up and lift away because guidance may come without words. Guidance may come because you feel peace. You don't know why but you suddenly realize, without being able to prove it, that all is well. And sometimes, in fact quite often, that is the central message of guidance. For you are on an even keel when you do not know it and when you cannot feel it. You may feel difficulties and chaos about you and feel that you are most confused and yet if you can but ask for help, that help is near.

Do you know the image from the tarot deck of the Fool that is stepping off the precipice into thin air? This is a helpful image to carry with you when you doubt your guidance. Doubt and fear take you away from your guidance. Take the image of this fool and, like the fool, step off into the thin air of faith. When you ask, invoke faith, and then wait for the universe to speak to you. To this instrument, with her long history of working with spirit, she actually converses with the Holy Spirit within. She will say, "Holly, help!" and immediately Holly helps. This instrument and the one known as Vara were driving here this day and they got lost, not once, but several times and Vara would look over and say, "You're praying again, aren't you?" And this instrument would admit it, so Vara would say, "And who is it this time?" And it might be Saint Patrick, whom this instrument invoked because Saint Patrick drove the snakes out of Ireland, so why couldn't he drive the confusion out of our roadmap? Or it might be St Alban. Why not ask St Alban to draw us to himself, to his seat within this beautiful land of Britain. And once, when [Vara] asked, this instrument was simply breathing. She was breathing in the love and the light of the one infinite Creator because she had forgotten to be herself and she was beginning to enter into fear. And may we say, from examining this instrument's mind, the possibility of having fear in the middle of the M25?

May we ask if there is another query at this time, my brother?

P: (Reading) "We were talking about the Earth being bombarded with vibrations and if there will be changes that will affect the Earth and its inhabitants.

Is this likely going to be a gradual process or it will be much quicker? And how will it be felt by its inhabitants?"

We are those of Q'uo, and are aware of your query, my sister. We realize that this particular question concerning the energy waves that are bombarding your planet at this time is connected to the question of "ascension." And as this instrument was saying earlier to one of those within this circle of seeking, there is the opportunity when viewing this question to enter into fear. And therefore the first thing that we would say to you is that we would encourage [you to] not to enter into fear. This instrument often quotes to herself from the *Bible* which she holds dear, "If I live, I am in Christ, and if I die I am in Christ, so whether I am dead or alive, I am in Christ and Christ is in me." [Thusly, she ceases to fear.]

However, we would also say that it is our opinion, and we could be wrong, that we believe that this process of "ascension," of coming into a sense of cooperation with these energies of the New Age, has already been gradually affecting your peoples for some time. In fact, the one known as Jesus the Christ was speaking about these energies two thousand of your years ago. The process of ascension [has] already begun, for in our ways of viewing the cycles upon your planet, the cycle that you are experiencing as what this instrument calls third density began over seventy-five thousand of your years ago in your measure. Therefore, the last two thousand years, spiritually speaking, are the very end times and you have been living in them since you were born. Much has changed quickly upon your planetary sphere. You have seen your civilization in two hundred years move from candles to the computer, from a donkey and a cart or a horse and a carriage, to the jet plane and the space ship. But has the heart of your people changed?

We encourage you to see this process of bombardment as a very positive and as a necessary thing. It is inevitable that the planet itself be born and we are happy to say that the baby is doing well, the baby is alive, the baby is coming through its labor just fine. Many of your peoples have caught on to the fact that things are changing and many among your people have talked about these bombardments of cosmic energy that are hitting the planet. How can one cooperate with something that often seems so uncomfortable? The challenge, my brothers and sisters, is to release control. It is not a process that is happening to you, it is a process that is happening to the planet and all of humankind. In and of yourself, you can do nothing to change it. It is what is appropriate for this planetary sphere at this time. Consequently, the goal that we may encourage you to follow here is to open yourself to the change that it calls forth from within you.

These energy waves are bringing up to you every bit of your shadow self that you do not want to look at. Look at them. Do not be afraid to gaze deeply into the mirror that they show you. Whatever your television tube shows you, look at it and say, "What have you to teach me?" And then let it go, release control. You have thought about it. You have responded to it. Move on. Allow these energies to work on you. They are transformational in nature and therefore they are challenging. Allow the challenging process to occur. Be naked and honest and vulnerable and if you must cry, weep; and if you laugh and feel joyful, dance and be like the leaves in the fall, and fall. Let things change, for change is occurring and the more you embrace it, the more you feel that you truly are a part of it, the more you will benefit from the transformation that is occurring among your peoples and upon your planet.

May we ask if there is another query at this time?

P: *(Reading)* "Firstly, are there other channels channeling this particular group and secondly, is that information going to be colored by the different culture that it comes into?"

We are those of Q'uo, and we are aware of your query. We thank you for the opportunity to speak to this question for it is often a concern of entities who are listening to channeling as to whether or not the source of such channeling is valid and whether or not they should consider it seriously.

The Confederation of Planets in the Service of the Infinite Creator speaks through many channels and, indeed, there are many within your inner planes who also speak through many channels. There are very many different ways to hear the message of love. Those of the principle of Q'uo who speak through this particular instrument speak only through this instrument. The reason is that this instrument tunes for channeling by asking for the highest and best contact of the Christ energy or consciousness that she can receive in a stable and conscious manner. She's very precise about that for which she asks, for she wishes to make the best use of her energy and her time in terms of offering clear and transparent information that may constitute a resource for those who are seeking.

Therefore, we as a principle have created ourselves specifically to speak through this instrument. Many other entities are less careful in their tuning and in their challenging of spirits and so you may find time and time again that you are reading a channeled source and you must put it down because it does not ring true. And this is not the fault of the instrument itself, which is service to others, but rather it is the fault of an unclear tuning. Perhaps the channel does not know precisely who she is and perhaps she has not challenged the spirit which is attempting to communicate through her in [the name of] that for which she lives and that for which she would die. When this occurs, [the unclearly tuned instrument] receives seemingly positive information which somehow turns into a fear-oriented channeling, so that you begin to hear ideas that have to do with exclusivity so that some are included and some are not, or so that some will reach the kingdom of heaven and some will not, or you may hear channeled sources that say you must believe this and this and then you will be enlightened.

If you can discriminate, carefully, you may read any source and find the good within it. So we would encourage you not to hew to this particular channel or to our source as a particular source but rather, as you read all material that is seemingly inspired, to listen for that resonance within of which we spoke when we began our channeling session through this instrument. Trust not the channel, nor the authority, nor the source. Trust yourself, for you know the truth that is yours when you hear it.

We find that this instrument's energy begins to wane and therefore we would ask if there is a final query at this time?

P: *(Reading)* "Do you think there will be a return of Jesus Christ or a Messiah? Or will it be a return of a particular energy?"

We are those known to you as the principle of Q'uo, and, my sister, we believe that you have begun to answer our question for us. It is our sincere belief that you are the Christ. It is our belief that each of you was sent forth from the Father, as this instrument calls the one infinite Creator, to be His daughter and to be His son. The tongues of flame have touched your lips, the spirit has descended upon your head and you have been created! And you shall change the face of the Earth.

We realize that you are young spirits. You are young co-Creators. And yet the power to create is yours. That which you forgive is forgiven. That which you lift is lifted. That which you reach forth to heal is healed. It is difficult to take ultimate responsibility for Christhood. And yet we say to each of you, that individuality that you see as yourself, that which you say is "I," is an illusion. The personality shell that you experience is very helpful for working within the field of Earth, for doing what you came to do, living and breathing and being and blooming. Yet it is not all of you. It is not the earth of you. And as you ask again and again, "In each day, create me to see who I am, help me to realize my true nature," you are opening the way, little by little, to begin to feel that essence, that "I" that is the consciousness of love.

The one known as Jesus did not wish to be worshipped. The one known as Jesus wished to be seen as one who was doing the will of the Father. We ask each of you, "What is your will? Who is your Creator? And how shall you follow the will of the Father for you this day?" This instrument prays every morning that she may hear the Word, that she may, in her flesh and in her mistakes and in her every movement, be used. If you but open yourself to the possibility of Christ within, you will understand that the "I Am" that is truly you is the way, the truth, and the life.

My brothers, my sisters, we are humble before you. The beauty of your seeking astounds us. Through so many difficulties and through so many trials, your courage and your determination to seek has carried you to this moment. May we send you forth rejoicing in the power of your spirit. May we encourage you to know that you are that which you seek and that you can do this that you came to do. And not by doing but simply by being who you are. We are there with you, as are so many angels and guides, to help you deepen your meditation and to help. In those little moments where you ask for inspiration, may you feel our presence when you ask. May you know that you are not alone. May you know how deeply you are loved.

We leave you, as we found you, in the love and the light of the one infinite Creator. We are those of Q'uo. Adonai. Adonai. ♣

L/L RESEARCH

L/L Research is a subsidiary of
Rock Creek Research &
Development Laboratories, Inc.

P.O. Box 5195
Louisville, KY 40255-0195

www.llresearch.org

Rock Creek is a non-profit
corporation dedicated to
discovering and sharing
information which may aid in
the spiritual evolution of
humankind.

SPECIAL MEDITATION
JUNE 19, 2005

Forest Row, East Sussex, UK.

(The session was being filmed by N.)

N: For the sake of the viewers, many of whom may find the concept of channeling weird, could you please explain why you are holding Vara's hand for this session?

Carla: Yes. I talked to you earlier about the contact I had with those of Ra in which we got the *Law of One*. This contact was unusual in that, unlike the rest of my channeling, which began in 1974 and is continuing on through to this very day, it was trance channeling. I never knew how I did the trance channeling but it was a very powerful experience and the material created was remarkably more concise and clearer than my other channeling and so that is the channeling that has been published and it is known the most. After my beloved companion, Don Elkins, died in 1984 I stopped doing the trance channeling because I had been told by those of Ra that it would be very deleterious to my health, not to say my life, to continue doing the trance channeling without both Don and Jim there as my batteries. So I did stop it but I found myself involuntarily going out of body and I experienced a couple of very difficult physical traumas because of people touching me because they didn't know I was out of my body, not just bruising my ribs or bruising my lungs but almost taking me out of this incarnation, having a heart attack and so forth. So I developed the technique of always holding onto someone else's flesh, someone else's body, to make a really good, solid contact so that I could not go out of body because the body won't leave itself defenseless. So as long as there is infringement with another body, the body will stay in the body and be guarded. So I do it simply for protection.

My best battery in the whole world, because we have been working together so long, is my husband, Jim, but Vara is second-best because I have been working with her for several years. Our bodies are very familiar with each other and our energies are used to blending. In fact, Vara's bedroom, when she is at the Magic Kingdom, at home[52], is next to mine and our heads are fairly close together through the wall, so our auras are touching all the time. It's very comfortable for me to swim in Vara's energy and she is not too much bothered by mine either. So, if it weren't her, it would be you, or somebody else in the group, whom I would be touching. It has nothing to do with my affection for Vara, which is great. It has to do with protocol.

I will squeeze Vara's hand when I'm ready and just talk to N.

N: So, may I thank you for agreeing to come through today and may I start by asking you what I may call you?

---

[52] The Rueckert-McCarty home near Louisville, Kentucky, is often called the Magic Kingdom by Carla.

(Carla, channeling)

We are those called Q'uo. We greet you in the love and in the light of the one infinite Creator, at Whose service we come to you this day. May we thank you for the great privilege of being asked to share our thoughts with you at this time and for the beauty of your circle of seeking, for to us, each of you is as beautiful as a gem. The colors of your energy are quite lovely. The way they interweave as you create this sacred circle of seeking humble us.

We would ask one thing of each of you, and of all who hear this voice, before we begin. And that is that each who hears takes responsibility for discriminating between those things which we may say that constitute helpful resources for you at this time and those things that somehow miss the mark and are not ringing true to you. If what we say does not resonate to you, we would ask that you lay it aside without a second thought, for we would not be a stumbling block before you or infringe upon your free will in any way. Thank you for this consideration

N: We are making a film called, *"Time of the Sixth Sun,"*[53] in the hope of helping to awaken more souls to the planet. I'd like to ask what would the message be from your dimension, from your density, direct to the viewers who will be watching this film? What would you want communicated to them?

We are those of Q'uo, and are aware of your query, my sister. We would say to the people of your planet that we and you are creatures of a certain kind. That kind is love.

We would say to you that all of us and all of creation are one thing, and that one thing is love. What does this word mean to you? How do you feel to express the truth of that word? Can you come into some sense of identity with the quality of unconditional love?

We would say to you that we have heard you. We have come to speak with those who wish to accelerate the rate of the evolution of their mind,

their body, and their spirit. We hope to give you thoughts concerning aspects of this journey of seeking the truth of life that may be helpful to you.

We come to tell you that you are not alone, that guidance is all about you, not only in the voice of instruments such as this one but in the voice of everyone who you meet, in the creation of the Father, in yourself, and in the moment.

May we answer you further, my sister?

N: We have previously received some channeled information about the nature of light for this film and I found this really, really helpful. I'd like to ask if you have anything to say to me about that quality and about the nature of how we use light, color and sound in this film?

We are those of Q'uo, and are aware of your query, my sister. We would say to you that your tendency to look for the dappled light that is streaming through the natural branches of the trees, shrubbery and so forth of our natural environment is very wise, my sister, for you are joining the dance of creation. You are asking.

You have spoken of elders in your conversation previous to this channeling session. You are calling forth the elders of the natural or second density. These entities have a great deal to offer to light itself. For light can be, as you have said, an illusion. It can also be quite false. But that light which is filtered through a natural environment like branches and leaves is that light which has been softened and yet not silenced. It has been colored and yet not created as false. You have invited the cooperation of a very powerful source of love and wisdom. We would encourage you to continue in your seeking for, may we say, the right light, feeling your way not only with your eyes or with your instruments but also with your heart.

May we answer you further, my sister?

N: I want to ask you about sound and about the key role that sound plays in the transformational process of humankind in the past, present and future.

We are those of Q'uo, and are aware of your query, my sister. What an interesting question you ask us! You delight us! The quality of sound is, in and of itself, sacred. Sound is produced in a certain medium and that medium is the wind or spirit. So all sound, developed or undeveloped, retains and expresses

---

[53] This film is a groundbreaking story enclosing a documentary involving dozens of people who are aware of information indicating that our planet is moving through an enormous period of transitions and are attempting to help the planet make that transition safely as well as trying to help people who are interested in transforming themselves along with the planet to do so.

various aspects of divinity or sacredness. Indeed, there are sounds and combinations of sound that are like keys that unlock dimensions of what this instrument would call the inner and outer planes and open doors that are otherwise shut.

The world of sound, then, is a temple, a temple unrestrained by the ideas of humankind. When moving into pure tone or sound, one is moving into a world where there is great healing, power and a potential for transformation. Sensitivity to and response to the quality of sound is therefore a tremendous asset for one who wishes to create a magical instrument that will move people's hearts. Perhaps you may have noticed that when people stop talking and begin singing, their ability to open their heart and to lift away from the limitations of the intellectual is greatly enhanced. Indeed, each entity is an instrument and each breath is an indication of the kind of instrument that you are as a human being. You are a wind instrument and you are played by spirit. May the sounds that you make to each other be those of kindness, compassion, honesty and truth.

May we answer you further my sister?

N: We have made a courageous leap in the past few weeks in taking this film from a documentary style to that of a full-length feature film where the main protagonist is a highly evolved being who strikes up a relationship with an unusual young boy. They guide us through the film, meeting and talking to elders along the way. Can you clarify for me whether we are on the right track introducing a story line?

We are those of Q'uo, and are aware of your query, my sister. We smile through this instrument because we hear through this instrument's ears the barking of the dog[54] [representing] the craziness of the world around that has keyed into this conversation and is commenting in its own way.

As you can see from all the conversation, when you bring in a story, you bring in a magical and mischievous spirit. The question for you is whether you wish to have that mischievous spirit! For we guarantee to you that the story shall tell itself with its

own mischief and its own magic and you shall not be in entire control of this process.

We cannot say to you whether this storytelling is a good idea. It is entirely a product of your own discernment and judgment. We can say to you that in choosing to tell a story you join a very long line of wise, magical people who have decided to access the realm of the archetypal by parable rather than by discussion. We encourage you to be fearless as you proceed to use your discrimination and your heart in the unfolding of this purpose that you have chosen. We encourage you to trust yourself and to have faith, absolute and unwavering faith, in yourself.

May we answer you further, my sister?

N: Could you talk to me about how you see the importance of this genre of filmmaking when the media in our society seem so intent on sending us into a permanent sleep with their choices of programming, rather than awakening the masses?

We are those of Q'uo, and are aware of your query, my sister. We find in this instrument's mind a great deal of agreement with your judgment concerning this matter. We would say that this created situation is part of a concerted effort of the "dying dragon" this instrument spoke of earlier, of governmental and international sources of control, to "dumb down," as this instrument would put it, or to keep asleep the entities of this planet. We would say to you that you are choosing to attempt to create a teaching instrument for those who wish to listen and those who wish to learn. We would ask you what better thing you could do to increase the harvest at this time than create an instrument of inspiration and information? We ourselves are extremely well aware of the near impossibility of creating truth without distortion through the medium of language and yet, in our desire to be of service to the one infinite Creator, our expression of being at this time is wrapped up in this communication.

May we answer you further my sister?

N: Earlier I spoke about a transcribed channeling from Hatonn in 1974 where they said that most on our planet were like children in the evolutionary sense of the vast universe and that children will never understand [those things] of which we speak, however we phrase it, prepare it, or wrap it up to look pretty. So therefore we must focus on searching out the adults, again in the evolutionary sense, those

---

[54] Somewhere in the neighborhood of the Brinch-Haghighi home where this channeling session was filmed, a dog suddenly began barking hysterically, creating a very noisy background noise.

that are seeking. I ask this question in regard to our film again. Should we target the adults as our optimum audience, those that will understand and use this information as a learning tool, rather than an awakening tool to those asleep who resist awakening?

We are those of Q'uo, and are aware of your query, my sister. We find that although we would love to serve you, we are not able to address this question for you. When you plant a seed, it is as it is. Its habit, its form, its bloom and its harvest are all present to see. We perhaps could ask you if you feel that the seed of your film concerns itself with the environment in which it shall grow?

May we answer you further, my sister?

N: I'd like to ask you, if the truth of love becomes more obvious in the higher vibration now coming through on our planet, is the experience of love amplified with the higher frequencies? And how might we see that visually in a way that is not cloaked by illusion?

We are those of Q'uo, and are aware of your query, my sister. In many ways entities are seeing the miraculous occur every day and are simply becoming used to seeing the miracles. There have been many new forms of healing which have become mainstream among your peoples, at least within this instrument's environment. There are those who have been able to develop methods of healing that have to do with the touch of one entity to another. There are methods of healing which employ sound. There are methods of healing that employ subtle forms of energy such as the Reiki energy, as this instrument would know it, where miracles have occurred and this is taken as simply another form of healing, such as the healing of an illness that occurs from taking a medicine. Perhaps more than any other form of visible sign, we would suggest that which occurs among peoples when they change their minds. People have been increasingly more able to take hold of their minds and change them; to choose with power to speak their truth. And for them the world has changed.

The difficulty with many of these entities is that then they wish to create, around this new-found beauty of truth, a structure by which they may teach others the same thing and then be teacher of this. They have hardened their truth, which is entirely subjective, into a new form of dogma, which in the end is as dead as the husk that is broken when the seed sprouts.

May we answer you further, my sister?

N: I have a question around the heart and love. My concern for the film is obviously whether it is visual. What does love look like? Does the opacity change? Are the colors different? As for myself, I imagine colors that don't exist on our three-dimensional plane and it is for me to get that over to the audience. So what else can you tell me about what love looks like?

We are those of Q'uo, and are aware of your query, my sister. How accurate you are, indeed, to make the comment concerning the difference between third-density and fourth-density color. Many of those who have gone through awakening moments of realization, many of those who have gone through initiation in the sacred mysteries, as this instrument would call white ritual magic, have had these moments of seeing what this instrument would call the golden orb.[55]

The experience of color in fourth density is different enough that it is as though you were, in the third density of consensus reality, in a black-and-white movie and suddenly walked out into the colored natural light. Color, like everything else, is alive in the creation of love. It is not held into limits by the physical limitation of the physical vehicle of your species.[56] Therefore, it flows like a river. It has dimensionality rather than being a flat perception.

To achieve that quality you have most well chosen this dappling effect of the sunlight filtered through the elders of beech, oak and maple. It creates that quality of moving, so that colors can be seen to be streaming, beaming and living. This is the quality that you wish to capture. This is the difference. Certainly if you could photograph fourth-density color it would be a powerful, poignant experience in

---

[55] The Q'uo source is probably referring to the Golden Dawn initiation, which is a specific event within the so-called Order of the Golden Dawn which has had a checkered career. In its positive aspects it has offered a powerful structure within which many have studied and learned. In its negative aspects it has sowed many seeds of confusion, in the opinion of Carla, who has studied the history of this material and its various and varied adherents.

[56] Carla: I believe they mean that the optical limitations of the human eye cannot see beyond their limitations.

which colors seem to get incredibly intensified as well as being living and moving.

We believe that there are many unseen and, shall we say, mysterious ways in which each aspect that is mechanical or technical can be enhanced by the devas or spirits of all of those entities whom you interview and all of those places that you choose to hold those interviews, so that you are in fact receiving a great deal of assistance in creating magical and enhanced qualities in your filming. By the purity of your focus, you create the capacity of your machines. You use their lenses to see what you feel. May we thank you for the love for which you have brought to the creation of this instrument of teaching, sharing and learning! It is a blessing for us to share with you at this time.

Is there a final query at this time?

N: Yes, my last question is this. When sound reaches a certain harmonic or frequency, as indeed was practiced many hundreds of years ago, does it reach a point along the vibrational scale where sound becomes light becomes color until it finally reaches the place where healing takes place?

We are those know to you as Q'uo, and, my sister, we would be happy to attempt through this instrument to speak of things of which she has does not know.

You are working at a certain place in the inner planes which we can only describe to you as the point of the capstone of the pyramid where energy changes from one kind to another. You are attempting to catch the spiraling upsweep of the light/love vibration as it moves from what we can only offer through this instrument as the final point of the indigo-ray center, where it spirals into fire and becomes the time/space continuum of the dimension or density of love.

Further, you have attempted to combine the work that you have done that enables you to be a catalyst for healing at this particular and precise time with an energy that is within the heart.

Now, in terms of this instrument's vocabulary, we can then say that you are working with the combination of the energy of the open and sacred heart, as it creates a crystalline-like effect of spreading out the light or the sound or the vibration or the mystery, so that an entity to be healed can live, dwell or experience for that momentary time in that environment, with your ability to hold in a steady state the point between space/time for the physical world and time/space for the metaphysical world. This creates a flavor or a kind to your ability to act as a catalyst for healing in which the person is not simply healed by his own choice, choosing a less distorted balance in mind or body or spirit or any combination of those, but also in which that entity can choose to spiral with that energy into that point at which he may gaze upon that world of the fourth density and, in complete freedom, if he wishes, to choose to take a part in being in that environment, thus bringing heaven to earth, within the momentary point of sound, vibration or mystery, which is the environment which you have created.

May we answer you further, my sister?

N: I have one more question on which perhaps you can give me guidance. It concerns more my world than your world. How am I most likely to find the full funding for this project or some advice that might help me in that area?

We are those of Q'uo, and are aware of your query, my sister. May we say that this instrument has also asked us this question and we are as hopeless answering her as we are in answering you. However, we ask that you have faith and that you know beyond a shadow of a doubt that what needs to occur for the manifestation of this idea shall be as you need it to be when you need it to be.

In a word, our answer is, "No." We can say nothing helpful except that all is well. Go forth in faith. Visualize what you need very precisely and then, my sister, realize that you have created a thing, for thoughts are things. Let it take wing! Let it work within itself, as this instrument has been studying.[57] Do not hold it to yourself and repeat over those things that you need. But, each day, form one complete visualization. Ask with all your heart. Then release it.

Did the one known as Jesus the Christ not say to pray, "This day, give us our daily bread"? It is important to keep the focus local, to keep the

_____

[57] Carla and Vara had been reading from a little book entitled *Handbook for the New Paradigm; A Personal Message for You*, no author given, published by Bridger House Publishers of Carson City, NV, and that book puts forth the concept that a "thought released to act upon itself will return in manifestation glorified and in a form more magnificent than the limited, focused mind can imagine." (Quoted from page 5 of that book.)

moment [as] that moment which is present and yet at the same time to know that, as a person of power, what you visualize you will create. We always say to this instrument … be careful what you ask for you shall receive it.

We find that this instrument's energy does begin to wane. She is not aware of it. She shall not be aware of it until she leaves our company and your company and returns to a more everyday existence in which she is distracted from her truth, her focus …

(The film runs out in the camera, and the channeling session ends.) ❧

L/L RESEARCH

L/L Research is a subsidiary of
Rock Creek Research &
Development Laboratories, Inc.

P.O. Box 5195
Louisville, KY 40255-0195

www.llresearch.org

Rock Creek is a non-profit
corporation dedicated to
discovering and sharing
information which may aid in
the spiritual evolution of
humankind.

ABOUT THE CONTENTS OF THIS TRANSCRIPT: This telepathic channeling has been taken from transcriptions of the weekly study and meditation meetings of the Rock Creek Research & Development Laboratories and L/L Research. It is offered in the hope that it may be useful to you. As the Confederation entities always make a point of saying, please use your discrimination and judgment in assessing this material. If something rings true to you, fine. If something does not resonate, please leave it behind, for neither we nor those of the Confederation would wish to be a stumbling block for any.

SPECIAL MEDITATION
JUNE 24, 2005

Bath Spiritualist Church, Bath, Britain

(Click here to read Carla's introductory speech that she gave prior to the channeling below.)

(Carla channeling)

We are those known to you as the principle of Q'uo. Greetings in the love and in the light of the one infinite Creator, in Whose service we come to you this day. We thank you each for the privilege of being able to share our thoughts with you this day. We want to tell you how beautiful you are to us. This instrument was speaking earlier about the colors of the energy bodies and, to us, those energy bodies are your true nature and your true identity. We would know you without knowing your name by simply seeing the bouquet and the bloom of the colors of your energy body. You are truly a beautiful bouquet of spirit and it is an honor and a privilege to share our humble thoughts with you at this time.

We would ask of you one favor and that is to listen carefully to that which we say with a skeptical and a jaundiced ear. If anything that we say does not seem right to you, we would ask you to discard it without a second thought. We do not wish to become a stumbling block to you, to impair your progress or to infringe upon your free will in any way. We are not authorities. We are seekers, such as you, who have, perhaps, walked a few steps further than you and have a few more experiences to share. You are the only person that knows what is true for you.

Your discrimination is accurate. Listen for those thoughts that we may share that somehow resonate to you and do not be satisfied with anything less. If you will do this for us, we greatly appreciate your kindness. It will enable us to speak our thoughts to you freely at this time.

We would ask the one known as Vara if there is a question at this time?

Vara: Thank you, Q'uo. We humans have a habit of thinking there has got to be a purpose or a destiny in our life. And we've heard Carla speak tonight about being as opposed to doing. Could you comment on how we learn to be and how we tune in to the authenticity of our being so that we know when we're, in fact, on the right pathway?

We are those of Q'uo, and are aware of your query, my sister. The one known as Frank Sinatra said it so well, "Do-be, do-be, do." It's a dance between doing and being and doing and being. When you take a breath in, when you give a breath out, you are being. When by mind or by instinct you take thought or action, you are doing. The difference is simplistic. Yet, does the doing inform the being, or does the being inform the doing?

This instrument prays each morning, "Show me the paths that you have prepared for me to walk in." That is doing.

She prays again in the same prayer, "Help me to focus on who I am and why I'm here." That is being.

When you move from an idea of what you should do or what you must do, you are letting your doing inform your being. When, as this instrument said earlier, you move from a point of saying, "Where is the love in this moment?" and you take the time, whether it is an instant or a real minute, to look for that love, to look for that point of infinite intelligence that informs the situation from the standpoint of spirit, then you have begun to see into the deeper levels of the present moment. And when your heart opens and you say, "Oh, I really see how I can be a part of that love in this moment. I see someone who needs help," or, "I see where a good word would make this person feel more comfortable," then you may, perhaps, be doing something very simple, but you are coming from a point where you have centered yourself into your deeper essence.

What does a flower do? Each of you is a flower. What is the worth of a flower? The worth of that flower is that is has grown from a seed. It is expressing its own kind. It has color, it has scent, and it has its moment in the sun. You, my children, have your moment in the sun. You are breathing the air. You are blooming in the sunshine of the Creator's love, and for this tiny speck of time, yours is the choice of how you shall spend that time of blooming. When you find yourself being pulled and tossed, ask of yourself, the consciousness, to stop the doing, to center into the heart, and to become aware of the moment. There is love in this moment. Where is that love? Does it not begin with you?

Is there another query, my sister?

Vara: Thank you, Q'uo. We have observed people suffering sometimes throughout their lifetimes. We wonder if you could speak to the nature of suffering, the purpose of suffering, and, perhaps, the attitudes in how we see the love in suffering?

We are those of Q'uo, and are aware of your query, my sister. What an excellent question! We thank that entity who created it. For, truly, there is a great point to suffering and yet it is not the suffering that is the point. It goes beyond the suffering to understanding the reasoning behind the creation of a structure that, almost inevitably, will cause each entity who enters incarnation to be brought to her

knees by pain, whether it is emotional or mental, spiritual or physical, or any combination of those.

The Creator is not interested in your suffering. However, you, as co-Creators, looking at your incarnation to come, thought long and hard about how you wanted this incarnation to go. How did you want to bloom? What service did you wish to render? And, as you looked at yourself, the soul-stream that you, as an incarnate being, are only a part of, you said, "Spirit, how can I better balance the forces within me? Do I have too much power and too little wisdom? Do I have too much love and too little power? Do I have too much love and not enough wisdom? How can I arrange these energies within me, in a more balanced form, so that I am truly of more service to the one infinite Creator?"

And you began to make a plan. You chose for yourself your major relationships, your birth family or those who brought you up, your spouse or mate and those lovers and friends that have been important to you. You carefully chose even your enemies and those who wish you harm because you did not wish to waste the relationships in this life. Rather, you wished to use them in order to refine that within you which is yourself. Just as that which is crude goes into the fire that refines it, you chose a certain kind of refining energy that would circulate throughout your life as if it were a theme or a motif.

In your suffering, begin to look for the pattern of it. It is a good thing on which to use your head, to a certain extent. Analyze the pattern of your suffering. You can even analyze it in terms of what part of your physical body might be suffering. Are you carrying too much on your shoulders? You might be expressing that with shoulder pain. This instrument does. This instrument is not carrying too much. She is carrying just enough to give her the lessons that she wished to learn. Her choice was to learn to love without expectation of return and she carefully chose for herself entities throughout her life [for this lesson.] [She chose] not just her parents, for parents die; their gift has been given. What is balanced between her and them has been balanced and they have moved on through the gate into larger life. Yet the need to work on this theme continues throughout the incarnation.

Now, each within this group has chosen for itself incarnational lessons. And, every once in a while, you get that theme popping up, whatever it may be.

And again we say that each lesson is different. Some have to do with the right use of power. Some have to do with love, and sometimes that moves into questions of worthiness and unworthiness. Some lessons have to do with the right use of wisdom. You can be very smart without being kind. Where is the balance? Whatever your incarnational theme, it is relentless. And you created it to be so.

This instrument has often heard the phrase, "You never get more than you can take." And we believe that, indeed, this is so. Consequently, the question then becomes, when you perceive patterns of suffering, how to start discovering ways to use this information, these motifs, without having the necessity to go through the suffering. It is not the body that created the mind. The mind created the body. Any suffering that you experience has come first, in a very gentle way, to your thoughts and you have had the ability to look at your thoughts and to try to find that pattern within your thoughts.

It is helpful, may we say, at the end of the day perhaps, or whenever you find it useful, to go back through the thoughts that you have taken this day. What thoughts have occupied your minds this day? What patterns of thoughts have caused for you concern, mental or emotional suffering and what triggered those reactions? Was it anger? Was it feelings of unworthiness? Was it jealousy? What is happening?

What damages are you still carrying from your childhood and your young adulthood that you are repeating instead of exploring?

If you use the gifts of your own thoughts to examine them and when you begin to see a pattern then to move into that pattern with an eye to working with it, then you begin to see that most suffering is a series of triggers that you have allowed to be imbedded deep within you so that when something happens on the surface it creates a reaction that is greater than it deserves. Look for those inappropriately large reactions and responses. Look for the hidden triggers that mask the suffering that lies deep within.

And then gently, ever so gently, a little bit each day, go after those triggers. See what you can do to mine them for the treasure that they represent. For they represent parts of yourself, and the infinite hall of mirrors that other selves represent, that you have taken into yourself in a distorted and untrue fashion.

Bring them gently to the surface. Look carefully at them and begin to forgive the other person and yourself for the damage that has been incorporated within your being as a falsehood that need not exist.

Let the healing of your suffering begin. Let the healing of your incarnation begin so that you can, as this instrument said earlier, stand on your own two feet and look the world in the face, saying, "I know I make many mistakes. I am heavily flawed. Sue me. This is who I am and I am still ready to explore the possibility that love is the answer to all suffering." Lift up off the cross of thinking it is necessary. Realize it is a training aid. When the training aid is no longer necessary, then you may spend your time rejoicing and giving thanks.

May we ask if there is another query, my sister?

Vara: Thank you, Q'uo. On the topic of suffering and healing, we know of a child who is suffering from cerebral palsy and is totally incapacitated at the age of eight. Still, this child seems to be a healer, and, in fact, able to communicate with God. Could you comment on this particular instance of suffering and healing?

We are those of Q'uo, and are aware of your query, my sister. It is very difficult, we are aware, to penetrate the mystery of why people choose to incarnate in such difficult incarnations. It is, however, our understanding, limited though it is, that there are many entities who greatly understand that their particular lifetime gift is about being. This instrument incarnated in a body which was carefully chosen to malfunction in such a way that the instrument would be able to live but would not be able to be, physically, very useful.

We do not have to express this instrument's discomfort with this particular lesson. Each of you has had times of illness when you were not able to do what you normally do and it is very frustrating. However, it was this instrument's judgment of itself that it was too active as a soul, as an energy, and that it needed to move its focus carefully inward, not at one particular part of an incarnation but throughout the incarnation.

It is not that she chose for herself the pain or the suffering. She chose the limitation. When she accepts her limitations impeccably, she is able to skate through her days and her nights without perceptible pain. She occasionally achieves this state.

For the most part, she slips off of the razor's edge and experiences a certain amount of discomfort because she is attempting to do too much. And why did she choose this but because she was a greedy woman? She wanted to express, in one incarnation, the power of love, and in order to focus her very active mind, she chose ways of limiting herself so that she would continue her internal process without a let-up or a rest for the incarnation.

This entity of whom this questioner speaks saw the power of his soul stream and the energy of the gift that he wished to give in his blooming and he chose a pattern that seems very difficult. But, as you see, in this entity's very being he expresses the worth and the value of the human soul in incarnation.

We know we cannot penetrate this mystery in a short answer but we hope that this will suffice to begin to offer resources by which you may find ways to think about the issues involved in the being and the healing wholeness of that beingness, regardless of how limited its avenues of expression.

May we ask if there is another query at this time, my sister?

Vara: Thank you, Q'uo. We've been talking this evening about learning to love and to see the love in the moment and, with regard to the exercise of looking in the mirror, the faces I have seen often appear dark and gnarled or as if they are earthy, or nature-like, in appearance, even decomposed. Could you comment on what it is that I am seeing?

We are those of Q'uo, and are aware of your query, my sister. To a certain extent, we find that we are unable to comment because, to this extent, there is an active part of your process which we do not want to learn for you. But we may say in general that what you are seeing in these dark faces is portions of the incarnations of other incarnational forms of your soul stream. You have the experience of coming through all the densities up until this one. This includes the experience of being rock, sky, water and wind. It includes the experiences of many inner-planes beingness energies which are spirits of rock, wind and fire, and so forth. You have experienced being trees, animals and plants. And there are energies within second-density nature, such as what this instrument would call fairies, gnomes and trolls, for instance, where the by-play betwixt rock and animal is expressed.

As you look into the mirror and you begin to move into the vastness of your own experience as a soul-stream, that upon which you are working within this incarnation and at this moment creates the atmosphere in which you see certain aspects that are going to be helpful to you in your process on any of a number of levels that go on infinitely in the inner planes of your experiences.

We would suggest that you gaze, first, at the nature of your interest in yourself, at this moment, whether it is in life or death, in power or in peace, in love or in fear, in sadness or in joy, and as you sense into the environment which you have created in your path of seeking at this point, and you see whether you're in the noontime of joy or whether you are in the darkness of the dark night of the soul, then you may begin to sense into the reason for your seeing those faces of some darkness and roughness as you look into the mirror that opens your subconscious process to you.

We would ask, at this time, for a final query, my sister.

Vara: Thank you, Q'uo. We have a friend who is a devout Christian and deeply dogmatic in her beliefs. She is fearful for her friends' well-being, especially concerning channeling and the interests outside the Christian church. Can you give us some guidance on how to deal with this, and, in fact, how to deal with [our feelings of] anger?

We are those of Q'uo, and are aware of your query, my sister. Indeed, this instrument has experienced many years of dealing with the dynamic betwixt an inerrantist,[58] fundamentalist Christian brother and herself. So, through this instrument's memories, we are very well aware of the pain that ensues when a beloved entity, who wishes only for your best interests to be observed, seems to turn into an enemy of your process and your truth.

Let us take a step back from personality and circumstance into that great hunger that this instrument was talking about earlier that entities do have to know the one infinite Creator. In many cases throughout the history of humankind spirituality has hardened into religion. Religion is something this instrument enjoys. This instrument has been an Episcopalian all her life. She loves the spiritual

---

[58] inerrantist: someone who believes in the inerrancy or literal truth of a particular writing or document.

community. She loves singing in her choir. She loves praising and worshipping and giving the Creator thanks in the distortions of her church. However, to this instrument, there was never any thought of believing dogma.[59]

(Side one of tape ends.)

(Carla channeling)

"We understand mystics in this church," he said. "I have trouble with the virgin birth, myself. But I don't worry about it because I am focused on the mystery of deity." He said, "Don't leave the church, because you love Jesus and you won't be able to talk about Jesus with people that aren't in the church. But don't expect the church to give you the truth."

This instrument was very fortunate. For many people, the only way that they have found to approach their love of the one infinite Creator is to buy, as this instrument would say, hook, line and sinker, the dogma of a particular sect of a particular religion. For those entities who wish to do this, we may say that it is a valid path to the one infinite Creator. We would point out, however, that it is trammeled and slowed by the dogma which it carries and by those entities which are excluded from the love and the light of their Creator, in their story of the Creator, by judgment.

When you see judgment, you know that you have, somehow, lost the way to a true understanding of unconditional love. The one known as Jesus, this instrument's Master, hung from the cross, unjustly judged, in the story of its Crucifixion. And, in that story, two thieves and murderers hung, one on each side. And one of those thieves said to the one known as Jesus the Christ, "I know I don't deserve it, but, Lord, when you come to paradise, will you think of me?" And the one known as Jesus said, "This day you shall be with me in paradise."

Does your Creator open Its arms and say, "Everybody in"? If so, my friends, you are on the right track. And if you run into an entity whose fear of not making that heavenly gate is such that it must

cling to judgment, then bless that entity on its way and find ways to relate to that entity as a soul and not as a personality. Lift up beyond the details of its judgment of you and focus on your total acceptance of it. For it, too, is the Creator. It may have descended into fear. It may have chosen to judge others. And so that entity is creating an old testament Creation. But for you, it is a completely different Creation and you get to judge.

Shall you open your heart in compassion or shall you close it because you can see something that might be amiss in another? You have the power! Forgive, and that entity is forgiven, that entity is lifted up. Choose your judgments well.

We thank each of you for being with us this evening and for asking us to join your circle of seeking. It has been a privilege and a blessing to us. We leave you, this instrument, and all unseen beings who dwell with you in this sacred space, all angels and ministers, guides and entities and essences of the unseen realms. We leave you, as we found you, in the love and in the light of the one infinite Creator. We are known to you as the principle of Q'uo. Adonai. Adonai.

(Carla also gave a concluding speech on this same day that followed the above channeling.) ❧

---

[59] The material missing in this lacuna is a story from Carla's youth. When she was thirteen, she was in an Inquirer's Class at her diocesan Youth Camp which was taught by Bishop Marmion. She told the Bishop that she thought she may need to leave the church, since she could not believe in the Virgin birth. The transcript resumes with the Bishop's response to this statement.

L/L RESEARCH

L/L Research is a subsidiary of
Rock Creek Research &
Development Laboratories, Inc.

P.O. Box 5195
Louisville, KY 40255-0195

www.llresearch.org

Rock Creek is a non-profit
corporation dedicated to
discovering and sharing
information which may aid in
the spiritual evolution of
humankind.

SPECIAL MEDITATION
JULY 16, 2005

For the Ranger Gathering

(Carla channeling)

We are those of the principle known to you as Q'uo, and we greet you in the love and in the light of the one infinite Creator, in Whose name we serve and in Whose service we come to you this day. It is our privilege and our blessing to be called to your circle of seeking. We would thank each of you for creating this moment in time in order to ask us our opinions and we are very glad to share our opinions with you with the understanding that your free will not be abridged. And in order for this to be so created we would ask of you that each of you take absolute responsibility for your own powers of discrimination. Truth, which we came to offer, is a tricky thing indeed. It is subjective and entirely personal. Therefore, we would ask of you that, in considering each of our thoughts, you check your own energy for resonance with these thoughts. If our ideas resonate to you then by all means feel free to work with them. If for any reason they do not resonate to you, we would ask that you lay them aside without a second thought. It is our hope to offer helpful comments but, even more, we hope not to be a stumbling block in your way. If you can take responsibility for this discrimination and realize that you are the one and only authority for yourself, that will enable us to speak freely. We thank you very much, each of you, for this consideration.

It is our understanding at this time that you would wish to have a potluck session of question and answer and so we would ask if there is a question at this time?

B: We're setting out on kind of an adventure ourselves between Avalon and our Rangers. I was wondering if you have some history on the Confederation and their founding?

We are those of Q'uo, and are aware of your query, my brother. The question that you ask is deceptively simple and the answer must be carefully considered, for there are elements of our creation and way of being that are easily shared and other portions that must remain to some extent hidden in mystery. The Confederation of Planets in the Service of the Infinite Creator is the loose designation that our group was given in order to render us a named group and is a created name. The naming that is so dear to your peoples is not used beyond your third density because words, as opposed to concepts, are quite rough and even primitive in their structure, being delimited by the association of words and letters and so forth with parts of your consciousness which are heavily tied into the third-density brain or bio-computer. Thusly, our Confederation sourcing, while quite real, has, let us say, a number of aspects to it.

Each of you, as you sit in this circle of seeking today, represents not only you, yourself, an unique and precious flower in the field of the Creator. You carry with you a family of unseen presences. Within this circle, for instance, there are overlapping groups. More than one entity within this group is not only an individual but also a family member of the community which is represented in fifth density and in sixth density families from which you came to serve upon planet Earth as wanderers offering, at great risk to yourselves, your very self in the hope that by your very being living in flesh and bone, strangers in a strange land indeed, you would be able to offer that energy of unconditional love that would help to anchor the fourth-density energies that now are being seated within the planet that is being born as we speak, that Gaia that is a fourth-density, positively-oriented planet.

Each of you, then, represents not only the self but an extended family, as it were, of beings that have allied themselves in various partnerships for this period of time and space. There is a time upon your planet that is ongoing wherein all of your energies have been called to bear witness to the light and the love of the one infinite Creator. We, ourselves, as those of the principle of Q'uo, are part of two of those groups: that of the fifth-density social memory complex known to you as the group Latwii—we are speaking through this instrument at this time—and those of the social memory complex known as the group Ra, which are part of this principle and with whom we of Latwii and also those of Hatton discussed matters before taking up the time of channeling through this instrument.

In addition to those of Q'uo, there are many social memory complexes or planetary or societal groups of entities who have, as a group, chosen both to offer wanderers to the Brothers and Sisters of Sorrow manifesting upon your planet at this time, and to offer ourselves as requested by groups such as this and by channels such as this one, or, alternatively, to offer ourselves to those who call upon us, whose vibrations are resonant with ours, for work within dreaming, work within vision, and work within what you would call times of inspiration.

The energies of this loose-knit but entirely harmonious Confederation have been called into being by the times that you now are experiencing upon your sphere. This entity has often prayed for that which she calls her "fragile island home"[60] of

Earth. We also are in a state of constant prayer in support of this fragile island home as it revolves into an entirely new area of space and time, one that has alternative characteristics to third-density space/time.

It is our hope, as regards the planet you know as Gaia or Earth, that we may be a tiny part of your own efforts to anchor fourth-density light by your very being. We hope to be responsive to your needs and to offer ourselves as requested. Each of six civilizations that are relatively near you in space/time are the founding members of this Confederation, with many, many others moving into alliance with us as the plight of your planet has deepened. We became concerned for your planetary civilization some of your time ago. The second of three harvest-times upon your planet, 25,000 of your years ago approximately, had come and gone, with only approximately 150 of your planetary beings achieving the right to move through the harvesting procedure and enter fourth density for the lessons of love. It is to be noted in humility and gratitude that, rather than move ahead as a small but significant social complex to take up the lessons of fourth density, all of these entities chose, as one group, to remain within third density and immediately to seek reincarnation as third-density entities, having only their hearts and their wills upon which to rely in order for their memories of who they were to return. These entities have been called by this instrument the Elder Race and it is to be noted that there are those within this circle that are also representatives of this group as well, Earth's first graduates, who have immediately and unhesitatingly sacrificed any future lessons of love that may be in their future in order that they may spend not one incarnation or two or three, but 25,000 years' worth of constant and unremitting reincarnation into the planetary miasma and confusion as the third harvesting cycle has proceeded.

We have called ourselves Brothers and Sisters of Sorrow because we are the Brothers and Sisters of the unremitting sorrow of Earth. And why do we describe it as sorrow, my friends? It is due to the increasing heartfelt suffering and woe experienced by those who have attempted repeatedly, over and over, to awaken within the dream of incarnation, to remember who they are and why they are here, and to take hold of their intention to become fully conscious and awakened creatures of love. The

---

[60] That phrase is part of the Prayers of the People in one of the instrument's Episcopal Holy Eucharist services.

yearning has not died at all among your peoples. It cries out in its yearning to be a part of the awakening to love that the very planet under your feet is experiencing. Yet again and again there has been the seduction from love to fear, from unity to disharmony, and from that incredible experience of working truly together for common goals to the voices of division and hostility.

You have, in fact, through repeated exercises which have ended in empire, warfare and division, been trammeled and beaten down by those which have seized power and leadership upon your sphere to the point where your entire planetary sphere has been placed out of the normal stream of time/space and space/time onto what this instrument calls a time lateral. It is a kind of shunt where a train can move away from the main track until it is repaired. Your planet, in short, is undergoing repair and this not simply from one or two repetitions of empire but from, let us say, at least half a dozen majestic and substantial experiments in empire. Again and again those entities within your population who are inspired by the one infinite Creator have called the people of this planet to the reality of your unity as humankind to their planetary responsibility, each for the other, in love. These clarion calls to ethics, virtue and the higher morality have been heard and many are those who have been inspired to seek the one Creator and service to that Creator. Yet again and again the forces of fear have seduced entities enough away from the hewing to the light that the light has been unable to establish the kind of energy within your planetary sphere which would begin to accumulate mass of a spiritual kind, of gravity of, again, a spiritual kind or metaphysical kind.

At this point, the time allotted for such a time lateral is through within the next very few years. The opportunity for graduation to be a part of fourth-density, positive Gaia shall be over. We rejoice to say that this final effort of those who are ruled by fear and who wish to create what this instrument would call Armageddon has failed. This time, although the vast majority upon the surface of your planet are deeply confused, they are not fooled any longer. They do not believe any longer in the truth of those who speak of division, hostility, control of resources, and the advantages of war. These forces are certainly disorganized and puzzled. However, on a planetary level, at the level of the heart, there begins to arise, as this group was speaking of earlier, a feeling that is growing throughout all of the continents and all of the populations of your Earth. There is a growing knowledge that humankind is truly one. There is a growing awareness among ordinary, everyday people that the leaders that have been given power have misused it and are not to be trusted.

This basic breakthrough is recent and is indeed a product of many groups such as this one which have attempted to speak their truth with power throughout the last forty to fifty of your years. Great waves of entities have come among you and have begun to remember who they are. They have shared humor, art, stories and songs. They have lived lives that have inspired many. They have loved in ways that are as individual points of light that have begun to anchor, in a very real way, fourth-density values even in the apparently hostile fields of your civilizations.

We are as those who represent your ties with the larger family of the creation of the Father, as this instrument has often called the creation that is metaphysical in nature. We have an energy that this instrument would perceive as feminine. The balancing energy that is critical at this time in anchoring the love and the light of the one Creator for this passage for Gaia is the Goddess energy, shall we say.

We attempt not to use words that have emotional overtones. It is very difficult to find a non-emotion-ridden word for the Creator that indicates the essential balance of the feminine energy which is the dynamic opposite of those forces which may be described by gazing at what this instrument would call the Old Testament Creator, the Yahweh or Jehovah figure from your Old Testament of your *Bible*. The energy of Mohammed the Prophet and the one Creator named Allah are equally energies of a masculine, towering and authoritative nature. There was a time upon your sphere when this energy was appropriate. That time is long past. Yet those who have incarnated, from Atlantis to Babylon to Rome and so forth, have tried again and again and again to hold onto this increasingly sterile and unproductive creator-energy that is what this instrument would call yang in nature, exemplifying aggression and control, those things that, in the process of evolution, have become representative of service to self rather than service to others.

You may observe many figures which have attempted to express this feminine energy. The one known as Jesus, the one known as Mary, the one known as Quan Yin, and many others have expressed that yin creator-energy which is all-compassionate, all-loving, and all-understanding, all-inclusive and without the faculty of adhering judgment. Our hope, as a Confederation, then, is to rest in the love and in the light of the one infinite Creator within the inner planes of this planet, which this instrument has often laughingly called the parking garage. Many of those who come from elsewhere within the creation dwell now within resting portions or parking garages of your inner planes, in the sub-plane which is resonant with our vibrations. We rest here with many allies, those essences of all of your densities, first, second, third and so forth, which animate and enliven your inner planes and help to create a fruitful Earth plane for those within third density at this time.

We are not comfortable in going into our planetary origins or those lessons which we have learned on our way to being who we are and where we are, for in many cases part of the awakening process for people such as yourselves is becoming aware of the incredible connections with a very substantial family group that takes in inner planes and outer planes and all densities of this octave in its system of family relationships, alliances and spiritually based relationships. The inter-connectedness of not only our group, but our connections with each of you cannot be overemphasized.

May we answer you further, my brother?

B: Yes. You said that the Earth's "plight" concerned you. But you're already aware that it's a fourth-density, positive planet. So why is there a plight?

We are those of Q'uo, and are aware of your query, my brother. The plight of your planet is in its lack of, what this instrument would call, the hundredth-monkey effect, up until this moment in time. There are a very few of your entities which have successfully moved through the process of choice and have chosen polarity. Very few of these entities will graduate fourth-density, service to self. There is a larger, but still quite small group in relationship to the total population of your planet which has awakened and, by making the choices that they have made, become very viable candidates for graduation into fourth-density, positive Earth. They will continue as pioneers of fourth density here. And so far, those two populations have succeeded or potentially are on the point of succeeding, as they naturally pass through the gates into larger life and go through the graduation process.

There is, however, an enormous number of entities who have been unable, so far, fully to awaken to who they are or why they are here. That is why wanderers have come among you and that is why we have come into the wings, shall we say, to wait our turn to speak through instruments such as this one, in hopes of helping somewhat to call people to remember, to awakening and to becoming part of that conscious portion of planet Earth which can form into first a social complex and then a social memory complex as the graduation is moved through.

The plight is very dear to our hearts, as it is dear to the hearts of wanderers and those Earth natives who have awakened at this time. It is as though you are extremely close to developing a large enough group of groups of entities which, together, remember who they are. But they are on the verge of being able to firm into crystals that choose to vibrate, as one, the love and the light of the one infinite Creator. When this is done with enough mass of intelligent, conscious, choice-making entities joining in, there is a speeding up or a multiplication effect. The crystal that each of you is can choose to become a great deal more powerful as commonalities merge entities into groups and those groups into light sources.

Efforts such as this group's Gaia meditations, occurring daily, are one such crystalline effort which has indeed, over a period of your years, begun to affect the planet. Its choice of a non-location-oriented, daily witness to prayer and meditation on behalf of the planet has created an energy which is common to many points upon or, shall we say, close to your planetary surface which are yin rather than yang, shall we say, in their energy focus, which have represented or created the opportunity for, shall we say, the infection of larger groups of entities by the enthusiasm felt by individuals in becoming a part of the Gaia meditation. These non-local points of love call in a way we cannot describe rationally to the awakening processes within those who have not yet made their choice, acting as what this instrument would call "snooze alarms" to bring them to some point of increased wakefulness where they are more close to being able to see what this instrument would call the bigger picture of who they are and why they wish to wake up and what they wish to do when they wake up. However, that point where the hundredth monkey effect is triggered has not yet occurred. There is not yet quite the mass of light workers awake. And so the plight, basically, is to call people to awakening without infringing upon their free will. May we say that those who are service-to-self oriented among your peoples and are in positions of leadership are attempting very consciously to entrain peoples' minds …

(Side one of tape ends.)

(Carla channeling)

… and hearts in fear, in anger, in aggression, and in fear-based actions such as attempting to control resources. The seductive qualities of these energies lie in the simple facts of high second-density values such as those known to the great apes which are that type of second-density vehicle within which each of you now experiences life. These service-to-self oriented entities are well aware that their stated values echo instinctual values of the great-ape body and, in and of themselves, do not trigger a warning to the mind of the second-density body. It is perfectly naturally and entirely instinctual behavior within the great ape to protect the clan and the family, to gather resources that it will need and to defend against those who would disturb it. To awaken into third density itself is the challenge for the consciousness carried by this second-density body.

The consciousness of third density is, by its very nature, not only aware of the self but its instincts are to seek love, to seek to be loved, and to seek to become one. However, by repetitive experiences in empire, your peoples have acquired habits of mind which mitigate against a full awakening into the awareness of self as the choice-making self. And so the tendency of your planetary population has repeatedly been to give its power away to those who are skilled at the processes of creating empire. Therefore, at this time, the plight remains to help those who have been repeatedly a failure at waking up to become a success this time.

The great challenge, then, is to be a force in helping people to wake up without in any way infringing upon their free will. The choice to leave the precincts of fear and to step forward boldly into the unknown territory of unconditional love, release of

judgment, and the embrace of all entities, is formidable. The habit of doing so is not there.

If you succeed and we succeed in creating that hundredth monkey effect, there is the opportunity in these next few years of awakening a larger number of your peoples to their possibilities and of bringing people fairly rapidly into a state where they are able to graduate. It is a possibility that has an increasing probability vortex. All of you and all of those who are awakening at this time have a tremendous potential to change the face of your planet and to help many, many entities to take hold of who they truly are. We can only say with great humility that we are very glad to be a part of this effort and we thank each of you who has dedicated the life experience to the awakening of Earth and its peoples. It truly does begin with each of you and this is a time when a relatively small number of entities can make a pivotal difference in the harvest.

You must realize how close many, many of your people are, not only to awakening, but also to embracing their creator-selves, that heart of love that they feel lies within them without really knowing what it is for which they yearn.

May we answer you further, my brother?

B: No, thank you.

This instrument is telling us we need to be aware that it is time to start wrapping up this session of working and so we would ask if there is another query at this time with which we may end this session?

B: Do you have any suggestions on how to help those that are confused or those that are about to awaken, to awaken, and to realize who they are?

We are those known to you as Q'uo, and are aware of your query, my brother. What we would say to you is, perhaps, seemingly unhelpful, yet it is the heart of our message to all and that is that the work that you came here to do is work upon yourself. You are an individual. You are a member of the group of Rangers. You are a member of the tribe of humankind and you are a member of the creative principle. When you act, you act for and by yourself and yet, at the same time, you act as a Ranger and as a human and as the Creator. All of these aspects of yourself are equally true.

The aspect upon which you consciously can do work is the individual aspect. We would encourage you, therefore, to work within yourself, bringing yourself each day and each moment to the most sharp focus you can, to the highest tuning that you can carry in a stable and conscious manner, to the highest picture of dedication and service that you are comfortably able to achieve. You cannot know, nor does it matter, that you are, at the same time as you work on yourself, working on your group, the Rangers, working on your tribe of humankind and working as the Creator. It is not necessary that you see into these deeper and wider parts of yourself. It is important simply to keep the focus of consciousness bright so that you are a candle. We have said many times through this instrument that it would seem that one candle is a very weak thing, yet one candle can be seen for well over a mile if a line of sight is unobstructed. And a candle in the darkness is hope. So you represent, knowingly, one person and one process and one offering of love to the infinite Creator; yet you also are the candle that the wind cannot snuff out, that the darkness cannot overcome, and that no amount of denial by those who would embrace the dark can deny. You exist, a point of light and love. Simply know that as you do your work, as you breath in love and breath it out again, consciously blessing that energy as it moves through you, you are affecting your group, your tribe, and the Creator Itself.

We would encourage you, in fact, not to crusade for those ideas which we offer you this day. It is not a matter of the sharing of information, this matter of awakening the heart of humankind. It is more of an infective process. You are the secret agent of energies such as faith and hope. As entities about you see that you are undismayed by the apparent chaos around you, that you are hopeful in the face of all that you do not at all deny but instead, embrace, there comes to light within entities which dared not hope before the attractive possibility of hope. As entities see you launching yourself into the mid-air of a fool, leaping into the abyss by faith alone and then, as they notice that you are riding that abyss in joy, there awakens within breasts to which faith was previous a stranger that possibility of another way of looking at the illusion of planet Earth. As you penetrate the illusion, your eyes seeing clearly the light and love of the one infinite Creator, those who look into your eyes know what they cannot express and see what they cannot describe, and, for the first time, they believe in the possibility of faith.

So each of you is as one who mounts the steed of desire and that desire, once pointed, aims you in your armor of light towards what this instrument would describe as a knighthood. You are forming your alliances. Go forth upon the quest for the truth. And what shall you share of that truth as you ride, my brother? What gifts do your eyes have as they gaze upon all that you see? It is time to imagine and to dream and then to solidify your imagination and your dream in the envelope of your flesh, your blood, and your living.

We salute each of you. We hope that you will remember to ask for help. We and all of those who stand ready to help cannot do so without express request from you. So please, open your communication within to ask for all the help that your guidance system is ready to give you. Remember to ask for help from those with whom you share the dreams and the hopes of Earth. For there are many angels in flesh that await a word of the question for help at this time.

Most of all we encourage each of you to be fearless in seeking the truth, in seeking the heart of yourself, in seeking the one Creator. We greatly encourage you at this time to bloom as the true flowers of your people that you are. Trust in your beauty and your goodness and in your nature.

At this time we would leave this group and this instrument, as we found you, in the love and in the light of the one infinite Creator. We are humble before you and we thank you with all our hearts for this opportunity to share. We are known to you as the principle of Q'uo. Adonai. Adonai. ✤

L/L RESEARCH

L/L Research is a subsidiary of Rock Creek Research & Development Laboratories, Inc.

P.O. Box 5195
Louisville, KY 40255-0195

www.llresearch.org

Rock Creek is a non-profit corporation dedicated to discovering and sharing information which may aid in the spiritual evolution of humankind.

SPECIAL MEDITATION
AUGUST 21, 2005

Living the Law of One Conference, Wooded Glen, IN

Group question: We have spent this weekend here learning about the Law of One. For our question today, Q'uo, we would like to ask you how the energy that we have created here has been of service to our planet and how can we take this energy back to where we live and continue to live the Law of One as individuals and together?

(Carla channeling)

We are those known to you as the principle of Q'uo, and we greet you in the love and in the light of the one infinite Creator, in Whose service we come to you this evening. It is our great privilege and pleasure to be called to this group. We thank you for the beauty of your being and for your great dedication in reserving this amount of time to come together to seek as a circle and to choose to call us to your group for this session of working.

We are glad to speak with you this evening concerning the efficacy of your work this weekend and of your queries concerning how you may continue in the group which you have formed. But before we address this question, we would ask of you that you take responsibility for discriminating carefully [among] those words that you hear through this instrument during this session.

We do not come to you in order to be believed. We are as are you: those who seek, not those who know.

We offer to you our honest and sincere opinions in the hopes that they may be a resource to you at this time. Therefore, we would ask you to listen to our thoughts, and if they seem fair to you and resonate, to work with them as you will. But dear ones, brothers and sisters of the light and the love of the infinite One, if they do not seem fair to you and do not seem resonant, please leave them behind. We would not be a stumbling block before you as you seek the truth.

Truth is, to the best of our knowledge, a personal thing. What is true for you may not be so for another at this time in his progress, just as what is true for you today may not be true for you at another time, for you are evolving, growing and learning. Do not be afraid to release old truth from its stricture. If you will do this for us then we will feel free to share with you our opinions without being concerned that we are infringing upon your free will and this will be a great service to us, for which we thank you.

We have been with this group during your time together, being called by several among you on a regular basis as the weekend progressed. We can only thank you for the sincerity of your dedication to seeking the truth and to serving together.

We assure you that the love and the light that you have created in this temple that you have made of your hopes and your dreams in your coming together has been most helpful. And as you had hoped, there has been a significant calming and reassuring effect in a non-localized fashion, in a helpful fashion, upon the planetary entity you call Gaia or planet Earth.

At the same time, there has been great work done in open communication, springing from open hearts, so that each of you has been teacher to each and each of you has absorbed love, wisdom and power from each other like thirsty sponges. The beauty of your coming together and of the crystal that you have formed humbles us.

And we offer you our gratitude. We thank each of those who attempted to speak on Living the Law of One.[61] Each of those who spoke has pondered long and thoughtfully, reflecting upon what to say, what to share, and how to say it. We assure you that the energy of your voices, far more than the words that you said, has done the work that you had hoped to do and carried, in the breath of your life shared with this group, the golden energy of loving communication.

We thank those who worked so hard and perhaps did not say very much or perhaps said nothing but whose dedication behind the scenes has brought an energy that otherwise would not have been carried by this group. We have heard it said several times this weekend that the more humble the service, the more profound, and indeed this is so.

We thank each of you who has come to learn and has stayed to teach. Your wisdom, love and beauty are also that which opens our hearts.

And we thank the devas and the spirits of animals, wildlife, trees, bushes, grass and all of those forces of nature, elementals and inner-planes [beings] who have gathered about this group this weekend. The very Earth beneath your feet has been singing with joy.

You ask of us our opinion upon how you may take this experience with you and be faithful to its memory, continuing that which you have begun in this place. Our first thought or impulse is simply to underline and underscore that which you have heard several times from speakers this weekend. That is,

that it is within yourselves, within your processes in the work that you are doing in consciousness, within your being, to put it another way, that the center and the heart of your service lies as you move forward from this time and this place.

It has truly been stated by several among the speakers of this weekend that your greatest gift is to be yourself. It is very simple to say and somewhat complex and challenging to accomplish on a day-to-day basis. But the heart of all service is being and allowing your being to shine. And we say to you, "allowing," because there is a tremendous amount of courage needed in order to allow yourself to be most deeply and truly yourself.

Each of you wonders what truth you have found yet and how much of what you think about yourself is indeed true. We would acknowledge to you at this time that indeed that of which you are able to be aware on a conscious level within incarnation in third density is but the tip of the iceberg and often a misleading tip in terms of who you are as a soul stream. For you have not brought into incarnation your entire panoply of gathered resources and assets.

Before incarnation, carrying a fairly small basket and having a huge inventory of stock from which to choose, you chose carefully those qualities of personality, those gifts and those limitations which you would carry into incarnation as the soul of your personality. You chose very carefully, conscientiously and economically. If you have sometimes felt incomplete, there is a reason for that. Third-density consciousness cannot carry the soul stream in its fullness. Neither body nor mind was designed to support the whole self in space/time.

And so you left a good bit of your clothing, shall we say, in the closet at home. For you are a creature who lives at home in infinity and eternity. You dwell in time and space for very good reasons, for a very short time, and for a very short space. Your concerns [in choosing to incarnate] were pointed, plangent and specific. And these concerns moved you into incarnation at this most interesting time upon your planet.

Some of your resources were chosen for the confusion that they would bring you. Many of your relationships agreed upon before incarnation were chosen specifically for the woe and the suffering they would cause because you wished with all your heart not only to be a light unto the nations and a priestly

---

[61] "Living the Law of One" was the title of this Workshop Gathering. This channeling session was the last event of the workshop, which went from August 19-21, with a trip to Avalon on August 22 for those who opted to stay for that optional extension to the weekend.

people but also to work upon the balance between love, wisdom and power within your soul or soul stream, as this instrument often calls the entire experiential nexus that is your individual soul in its totality.

Each of you chose gifts that you hoped to share and these constitute possibilities for your outer service. Indeed, most of you have given yourself far more gifts than you need because so often plans go awry. So there is redundancy built into your system. If one path is closed, there are others that are set in place.

You shall not fail, within your incarnation, to serve. If you seem to be, at this point in your incarnation, at liberty, as they say in show business, and seemingly unemployed in your deeper, outer service, do not despair. Do not be discouraged. Be lighthearted, confident, at peace and at rest within your heart. As the ones known as Ra said through this instrument some time ago, there are no mistakes, although there are surprises.

This instrument has talked during her times of speaking as a human being and not as a channel concerning the nature of your being, your crystalline and powerful nature, your ability to do work in consciousness that might even seem miraculous. This is not a time to be proud nor is it a time to be overly humble. It is a time to rest in quietness and confidence, knowing that your guidance system planned an incarnation that you can accomplish and that you are accomplishing.

We encourage you to think of yourself, however, not as those crystals that must freeze into place and remain precisely as they are, such as your gems, your granite, and your rocks. For change is washing over your planet in wave after wave. We urge and encourage you to allow yourself to respond in cooperation and with a lack of fear to the changes that you now are experiencing and that you shall experience in the future.

We cannot tell you what those changes will be for you are writing the story of planet Earth. We can only tell you that groups such as this one, seemingly few in number, seemingly inconspicuous in the extreme, are in fact capable of creating very positive and very substantial change on a planetary level.

We have said many times through this instrument that each of you is as a lighthouse. Tend your light and let it shine. Polish the glass walls of the house of

self to be sure that the light that is flowing through you may cast itself out into the world around you without impediment or smudge. You are not the light. You cannot control the light. You are an instrument that allows the love and the light of the infinite Creator to flow through you and out into a dark world.

It is said in your holy works, "The light shined in the darkness and the darkness knew it not. But the darkness could not overcome it." Trust in this bit of wisdom. You cannot be stopped or overcome by anything but your own fear. Therefore, do not be discouraged, but simply persist, sensing into the present moment for the center of your desire and then pursuing that desire with passion and singleness of thought, as this instrument would say.

You have done your planetary work with exemplary zeal this weekend, coming together often to meditate upon behalf of Gaia in the cause of personal and planetary peace. We might encourage you to [continue that work] by joining the Gaia meditations whenever and however you can, for this is work that is well begun and you join a large number of people around the globe who are already dedicating time and heart energy to lightening the planetary energy in a non-local and reassuring way.

This instrument was warned by the one known as B before this weekend to encourage people not to focus upon local problems, not to focus upon politics, religious structures or any perceived points of difficulty within third-density planet Earth, for this kind of concern is that which crystallizes and focuses back into third density in a way that could be damaging to the development of fourth-density planet Earth. There is no need to break structures in order to create new ones for the simple reason that you are not attempting to fix third-density planet Earth when you work upon the grid of fourth density. You are simply joining angelic forces that have already been weaving golden threads into a net of love and light about your planet at this time.

This instrument has often seen the angels with their golden threads blending more and more substance as they ply their needles to intensify and strengthen the web of love. This is an image you are welcome to use. It is a true one. There are many ways to visualize turning your attention and your love to the cause of Gaia. You may visualize color and many have seen a violet color as the best way to strengthen the web of love. Others have seen golden light itself as a means of focusing your own love and pointing your attention.[62]

Whatever image or icon serves you, that is what we encourage you to use. For you are truly unique, an individual who is not built like any other entity in the universe. May we say that absolutely each [and every one] of you is essential in this work, for each of you is unique and your contribution can not be replicated. Trust that uniqueness and do not try to copy someone else, but go with your own feelings, your own resonance, and your own heart in doing the work that you came to do.

This is something that you seem to be doing, individually, and yet you now carry an identity as part of a family. This group has become a clan built of love and dedicated to service. In jest, an entity called this the "Wooded Glen Family." You may name it as you will, but we assure you that the nature of your bond is substantial and real.

And because you are who you are, you have brought with you your guidance system and those social memory complexes which some of you represent, which are millions and billions strong in some cases. You have brought with you angelic forces which have family connections as well. You are now a family with many, many in-laws, cousins, uncles, aunts, grandmothers, grandfathers and children, most of whom are unseen and many of whom are completely unknown to you.

Perhaps your greatest accomplishment as a group this weekend has been to turn to commonalities. And as you supported each other and listened to each other, you have turned the compass of your intention in one direction and that direction has been unerring. Continue to trust in the energy that brought you here and let it send you forth rejoicing.

We would at this time open the meeting to questions. Because this instrument does not have excellent ears at this point in her life, we would ask the one known as Jim, who is holding this instrument's hand at this time, to repeat questions and to act as the master of ceremonies for providing this instrument with those questions. We would at this time ask if there is a query in this group.

P: Would there be an auspicious time for us to meet next year?

We are those known to you as Q'uo, and are aware of your query. That which is auspicious to spirit is the now, the present moment. We do not know what present moment shall be auspicious to those who are responsible for the production of weekends such as this one.

It is, in some ways, helpful to consider such cycles as those connected with your lunar calendar and your astrological calendar, for there are cycling energies that surround your planet. And yet we would point out to you at the same time that this particular weekend took place when, as this instrument would say, Mercury was retrograde, and it did not stop or even hinder you in that which you hoped to accomplish.

There were those who had to move heaven and Earth to find the time to come here this weekend, as was certainly true of the one known as Jim, who was mowing grass up until the last minute and got to this conference with ten minutes to spare before its beginning. He was amazed that the grass started to grow after two months of drought, the very week that he was hoping for a little extra time! So we cannot express to you some favored moment for meeting but shall leave it to the free will of those who seek very humbly to serve by planning such weekends and such times together.

We would ask, as this instrument asked before this particular session of working began, that each of you spend time pondering what you would like to learn to investigate and to discover at this reunion what you hope will take place next time, so that as you enter again the clan atmosphere and come home to each other for more work together, you will have the feeling of a progressive investigation of love and light and living the Law of One.

May we answer you further, my brother?

P: No.

Is there another query at this time?

L1: For those of us such as myself that are interested in working more closely with the deva kingdom but who have not really had the experience of being introduced to a way to be able to communicate with them, do you have any suggestions as to how we

---

[62] For more information about the daily L/L Research Gaia meditations, you can go to www.llresearch.org and click on the Gaia Meditation navigation button.

might initiate that process in order to be able to do planetary work?

We are those known to you as Q'uo, and are aware of your query, my brother. We would say to you that, first of all, before we say anything further, we would encourage you to listen to those known as V and B as you visit that place known as Avalon Sacred Growth Center, that part of L/L Research dedicated to harmonizing the densities and creating a safe place for them all in the valley of Avalon. These two entities have had much experience working with the deva kingdom and they are glad to create a teach/learning circle as you walk that sacred ground that has just begun to be given full permission to thrive and to speak truth to those who walk upon her meadows and hills. After you have heard a few thoughts from these very dedicated lovers and stewards of Gaia, you shall perhaps feel an inspiration that has a vector that points you in a direction that you may understand.

Beyond that we would say to you that the universe as a whole in general, and the locality of any place upon which you set your feet in particular, is already communicating with you to the extent that it feels you will hear it. In order to intensify and enhance this communication you have only to ask, in humbleness and in sincerity, and with a mind empty of presupposition, and then to listen to that which occurs.

The one known as V was talking earlier of noticing and paying attention to the little things that nature expresses. She spoke of the march of three spiders walking in a row; "What," she said, "could this possibly indicate?" We think of many times this instrument has taken one blossom, a convocation of birds, or a visitation of a deer with two fawns and had information flow into her perceptive web and into her archetypical work because she simply noticed …

(Side one of tape ends.)

(Carla channeling)

… the gift of the moment. It is a matter, first, of simple faith, and then of focus. How easy it is not to pay attention, to let the mind drift and dream its way back into the world of commercial jingles, fast food, and the concerns of the moment.

If you wish to work with the devas, they are everywhere and are most thrilled at the opportunity

to be heard. Naturally, for most of you, it will be difficult at first to feel with surety that which the devas wish to express. Yet sheer repetition of asking brings its own results. We assure you that simply knowing that you stand in the kingdom of the devas and expressing that knowledge to that kingdom will yield tremendous and efficacious results.

It is not necessary even for you to know the nature of the communication that has taken place in a conscious manner, for much of the work of the devic kingdom is accomplished in an unseen and inner level. Yet the results of that partnership and that coming together of human and devic creates the environment for the thriving of those plants and animals for which the devas stand. This instrument has often said that her husband only seems to be mowing lawns and making gardens. In truth he rides upon his chariot into the kingdom of the devas and does his dance with them. And those portions of the creation which have the blessings of his dance with the devas do indeed shine.

When you are in your focused state of mind and you are walking upon the ground, feeling the wind, living in the kingdom of the Creator with awareness in a conscious manner, you cannot help but interact with the devas. Come to them with joy and know that they come to you with joy. And if you cannot whirl and spin with the joy that you feel, let your spirits reel and whirl and do that dance that is so helpful to you and to them.

May we answer you further, my brother?

L1: I thank you very much.

We are Q'uo, and we thank you very much, my brother.

L2: Can you tell me how best to focus my energies to increase my psychic awareness?

We are known to you as Q'uo, and are aware of your query, my sister. We examine this question for that which we may say to you, for there are many things that we cannot say to you. You are working to make choices as part of your process at this time and we would not infringe upon your free will at this time by making specific suggestions. We can say, without hesitation and with absolute sincerity, that you are doing a wonderful job. You are listening and seeking with all your heart. You who seek shall find. To those who knock, the door shall be opened. Do not doubt your process or your intuitions. We have perfect confidence in you. We believe in you and love you for that which you are hoping with all your heart to do, to serve.

In looking at the general question of opening to a more profound use of subconscious material by the conscious mind, which is the essence of that which is psychic, we would ask you simply to stay humble and empty and quite secure in the knowledge that you do not know and cannot know the efficacy or the success with which you serve. Indeed, you should mistrust those easy feelings fed to you by those who would flatter you and tell you how psychic you already are and so forth. Allow time and silence to nourish you.

And when you feel resonant and powerful and you have moments of realization, rest in that moment as long as it will last in a natural fashion, not holding it, not trying to glean more from it than is there, but allowing the process to work.

Resources for those who would improve the depth of their psychic nature and their awareness of their own process have been spoken about quite a bit this weekend. Depending upon your nature, your personality, and the way that you have worked in the past, you may be more or less sensitive to various kinds of work in consciousness.

For one entity, a dream journal is the very best way to proceed in a safe and stable manner into work in consciousness. For others, such as this instrument, the oddities and quirks of psychism within her personality are such that when she opens that door and begins to journal her dreams, she stops sleeping and creates so much material that it is impossible to work with it. Consequently for this instrument, the best way to improve her psychic abilities is to take time off on a daily basis and to chill out, as this instrument would say, resting from her labors and not pressing forward with any degree of impatience but rather trusting that, for her own process, the material of a consciously lived day is more than enough to stoke her process.

We would suggest that you play with the various ways of investigating the archetypical mind. We would suggest that, among other things, meditation, walks in nature, discussion with those of like mind, the reading of materials may be inspired and inspiring. This does not exhaust the long list of ways to seek in this way but it gives you an idea of the kind of focus that may be helpful to you.

The life that supports such work is a life that continually investigates the possibilities for seeing sacredness in everything, every thought, every chore, and every moment. The work of deepening one's psychic abilities is not divorced from the work of shopping and cooking, child raising and cleaning. It is inextricably intertwined with the nuts and the bolts—as this instrument would put it—of living the simplest form of life, perceiving and accomplishing the duties that you see before you.

In truth, all things done with love are sacred. And when you are dwelling in the universe that you create of the actions and thoughts of love to the best of your ability, you are creating for yourself an optimal environment in which, in a stable and conscious manner, to deepen your psychic abilities.

To be mistrusted are those ways of deepening psychic ability that take you away from the heart of your family, your work, and all of those mundane concerns that are considered worldly. We do not encourage going apart and considering yourself to be on a special mission.

Rather, we would encourage your allowing this gift to develop in the midst of your daily life. We would, however, specifically encourage your seeing the value and the giving yourself the opportunity of time for yourself. We do not know what you would wish to do with this time. For this instrument, with her great love of ritual, the time that she gives to herself is time dedicated to what she calls her morning offering and her Gaia meditations. Further, she is very fond of working on tuning herself as she goes through her day, taking the time before answering the door or the telephone or starting a letter to ask for help to be sent to herself that clear her own energies so they do not pollute and spoil the environment in which the moment is met.

If these thoughts are resonant to you, we encourage you to attempt to follow through with some of them but we say, do this playfully, lightly, with an eye to seeing what makes you joyful and what makes you laugh. For it is not a burden that we would put upon you.

It is said—and we apologize for using the contents of this instrument's mind which are strictly and profoundly Christian—"His yoke is easy and his burden is light." This is the energy that we would transmit to you at this time in the way of saying that, as you pursue the most serious and profound of attempts to dedicate yourself, your life, and your service to the one infinite Creator, balance lies in achieving a lightness of purpose that equals the profundity of your determination to move forward.

That which unbalances those with psychic gifts is eagerness, a feeling of intense urgency, and other such energies which pull you away from the slow and steady progress that keeps you within your body, your mind, and your emotions and that unbalances that integrity of self which for many who are gifted psychically is somewhat fragile.

When you are working with psychic gifts, you are working with a vast multitude of energies that are unseen, essences and entities who are not necessarily friends to your service but who would do mischief to you, distract you from your path, and even drive a wedge into your personality shell that completely unbalances your waking personality.

Therefore, we encourage you not to work in a consciously psychic manner without either [having with you] an experienced psychic along the lines of that service you wish to perform or working within your guidance system. If you stay within your guidance system then you cannot be infringed upon by outer influences that do not belong to you and do not have your best interests at heart. Those ways of working within your guidance system include many things that you have heard this weekend. The journaling is a waking way of creating a safe dialogue with the self that deepens an awareness of one's psychic abilities. You may simply write down a question and then wait and when thoughts come into your mind, write them down. Do not attempt to share this wisdom with others but listen to it yourself.

May we answer you further, my sister?

L2: No, thank you very much.

We thank you, my sister, with all of our hearts. And we thank each of you, for we see this determination and dedication and the love that you have for the Creator, for the work, and for each other. And we are humble before you.

Is there a final query at this time?

M: I have a question about the conscience and how it relates to the guidance system. I don't know if it's too broad a question. What is the conscience?

We are those of Q'uo, and believe we are aware of your query, my brother. You are asking about the conscience, not consciousness, is that correct?

M: Correct.

"Conscience" is a word that can be used interchangeably with "ethical awareness." Conscience is a very personal thing, as are ethics. Much has been said during this weekend concerning becoming aware of the self as a choice-maker, and certainly this instrument is a prime example of one whose life has been absorbed from a very early age with fascination for the dilemmas of conscience.

We would say to you that conscience is a very personal thing. It is part of the instinctual web of self that defines third-density awareness. And by that we do not intend to mean, by "third density awareness," the simple awareness of life, but rather that which awakens during incarnation because of a growing desire to penetrate beneath the surface of questions such as, "What is right? What is wrong? What is fair? What is unfair? What is just? What is unjust?" and so forth.

Each entity moves into incarnation with a slightly different set of sensitivities to moral or ethical dilemmas. Some entities are roughly or insensitively wired so that it takes a great deal to awaken the pangs of conscience. Others are wired with such delicacy that there is almost nothing that does not awaken the conscience, does not awaken the questioning process. It is a very personal thing.

When you as an entity perceive that there is a question as to what is the right thing to do, you may trust that you have awakened your conscience. We would simply encourage you to follow the thoughts that you have when these concerns arise.

But we would also encourage you to remember that you came here with the desire to love and to serve, not to judge. So in pursuit of ethical and moral action, we would encourage a dispassionate, compassionate and systematically passionate attempt to be an agent of love.

We would encourage you to invoke your own creativity and to ask for guidance. For there is always a bigger picture to see, a wider point of view upon which to plant your feet, so that your conscience awakens in you your highest and best response.

May we answer you further, my brother?

M: Thank you very much.

We thank you. This instrument's energies wane and we have been careful to allow our energies to flow in a particularly slow and careful way through her this evening. We thank each of you in the circle for lending your love and light to the circle. It has enabled this instrument to end this channeling in a far better situation than she entered it. And that is part of the power of a group such as this one. The combined energy of the group is such that, though each is imperfect and has many flaws, the combined energy of the group is far more powerful than any one of its members and far more efficacious to serve.

We leave you in the love and in the light of the one infinite Creator. We are known to you as the principle of Q'uo. Adonai, my friends. Adonai. ✿

L/L Research is a subsidiary of
Rock Creek Research &
Development Laboratories, Inc.

P.O. Box 5195
Louisville, KY 40255-0195

L/L RESEARCH

www.llresearch.org

Rock Creek is a non-profit
corporation dedicated to
discovering and sharing
information which may aid in
the spiritual evolution of
humankind.

SPECIAL MEDITATION
AUGUST 24, 2005

Question from J: Q'uo, please offer me any information regarding my spiritual journey which you feel may be helpful to me at this time.

(Carla channeling)

We are those known to you as the principle of Q'uo, and we greet you in the love and in the light of the one infinite Creator, in Whose service we come to you this day. We are most pleased to speak with you and we thank you for setting aside this time to ask for our opinions.

It is a great privilege and pleasure so to be asked and we would, as always, simply request of you that you listen most carefully and with discrimination to those things which we have to say. We are not authorities over you and all we are doing is offering our opinion. Informed though it may be, it is not always on target for a particular person at a particular time and consequently it would enable us to speak far more freely if you agree to listen with great care to those things which we say, following only those thoughts which seem resonant and helpful to you and disregarding and leaving behind the others. We thank you for this consideration.

To those one known as J, we would say that the spiritual path upon which his journey is being taken is fair and bright. Sometimes when entities ask us to examine the path of their seeking, we see a certain amount of distortion and confusion. In your case, my brother, we see steps being made with care and

with joy, with a sense or feeling of great spaciousness and a lack of concern about the opinion of others which greatly frees you to examine, in a measured and leisurely way, the material that comes before the face each day. The eyes and the ears and the sensibilities report to you and you take the time and offer the attention to follow the threads that you receive. We congratulate you on having achieved a great measure of maturity, especially when one considers that you dwell within third density with its seemingly endemic and chronic rush and hurry.

We would also say to you that these characteristics have been achieved at some cost. As you continue on your path, we would encourage you simply to continue to follow the threads that are offered to you in the moment, whether they be treats of the eye, visitations by, shall we say, your totem, or those many synchronicities of number, name and word that one discovers in moving through the normal day-to-day experiences of, as this instrument would say, the street signs, the billboards, and the conversations with strangers as one goes about one's chores.

There are doors which, without realizing it, you have closed in the very focused and concentrated seeking for the widest possible point of view, speaking in a metaphysical fashion. These are doors that you perhaps did not intend so thoroughly to close. We assure you that it is a matter not of retrieving something that has been lost but of balancing and therefore bringing into a more harmonious configuration the various characteristics which are part of the dynamic of your deeper self. The day-to-day experiences are ample for providing you with the clues and the inklings that will guide you in terms of how to become more and more able to open your wings and feel that you truly are balanced and that there is no characteristic which is precious to you that you have left behind.

All in all, we offer you our esteem for the work which you have put into creating and sustaining a spiritual seeking and we can only encourage you to move on as you are now. We do not have specific suggestions to improve your walk at this time.

At the end of this series of questions with which this instrument is familiar, we will ask if there are follow-up questions. If it is satisfactory to the one known as J, we would move on to the second question at this time. May we ask if the one known as J would speak the second question at this time?

J: I've spent over two decades working with the Rotary Club organization and I feel this is service-to-others work. Can you confirm that this work is service to others?

We are those known to you as Q'uo, and we certainly can confirm, my brother, that such work as that estimable organization, with which this instrument is also familiar, is indeed service-to-others work. Indeed, any organization such as the Rotary Club which attempts to give back to the community which has given to the members their livelihood and their life is an estimable and honorable mission.

There are indeed many, many ways to serve others. A wide variety of choices awaits those who attempt to survey the possibilities for service within your community. There are many things one may do as an individual and they are all most worthy.

Yet when one is working within a group, one has a much expanded opportunity to investigate what it is to be of service to others. The great value of groups that come together in order to serve is that they reflect two ways. They reflect out into the world, as is the conscious intention of such a group. One is able to create, as an offer to the community, projects and systematic attempts to serve that are able to be offered over a period of time with steadiness and stability. This takes a group of people out of

themselves and lets them have a look at living their beliefs in such a way that they are truly of service to others.

The hidden benefit of such a group is the opportunity that the members of such a group offer to each other for learning about themselves. This instrument has spoken often about the mirroring effect of other people in her life. And certainly, this mirroring effect is greatly enhanced when a group which is conscious of wishing to be of service comes together in commonality of purpose and offers friendship and companionship, one to the other.

Each entity becomes a mirror that reflects back to the self what the self is creating and expressing within that group. Certainly, many of the reflections which one receives from such a hall of mirrors, as this instrument has called a spiritually-oriented group, may be warped or distorted in some way, therefore not offering a completely accurate image. However, the colorations and distortions offered by each entity within the group are in themselves interesting and offer in some cases that precious item which is so often under-appreciated by your peoples; that is catalyst. Even those who may see you in a critical or otherwise distorted fashion are of benefit to you in that they offer you material upon which to work both by using your powers of analysis and your powers of intuition and insight.

May we ask for the third query at this time?

J: I feel I am more than 51% service-to-others in polarity. Could you confirm this and offer any comments you feel would be helpful?

We are those of Q'uo, and are aware of your query, my brother. We can confirm that you at this time are at a level of service which commends you well towards the energies of the graduation process. Naturally, until you walk through the gates of larger life, the picture that we see of you is a picture that is yet unfinished. The signature of your life shall only be written at the corner of this picture as you walk through that gateway. That shall be your final reading. However, we would dare to say without infringing upon your free will that the likelihood is that you shall continue to hold this level of service-to-others polarity or improve upon it, given your distortions and your dedication towards seeking at this time.

We would have some general comments to make upon this basic concept of polarity and graduation. It is not often understood among your peoples that it is extremely difficult to achieve a service-to-others rating of 51% or greater. Indeed, in our opinion, it is as difficult to achieve that rating as it is to achieve the obviously difficult rating of 5% service to others which is the standard for graduation from third density for those who are seeking along the path of service to self. In the case of service-to-self polarity it is overtly clear as to why it would be difficult to achieve such a rating. The purity of thought necessary to achieve the level of self-discipline and control inherent in seeking to control others 95% of the time is patent. There is no one who would argue that it is an extremely difficult and challenging feat to achieve such a polarity.

It is far more difficult to see into service to others to understand why it would not be equivalent to attempt to obtain a service-to-others polarity of 95% service to others as a balance to 95% service to self in the opposite polarity. However, the orientation of third density is geared towards a world that is not neutral but that is outwardly biased towards service to self.

To an extent, this was done on purpose in that it was taken as given and accepted by the Creator of this planetary experience that the end of second density contains within it an orientation which, when translated into third-density terms and elements of consideration, is inherently, seemingly, service to self. In terms of second density and the instincts of the higher apes—of which your body is, shall we say, a development or a greater ape, but still containing the orientation of the great apes—the instinct to protect the clan and to defend the clan and the supplies needed by the clan for survival are neither service to self nor service to others but simple pure instinct.

When this instinct is brought through into the beginning of third density, it cannot immediately be said in the innocence of a first incarnation in third density to be service to self, but rather to be the first experience of the inheritance of, shall we say, the gene pool, the inheritance of the body. These instincts and this body are part of third density in order to offer entities of consciousness the best possible chance to have an experience in space and time that is rich with material to work with in order to investigate what it is to be the self.

In one way, and we do not say this to confuse you but simply to give you, as the one known as Vara would say, a baseline, the life experience is satisfactorily accomplished if one is a responsible observer; if one observes and notes all desires, and if one follows through on all of the desires that are felt until those desires are satisfied. In another sense, and on another level, this degree of participation in the experience of consciousness within incarnation is not sufficient, and that is where the being of the self, once investigated, becomes paramount. For that beingness is beingness which is constantly being invited and invoked by the being.

Each entity has the choice of what level shall be investigated within the self. There is a surface aspect to the entire question of selfhood in which the experience of many within your consensus reality lives and moves to the exclusion of any other level of awareness. This is the level of your consensus reality where the attention is caught up in the affairs of the day. It is possible, and indeed probable within your culture, for entities to rest comfortably within this level of awareness and to participate in what seems to be a full and rich life without ever waking up to the drama of infinity, eternity and timeless themes of investigation which, when pursued, offer to the discerning entity an infinite array of opportunities to plunge into the depths of the infinite and eternal self.

This infinite and eternal self has various aspects. One aspect is almost completely chaotic and it is maintained as chaotic and over against any attempt to organize or structure these deeper truths of being, in order to offer a continuing freshness and originality to the investigation of self by self.

However, it is usual for entities to find ways to structure or organize this deep well or kingdom, shall we say, this realm of information which can fruitfully be plumbed or mined in order to work with the dynamics of various threads of interest which have sprung naturally from greeting life experience and the coincidences of everyday life. This instrument, for instance, finds it useful to use the structures of philosophy and religion as it works with its own attempts to note down and to follow observations it has about itself, its feelings, its thoughts, and its deeper beingness.

These efforts to know the self dwell within a life that, in its outer characteristics, must continue to cope with and address the societal and cultural overview or environment in which the seeker dwells. And if looked at with some care, it can be seen that the societal constraints have a strong tendency towards a service-to-self concept, theme and orientation.

Consequently, the default position, shall we say, of one within your society or culture, entrained by the authority figures of parents and teachers of childhood, is quite mixed and is perhaps at a balance point or a resting point, if one pictures a swing of a pendulum, at approximately 25% service to others and 75% service to self. This may seem to be quite cruel, and yet it is the natural result of the interactions of those who are dealing with consensus reality issues, such as survival, making a living, and defending the family against what it perceives to be situations and elements which may tear it apart.

Added to this is the situation which is unusual upon your planet, in terms of planetary entities as a whole throughout the infinite creation of the Father, where entities have come to this third-density experience upon planet Earth having already made service-to-self choices repeatedly within other planetary experiences, so that unconscious and yet very well established habit acts as a passive force which pulls unconsciously at an entity's ethics or conscience saying, "Please be sure that you have taken care of the self, the family, and the structures that you wish to defend." This tendency pulls the natural default position or the resting position of the pendulum of service to self versus service to others down to about 20%.

Further complicating the efforts of one who wishes to polarize [towards] service to others is what we would call a lack of concentration that is endemic to your peoples by virtue of the culture in which you live. It is difficult to sustain complete focus or attention. Therefore a very genuine and sincere effort to make a foundational choice of service to others may be made with the utmost purity of intention and utmost and complete dedication to sustaining such an effort. However, the natural tendency is to lose or be distracted from that focus.

This does not occur in obvious ways sometimes, but it is a natural occurrence which is preordained by the tone and the nature of the surrounding environment in which you are doing spiritual work. In order to persist in polarizing efforts, it is necessary to be quite unnaturally focused, compared to your societal norms. And entities may even say to you that you are driven or that you are obsessive concerning the spiritual walk when they observe the degree of effort in you which is necessary to continue making choices which back up your foundational choice of service to others.

With that said, you may perhaps begin to see into the ways in which you have been challenged throughout your long process of attempting to become more and more a creature of conscience and ethics. It is not that you have insincerity or that you lack focus but rather that there is the very deep tendency from old habit in previous lifetimes and the childhood of this lifetime that tend towards creating many instances in which there is a very natural and seemingly open door which one may slip through and lose focus and lose that purity of intent.

The challenge, of course, is to find them and shut those doors so that one continues on being very conscious of one's tendency of losing focus so that one is encouraging oneself constantly to pay attention and to increase the level of observational accuracy in moving beneath the husks of outer experience into the seed and the fruit of inner experience.

Is it any wonder, then, that 51% service to others is enormously difficult to achieve? That you have achieved this rating is an estimable thing for which we offer you our respect and thanks.

As you continue to work with yourself in this hall of mirrors upon planet Earth, we simply encourage you to balance focus and sustained effort with a lightness of touch which enables you to thrive and to experience joy and laughter as well as a good conscience. We offer this instrument the figure of Kokopelli, in order to attempt to make the linkage between humor and even mischief more obvious.

In spiritual seeking, to be without humor is very easy when one is focusing with all one's effort and intent upon the spiritual path. Yet for one who does this it is as if one is carrying all of the seriousness of this intention upon the shoulders and it is a difficult thing to carry such intention.

In working with lightening this load for the self, it is well to investigate the faculties of faith, trust and hope. This instrument has often used the term "grace" to indicate that there are times when she feels that only through grace has she been able to sustain an effort or to be successful with an intention. And this term grace is a general term indicating that the Creator cuts one some slack, as this instrument would say in a slang way.

We would say it in another way which is yet equivalent to this image of the Creator cutting one some slack and giving one some grace. If you can internalize the voice of the Creator within the self, it becomes the voice of hope, faith and trust. If you internalize grace and you are not looking outward towards a figure that is the Creator, but rather are looking at the consciousness of the self, that consciousness has the power to give or to withhold any aspect that you may wish to give or withhold.

The aspects one is tempted to withhold from the self of the one infinite Creator, when internalizing these voices of self from the Creator's level, are those aspects that may positively be seen as trust, faith and hope. It does not seem entirely humble or natural to trust the self, and yet it is that trust in the self that enables one to take a deep breath, let it out, and relax.

It does not seem entirely profitable to spend time in hope, for hope is intangible, having to do with a future that is not yet, or having to do with assigning value to the present in a way that cannot be said to be provable at all. Yet it is of great value to encourage hope within oneself; not hope in anything in particular but simply that faculty that always hopes for the best outcome.

For this faculty of hope colors the energy with which one meets the present moment. It is perfectly natural to be skeptical and we encourage those energies of skepticism. But skepticism is endemic to your culture whereas hope is not. In order to balance the self, it is precious to realize that hope is as real as balance and is much to be trusted within the self as an energy that has honor and virtue.

And when we begin to talk about the faculty of faith, we find ourselves up against the full stop of our ability to speak in language, for faith is not only an aspect of the Creator's internalized voice. It is the very Creator, seen in the hall of mirrors that projects infinitely, just as the hall of mirrors at Versailles reflects the reflection which reflects the reflection, infinitely. This faculty of faith is not only an aspect of the Creator; it is the very gateway through which the self meets the Creator and the Creator meets the

self. Faith and intelligent infinity may be seen to be one thing.

We hope these comments help you as you ponder what it is to be J moving through the experience of a lifetime in flesh!

(Side one of tape ends.)

(Carla channeling)

We are aware that you are clear about your true nature as spirit but less clear about precisely how to bring forth, through the flesh, into manifestation, the deeper self and the deeper truths.

May we have your next question at this time?

J: How can I use the knowledge I have gained to help others now that my voice is not able to hold up to sustained teaching?

We are aware of you query, my brother, and we thank you for it. It is the question of a person who is accepting of the changes wrought by age and life circumstance.

We would respond in two ways. Firstly we would say that a teach/learning circle does not have to be large in order to be helpful. As this instrument is very fond of quoting from those known as the Ra group, "If one is illuminated, are not all illuminated?" There are those within the circle of people you know already who may ask you questions. When the questions are asked of you, we encourage you to feel free to share those things that come to you. If you speak with only one person and that person is helped, then you have accomplished as much, as far as metaphysical concerns are valued, as if you were speaking to a great multitude.

Further, there will show up in your life those circumstances in which you may see an opportunity to offer your help to a new person, whether it is a person who is asking your opinion about a business concern or asking for mentoring in one of several different ways. See these opportunities also as opportunities for a small teach/learning circle, one-on-one, as this instrument would put it, and know that these are very valuable opportunities when you are offering all that you have to offer for what seems to be a very small audience; yet this audience is a hologram of all that there is.

As you teach one you are, indeed, teaching humankind and that entity, as one who is presumably learning from you, is also teaching you. For indeed, in any teach/learning circle that entity which is presumed to be the teacher is inevitably that entity which is learning the most.

The other way in which we would respond to your query is simply to say that the fundamental service of all of those who polarize towards service to others is the service of being yourself, most deeply, most honestly, and most humbly. The beingness of one who has achieved a clarity within is a beingness which radiates according to the amount of energy that you allow through your chakra body or your electrical body.

You are constantly doing energy work on behalf of the one infinite Creator as you breathe and be who you are. This is the fundamental and central gift that you are giving in this life. This instrument has said many times that the outer gifts pale in comparison to this central gift.

May we ask for your final query at this time?

J: I feel I struggle with being able to feel emotions and compassion. How can I improve or increase my compassion? Or is it a perceptual problem? Am I full of emotion of compassion but unable to contact that part of my inner self? If so, how may I increase my perception of my feelings, emotion and compassion?

We are those of Q'uo, and are aware of your query, my brother. We see in this query more than usual the efforts of this instrument to clarify and to make available to us the best possible chance for answering your question. And we would thank this instrument for including that last phrase concerning the perceptual problems inherent in your particular personality shell's being aware of what is actually going on at a deeper level within the beingness of the self.

It is quite accurate to say that you are indeed full of the deepest compassion and the most finely wrought emotion. You have, however, at times now fairly removed towards your past within this incarnation, made choices in order to be able to carry on within the consensus-reality world of business and family which effectively shut down some perceptual windows into the self.

It was not a bad decision that caused this distortion within your energy body but rather a sound and pragmatic decision which enabled you to fulfill your responsibilities and to do that in a way which did not trouble you.

This instrument's father was also one who could never perceive the very deep wells of emotion and compassion within himself and towards the end of his life he lamented to this instrument that he had sadness about not being able to feel either joy or deep sorrow. This entity also, at a very early point in his life, being a child of the Depression and having to go to work at the age of five in order to help the family sustain life and make enough money to eat, created within himself closed doors so that he would not need to deal with the deeper plangencies and sadnesses of his situation but rather simply be able to get up and do his work.

This entity's father was very successful in achieving the goals set out by himself at a very young age, whether it was the selling of newspapers or any other job which this entity undertook. This entity was always able to meet his responsibilities and to do it with no bitterness or sourness of spirit but always with a smile and gladness to be able to help.

As this attitude opened the way to service to others on one level, just so did it close some perceptual doors on other levels, making it nearly impossible for this entity later in life to abandon caution and open those doors which would allow him to experience the full range of emotions further. The deep wells of compassion that were within him were blocked from his own ability to experience them because, rather than allowing himself to experience anger, frustration, and even rage at the necessities of his life his conscious desire was to serve others and by that he intended to mean his family group.

Therefore, his only option at that young age was to choose an attitude which allowed compassion towards others but no compassion towards the self. To have compassion upon the self would have been to say, "I want to be a child. I want to play. I want to have a life that has nothing to do with anyone else." And because this instrument's father was a man of great integrity and high intelligence, these thoughts, even at the age of five, were unacceptable to him.

We tell you the story of this instrument's father in order not to infringe upon your own free will. We cannot go into your own past and pull out the experiences that have caused you to make decisions which have locked perceptual doors behind you at an early age. However, by offering the narrative of this particular entity, we hope that we have shown you the way that entities with a very high level of conscience and a great desire to serve others, can, inadvertently and innocently, shut perceptual doors behind them.

We hope that this will give you some feeling about how, with great care and patience, to move back into some of those earlier decisions and experiences and give yourself permission at last to experience the rage, the anger, the fury and the concomitant guilt at having those feelings that may have indeed caused you to block your own perception of the great range of emotions to which you indeed do have access and which you have used throughout your life in a very full manner on the unconscious level.

It is as if you stand upon the surface of a desert, not aware that there are very deep wells into which you may dip and bring out one bucket-full at a time of experience of these lost emotions. Stand in the oasis of your own reflections, musings and process, and as you are able, dip into the deep well of that oasis, knowing that the crystalline waters therein are good and come from a true and authentic part of your being that is not a desert at all but, indeed, the Garden of Eden.

We would at this time ask if there is one or possibly two follow-up questions that we may answer before the energy of this work session is exhausted. Is there a further query at this time, my brother?

J: You mentioned earlier that I had closed doors unknowingly and could work to open these doors to continue my spiritual growth. Can you elucidate shortly on that, please?

We are those of Q'uo, and are aware of your query, my brother. We cannot elucidate further. We spoke in a roundabout manner specifically because of our being unable to elucidate in a direct manner upon your process. We are apologetic concerning our reluctance but we wish to be completely free of infringing upon your powers of choice. This is an active part of your process at this time. We simply encourage you to proceed and to go after opening those doors using creativity and your keenness of observation.

We are with you at any time that you would ask us to be with you as you meditate and reflect, not to offer you thoughts of insights but simply to be as a battery to you so that any bumpiness or roughness in your own energies may be sustained during the weak spots by our foundational energy underlying yours.

May we say we believe in you. We love you. And we are most glad to assist you in that way. You have only mentally to ask us to be with you and we are glad to be a resource for you by helping you to be stronger in having a stable, conscious process.

We would leave you at this time, with many thanks for your beauty as a person and your integrity as a seeker. It has been a pleasure to share energy with you at this time. We thank the ones known as Vara and Carla, also. And we leave you in the love and in the light of the one infinite Creator. We are those of Q'uo. Adonai. Adonai. ♣

L/L Research is a subsidiary of
Rock Creek Research &
Development Laboratories, Inc.

P.O. Box 5195
Louisville, KY 40255-0195

L/L RESEARCH

www.llresearch.org

Rock Creek is a non-profit
corporation dedicated to
discovering and sharing
information which may aid in
the spiritual evolution of
humankind.

SPECIAL MEDITATION
SEPTEMBER 5, 2005

Question from V: I have experienced substantial changes in my health and am currently unable to drive long distances or live as I used to do. I feel a huge sadness in these changes, as though I had lost my life. I feel trapped like a mouse in a laboratory maze, unable to break out as my husband does not fly and so I no longer feel free to travel. How can I avoid feeling self-pity? How can I deal with the despair I feel as my doctors find no cure for me? How can I shore up my trust in myself when my memory is faulty and my self-confidence has been completely undermined? How can I come to terms with these changes in my life?

(Carla channeling)

We are those of the principle known to you as Q'uo. Greetings in the love and in the light of the one infinite Creator. We thank the one known as V for requesting our opinion upon the question of life changes and ways of adjusting to such changes. We are more than happy to share our energy and our thoughts at this time. We also thank the one known as Carla and the one known as Vara, for they too have set aside time during their busy lives to create this circle of seeking.

We would ask them and any who may read these words one thing before we begin and that is simply that each who considers what we have to say use his discrimination in choosing whether or not to listen to any particular thought of ours. Some thoughts may seem to be very helpful, and, if so, we would be glad for you to work with these thoughts. However, some thoughts may not seem to be helpful. In that case, we would ask that the thoughts be simply set aside and discarded as not being useful at this time. In this way, your responsibility in taking charge of using your discrimination in order to work with our material creates for us the opportunity to share our thoughts freely without being unduly concerned that we may inadvertently disturb the process of your own spiritual evolution. We greatly thank each for this consideration.

Our hearts are most sympathetic to your question, my sister. And, indeed, we find many resonances within this instrument's mind, thoughts and experiences which relate directly to the issues which your question raises.

This instrument, for instance, just this morning chose to write a letter to the rector of her parish where she has been a member of the choir and a regular attendee for thirty-seven years. However, this instrument has experienced changes in her health and just this day she has chosen to make the corresponding and appropriate changes in her lifestyle that reflect the fact that she is not able to spend long periods of time sitting up as opposed to reclining somewhat in her seat. Therefore, she has changed from a parish that is half an hour from her by car to a parish that is two blocks from her house, to which she is able to walk or to ride her motorized wheelchair.

There is a tremendous burden, shall we say, of grief [that] this decision has created as catalyst for this instrument to use as a gift as she works through it and acknowledges and processes her legitimate and authentic feelings and emotions. Change is difficult to accommodate. This instrument, herself, is not yet aware on a conscious level of this burden or gift of grief or the other attendant and seemingly negative emotions connected with this decision to change churches. There is anger and frustration and it is directed not at others, but at herself. How could she be so foolish as to become weak in the body? How could she be so poor in worth as to be unable to carry on with a pattern that fit her life and suited her personality for thirty-seven years?

Yet, because this instrument is one who tends towards dealing straightforwardly with perceived catalyst, the instrument has started the process of moving through the evolution that such change as she has instituted requires.

Just in such a way, my sister, have you faced, at last, the changes that have taken place in your life and the burden and gift of catalyst that these changes have brought to you. And so we would begin [by speaking] about change itself.

The nature of your present experience of life on planet Earth is that of having to deal with change repeatedly and cyclically. There were changes from babyhood to being a schoolchild that were most difficult. There were similar changes from childhood to being a teenager, from being a teenager to being a young adult, and so forth. Every cycle of living has a natural periodicity.

There is that time when a new cycle of living is brand new and everything is exciting. There is the blooming or thriving part of a cycle when the first flush of joy at the new cycle is gone, and, similarly, so are the difficulties involved in making the changes to accommodate the new cycle over with, processed and done with. In this time of the heyday or the summer of a cycle, there is a wonderful feeling of settling into a new environment and making it your own. While this season is occurring, it can easily seem as though this situation of life were in a state that could be sustained comfortably and joyfully the whole rest of one's life on planet Earth.

Yet inevitably, in time, that cycle, too, has its season of waning days and early nights. Eventually there comes the time when that cycle has come to an end and another cycle has begun.

It is those times that are frequently called the dark night of the soul. For as one undergoes the death of oneself as known within one cycle, it is not at all easy to retain enough confidence in the underlying sturdiness of the self to have faith in the fact that this new cycle that is just beginning has benefits as well as causing changes that are more uncomfortable and seem to indicate, in a way, the death of the self.

Change and all of its concomitant gifts of struggle, pondering, adjustment and all of its emotional burdens or gifts such as frustration and anger at having to change and that lack of self-confidence as to whether one will be able to weather the change satisfactorily, do not feel either helpful or comfortable. One is very tempted to ask the self why one must go through these changes. The basic question here, my sister, is why life is all about repeated times of change. We would answer that by asking you to consider yourself in a way that you perhaps have not considered yourself before.

We ask you to consider your physical body as a spiritual refinery, an oven, if you will, or a furnace in which old things are burnt up and changed into new things. The nature of transformation in the physical world often contains an element of destruction. If one wishes to process ore to refine the metal that is considered precious out of the basic ore, one must place the ore into the refining fire. There, the original material is actually transformed by melting it, reducing the ore to its component parts and, through the processes of refinery, taking away the slag or waste products and collecting the pure and precious metal.

My sister, within your body you carry the precious gift of consciousness. You hoped by placing this enormous and magical consciousness into the cup of your body to carry into an environment which is rich in the sense of time and place, your entire consciousness held within a tiny cup which is your body.

You gave yourself gifts of personality and as well you gave yourself gifts of limitation and even confusion. Before incarnation, it was your judgment that the love, the wisdom, and the power or will within you may not be completely in balance, according to the highest and best vision that your infinite and eternal spirit would judge. And so you sat down with your higher self, or, as this instrument sometimes calls it, your guidance system, before incarnation and planned carefully the shape and the general themes of an incarnation within this system of illusions that you call reality or life.

Having only your faculty of faith at your side, you wished within this fiery furnace of life on Earth to take an incarnationally long look at this balance that you have within your self, largely [the balance] between love and wisdom.

For many entities coming into incarnation and already qualified for graduation to fourth density—which is your case, my sister—the balance between love and wisdom [is], by your own judgment, that is, to be long on love and short on wisdom. It is, in fact, one of this instrument's incarnational lessons. And so we speak to you both when we say that many of the changes in both of your lives have to do with reining in this tremendously large heart that you have and this enormous desire to serve and finding a slightly enhanced balance between love and wisdom in which you have granted to wisdom a larger portion of the value that you place upon your thoughts.

Wisdom does not seem to be as important as the open heart [to you both] and the absolute love that you both so value. Yet love without wisdom creates a sense of martyrdom and often an abbreviated end to an incarnation as an entity keeps giving beyond [that] which she can give, until she literally breaks her health and is therefore taken out of the incarnation by illness. Therefore, this instrument has worked long and hard on a very conscious level for some years at attempting to be more and more aware of the importance of asking for the gift of wisdom.

There are a number of ways to ask for wisdom. This instrument's way is to move into a state of meditation and then simply ask the self, "What would my highest and best self do in this situation?" Often, the suggestion that comes into the mind at this point is one which is not attractive to the waking personality. For instance, when this instrument first considered moving her letter of membership from one Episcopal parish to another, her warm and loving heart which passionately adores her present church, simply shut off the conversation. It was not until repeated experiences of pain and suffering caused this instrument to revisit her inner conversation that she was able to acknowledge the

gift of wisdom and to move into the fiery furnace of transformation and to ask, in all humility, "What does my highest and best self guide me to do in this situation?"

When this instrument finally asked the question in that way, the answer was immediate and simple: it was time for a change. And not only that, it was time to embrace that change, to look forward to that change and to run towards that change, even though she did not know and still does not know what will happen next.

We would suggest to you, my sister, that you have encountered the beginning of a cycle in your life at this time. That cycle can be identified as that time of transformation that moves from middle age into old age and from vigorous health into declining health. We ask you to be consciously aware at this moment that this is not, in and of itself, a negative change. It is a part of the natural progression of your body, your mind, and your spirit within incarnation on planet Earth.

We would suggest to you further that, as the body begins to fall away, the gift of that seemingly negative occurrence to you is that it has become obvious to you that you are not your body, if you have the courage to grasp this gift and use it.

Within your question you stated that your memory is faulty and yet we would greatly expect, as is the truth of most entities, that your memory of how it feels to be yourself is intact. You have not lost one iota of your identity. And you shall not lose any portion of meaningful identity throughout this cycle.

As you enter into the gates of larger life at the end of this cycle, your identity will still be intact, just as it was when you entered through the gates of birth into this that you call incarnation or life.

Indeed, for all the seeming changes that you have experienced throughout your life, we would say to you that your actual, internal identity has shifted very little. This is to be expected. You are a citizen of eternity. This incarnation was designed to enable you to work on subtle points of balance within your eternal nature and to give you the opportunity to serve.

Now, service to others is in part service to perceived other selves. It is in part service to the greater consciousness that lies within you in that you are serving the Creator as you dig down deeper and deeper within yourself to discover the true nature of who you are. And further, it is service to the infinite Creator.

As you enter into the gates of larger life, move through the death process, and begin to review the incarnation you will find that this review, when finished, is the most precious gift that you could possibly give the Creator. You have worked tremendously hard in your incarnation to observe accurately and think deeply upon the experiences that you have undergone. Your heart has been opened and made joyful by many things within your incarnation, and that same heart has been sorrowed and broken by many other things which have occurred within the same incarnation. Both the joys and the sorrows have etched patterns within your energy body and have created for you a sharpening, a focusing, and a clarity of the colorations of that energy body. You have learned much and you have earned those lessons learned. And everything that you have learned is part of your gift to the infinite Creator.

The Creator sent you forth, at the beginning of this creation, as a collector, observer and transmuter of experience. Your job has been, and continues to be, to observe all things; to create within yourself an awareness of how you feel about those things; to create questions and find the heart of your desire as you look at how you feel, and then to move yourself forward along the paths that you have chosen in order to respond.

Again and again you have been called forth from contentment into discontent, from sameness into change, from stability into the seeming chaos of transformation. This is such a transformational time for you as well as for this instrument. We would ask simply that you approach the changes that this time in your life calls forth from you with a stubborn and fearless faith that all is well and that these transformational changes are not to your detriment although the world may see them that way.

We ask you to have the faith to know beyond all telling and beyond all doubting that what is happening to you is perfect. It is precisely what should be happening at this point in this incarnation. The material of loss is rich material, my sister.

We would speak a bit about the issue of self-worth. For loss is experienced in an entirely different way by a self-confident person from the way it is experienced by a person who is suffering a feeling of a loss of self-worth. You and this instrument, once again, have a great deal in common in that both of you have repeatedly had your self-confidence undermined almost completely. In this instrument's case, it has occurred largely within childhood and not so much within any portion of adulthood. However, this instrument tends to spend time inadvertently moving into the precincts of low self-worth and lack of self-confidence on an instinctual or knee-jerk-reaction basis.

And we find, my sister, [that you], both in childhood and in adulthood, have been challenged by those who do not give you respect and do question your worth. This is very difficult catalyst to ignore and it tends to be internalized so that those voices from outside you that say, "You are not worthy," become that voice within you which says, "You are not worthy. You are faulty. You are in error."

We suggest to both the one known as V and the one known as Carla that whenever you find yourselves speaking to yourself in tones that have internalized this judgment of the self, that you—verbally, consciously, and out loud—correct the statement. If you say, "Oh V, you are so stupid! You forgot the phone call," stop right there, my sister! For you have the work of the refining fire.

For you are not stupid. You are a woman with a faulty memory. That does not make you unworthy. It makes you a woman with faulty memory. Pick yourself up, as the song says, dust yourself off, and say to yourself, "You are worthy. You are perfect. Now, what shall we do about the late phone call? Let us correct that error. Let us move onward. Everything is okay. All is well." It is much more important for you to achieve that feeling of self-worth within yourself than to worry or fret because you have forgotten a telephone call.

This instrument also has faulty memory and this instrument and the one known as Vara were laughing together at that fact when they realized that the time for the call had come and gone[63] and

---

[63] V called for her appointment a half-hour later than she intended, as she had temporarily forgotten our appointment for

perhaps it would be necessary to call the one known as V and create the contact in that way. And the one known as Vara said to the one known as Carla, "You wouldn't know anything about faulty memory, now would you?" And both entities laughed heartily, for indeed the one known as Carla has terrible memory and has created innumerable occasions where she has inconvenienced not only the one known as Vara but all of those within her vicinity.

The circumstances of the present moment are neither positive nor negative. They are the perfect conditions for the evolution of your spirit at this time. What is the goal that you may pursue in the knowledge that you are doing the very best that you can so that you may indeed feel, in a very legitimate and rightful sense, that self-worth and peace of mind that you so crave? It is to realize that your job at this time is to be present with yourself, to encourage and support yourself.

This is the time within your life where you are collecting all the loose ends of self up. You are having the opportunity to love all of them and accept all of them as parts of yourself. If you look at yourself with judgment you shall cut up your peace and you shall be forever in a state of distress and sorrow. If, on the other hand, you start from a standpoint of absolute faith and the point of view that all is as it should be and all is well, then each thing that occurs to you can be looked at with an eye to examining how that makes you feel and what messages you are offering to yourself because of those emotions. And then you are able to examine those emotions to see if you are judging or loving yourself.

(Side one of tape ends.)

(Carla channeling)

You will then be able to deal with each thing that occurs to you from the standpoint of acceptance and the encouragement of those processes through which one goes when one is examining a situation with an eye to solving any problems that the situation has brought up and then, at a deeper level, with an eye to collecting, within the self, the full harvest of information gained from the examination of those emotions and feelings that have been brought up by any given point of difficulty.

the channeling session. We were able to go ahead and have the session.

Many things will fall away during each part of an incarnation. The refining fire removes the waste of unneeded material. That which is not needed does fall away. That which remains is gold.

Lastly, before we open this session to further questions, we would like to take a look at what gold you contain and what treasure you have within you. As we said at the beginning of this conversation, the ore within you or the self within you that you brought into incarnation is huge, much greater than can be imagined in terms of a personality or a human selfhood. You, and all sparks of the Creator, are a portion of the one infinite Creator.

You are a Creator, furthermore, who, though very imperfect in its realization of itself as Creator, has hands and a voice with which you can reach out and make a change in the environment and in which you speak up and express truth as you see it in this environment of mirrors and illusions that is consensus reality. You can be, therefore, the hands and the voice of the one infinite Creator.

The gold that is in you is your deepest self and as you have moved through many transformations in your life already, you have perhaps noticed that as things fall away from you and as you mature, you have become less and less a creature of personality and more and more a creature of the open heart, a creature whose selfhood is not bounded by what she does, what she wears, and where she goes, but who she is.

This is the part of your incarnation where you are most directly in contact with the ultimate question of, "Who am I?" If you identify yourself with the slag and the waste products of evolution, you shall stay with your body, your personality, and your former habit and you shall be mourning and grieving for your loss.

If, on the other hand, you have the fearlessness to embrace the changes that have taken place within your body, you may see that they are in their way a gift that lets you see more deeply into who you truly are.

What is the true nature of V? What manner of being is she? Recently, an acquaintance of this instrument said to her, "I have always thought I was a physical person having a spiritual experience. I am now, at last, coming to realize that I am a spiritual person having a physical experience." The shift from the self as a person, a wife, a mother, and so forth, to realization of the self as a part of the infinite Creator is a huge shift. Further, it is a shift from doing to being.

When this instrument, for some three years, was unable to sit up in her bed, or to work in any way, the emotions that this raised within her breast were most bitter. In order to work with this catalyst, this instrument did something which we would encourage you to attempt to do also. She put in front of her eyes, where she could not fail to see it, some personally meaningful language. She made herself two signs. One sign read, simply, "Faith: The Final Frontier." The other sign was a quotation from the letters of St Paul. The quotation read, "For if we live, we live in Christ, and if we die, we die in Christ. Whether we live or die, therefore, we are in Christ, and Christ, is in us." When everything was taken from this instrument except being, after many tears and sessions of hopelessness and helplessness, this instrument finally emptied herself of all self-pity and any judgment whatsoever and applied herself to the business of being empty.

And what she found when she was truly empty was that angelic hosts were around her. The holy spirit was with her. And light poured into that empty cup so that she lay there on her bed, glowing and vibrating with joy. She had nothing to do but be that which she believed was her deepest self and she found that deepest self in her open heart and in her desire to follow Jesus the Christ in living the life of absolute faith.

Faith is the final frontier. When you lay hold on that faith, even though you have had to leap into the abyss of not knowing in order to lay hold upon it, you will find, my sister, that you are firmly supported in the mid-air of not knowing. Those energies that you cannot see are with you. Angels are all around you and all they wish to do is love and support you. You are loved and you are most worthy to do this work.

We also are with you. You have only to ask for those of Q'uo, mentally, in your meditations, and we shall be with you to strengthen your meditation and lend you the stability of our belief in you as worthy, beautiful and perfect. For we see you as you truly are: a child of the one Creator, a portion of the creative principle, and a giver of tremendous gifts in all that you are.

This instrument is requesting of us that we open this session to any further questions [you may have] at this time. My sister, do you have a further question at this time?

V: I don't think I do. I've never felt so full of love like this before, I feel really tearful, because it was just perfect. I just look forward to having the tape and being able to go through it all and I feel really blessed. I don't, I think ,have anything to say but thank you.

We are those of Q'uo and are aware of your statement, my sister. And we feel similarly blessed in sharing this time and this space with you. We are those of Q'uo. And we leave you in the love and in the light of the one infinite Creator. Adonai, my sister, Adonai.

V: Thank you so much. ☙

L/L RESEARCH

L/L Research is a subsidiary of
Rock Creek Research &
Development Laboratories, Inc.

P.O. Box 5195
Louisville, KY 40255-0195

www.llresearch.org

Rock Creek is a non-profit
corporation dedicated to
discovering and sharing
information which may aid in
the spiritual evolution of
humankind.

SUNDAY MEDITATION
SEPTEMBER 18, 2005

Group question: The question today, Q'uo, has to do with the fact that so many of us who are here on Earth at this time wishing to be of service to others have found a great deal to do. We live at the speed of computers, jets and commuting. The problem seems to be, for many people, how to get everything done that you want to do. It seems like some things have to be left off! There isn't enough time in the day for one person to do what that person has set beforehand for herself. How do you go about prioritizing your expenditure of energy in the area of serving other people? Do you listen to your heart that says you give everything you have got to each person that comes your way one at a time? Or do you try to use some wisdom; do you try to tear down, logically, the load that you've got so that it's more manageable? We would appreciate any thoughts that you have in this area of organizing our energies, being of service, and not wearing ourselves out with trying to do everything that's in front of us.

(Carla channeling)

We are those known to you as the principle of Q'uo, and we greet you in the love and in the light of the one infinite Creator, in Whose service we are privileged to come to you this day. We thank each of you for the beauty of your being and the power of your dedication to seeking the truth. We thank you for forming a circle of seeking and for calling us to speak with you concerning the use of your time in the time of your usefulness.

As always, we would ask of you one clarion thing and we would be as clear as a trumpet as we say to you to take responsibility for discriminating as you listen to our thoughts. Do not take them into your being if they do not resonate to you. If you will guard your own temple, then we shall feel free to offer our opinion without being concerned that we may infringe upon your free will. Your process of growth is precious and it needs not to be disturbed but to grow very organically.

Your query this day concerns how to maximize the use of your time. It is understood in this question that you are on the path of service to others and so this is not a talk about how to choose between service to self and service to others, yet it is a talk that encompasses the question of how service to others works.

Your group has asked us many questions in the last little while concerning the nature of being, and, as we hear this question concerning the use of time, we find ourselves relating this question to the question of being. In the best of all possible worlds, that which you do flows from the fount of being within you.

The one known as Jim has made a vow to invoke the mantra to "relax and enjoy" whenever he becomes aware that he has lost his balance and is no longer resting in his own peace and power. We would begin by saying that this mantra is very apt for anyone who wishes to serve others well. It is not to the fleet of foot that the race against time goes. The winner of that race is the one who remembers to stop running and to rest. Clearly, we do not mean this literally. Even the most abstruse and abstract work involves movement. Once the choice of tasks is made, the fingers move across the computer keyboard, the mind and the body working together to create patterns, thoughts, and ideas where before there was nothing.

Those who work in more physical ways must do their work working with machines or using their bodies to create more order out of the chaos of nature's bounty, as the one known as Jim does in his gardening. Certainly the one known as C must take many steps, climb many ladders, and investigate many malfunctions and difficulties as she goes about creating order and beauty in the pattern of her rental business. Whatever the kind of work that you do is, the gist of your query to us this day concerns not the work itself but your choices of two things: precisely what task you shall choose in any given day or moment, and what attitude or point of view you shall choose as you offer yourself in service.

Energy expenditure is little understood among your people. You do not understand where your energy comes from. There is an abiding belief that energy is personal and that it belongs to you. When you go to sleep, you are thinking in terms of restoring your energy. When you make an effort you think of it as your effort. This is entirely understandable.

Nevertheless, your energy is the energy of the Creator. Your life is the life of the Creator. Your path is the path of the one infinite Creator. You are a miracle, astonishing in your perfection, breathtaking in your brilliance, and unknown to yourself.

You are a nexus, a crossroads, shall we say. You have offered yourself to incarnation in order to create this nexus or crossroads of illusory reality within an environment of third-density existence. You chose to enter third-density existence and create this point of potential because you realized, in gazing upon the Earth plane, that you wished to express the love and the light of the one infinite Creator within this precise environment.

We do not have to paint the stark picture of your environment. For all of the surpassing beauty of the world of nature that makes up the vast majority of this environment, the passion play of humankind has created a drama that unfolds before you in details and patterns of outworking expressions of the distress and confusion of a lost humanity. You did not come to add to the sorrow and the distress of this environment. Rather, you entered incarnation with a firm intention of being a part of the lightening of planet Earth at this time. You came to offer a local habitation to the ineffable and illimitable values of compassion, wisdom and unconditional love.

It could be said in a way that you came to save the world, and yet you did not in any way say to yourself, "I have to come to save the world." What you said to yourself, was, "I come to bear witness to the light and the love of the One whom I follow, that Logos that is the Creator."

What is it to bear witness to the light? What is it to follow the embodiment of love? It is certainly no tangible thing. It is, however, more real to you than your body and closer to you than your breath.

Energy expenditure is only possible, in terms of your present illusion, when there is a local habitation for that energy. Thusly, have you come into manifestation as a mind, body and spirit which serves the Creator. To move to the depth of such energy expenditure and to investigate its source, one must apply to the Creator Itself.

This instrument has been studying the nature of the archetypal mind as set forth by those of Ra in *Book IV* in the *Law of One* [series] in order to respond to questions in one of her forum e-mail groups. She is aware of the Ra's statement that the archetypical mind is the blueprint or builded structure of all energy expenditures within incarnation in this local habitation of third density. Therefore, logically, an investigation of the most appropriate choices of energy expenditure would turn to the study of the archetypes.

Dear brothers and sisters, we realize that the depth [of the gap] betwixt your present ability to contemplate the archetypical mind and a skillful use of that vast and powerful resource is tremendous. You may perhaps even feel that it is impossible to bridge that gap. We would say to you that in some ways it is literally impossible for you, within incarnation, to be able to have a grasp of archetypal processes, especially as they are ongoing within your energy system.

However, the gift of story and myth is that, without knowing what you know or how you know it, in telling each other your story you inadvertently touch upon various aspects of your archetypal mind. It is very helpful, for instance, that this group met today, not simply to ask us a question but also to tell each other your stories.

The listening ear and the understanding heart of those who hear your story create resonances that support and validate your archetypal process. You are not aware that you have solved any problems by sharing your stories, yet you have expended the Creator's energy in ways that have built up each of you as well as building up the adhering and abiding energy of the group itself in sharing your essence.

Moreover, you have alerted vast sources of energy which are unseen within your plane of existence, yet which add tremendously to the available energy within the system that this group creates as it sits in this circle. Any two entities listening to each other in an atmosphere of support have much the same dynamic. Any entity conversing with its guidance system, moreover, creates this same dynamic if the guidance that is requested is then listened to, heard and responded to within the context of the ongoing, daily life. You do not pray into a void. There is in every prayer a conversation with the divine within you.

We realize that your query is about how to choose what tasks to accomplish in any one day. Perhaps you may begin to see that, to our way of thinking, that question lacks priority. To our way of thinking, the priority in any day needs to be first, "What is the Creator's will for me this day?" We wish to move your thoughts away from the specific and into the underlying nature of your being who is the self that comes to the moment and begins to do the work of the day.

Look deeply into this question in order to retrieve your self in your entirety and wholeness from the shredding influence of detail. When you begin to work, let the self that begins that work be that self which has come to bear witness to the light. Let that self rest in its own nature. Indeed, dear ones, be intransigent in your determination to retain your identity. Then, that which you do shall be flowing through you and not from you. Your personality may flow and bubble along behind the essential self that you are and enjoy the light.

But that personality shell needs not to be the one doing the work. Know that the Creator is working through your nexus. This instrument, as part of her tuning process, prays, "Fill the heart of your faithful and kindle in her the fire of your love. Send forth Your spirit and she will be created and You shall renew the face of the Earth."

Whether you work at mowing a lawn, writing a paper, fixing a window, or responding to a correspondent, you work as an agent of the transformative power of the one infinite Creator. You are magical. And what you do is effortless when you remember that you are only here to bear witness to the light. You are here to dance, to play the pipe and timbrel and to be a part of the whirling, rhythmic pattern of all that there is.

If you can retain this basic remembrance of your point of view, then we do invite you to use your conscious, intellectual, analytical mind to make those choices of what task you shall pick and how you shall proceed. As you make those choices, open yourself to those sacred impulses within you which sense the rightness of the present moment.

This instrument, for instance, has expressed her feeling that each entity that contacts her is a spirit which has a need to be heard.

(Side one of tape ends.)

(Carla channeling)

Yet, as this entity becomes aware of the cry for help of that one who wrote in to her, she is that entity which is bearing witness to that help that has already been received, not because she responded but because the universe itself responds to every cry for help. The act of asking this instrument for validation activates for the one asking for help a chain of events that is completely independent of her and whether or not she responds to the correspondent.

In the moment of asking, that correspondent has created channels for energy to move within him or her from the guidance system within him or her and from the environment, spiritually speaking, which surrounds that correspondent.

Things are not as they seem to be. They are not linear, nor are they bound by space and time. However, it is because each of you has become a location in space and time by virtue of incarnating that these non-local processes may work.

We would suggest to each of you that you breathe deeply, in and out, knowing that life is one breath at a time; yet it is infinite.

We suggest that you look at yourself with that same double realization that you are local, flesh and blood, a gathering point at a crossroads through which spirit may speak and move and, at the same time, you are all that there is: non-local, not bound by selfhood, bound only by the awareness of the harvest of all the energy that you have processed, harvested and developed into the flower that you are at this moment.

We would at this time ask if there are any further queries from this group? We are those of Q'uo.

(No further queries.)

My friends, it is rare when there is no question at the end of our speech! But we hear only silence through this instrument's hearing apparatus and so we assume that the fund of questions for this day has been exhausted. May we say what a privilege and pleasure it has been to share our humble thoughts with you at this time and to rest with you upon the waves of consciousness as they flow from the Creator to the Creator. We leave you as we found you, in the love, the light, the power, and the peace of the one infinite Creator. We are known to you as the principle of Q'uo. Adonai, Adonai. ✦

L/L Research is a subsidiary of
Rock Creek Research &
Development Laboratories, Inc.

P.O. Box 5195
Louisville, KY 40255-0195

L/L RESEARCH

www.llresearch.org

Rock Creek is a non-profit
corporation dedicated to
discovering and sharing
information which may aid in
the spiritual evolution of
humankind.

SUNDAY MEDITATION
OCTOBER 9, 2005

Group question: The question today has to do with the seasons of change that we go through as conscious spiritual seekers on the path. We're wondering how these might manifest in our lives. We know that there are initiations we go through when times are kind of difficult and we learn specific lessons and if we do learn them then we're a more advanced neophyte and we're working our way to adept and pointed towards mastery someday. How do these changes manifest? When we feel blockages or difficulties on the path, is that a part of the process or can we actually make things more difficult for ourselves?

And the way we face the blockages or go through the difficulties seems to be important. Could Q'uo talk to us about the seasons of change in the spiritual seekers life?

(Carla channeling)

We are those known to you as the principle of Q'uo, and we greet you in the love and in the light of the one infinite Creator, in Whose service we come to you this day. It is a great privilege and pleasure to be called to your circle of seeking. We thank you for this honor and are most happy to speak with you concerning the various considerations of the conscious acceleration of one's own spiritual progress and the issues that that raises within one's seeking. It is what this instrument would call a juicy question and we look forward to working with it.

But before we share any thoughts upon that subject, we would share our request of all of you to be diligent in the use of your discriminatory powers. We offer you our thoughts. They are not the thoughts of those who are more advanced than you or those who have more authority than you.

In truth, each of you is the sole authority in your universe in terms of metaphysical work. In the world of humankind, in your consensus reality, shall we say, there is indeed a perceived system of authority and a perceived level of truth which can be assigned to various aspects of your seeking. We are not asking you to seek in the world of humankind or consensus reality, nor are you asking us for our opinions within that context.

You are asking for our opinions in the world of thought, in the world of time/space. And in that world, thoughts are things. And if you do not take full responsibility for the magical nature of your own being, you are then at the mercy of the small magic of each thought across which you come.

We would ask that you assume the sigil[64] of power, whatever it may be for you. Switch on that knowledge that you have within yourself, of yourself, and know that you are a powerful and magical being and fully capable and worthy of doing this work. You and only you can be or should be in charge of

---

[64] sigil: a sign or an image considered magical.

deciding what thoughts you will entertain and what thoughts you will pass up.

When you listen to what we have to say, be very ready to pass up our thoughts. Be a tough room, as this instrument would say it. Do not be overly pleased with us but listen carefully for that inner resonance that says, "This thought may be a good resource and I will pursue it."

If you will take that care with what you allow into the deeper regions of your thoughts, then we shall be completely free to share our humble thoughts with you at this time. We thank you greatly for this consideration, my friends.

The process of following one's thoughts is a never-ending and constantly beguiling process. Since your mind and your consciousness share the same space within your brain, you are constantly toggling between the two worlds of which the one known as M spoke earlier. It is not precisely that they are parallel universes, but they are certainly alternate universes. They are, in fact, reciprocal.

Toggling between two universes is at once a simple and a subtle process. It is simple in that there are two clearly defined universes separated by the shuttle of the spirit. You, in your body, your mind, and your spirit constitute a nexus or meeting; a place where those two worlds coincide.

In every cell of your body you carry the imprint of the one great original Thought of unconditional love. Every cell of your body is fully aware of the love and the light of the one infinite Creator at a level far beyond conscious thought. In fact, it is far enough beyond the reach of conscious thought that this precious, infinite and sustainable resource goes unnoticed and unused by most entities.

We would encourage each of you to become more and more aware of the intimacy of the one original Thought. It is not far from your body, from your mind, or from your spirit. It is inherent in every cell of your body, every cell of your brain, every iota of your consciousness, on whatever level and in whatever universe is, replete, teeming, and overflowing with love and light. The energy held within your system or energy field is infinite.

You are protected from the infinity of this resource by the degree to which you attend to transient thought. It is not needed or desired that you be at all times in full, conscious awareness of your metaphysical mission on Earth. Your goals within that metaphysical world in which thoughts are things and questions such as, "What is my mission on Earth?" have a degree of meaning that is substantial. There is a handsome portion of your life experience that is perfectly appropriate to reserve for what, in metaphysical terms, might seem meaningless activity.

It is well that you reserve a substantial portion of your life for such questions as, "What shall I eat?" "What shall I do?" And, "What shall I put on my body this day in order to keep me from the heat or the cold?" There is neither shame nor bad judgment involved in the choice to pursue earthly and worldly matters.

When you have achieved a certain degree of comfort and facility at blending or toggling between the physical and the metaphysical universes which come together and share space within your mind, body and spirit, then you can begin to allow those universes to coalesce through the shuttle of the spirit so that the simplest worldly duty begins to have the potential of becoming replete with meaning that is purely metaphysical.

Reciprocally speaking, as you become more able to enjoy both universes without giving preference to one over the other, you may gradually become more able to embody the progress that you are making in following the metaphysical nature of your thoughts.

This, my friends, is subtle work. It cannot be done quickly. It cannot be done conveniently. The process of evaluating one's progress is fraught with difficulty. This instrument was speaking earlier about this difficulty. She was sharing with this group, in the conversation preceding this channeling session, her blind spot in recent work in consciousness which she had been doing. Her particular stumbling block happened to be a mental and emotional mind-set, as this instrument would call it, which assumed, without examining the assumption, that the work that this instrument had been doing for some time was the appropriate work to do and therefore the only consideration was how much she could accomplish within a twenty-four-hour period. Fortunately for this instrument, she had not only the counsel of those who cared for her soul's health, but also a willingness to listen to those messages which she might not wish to hear, which is characteristic of this particular entity. She listened to those who suggested that she was stumbling over her own devotion and dedication. It was out of balance. This was impossible for this instrument to see on her own.

So let us look at that dilemma, for it affects everyone who is upon the path of seeking which she has defined for herself. When a seeker grasps the baton of work in consciousness and accepts the fact that there is power available to that entity to accelerate the rate of the evolution of mind, body and spirit, that seeker enters into a world which is completely and utterly metaphysical.

The metaphysical universe is a universe in which time is a field. All of time—past, present and future—becomes unitary. It is a world that is specifically non-physical. The things or objects of this world are thoughts which carry vibration.

A thought is an object but a thought is not a flat object. A thought is rounded by various subtle and etheric attachments that are not abstract but rather are wrappings or colorings of emotion that create a certain vibration. You can say a thought or a concept and in saying that thought the words themselves carry a certain roundness or vibratory coloration.

However, the state of mind in which you find yourself as you come to that thought, and all of the emotions that are wrapped into the creation of that thoughts or concept, create the specific vibration or coloration or roundness or shape of that thought. On no two days and in no two repetitions of that thought shall that thought be the same shape.

This is why the work is so subtle. You are part of every thought that you think. How you come to that thought, how you feel about the thought and how you respond to the work you have previously done on that thought all create for you the unique moment in which you are the creator of a vibration and a field that is not only a thought or concept but is also that which has brought it to life so that it is a creature. It is a creature that exists in your universe.

And it then becomes an essence that, as you work with this thought, as you stabilize this thought, you become able to use as a building block for the further creation of developing thoughts or concepts along the lines of the process that you have begun by focusing on this particular thought.

The stumbling blocks involved in this process begin with the fact that it is your universe and no one

else's. To an extent, you can share your concepts with each other. But this extent is not on the level of open communication using words, a generally satisfactory component of companionship with others. You cannot successfully, directly, share the full vision or vibration that lies behind the words that are flat upon the air or upon the paper as you speak or write them. You are blindsided, in short, by the isolation of your process.

Therefore, your first blessing as spiritual seekers is guidance.

Your second blessing is the willingness to listen to the guidance that you receive.

There are many sources of guidance. For one such as this instrument, who spends a great deal of her time communicating in correspondence, e-mail and personal conversation with those within her extended family of spiritual community, the sources of guidance are many. Each person with whom this instrument corresponds comes in at an unpredictable and unexpected angle and may ask any number of questions or may offer advice. In each and every contact there is the possibility of inspiration and guidance. It is a matter of applying those powers of discrimination of which we spoke earlier and listening for resonance.

Perhaps you could visualize, as this instrument does from watching so many World War II war movies, the ping of the sonar as a searched for underwater object becomes closer and closer and the pings become louder and louder. Listen with your sonar for the hidden resources of guidance from without your energy system.

It does not matter whether or not you know the person that is interacting with you. That person is a part of the creative principle and is a mirror to yourself. It may be a casual mirror. It may be a very distorted and basically useless mirror.

On the other hand, anyone, anywhere, can be an angel that you behold unawares. That is the nature of our shared universe. It is unified. Everyone can communicate with everyone.

The question is how deft and dexterous you are at listening for the guidance that is yours out of the tremendous bulk of communication you receive which, indeed, is not helpful. Where is the signal and where is the noise? Let your sonar work. Listen for the ping.

It is important not to scorn the company of those who do not seem to be awake and seeking. All entities are moved by the tides of creation and whether or not they have any knowledge of being a part of your guidance system, as they pass you they are, by virtue of their being, for that moment, a part of your guidance system. Honor, respect and cherish these strangers and listen for that ping.

Indeed, we would urge you to listen even to inanimate sources such as the inevitable synchronicities as you pass signs, advertisements on the road, and things that are announced upon the radio or television as you pass that noise. Anything can be a source of hints and revelations. Listen for the ping.

There are precincts of despair and other involutional emotions that tend to isolate the dedicated spiritual seeker from outside guidance. And many are the seekers who basically feel that they seek almost inside a bell jar, that glass surface that keeps the dust of ordinary living away from the process of seeking [and] also works invisibly but effectively to create a sense of inner isolation. The emotional feeling that one is alone can build up within that bell jar of intense seeking. This in itself can be a stumbling block.

When you sense that feeling of inner isolation, we encourage you to find the energy within yourself to ask for the guidance system that lies within your heart to come into play. Indeed, this instrument has at times of deep distress found it helpful to sit down with a pad and a pen and write down her question. And this instrument addresses her guidance system, whom she calls "Holly." And her opening mantra is, "Holly, help!" She will then either speak aloud or write down her dilemma and she receives an impression, when she has asked a question, which she also writes down.

This process is a valid and meaningful conversation. We would especially encourage those who feel that they do not have much help in the outer world, as far as companionship and the ability to communicate openly, to use the guidance system that lies within.

Whether your guidance is from a source that is apparently outer, or apparently inner, its effectiveness is bounded by the choice that you make as to whether or not you shall listen to this guidance.

It is essential that you listen to the guidance that you receive and follow it.

That is what this instrument did within this last week, responding to the request of those about her that she contemplate whether or not she was using her time wisely by working at her perceived tasks for each week on all seven days for all the time available. The suggestion was made to this instrument that she was not valuing herself and that she should take some time, perhaps a day in each week, to honor and respect her own private concerns, whatever they might be, disconnecting completely from the self-perceived work of being facilitator for a spiritual community.

To this instrument's surprise, there was substantial resistance within her to disconnecting from the work at hand. To her further surprise and delight, she found that upon achieving a state of disconnectedness from her perceived work, she opened up within herself a tremendous source of energy which she has not yet come fully to understand. Nevertheless, she is aware of it and is aware that new life and new growth are available to her because she heard the ping of resonant information and she changed her actions and her thoughts in response to that resonance.

What constitutes a stumbling block? In each seeker, that answer will be different. In general, entities create their own stumbling blocks. It is not an energy that is imposed from without. We might say to you that a keyword here is balance.

Some stumbling blocks are easy to identify. When one sees that one's prejudices or biases have limited one's thinking, it is easy to assign blame. As the one known as T was saying earlier, his dislike of religiosity and dogma had been a stumbling block that had kept him from thinking deeply about the nature of true Christhood or that thought that encompasses unconditional love within this meeting place of flesh and spirit that each of you is. He could not think of the nature of unconditional love as embodied in the one known as Jesus the Christ because he had been so punished by a childhood within which Jesus, Mary, the Saints, the Pope and other mythical figures were woven into a seamless prison where ideas could not flourish and where love died, gasping for validation.

He found judgment, guilt, and death in the church. He did not find the Christ.

So it is with each perceived dogma that seems to limit one's creativity. And we encourage and urge you not to accept those limitations that do not feel resonant to you. We encourage you, however, to look beneath the surface where you run into a situation where there are ideas offered to you that have potential. Look beneath the dogma and the limitations implied by those who believe dogmatically to hear the melody that gives life to a flat fact or color to a flat piece of writing. Search out those moments of inspiration that dogma is attempting to stamp out in the way it says something that has potential.

(Side one of tape ends.)

(Carla channeling)

Do not be afraid to separate the melody that dances in your head from the imprisoning words that seem to limit that melody's usefulness. Allow yourself to become a non-literal singer of the song of feeling and thought.

We tread very delicately here in speaking of stumbling blocks in the spiritual process because while it is true that you create your own stumbling blocks, it is also true that stumbling and falling are a needed and valid portion of the process of growth.

Since it is your universe, who else can create the opportunities to fall but yourself? Therefore, in your every error, as self-perceived in hindsight, lies an astonishing and unexpected gift. Falling is a gift. As you rub your spiritual posterior and contemplate your bruises, you may not appreciate that gift. Yet every stumbling block is information.

We encourage you, then, to retain your sense of self, your sense of proportion and your sense of humor. Do not use the occasion of self-perceived error to scold yourself or to shy away from that error, looking for its dynamic opposite. There are reasons that you erred in just such a way. Gaze upon the pattern. Try to see into your own biases. Were you proud? Did you assume? If so, what were your assumptions?

We do not wish to seem to disrespect this process overly [much]. But in a way it is very much a game. It is a game in which it is supposed that there is a linear progression from being a novice to being a master. In many ways there is indeed a progression that is linear that can be seen, especially in hindsight, when one is looking back on a spiritual process that

has been played out, or, to say it another way, a song that has been sung to its natural conclusion. Hindsight is a wonderful thing.

In another way, there is not such a progression. Rather, there is the stitching together of a pattern much as the process of weaving would eventually create a complex and beautiful pattern upon the loom. There are various thoughts that create the work and there are various techniques of moving with the energies that are available to you at a particular time for you take those energies in hand as if they were thread and you created by that pattern of your weaving the finished woof.

It is as if your concepts were the "A axis," shall we say, the vertical threads. Whereas your sensings, intuitions and feelings are the thread which you weave on the "B axis," or the horizontal axis, through these preexisting concepts which you are using.

The patterns of the weaving that you choose are heavily influenced by the work in consciousness that you have chosen, whether it be meditation, visualization, contemplation of inspirational texts or any other technique that seems useful to you. What you are creating in doing this work is a piece of material that then is your momentary creation, a thing of color and shape and texture, a gift to yourself and to the one infinite Creator.

It is certain that these prayer rugs, shall we say, that you create for yourself are in and of themselves things of great beauty and usefulness that may constitute for you a resource as you move forward. At the very least, they are mementos of where you were and who you were at this particular moment. They may well reflect back into your momentary, everyday, ordinary experience and in turn, as you become more facile at toggling between the two worlds, your ordinary experience may give you inspiration to create your next prayer rug, a concept, question or love.

We thank you for this question which has been a delight to work with and would ask you if there are other queries that you may have on your mind at this time? We are those of Q'uo.

R: I had a question, Q'uo. To follow up on your explanations at the beginning when you were speaking of the love of the Creator being in every cell of the body and that being a resource that is close to us and yet often unused, when I look at it, I see no entry into that subject or suggestion, at least with my intellectual mind. Could you speak on that love of the Creator vibrating in every cell in some way that we could work with?

We are those of Q'uo, and are aware of your query, my brother. We can make a beginning, my brother, and welcome your querying concerning the implications of that beginning at a later time. Indeed, much of what we have said is heavily implicatory and open to further questions and we would welcome them.

Every cell of your body is made up of atoms which are fields that are held into greater fields as molecules and then bound into combinations in the development of organic life that creates the cell. These atoms and molecules and so forth have energies of rotation and field values that are unique to those particular atoms, molecules and so forth. Each of these atoms is the outworking of the impression of the one great original Thought of unconditional love upon space and time in its progression.

This concatenation or combination of love, space and time creates light acting in ways that are impressed upon it by love which then creates the particular kind of atom, molecule and so forth that constitutes the field of the self.

Your body is made of love and light. That is why we greet you in the love and in the light of the one infinite Creator. We are marking this moment in time and in space in such a greeting and when we leave you we are leaving you in the house of oneness in which you shall reside in infinity and eternity.

The light that is held in just such and such a kind of field is relatively undistorted, bearing in its information, shall we say, the "factory specifications," say in the infant body, the imprint of the Creator's design. Thusly, every cell in your body is instinct with the truth.

Mark the power of the human mind. You can overwrite the instructions or the information at the cellular level and often you do so to your detriment as far as the integrity of your health [is concerned] by the way that you think habitually.

We have talked often to this group concerning the power of thought and the power of the things that you tell yourself. If you give yourself information concerning your environment from a place that is governed by fear, that is, if you are afraid for your health, for your source of supply, or for anything at all, you will eventually, as these repetitious thoughts continue, begin to affect your body systems at the cellular level, weakening them and making them sensitized to environmental input.

For instance, if you are habitually concerned in such a way as to arouse fear and if your body has sensitivities to allergy or illness of some kind, be it cancer, heart disease or whatever is in your genetic predisposition, you can gradually build up for yourself at the cellular level a tendency towards grabbing those inputs that are fear-based and rewriting your cellular information so that you become more and more able to become sick.

Similarly, if you think conscientiously and constantly to the best of your ability in a fearless manner, affirming your self-worth, affirming your health, or affirming the sufficiency of your physical supply, you gradually inform your body at the cellular level that it does not have to respond to environmental inputs of this fearful nature, thereby beginning to make you less and less pervious to the damage done by habitual fearful thought.

What you believe and how you believe it are not abstract things. They are powerful inputs that go down into every cell of your body. When you assume that your body, at the level of being fresh from the factory, shall we say, being newborn and completely free of the benefits of life on planet Earth within incarnation, [is] appropriate and correct, then you have established for yourself a default which you can trust.

Then your conscious mind simply needs to go back to that default position of the newborn, undamaged factory specifications with which you entered into the incarnation. Affirm those defaults. Ask for the body to reprogram itself to those default settings, losing the overwriting of the cultural miasma.

Trust and faith are all-important in connecting the consciousness with the goodness of your physical vehicle. This is also true in the more subtle and etheric form of connecting your consciousness with the goodness of your basic thoughts and feelings, whatever they may be.

May we answer you further, my brother?

R: No, thank you, Q'uo. There is more that we can follow up but I think the group grows tired and the energy is low.

We are those of Q'uo, and we thank you, my brother. Is there a final query at this time?

T: I have question which has come up before. I often feel that I'm not making progress in meditation. Could Q'uo talk about perception of progress versus actual progress?

We are those of Q'uo, my brother, and are aware of your query. It may seem that we are far in advance of you in terms of our progress, and yet, my brother, this question has great resonance for us because our rate of progress is considerably slower than yours within third density. Indeed, your progress seems to us to go by at a blinding speed, for in the very heaviness of your outer environment and your experience of seeming to have to slog through physical life in order to get to the metaphysical portion of life you are truly in an environment which is incredibly rich in the opportunity to make changes in consciousness.

We have been going through a refining process for some time, as you would say, and at our level of development our progress is very difficult to see, even in hindsight. We must, more than you, take on faith the goodness of the process through which we are going. We must maintain faith that that which we do is bearing fruit. We can only encourage you to do the same.

Every once in a while, my brother, there is a gift that is given from spirit. It is a gift of realization. And in that moment, your progress is clear and the worth of the efforts that you have put into coming to this moment of realization are also very clear. Treasure those moments and give thanks for those gifts. They are rare.

For the most part, one's sense of one's progress must be left to faith. In the world around you, much of spiritual progress is rather pushed upon one from behind, by the context of guilt, sin and correction of that guilt and sin, by doing something perceived as virtuous or good. This has almost nothing to do with spiritual progress.

In truth, we believe that progress is an organic process that uses everything that you are, weaving and reweaving context on the one hand, and every thought of substance that you think on the other hand, to create a shifting kaleidoscope of color, texture and form.

Therefore, as you meditate, trust that you do not need to be pushed from behind to make progress. The Creator is calling to you from the alpha and the omega of the circle of oneness. Spiritual gravity is building up within you and you are called from beyond yourself ever forward with the inevitably of weather, taxes and so forth.

You cannot help progressing. Your only question is whether or not you wish to progress faster than the surrounding ambience or environment out of which you come.

Naturally, you wish to progress faster than humankind as a tribe is progressing, for the humankind that is your tribe upon planet Earth is having systemic difficulties that are deep and substantial. They need not concern you, yet you must and you do make a conscious decision to separate yourself from that ambience and to move into a far more individualized and creative personal environment.

You create for yourself a hotbed, a greenhouse, an enhanced growing environment by doing the meditation, the contemplation, the reading, and the daydreaming. You are continuing to create growth conditions for yourself.

Focus, then, on those things over which you have control. Give to yourself the gift of reading inspired thought. Give to yourself the gift of silence. Do those things which you feel have resonance for you. Place yourself, in other words, in the deepest, richest soil of which you know. Ask of yourself that you empty yourself of preconception and pride. Let yourself be planted. Let your soil do its work. Bring the water and the sunshine to yourself by those things which you call into your environment. But do not second-guess the growth. It is occurring not on your time but on the Creator's.

May we answer you further, my brother?

T: No. Thank you again for your usual clarity.

My brother, we thank you as well. It is a great pleasure to share energy with you. This instrument informs us that indeed we must leave this group as the energy does wane and we do so with great love and with many thanks for the privilege and the pleasure of your company. May we comment on your beauty and on the joy that we feel in sharing these moments with you.

We are known to you as those of the principle of Q'uo. We leave you in the love and in the light of the one infinite Creator. Adonai. Adonai. ☙

L/L Research is a subsidiary of
Rock Creek Research &
Development Laboratories, Inc.

P.O. Box 5195
Louisville, KY 40255-0195

L/L RESEARCH

www.llresearch.org

Rock Creek is a non-profit
corporation dedicated to
discovering and sharing
information which may aid in
the spiritual evolution of
humankind.

© 2009 L/L RESEARCH

SPECIAL MEDITATION
OCTOBER 11, 2005

Question from K: I have felt very frustrated in that I do not seem to be able to more directly access my own inner guidance, intuition or spirit in a more specific way. Could you please comment and provide any advice on how to increase this aspect of my knowingness? This issue leaves me feeling somewhat devoid of a guiding influence in attempting to do service to others and feeling unsupported at times.

(Carla channeling)

We are those known to you as the principle of Q'uo, and we greet you, my sister, as well as the one known as Carla and the one known as Vara, in the love and in the light of the one infinite Creator, in Whose service we come to you this day. As always, we are delighted to be called to your circle of seeking and are glad to speak to the one known as K on this interesting query and others that you may have.

However, in order for us to feel completely free to share our thoughts with you, we have a request to make of you. We would ask that each of you who hears our words retains a very firm awareness of your responsibility as the sole discriminator of what questions you will consider and what questions you will not. That is to say that we may offer many thoughts. Some of them may create avenues of questioning for you which are not desirable to you. We would ask you to listen to your discrimination and drop any of our comments that do not seem resonant to you. If any comments of ours do make

sense and do seem to lead to helpful work in consciousness, then we would be happy for you to work with them.

Our concern is simply not to interfere with your natural and spontaneous process of spiritual development. If you will abide by this request then we can feel completely free to comment with our thoughts. We would not wish to become some sort of outer authority that might create for you a stumbling block at a future time. Thank you for your cooperation in this regard.

K: Yes, I understand.

We are those of Q'uo, and we thank you, my sister. As we take up your query on guidance, we would note that the guidance system which belongs to you and indeed that guidance system which belongs to each entity who seeks is both a very substantial and firm part of your system and one that is closer to you than your breathing and nearer to you than your very heart and also a delicate and subtle influence. So we would comment in various ways.

Our first comment is that the system of guidance that is yours is not an importuning or encroaching presence, it does not, of itself, shake you or act as a kind of alarm clock that will, on its own, awaken you or alert you. It must be sought and asked for its help. This is a simple fact and yet it is one which has often been that which is overlooked by those who seek.

Guidance is an energy which is so much a part of you that it came into incarnation with you. Yet it comes from what this instrument would call the time/space or metaphysical universe or creation that interpenetrates the physical universe which your body and your mind enjoy at this time. It is not a part of space/time or consensus reality. It remains firmly fixed in the metaphysical or spiritual universe. Consequently, a short prayer will alert the guidance system that you are ready to receive information. Indeed, it is a good idea at the very beginning of each day to ask for the guidance system to get turned on and left on for the day.

It will, naturally and as a part of the experience of sleeping and dreaming, work with the dreams and the impressions that you receive upon awakening. You do not have to ask for guidance to speak with you in order for it to work with you during the dreaming and sleeping processes.

However, when you are awake and functioning with the brain that is a part of space/time, working in problem-solving mode, then it is well to request that guidance be able to speak to you. A simple request is all that is needed. It does not have to be said out loud. It can be strictly mental as long as your mental processes are such that you are able to make a clear and distinct request without speaking out loud. If there is any doubt within you at all concerning this point, then we would suggest that you go ahead and speak out loud.

This instrument often does so because she is aware of the power and strength of her mental processes in terms of her intellectual mind. So she will say, "Come Holy Spirit! Fill the heart of your faithful and kindle in her the fire of your love. Send forth your spirit and she shall be created and you shall renew the face of the Earth."

This is a prayer that she uses frequently in order to tune. We offer this text to you as a possibility for you to consider if it seems to have resonance for you.

A shorter form of this which this instrument also uses upon occasion is, "Come Holy Spirit. And that right quickly."

You can also simply say, "Help." This instrument sometimes does that, saying to her guidance system, "Holly, help." She calls her guidance system, "Holly."

Any way of expressing this request that seems most natural and resonant to you, my sister, is the one that we would suggest.

It is not only at the beginning of the day that this request may be made effectively. At a time of your choosing, when you have a bit of spare time, shall we say, that can be used to make more firm contact with your guidance system, you may sit down, rest and clear your mind, and then repeat any of those prayers which we have offered as examples for your resources in this wise.

When you wish to inaugurate an actual conversation with your guidance, we have two suggestions for your consideration. They may be taken literally. They also may be taken figuratively and the essence of the suggestions used, rather than the form.

The first suggestion is that you sit down with a pad of paper or a computer keyboard handy, and, after clearing your mind, inaugurate a conversation with your guidance. It helps in terms of feeling natural in doing this for you to identify for yourself the name that you wish to call your guidance system. This instrument, for instance, as a mystical Christian, identifies her guidance system as the Holy Spirit, whom she long ago nicknamed "Holly," feeling that it is more respectful and more personal to have a human kind of name rather than simply calling the guidance system, "The Holy Spirit," which is a generic term.

Each person's guidance system is unique and so consequently, when you simply call upon guidance, you are calling upon the generic version of guidance, which is helpful but not as helpful as calling forth or evoking your personal guidance.

The invocation of guidance having been done, we would then suggest that you write or type your basic concern. You come to the moment of asking for guidance because of a certain concern. Identify that concern to guidance and ask for any information, resources or comments that guidance may offer you at this time.

Keep your fingers on your pen or poised over the keyboard and no matter what your next impression is, write it down.

Upon reading what you have now written, you will form a further comment to guidance. Type that or write that down. And again, await the next thought that pops into your mind.

When you begin getting that thought, again, without comment, criticism or questioning, write down what you are impressed with.

Again, read what you have received, form your next question or comment and write that down.

In this way you are staying safely within your guidance system, which is protected and is completely within your etheric or electrical body. It is a protected and safe procedure as long as you are focusing completely within these parameters.

This is the first way of becoming able to feel more concretely anchored within your guidance system and more specific in your ability to receive information from guidance.

The second way we would suggest to you is somewhat more complicated but we feel that in your case, my sister, it may be well to take the time to go through the basic procedure for creating for yourself a place for inner work. This instrument has done so and has found it helpful. It is a procedure that she learned from an entity who was teaching principles which he had learned from the so-called Silva Mind Control Technique. It is not a faithful reproduction of such techniques but is in fact an alteration of those techniques that this instrument has found helpful. We will use this instrument's technique in explaining to you the basic process of creating what this instrument would call a place of working.

Step one is to ask yourself where upon this Earth, in terms of location and geography, your favorite place resides. Where do you feel most at home, most protected, most safe and secure? When you have that location firmly in mind, then we would proceed to step two.

Step two involves creating for yourself, in that place, a place of working. If the place that you have chosen is a building or contains a building, then we would suggest that you create for yourself within that actual building a mentally constructed room. It can be a copy of an actual room in that dwelling or it can be a room that you have created completely out of imagination. It is, however, attached in your mind to that safe place, created very consciously as a sacred place.

Create it as you would wish it. If you feel it needs a kitchen, make yourself a little kitchenette. If you feel it needs a bathroom, make yourself a bathroom. If you feel you need an office, make yourself an office, and, most importantly, if you would like to have an inner sanctum where you go after you enter this basic sacred space, create for yourself the sanctum sanctorum, which is where you shall do your actual working.

Before you go any further, create for yourself every comfort, every convenience, and every amenity. For instance, this instrument, feeling that she wanted the comfort of all of her information at hand, created for herself a room in which there were office files, a desk, a computer, and so forth, so that she would know that all the information that she needed to do her work would be on hand and if at any time she wished to consult any of that information, she could mentally go to the filing cabinet and ask for the appropriate documents to be given to her.

In fact, this instrument has never opened that filing cabinet, for in spirit there is no literal need for such. However, because it helps to create a sense of safety and security for this instrument so that she can do her work better, she has this office which she has furnished with her favorite kind of rug and her favorite kind of office furniture, her favorite kind of lighting, and so forth.

The goal here is not to create a specific kind of work space but to create your ideal work space. So let this ideation and visualization process be as long as it needs to be and as careful and detailed as it needs to be in order for you to create a very recognizable, safe and sacred working space.

When you have all other details attended to, we would ask that you create in your working space, whether it be one room or whether you have created an inner sanctum, two doors, one on either side of a central screen. The screen is a way of objectifying within your mental processes the visualization process of doing your spiritual work. The doors on either side of this central screen represent the openings to the Holy Spirit, as this instrument would call this energy, or your guidance system.

In order to balance your request for guidance, the door on the left of the screen represents the masculine energies of guidance. The door to the right of the central screen represents your access to the feminine portion of the energy of your guidance system.

Create for yourself your most comfortable sitting, resting or standing position for doing work. This is entirely up to your discretion. Many are those who visualize doing their work in the seated, cross-legged position that is often used by those who are working with oriental meditation systems. This instrument uses a recliner as her visualized, most comfortable seating.

Visualize two places, one on either side of you, for the guidance that you call forth.

When you are ready to do your work, stand in front of the seating that you have created for yourself. Mentally turn on the screen so that it is alive and lit and ready to receive impressions and to give forth images. Then call forth your guidance saying, "I call forth guidance," or, "Come Holy Spirit," or whatever phrase most satisfies you as expressing your desire for your guidance system to manifest itself to you.

It is well when beginning this practice to call one aspect of guidance at a time. When you first call your masculine guidance, you may extend your hand to the door and ask that guidance to come forth. You will receive the impression of an entity who is walking toward you. Observe that entity insofar as you receive impressions. This entity may have a name. It may have a face that is familiar to you. Or it may not be familiar to you.

Become familiarized with this entity. You may ask its name or you may simply greet it and thank it.

Then turn to the other door and, by gesture or word, invoke the other portion of spirit. Again, take the time, initially, to look at, familiarize yourself with and become conversant with this entity. It may have a name. It may have a recognizable or an unfamiliar face. Welcome it and thank it.

When you have greeted these two aspects of your guidance system, invite them to sit with you. It may be helpful for you to ask them to take your hands, as this instrument does, so that you are physically, in terms of your visualization, linked with and connected to your guidance system.

This is the procedure for becoming ready in this visualization to do work in consciousness in your place of working.

Before we move forward with a discussion of how to proceed from this point, we would move back into comments concerning your own inner work as you come to the moment of entry into the place of working.

It is very helpful for you to determine for yourself a method of tuning your being to do this work in consciousness. The normal and everyday state of consciousness of what this instrument would call even the best of us is less than the optimal tuning position or rate of vibration for doing work in consciousness. Depending upon what you have on your mind or on your schedule, you may well be in somewhat of a scattered frame of mind, which you would describe to yourself as not being your best or highest self.

Your goal, then, is to tune this very powerful entity that you are up from its present, everyday and ordinary state of mind to the state of mind that would be the highest and best tuning that you can carry in a stable and conscious manner. You do not want to go beyond that which you can carry, being quite awake and quite alert. But you do wish to do the work necessary to sharpen and hone your true self so that you are expressing the highest and best version of who you are when you come to the moment of contact with the spiritual guidance that is yours.

When you have achieved this, you then may approach the door to your dwelling. If you do not actually have a dwelling in your favorite place, then you simply need to construct the outer walls of the sacred space, as a boat on the water, a cabaña on the sand or whatever fits in the environment you have chosen for your magical work.

When you are satisfied that your tuning is complete, you may then ask for the keeper of your sacred space to come forward. This is a convention which this instrument has learned from the practices of the Spiritualist Church.

We are not suggesting that you are creating a séance atmosphere or that you will be speaking with inner spirits of any kind. However, the convention of having a gatekeeper is a powerful and a helpful one to our point of view. It is to this gatekeeper that the responsibility for guarding your back is given. Therefore, when you are tuned, ask for your gatekeeper to appear. You will not know what this gatekeeper is like until you ask.

Depending on your personality and your training, this gatekeeper may be virtually anybody or anything. If it is an animal, however, it will have the capacity for communication with you. If it is a color, it will have the ability to share information. For most entities who do this kind of work, the gatekeeper turns out to be a human, whether of this world or of the inner planes. It is not necessary that this entity have a name. The one known as Carla calls her gatekeeper, "Mrs. Gatekeeper," because when she created her place of working, she created it in a place which already had a woman who lived there. She was the wife of the head of a school and this instrument's favorite place happened to be one of the buildings on a large campus. Therefore, she simply calls her gatekeeper, Mrs. Gatekeeper, but she sees the pleasant and careworn face of a middle-aged woman who acted as housekeeper and mother to the students of this particular school.

When you address your gatekeeper, simply ask if you are in a good position to do work in consciousness. If you receive a "yes," then you may proceed inward, after thanking the gatekeeper and asking this gatekeeper to remain on duty and to alert you if there is any problem whatsoever. If the gatekeeper has concerns, that entity will express them to you. Listen to the gatekeeper, and insofar as you are able, address the concern. Once you have been okayed for work, then you may step into your dwelling or your sacred space, close the door behind you, and begin the protocol we described previously.

When you have concluded your work in consciousness, remember to thank and dismiss the spirit in its two manifestations, to turn off the screen and physically to leave the sacred space. While the screen is on and you are working with spirit, the procedure can be precisely that which we described above, with the pad of paper and pen or the computer and the keyboard being your method of communicating and recording that communication.

It can also be completely mental.

The asset of having your words written down and the suggestions from spirit also written down is that it is objectified and can be referred to in your future. This becomes more important to you when you wish to follow the suggestions of your guidance. And we would suggest to you that, once you have received suggestions from guidance, it is extremely helpful to the process of following guidance to refer back to suggestions made during this process and to follow them insofar as it is possible for you to do.

Guidance has interactive qualities and those qualities are sharpened and articulated or made more detailed by the process of listening to guidance and following instructions. This does not mean that you must follow orders of any kind. What it means is that you are as active after a session of communication with guidance as you had been beforehand in asking for guidance.

We would comment further before we leave this subject on the general nature of guidance. You come into incarnation with a guidance system that is composed of three parts. That tripartite nature of guidance is, in a way, a convention but it is very helpful to realize that the energies of guidance are not simplistic or unitary in terms of the kind of information you are getting. There is what this instrument would call a yin or feminine side to guidance having to do with nurturing and the immediacy of unconditional love.

There is the yang portion of guidance which could be called masculine which has to do with power and the right use of power and can also contain the energies of wisdom and discrimination.

In many systems of magic, philosophy and religion, these two energies are switched and what we have described as feminine energies are assigned to the masculine or negative or yang energy and vice versa.

It does not, to our mind, much matter how you define the qualities of masculine and feminine, yang and yin, negative and positive. It is more important by far that you see the dynamic between love and wisdom, and so forth.

The third aspect of guidance with which you are naturally endowed could be described as androgynous or sexless in that it is that common ground which unifies guidance. It is also that energy which is most closely aligned with the process of moving within that shuttle which is your spiritual nature to bring to you, from the resources of your deep mind and the inner planes in general, those energies which are most helpful to you at a particular time.

It is not necessary to give this third entity a habitation, a place, a seat with you, and so forth. It is far more necessary that you come into contact with the dynamic of masculine and feminine, yang and yin, positive and negative. In your very body, mind and spirit you unify this dynamic. But it is well to invoke spirit, if so you do, in a way which specifically honors and respects the dynamic of love and wisdom in your guidance system.

You have other aspects of your guidance as well which you have accreted to your essence within incarnation because of the work that you are doing, the service that you are providing, the purity of your intentions and the sheer beauty of your soul. It is unknown at the beginning of an incarnation what your guidance shall blossom into by its end. This instrument, for instance, has well over a dozen entities and many, many essences which have attached themselves to her because of appreciation either for her nature, her dedication, or the work that she has done within incarnation as a service to others.

You, my sister, also have a multi-faceted guidance system. It is not necessary for you to identify or know all of these different layers of guidance. It is only necessary for you to know that they are, by their very nature, incapable of harming you or giving you poor information.

They also will work once you have asked for help. When you are outside of this sacred space that you have created, they will work for you in your car, during conversations in stores and shops and at the roadside. Therefore, all that you see once you have invoked guidance for the day has the potential for being full of messages from guidance.

Therefore, we encourage you to pay attention as you pass the street signs, the names of businesses, the advertising billboards, and other sources of information that are completely random. Note those street names, business names, and so forth, that resonate to you or that jump out at you.

(Side one of tape ends.)

(Carla channeling)

Consider them and the implications of the phrases or the words involved. Note birds and animals that cross your path and ask yourself how they make you feel and what, if anything, they may have to suggest to you in terms of the way that you feel.

This instrument informs us that we need to move along as this session otherwise will grow unmanageably long and we will run out of energy before we reach the end of your queries.

Consequently, we will ask if there is a second query at this time? We are those of Q'uo.

K: I recently experienced a very trying time emotionally. A healer that I work with and whom I trust determined that I was being infected both by dark energy and by a dark entity, the latter having come in or attached during my birth process in this life. Once we identified this it did feel right and resonate with me. Is it possible for you to confirm this and comment further to help me to understand this dark energy and the attachment of entities in general and why I specifically manifested such an experience in my life?

We are those of Q'uo, and are aware of your query, my sister. We find that it would be crossing the line and infringing upon your free will specifically to identify the source of such a specific attachment as you describe. However we find ourselves wishing to express both to you and to the one known as Carla that the reason for such attachments of an entity as opposed to a general energy have to do with one of two things.

They may have to do with a dedication on your part to working through a specific issue with a specific entity; that is say, a parent or someone within your incarnative process with whom you will have a continuing relationship. It also may be a connection that you pick up because of work that you have done in consciousness or in service in which you have created for yourself the characteristics of what this instrument would call a "lighthouse," where you are consciously and with dedication and persistence standing very close, as close as you can, to the light and the love of the one infinite Creator.

It is often said that when you stand in a stronger light you cast a sharper shadow. In that strong light your shadow self becomes glaringly obvious. The entity, seeing this sharper shadow, sees, then, its best route of access into your energy system. Any shadow that you cast, or to say it another way, any nicks in your armor of light that offer erroneous thinking or an immature understanding of love, light, wisdom, truth and so forth, can constitute such a point of weakness which makes it possible for entities to enter the energy system.

Whether or not there is an entity involved, the process of dealing with darker energies remains precisely the same unless you wish to engage specifically with an entity by knowing its name, working to control it or its power, and so forth, We would not recommend this avenue of control for it is not ever entirely service to others to attempt to control any essence, entity or energy.

We would suggest simply that you realize that whether an entity is involved or not, the reason for your having attracted this energy is your very loving and light-filled nature. It has called forth your shadow side or a mirror of your shadow side, for are not all things one? Therefore, even if it is an entity with a name, a background, and so forth, yet still, in its essence, it is yourself and, more specifically, it is mirroring to you a part of yourself that is unredeemed by your own acceptance, forgiveness and love. Therefore, sending such an energy or entity your deepest understanding, acceptance and love is, in our opinion, the most efficient way to deal with what this instrument would call psychic greeting.

May we ask if there is another query at this time?

K: Can you please comment on the following. In our world there are various moral and societal expectations for behavior on the level of personality or ego which sometimes seem directly to contradict what one needs on a soul level. Example: I was married and now am divorced. My husband and I both felt that our marriage had died and despite our efforts to revive it, we were unsuccessful and decided to separate. I felt very strongly that in some way my soul would have died had I tried further to remain in that relationship. Yet in leaving my marriage I broke a vow I had made. And my issue is not so much a religious one, although that also has meaning to me. It is a question of how to manage it, when what one should do seems to contradict on a soul level what is expected on the everyday personality level.

We are those of Q'uo, and are aware of your query, my sister. May we say that this is a question which resonates greatly to this instrument as well and in answering this query we will use her example in terms of the way she approached solving the same paradox.

The paradox involved in making a promise that is both in consensus reality and intended to be sacred or in metaphysical reality is that the promise in space/time and the promise in time/space are two completely different animals or creatures.

A promise within space/time is, in actuality, and in terms of energy expenditure, connected to the yellow-ray chakra, that chakra which works with the energies involved in dealings between yourself and groups. When you make a promise such as marriage within consensus reality, you are in effect making a contract.

The ways of contracts are binding within the limitations of those contracts and can be unbound in the ways of your worldly or cultural systems. You have obeyed those conventions in becoming disentangled from the agreement that you made. This completely eliminates any problem on the level of your energy as it has connected with the doings of the planetary culture.

What remains and what you are attempting to resolve, we believe, is the sacred promise that you made or the sacred aspects of that promise. The philosopher known as Emanuel Kant to this instrument created a body of literature in which he suggested that there are some rules that cannot be broken, or rather, that there are some rules that can be categorical, so that they would never be broken by their very nature.

This suggestion has been quite destructive in terms of its interaction with those who have been responsible for actions within consensus reality. In truth, within consensus reality, we do not believe that there are any categorical imperatives, as the one known as Kant suggested that there might be. It is our understanding that those who attempt to create immovable or immutable rules shall find themselves impaled upon the points of those rules. It is acceptable for such a decision to be made and it is in that wise that we cannot criticize any who remain married, for instance, when there is no hope for health for either soul in the contract of marriage.

It is understandable to us that entities would wish to martyr themselves in order not to break such a promise in order that they might be stainless and without any perceivable sin. However, we use this instrument's own experience to illustrate the possibility of another way of observing such sacred promises.

This instrument, in attempting to honor the sacredness of this promise of marriage with her first husband, found that she was only able to experience profound relief when her first husband asked her for permission to dissolve the bonds of marriage.

However, this instrument asked for permission to talk it over with the first husband and to change the agreement on the level of sacred agreements and specifically to address the change in sacred terms.

They therefore went through the necessary verbal means of acknowledging the sacred obligations of such a promise and freeing each other not only from the legal promises but from the sacred promises. They then knelt together and asked the Creator to bless the changes in their agreement.

We believe that it may well relieve your concern at this time to go through the additional process, whether with your partner or simply between yourself and the one infinite Creator, in acknowledging the sacred aspect as opposed to the legal aspect of breaking such a promise; of detailing to the Creator, and if you wish, to this entity in your life with whom bonds have been dissolved, the details of your dissolution of these bonds, and then asking for the blessing of the one infinite Creator on this change of agreement. In this way, what this instrument would call situational or relative ethics may be invoked without ignoring or abnegating the responsibility of honoring sacred vows.

May we ask if there is another query at this time?

K: This question concerns a relationship. A man whom I love very much seems to be oriented to service to self and to be fairly polarized in that direction. He is also very powerful in the psychic realm. I see myself as being more oriented to service to others. When we started to become closer, he seemed very much to back away and I felt that this was because our connection was depolarizing him or generating fear or a sense of losing power. Is this an accurate understanding? Also, is this person possibly being influenced by fifth-density entities unbeknownst to him? This has been a concern of mine for some time.

We are those of Q'uo, and are aware of your query, my sister. We find our ability to speak severely limited with regard to this question. The reasons are multiple. Firstly, this is an active point within your spiritual process at this time. We do not wish in any way to do your learning for you.

Secondly, we can comment to you concerning yourself with far more of a sense of remaining free of infringement on your free will than we can in terms of commenting on another entity who is an other self outside of your energy system.

What we would wish to do, then, is simply to comment on your own way of dealing with your perceptions at this time. We ask you to lose all fear and to realize that, in terms of energy work, this entity has no beingness within your system but is acting as a mirror or reflecting surface, reflecting to you those energies within yourself which your dynamic with this entity bring forth in your process.

Therefore, if you are experiencing negativity or the results of negativity from your dynamics with this entity, they are there, in terms of your energy work, not for you to deal with this entity, but for you to work within your own energy system, using the information about your shadow side that you have been receiving as the mirror-images back to you from this entity yourself as he sees you or as you evoke his own nature in reaction to the dynamics with you.

Take this information in as if it were a psychic greeting. Ask yourself what you can learn from this picture of yourself. What can you learn from the picture of yourself as one who has pride or one who has impatience or one who has vanity? And so forth. Whatever aspects of self that are being brought up to you that you would rather not look at, these promptings from this entity create the opportunity for you to choose finally to look at them squarely. Find out, firstly, precisely what the nature of this shadow image is and then ask yourself if you can love, accept, forgive and transmute these energies. In terms of dealing with the other entity, that is an entirely different subject.

In terms of your own work, use this and every relational dynamic as information concerning yourself and look always with eyes of the deepest and most sacred love and compassion upon the issues raised by this imaging process.

We find that we have a certain amount of energy and would ask the one known as K if there are any questions remaining upon her mind or any ways she would wish to follow up on these questions? We are those of Q'uo.

K: Thank you very much for all that you have shared in your great service and kindness. On the last question about the relationship, I do have one follow-up, which is to ask, as I've been doing this work and attempting to do what you are suggesting, what has come to my awareness is that, in some ways, the mirror-image is about my feeling like I know what is better for this entity. This is something I accused him of doing for others. Would this be a correct understanding of my shadow?

We are those of Q'uo, and can confirm this understanding for you. May we say that it is rare that an entity is so able to pick up the subtlety of how the mirroring effect works. It is indeed very helpful that you have come to this conclusion.

May we answer you further, my sister?

K: I think that's it. That's all I can take in today and I thank you so much because it's been very helpful and your services are most appreciated, today and in all the various channelings. And I also thank the one known as Carla and Vara and all the guides and other assistants that I feel have been present today, and I send you light and love.

We are those of Q'uo, and are aware of your comments, my sister. We cannot tell you how much we have enjoyed this opportunity to share energy with you at this time.

We are aware that the one known as Carla had a query but at this time we would suggest that she retain this query and ask it at a later time, as the energy does wane at this time. Therefore, we would leave this instrument, those present, and all, as the one known as K has said, of the unseen friends that have attended this session, in the love and in the light of the one infinite Creator. May you go forth rejoicing. We are known to you as the principle of Q'uo. Adonai. Adonai. ✨

L/L Research

L/L Research is a subsidiary of
Rock Creek Research &
Development Laboratories, Inc.

P.O. Box 5195
Louisville, KY 40255-0195

www.llresearch.org

Rock Creek is a non-profit
corporation dedicated to
discovering and sharing
information which may aid in
the spiritual evolution of
humankind.

Special Meditation
October 14, 2005

V: *(Reading question.)* "E's first question today reads, "I feel I have made significant progress in my spiritual growth over the last couple of years. Can you confirm this? Please comment in any way you feel helpful concerning what specific things I could consider or do to continue in this growth."

(Carla channeling)

We are those of the principle known to you as the Q'uo. Greetings in the love and the light of the one infinite Creator. We are most privileged to serve the infinite Creator by offering our humble thoughts through this instrument and we thank the one known as E for setting aside time and energy to request a circle of seeking at this time.

We are most happy to respond to this query. However, as always, we would request, not only of the one known as E but of all who may read or hear these words, that each take the responsibility for his own powers of discrimination. The issue here is our desire not to infringe on the free will of any person or to become inappropriately engaged in the process of spiritual evolution for another.

Therefore, if it is well understood that we are asking that you listen to each thought of ours carefully and be very ready to reject it if it does not seem resonant to you, that will free us to speak our minds without being concerned that we will infringe upon your free will inadvertently.

We have found in the past that there are those who would take our words to be those of an authority and we would not wish them to be perceived in that light. We, as you, are those who seek a greater understanding of the one infinite Creator. We do not wish to be perceived as authority figures or as those who could give you words that would be taken without question. Please do question each and every thought that we offer you this day. We thank you for this great consideration.

We can confirm that the one known as E has made significant progress in his spiritual evolution in the last couple of your years. We would comment on the request for suggestions for further work in this wise in two ways.

Firstly, we would comment on the basic nature of what it is to come to graduation at the end of your third-density experience upon planet Earth.

Your tuning, as of this pleasant autumn day that we enjoy seeing and listening to through this instrument's ears and eyes, has almost nothing to do with what will occur when you or anyone else in this situation actually enters the gates of the larger life and so becomes eligible for graduation. The only consideration for graduation at that time will be your tuning at that time.

It is very helpful to do work day by day, week by week, and month by month. That kind of dedication and persistence is always fruitful in accelerating the pace of your spiritual evolution.

However, graduation is not a test that can be taken beforehand. Nor is it a test that can be studied for, in the sense of cramming for a final, as this instrument would say.

When we speak of the word "tuning" or consider the vibratory energy that you hold at a certain moment, we are not speaking of anything physical. We are not even speaking of the weak electrical charge of your thoughts. That is an artifact of third density and space/time.

We are speaking of that tuning which is a true reading or readout of your state of mind at any particular moment. The tuning that you have at the moment of your entry into the gates of larger life may be radically different from your tuning at this time. We are in no position to know your future.

Each choice that you make between now and the moment of your death, whenever that is, will readjust the vibratory energies of your energy body and will change your readout. This process will go on in a completely open and fluid manner until the point at which your consciousness separates from your physical body and enters through what this instrument has called at times, in a somewhat joking manner, the Pearly Gates. We call them the gates to the present moment, the gateway to intelligent infinity, or simply, as this instrument terms it, the gateway to larger life.

This is not to discourage the one known as E from taking pride in the accomplishments which are his and in the changing of his vibratory rate as it has been changed by his seeking, suffering and entering of the silence. It is rather to orient the one known as E to a deeper realization of what it is to enter the graduation process.

In truth, the vibratory levels with which you entered incarnation upon planet Earth will most likely not have altered tremendously when you leave the planetary environment of Earth. What will have changed is the readout of your energies within each of what this instrument would call your chakras and the overall balanced readout of all of your chakras that together make up your ultimate vibration as you leave Earth and space/time through the gateway to intelligent infinity or to larger life.

Each time that you perceive an ethical question and move to respond in a heartfelt way to that ethical question, the choice that you have just made

rebalances your entire energy body as well as altering the vibratory readout on the chakras to which these decisions apply. Unfortunately, for those who would like to see their progress as an unending upward climb, one day's good work can be completely undone by another day's error in thinking. Polarity is very fluid. It changes from moment to moment and from day to day.

Each day we would encourage the one known as E to awaken with the realization that this is a new day. This clears the way for you to make the most use possible of the catalyst that is offered to you during this day. Each day you will receive various elements of catalyst that create in you various thoughts in response. Examine these thoughts to see where your point of view leads you in responding to catalyst.

Again, this is not to discourage you from making a concerted effort to progress. It is simply to say that the work that you do is a work in progress and that you are not building precisely the way entities build buildings in third density. You cannot and do not, in spiritual work, build your footings and then your walls and then your roof and so forth. In actuality you are building parts of all elements of your building of self. You are creating elements of the structure of your self by the decisions and the choices that you make.

The most helpful way to progress quickly is never to unmake a choice. However, we have found that it is almost inevitable in third density that entities will make and unmake choices repeatedly, not always being consistent. And each time that the inconsistency occurs and the choice to love without condition, or whatever choice of an ethical nature that you have made, is then rescinded, this changes your vibratory level.

It is not possible to hold on to past glory. Rather, the most helpful thing to be before your mind is always the moment and the choice of this moment.

Secondly, in this regard we would note that to those who perceive, at the heart level, the absolute centrality of service to others as a polarized choice, it is close to inevitable that at the moment of death and the entry into graduation, your vibratory level will reflect that basic choice. Once you have awakened and begun the process of spiritual seeking, the odds are heavily in your favor that your vibratory level at that time will reflect a satisfactory level of service-to-others polarity for you to be able to have the opportunity to graduate.

We say this in order to take away that feeling of needing to pass a test. It is the essence of the grasping of the centrality of the choice of service to others as a polarity that is the most substantial part of how your energy body will be vibrating at the time of your passing through that gateway, rather than the day-to-day details that vary according to those transient and ephemeral circumstances that come and go, rise and fall away again in the course of any lifetime.

Therefore, rather than being overly concerned about any one choice, any one day, or any one action, keep moving back in your mind to the central point and to your first faithful choice of polarity. Affirm and reaffirm that choice. This is your fulcrum. This is the source of your power as a choice-making spiritual seeker.

Then, each day, let the day be a new one and see what you can do to make this day a day in which you have upheld that basic choice to the very best of your ability as a spiritual seeker.

As to what you can do from this point onward to keep moving in the direction which you have started, we would simply encourage you in two ways. Firstly, we would encourage you on a conscious, mental and intellectual level to engage your powers of analysis on a daily basis. Perhaps the evening is your most convenient time for this exercise but it can profitably be done at any point during the day that is convenient to you. Take time to analyze those thoughts that have been uppermost in your mind. It may even help you to jot them down on a computer or with pen and paper. Where has your mind been today? What are your thoughts? What emotions occupied your attention? Ask yourself this on a daily basis. It is an efficient and not a time consuming way to respect and honor your own thoughts.

It is notable how many good thoughts entities who are seeking have, to which they do not pay attention. Pay attention to your thoughts! Spiritually speaking, your thoughts are the objects that furnish the rooms of your consciousness. Furnish well, my brother, that room of consciousness.

And if you are not satisfied with the quality of those furnishings, analyze with that excellent intellect of yours precisely where you are dissatisfied with your own performance and muse, asking yourself how you might encourage yourself to be more focused and more centered when those same themes of thought and feeling come up tomorrow.

Secondly, as always, we encourage any entity who attempts to live a spiritually oriented life to make time on a daily basis for silence. The distracting and seductive power of noise and activity is remarkable in your culture for its constancy. Even in the midst of seemingly rural circumstances there is busyness and noise, distraction and seduction.

Entering the silence, one at last closes the door on distraction and seduction. We always recommend meditation, which is a very straightforward thing in our minds, consisting of sitting, lying or walking while keeping inner silence. If thoughts arise, allow them to arise but do not following them. Let them fall away. When more thoughts arise, be just as tolerant of them but do not follow them. Let them all fall away.

It may be that your experience of meditation is nothing but watching your thoughts arise and then fall away. That is acceptable and will be helpful to you. It is not to the one who meditates perfectly that advancement and awareness are given. It is to the one who is persistent.

There is a tremendous cultural bias towards looking for some kind of result from any action that is undertaken. Sometimes in the life of the spirit meditation seems to produce moments of great realization and that feeds into the spiritual materialism of thinking that the meditation has produced a result and therefore is a good thing. In fact, it is the discipline of submitting the body and the mind to being shut down and to entering the sacred space within your own heart in a conscious manner that creates the environment in which what this instrument would call results are recorded or are seen.

Therefore, as you choose your manner of meditation, see what you can do to find for yourself a time of day and a place which is as much as possible stable for your time of silence. Like anything else, such times are a habit. When you have established a habit, it is much easier to continue a spiritual practice. Until you have established a routine, shall we say, your practice does not have a convenient nook or cubbyhole in which to park itself and so each day there is a moment of anxiety when you realize that you have not yet provided for yourself the opportunity either to enter the silence and to listen for that still small voice within the silence that is the Creator or to analyze and think about your thoughts of the day and of the previous day. Finding a place in your daily routine that works for you for these disciplines is, to our way of thinking, very helpful in that it allows you the daily opportunity to fulfill your basic goal of attempting to accelerate the pace of your spiritual evolution.

We do not insist upon any particular kind of meditation and believe that there are many different variations on meditation that are equally helpful. There are some who find working and walking in nature to be their most effective visit to their own heart of hearts.

There are others who find open-eyed meditation, gazing, for instance, at a white sheet or white wall, to be the most helpful form of meditation.

There are others who find visualization a very helpful focus for meditation and others who find chanting or mantra helpful.

We encourage you to follow any and all of these variations in entering the silence until you have found one that you really feel is your own. Then, my brother, make it your own. Create a rule of life for yourself that includes the daily observance of these disciplines. This basic reserving of time is a tremendously powerful resource and creates an environment for enhanced spiritual growth.

May we ask if there is another query at this time?

V: Thank you, there is. E's second query is, "Do you see my work with DNA activation and Ormus as beneficial to my spiritual evolution?"

(Carla channeling)

We are those known as the Q'uo, and we are aware of your query, my brother. The one known as V and this instrument were speaking earlier concerning this very question, and it was mentioned that almost anything is helpful to spiritual growth. We would agree with this assessment. We cannot offer you a general estimate of the value either of the DNA Enhancement study or of the Ormus study, although we grasp the excellence of the energy connected with those who do this work. Moreover, we grasp that in both instances entities of considerable spiritual polarity and power are

working with valid and legitimate principles within the natural world and producing provocative and helpful material.

What we can say is that when working with such concepts and areas of study as these it is well to question that which you are studying with the same kind of trust in your own powers of discrimination that we have asked you to invoke when looking at our thoughts. Do not assume that any so-called outer authority can be trusted.

It is not that entities would wish to produce untrustworthy material. Rather it is that all material must come into the energy system of one particular individual. It is not a one-size-fits-all world at all, in terms of truth. That which would simply be truth to one person might become a very unbalanced truth that for a particular entity could be overvalued as being something that is true for all people, whereas this is never the case. Something that is helpful to you on one day may not be helpful to you on another. Something that you work with very usefully at one point may need to be put down and forgotten entirely as a higher truth comes to you along the lines that you were studying.

Therefore, we ask you to remain sensitive to the present moment and to the person that you are as you approach the material as it appears to you today. Do not be afraid to let go of something that has seemed to you to be the truth in the past. Rather, lift up that which you are studying this day to the light of your present mindset.

And if you sense that there is any lack of resonance in that which you are studying, then we would ask you to put that resource down for the present. For this day it is not helpful to you. Take it up again another day and see if the resonance has returned. Either something about the material has changed, or something about you has changed. Allow those things to change. But you may always reinvestigate any body of material to see if you may reenter it at a different level and find use for it once again.

Try to remember that everything in the process of a spiritual evolution is in flux. You are dancing with the various influences and energies in your life. Blessed is the entity whose dance is not completely bogged down in the dance of relationships, the dance between the self and groups and so forth. Blessed indeed is the entity who has balanced these energies to the point where the life in its totality may be viewed as a spiritual experience.

When all things are seen as sacred, then the potential for accelerating the pace of your spiritual evolution becomes ever greater. We encourage you to see all things as grist for the mill.

May we ask if there is another query at this time?

V: Thank you Q'uo. That response also spoke to E's third question. So I will move on to number four: "I feel that I am a wanderer. Can you confirm? Please comment on where wanderers return to after graduation from third density."

(Carla channeling)

We are those of Q'uo, and are aware of your query, my brother. We can confirm indeed that you are a wanderer. The choice of where you go after you have completed graduation from third density is a choice that will not be made until that moment.

Upon the physical death of the body which is connected to your spirit complex there is a period of unknown length during which you finish that business that is yours within third-density life. This includes a carryover as you stand in the gateway where the expectations that you have of the life to come or what this instrument calls the larger life meet the actuality of that larger life.

For many people there is a time of clearing away of expectation of an unknown duration depending upon the tenacity to which certain expectations are held to the self.

(Side one of tape ends.)

(Carla channeling)

For instance, if an entity desires or expects to see the one known as Jesus or the one known as the Buddha, then there will need to be a certain amount of time during which these expectations are fulfilled.

When an entity's mind and consciousness are clear at last of expectation, then that entity is ready to go through the process of actual graduation. That process is as simple as moving into the light and stopping at the place that feels the most comfortable, neither too much light nor too little light.

It will not be obvious at all as to whether that final destination, that place of stopping, is in third density or fourth density. Once you have stopped, then you will discover, along with your higher self, what your point of destination has been. If you are still in third density, then you and your higher self will talk together, looking over your incarnation that has just taken place and choosing the next location for third-density work. Once that location has been chosen, then you and your guidance system will move into discussions concerning the actual setup and shape of the incarnation to come.

If, on the other hand, you have stopped at a point that is further than third density, whether it be fourth, fifth, or sixth density, then it may be assumed that that location is your embarkation point for your next incarnation. It may be that you will not move back to your previous destination, in other words, that destination from which you came to offer yourself to service upon planet Earth. It may be that there will be incarnations that simply rebuild and rebalance parts of yourself that in some way were damaged during the sometimes very rough and tumble processes of third-density incarnation.

In the end, when all impediments to your returning to your place of origin have been met and balanced, you and your guidance system, or your higher self as this instrument calls it, will then do the same kind of thinking and planning that we were speaking of an entity doing in third density when they do not get to graduate and when they are simply planning their next incarnation.

For one who has wandered, such as you, the universe is quite open. You and your guidance system will discuss the needs of your beingness for rest, for learning, or for further service. These discussions and considerations will take in the full range of your beingness in a way that it is difficult to share with you with words.

Were you to attempt to write down the fullness of these considerations you would discover that the document that you produced would be thousands and thousands of pages long. It is no inconsiderable thing to choose the manner of your expression when you have cleared service as a wanderer in a lower density and you are now contemplating your next move.

Generally speaking, you will be consulting not only with your guidance system as a person, but with the guidance system of the group of wanderers of which you are a part. And while it is not certain, it is very likely that you, as a member of that group, will choose, after due consideration and deliberation with other members of that group, to serve again as a group in another situation in which you become wanderers once again and enter into becoming natives of a lower density in order to serve as light bearers and lighthouses, as this instrument would say it.

May we ask if there is another query, my sister?

V: Yes. "Please assess the probability of a pole shift in this planet's near future. Please comment in any way you find helpful about the end of the Mayan calendar and 2012."

(Carla channeling)

We are aware of your query, my brother. We are those of Q'uo. That which we have to share with you on this subject is somewhat limited because of the fact that these considerations are part of your process at this time. We would say three things:

First of all, the likelihood of planetary pole shift is nearly certain. The only question is when that shift shall occur. What entities such as L/L Research hope to accomplish with their service is the delaying of such a time of planetary annihilation and, if possible, the softening of that blow so that it is possible to have the shifting occur in stages which the planet and some of its population can survive. This is simply in order to create the continued environment within which third-density entities have the continuing opportunity to make the choice of service to others or service to self.

Secondly, the Mayan calendar and many other systems indicate that 2012 is the end of an Age. Indeed, the Mayans end time is in 2012, at the Winter Solstice. This is an accurate assessment of the movement of the planet itself into the Age of Aquarius. This Age begins a kind of octave and is a tremendous shift. It is occurring very much on time and on schedule. It is, however, to be noted that this event is metaphysical rather than physical. There is nothing inevitable, in terms of physicality, about what is going to occur at the Winter Solstice of 2012.

It is the hope of many entities such as this instrument that in between now and 2012 it will be possible to continue to create an environment in which entities may awaken as to the choice of polarity that they have to make. It is equally hoped by this instrument and many others that they will be able to serve by helping the planet itself, and in this case we are speaking of the third-density Gaia, after 2012. There is a considerable amount of restitution and rebalancing which entities such as you and this instrument may do in order to help the planet itself to heal after the grievous wounds inflicted upon it by the humankind that dwells upon this planet.

Third density itself is waning. The need for wanderers and their lightening of the planet will cease in 2012. However, the need for all of those who live and who dwell on planet Earth as natives, which includes all wanderers, continues to be that of being loving stewards of the planet itself.

It is possible, when you search your heart, that you may find great resonance not so much in your service to the people of planet Earth as to your determination to serve the planet itself. And that is something you may ponder.

In leaving this subject we would take note that we found this instrument's vibration dropping considerably when this question was asked. And that indicates to us, since we know that this instrument herself is not fearful concerning the times to come, that the query that you asked held a certain amount of fear.

In an atmosphere of fear, it is difficult for the truth to come through. If that fear is held and if the focus of that fear is gradually intensified with each new specific piece of information found, then we would observe that you are creating the potential for undoing the work of polarization in consciousness that you so carefully and persistently have pursued.

If you find yourself dwelling in the precincts of fear, cast your minds immediately to the grave. Lie down in your grave and realize that this is the end of your body. When you have gotten very clearly in mind the inevitability of physical death, arise from that grave. For today you are alive! Today the sun shines upon you and you bloom like a flower. In your blooming, praise the one infinite Creator and know that both in life and in death your consciousness is unchanged.

Is there a final query at this time?

V: Indeed there is. "Please tell us about the nature of physical life in fourth density, including details about jobs, home and family, those things that seem to make up the mundane part of third-density life."

(Carla channeling)

We are those of Q'uo, and are aware of your query, my brother. In a way, it is not at all difficult to answer this query, my brother, for in fourth density you will have a physical vehicle and you will occupy yourself with various activities.

What is almost impossible to convey to you is the changed nature of your awareness in fourth density. In third density you have been dealing with life in the dark. Having to make the choice of polarity in an atmosphere of absolute unknowing created the necessity for third density to be a life lived in the dark. Faith is not faith unless it is grasped without proof. Therefore, you have been veiled of all possible ways of proving in any objective sense the truth of those spiritual principles you have chosen to hold dear.

When you have come through the refining fire of this furnace-like existence of third density, you will find yourself in a much different environment. But it is not an environment which you would think of as idyllic. You will be living in a completely open environment in which everyone knows all of your thoughts at all times. You will know everyone else's thoughts at all times. It will no longer be possible for you to put others on a pedestal or for others to put you on a pedestal.

However, fourth density is life lived in the daylight of the awareness of the one infinite Creator. There is no need for faith in fourth density because the situation is eminently clear. It is very clear that all are one being. It is very clear that the elements of what you think of as personality are bits and pieces assembled like the change in your pocket or a collection of bibelots[65]. Whatever you do choose in fourth density, you will be aware that it is not adhering to you because it is you. You will be aware that you are wearing it as you wear a piece of clothing. You will be aware of the roles that you play. You will embrace them. But you will also realize that that which is most essentially yourself recedes infinitely and ever before you. The shadows that you chase in the daylight are the shadows of paradox and mystery.

In fourth density it is not necessary to earn money. It is, however, an absolute imperative of your very nature that you serve, love and give and that you allow entities to serve you, love you, and give to you. Consequently, you shall move where you wish to move in thought and in physicality in order to fill the niche that most beautifully fits your needs and your gifts. The overriding energy of those days will be to discover how you can create wealth in terms of multiplying your gifts.

You shall certainly continue to choose a life partner as a way of serving the Creator and you shall choose most likely to live in families. It is however, likely that these families will be clans rather than nuclear families and they will sort themselves out by what this instrument would call the "birds of a feather" plan.

You have already found in this last bit of third density that entities find themselves grouping themselves by common interest. This will continue and will intensify. It will be, however, exponentially more simple to choose one's group and to work within that group because there will be that awareness of the thoughts of others so that a very deep level of certainty may be yours as to the true compatibility of yourself and the rest of your clan.

We find that the energy wanes. We thank you, my brother, for the opportunity to spend this time with you. It has been a pleasure and a privilege and again we thank you for setting aside this time and we thank the ones known as Carla and V as well. We leave you in the love and the light of the one infinite Creator. Adonai. Adonai. ✤

---

[65] bibelot: a small household ornament or decorative object.

L/L RESEARCH

L/L Research is a subsidiary of
Rock Creek Research &
Development Laboratories, Inc.

P.O. Box 5195
Louisville, KY 40255-0195

www.llresearch.org

Rock Creek is a non-profit
corporation dedicated to
discovering and sharing
information which may aid in
the spiritual evolution of
humankind.

SPECIAL MEDITATION
OCTOBER 15, 2005

Question chosen by PLW poll:[66] Can you talk about the concept of densities and/or vibrations levels? We hear a lot about these terms. What do they really mean? How do we apply them in our daily lives here?

(Carla channeling)

We are the those known to you as the principle of Q'uo. Greetings in the love and in the light of the one infinite Creator, in Whose service we come to you this day. It a pleasure and a privilege to be called to your circle of seeking and we thank you. We are most pleased to be asked to share our thoughts with you on the subject of densities and rates of vibration.

We would ask of you, as we always do, that each of you who considers our words be very careful to employ the full power of your own discrimination as you listen to or read these words. Be aware that you are the sole arbiter of what comes into your mind and what is released from being considered by you. Each entity's universe is unique. Each person is a being that creates their own universe. Consequently, what is true for you at one time may not be adequate for you at another time. And what is true for you may not be true for someone else.

Therefore, as you listen to those things that we say, we would greatly appreciate your being very careful to listen with an ear for the resonance of any particular thought. If a thought seems resonant to

you, then please feel free to explore it. If it does not seem right to you, for whatever reason, we would ask you to lay it aside. In that way we will feel much more able to speak our thoughts freely, knowing that we are not infringing upon your process. We would not wish to become a stumbling block in the evolutionary process of any. We thank you for this consideration.

In speaking about the terms "vibration" and "density" we are to a certain extent limited by the concepts of your culture. In terms of the standard cultural concepts of these terms, they represent terms speaking of one system only. It is our understanding that we are speaking of not one but two types of systems when we use these terms.

One system is the classic system that your Newtonian physics represents or discusses. It is consensus reality, or as we might put it, it is the world of space/time. It is the physical universe. The other system to which these terms applies is the metaphysical universe, the universe of time/space.

The universe of space/time is the universe in which your intellect functions. Your brain is a tool that is limited to the space/time considerations of analysis, the solving of problems and other abstract functions of reasoning and rationalization.

The world of time/space is the world of the unseen realms or the inner planes. It is the realm of your consciousness and your heart. If you sometimes feel that you have a divided mind, you are perceptive

[66] Planet Lightworker Magazine (www.planetlightworker.com).

and literally correct. For you have two kinds of mind. You have the mind of the brain and you have the mind of your heart. The brain is an excellent tool for solving problems of your consensus reality. The mind of your heart is the province of intuition and insight. It receives promptings, visions, dreams and inspiration from the spiritual realm.

This instrument has often said that the longest distance in spiritual work is the fourteen inches from head to heart. Neither kind of thinking is to be rejected or disrespected, and the goal that we would suggest to each of you is to combine the two ways of using the faculties that have been given to you as a person or a soul.

The terms vibration and densities are equally applicable to both universes, the universe of space/time and the universe of time/space. However, it is necessary to remember that there are two reciprocal creations that interpenetrate each other and create your inner and your outer worlds.

In order for you to be able to use these concepts most efficiently, let us look first at the concept of vibration. Everything that exists within your universe, both in space/time and in time/space, has a rate of vibration. Your body, for instance, is composed of various energy fields. Each of your cells is an energy field, and the atoms that make up those cells are small but are very powerful energy fields. Each atom and cell has a rate of vibration. The cells come together to create the systems of your body which in turn have an overarching unitary field of energy which has a rate of vibration. Your body as a whole, sitting or standing or riding in your car, has, similarly, a composite field and rate of vibration.

In the space/time world you have instrumentation that is capable of measuring many of these rates of vibration. The way that vibrations are expressed in your system of physics is that which is called a sine wave. That is [in] a shape of an unending "S." The vibration moves above and below a center line which is the center point of that vibratory expression. When you think a thought, the process of thinking creates a weak electrical vibration.

The planet upon which you live has a composite rate of vibration as well as a composite energy field. Every object in the space/time universe has an inherent field and rate of vibration. This is important to remember when you consider that your universe is made up of mostly empty space. It is

these fields that create the illusion of solidarity in your field of view.

When you look at your chair, it seems as though you are looking at something very solid. However your scientists will explain to you that you are actually looking at an illusion that is mostly empty space. The system of one atom looks a good deal like a very small sun and its planets, with the electrons functioning as the planets.

In so-called matter, scientists have never been able to see any matter. They are able either to locate the path of energy that is going on in the electrons of an atom or they are able to identify a position that the atom is holding in the space/time continuum. In terms of being able to nail down something called matter that has mass, they have not been able to do so. In fact, your space/time universe as well as your time/space [universe] is a universe of energy.

Consequently, when we speak of densities we are not speaking of something that is dense in terms of matter. Rather, we're speaking of various levels of the density of that which we would call light. If you can accept that everything, including your thoughts, has a vibratory level then you are conversant enough with this concept in order for us to speak of density levels.

As you think of yourself, you think of your physical body with your eyes, your nose, your mouth, the way that your body is, how much it weighs, what color the hair is, what kind of texture your skin has, and so forth. These are the considerations which come to your mind when you think of who you are.

In fact, there is a part of your body which exists in time/space. It is the metaphysical or the time/space portion of your physical body. In some systems of philosophy it is called the chakra system. In others it might be called the electrical body. There are many names, in fact, if one examines the terms used in religions and systems of spiritual seeking for this unseen but causal body. It is, shall we say, the repository of the default settings for the body which was born into incarnation at your birth. The chakra-[body] or the electrical-body contains the ideal or perfect system settings for your entire body system. These settings exist in the memory in each of your chakras.

Within the system of chakras known best by this instrument, there are seven chakras and each of them is a part of the energies of the body.

The red-ray or root chakra deals with issues of survival and sexuality.

The orange-ray chakra found in the [area of the] lower intestines deals with the relationship of self to self and the relationship of self to people around you on a personal level.

The yellow-ray or solar plexus chakra deals with issues of groups and the self. If you have married your mate, for instance, that energy has moved from an orange to a yellow-ray vibration. Family, work environment, your relationship with groups such as churches and other communities, all have the characteristics of yellow-ray work.

The heart chakra or the green-ray chakra is the first chakra at which there is the possibility of energy transfer and it contains that energy which this instrument calls Christed or that energy of unconditional love. The green-ray energy system is the springboard for the remaining chakras of your body.

The throat chakra or the blue-ray chakra deals with open communication and inclusivity.

The indigo-ray or brow chakra deals with issues with work in consciousness. If you are a person that enjoys meditation, for instance, you are doing indigo work. If you enjoy walks in nature, the reading of inspirational materials, or work in visualization, these are also indigo-ray works.

The remaining chakra, found on the crown of the head, is the violet-ray chakra and is a simple readout of your system-wide rate of vibration at a particular time.

Altogether, this chakra system is not only yourself in the unseen realms, that self that came to incarnation and that self that will leave incarnation with you. It is also your identity as far as energies and essences such as we ourselves are concerned. When we look at those who are sitting in this particular circle of seeking, we see not your physical bodies but the rainbow of your chakra system. Each of you is completely and utterly unique in your coloration and your energies, and that readout, shall we say, of the rainbow being that you are in time/space identifies you much more accurately and completely than your name or the way you look in space/time or consensus reality.

This system of space/time and time/space, outer and inner self, is who you are at this moment in your incarnation on planet Earth. It carries with the chakra system all that you are as a citizen of eternity and infinity. At the same time it carries the very ephemeral and transitory energies of your physical body. Your physical body was born and it shall pass through the gates of death and be no more. Your metaphysical body or the chakra system will travel through the gates of death into larger life with you; and in terms of your own experience or consciousness, your consciousness will not know any stoppage nor will it cease in its being for an instant at any moment during the death process. When you leave this incarnation, you shall be leaving what we would term a third-density incarnation. And that brings us to the discussion of the densities.

The densities repeat at a macrocosmic level the chakra system of your body.

The first density is equivalent to the red-ray chakra. It is the elemental density of earth, air, wind and fire. It is out of this elemental red ray or first density that your planet was formed and that your body was formed. The elements within your body vibrate at first density.

First density is interpenetrated by second density, and the denizens or inhabitants of second density are governed by that energy which seeks growth, movement and light. Second density includes the plants and the animals that are not self-aware. The world of nature is the world of second density. Neither first nor second density is at all or in any way separate from the love that created it and so all aspects and each iota of first and second-density entities and essences have a full awareness of the love and the light of the one infinite Creator.

Third density, however, is a density in which the inhabitants are veiled from that primal, instantaneous and instinctual awareness of this love and light. It is not obvious to the inhabitants of third density that there is a Creator or that they are one with the Creator. The third density is inhabited by those animals of second density that have become aware of themselves. If you gaze upon your pet you will notice that the entity that is your pet is not self-aware. Without self-consciousness it goes about its life.

You, on the other hand, are endlessly self aware. You are always looking into yourself, asking yourself what you think, how you feel and who you are. You are aware that other entities are looking at you and you can become self-conscious and create all manner of concerns having to do with how you are coming across to other people. Second-density inhabitants are never troubled by concern as to how they are coming across. You, on the other hand, are self-concerned.

The third density is a density which is veiled from direct knowledge of the one infinite Creator in order that you may choose the manner of your being in perfect freedom. The Creator, in creating the universe which you enjoy at this time, wished to know Itself. And you are the sparks of that Creator which are going about the business of getting to know who you are. The harvest of this observation, with its processes of learning and realization, are the gift that your life will offer up to the one infinite Creator at the end of your incarnation.

That harvest is your crowning achievement. All that you have thought and felt, chosen and decided become a system of thinking that has a coherence and exists as a vibratory essence. It is this that remains, not your personality, not anything to do with your physicality, but this very bouquet of thoughts and feelings that you develop into the self that you are. This is your highest achievement. So it is very valuable to yourself in terms of the process of evolution of mind, body and spirit that you are engaged in as a seeker; that constitutes your basic vibration within third density at this time.

It is interesting to note, before we move on to fourth density in our discussion, that your third-density world at this time is giving birth to its fourth-density self. The Earth or Gaia is exhausting its third-density identity at this time. And in unseen realms interpenetrating with the third density planet, or Gaia, is a baby Gaia. It is being born full-grown and is swimming into coherence with the inevitability of the striking of the clock upon the hour. It is time for fourth-density Earth to be born.

We are happy to say that the birth is going well, and the baby is alive. The challenges that you experience in your third-density planet at this time, having have to do with wind and weather, are the birth pains of third-density Gaia as she adjusts her rate of vibration in order to bring forth the fourth-density Earth in both its space/time and its time/space aspects. At this time, however, it is a time/space phenomenon and it will not become a fourth-density space/time entity until the third-density inhabitants have been thoroughly cleared safely from the planet.

It is worth noting at this time that the planetary evolution is separate from your personal evolution from third density into fourth density. And one of the reasons that you were so happy to come into incarnation at this particular time is that it is a challenging time for your planet. Your heart went out to the planet as it entered this period of transition and you hoped to be a steward and a lover of the planet itself in that you may help it to achieve a soft landing, shall we say, into fourth-density beingness. When a planet changes densities it is then time for the entities that have had incarnations on the planet also to choose the manner of their beingness. So you are, as a third-density being at this time, in an incarnation at the end of which you shall be given the opportunity to graduate from third-density experiences into fourth-density experiences.

The person that will decide whether or not it is time for you to move on into fourth density with your planet is yourself. Upon your death you shall walk what this instrument is being shown as steps of light, each step being of a slightly fuller vibration of light than the one before it. There is a quantum break between the top level of third density and the lowest level of fourth density. At that point the light changes in its nature. If you are comfortable with fourth-density light, then you shall continue walking up those steps of light into fourth density. Wherever you stop is where you shall find the manner of your beingness when next you take flesh and incarnate.

If you remained within the third-density range of levels of vibration, then you shall need to move to a third-density planet elsewhere in order to continue your learn/teaching, your teach/learning, and your process of seeking. If when you stopped walking in the steps of light, you were standing in fourth-density light, then your next incarnation shall be on planet Earth as a fourth-density being. There are exceptions to this statement into which we shall not go into at this time. In general, this is correct information.

Fourth density is a density which has been called the density of love or the density of understanding. In fourth density the lessons of love will be explored.

All of the thoughts of all of the entities within a fourth-density planet are known to each other and work is done in groups rather than being done singly.

The fifth density is a density which has often been called the density of wisdom.

The sixth density has been often called the density of unity. It is a density which explores the balance between love and wisdom.

The seventh density has been called the density of foreverness. In this density the energies of spiritual gravity begin to take hold of you as a spark of the Creator. The Creator shot you forth into first density with the understanding and the knowledge that within an infinite reach of time/space and space/time you would once again be drawn up into the Creator completely. The seventh density is the density where you prepare for and then go through the final stages of return to the one infinite Creator.

At the end of this density, it is as if you have entered a black hole, and, indeed, the physical black holes that your scientists have seen are physical aspects of this metaphysical process of spiritual gravity and the return of all that there is into the heart of the one infinite Creator. The end of this density system has been called by this instrument the "octave" because she is a musician and sees that when the seven tones, or colors, of creation have been completed there is a return to the original creation of the Father, as this instrument would put it. As the Creator's heart beats, shall we say, the entire process begins again. It is an infinite cycle.

The Creator is endlessly curious.

Now, each of these densities take a considerable length of what this instrument would call time. Your density, the third density, is the shortest of all densities, being a bit over 75,000 of your years in length,[67] and if you are familiar with the study of astrology, it is equal to the age of three of the signs of the zodiac. You are now ending one age and beginning another. The age of Pisces is giving way to the age of Aquarius. This 75,000-year cycle is called a density of choice.

You asked, "How can I use the concept of densities?" The most important way that we know of to use this concept is to realize the purpose of the density which you now inhabit. The purpose of the density you now inhabit is to create an environment within which, with complete free will and no compulsions because of knowledge that you have but only through those realizations that come from within, or as this instrument would say, by faith alone, you make a certain choice upon which hinges your path through fourth density, fifth density, and part of sixth density.

The choice is the one of your polarity.

There are two choices of ways to go or paths that you may choose within third density. One path is the path of service to others. The other path is the path of service to self. Either path, followed persistently and with dedication will lead you to graduation from third to fourth density.

In order to graduate from third density in the path of service to others it is necessary for you so to make choices that you end up being the kind of person that will choose service to others over service to self over half the time; that is, 51% of the time or more. A grade or level of choice of 51% percent or higher is that level of polarity which will qualify you for graduation to fourth density on the path to service to others.

If you choose, on the other hand, to follow service to self in order to graduate in the negative polarity it will be necessary for you to make choices that create a person who ends up choosing to be of service to the self 95% of the time or higher; that is, to have a level of service to others that is 5% or less.

We realize that it may seem to be off-balance that such a low positive grade would guarantee graduation, since 51% is not usually considered a passing grade, whereas in order to graduate service to self, an entity must have an almost perfect score of 95% or more of service-to-self [orientation.] However, we assure you that it is as difficult to achieve unselfish choices over half the time as it is to achieve selfish choices 95% of the time.

The reason is that the culture in which you are embedded is basically a service-to-self culture, thereby creating an outstanding and substantial bias

---

[67] This figure is closer to 78,000 years than 75,000 years, being the equivalent of three astrological cycles. The Confederation sources seem to "round down" to 25,000 years rather than up to 26,000 years for a minor cycle. There are three minor cycles in a major cycle which ends in a Graduation. So in fact the Ages of Taurus/Aries/Pisces are giving way to the Ages of Aquarius/Capricorn/Sagittarius.

which must be overcome by those who wish to vibrate in unconditional love, or service-to-others polarity. Choosing to be of service to others at the expense of the self is difficult to speak about and, within the confines of this question and this session of working, we would only point in the direction of speaking about it by saying that there are many examples of those who have chosen service to others at the sacrificial level.

Every parent is an example of those who have chosen to love unconditionally at the expense of their own comfort, time and convenience. Certainly exemplars such as the Buddha, the one known as Jesus, and other gurus and masters of the spiritual path exist as obvious examples of those whose lives exemplify the choices of unconditional love.

It is equally obvious, when one thinks about it, that there are exemplars of service to self. This instrument thinks immediately of the one known as Hitler, and there are many other examples whereby the principles of service to self were invoked. Principles of service to self suggest simply that the self is worthy and that others exist to serve the self. By serving the self those other entities will learn that purity of thought and singleness of mind that will enable them to become service to self in their polarity.

Whether one chooses service to others or service to self as the path, it is a choice in how to love. If you are offering service to others you are expressing the love that is at the heart of your being by offering that unconditional love as your vibratory gift. You are allowing light to shine through you in just the way that a light house would.

If you are expressing service to self you are attracting the light to you rather than allowing it to radiate from you. So you might say indeed that the service-to-others polarity is the path to radiation whereas the service-to-self polarity is the path of magnetism or attraction.

It is your choice. How do you wish to express the love that created you? What do you feel is the truth and the heart of your being? Do you wish to follow entities such as Jesus the Christ, Gautama Buddha, or that guru that speaks to you of unconditional love? Or do you wish to follow those exemplars of the negative path which will teach you how to purify your ego and create a universe in which all things lead to you, and all other entities exist to serve you?

The point is to make a choice. If you do not make a choice, then you shall, along with your culture, take one step forward and then one step back. [You will] do a service-to-others act and then be selfish. You will never gain power until you begin to make, not only that first choice, but then to hold to the determination to live in such a way that your subsequent choices build on that first choice. With every choice that you make which is consistent, you are building polarity. You are strengthening your ability to do work in consciousness, and you are becoming a magical, powerful being; the being that you were meant to be; the being that you hoped to be when you took the bold and unimaginably brave step of casting away the memory of who you are in order to enter into the world of illusion that is third density so that you could, by faith alone, choose the manner of your expression.

We would ask the ones known as S1 and S2 if they have any questions to follow up our initial statement. We are those of Q'uo.

S1: Actually, we do. In the last few days, we have this, what S2 called miasma, a fog or a depression that doesn't seem to be focused on anything in particular. We have had various expressions and ideas of it. Q'uo, please give us your take on this recently energetic feelings that we have.

We are those of Q'uo, and are aware of your query, my brother. The one known as Willie Nelson once said in an interview this instrument heard that he did not understand why people were so complimentary about melodies. He said, "The melodies are in the air. When I need one, I just start listening and I pick one up."

In just that way, as planetary influence in all of its inner and outer expressions goes through the tremendous alteration necessary to create fourth density Gaia, it is singing many melodies.

Some of the melodies are coming from the planet itself.

Some of those melodies are coming from those who are here to assist those who are attempting to graduate along the lines of service to others.

Some of the melodies are being created from the unseen world who are here to assist those calling for help on the path of service to self.

Therefore, some of the melodies are unimaginatively light and beautiful, while others are difficult and dark. These melodies all have the right to sing their song within the influence of Earth at this time. Each of them has a beauty. And there is a certain seduction or persuasion involved in both the light and dark melodies.

It is, as always, the choice of each of you as to what melodies you shall pick up and hold to your hearts, and which of those melodies you will choose not to focus upon. Now, each of you is familiar with the process of choosing what melodies, in a purely physical sense, to listen to, and what melodies to ignore. Every elevator that has Muzak is offering you a melody that you hope you will forget, most probably. Each store that you enter, particularly in the time of year which is coming up for you at this point, is going to offer you melodies that you may hum, or you may decide to forget. And so it is with these incredible waves of energy that are hitting your planet at this time, whether they come from the planet of whether they come from the unseen realms surrounding your planetary influence.

We suggest firstly that you respect and honor all of these melodies.

Secondly, we suggest you make a point of choosing which waves of energy you shall cooperate with and which waves of energy you shall not resist but simply not take seriously. The dark energy of which you speak is one which, as each of you has expressed, has been felt by not only you but also by many, many others with whom you have spoken in the last few days.

If you follow these waves of energies and ask entities with whom you come in contact about them, you will discover these waves of energy are system-wide. They are global. Entities are feeling them all over the planet. And so we ask you, "What shall you choose?"

We would suggest to you that there is no need to have any fear simply because dark melodies are being played. Choose instead to sing, "Alleluia, alleluia," and you shall tune into the more positive melodies. Even if you do not feel you can sing a note, let your heart sing for you. The unheard songs are the sweetest.

May we answer you further my brother?

S1: The last one will be a very whimsical question, for a dear friend of ours. Does Q'uo like chocolate? E would like to know.

(Laughter)

We are those of Q'uo, and if the instrument will stop giggling we shall attempt to answer your whimsical query, my brother. Let us say that the metaphysical aspects of chocolate are a delight to us.

(Laughing)

We leave you as we found you, in the love and the light of the one infinite Creator. Adonai. Adonai. ✤

L/L RESEARCH

L/L Research is a subsidiary of Rock Creek Research & Development Laboratories, Inc.

P.O. Box 5195
Louisville, KY 40255-0195

www.llresearch.org

Rock Creek is a non-profit corporation dedicated to discovering and sharing information which may aid in the spiritual evolution of humankind.

© 2009 L/L RESEARCH

SUNDAY MEDITATION
OCTOBER 16, 2005

Group question: The question today has to do with what I call a dedication to an outcome. When we expend our energy; when we do things, we hope that it will produce a certain result. By dedicating ourselves to this result, we focus our energy. We make it more likely that we will accomplish the result. However, if we happen to fall short, it gives us a reason to doubt ourselves, to be angry at ourselves, to feel unworthy, and so forth. I'm wondering if this dedication to an outcome has anything to do with the creation of the emotions or how the emotions that we feel play into our dedicating ourselves to certain outcomes. Could Q'uo speak to us about that?

(Carla channeling)

We are those known as the principle of Q'uo. Greetings in the love and in the light of the one infinite Creator, in Whose service we come to you this day. What a blessing and a privilege it is to share this time with you! Thank you for calling us to your circle of seeking. We are delighted to speak with you this day concerning your query about the issue of how dedication to an outcome affects you and how this dynamic works within your process.

As always, we would ask of you one simple thing that is most important in terms of our ability to speak freely to you without being concerned that we will infringe upon your free will. We would ask each of you to take responsibility for listening to what we have to say with a jaundiced and a careful ear. Do

not be too quick to think that we are right. Do not take our authority as if we had authority over you simply because we speak with a voice that has the authority of our own experiences. Truth is a very personal thing. Realize that and realize that you are in charge of what you will work with and how your process will go. So listen for those thoughts of ours that seem really to resonate to you, to inspire you, and to make you want to take them further. If they do not have that effect upon you immediately, then they are probably not for you at this time and we would suggest that you leave them behind. If you will do this then we will greatly appreciate your care.

We thank the one known as Jim for this query concerning the dynamics of dedication to a result or an outcome. You speak of the dynamics of will and power in asking this question. It is a delicate matter to direct focus and create a pathway for the will. The amount of power that you have within you as a being is immense.

There are some personality shells whose ability to direct power, to direct their will, is limited. There are other entities, such as the one known as Jim, and to a certain extent, both the one known as C, the one known as Carla, and the one known as T, who have an innate capacity to focus their will on a continuing basis. And so they are familiar with what it feels like to be powerful. However, the question of the polarity of that power is troubling, shall we say, to each of you, and probably to every person who has ever been able to direct the force of their will and therefore who has become aware of the power that they do inherently possess.

One needs to be alert and sensitive to the feelings involved as one gathers one's will to direct it, sensing into the polarity of that will and the feelings having to do with the appropriateness of the gathering of that will and the use of the will. Dedication to a result is a basic human decision. Third density is full of such choices. They are the stuff of which your density is made. We would not want to interrupt the use of that power or to suggest in any way that it was inadvisable to use the power of the will.

If we look at the use of the will within those who are sitting in this circle of seeking, we may say that for each entity, the use of will and the dedication to a result has created solid worth in each of your lives.

For the one known as Jim, the lawns have gotten mowed; the business of Jim's Lawn Service has thrived. The various concerns that this entity has towards home, family and relationship has similarly blossomed under the careful tending and the persistent care given because of dedication to these outcomes. A good deal of sacrifice has gone into applying the will and disciplining the self in order to use time and energy to the most effective and creative ends.

For the one known as Carla, the use of the will in dedication to the outcomes has resulted in much useful work being done that has moved on from her desk to the desk of those who place the material on the internet and, therefore, entities from all over your world have found use in the thoughts that have been shared by this entity's editing and preparing this material for internet usage.

For the one known as C, dedication to the outcomes that she feels are important has resulted in her being an effective and loving manager of her family and her business.

And for the one known as T, dedication to the outcome of those things which he feels are valuable in his life have resulted in a well tended, loving relationship with his mate and creative and effective work at accomplishing a long-term and substantial goal and in writing the thesis that this entity is now finishing up.

Without being dedicated to these outcomes, and without engaging the will, none of you who sits in this circle would be sitting in the circle with the present feelings of comfort and peace that doing your best creates. We commend each of you for the excellence of your dedication to your outcomes and of your care in pursuing that dedication and backing it up with the force of your will and the persistence of your grit and determination.

What we want to explore with you is somewhat difficult and therefore we ask your patience as we look for ways to share our thoughts.

There are challenges involved in being a magical person, in being dedicated, being committed, and being powerful as people. If you create a world in your mind and you see it whole and perfect, there is the tendency to focus that fire hose of the will on maintaining that structure. We have just said that each of you, to some extent, does this and is successful at doing so.

If you are too successful at doing so you tend to create for yourself a stumbling block that is difficult to see. That stumbling block is that you have created a crystallized and static environment which you are working to maintain. In that visualization there is no room for the free rein of spirit.

Spirit has a predictable and useful tendency to want to change the visualization of that creation to which you are dedicating your will. There is the predictable and cyclical desire of spirit to take down the structure of that visualization. Spirit wishes to undo and rebuild your universe day by day; even moment by moment sometimes. And over-dedication of the self to specific outcomes can hinder those energies of spirit that would like to help you grow, change and become more loving, more wise, more powerful, and more self-aware.

This creates a dynamic of two polar opposites, for you see clearly the desirable shape of your universe and wish to bend every effort and offer every excellence of your being to continuing to create that visualization of the ideal process of your life at this time.

At the same time, paradoxically, there is an energy that moves through you that would very much like for you to maximize your opportunities for growth. This energy of growth can sometimes seem like an energy that is deconstructing your reality and making chaos out of order. Therefore, one's first reaction to such growth energy is distaste and irritation. "Why does something that works have to change?" you may ask yourself. "Why does such a useful structure have to be taken down and rebuilt? Why does the function of this energy seem to be working at cross-purposes to living an orderly and understandable life?"

And yet the energy of growth is an energy that is driven by the deepest quest of your heart. For you are part of the Creator. And as part of the creative principle you desire to know yourself. In that quest lies your nature, and to an extent, your purpose. It is an irresistible force in your life and whether change and growth come slowly or quickly, that such a process shall occur is inevitable.

Your choice is whether you wish to exist in that lane of traffic that is moving slowly towards the octave and eventual return to the Creator or whether you wish to be in one of the faster-moving lanes. Each of you within this group tends to want to be in the fast lane. You want to grow. You want to refine the ore of your being and to find the jewels and the gold within your nature.

And you want to share that gift back with yourself, with the world around you, with the people around you, and ultimately with the Creator. Consequently, you have a continuing desire both to maintaining the visualization of the ideal which you have now and to creating new ideals and new creations and universes which are even better than the universe that you have created at this moment and the ideals to which you have sworn allegiance at this time.

We would never say to you, in any way, shape or form, that [it] is unwise of you to feel passionately concerning the performance of the duties that you see before you. Your dedication to fulfilling each and every duty, each and every chore that is perceived by you to be yours, is commendable and ethically appropriate, in our opinion.

We would say to you that it is most helpful for powerful entities such as you are to realize where your power comes from. Your power does not come from you except insofar as you choose the manner of your being. Your basic source of power comes through you and is a function of your awareness of the Creator within.

If you are attempting to fulfill your obligations and pursue your ideals from a concept of self which involves the self by itself as a powerful thing, then your power will not last long. You shall run out of available power, exhaust yourself, burn yourself out as this instrument would say it, and find yourself empty and hollow, weary and exhausted, sitting by the side of the spiritual road gasping for breath.

It is the entity that realizes that the source of the magic within is that energy which is coming from the infinite Creator that will have the staying power to persist through these cyclical times of deconstruction and re-imagining your universe.

Perhaps we would say that one could imagine oneself to be one who was collecting items and putting them in their hands as they went along doing their work. They would see this to do and that to do and each item on that to-do list would become, say, an object which was held in the hand. Periodically, then, we would suggest that it is well to empty the hands completely and to rest and ask very consciously for spirit to prune you back and take away all of those concepts that are no longer useful.

Spirit might take away one or two of those objects from your hands, or they might take most of them away, for the spiritual guidance system is unpredictable but unerring in its instincts for that which you truly need and that which you do not need.

You need to make room for things to fall away. Because you have done something for a substantial length of time does not necessarily mean that you must go on doing it for the rest of your life. There is a time and a season for every passion that you feel.

Be sensitive, therefore, to your feelings about the things that you have dedicated yourself to doing. Is your passion concerning this effort fresh as if it were bubbling forth from an unending source or spring? If a fountain seems vital and powerful, then you may trust that what lies beneath that passion and that energy is fresh and vital within your process.

You might pick up other items that represent issues about which you have felt passionately in the past. And as you pick that one up you discover that it feels tired to you. Do not brush away that feeling but examine it, note it, and follow it.

Reexamine this issue several times, on different days, at different times of the day, at different points in your own energy expenditure, so that you are not always weary when you think about the issues involved. See if you truly have begun to be weary of carrying this particular chore or duty.

It may be worthy. Indeed, it must be worthy for you to have chosen it. The question always is is it still part of that which makes you vitally alive? Is it still fresh and bubbling forth from within you in that way which suggests that it is powerful within your heart? If the answer, over a period of time, continues to be somewhat negative, then you may safely begin to explore ways that you may disentangle yourself from that particular dedication to a result. That, then, becomes something that you are ready to put down and let go of, it is no longer working for you.

This may be something that is small, such as a hobby, a volunteer possibility that you have done in the past or a relationship, a friendship perhaps, that is no longer functioning for you. Or, indeed, it can be quite large and substantial such as those times when a major relationship such as the mated relationship has fallen into disrepair for reasons that are beyond your control and you find that even with prayer and supplication to spirit, Humpty Dumpty cannot be put back together again. It is very easy to feel, when such a relationship fails to persist in its integrity, that you have failed. And many are the souls that have battered themselves into insensibility in their attempts to preserve that which cannot be preserved.

We do not say that it is wise or appropriate to release such major relationships lightly. Along with more conventional sources of advice such as marriage counselors and authorities within your cultural systems, we also feel that it is very important to go to the very furthest possible effort in the attempt to repair, renew, refresh and revitalize relationships that have fallen into disarray, especially when they are the mated relationship. The value of a strongly functioning mated companionship is infinite for those who wish to do spiritual work.

For in many ways you dwell in an environment which is closed to you in terms of direct sources of information concerning who you are and what your nature truly is. The closer your companions are and the more spiritually oriented your relationships with these companions, the better the system of mirrors will be in which that entity reflects back to you who you are and how you are coming across. Having honest, compassionate mirrors around is perhaps the single greatest asset that a spiritual seeker can have.

Someone to talk to about the puzzlements of life is endlessly valuable. Someone to share energy with creates the best environment possible for your growth as a servant of the light.

Yet there are times when such substantial relationships come to an end. The one known as Carla has experienced it and we would say to this instrument that when she made the decision, nearly forty of her years ago, to allow that relationship with the one known as D to die a natural death, she made a wise and loving decision for herself and the one known as D.

It went against her cultural conditioning and she was dedicated enough to keeping her promise that she held onto what was a dysfunctional relationship for several years strictly because she felt that she needed to keep her promise. We cannot say that that decision was a mistake, for it taught her many valuable lessons and it showed her that she was capable of maintaining a difficult situation simply because she felt it was right.

We will say that she created for herself an extensive period of suffering which was not strictly necessary. Had she been willing to let go of this promise earlier, she would have shortened her period of Lenten fast and created an earlier Easter feast in terms of the energies of that relationship, and, indeed, the energies that were released when the relationship was released.

Sometimes it is necessary to empty one's hands and to hold them out and share in simple supplication to spirit, asking to be pruned. This instrument was recently told that, in the fall, a grapevine is pruned back 90% in order that new growth may occur the next year.

As personalities or egos, that process of pruning sounds bad. Therefore, we encourage you to transcend that level of thinking; to reject the fear involved in shrinking from the pruning shears and to invite the bite of those health-giving shears in your life. If things are taken away from you, we would suggest that you might consider the possibility that spirit's pruning shears went to work because it was necessary for your own growth that the pruning take place.

Certainly, a pruning does not feel like growth, it feels like exactly the opposite. It feels as though you are losing valuable parts of yourself. We assure that each step in your life, whether it seems like loss or gain, is useful and necessary; not in terms of a human or a linear point of view; not in terms that make sense to the intellect.

However, we are suggesting that there is a great deal more at work here than the forces of this world that you call consensus reality and the powers of the intellect. You dwell also in the realm of infinity and eternity and the power of the spirit is that power that wishes to renew, refresh and revitalize you day by day and moment by moment.

Let your awareness of this dynamic make you fearless. And when you perceive that your hands are too full, empty them. Put it all down and ask for the pruning of spirit.

Your question suggested that the one known as Jim has become aware of the interplay of emotion and will. My brother, may we say that your perception is acute and it takes us to a place where what we would say to you is almost beyond the capacity of words to express.

You are so much more than your words. Conceptually, you are so much more than what you can think or imagine. Yet you are entirely accurate in sensing that there are desirable and useful aspects to the present moment that you are not picking up because too much of your beingness is invested in that which you already understand. Again the entering into silence and the fearless embrace of emptiness are your best allies.

Allow yourself not to know what is true, what is right and what is adequate. Allow periods of times where you aggressively pursue not knowing.

(Side one of tape ends.)

(Carla channeling)

Become empty and know that this, too, is an entirely fruitful and helpful energy and environment in which to dwell.

Emotion begins to express truth as the seeker has the courage to pursue feelings and emotions beyond the surface. We cannot say that surface emotions are wrong. But we would suggest that the easier an emotion is to feel, the less likely it is to contain any purity of emotion.

Indeed, surface emotions are energies that we might wish for another word to use to describe! Because

emotion itself is enormously valuable. As you are able to purify the emotions of anger, love, discouragement, despair, grief, jealousy and so forth, you begin to enter archetypal rivers that flow deep within your mind, taking you to truer and truer places within your being and to places where power is gathered as water is gathered into a cistern.

You can blunt your emotions by holding onto patterns and creations in your life into which you have poured energy, time, talent and will previously. Therefore, emotion itself is something to be examined, just as you intellectually examine your abstract thoughts.

Allow your heart to examine the quality and the shape of your emotions. See what you can do to get past the cyclical ups and downs of your personality so that that which drives you emotionally is as stable and as true to yourself as your ideals.

We would at this time allow this conversation to change in its nature for this instrument is informing us that we have used up our available time and the available energy of this group on this question. We have barely scratched the surface of a whole constellation of concerns which are raised by this very provocative and interesting question and we thank the one known as Jim for his thoughts.

Is there a follow-up question or another question that you would like to ask at this time?

T: Q'uo, I have a question from the one known as F, who is experiencing a kundalini awakening. Can you advise on how best she can cope with these intense energies she experiences in the head and crown chakra and the pain from intense headaches? Is there any change, is there any danger to the physical vehicle?

We are those of Q'uo, and are aware of your query, my brother. We would say to the one known as F that there are, indeed, times in the development of the reconnection of self with self that is represented by the rising of the kundalini where there is the potential and the capacity for a good deal of physical discomfort. Naturally, there are limits to those things which we may offer at this time. We would offer three suggestions.

Firstly, we would suggest, for the satisfaction of those concerns that are natural, especially in those around the one known as F who care about her, that there be a continuing medical presence, being absolutely sure that there are no systemic problems that are a portion strictly of the physical body that need to be looked after in order to be sure that there is no physical breakdown of the system.

There are times when, as weak as your medical systems indeed are in terms of dealing with the whole human being, shall we say, there is help that is available that is helpful. As this instrument was saying earlier, in talking about her own physical difficulties at this time, she has gratitude for the medicine that has alleviated the physical pain that was making it difficult for her to breath. She finds it unfortunate that this medicine has side-effects that she must cope with in turn. Yet at the same time it is physically easier for her to think and to move about without having to fight for every breath.

In the same wise, it is good simply to touch into the best advice that you can get from the medical persons whom the one known as F trusts the most and simply be sure that there are no purely physical problems that cannot be addressed.

Secondly, we would suggest to the one known as F that the rising of the kundalini, as powerful a process as it is, needs to be seen not in terms of personal development alone but also in terms of a system that is larger than one person or even one energy system, such as the chakra or electrical body. The rising of the kundalini is an expression of the Creator to the Creator. It is a movement within a tiny portion of the Creator of the location of where the Creator in space and time is meeting the Creator which is outside of space and time.

If it can be seen that these energies begin before the chakra system begins and end after the chakra system ends, it can perhaps be seen that there is no need to visualize the energy within a closed system. It is indeed an open-ended system.

There are no limits as to where this energy can reside. For as the entity in time and space which is the human being meets the self that is without limitation, it has literally no limit to how the tuning of that system can be affected by the appropriate placement of the will and the faith of the entity and its openness and hunger for the love and the light of the one infinite Creator.

It may even be helpful to visualize the chakra system opening up so that the crown of the head is not the limitation that it may seem. Allow that energy to shoot above the crown of the head if it so desires, for the stars are not even the limit! There is no limitation to where that energy can be taken.

We are not suggesting that you push the energy or prod it in any way. We are simply suggesting that you take any thought of limitation away from your visualization of how this process is working. It is not only working within the one known as F. It is working within the Creator and the one known as F is a location in space and time which is allowing this process to take place. Therefore, it is not simply her process and she is in safe hands in allowing the energies to flow as they will.

In terms of safety, there is a natural energy field within which, metaphysically speaking, this process is taking place. And certainly, in that wise, it cannot move out of that energy field and we would refer to this energy field as what this instrument would call the visica piscis[68]. But that is not the end of the story.

So what we are suggesting here is that, beyond all thought of limitation or even trying to understand this process, it is helpful in a way simply to let go so that you may allow the energy to move in a way that is not limited by your concerns.

Thirdly, we would encourage the one known as F to treat this time of growth in the same way that you would treat a time of physical growth. In a time of physical growth, you would feed yourself more vitamins. You would be sure that you got enough exercise. You would watch the quality of the food that you ate. In all ways, you would encourage this process of physical growth by giving yourself every advantage that you could in terms of nutrition and good, healthy exercise.

In just the same way, when you have entered upon an intensive period within your process of seeking and evolution, it is well to pay particular attention to the regularity of your arrangements for nutrition and exercise in the spiritual sense. If there is a preference in you for a way to enter the silence that you have not followed up as you might wish to do, this would be the time to regularize the practice of this way of entering the silence, for this is your food.

---

[68] visica piscis: a pointed oval shape used in medieval Christian art as an aureole to surround a sacred figure. It is used by Drunvalo Melchizidek to mean the sacred geometrical shape of a soul's spiritual body, thought body or "flying saucer."

Ask yourself what exercise, spiritually speaking, is that exercise that most appeals to you. For some entities that exercise would be, as the one known as T has stated recently, to do more work with the dreaming.

Other entities might prefer to regularize a conversation with the guidance system within. This is done by taking a pad of paper and a pen or sitting down at a computer and deliberately and consciously entering into a conversation with your guidance system by writing or typing out a question and then, when an impression comes to you, writing or typing what you receive as answer. Then respond as yourself, by writing your next question and then listening for your next impression and then typing that out, reserving the evaluation of this conversation for a later time.

If this appeals to you, then we would suggest that you remember that after this conversation is over, the energy has not been appropriately addressed until you have followed whatever instructions you have received during this session with your guidance system. Follow through on whatever suggestions you received. Pay attention to the wisdom and the love that your guidance offers you and take it seriously.

Remember, my sister, most of all that the energies of spirit are light, glad, joyful and free. Attempt insofar as you can not to become mired and bogged down in the importance of your work. Rather, maintain a sense of proportion and the light touch. Remember that you dwell in the density of unknowing. It is very helpful reminder that not only do you not know any ultimate answers but in this density you cannot know any ultimate answers.

You can come to realizations and glimpses that are quite profound and authentic, but like the glimpse of the mountain that is seen by the seeker in all of its glory and beauty, that glimpse does not endure. It is momentary. First there is a mountain; then, there is no mountain; then, there is. That is the cliché known to this instrument and it is very true when it comes to realization and the process of becoming in which you are now involved.

Remember to factor in that light touch that allows you to laugh at the whole process and to take it lightly at the same time that, with all your heart and with all your soul and with all your mind and all your strength, you dedicate yourself to becoming who you really are. There is that paradox again of

dedication and the release of all dedication to the overarching dedication to the Creator Itself. Trust in this process. Relax and let go.

May we ask if there is any further way we may respond to this query, my brother?

T: No, thank you, Q'uo. That's a comprehensive answer and I will relay it to F and see if she has any other questions.

We are those of Q'uo, and we thank you, my brother, and that is very satisfactory with us.

Jim: I have one [from] the instrument. What's happening when the instrument asks spirit to balance her chakra system to meet the energy of the weakest chakra? Is there anything that can be done to better bolster that weakest chakra?

We are those of Q'uo, and are aware of your query, my sister. We would say that we feel that you are correct in your reading of the adequacy of this adjustment to your chakra system during the tuning process when you request that the energy be rebalanced to balance with the weakest chakra. We find this to be a wise adjustment to your tuning process, my sister, and are glad that you have undertaken to take care of your entire system rather than leaning on your strengths and dragging your weaknesses behind you like chains. It is far better for the entire system to maintain less system strength and yet to be far better balanced internally.

As to ways to bolster the weakest chakra: this is active work upon which we cannot comment except to say that there is no shame in having a weakest chakra. It would be remarkable in any of those among your tribe to discover a system in which there were no variations in strength from chakra to chakra within a chakra system. Each entity will have strengths and weaknesses that are endemic to that system.

Certainly it is well to pursue the work in consciousness necessary to allow fear to drop away and allow the energies of growth to be strengthened.

It is also very helpful to accept oneself just as one is, with one's strengths and weaknesses intact. Work with the system that is yours. Allow the weaker chakra to be weaker, and then accommodate that situation by requesting that spirit rebalance the chakras in order to protect the system and make it safe for that system to do work in consciousness.

That is what you are asking of your system when you tune in order to do a channeling session. Would you not wish to work with the system that you have without judging yourself for having that system?

Therefore, we encourage you to continue to work to bolster that weaker energy which we are well aware is known to you; those energies of low self-worth or low self-esteem which the one known as Carla has carried since very early childhood. Do not waste time attempting to brush up that chakra or get rid of low self-esteem or low self-worth.

There is value in every distortion in a system. It should not be excised as if it were a growth that needed to be removed. If there is use in low self-esteem, find it. If there is value and information in low self-worth, dig for it, not with an idea that you will find it to get rid of it, but with the idea that you will find it to treasure it, appreciate it, and love it.

Is there a final query at this time?

(No further queries.)

We are those of Q'uo, and find that we have exhausted the questions in this group for the present moment. This is well, for energy begins to wane within this instrument and this group. May we thank each of you for the pleasure of your company. May we express our appreciation of the beauty of each of you. It moves us more than we can say to share energy with you and to appreciate every petal and fold of your amazing and courageous beings. Thank you for this time together. It has truly been a privilege.

We leave you in the love and in the light of the one infinite Creator. We are known to you as the principle of Q'uo. Adonai. Adonai. ❧

L/L Research is a subsidiary of
Rock Creek Research &
Development Laboratories, Inc.

P.O. Box 5195
Louisville, KY 40255-0195

L/L RESEARCH

www.llresearch.org

Rock Creek is a non-profit
corporation dedicated to
discovering and sharing
information which may aid in
the spiritual evolution of
humankind.

SUNDAY MEDITATION
NOVEMBER 6, 2005

Group question: The question today has to do with the kind of problems that we run into in our daily lives that seem to be repeating. After a while they seem to be unsolvable. It looks like the best that you can do is to keep dancing and working with them. We're wondering if Q'uo has any comment to make that could shed some light on what goes on in a seeker's life when you run into these problems that may be in relationships and may be with yourself. Is it psychic greeting? Is it something within yourself that wants to show you the dark side so that you can work on it? Could Q'uo comment on these problems that keep recurring in our lives that don't really seem to go away?

(Carla channeling)

We are those known as the principle of Q'uo. Greetings in the love and in the light of the one infinite Creator. We are in the Creator's service as we speak with you at this time. Thank you for the privilege and the pleasure of being called to your circle this evening.

As always, we would ask of you that you employ your discriminatory powers in listening to what we have to say. Use that material that is helpful and seems resonant to you while leaving the rest behind. If you will take responsibility for doing this, it will enable us to speak freely without being concerned that we might infringe upon your free will.

The gaudy jewel and earth tones of your autumn leaves are swirling around in this instrument's mind as we settle into her question this day. And, indeed, the gaudy and earth tones of your question swirl about as we contemplate our response. We thank you for this query concerning the seemingly insoluble and cyclical challenges of each of your incarnations.

It is a characteristic of the density which you now inhabit that nothing is known. Everything is an illusion. The rainbow colors of your supposed problems and challenges have the same seductive value as a display of beautiful clothing in a department store window has to this instrument. The way the human mind works is to gather these garments of thought as if they were apparel and coordinate the garments, one with the other, so that one is wearing a mental and emotional outfit that goes together.

It is to be noted that much of the way patterns of thinking develop is as simple as that habit that entities such as this instrument have of going into the closet and selecting an outfit for the day that coordinates in terms of color and pattern.

There is a surreal aspect to reality that cannot be shaken off or gotten rid of. It is part of the human condition. It is a big part of the human condition. It was created that third density be a density in which nothing can be known in order that those who entered into the density would be able to do work intended for this density. That work is the seemingly simple but in fact endlessly painstaking work of choosing what shall be the manner of your being.

It is a very helpful thing to lose the beliefs of all kinds of thought, feeling and emotion from time to time and to strip oneself down to the bare branches of one's true self. This instrument spoke in her journal[69] recently of this need to be naked of the clothing of those garments of emotion and personality that did not seem to her to be very indicative of any real beingness within herself. She was looking for the bare branches and the roots and trunk of her personality to find out more about who she really is. We would suggest to you that it is well to look at these cyclically recurring thematic challenges in this extended context of that image of the essential tree with its many-colored leaves which must fall and come down from time to time to be lost, in order that change and growth may take place.

This is true for all entities regardless of when they come to third-density incarnation. It is especially true of an entity such as this instrument or those within this group, for each within this circle of seeking has made conscious agreements with the self to accelerate the pace of spiritual growth. Therefore, it is to be expected from such entities that these cycles of the self meeting the shadow self, shall we say, would be intensified.

And there is another factor, offering another layer or level of intensification. That extra factor is the times in which you are now living.

Let us contemplate the times in which you are now living from our point of view. For we believe that this may add a dimension to your own thinking at this time. We have said before that at this time your Earth is being born as a fourth-density planet and indeed is alive and well.

The third-density planet which gave birth to baby Gaia, that entity which we may call third-density Gaia, has expressed a great deal of her energies in the nurturing of all of her third-density tribe and family. The Earth being that you call Gaia or Terra is a

mother in love with her children and blissfully nurturing of them, always protective of them and yet, at the same time, in harmony with the desire for growth and transformation that exists within the heart and the soul of each one of her children.

As she has approached this last decade of her appropriate time to be alive, she has seen that the harvest of those who have chosen is still a slender one. Those who have taken incarnation at this time have taken incarnation knowing full well that time is short upon your planet for making the choice of how to be.

There are those of you who traveled from other densities and other planets to this density and planet Earth in hopes of being a part of that energy which would create the expression of light on planet Earth that would help entities to awaken to the realization of who they are as spiritual beings and of what they are here to do in terms of making the choice of the manner of their being.

There are other entities whose hope is to wake up, having been unable [to do so] within third density in other third-density cycles.

The thing that each of you has in common with the other is that, whether you are attempting to awaken from within the third-density dream or whether you have awakened within the dream but now are hoping to help others to awaken, your awakening is precious to you and central to your reason for choosing to take incarnation at this time. It is as if all of you are under pressure to graduate.

If you will cast your minds back to your last graduation, you may remember the kind of pressure that this situation creates. There is the feeling of being tested and wondering if you have the knowledge to answer the questions on that test appropriately. There is that frantic feeling of not having enough knowledge and knowing that you do not have the time that you would like to have in order to organize your thoughts. It seems as if a great deal is compressed into a very short amount of time.

Your entire incarnation has this intensity at this time, and as we said, there are several layers to the reason for this intensity. It is intense because you are intense. It is intense because the Earth is at an intense place. And it is further intensified by the great desire of each of you to do well at this time so

---

[69] Carla keeps a journal of her daily work on www.bring4th.org under Camelot. It is called the Camelot Journal. Camelot is the home near Louisville where Jim, Carla and Don Elkins settled in 1984. The companion property is the farm, Avalon. The Camelot Journal and the Avalon Journal are kept on line in order that readers can keep up with L/L Research's doings.

that you are in effect your own parents, encouraging and urging you to study harder and get good grades.

The one known as C was correct in saying that the cycling, thematic challenges of an incarnation are not intended to be solved. And the one known as Carla was equally correct in describing the condition of being as that of dancing with the situation without any hope of solving or affecting the situation. These are positive and loving perceptions of a situation that might otherwise seem to be very frustrating.

It seems frustrating when one attempts to solve a problem that will not solve. There is the natural desire to create order and beauty in any pattern of living or thinking. And we encourage your efforts to beautify your thoughts, your emotions, and your being as you can. We would ask you to remember that your goal is growth, progress and transformation. You are asking yourself to change and to become that which you do not yet understand.

When you ask spirit for the opportunity to grow, change and transform, spirit is ever ready to offer you those opportunities. When the opportunities to grow are offered to you, they will tend to express themselves in terms of your thematic, incarnational lessons.

It is not that you are getting a direct repetition each time that such cyclical problems come up. Each situation that you experience, no matter how closely you can identify it in kind with previous occurrences with this same theme in your life, the consciousness that takes in this current, fresh, new version of the thematic challenge is a new being facing a new problem.

Fortunately, you have the tremendous advantage of having identified the recurring and thematic incarnational lesson or you would not have asked this question. Simply realizing how growth works and what its mechanisms are is an extremely powerful resource.

Becoming comfortable with this discomfort is a very helpful resource as well. We enjoyed the conversation which took place before this channeling session began for there was genuine laughter as the ones known as Carla and C spoke of their recurring difficulties. That laughter was not angry or hysterical but rather was the relaxed enjoyment of that which

is truly funny. One of your most powerful resources in doing spiritual work of this kind is a sense of proportion or a sense of humor. And we are very glad that you are able to relax with each other and feel comfortable in your discomfort. We acknowledge and sympathize with that discomfort.

It is not a comfortable or easy thing to create within the self that environment that welcomes growth. We have talked recently with this group about the tremendous courage it takes to put down the current pattern of one's life and thoughts, to empty the mental and emotional pockets of all preconceptions and to say, "I am empty and I would ask what spirit would like to say to me now. How may I serve? How may I learn? How may I grow?" Casting those requests to the wind of spirit is a wonderfully powerful act.

What occurs thereafter is often what this instrument would call the silly season. The sky seems to fall in on one. All patterns seem to fall into chaos. Entities which normally behave in such and such a way suddenly seem to be behaving otherwise.

Whatever the shape and nature of the challenge that you experience because you have asked to grow, it takes you from the precincts of tidy and orderly living into a seemingly darker and much more shadowy atmosphere where it is impossible to see around corners or very far ahead. There is the feeling of being in darkness and unable to discern the shape and true form of the thoughts and feelings of others, and, indeed, of oneself. There are feelings of isolation and even of being stranded in a place far from comfort, with the ghosts of one's past crowding around, making rude comments upon the current situation.

We would ask you to step back when you begin to feel blocked in by this darkness, for help is near. That help does not exist within third density and its world of illusion. That help comes from a world which interpenetrates your third-density illusion. That [is a] world in which truth, beauty, wisdom and justice walk as entities. That is the world of time/space or the metaphysical world.

It is that place from which your inspiration comes. Your heart dwells at all times in this metaphysical world. The safe place that you need in order to move through these cyclical times of difficulty lies within you. And yet you must journey to you as if you were a stranger coming from afar to the city gates of your own heart.

Your inner heart is a world unto itself. It carries your truth. It carries your identity. It is the resting place of the one infinite Creator. When you sleep, your personality shell curls up for some rest and the truth of you comes out to play, to express, to stretch its muscles and its sensings. And in dreams and visions, this true self of yours communicates with its surface self as best it can. When you meditate and enter the silence, you can hope to enter those precincts of sacredness and truth.

We find the phrase or the image of dancing with your incarnational lessons very apt because, in a way, your entire life is truth dancing with the illusions necessary to create an environment in which the shadow of truth may be visible. In a way, that is the nature of third-density life. It is a shadow life. And yet that shadow contains as much truth as is bearable in a learning environment.

You have placed yourself in an environment which can be anything you wish to make of it. For many people, so great is their desire for comfort that their every concern is simply to seal up any possibility of letting the light in so that they may remain safely asleep.

We are not speaking to those who wish to remain asleep, however. We are speaking to those who genuinely, authentically wish to awaken, to greet the day that has been given them and to take hold and make of the incarnation that which they intended before they set out on this journey from birth to death in third density.

We feel the truth of your great desire to fulfill this pattern of growth and service. We cannot find enough ways to express to you how exciting we find your adventures. We see all too clearly the perfection of the Creator's plan. And we are aware of your blindness. It is therefore very exciting to us to see how you step forth so bravely into the arena of everyday life, armed only with your faith.

Certainly how to find that faith is a question unto itself, for faith is created out of nothing. Perhaps you are aware of the figure of the twenty-second archetype of the tarot deck of the fool stepping out over the [edge of the] abyss into nothingness. That is how you find faith, my friends. And so it is with the dance that you do with the incarnational lessons.

When you hear the music and recognize that your leitmotif[70] is playing for you once again, we encourage you not to be concerned that you do not know the steps. Arise and join the dance. The steps will come to you as you free yourself to experience them by giving up the safety of your seated position.

May we ask if there is another query at this time?

Jim: We have one from G. He says that Book I of *The Law of One* has a quote from Ra that says:

The mystery and unknown quality of the occurrences we are allowed to offer have the hoped-for intention of making your peoples aware of infinite possibility. When your peoples grasp infinity, then and only then can the gateway be opened to the Law of One.

Could Q'uo offer any thoughts as to what Ra meant by this infinity that needs grasping in order to open the gateway to the Law of One? What is it and what is it not?

We are those of Q'uo, and are aware of your query, my brother. As we were speaking of the difference between consensus reality or the world of illusion and the metaphysical universe or the world of time/space, we were speaking of a finite universe as opposed to an infinite universe. Your everyday, consensus reality is measurable. One can measure the terrestrial ball upon which you walk. One can measure the beat of your heart and the pressure of your blood.

(Side one of tape ends.)

(Carla channeling)

One can use instrumentation to measure the exact electrical charge of each thought that you think.

The world of metaphysics is not measurable by such instrumentation as you are aware of in your everyday world. It is a world in which anything is possible because you are unbounded by any limitation whatsoever except those you create for yourself.

The world of time/space is the world of consciousness. It is the world of infinity and eternity. The reason it is difficult for us to describe this to you is that your mind is a space/time artifact. The intellectual brain, that marvelous problem-solving

---

[70] leitmotif: a melodic passage or phrase, especially in Wagnerian opera, associated with a specific character, situation, or element; a dominant and recurring theme, as in a novel.

bio-computer, is not capable of grasping the infinite. It can only grasp it by saying, "Oh, it is that which goes beyond that limit." But since the mind thinks in finite terms, there is always an end to that place that is beyond. And then infinity must again be invoked so that that limit too is transcended.

As far as we know it is not possible intellectually to conceive of infinity. It is, however, possible to experience the infinite. The infinite is that world in which you exist without masks. You have journeyed to the world of finity in order to do work in consciousness that must be done without recourse to that point of view that is full of love, wisdom and knowledge.

So we would say to you, my brother, that the value of the infinite can only be known by you in experiencing the infinite directly. That is what work in consciousness concerns itself with.

You are a living and breathing meeting place of the finite and infinite, in every cell of your body. There is that aspect which experiences life and death and there is that aspect which was never born and which shall never die. That infinite aspect does not know itself for it is wrapped up and lost in the Creator itself.

You, as a finite being, are the place where great truths and infinite values meet; that environment which creates form and gives shape to the dance of the Creator learning to know Itself.

Seen from a certain point of view, all of creation can seem whimsical. Why would the Creator wish to know Itself? It is already Itself. You are proof positive that the Creator has a whimsical side.

We offer these thoughts, my brother, and we are glad to welcome further questions on this point at a later time. Is there another query at this time?

Jim: This is a question from the instrument, who asks, "Two of our community have fallen painfully in the last week and people have expressed disharmony in an unusual manner. Can you comment in any way that you think might be helpful concerning these disharmonies?"

We are those of Q'uo, and are aware of your query, my sister. The one known as Carla, when speaking of the experience of tripping and falling in the dark, said that she thought it was highly symbolic that the mishap occurred in the dark. We would agree with her statement. Sometimes the simplest and most obvious points about a symbolic event are also the most helpful when thinking about the nature of such an event.

There is a certain amount of pride in the creation of any group. Those who create such a group supposedly have created the group because they have a certain vision. When such a group gathers, the question of vision becomes central. For each person in the group is the Creator and each person is seeing the other people more or less as the Creator.

Daylight for such a group is that climate in which it is remembered that all entities are the Creator. Darkness for such a group falls when entities within the group forget the absolute identify of other self and Creator.

When a community such as L/L Research gathers and begins to attempt to work as one, the original impetus that drew entities together must be tested. And so the mirroring effect sets in. Each looks into the mirror of the others' perceptions and begins to see all of those parts of the self that the self least wishes to see. That is because it is a very positive and helpful function of the community that is operating on a spiritual level to help each other to grow closer to the one infinite Creator. And the way that this is done is by bringing up all these lost sheep of self, all these parts of self that are not redeemed, loved and accepted.

There are many occasions, for each member of such a group, when the information given about the shadow side simply overwhelms sight. The world darkens and the shadows lengthen. It is easy to lose one's way, to trip and to fall in the dark. It is a somewhat painful experience, literally speaking as well as figuratively, to fall. And falling is a rather drastic way of saying, metaphorically, that sometimes it is necessary to let go of what you think you know.

While you are fallen, touch the Earth. Reestablish contact with the ground underneath your feet, both physically and metaphysically. Realize that you are always safe within the context of having fallen down. The ground of being is very real and trustable, as is the ground beneath your feet. In the process of all this growth, you can always find the ground of being by letting yourself fall down. Indeed, rejoice in having fallen down! Rejoice in having expressed some of this energy that was previously being expressed in mental and emotional frustration.

How shall you dust yourself off and begin again? Shall you simply assume that you are now standing up in the same world in which you fell down? We encourage you to open up your mind to the possibility that you stand up in a new world. What shall you make this new world to be? How shall you grow?

Is there another query at this time?

(No further queries.)

We are those of Q'uo, and are aware that we seem to have exhausted the supply of questions in the circle of seeking at this time. It has been our pleasure to work with these questions and we thank each of you for putting aside the time and the energy to spend time in seeking and questing of the truth. We hope that our poor thoughts have been of some small value to you and we can assure you unequivocally that your questions have been very valuable to us, as has been the experience of your beauty, which always takes our breath away. We thank you from the bottoms of our hearts and we leave you as we found you, in the love and in the light of the one infinite Creator. We are known to you as the principle of Q'uo. Adonai. Adonai. ✲

L/L RESEARCH

L/L Research is a subsidiary of
Rock Creek Research &
Development Laboratories, Inc.

P.O. Box 5195
Louisville, KY 40255-0195

www.llresearch.org

Rock Creek is a non-profit
corporation dedicated to
discovering and sharing
information which may aid in
the spiritual evolution of
humankind.

SUNDAY MEDITATION
NOVEMBER 20, 2005

Group question: We have two questions today for you, Q'uo. Here is the first one: Could you comment on the effective ways of bringing people in their teens and in their twenties physically together to grow into the fourth-density consciousness?

(Carla channeling)

We are those of the principle known to you as Q'uo. Greetings in the love and in the light of the one infinite Creator. It is in the Creator's service that we come to you this day to share with you our thoughts on the subject of effective ways to invite people to gather together to explore ways of growing in a fourth-density manner. We thank the one known as P for this query and are happy to address it.

Before we begin, as always, we would ask each of you to take full responsibility for listening to our thoughts with careful discrimination. If a thought appeals to you and seems to have use, by all means, work with it. If it does not immediately appeal to you than we ask you to put it aside. Truth is always a personal and even an intimate matter. We would prefer greatly that you were able to do this simple thing for it will enable us to speak freely without being concerned that we might infringe upon your free will. We are not those of authority over you but rather those who share conversation with you at this time as fellow seekers of truth. We thank you for this consideration.

The elements of this query are such that we shall need to discuss some of the words before we can discuss the concept and the question. The first word that we would take up is the word "growth." What is it to grow? As the one known as P himself said, it is inevitable that entities grow. That growth develops according to the nature of the entity. Each entity comes to life from a seed. That entity has, written in its seed, the nature of its growth and indeed the path of its life through budding and blooming, yielding up its fruit, and dying.

Growth, then, is not simply then becoming ever larger and ever more developed. There is a roundness to growth which involves not simply the growing portion of a cycle but also the ripening, the harvesting, the dwindling, and the dying of the organism that has done the growing.

Growth, then, in the physical sense, is bound carefully and specifically by the type of seed which you are and the environment in which you are planted. From the physical standpoint, then, your query involves partially a discussion of the seed and the nature of that type of seed that you are and that entities such as humans are. And partially it involves a discussion of the best environment for growth within incarnation.

Metaphysically, growth may be seen in a far more spacious context. You as an individual have been growing, not simply through one incarnation but through many, not simply in one density but in all of them within your octave. Speaking metaphysically and in a non-local manner, you are growing in all densities simultaneously and creating a non-local harvest which is being developed over a period of billions of your years, speaking from the standpoint of physical terms.

It is very difficult to speak of metaphysical-scale growth within your numbering system. However, let us say it is a very large-scale project to grow metaphysically. We would, however, point out that within the context of this infinite environment, growth, again, consists of the seed, the environment, and those cyclical experiences of learning, assimilating the learning, and responding to that which you have assimilated.

In the first case, that of physical growth of a human being through incarnation, the seed is that which is produced by sperm and ovum from the dust, metaphorically speaking, out of which your Earth has created a local habitation of flesh in which you as a metaphysical being have chosen to place your consciousness for that cycle known as an incarnation in order that you may have being within the environment of third-density Earth.

We will allow you to name the nature of the seed of flesh, saying only that it is steeped in illusion and rounded in mystery. Each life is a gift, a miracle, an incredible circumstance, which happens only once. The being that you are is unique. This incarnation you experience shall not be experienced again. The song that you sing in flesh shall never be heard again. The colors of your emotions as they flash and change and transform are an experiment in beauty and dynamic that shall not recur. You are precious beyond description within the folds of your dailiness.

As infinite and eternal beings, the seed from which you sprang is the infinite Creator. And in this metaphysical creation, although growth indeed does take place, it is rounded just as a [physical] incarnation is: in the birth and the death of one beat of the Creator's heart, one unit or creation of the creative principle.

That which this instrument calls an "octave" [includes] the seven densities moving into the eighth density and therefore back to the first.[71] It is the

measure of your measureless life as a metaphysical being. It begins with birth which is a being cast out of the womb of the mother that is the Creator. Not to be abandoned; a mother does not birth a child to abandon it. It does allow the child to grow and in this case the entire purpose that your parent had in mind for you is for you to teach your parent about the nature of itself.

"What seed do I cast forth into beingness?" You are spending your energy and your time exploring at your leisure and at your pleasure the ramifications of this question.

In the fullness of this moment within the Creator's beating heart, you shall return to the infinite Creator with your harvest and your burden of awareness and beingness and in offering up the essence of all that you are, you shall once again be lost up in the Creator Itself, and the Creator shall be full of all that which it has learned from Its child. And in that diastolic moment, when the Creator's heart rests between beats, all shall be measureless, unified and without any kinetic [component].

And then the Creator's heart shall once again beat and you and all of the tribe of those who share consciousness shall once again start their immeasurable journeys.

When you asked your query, my brother, you asked what effective ways there may be to bring entities of your age group—you yourself, we find in this instrument's mind, being 19 years of age—together, physically, in order to seek new ways of relating to each other and to the creation.

You spoke specifically of learning to live according to fourth-density ways. And so we would look secondly at those words, "fourth density." As we have said, entities grow according to their nature. That which an entity is does not change because of a desire to change. The change that is desired needs to be physically and metaphysically possible for the entity doing the growing. A frog cannot sprout a

---

[71] In music, an octave consists of 12 half-tone notes in sequence or a scale of eight notes in a major, minor or modal

configuration. We know the major scale as "Do Re Mi Fa So La Ti Do" from the musical of the 1950s, The Sound of Music. Whether we are speaking of the 12-tone scale or the 8-note scale, the last note, "Do," is the same tone as the first note, but an octave higher. In the same way, first density starts in timelessness and as the densities proceed, at the end of perceivable time in seventh density, timelessness sets in again. When time emerges again, it is the mid-first density of the next octave.

rose from its head. Your scientist may find a way to clone a frog that grows a rose from is head, but in the natural environment of Earth, this shall not happen.

Therefore, we would say to the one known as P that there is no other way for a third-density entity to grow than to begin to explore elements of the self that will continue to be developed in fourth density. Therefore, we would redirect your query in two ways.

Firstly we would suggest to you the great centrality of grasping polarity. For growth is a matter, within third density, of choosing the manner of its beingness. Shall it be of service to itself, primarily? Or shall it be of service to others? Graduation is possible using either path. Entry into fourth density is possible only through graduation using one of these two paths.

Therefore, grasping the importance of polarity and determining to pursue with persistence and devotion the path that you have chosen is very important in accelerating the process of growth. Until this central point is taken and internalized, it will not be at all apparent to you as to what disciplines you need to persist in learning in order to accelerate the pace of your growth.

We understand that there is no equivocation on the part either of yourself speaking personally or of yourself speaking as a representative of the group of which you are a part. As to the polarity you have chosen, you and your group have chosen service to others as your polarity.

However, my brother, the progress of a life that is polarized in service to others is measured not by that which you may see, although certainly the results of your efforts to serve are indicative of much and can be assumed to infer progress along the lines of polarization.

Habits of thought and ways of relating to yourself and to other entities are infinitely subtle in the lessons that they hide and partially reveal as you experience interaction with yourself and with others.

Pure service-to-others polarity is very difficult to achieve within your density. The biases of our culture and those internalized biases that are part of your net of assumptions and things that you feel that you know are incredibly invasive and prevalent within the habitual mindset that you experience as

being yourself. Consequently, there is an ever deeper element of honesty with yourself that is very helpful for you to pursue.

It is well to do this within your internalized self. The more that you work with your own thoughts, the less that you shall need to use what this instrument has often called the hall of mirrors, which is what occurs when you do not do the internalized work of exploring the nature of your thoughts and your being and are instead given projections or images of your being and your thoughts in the face of those about you.

When you receive those images from those about you, you may assume that these images are to some extent distorted, just as a bad mirror will make you thinner or taller or curvy and wavy in the way that the image looks back at you.

You can do the same endless imaging within yourself or you may choose at any time to pull away masks, attitudes and assumptions and enter into the present moment and the freshness of now.

We realize that this is not exact language but there is a membrane separating you from what this instrument would call the fast track. It is an invisible membrane, a kind of meniscus, which is made up of your self-awareness and whatever energies you have that are holding you to your present way of being.

What hidden resistances do you have to releasing yourself to the possibilities of the present moment?

This instrument as a part of a group has found that it is very useful to work with the mirroring effect of being a part of a community. And we are aware that there are others within this group who have also found the mirroring effect very useful, if challenging. And we would suggest to all of you that in order to use this mirroring effect better, you use the internal mirrors of self first. If you can, do this internal analysis each day. We would suggest doing it in a private environment, working with pen and paper or on the computer or in the privacy of your own mind.

We have spoken of the nature of growth and the nature of the entity that attempts to grow into fourth density, attempting to draw a three-dimensional picture of the environment which is helpful for growth. You cannot, within third density, be a fourth-density being. You can, however, be a third-density being who has become mature and who is no longer holding onto that which has been assumed to be the limitations of the possibilities of growth within third density.

By the very nature of the being that you uncover by doing spiritual work, you are aware of the direction in which you are going. You know that as you learn the ways of unconditional love, you shall prepare yourself for graduation into an environment in which unconditional love is manifest, obvious, overt and apparent.

Can you live in a private universe: the universe inside your own being and inside your own heart where unconditional love has become the order of the day? Can you love without expectation of return? Without blinking at those who detract or scorn or ridicule you?

This instrument was speaking earlier of attempting to create a home upon the website which she calls bring4th[72] for entities who specifically wish to criticize and scorn either this instrument or concepts in which this instrument has had a part in putting forth. This instrument did see the paradox of wanting to give a home to those who would wish to tear her apart and tear her ideas down.

However, in this instrument's humble opinion, the ideals for which the organization stands and which it holds dear are sturdy and are in no danger of being torn down by criticism.

Nor is she overly concerned that ridicule or scorn of her would make any difference in her ability to love the entity who is scorning her. She has earned the right to her opinion. She dares much in attempting to express, awkwardly and in this shadow world, an atmosphere of unconditional acceptance and love.

How shall you dare this *beau geste*, my brother? For it begins with you. It begins with this instrument. It begins within each of you as individuals.

The manner of your being becomes a seed. At any given moment of Now, you have become a seed to be planted that others may watch you grow, may see you bloom, and as you perish and offer your harvest to the autumn winds and the reapers, others shall be able to use the light that you have gathered within yourself as if it were food, fueling their own growth by the inspiration of your being.

You have said that you wished this group to gather physically but we find that effective ways to create physical gatherings are non-physical in nature. It begins with your dedication to being a seed that buries itself in the ground of the group that you wish to create.

This is very resonant for this particular instrument and certainly for the one known as Jim as well, for many years ago they, in moments of deep, personal humility and focus, offered themselves and their entire life, first apart and then together, in an attempt to serve the one infinite Creator by creating, if possible, a spiritually-oriented group. This group is that now known as L/L Research and it is a group with which we have had, in one form or another, a continuing contact to our mutual benefit, we believe, for some of your time.

You are not starting from scratch, then. You can build on the work that has bloomed and been given to the environment of L/L Research.

But that which moves your vision into manifestation is not directly under your control. What is under your control is your own integrity and honesty and your persistent effort in seeking to uncover the nature of your true self. As you dig deeper into this supposedly homogenized and coordinated self, you will find that many things fall away and that you as a person begin to fall apart. This falling apart is a necessary portion of that which prepares you for meeting the essence and core of self.

This essence is not trapped in third density or within incarnation. Where is it?

(Side one of tape ends.)

(Carla channeling)

We suggest that you seek it in the sacredness of silence. Within that silence, when you have come to the end of your time with the Creator, round out that time of meditation or contemplation with a visualization of that which you wish to make manifest in your future with regards to this gathering of entities.

Do not visualize as one who is attempting or trying or making an effort. Rather, spend time knowing and praising and celebrating and giving thanks for that which is naturally gathering because of the energies of yourself and the infinite One. Spirit has

---

[72] www.bring4.org

brought you to this moment. It is well to trust both in yourself and in spirit.

There are many within your age group who are ready to awaken to this common and shared vision of living the ways of love. This is why we said to you that it is well to realize that much of the work of bringing entities together physically is contacting them in ways that are not immediately physical. The technology which your people have created which this instrument calls the internet offers ways to communicate globally.

Therefore, we encourage you to use the simple, ordinary and everyday aspects of your life to create ways of communicating via the internet with those entities which you are faithfully and peacefully sure exist, sharing in the ever imperfect ways of words the love that is held in your vision.

This instrument is informing us that we must move on and therefore we would ask at this time if there is another query?

Jim: *(Reading P's question.)* Could you discuss ways to decrease distortion within the learning environment based on your experience?

We are those of Q'uo, and are aware of your query, my brother. Indeed, to decrease a distortion is a thing greatly to be wished for us all.

It is to be noted, however, that without distortion there would be no expression. Without distortion, in an absolute sense, there would be no creation. You are necessarily and permanently, as far as we know, dealing with distortion.

You yourself are a distortion of the one infinite Creator in that you have been given a locality. Yet within you lies absolute clarity on an unconscious basis or level. Can you accept the paradox of distortion and clarity indwelling, interpenetrating each other and blessing each other with the gifts that each has to offer the other?

It is always helpful in attempting to decrease distortion to rest in silence in the environment of your own private time, when you gaze inwardly at the depths of your being and outwardly at the depths of the day or the night sky. There seem to be greatly enhanced opportunities for that seeking self to become able to contact the gateway to intelligent infinity, to come into the present moment, and to rest at last in the peace of no time and no space.

Each moment that you are able to live there fills with you the love and the light of ten thousand years spent in the hurly burly of normal living. And yet it is very difficult, perhaps nearly impossible, to live day to day and moment to moment resting in the present moment. Distortion will call you forward. You will be pulled one way or another and you will be lost to that clarity that you had when you were undisturbed.

My brother, we would encourage you to embrace the colorations of distortion as they pass before you. Love them all. Look at them carefully and let them go. Do not be overly impressed with any of your distortions, be they seemingly negative or seemingly positive. They too are masks and that which you discover when you take that mask off is also a mask. There is no end to the roles that you are playing while upon the stage of what this instrument would call earthly life or third-density existence.

But you have an incredible amount of power over the situation if you are able to let go of every vestige of control. You have forgotten that you wrote this play. Yet you did and you can rewrite it as you go. There is nothing holding you or anyone else from rewriting the play that you unfold day by day.

You are also the audience and we encourage you to watch with appreciation.

And since you are a critic, as well, we ask that you sharpen your wits and review the passion play that unfolds within and around you. Play with your play. Let it become play.

The one known as V spoke to this instrument recently of the story of the Dalai Lama, an entity who is much revered in certain quarters among your peoples as a highly advanced spiritual being. This entity sat down on a tussock that had been prepared for him to sit on and discovered that it was springy and soft. So this entity, in front of all these people who were waiting for the next pearl to drop from his lips, celebrated the bounciness of this soft tussock and spent a considerable number of seconds enjoying bouncing on his seat. He remembered to take life lightly and to introduce a comedic aspect, something to laugh at, something to enjoy "just because."

Introduce whimsy and lightness and all of the aspects of the fairyland and the kingdom of the devas that you inhabit, as well as the overarching seriousness and driven dedication of your hopes and your intents. It is a matter of staying in balance while moving as fast as you can along the upward spiraling light that is spiritual evolution.

We find that the energy begins to wane within this group and so we would ask for one more query at this time. Is there a final query before we leave this instrument?

B: I have one. You referred to "non-local harvest." I was under the impression that harvest was located in space/time and resulted in physical and environmental change. Could you clarify that?

We are those known as Q'uo, and are aware of your query, my brother. We thank you for that question. The non-local harvest is the harvest of the one infinite Creator. The harvest that is non-local is that which is drawn into the Creator Itself through the processes of increasing spiritual gravity and it is a portion of the life cycle of you as a metaphysical entity within this octave of the creation.

May we answer you further, my brother?

B: I understand. I just had not thought of that before. Thank you.

We thank you, my brother, and may we say what a blessing it is to share energy with you at this time. It is a blessing to share energy with all of you.

We are aware through this instrument's mind that you gather together to give thanks at this time and to feast together.[73] May you feast not only on food of the physical [kind] but on the food of your laughter, your love, and your shared energy, for you are blessings to each other, dear brothers and sisters, and together you truly are beautiful to us.

We thank you for your presence, for calling us to you at this time, for enabling us to serve and for the beauty of your being. It humbles us and it blesses us greatly.

We leave you as we found you, in the love and in the light, in the power and in the peace of the one infinite Creator. We are known to you as the principle of Q'uo. Adonai. Adonai. ❧

---

[73] The group celebrated Thanksgiving together at Camelot the Sunday before the actual holiday, immediately following this meditation.

L/L Research is a subsidiary of
Rock Creek Research &
Development Laboratories, Inc.

P.O. Box 5195
Louisville, KY 40255-0195

L/L Research

www.llresearch.org

Rock Creek is a non-profit
corporation dedicated to
discovering and sharing
information which may aid in
the spiritual evolution of
humankind.

Special Meditation
November 21, 2005

Question chosen by PLW poll:[74] The Mayan calendar system indicated 2012 as the end of their calendar and therefore the end of time. Please comment in any way you feel helpful concerning this concept of the end of time and why 2012 was chosen by the Mayans as the end of the calendar.

(Carla channeling)

We are those known to you as the principle of Q'uo. Greetings in the love and in the light of the one infinite Creator, in Whose service we come to you this day. May we say what a privilege and a pleasure it is for us to blend our vibrations with you at this time! We are extremely thankful, in this season of thanksgiving among your people, for the opportunity to share energy with you and to be asked to share our humble opinions as well.

We would ask each of you to use your powers of discrimination carefully in listening to our opinions. They are not intended in any way to represent authoritative statements which you must follow or which contain dogma of any kind. They are our opinions and observations. In order for us to share them without being concerned that we will infringe upon your free will we would ask you to take responsibility for guarding the precincts of your own thoughts. If any thought that we share with you does not seem resonant to you, please drop it and move on. If any of our thoughts do seem to ring a bell,

that distant bell of a memory that was half-forgotten, then by all means take it up, it is yours to work with. We thank you for this consideration as it will enable us to speak freely.

It has long been seen among many of your cultures that there is a periodicity to the energies which create the environment for your incarnational experiences.

Various cultures and civilizations have categorized and organized these periods, eras or times within the energetic progression of what this instrument would call the time/space or space/time continuum. The particular age of which you speak is a space/time era primarily, although it certainly has corresponding shadows and equivalencies in time/space.

Indeed, in time/space you are already solidly and completely within fourth density.[75] You dwell in a third-density energy that is now completely interpenetrated with unconditional love and complete understanding of your true nature.

You dwell within powerful times in which you, as a third-density entity, dwell in a body that is capable of living and thriving within such fourth-density

---

[74] Planet Lightworker Magazine (www.planetlightworker.com).

[75] Fourth density is a term that the Q'uo use to indicate the next density of life after our present environment of consensus reality, which they call third density. Second density refers to the world of nature with its plants and animals and first density is the density of earth, air, wind, fire and the elements.

energy as you can meet with a sense of cooperation, faith and trust.

You cannot, however, join fourth density. Dwelling within your house of flesh and bone, you cannot know beyond a shadow of a doubt that all is one. You cannot know that that one thing is love.

Indeed, you have volunteered for an incarnation at this time because you wished to experience and be a part of the tremendous times that are at hand. [These are] times when a few people who discipline their minds and their thoughts can make a tremendous difference upon your planet not only in terms of the people of your planet but in terms of the comfort in the planet itself as it moves through the last of this birthing process.

The Mayans are among those civilizations which became aware of a cycle that stretched across long eras of your time. They saw that the planet itself would move through a very decisive change from the Age of Pisces to the Age of Aquarius. The Age of Pisces is at its end. The Age of Aquarius is in its dawn. Energies are shifting and the time of energy being as it has been for thousands of your years is rapidly coming to a close.

That time will end during what this instrument calls the winter solstice of the year 2012.

We would ask each who reads or hears our statements to pause at this time with us and release all fear.

(Pause)

It is easy to fear a concept as powerful as the end of time. We would say several things concerning this concept. Firstly, it is a metaphysical rather than a physical ending of time. Your planet as you know it shall move serenely on. Time will not seem to end to the physical eye.

The quality of time shall be different. In third density the differences will be only statistically perceptible. In metaphysical terms, in time/space terms, shall we say, that difference will be far more powerful.

For entities who are sensitive to energy, it is already thoroughly apparent that wave after wave of energy is crashing upon the shores of Earth. The planet is changing and the changes will continue. There is a necessity, having to do with the difference between third-density energy and fourth-density energy, for

the planet to realign its magnetic pole. This shift is occurring.

Thanks to the many loving efforts of lightworkers such as this group all over your globe, working in relatively unconscious unity, but nevertheless being very effective in increasing the light on planet Earth by their loving affection for it, it is as though this change in magnetic polarity is being accomplished step, by step, by step, rather than all at once.

As you see your planet experiencing many weather-related phenomena, you can see your mother, Gaia, at work, doing what is necessary to shift vibrationally and magnetically in order to align with fourth-density energies. The mother suffers in order that the child may thrive. Such is the labor of Gaia.

As these inconveniences continue, we would ask that each of you refrain completely from fear.

It will seem to be an increasingly logical response to the news of the day to experience fear. When these natural feelings of fear arise, we would ask you to remember that you are the light of the world.

Each of you, by your very nature, is a crystal that receives, transmits and transmutes energy. That energy is the infinite love and light of the one Creator, which streams in infinite supply from the heart of the planet itself into the energy bodies of each of you and out through the crowns of your head, where you function just as does a pyramid.

The energy that you create, bless and give to the Creator by keeping your heart open and your love and faith strong winds itself into a golden net that surrounds the planet with love.

Angels guard this work and join you in weaving this net of love. This works by blending third-density energies with the fourth density that is birthing at this time.

We thank each of you for creating within yourself the capacity for increased faith. We ask you to attempt, in each moment where fear might be a logical reaction, to move into your heart and find that place of faith in which you know that whether you are in life or in death, the Creator is living through you and you are the Creator or part of the creative principle within flesh. You are not an entity that shall be stopped by death in any way.

Nor do we suggest for a moment that all of you shall die in one dramatic planetary cataclysm. Indeed, once 2012 has come and gone, we are hoping that third density will have a considerable number of years, perhaps even centuries, in which those who choose to dwell in third-density [physical] vehicles may see to the continuing restitution or healing of your planet.

Many are the entities on your planet who have destroyed other planetary vehicles for existence such as Maldek, Mars and other [planetary] entities outside of your solar system. We ask that you become more and more aware that you have the opportunity, at this time, within this incarnation, to turn that energy within yourself around and to become stewards, loving and wise, of whatever little acre or square foot that you may have of planet Earth.

What does your space need? If you are one who has property, we would ask you to commune with your land. And not simply with your land, but with your local situation. What local situations having to do with planet Earth have gone awry on your watch, in your neighborhood? And what can one person do to bring them gently into more harmony with those things which the planet itself needs?

Are you waters foul? What can you do? Is there a lack of sustainable practice amongst your businesses? What can you do?

We could go on and on, listing the kinds of simple, down-to-earth, human, local problems to which you may address yourself. Whether you do have land or whether you live on the thirty-seventh floor of a high-rise, yet still you are part of planet Earth.

What can you do? What are your gifts, and what kind of problems do you see?

You are potentially one of those who is able, as one simple, single being, full of flaws, and yet full of good intentions, to join in groups that have a hope of coping with and creating solutions to those imbalances that have resulted in pollution and illness within the planet itself.

The healing begins within your own heart whether you live on a large parcel of land, a small parcel of land, or in that high-rise of which we spoke earlier. Heal the pollution within yourself. Love yourself. Be a steward to your own body, your own mind, your own nature and your own advancement.

As you see your own advancement, do not take someone else's word for what constitutes healing and advancement. Move within your own being where sources of guidance are thick on the ground and begin asking for that guidance to speak to you.

Let that guidance spring to life from the world around you. Observe synchronicities and listen to words, phrases and thoughts that take you and make you imagine, hope and dream. For your imagination is the key to forming a new paradigm for living in a new time, on a new Earth, and in a new dawning of possibilities.

We would ask at this time if there is a follow-up that either the known as S1 or the one known as S2 would like to make in order to further direct our response to this query. We are those known as Q'uo.

S1: There are several variations of the Mayan calendar and the different native tribes that have kept information to be brought forth at this time. They are different perspectives, some seemingly different, some very similar. Could you comment on the similarities and the differences of these different messages?

We are those of Q'uo, and are aware of your query, my brother. We do not find it useful to comment upon the various differences of stories among your people which attempt to speak of events that beggar the imagination not only of those upon third density but those who have the full potentiality of the one infinite Creator.

There is a mystery involved in the way densities change. That way of changing is as the movement betwixt one quantum and another. There is not a direct movement across a quantum boundary. We show this instrument, who knows nothing of science or quantum physics, the image of the meniscus that is liquid in nature. This entity has directly experienced this liquid environment betwixt densities.

She has called it the gateway to intelligent infinity, for it is, in the terms of the *Law of One* material which this instrument has studied, that which she understands as being the point at which one may move from the quantum of third density to the quantum of fourth density.

And she has rested there at times in those moments when she has by unconscious processes been placed in a mystical state of awareness which contains unity.

In this environment this instrument becomes aware that all is well and that all will be well. She sees a perfection of the outworking of the pattern of time and space.

She cannot bring any quantity of this awareness back from this state. It is simply a gift. It has been noted by the one known as Saint Paul, in his writings in your *Holy Bible*, that such gifts as this and so-called speaking in tongues have very little human use. They are gifts only.

Nevertheless, because this instrument has been given gifts of this nature in times of vision and awareness that are heightened, she is able to understand what we show her, and that is that there is a very discernible, real place of no-time in which, just as in your dusk and in your dawning, or as in energy shifts as you have just experienced in your All Souls Day, one kind of light is leaving and another kind of light is arriving.

The spirits of day and the spirits of night are quite different. In the dusk and the dawning there is a very perceptible shift and it is a time of waiting and hush. [It is] an excellent time for doing work in consciousness.

The differences between the stories of various cultures are differences related to those cultures' relationship with the quantum edge that this instrument calls "the gateway to intelligent infinity." Were we to begin to focus in on specific details of this shift, we would, we believe, be detracting from the intention of the question to discover the heart of what the so-called end of time is about.

What that time is about is spiritual evolution. It is amazing to consider what occurs in any lifetime. From the beginning of your lifetime to this present moment, how many things have changed in your world? What progression has there been? And as you approach this present moment have you not seen how these energies of progression have intensified and speeded up? As this time approaches, these energies will continue to intensify.

What we would wish to do, then, rather than focusing on any detail, is to focus on the general nature of this cosmic moment. You dwell in a time that is coming to an end and yet in your body, in your mind, and in your heart you carry the seeds of the future within you.

As live your life, breathe in and breathe out, you are planting seeds that shall be reaped by those that come after you. We ask you to plant the seeds of love and faith with a happy heart and a peaceful mind.

As you see suffering from the energies of war and from the energies of a planet that is adjusting itself as it must to new energies and new life, we ask you to become ever calmer, reaching deeply down into your store of faith and hope.

We do not see at this time the probability of planetary destruction from nature. We do see the possibility of planetary destruction from the toxic nature of the human tribe. If those who have chosen to fear are allowed full sway they may well bring about planetary destruction, as has happened with many of those entities now in power upon your planet on other planets and even on your own planet, to a certain extent, for those who are among your leaders at this time are often those who brought about the destruction of one of your continents, the continent of Atlantis.

If these words resonate to you, my children, pay attention. This is the hour in which you can choose another way.

In the face of fear, remember love.

In the face of anger, remember compassion.

In the face of disunity, remember union, for are you not part of everyone and everything that you meet?

In the face of seeming dearth, lack and limitation of resources, we ask you to dwell in thanksgiving and joy upon the unlimited possibilities that dwell within your imagination.

We say to you this: for every problem that faces you this day, there is a solution.

We have no way of knowing what you face and what you shall face, but we do know that your peoples have been given not only great challenges but also great gifts and unlimited resources.

The challenge that lies before you is not to husband dwindling resources but to begin to see the resources that are available to you that are not now properly valued and to realize that the greatest resource of all is the compassion that lies within your heart.

It is hard sometimes to see how in times of distress the answers lie within you rather than outside of you, for all of the distress seems to be coming from outside of you. However, we say to you at this time that in our opinion that which shall heal you and your planet and bring you through the end of time to greet the dawning of a new day is that which lies within you waiting to be acknowledged.

What is in your heart? What lies waiting within that mighty resource? Go into your own heart in humility, on bowed knees and with empty hands, and ask for help. It is waiting for that asking and the help that comes will be instantaneous. As you ask, so shall help be present.

Listen, then, when you have asked, for that still, small voice, as this instrument would call the voice of spirit, to speak in the power of silence within you.

And when you come from that room of prayer in silence and contemplation, may you sing with joy and may you illuminate your world with thanksgiving, peace and power.

We would at this time thank each of you and leave you, as we found you, in the love and in the light of the one infinite Creator. If there is a desire to pursue such queries as you have put to us on these details, comparisons and ways to contrast stories of the end of time, we invite them at another session. But we would ask that you rephrase the query in such a way that we may be speaking of known quantities within your query in order that our response may be clearer.

Meanwhile, we thank each of you for setting aside this time in order to seek the truth. We thank you for the beauty of your beings and for the light that you as a group have created within this circle of seeking. We are known to you as the principle of Q'uo. Adonai. Adonai. We are those of Q'uo. ❧

L/L Research

L/L Research is a subsidiary of
Rock Creek Research &
Development Laboratories, Inc.

P.O. Box 5195
Louisville, KY 40255-0195

www.llresearch.org

Rock Creek is a non-profit
corporation dedicated to
discovering and sharing
information which may aid in
the spiritual evolution of
humankind.

© 2009 L/L Research

SUNDAY MEDITATION
DECEMBER 11, 2005

Group question: The question today, Q'uo, has to do with just what language is and how it works. Whether we are communicating with a rock, a tree, with each other, or with a fourth-density entity, how does it work? It is said that Solex Mal is one of the basic languages. Ra said that Hebrew and Sanskrit were very basic languages. What is the basis of language? And after we have communicated, after we have attempted to use words to describe thoughts, feelings, ideas and so forth, how do these thoughts, feelings, ideas and words sink in and have an effect upon us so that we grow, so that we're more than we were before we heard them?

(Carla channeling)

We are those known to you as the principle of Q'uo. Greetings in the love and in the light of the one infinite Creator. We come in the service of the infinite Creator to share our humble opinions at this time. We thank the circle of seeking for calling us. We thank this instrument for tuning to secure us specifically. And we thank all of those unseen presences whose energies add so much to the richness of the experience of all of us who experience this circle together.

It is our pleasure and our privilege to offer you whatever thoughts we have. As always, however, we would ask each of you to be very responsible about maintaining a guard upon your own temple gates. Please be careful about what you accept for material for thinking. If an idea seems helpful or valid to you,

by all means follow it. That is why we are sharing the information. However, we are not always those who hit the mark. Be aware of this. Not all of our thoughts may be specifically for you. If one does not seem to be helpful, then we ask you to leave it behind without a second thought. We thank you for this favor for it enables us to speak freely and not be concerned that we will infringe upon your free will.

By the very words that we have just spoken through this instrument, we have indicated that we consider your words to be instruments of communication that are efficient. We would like to make that point first for much that we have to say about words seems to denigrate the power of the spoken word or the heard word. And we would not in any way suggest that there is little or no power in that which you hear and that which you say.

Remember that you are creatures whose only access to life is through breathing in and breathing out. The train whistle that you hear outside of the dwelling place in which each of you sits at this time is also a wind instrument expressing noise or signal through the expression of air. Each of you, similarly and hopefully with more sense, is a wind instrument. You have far more than one two-note dyad to sing your song. You have all the colorations of the voice before you ever come to say a word.

The simple expression of your voice is enough to let someone else sharing space with you in a house or home, an office or a restaurant know that there is another entity dwelling in the same space with them. The simple sound of your voice humming a tune is enough to tell them who you are and to awaken in them the emotions created by the dynamics of your energy exchange. We encourage you to have great respect and give great honor to your breath. With it you ride the surf of life within the environment of third density. And with that voice, with that breath expelled just so, you begin to make patterns at a very young age.

What are your first words? For most entities the first words are those recognitions of entities that share space with them: "Mama," "Papa," Grandpa," "Grandma." We discover within this instrument's mind—and perhaps it is not too far a detour to take—that this instrument's first words were, "Put me down," spoken to her dear mother. There is in the human energy almost an equal need to recognize intimacy and to create individuation or individuality. Words are used for both purposes. Therefore, before you speak your first word in a conversation, ask yourself, "Is this a pattern of words designed to increase intimacy or is this a pattern of words designed to increase individuation?"

You have asked, "What is language?" And you have indicated by the way that you have asked this question that you are not speaking simply of language such as we are using through this instrument but rather the whole concept of modes of communication. Moving into a lucid discussion of the fundamentals of language is a bit like attempting to pluck the middle out of a system which is involuted to an extent where the middle is difficult to reach directly. Therefore, let us be somewhat relaxed in our logic and approach the question from a couple of different angles.

Firstly, the basics of language—or as the one known as R pointed out, the basics of its synonym, communication—are two: love and light.

The very nature of nature, Creator, and created is a living Thought. You are a thought. That thought translates into your language as love. This instrument was speaking recently of the hopelessness of using language and especially of using the word, "love." We would agree. Yet, we have no choice. We can attempt to throw up a hedge of adjectives and qualifiers to indicate the kind of love of which we speak when we speak of the one great original

Thought. It is a Thought of unconditional, absolute love.

In and of itself, love is pure being and being is pure love. There is no vector implicit in love itself or in you as a being, purely considered. The vector is provided by that thought that you are, with all of its distortions, as you exist in incarnation in third density acting upon that love that you are.

It is light that has molded itself into each atom of your body, into the various energy fields which control your various organs, your elements of sense, such as sight and smell and taste and hearing. It is light molded in the ways of energy as it is received from the infinite energy of the one Creator that the love which is you molds into your distorted pattern of energy expenditures. That use of energy, endlessly creating and recreating itself as unique catalyst and response to it, is at any moment the sum total of expression of who you are. You are love using light to experience the incarnation you now experience, to process the catalyst that you are now receiving, and to explore those regions of feeling and concept which are sparked into awakening within you.

The most potent information that you will ever gather is information concerning your thoughts. This is entirely interior to your process. We cannot say how much of your own internal processing is done in words, how much of it is done in feeling and how much is done in various idiosyncratic ways or uses of energy such as visualization, meditation, what this instrument would call prayer and other tools and resources of an entity who decides to go deeper and look further than the entities in consensus reality around one tend to go.

You were speaking as a group of staying on the surface of things. It is indeed a wise plan to skate on the surface of life for awhile, to allow for whatever patterns that have occurred to settle and to clarify themselves. Sometimes the hardest thing in the world is to realize that one is in the middle of a confused pattern and that waiting is indicated. That is a waiting without words, a waiting that is full of knowing.

Another way of looking at language is to look at what actually occurs during a communication. The one known as B was asking about how one talks to a rock. This is difficult for us to communicate through this instrument but we will attempt it. All entities besides humans in third density speak and understand the thought behind the words rather than understanding words. It is to the human mind that words are necessary, not to the consciousness that indwells all of the other densities and, indeed, the inner planes of your own density. It is not the rest of creation that is odd, it is you.

Words are a very special artifact of your density. They are necessary because there is a carefully placed veil that blocks the conscious mind of third-density entities within incarnation from being fully aware that all is one, that all are part of one infinite creation and are part of the principle of that creation. Each of you is a shaft of the sunlight of the day that the Creator has made.

And so for you, words were created as if rolled out by a great rolling pin from the roundness of concept and then stamped with cookie cutters to make this and that shape in the mouth and in the ear so that you could stumble your way through communicating what you are perceiving to each other and to yourselves.

In actuality, when you are truly communicating, even within your third-density, illusory bodies, the concept that lies behind the words creates points of unification that make the energy of the words that you use more coherent. To a rock, however, there is no need for a word, although it is very helpful to an entity within third density communicating with a rock to use the words. But the visual and auditory aid is not useful in communicating with the rock. It is useful in letting the human know that the human is indeed attempting to communicate with the rock.

Now, this being said, it is helpful to realize that the first communication that you give, in terms of metaphysical—not physical—discussion, is being or love. The precise distortion of love at which you are vibrating or expressing at this moment is the beginning of all communications from you. Admittedly, in human conversation, the beingness aspect may or may not have much impact depending upon the quality of the entity to whom you are speaking, the quality of yourself as a self known to itself, and the quality of the conversation itself.

That beingness is information that is as the matrix for the movement of concept that constitutes the formation of a communication. If you are speaking to a rock, your first communication is, "I am here." Your second communication is, "I recognize you." Your third communication, given that you wish to speak to the rock is, "Listen to me." You are setting up a way for the rock to grasp the fact that you are in communication with it. That rock is immediately aware of your being and of your desire to speak with it. It is variably interested in listening to you, depending upon the nature of your being. The more you come to an entity not of your own density resting comfortably in your own skin, energetically speaking, the more accurate and eloquent your communication may be.

Therefore, the skill of communication begins with the ongoing business of discovering ever more deeply who you are. What you wish to communicate to a being such a rock can, in your mind, be very complex, having to do with a good many details. To the mind of a rock, the details will be lost. It is your honest and clearly felt emotion and desire that are communicated to such an entity.

The qualities of self and feeling are ever blended, just as love and light are blended constantly throughout your incarnation, playing and dancing back and forth so that you have an ever new opportunity to explore the present moment as if it were a brand new thing, and, indeed, every moment is a brand new thing.

The reason that entities respond so clearly, and for the most part, so positively to that which is perceived as euphonious music as opposed to speaking is that the energy of speaking has a good deal of limitation depending upon the habits of speaking of the entity who is using words. An entity such as this instrument who spends a good deal of time singing creates a certain musicality even when it is not singing, which enables entities listening to singers such as this instrument to carry away the gift of feeling as well as the words themselves. And perhaps you have noticed how differently you have responded to precisely the same words offered by different people in different kinds of voices with, you suspect, different motives and agendas behind the words.

The universe moves along orbits described by energies that this instrument recognizes only as color and tone. However, those colors and tones are shadows within third density indicating the substantial existence in metaphysical or non-local systems or structures of entities and essences of great power and beauty. So if this instrument says, "Oh taste and see how gracious the Lord is," there is one reaction based on the words. If this entity sings—

(Carla sings) "Oh taste and see how gracious the Lord is!"

—there is another reaction based primarily not on the words but on the coloration of the wind instrument of this instrument's voice.

There is a tremendous relief in escaping into the color and tone of music, storytelling or the more stringent disciplines of non-spoken art, where only color, shape and texture can be used to catch those shadows of substantial truth that are unseen within your density. This is some of what we can say about the nature of language and communication.

At this point we feel that perhaps it might be useful to open the discussion to further questioning. Is there a question at this time? We are those of Q'uo.

B: When you are speaking about song, how does the song communicate directly to the feelings? I'm not understanding the connection there. I can understand the words talking to the intellect, being processed into concepts, coming through the auditory canals, but what's different about music?

We are those of Q'uo, and we believe we understand your query, my brother. We were speaking earlier of the cookie-cutter approach to concepts that words use. They take a roundness that is the gift of consciousness. They take that concept that is a metaphysical, living unity. They take that marble rolling pin of the intellect to it and press it flat into conformable, piecrust-sized dough, and they cut words out of it. And so you have created many a language in your sojourn upon this planet.

Yet, underlying this cookie-cutter approach are some guiding principles having to do with sound. This instrument was speaking in a former conversation with this group concerning the value of certain sounds such as the sounds of the letters themselves in the Hebrew and Sanskrit alphabets, where the simple repetition of certain sounds uses the shadow power of those particular sounds to unlock the substantial entity that those shadows of sound represent so that they may come into contact on an unconscious level with those aspects of your archetypical mind or your deep unconscious or your frontal lobes, to give a habitation and a name to what we are talking about.

So as you hear certain words, the energy body reacts at an unconscious or pre-conscious level. There is no effort involved. When you hear the sweet sound of the human voice, or a well played instrument of any kind, whether it be a wind instrument or a percussion instrument like a piano or an instrument like the violin that creates music from vibration, you are creating sounds that in themselves are sacred and that have the ability to awaken, at the preconscious or subconscious level, streams of emotion.

Further, the ability of those gifted musically to create not only a tone but a melody is a gift of unseen clarity. Again we are speaking of things that are, to the intellectual mind, simply shadows. Yet those shadows are the shadows of enormous, enormously powerful energies. So when you are able to experience not simply tone but melody, then your emotions are literally being played upon as if they were the instrument that music plays. When you add words, especially heartfelt words, to the stream of melody you have created a powerful instrument for waking an entire orchestration of thoughts and feelings created in a coherent pattern that is evanescent but yet, while you are hearing and experiencing this stream of sound, you are able to perceive entire universes that otherwise would be lost to you.

May we answer you further, my brother?

B: Yes. The song, as I understand it, is kind of like a non-local representation that talks to the unconscious, whereas the words are more localized, conceptual representations like indices in a book. When they combine together, song and words, words being sung, it basically is talking to both halves [of the brain] at the same time, is that correct?

We are those of Q'uo, and, my brother, you are perceptive. This is correct.

B: Then would you equate the music to love and the words to light? In the relationship you indicated earlier we're love moving toward the realm of light.

We are those of Q'uo, and, my brother, we cannot entirely agree with you on this point. From the standpoint of you as a collector of information, both words and music to some extent have elements of both the love and the light vibration. However, we would say that it is certainly accurate that there is more beingness or non-local-ness in the musical portion of a song with words than there is in the words.

There is another element that may be seen here that is very important in understanding your and every entity's value to the Creator and that is that as you hear the words and the music, by the entering of your heart into the words and the music you bring to it a life that it has not previously had and color it in a way that shall never come again.

When you react and respond and especially if you are able to hum or sing along with a song you entirely agree with and with whose words you also agree, then you have created an instrument of transformation that is local to yourself and yet which contains all of the richness of all those essences of great power that have been called forth into life by you hearing and feeling and experiencing.

May we answer you further, my brother?

B: I think I understand you now. I have another question. Words can cause a great deal of pain. But pain tends to be more of the thing you communicate via the song. Why is this?

We are those of Q'uo, my brother, and we believe that we grasp your query. The ability of words to heal and harm has been something that this instrument has also thought upon a good deal lately. You must understand that you are not simple beings. You do not come to the present moment without carrying burdens.

Would that you could come to the present moment completely unburdened! There are whole disciplines of the personality that are devoted to clearing one of one's burdens so that one actually approaches a few precious, present moments untrammeled by anything but pure being. However, for most entities in the midst of the passion play upon planet Earth …

(Side one of tape ends.)

(Carla channeling)

… there is a burden. It is a burden that has been stacking up for as long as you have been carrying pain. For most entities that begins to occur fairly early within incarnation. Imprinting pains occur at a fairly early age, usually. And then after the original imprint of that pain or that type of pain, there forms a pattern not only of experiences of that kind of pain but experiences of how you have coped with that

kind of pain. It can get to be a very rococo[76] structure with great embellishments, gargoyles[77], flying buttresses[78], and the occasional crenellation[79].

When an entity speaks a trigger word to you, it may simply hit the edge of a crenellation. And you can certainly stand at that crenellation and loose an arrow that destroys the entity that spoke that word. But that word has hit its mark and the entire structure of that pain is brought forward. You perhaps did not know that you had this buried treasure of unexplored catalyst. That one word that triggers all of those painful feelings makes it entirely clear that that gift has yet to be unwrapped, that work is yet to be done.

For the goal is not to collect pain but to receive it, explore it, balance it, redeem it, and increase the store of your compassion.

For everyone else is also experiencing this kind of pain, in one way or another, according to their personality shells and their way of processing material. You are never alone when you are suffering. You are never alone when you are in absolute joy. When you are feeling, you are feeling a non-personal but entirely valid feeling.

We have spoken through this instrument before concerning the rivers of emotion that you are purifying as you dip into them. You hit a surface emotion and it is muddy and unclear. But through time, through the loving perception of your own pain and through your working with that pain, you begin eventually to have sympathy for yourself. There is a sympathetic vibration that is set up so that when you encounter these fell and swift pains in your daily existence, you do not simply react to defend or to seek revenge for painful feelings, but, rather, you ask for clarity. You ask to sit in the fiery furnace of that suffering and ask for clarity. "What is

---

[76] rococo: a style of art, especially architecture and decorative art, that originated in France in the early 18th century and is marked by elaborate ornamentation, as with a profusion of scrolls, foliage, and animal forms or a very ornate style of speech or writing.

[77] gargoyle: a roof spout in the form of a grotesque or fantastic creature projecting from a gutter to carry rainwater clear of the wall or any grotesque ornamental figure or projection.

[78] flying buttress: an arched masonry support serving to bear thrust, as from a roof or vault, away from a main structure to an outer pier or buttress.

[79] crenellation: a rampart built around the top of a castle with regular gaps for firing arrows or guns.

this about? Where did this come from? And how can I use this gift to grow?"

May we answer you further, my brother?

G: I have a question, Q'uo. In my process of seeking there have been obstacles. There's been a recurrence of a variety of problems, imbalances and distortions that I feel have their roots together in one single source. In working with this problem, whatever it, is unidentified within me, it feels as if, over the past few years now, that it is still a boulder that sits within me. With all of my efforts and strength I have removed but teaspoons of it. I cannot seem to understand this boulder, to remove it, to drop it, and let it go. And I was wondering if there are any key concepts that might help me in—whatever the analogy—removing the boulder, freeing myself from my imprisoning mind, or walking permanently out of this desert experience with which I am all too familiar?

We are those of Q'uo, and are aware of your query, my brother. We examine this question for those things which we may say without interfering with your process and we find a fair supply of words with which we shall shower you at this time, my brother, with utmost affection in our hopes that they may be of help.

Firstly, as we have said before in this session, you are not alone. It is helpful to focus in on the emotion that you have uncovered and to sit with it as a student would sit with a teacher, knowing that you are not the only student in this classroom. You do not know what entities are sitting with you, looking at the same boulder. But we assure you that you have great and good company, the company of fine, seeking people that are equally as stumped as you and as equally isolated in their inner process.

To escape from the isolation of this process, it is helpful simply to sense into the non-isolated portion of your experience. You are experiencing a real emotion. It is to some extent muddied. That does not mean that it is not legitimate or worth looking at. Whatever distortions you are experiencing, they are entirely worth looking at. But they cannot be so threatening if you know that you are not alone, if you know that you are in a place as safe as any other, in terms of energy work, when you are experiencing powerful and frustrating emotions. The emotions themselves, if you simply let yourself get wrapped up in them and let them sweep you away from yourself,

may not be helpful because they may be too strong for your system.

It is helpful in terms of gaining a perspective and at the same time allowing intimacy with these feelings to come at them from a place of sacred commonality, knowing that you and all other beings that dwell upon this sphere that you call Earth are going to be in the situation of gazing at that boulder. And when you are there, you have not only the company of fellow sufferers, but the company of the guidance systems of your self and all fellow sufferers that are involved in dipping into this stream of this particular river of emotion that runs through the archetypal mind.

Secondly, we mentioned guidance earlier and we mention it on its own hook now, because help is available. In order to get to that place within yourself where you can actually ask, it is necessary only to be real and authentic within yourself. Whatever rationales, intellectual thought, or logic that you are using to try and analyze such a situation, when you are asking for guidance is not the time to use those tools.

Asking for guidance is a matter, as you were saying earlier, my brother, of becoming humble and realizing that you need to ask for help. And when you ask for that help, it almost doesn't matter what entities say to you. Asking for that help has opened the springs of your own compassion so that you yourself have become a friend to yourself where you were not before because you were too busy defending what you thought you already knew.

Thirdly, and this may not seem to be very much of a gift from us to you, we would offer you the concept of a boulder inside a very larger processor that does nothing but crush boulders. We do not know what in your life will have the power to act as the machinery that breaks up paint in a paint can. In a very, very large way such a shaking and rattling contraption breaks down ore and refines the basic ore by taking the dirt out and leaving the jewels, the gold, the precious metals.

That which has the tendency to create that shaking-up, breaking-up action is love.

You are at this time, as this instrument heard earlier, enjoying a deepening relationship, such as you have hoped for for a long time, with a mate, at least a potential mate. It is no wonder that you have reencountered the boulder, for that boulder is, to a part of yourself, an object of great safety. It blocks you from moving through a door on the other side of which is the unknown, and more than that, on the other side of which you are completely undefended.

Remember that your experiences within your birth family of what love is have not been those experiences which were very encouraging in terms of the safety of one being in the arms, the heart, and the words of another. That safety, that intimacy, those great possibilities do exist but not in your personal memory.

You shall need to create that safe place where you may be true, vulnerable and loving. This is new territory. We wish you every good fortune but must say to you, my brother, and to all who seek to press through pain to the land beyond, that it takes courage, persistence and raw faith.

May you fly and soar through the door that is now blocked. And may every effort that you make to get to the point where you are ready to fly be made in the faith that what you desire is entirely and absolutely possible.

We find that this instrument's energy begins to wane and at this time we would suggest an ending to this circle of seeking. We leave each of you marveling at your beauty and your courage. We thank you for your company and your questions. It has been a true blessing to us to be with you.

We leave you, as we found you, in the infinite love and light of the one Creator Whose name is unconditional love. We are known to you as the principle of Q'uo. From our hearts we are with you and we will be with you whenever you would request that our energy be a part of your meditation. Adonai. Adonai. ❧

L/L RESEARCH

L/L Research is a subsidiary of
Rock Creek Research &
Development Laboratories, Inc.

P.O. Box 5195
Louisville, KY 40255-0195

www.llresearch.org

Rock Creek is a non-profit
corporation dedicated to
discovering and sharing
information which may aid in
the spiritual evolution of
humankind.

SPECIAL MEDITATION
DECEMBER 12, 2005

(J attended this session by telephone. Jim placed J's questions on the tape for her, reading from the text that J had prepared beforehand.)

J: Q'uo, I thank you from the depth of my being for the gift of your shared thoughts, which have helped me open my heart, free my mind, and find my truth. I most humbly thank you. I seek whatever thoughts, observations, comments, words of encouragement, etc., which from your view would be most helpful to me at this point in my journey, that journey being on the path of service to others, service to the one infinite Creator. Under this umbrella I'm particularly interested in the following. However, I defer to you to address whatever you choose.

The first question. Have I missed the point of service to others? My focus is service to all or service to the whole, which includes self. I am uncomfortable with the idea of sacrificing myself for another self but I am willing to sacrifice myself for the whole. Is this keeping me from progressing on the path of service to others? I believe that I have made the grade, that I've achieved 51% or higher polarity. Can you confirm? Please comment in any way you feel might be helpful.

(Carla channeling)

We are those known to you as the principle of Q'uo. Greetings in the love and in the light of the one infinite Creator. We are in the Creator's service as a source of information for those requesting it and we greatly appreciate the privilege and the pleasure of your forming a circle of seeking at this time to ask us to share our thoughts.

We would request, as always, that as you hear our opinions you remember that we are not authorities but fellow travelers who may have had a bit more experience than you in some ways and therefore may have some suggestions that might be helpful. If our thoughts seem helpful to you, then please do use them. If they do not, please leave them aside without a second thought. If you can do this we would greatly appreciate it, for this will enable us to speak freely without being concerned that we will infringe upon your free will.

Firstly, my sister, we can confirm that you have achieved a harvestable grade. The achievement is not permanent in that the energy which you express at the moment of your transition through the gate into larger life is that momentary tuning or expression of your self that will be considered and it cannot be known ahead of time what that tuning shall be, as it is not something that one earns at a certain point and then has no more concern.

Indeed, when one is attempting to polarize in terms of service to others, it is easy for the tuning to vary somewhat and so we would simply encourage all entities still within the illusion of third density to look to the day and the hour and the moment. For it is in this moment that your true self and your true presence lie.

That which you have achieved is excellent and we do not warn you in the sense of feeling that there is some great danger that you may fall below harvestable grade. We simply wish to make the point that the lifetime continues on, moment by moment, until that point at which the pattern is finished at last. And it is that tuning, at the point where the pattern is finished, which shall be the tuning with which you enter the process of graduation.

We find that we have difficulty in gauging the entire mind of this instrument at this time for the simple reason, my sister, that her lessons and yours march hand in hand at this time. She also is dealing with how much service to others is about service to the whole and how much it is about seemingly sacrificial offerings made to one other person. We shall move forward with our response but we do wish you to know that there are conditions having to do with this instrument's progress and process which make it more difficult for us to be entirely candid because of the fact that not only you but she are dealing actively with these questions. When a question of this kind is active in the process, then we must look at the spiritual principles involved and this is what we will do in this case.

The principle of service to others is to love the neighbor as the self, as this instrument would put it from her Christian background. To pull back and look at it from a wider point of view, service to others is always service to the Creator and in that sense we believe that both you and she have a firm grasp upon the highest and the best service to others that is possible within your third density.

Indeed, we would say unequivocally that service to the whole is that ideal which, in its very nature, is greater than service to any one entity. However, the unfathomable challenge of incarnated life is that often it is difficult to see how service to one person becomes a symbol or a story that, in its telling, inspires the whole, or creates an awareness in some way for the whole of the human tribe.

Therefore, we must ask both of you to move into a path where you ask for guidance daily and even hourly, attempting to keep the lines of communication to your guidance open. For there are opportunities hidden in this question for realization and a greater understanding of service to others. What is it to be an individual? What is it to be part of the whole? These are very legitimate questions and we leave them with you to ask yourself and to ask your guidance.

The one known as Carla, who acts as instrument at this time, said recently to the one known as Jim that perhaps in order to be of service to another entity, she could make a large change in her personal situation, the one known as Jim responding by saying that this was an overreaction and tended to bring out her martyr tendencies. It is easy to move into a mental zone where the desire to be of service is so marked that an entity will move into the position of a martyr, or as this instrument would call it, a doormat.

We simply suggest a continuing relationship with your guidance that is very close and that is renewed at least each day. Something trembles close to triggering a step within awareness that is a powerful one for both of you. That step will come when it comes. Yet your work at this time on this subject is extremely helpful. The fact that you are asking the question and continuing to ask the question so that it stays in the forefront of your mind is a good idea and we would encourage your attention and your devotion as you have showed in the past.

Is there another query at this time?

J: I feel a deep and abiding love for the animal kingdom, especially the felines. And I wonder if you can share anything about the meaning or significance of that and particularly about the beautiful and most instructed relationship I had with my beloved cat, MaxCat?

We are those of Q'uo, and are aware of your query, my sister. The relationship of what is called within your culture "owners" and "pets," has several layers, all of which are very helpful to you as an entity as well as to the pet involved.

The first layer is simply that of a person whose life is such that there are many times when the unjudging, unguarded affection of a living being is a very healing and comforting thing. It is as healing for the pet as it is for the so-called owner. This instrument is also a lover and a keeper of cats and we find from gazing within her mind that it is her opinion that the cat owns her rather than the other way around.

Certainly, it is a partnership of a very special kind and it begins with the simple creature comfort of two second-density animals that have agreed to make each other part of their family. There is a tremendous comfort in coming into the presence of one for whom you feel affection and one who feels affection for you. It is the gift of several species, cats among them, which are normally treated as pets among your culture, that there is the gift of affection which is part of the natural mentality and emotional makeup of that second-density animal that is the cat. Such animals are extremely well suited to creating a healing and comforting partnership with their humans.

The second level of helpfulness between pets and their owners has to do with the energetic balances and rebalances of your system as an evolving human being and the sensitivity and accuracy of the pet in its ability to pick up and to deal with the ongoing energy situation as it fluctuates within your process. The pet is able to act as a kind of guard, becoming alert when there are difficult vibrations around an entity, becoming aware that there is physical or mental or emotional illness, and wishing to move into that energy and help balance that energy; so that there is a natural tendency of the pet to create an atmosphere or to help to create an atmosphere of healing for the human involved.

Certainly this instrument has told many tales in her time of her cats and the ways that they have been aware of her emotional situation and sometimes her physical illnesses and have been faithful and devoted to an amazing degree in responding to the needs that are felt.

This energy balancing factor is extremely helpful when one is going through the rapid changes that are occurring as a matter of global nature at this time among your people. The waves of energy that are moving through the planet at this time are many and intense, as befits that time in which you are now living, where fourth density has completely interpenetrated third density and there is a strong energy of unconditional love that is flowing through the inner planes and effecting sharp shadows when energies within the third-density existence are experienced that are not in harmony with fourth-density values.

Entities living in third density cannot help but be buffeted by the more or less developed light within third-density people that they meet, whether on errands, on the road, or wherever you might go. Consequently, that stability that the second-density creature offers with its affection and its awareness of

what you are going through energetically is tremendously helpful.

The third level of aid that your pets are to you or can be to you is that they can function as guides and totems[80], if you will, in the shamanic or Native American sense of those words. In that sense, they become messengers and may show up in your visions or your dreams.

We encourage you, therefore, to open your senses when you have the opportunity to share time with a pet and to have that awareness that the possibilities do not begin and end in simple affection and shared love but they penetrate that level of the subconscious where thoughts become things and where an object that is seemingly physical like a cat can become a spiritually wise and very aware messenger that brings to you information from deep within your own subconscious process, thereby acting as an archetypal force within your process.

Is there another query at this time?

J: I found love by seeking the truth and it's been my perception that truth and love are different experiences of the same energy—like two sides of an energy coin. Is this at all accurate?

We are those of Q'uo, and are aware of your query, my sister. We would say that this concept is quite accurate, my sister, and would add to it the suggestion that there are other words as well that fit within this basic unity of meaning that goes beyond words. This instrument was speaking yesterday about the relative uselessness of a word such as love. It has been robbed of its meaning by being overused and used for trivial emotions and those ephemeral feelings that run along the surface of life so that one is perfectly able to say that she loves a certain type of food or a certain type of activity using the same verb that you use to say that you love the Creator or that you love service to others or that you love a friend or a mate that has shared history with you throughout your lifetime.

In such a trivialized landscape as that which your language offers, it is difficult to get a grip on words like love and truth. We would add several other words to this short list of concepts that represent

[80] totem: an animal, plant or natural object serving among certain tribal or traditional peoples as the emblem of a clan or family and sometimes revered as its founder, ancestor or guardian or a representation of such an object.

powerful essences that have a life of their own within fourth density and higher densities in general. Those words are beauty, wisdom and peace. We might add the word faith to that as well with the understanding that faith is not belief nor is there any content to faith.

What these words have in common is that they represent a pure vibration. The vibration of love, in the sense of unconditional love or Logos, is a particular vibration that has created all that there is. Consequently, we cannot say that love and truth are absolutely equal. For in the sense of the Logos, that is a way of describing the Creator Itself.

However, if one steps down from considering love as the Creator to considering expressions of love that are pure, then we find true evenness of equivalency of meaning. Then, such words as truth, love, beauty and faith become separate, shall we say, or recognizably different but equal in the purity of their vibration.

When you come upon a moment within your process in which you sense the presence of absolute love or absolute beauty, absolute truth, or absolute faith, you know that you have found the guiding star by which you can set your rudder and steer the ship of the progress of your process.

We pulled in those other words so that you might see how different personalities and people at different points in their process will find one star to be more helpful than another, truth at one point, beauty at another, and so forth. There is a tremendous amount behind this question and we would appreciate your following up with questions if you wish to when we have exhausted those queries that the one known as Jim has on his piece of paper.

We would at this time ask if there is another query.

J: A few years ago, I began seeing beautiful colors in my mind's eye while having what I would call a spiritual experience and connection, as in meditation or in spiritual healing work. I would appreciate anything that you would care to share about this phenomenon. Is it chakra related? Is it a visual greeting of some sort? The colors feel so beautiful that I'm often moved to tears.

We are those of Q'uo, and are aware of your query, my sister. The experience of seeing certain colors is an experience which moves an entity beyond the limitations of language. It is not that the colors

within themselves have a reality as colors, alth[ough] certainly the study of colors is very interesting each entity has relationships with various colo[rs] ... terms of the way they make you feel.

However, we believe that it is quite possible that what you are experiencing is the overshadowing of the comradeship, shall we say, of essences which are drawn to you because of your healing work and which wish to accompany you as you set out to create a healing atmosphere for others.

The color itself is, say, the name or the nickname or the shadow of this powerful entity that the color represents. So you are being accompanied, greeted and embraced by those unseen energies and essences that appreciate you and are drawn to the work that you do in service. It is their service to lend their energy to entities such as you who stand within third density in incarnation and are therefore able directly to offer help. For they would, in and of themselves, be unable to, and not even have the right to, offer help.

Therefore, it may seem to you that you are very blessed in receiving these energies. And, indeed, this is so. But we would say to you also that you are a tremendous blessing to these entities represented by these colors. We feel that the relationship is entirely helpful in strengthening and encourage you to embrace these sensations and to use them with confidence and thankfulness in your work.

Is there another query at this time?

J: I would appreciate hearing your thoughts, observations, comments, etc, about what I perceive to be my unmet and deep desire for human community. I have had the feeling all my life of not belonging anywhere. I continually sought for that feeling of being part of a community and a real home. Is this because I am a wanderer?

We are those of Q'uo, and are aware of your query, my sister. My sister, in part it certainly is an experience you have had because you are a wanderer and we say this because it is peculiar to wanderers that they bring forward from their deep memory a memory of times within clans or families or tribes which are not related necessarily by what you would call blood but are related because of common beliefs, concerns and desires to be of service.

In higher densities and especially within the fifth density and the sixth density, the refinement of the personality shell and its discipline has moved through so many cycles of refinement that it is no longer the tremendous challenge that it is within third density to pull away from the details and the minutiae of a relationship with another entity to see into the deeper threads of commonality in love, in devotion, and in service to others that truly bring two people together.

Within third density there are heavy cultural overlays which make it difficult for any two entities to unite as one. As soon as there begins to be the building up of trust, there is nearly always an energy which is offered by the shadow side of self which encourages individuals to increase their individuality and to pull back from true intimacy. There is the feeling of the need to defend and protect the self from the pain that it is possible for another entity to inflict.

To move beyond these cultural and instinctual guards into a state of true vulnerability to another person is very difficult. Entities attempt it in many ways. There are the natural bonds of friendship. There are specialized communities of all kinds throughout the entire spectrum of religiosity and spirituality where roots indeed have formed which are based upon ideas and ideals that are supposedly larger than the self so that the community is brought together by a need to worship or to serve.

For any person incarnate upon Earth, there is the natural instinct for community. Consequently, it is not entirely because you are a wanderer that you crave community. It is, however, because you are a wanderer that you have high hopes and expectations for community within third density. We can only say to you, my sister, that such hopes are not in vain. It is a matter of being willing to be very patient and to wait for those entities which seem to you to be trustworthy and of the proper vibration for you to find commonality with them.

When you do find such people, humbly and gently keep them in your heart and await those opportunities to come closer, to share ideas and hopes and to create together what service you can from the dynamics of your relationship.

The power of groups as opposed to individuals is that there is a tremendous creative potential in the dynamics between people and how, together, they are much more than any of them is apart.

So the challenge, my sister, is to keep hope, faith and affection constant while being aware that there are energies endemic to your culture that will constantly offer challenges whenever you attempt to become closer to another human being.

Those energies will simply use the dynamic of your relationship to show you, not the commonality between you, but the dynamic between you which shows to both of you your shadow side, so that in seeing another for whom you feel affection, you may also see shadow characteristics such as selfishness, self-indulgence, greediness or other unfortunate aspects of the self which have not perhaps been entirely balanced within your own energy system at this time.

Since they have not been balanced, they represent that which can be a stumbling block that will discourage you from pursuing relationship. We do not ask you to ignore such stumbling blocks but to work with them and to see them not as that which stops you from community but that which enables you to be able to become more able to offer yourself in community. That energy with which you work to heal the shadow self, as you perceive it within yourself, becomes then that compassion which enables you to love that same energy as you see it in another, not condemning it in any way but holding it in honest affection and trust and waiting for that development which will enable you to move forward in commonality.

Is there a further question at this time?

J: I find myself uncomfortable praying for a specific outcome. Even if someone has asked me to pray that their cancer be healed or something of that nature. I'm more comfortable praying for divine order or divine will, like, "Thy will be done," or that the individual see the truth about who they are in terms of the love and light they are. My mind gets all muddled trying to sort it out. I guess it's that I don't trust that anything that I could pray for could be better than praying for divine order or divine will. I believe that we have a lot of power in our prayers and I get lost with how to apply that.

We are those of Q'uo, and we are aware of your query, my sister. It is an interesting point which you bring …

(Side one of tape ends.)

(Carla channeling)

We are those of Q'uo, and are again with this instrument. We quite agree with the one known as J that it is a far more pure and undistorted request of spirit to ask, "Thy will be done," or, "May divine order prevail," than to ask, "May a certain condition be healed."

So let us look at that a bit to see why that would be a more satisfactory prayer. As the one known as J states, prayer is a very powerful tool. Spirit is ever ready to hear prayer and it will respond to prayer instantly, as best it can. If the prayers are enough distorted, however, there become more and more limits upon what spirit can do in response to this specific prayer.

In actuality, working backwards from a symptom or an illness, it is impossible to know, from the standpoint of being in third density and incarnate, what the precise structure of that illness or situation might be. It cannot be seen except by insight, intuition or guidance whether the illness is actually an asset or a negative in the book of debits and credits, [speaking] in a metaphysical sense. Very often there are structures placed in peoples' lives which have the simple logic of "IF the situation of my life departs sufficiently from these parameters, [THEN] I will set in place an illness that is limiting in nature in a certain way that will encourage me to rethink and reimagine my life and my process so that I am more actually in balance with myself."

To use this instrument as an example, this instrument has a variable degree of wellness from year to year and from decade to decade but has been in fragile health her entire incarnation. And as she is already aware, which is why we may use her as an example, she has set in place the structure of illness that limits but does not end the incarnation, so that if she is drawn too heavily into physical activity, she will be brought up short and forced to move inward in order to persist in her inner work.

This instrument is extremely fond of the outer work with its details and its easiness. It is easy for this instrument to weed the garden, to cook the meal, to do the outer service that stares one in the face. It is less easy for this instrument to spend the time needed to do inner work, especially work strictly within silence and within what this instrument would call worship or prayer. There are so many wonderful things to do and so little time to do them

that it is this instrument's tendency to stay very busy and not to take thought. Structures within this instrument's life, therefore, were set up in order to encourage her to take thought.

When these illnesses occur to this instrument, she is not pleased. Nevertheless, because she is unable to do the things that she normally does to distract herself, she involuntary and quite naturally moves towards doing the spiritual work which she and her higher self before incarnation felt was very important as a part of the structure of her process within incarnation.

Therefore, when someone asks you if you will pray to heal a cancer, they may well be asking you to pray to remove a structure that the higher self of that entity put in place before incarnation for the very purpose of advancing awareness within that entity and decreasing distortion.

Consequently, it is very wise and very loving of the one known as J to be aware that divine order is not necessarily that which looks like order to the physical eye.

May we answer you further, my sister?

J: I recently started using a process known as voice dialogue, a technique originated by Hal Stone. It appears to me that the better I am at embracing my various inner selves, the better I am at embracing all of humanity. And I find this a very valuable technique. I'm wondering if you can confirm my perception or add any comments.

We are those of Q'uo, and are aware of your query, my sister. We can indeed confirm that this is extremely helpful technique for you to use at this time. And certainly in general it is a helpful technique for anyone whose process has brought them to a degree of sensitivity at which they are actually able to be aware of this. It is helpful in general to any as a resource for advancing their spiritual evolution as they wish.

The elements of your own personality may seem to be a seamless whole or a unity. To the psychologist's or philosopher's eye, it may seem that each person is, as this instrument would call it, a monad, a complete, atomic being, whole within himself. And to a certain extent this is so.

However, the personality shell of entities is created almost the way that you would create the packing of a suitcase to take on a trip. You have packed for this incarnation the elements of personality that you feel would be helpful or that you felt at the time, before incarnation at which you packed the suitcase, would be helpful.

You packed some items that are for your upkeep and your health. You packed some items that would enable you to serve and share your gifts better. And you packed some few seemingly less attractive items in your personality, realizing that you would need a certain amount of these shadow energies as a point of departure and a point of reentry so that you could go beyond your comfort zone in various ways, looking for ways to balance dynamics within you.

Some entities have dynamics which have to do with truth and justice, as opposed to love. Some entities have issues about the dynamic between wisdom and love. Some entities have dynamics with even more complicated structures such as truth, power and love.

However, all of these characteristics that you packed are what this instrument would call integrated rather than unitary. They have formed a personality shell for you but they are actually made up of components, each of which is shared by all beings whatsoever who are moving through spiritual evolution. It is not that you are just like everyone else, for you are not. You are quite unique. Rather it is that your component parts are each shared throughout the system of the human tribe.

Therefore, as you become aware of the various aspects of your personality shell, you are able to see how they have amalgamated in structures that surround each of your energy centers so that your personal or orange-ray energy center, for instance, has a certain individuality that is unique to it and yet which works in harmony with and in concert with those energies which surround other chakras and other portions of your energy system in which various chakras and their dynamics are considered.

May we answer you further in this query, my sister?

J: Yes, actually. I'd like to pursue several queries before with the words of truth and wisdom and beauty. You mentioned the phrase of the vibration of purity, I think is what you said, and I am more and more becoming aware of the importance of purity in all things. I guess I'm wondering if there is a difference of importance in pursuing purity at the spiritual level, the emotional, and physical and mental. Most recently I've been really concerned about the purity of my food and it seems that purity has a special vibration or resonance for me right now.

The question would be: is purity more important in some areas of life than others?

We are those of Q'uo, and are aware of your query, my sister. The concept of purity in and of itself is extremely helpful and we would agree with you that there are many different ways to express this purity. The underlying purity, of course, is that purity of self where the self has met the self, knows the self, and stands naked in its truth as it knows it at that moment.

In terms of estimating the value of purity at different levels of the personality or the life, we would say that the teaching of the one known as Jesus is helpful in this regard. This entity said that that which comes out of the mouth is that which is of interest in terms of purity rather than that which enters in the mouth.[81] The one known as Jesus was basically saying that those outer considerations, as important as they may be, pale before the value of the awareness of your own thoughts.

When you are able to express a purity and single-mindedness in that which comes out of your mouth or comes out of your thoughts, that is perhaps the highest degree of purity in terms of value to your process that we could offer. It is, however, to be noted that no matter where you look to create a higher degree of purity, the attempt to create that purity has a powerful and positive effect on the process of evolution.

For instance, you were talking concerning your desire to purify your diet. As you focus on the purification of what goes into your physical vehicle, you are offering yourself your own affection, respect and honor. You are considering yourself as a sacred temple rather than a convenient physical vehicle that you have hung your consciousness on or in for the duration of the incarnation.

And therefore you have come into a far more balanced and correct relationship with yourself

---

[81] *Holy Bible*, St. Mark's Gospel 7:15-16: "There is nothing outside of a man, if it should enter into him, which can defile him; but what goes out of him, that defiles the man. Who has ears to hear, let him hear."

simply by attempting to consider what is best for you. It is extremely helpful to consider such things and certainly this instrument has spent a good deal of time in the last five years or so gradually attempting to acquaint herself more and more with how she can most effectively nurture and love herself. The slang phrase that she uses to express this is "the protection of the package."

And it seems, in a way, a very glib way to consider such things as how to exercise and how to eat and so forth. And yet you are a package of consciousness which has been all wrapped up at the factory at birth and sent forward into the world. So protecting that precious package of selfhood is protecting that which truly is sacred and that which came here for high and lovely reasons.

So we encourage you by all means to follow that inclination which has taken your mind recently wherever it may lead you and to realize certainly that what you are looking for always is not to be perfect but to be as pure as you can be. There is a natural limitation within humanity that eliminates the possibility of any self-perceived perfection. So, consequently, realize that what you are attempting to do is not to perfect yourself but to work at loving yourself, accepting yourself, and respecting yourself.

We find that this energy of this contact is waning and therefore we would ask if there is a final query at this time.

J: Yes, there is. I loved the cat that I mentioned earlier, Max. I believe throughout our relationship, the message I kept getting back from him was to love myself equally. And I very much want to give the four cats who now share my home the best experience I can. But I'm not sure what that is. It is my conscious intent to give them the experience of being cherished, enjoyed and loved but I'm wondering if there is a better way that I could serve them than that?

We are those of Q'uo, and we believe we understand your query, my sister. The sharing of love, when it is felt from an honest and open heart, is that which does not need to be planned or guided or angled in any way. We suggest that you simply let the love that you have for these precious beings radiate naturally from you to these entities, [knowing of] their ability to grasp emotions and unseen energy. That energy in and of itself will be the gift that is yours best to give.

Naturally, it is always helpful to attempt to come into individual relationship with each pet, for each pet may require a different amount of affection or a different way of expressing affection. Yet the underlying knowledge that they are loved and welcomed is that which they crave.

They are basically entities which look for the feeling of the nest or the tribe and you are their chief nester, the leader of their tribe. They therefore, no matter how they express it, have the desire simply to belong in your environment. When you share a word with them or simply mentally speak to them, acknowledging them and including them in your affection, that is the essence of the best service we feel that you could offer to such entities as these pets.

We thank you, my sister. It has been an unalloyed joy to speak with you this day and to share energy with you. The beauty of your being is great and it has been a real pleasure. We leave you, as we found you, in the love and in the light of the one infinite Creator. We are those of Q'uo. Adonai. Adonai. ☙

L/L RESEARCH

L/L Research is a subsidiary of
Rock Creek Research &
Development Laboratories, Inc.

P.O. Box 5195
Louisville, KY 40255-0195

www.llresearch.org

Rock Creek is a non-profit
corporation dedicated to
discovering and sharing
information which may aid in
the spiritual evolution of
humankind.

ABOUT THE CONTENTS OF THIS TRANSCRIPT: This telepathic channeling has been taken from transcriptions of the weekly study and meditation meetings of the Rock Creek Research & Development Laboratories and L/L Research. It is offered in the hope that it may be useful to you. As the Confederation entities always make a point of saying, please use your discrimination and judgment in assessing this material. If something rings true to you, fine. If something does not resonate, please leave it behind, for neither we nor those of the Confederation would wish to be a stumbling block for any.

SPECIAL MEDITATION
DECEMBER 18, 2005

Question chosen by PLW poll:[82] I read Q'uo's response in PlanetLightWorker magazine to the question about densities and vibrations. The Q'uo group spoke about seven densities in an octave. Others in the esoteric world speak of twelve dimensions. Can you explain the difference?

(Carla channeling)

We are those known to you as the principle of Q'uo. Greetings in the love and the light of the one infinite Creator. We come in the Creator's service to respond to the call of the circle of seeking this day. May we thank each of you for setting aside the time to create a circle of seeking and for calling for us to share information with you. It is our pleasure and our privilege so to do.

As always, we would ask of you that you are very careful in your discrimination. Set aside any thought of ours that does not immediately appeal to you. If you will take care to guard the gateway to your own thoughts then we shall feel free to share our opinions without being concerned that we might infringe upon your free will. It is crucial to us that we share information without such infringement, so we thank each of you for this consideration.

The query this day concerns the system of chakras that is used to structure the way that you think about your energy body. The question itself actually used the terms density and dimension. However, we

believe we grasp that the actual intent of the query is more in terms of the internal workings of the body system rather than the macrocosmic point of view in which densities of the creation are considered. We apologize if we misunderstand or mis-speak because of this misunderstanding. However, we believe that the point of interest of the query has to do with looking at the system of the physical vehicle and its connections with the metaphysical universe in the form of the energy body that interpenetrates your physical body, and so we shall answer according to our understanding of this question as somewhat revised from the original statement.

We would take note of the way the question was phrased in simply saying that there is no true difference in the way that density and dimension are used, so that whether you are talking about the third dimension or the third density it is, in general, understood by students of metaphysical work that one is speaking of a quantum or certain kind of energy. The more appropriate of the two words for working with the concept of the octave of densities in creation is the word density rather than dimension. However, these two words are used interchangeably for the most part, not only by this instrument but also by many others whose works this instrument has read.

The densities, macrocosmically speaking, are reproduced faithfully within the energy of each and every entity that is in incarnation on planet Earth at

---

[82] Planet Lightworker Magazine (www.planetlightworker.com).

this time. Each of you has an energy body which contains elements that are as true in pitch as the notes of a scale.

The difference between conventional octaves within your Western modalities of physical notation creates a choice of various scales among the twelve notes that make up the diatonic scale, so-called, within one octave of one your [musical] instruments. In music this twelve-tone scale is a creation whereby in twelve half-tones the tones are created from octave to octave so that the twelfth tone is the same as the first.

That diatonic scale sounds like this.

(Carla sings the twelve-tone scale of one octave.)

In contrast, the major scale chooses eight of those twelve notes and sounds like this.

(Carla sings the octave with an eight-tone scale.)

There is a minor scale and there are modal scales within the Western system of musical notation, all of which have eight notes. It is to be noted in this regard, still speaking of music, that in the Eastern or Oriental ways of producing tone, there is no precise way of grading notes. Not only are quarter-tones appreciated and differentiated but also those who are gifted musically can produce by their voice or upon an instrument that is unfretted[83] an infinite number of gradations which have values less than a quarter-tone.

This is why Eastern music is fundamentally different in its effect upon the listener than Western music. Western music lives in modular boxes of differentiation that have neat and regular borders, whereas the Oriental approach offers an infinite landscape in which to create tone.

If one gazes into the thinking and the culture of the West and the East, we would suggest that many inferences could be drawn by this difference. The tendency of the Western or Occidental orientation of mind is to choose the major scale or one of the eight-tone scales to listen to in music. It is not by chance that this choice is natural to the Occidental culture.

The reason for the use of an eight-chakra system, which is the seven chakras and the octave chakra, or the eighth, being the same as the first, only an octave higher, is that the Occidental culture is like a younger version of the older Oriental twelve-tone system. There are fewer gradations, fewer differentiations, and a clearer, simpler, plainer structure for looking at the self and structuring ways to interact with one's own energy system.

On the other hand, the twelve-chakra system is indicative of the further articulation of energies and the use of energy which is more typical of Asian, Eastern or Oriental thought.

The eight-chakra system has been discussed previously, and so we will very briefly review that system. The red-ray chakra is concerned mostly with survival and sexuality. The orange-ray chakra, located in the lower belly, is associated with issues of personal relationship. The yellow-ray chakra, or the solar plexus energy center, is associated with the energies of interacting with groups. The green-ray or heart chakra is associated with opening the heart and discovering one's own sacred nature. The throat chakra or blue-ray energy center is connected with communication. The indigo-ray center at the brow is associated with the disciplines of the personality and work in consciousness, and the violet-ray chakra, which is the crown chakra, is associated with that readout of momentary reality that is expressing at any given moment and is a system readout for the entire energy body that is what we would call the Occidental or Western chakra structure.

The subtleties of the twelve-chakra system can be very helpful to students of metaphysics. It begins the same way as does the Western system, the first chakra being connected with issues of sexuality and survival.

The second chakra, however, is divided in the Eastern system into two energy centers, one of which deals strictly with the self relating to the self. The second of these so-called orange-ray energy centers deals with the self in relation to other selves.

The solar plexus chakra remains unified in the Eastern system. However, after the solar plexus is left, and before one reaches what in the Western system is the heart chakra, there is a chakra which this instrument has often spoken of as the outer court of the heart.

---

[83] An unfretted instrument is one, like a violin or a sitar, which does not have frets, the tiny bars that go across the neck of an instrument and against which the fingers may be pressed to depress the strings to create a note or chord.

It is helpful to realize that moving into the heart is not an unalloyed and simple joy. It is a process that in its inception can create a great deal of difficulty for the student and the seeker. The difficulty of moving into the heart is that one must bring all of the self into the heart in order for that space to become truly sacred. Most seekers are quite astonished when they first enter their own hearts to discover that there is a real perceived problem with meeting one's shadow side.

After all the work of realizing that we are spiritual beings has been done, after clearing issues of personalities, sexuality, survival, personal relationships and all of the work that each entity is doing with groups, an entity that is seeking feels balanced and eager to enter that spacious holiness of the open heart.

However, the first thing that most entities find upon entering this space is that, just as in the story within your *New Testament* of the entity known as Jesus the Christ walking into the temple and seeing all the sellers of doves and so forth which entities could buy for sacrifice, entities walking into their own hearts find that there are sellers of doves there hawking busily away with their own agendas.

Little do most seekers know just how much of their personalities have been subverted and taken over by cultural expectations, parental teaching, and other sources of information which create assumptions and theories of how things are that simply do not meet the standards of purity that the particular space of the open heart requires in order for the seeker to penetrate from the outer courtyard to the inner sanctum.

This is related to that concept or idea of that which is called psychic greeting or psychic attack. The outer courtyard of the heart is that place where those portions of your personality shell that have been allowed to express themselves without your being aware of their presence make their presence known.

In many cases, entities will experience these energies as attacks. Perhaps they will feel that there is an entity that is attacking them from the outside, with some sort of overshadowing or attacking going on. Others have more sensitivity in discerning the source of such seeming attack and can pinpoint the energy as being within the system of the self. Whether these attacking energies are seen as part of the self or as coming from outside the self, fundamentally

speaking, we may say that in our opinion they are part of the self in that all things are one and you as individual selves are actually tuning into the space and time that is articulated by the parameters of one particular kind of energy.

Therefore, that which seems very personal and very threatening in many cases is in actuality not a threat but simply that portion of self which has gone unnoticed and, therefore, undeveloped.

There is great virtue in being willing to spend time in that outer courtyard of the open heart and to see that as a separate chakra or energy center; to spend time with those sellers of doves for sacrifice to discover why your culture felt that sacrifice was necessary, and why certain elements or essences within your personality have been chosen to be sacrificed.

We speak in extremely non-literal terms here, and are basically speaking of all of those energies of self that have escaped your attention up until now. Perhaps they did not so much escape your attention as that you felt that they were unworthy of attention. There are energies such as shame, guilt, jealousy and anger that are systematically and ritually downplayed and discouraged in terms of outer expression within your culture. Nevertheless, these too need to be taken up, brought up into the light of attention, and given respect. These, too, are ways that you feel. These, too, are worthy to be examined, inspected, analyzed and accompanied in whatever amount of time it takes for you to begin to be able to see their virtue and their value.

Many seemingly rough and negative aspects of character and personality are precisely those energies that create a true depth to understanding any genuine stability and steadiness of attention.

The quality of anger, for instance, once translated into unquenchable stubbornness in dedication to service, can become the powerhouse that it was intended to be, but this cannot occur until the virtue of anger is seen straight on, for its own self and its own essence.

The outer sanctum of the heart chakra is therefore a really powerful and very hurly-burly sort of energy. And to move from the outer courtyard to the inner sanctum of the heart becomes a much more clear and focused movement when that outer heart is given its own private place.

Another difference between what we would call the Western and Eastern chakra system is that immediately after the heart chakra and before the [throat or blue-ray] chakra of open communication there is an added energy center in the Eastern system. To explicate why this becomes very helpful, it is well to point out that the green-ray or heart chakra is the first energy center in which the possibility of a true energy exchange exists.

The lower chakras, having to do with the self, its survival issues, its sexuality, its relationships with self and other selves personally, and its relationship with groups, are all energies that may seem to be in need of balancing and clearing so that they are neither under-activated nor over-activated. But one cannot share energy between red ray and red ray, or orange ray, or yellow ray.

One may impress those energies upon another self, and because of the strength of your energy system, it is possible for energy to be impressed from you to another person, or for another person to impress you with their energy. It is, however, an overlay. It is time-bound in its effect and will wear off naturally. Many of your faith healers, so called, are those who are healing either from the orange or the yellow-ray chakra and they are impressing their understanding and their environment upon another. Those who are able to accept those impressions are able to experience quite a bit of release from various ailments for a certain time period. However, in every case where it is at the level below the heart, those energies will not persevere and will fade away naturally.

Only when one moves into the open heart can one begin to share energy; to exchange energy with another; to give love and to receive love. The great blessing of opening the heart and keeping it open is that, working from the open heart, all of the functions of the lower energy centers are recreated as sacred.

The chakras above the level of the heart are also energy centers from which energy exchanges can be made. The reason that this information is helpful in discussing the chakras that come after the heart chakra in the Eastern system is that there is this [additional] energy center [which] captures a structure that is missing completely from the Western system. There is a subtlety here that can only be appreciated by those who {have] done quite a bit of work in consciousness. It involves what this instrument has termed a 90-degree phase shift.

These are not words that have an objective referent for this instrument, but they represent a phrase she has heard many, many times in speaking with one known as Don Elkins, who was largely working from concepts created by the one known as George Williamson. The key concept of this added chakra is that in this turning after the heart chakra, the turn includes the whole of the unseen realms of the metaphysical of the time/space universe.

It is an energy center that is focused upon right relationship with the extended family that one has in the unseen realms. The greatest part of this family for seekers is that portion that is connected with guidance. Each entity has a guidance system and access to this guidance system is extremely helpful. If one focuses upon this particular energy center, one can do very precise work in opening oneself to the guidance that lies within.

The other differences between Eastern and Western chakra systems has to do with subtleties within work in consciousness in communication, which is the blue-ray energy center. There is a division in the Eastern system between the communication of self with self and the communication of self with other selves.

Further, there is a third division which deals with the communication of the self with the extended family of guides, presences, essences and entities that are connected with the self.

We say this realizing that the subtleties are such that we cannot say to you in general what those various essences are. Each individual creates a web of family throughout not only the incarnation which you are enjoying at this time, but also those entities with whom you have worked between incarnations, those entities that you have worked with in past incarnations, and the known planetary, non-local energies which have been drawn to you as a local entity within incarnation because of your work within incarnation and work you have done between incarnations.

Each of you within this circle and each to whom we speak in the extended family of internet and listener and reader-ship that is constantly growing contains a large, loving, extended family that awaits your focus and your request for help in order to become more within your life. It is important to remember, ...re, to request help from your guidance system.

The other added chakra in this Eastern system is very difficult for us to express to you. Once the readout of violet ray has been cleared, there is an additional chakra in the Eastern system which is dedicated to that point where the energy of self spirals from the now into the possibilities of the future. It is the point which this instrument would call the gateway to intelligent infinity.

We are aware that this information, by itself, is sterile and barren. We speak here of structures. It is you who draws the infinite love and light of the one Creator up into that structure, up into that energy body. It is you, by prayer, meditation and other forms of requesting guidance, insight and vision, who draw from the energies of the one infinite Creator teaching entities such as we and many, many other types of entities that do not speak at all but who stream from the point of entry at the gateway of intelligent infinity down into the energy system that determines what kind of life your energy system has.

Picture with us, if you will, the creature that you are. You receive this information along your spine, in the physical lines of a system of energy, reception and usage. It is fed infinitely, in an unending supply, by the love and the light of the one Creator.

That light is literally sent down into the heart of the Earth, your mother, who then pours it from the center of the Earth—or you might even say the womb of the Earth—up through the Earth into the soles of your feet, into your body system, so that it is constantly streaming into your energy system at the red-ray level and rising as it will up and out through the top of your head to the gateway to intelligent infinity.

Meanwhile, according to your desire and will and your requests, guidance and teaching is being pulled into your energy system from the top through the violet ray, then the indigo ray, and so forth, until it reaches the blue ray or the green ray, depending upon whether you are using those energies in communication or whether you are using them in healing, basically.

Realize that the point at which those two energies meet is the point at which your kundalini is now focused. If you wish to raise your kundalini you have two things to work on. Firstly, you have the clearing of the lower energies so that you get full creative energy up through the soles of your feet and into your energy body.

Secondly, you are attempting to focus your will, discipline your personality, and call forth the most helpful energies that you can to teach and guide you as you seek the truth.

We thank the ones known as S1 and S2 for this query and would at this time open this meeting to other questions. Is there another query at this time?

B: Earlier you mentioned the rise of kundalini. Could you clarify that?

We are those of Q'uo, my brother, and are aware of your query. That which is rising, or not, is the point of contact between the natural energies available to all within creation and the energy of the creative principle called to the self by individual work.

That point of contact begins, roughly speaking, within that point where the outer courtyard of the heart yields to the inner sanctum. The kundalini cannot be pulled lower than that as information of the creative principle cannot be understood by any energies lower than that of the heart.

However, the point of the kundalini rising, in terms of entities' desire to progress spiritually, is that as one begins to be able to pull the full energy of that open heart up into work in consciousness, each place to which it is raised opens up vistas of opportunity for various types of work in consciousness, not simply moving upwards as one aiming directly for the Creator, but, in terms of [working] at any level—for instance, in open communication—there is the opportunity to spread out one's discoveries and one's services by creating more and more layers of understanding or awareness of subtle energies involved in the sub-density, shall we say , of open communication. Once the kundalini has been pulled from the heart up into the throat, then more articulated work can be done in communication. And this is also true as the kundalini continues to be pulled upwards by seeking and the careful development and discipline of the personality.

May we answer you further, my brother?

B: What aspect of the self is doing the pulling?

We are those of Q'uo, and are aware of your query, my brother. The aspect that pulls the energy forward is desire, or as it is sometimes called, will.

May we answer you further, my brother?

B: That covers it. Thank you. ⚘

L/L Research is a subsidiary of Rock Creek Research & Development Laboratories, Inc.

P.O. Box 5195
Louisville, KY 40255-0195

L/L Research

www.llresearch.org

Rock Creek is a non-profit corporation dedicated to discovering and sharing information which may aid in the spiritual evolution of humankind.

Special Meditation
December 19, 2005

Group question: What exactly is a time lateral and how is it created?

(Carla channeling)

We are those known to you as the principle of Q'uo. Greetings in the love and in the light of the one infinite Creator, in Whose service we come to you this day. We want to thank you for creating this circle of seeking and for asking us to share our thoughts with you.

As always, we would ask that you be extremely vigilant in monitoring your reactions to our thoughts. If there seems to be resonance to what we have to say, please feel free to use our thoughts in any way that seems helpful to you. If there does not seem to be any resonance to our thoughts, please abandon them and leave them behind. This will enable us to speak freely without being concerned with infringing on your free will or the integrity of your spiritual process.

You ask this day concerning the nature of the time lateral that we have talked about previously with this group. The creation of such a shunt or rail for an alternate track along space/time within your local sector, which you call your solar system, was created for the same kind of reason that a railroad switching station would employ shunts or lateral track systems to hold trains that have, for one reason or another, lost their initial engine. The formation of this sidetrack is that which is created to be precisely parallel to the main track of the solar system which is now finishing an important part of its evolution through its own part of the densities of creation. It was intended to last until your year, approximately 1998. It was provided with the opportunity to link back to the main track of your solar system's development at that time.

Because of the energies of groups such as yours and many others across your planetary sphere, the ability of this shunt or time lateral to maintain traffic across the normal boundaries of your solar system's and your planet's development [has been enhanced.]

There have been energies which have been called forth amongst many of those upon your planet who have been inspired to help in the goal of maintaining the openness of this reconnection point which this instrument feels comfortable calling a bridge. It is a bit easier for us to give her images of a bridge and the way that bridges can be closed because of incoming traffic. For instance, if a bridge is across a river and is split in the middle, it may raise up and allow a tall ship to come through. This is the basic situation with your shunt at this time. It is on the verge of becoming time to raise that bridge and to allow other traffic and other energies to pass athwart or in such a way that that bridge cannot endure.

And let us be specific concerning the nature of this time lateral. It is not a time lateral that concerns the planet as a whole. The planet as a whole is unimpeded in its entry into fourth density. The energies of a living third-density system have been encouraged to continue for the approximate ten to twelve years further that this shunt can stay physically open in terms of space/time. This is to say that, by the energies of unconditional love which are generated by the prayers, meditations and visualizations of groups such as this one, the bridge or reconnection point has been maintained for those who would wish to awaken and make their choice of polarity by the date which has been set as the last possible date to keep this connection point open, which, as we have said before and still find to be true, is the date of the winter solstice of the year 2012.

This cannot be said to be precise. It is not known to us just when the last entity will be able to cross that bridge. The choice of many entities is involved in maintaining such a bridge. And indeed the traffic across the bridge of those who awaken and make their choice also has its part in keeping the bridge open until the last possible moment. The more traffic upon that bridge and the more guardians who stand watch along the bridge, holding and anchoring the incoming light of fourth density on the one hand, and acknowledging, honoring and blessing the waning light of third density on the other hand, the fuller the harvest may be. This is the entire core of the exercise of creating this time lateral.

Let us talk to a certain extent about this time lateral and how it came to be necessary. As the ones known as P and B are far more aware than this instrument, there is a separation that is inevitable between higher and lower energies. As fourth density has now completely interpenetrated [third density] and is as active as third density and indeed gaining in energy while third density wanes, the vibration of each of the entities upon planet Earth becomes more and more critical in terms of being able to physically remain viable and functional within the third-density energy that is so heavily overarched and under-girded with the interpenetrating fourth-density energy.

In this environment, third-density entities who have not made their choice become buffeted by the energies that are crashing upon your planet in waves at this time. These waves are all perfectly normal and completely benign: they are a part of the awakening of the morning of the fourth-density day. Nevertheless, these energies have the side effect for the people of the planet of encouraging polarity. If

there is a slight choice for service to others, it creates enhanced opportunities to make deeper and firmer choices of service to others and the same is true for those who are service to self. There are increasing and markedly more attractive or seductive opportunities to choose the ways of service to self.

For those who do not wish to make either choice, there is the life[-style] lived precisely as the fifth-density entities who are enthusiastic about maintaining this time lateral wish to keep in place.

So on the one hand you have a well-meaning set of guardians of your planet who, gazing at the difficult time that your planetary tribe has had in achieving graduation, chose to create an enhanced opportunity for a last-ditch effort, shall we say. Wanderers came forward, some of whom have been here for fifty of your years, some forty, some thirty, and so forth. In addition you have entities who have come in the last twenty years or so who are approaching this problem from the fourth-density angle, sending entities such as the one known as P, who have certain activation within fourth density as well as having third-density activated energy. These entities also are those who would wish to maintain this opportunity for the harvesting of as many entities as possible before the time literally runs out.

On the other hand, you have opportunistic entities of a negative polarity from fifth density who have discovered that there is a characteristic of this planet which is unusual and of which they may take advantage. They are busily doing that and have been doing so for some of your time.

The situation about which we speak is this: as we have said before, the planetary population is made up not only of those entities who are native to your planet. For the most part and for the great majority, your planetary population [consists] of those who have been imported from other failed third-density planetary cycles. Many of those upon your planet, then, are those who have either destroyed their planet completely through acts of war using advanced technology or are those who have for one reason or another been unable to finish out their normal cycles upon their native earths. Therefore, you have adopted each other as a kind of mixed bag, shall we say, of many differing planetary origins.

This means that you have the attempt to integrate many differing subconscious or archetypical systems of looking at and structuring information. You do not have a homogeneous population. You have a population that has enormous difficulty in communicating because of the great variety of those groups, speaking in terms of planetary origins, among its tribe.

Nevertheless, the entire gamble of Earth in third density was to see if such a polyglot group of entities could mold themselves into a tribe [with] all embracing planet Earth, all becoming aware of their true situation as regards the need to make a choice of service to others or service to self, and all having a great desire to restore or reconstitute the planet Earth where there was a group karma, shall we say, to be balanced, as so many entities had been involved actively in previous planets where, by their own choices, the planet was damaged, as in the case of Mars, or completely destroyed, as in the case of Maldek.

The first and perhaps the most disastrous of the experiments of rebuilding the tribe of Earth and creating or recreating a level of technology which was well remembered by many entities from previous planetary experiences was that of Atlantis. In this pattern's outworking, those within Atlantis came to power at a time when their technology had grown sufficiently to offer the opportunity for advanced applications such as crystal technology.

These leaders, instead of embracing the ideals of service to others, embraced what can perhaps be called the path of conditional service. This is a path of service to self which is overlaid heavily by the rhetoric of service to others. It is a situation which initially was innocent. Those involved did not see that rather than polarizing fully service to others there was a good deal of rationalizing and sophistic thinking which justified exceptions to various rules of ethics and [which] involved infringing upon the free will of entities which were considered less valuable or intelligent than others.

This pattern of exclusion and manipulation of entities considered as lesser is the initial point of departure from service-to-others polarity.

Because of these choices, eventually those who had previously created disasters on other planetary spheres created the first disaster upon the sphere of Earth, sinking the continent known as Atlantis. The wise and the clever—that is, those polarized positively and those polarized negatively—managed to remove themselves to other continents in

sufficient number that these energies never left your planetary vibration. And if you will examine your written history, you may see a pattern of empire: its building, its maintenance, and its eventual and inevitable destruction, played out again and again.

Into the pattern of this repetitive, self-destructive behavior among the population of planet Earth came those who were watching for the opportunity to present itself to make use of this time lateral. For if entities such as your group are unable to clear the population of your planet from this lateral, there are ways in which the negatively-oriented entities have every hope of keeping the time lateral viable. It would no longer be attached to the main track. That opportunity shall soon be closed. Nevertheless, those that believe that they are in the appropriate place for themselves could choose to remain not polarized either positively or negatively but simply as those who would remain on third-density Earth as it reverts to late second density.

These entities would no longer be enlivened by third-density entities who have the power of free will that could make the choice of service to self or service to others. They would be instinctual, great-ape-type beings who look like you do because that is the genetic pool that now exists upon planet Earth. However, these entities would simply be slaves of a kind that spent their lives living a life much as you now experience it: a life without a good deal of variety, a life that is not concerned with coming into harmony as a planetary system but is only concerned with the tribe of its family and its clan, with protecting the resources of that family and clan, and of defending that family and clan.

What the fifth-density entities, which you may call, as this instrument has jokingly done, "space pirates," have in mind is simply to have a continuing harvest of food, that food being fear. You may see [the creation of an atmosphere of fear] in your governmental systems in your present culture. Indeed, we find from this instrument's mind there have been several conversations concerning this precise point recently among those who sit within this circle.

The goal, therefore, of those who wish to aid planet Earth at this time is firstly to express the situation of the choice, without concern for numbers but only with concern for making an appropriate effort to, as this instrument would say, get the word out globally;

to share the information of the Confederation as regards this being the density of choice and there being time yet for making that choice.

A secondary effort at this time, but one which will grow increasingly stronger and which will, within the next several of your years, become more important by far than alerting the population of this planet, is the concern for the planet itself. For there are many, many entities upon this planet whose route or road to realization of their true situation involves becoming aware of and responsive to the sad plight of the planet itself and the fact that your culture and your way of life are gradually destroying the viability of this planet.

The desire to change this pattern is a key to the activation of the will to choose in many entities whose energies are unconsciously but deeply involved with connecting with restitution and the energies of stewardship and unconditional love, not so much to the people of the planet as to the planet itself.

That is the situation as we know it with the time lateral at this time. It is not a situation that will endure. We would, however, emphasize that there is no serious disturbance that is even possible to be balanced, either of the planet or of the solar system. There is in progress a desperate gamble on the part of negative entities, as we had mentioned before, to attempt to hijack the time lateral.

Getting information more globally available is the best means of creating a balance to the situation that makes it impossible for this gamble to work. The best help the negative entities have, however, is not negative entities as much as it is the deep sleep of those who are unawakened at this time. It is to the interest of the negative entities that that sleep be continued as untroubled and peaceful as possible.

Energies such as your religious bodies and what this instrument calls the "religious right," those entities who lean heavily upon dogma and whose teachings are based on fear and judgment, are the leaders of the pack in maintaining the lack of choice among entities who indeed have translated spirituality into a religiosity in which the concern is simply to belong to the appropriate pack and to be a part of that pack by following blindly any directives given by the leaders of that group.

We realize that gazing at this situation, there is the possibility of creating within oneself an easy and seductive anger, or even rage. We would encourage each of you to take this entire situation lightly, to let it slide off your back. This is not a burden for you to pick up. This is not something for which you can be responsible or over which you have any control.

What you have, in terms of your ability to serve at this time, is primarily your own deepening awareness of what it is to choose; what it is to choose so deeply that the rest of your life becomes a joy. What it is to choose so completely that there is no longer the need to spend time questioning whether faith is the answer, whether service is the answer, or whether one particular kind of service is better than another, and so forth. When the choice for service to others has been absolute, there is a knowing that comes. It is a knowing that transcends planning. It is a knowing that includes the awareness that you really do not have control over anything but your own desires, your own will, and your own persistence.

We ask you who wish to serve at this time to look to your own self-awareness and self-knowledge and to be aware and trust completely in the fact that you are part of a web of love. Your work has been effective because you have chosen the very difficult path of working in groups. The energy of the group and the energy of groups of such groups is now that which is challenged to undertake what this instrument has called a new paradigm.

What is that new paradigm, you may ask. But it is not for us to answer the question. It is for you. It is certainly not building upon anything that has been seen before, for the old ways have failed. Yet there stirs within the hearts of so many the sure and absolute knowledge that there is a way to create harmony, power and balance once again at the dusk and the evening of third density. This instrument is fond of saying that she likes to leave a room tidy when she leaves it, as good as it was when she came into it or perhaps even better. That is your work at this time.

You are those who stand as guardians and anchors of light, holding that bridge open, and, by your vibrations and your thoughts, radiating the love and the light of the infinite Creator with your own coloration out into the ambient atmosphere. You are an agent of infection. You are infecting people with the highest and the best of your love. Witness your opportunity to offer your love. You will find, as you attempt to do this, that there is resistance down every path. This is inevitable and ever more inevitable at this fairly radical and extreme point at the end of your cycle that you are now experiencing.

We find this to be sufficient information from that question and would ask if there is a further query at this time.

P: What you were saying sounded a bit synchronistic with *Psi-Corps*[84] and I wanted to know, first of all, about the free will aspect. It would seem like a major violation of the distortion of free will for a time lateral to be created. In conjunction with what you were saying about the time lateral being created, it sounded like an experiment almost on planet Earth. Could you elaborate on that?

We are those of Q'uo, and are aware of your query, my brother. The Confederation of Planets in the Service of the Infinite Creator has indeed experimented repeatedly with the planet which you call Earth and which this instrument calls Gaia. There was a realization that entities would need to begin with an entirely new planetary and solar system if the experiment of Earth did not succeed. And so it was proposed that this time lateral be created and that what this instrument would call a kind of reform school be instituted upon the planet. The idea was simply to increase the harvest and to break some significant knots of fear that had occurred in unusual quantities within your fairly local area of space/time.

It was felt that there was a lot of risk involved with the experiment but it was felt that there was the possibility of bringing many, many entities into a configuration where true choice would become possible. And, in terms of this basic intention, the experiment has been a roaring success.

(Side one of tape ends.)

(Carla channeling)

There has been a genuine, authentic time of choice that has been created out of the nothingness of previously impossible lack of time. However, like any experiment, it has a period: a beginning, a middle, and an ending. The beginning was before history began upon your planet. You have a fair view

of the history of the middle. You gaze now at the end point of this experiment.

It is impossible for us to say how many souls or spirits or beings shall have been harvested that were not harvested before [because of the creation of the time lateral.] But we can say that there has been an additional harvest because of the efforts of all entities involved, whether they be Earth natives, elder race, walk-ins, wanderers or other categories of those who walk upon your Earth.

The end point is at this time rapidly approaching because the energies are precipitating out of third density, either moving on to fourth density or moving back to late second density, getting ready for removal to another solar system for the beginning of a new effort in moving through third density.

The likelihood of the negative entities that this instrument has called the space pirates being successful is almost nil. It is extremely doubtful that they would be able to bring through enough intensity of fear to create, again, such a knot that it would be the choice of those entities remaining to refrain from being at all aware as third-density entities. This would have to be a choice made by each entity. The energy that attracts entities to choices like this is that energy of fanaticism which creates situation in which people would rather die for a cause than live in freedom.

The tendency of your planetary people is not to make such a choice but rather to maintain enough confusion to allow the normal harvesting procedures to precipitate them out of the time lateral and into a beginning class, shall we say, for a new third-density experience.

Whenever entities are attempting to serve and lend their aid there is the possibility of infringement upon free will. Looked at from a system-wide point of view, there is certainly the possibility of feeling that the Confederation, choosing to make this experiment occur, were in error. In the ways of all energy, such errors shall and will be balanced and it is our intention to be part of the energy that loves, accepts and embraces all of those who are engaged in this experiment on all of the inner and outer planes connecting with this planet.

May we answer you further, my brother?

P: A friend of ours has started hearing voices in his head and is concerned that it might be a sign of

---

[84] Characters on the science fiction television series *Babylon 5*.

schizophrenia or multiple personality disorder. Are there any comments you can offer to help him through this process?

We are those of Q'uo, and are aware of your query, my brother. We find that this instrument has every intention at the first possible moment of working with this entity by e-mail. And because of the fact that her service is soon to be manifested, it would be our request that the entity to whom you refer read and digest the gist of the material that this instrument will make available. And then, when it has processed that which may considered a starting load of information, which we would as soon not repeat through this instrument at this time, have this entity ask questions of us which we may address at a future session.

If that would be acceptable to you, that is what we would prefer to do, for we would not wish to tire this instrument, whose energy is already waning, with the repetition of information that is readily available. Is this acceptable to you, my brother?

P: Of course.

We are those of Q'uo, and we thank you for this. We find we have energy for one more question at this time.

P: This one concerns how a social memory complex such as yourself would express creativity. How do you express creativity, such as an individual expresses beauty through artistic expression?

We are those of Q'uo, and are aware of your query, my brother. We find it most humorous that you would ask this question because of the burden of our comments today. They have been about an experiment in beauty and truth which is called planet Earth. The time lateral experiment, which is your planetary school of learning, was crafted by us with tremendous creativity, love and caring.

The intentions of all of those involved in the creation and maintenance of this planet in its special circumstances is a very good example of the kind of beauty that social memory complexes might create if they have chosen as their role the guardianship of a space/time continuum such as that of your solar system.

In general, let us simply say that when groups of entities create, the energies of creation are very much the same as when individuals create. The time that it takes to create is extended dramatically, for the commonalities of all of those within the group must be gathered and balanced in a continuing cycle of increasing self-awareness and increasing focus so that when choices are made as to how to proceed along the lines of the preservation or the creation of a thing of beauty, or a thing that has form and function, there is the fullest possible realization on the part of all entities involved.

Each entity within a social memory complex is known to the other entities in terms of the contents of that entity's mind. What is not known until the entities engage at a very deep level with each other is what the dynamics of connection between each and every member of a social memory complex shall create as a pattern. It is from that pattern of commonality that the creations of a social memory complex come.

We realize that we have only scratched the surface of any of these questions and are more than happy to continue to offer our humble thoughts through this instrument at a future time. You have only to create the opportunity and we shall make every attempt to be with you.

We thank this instrument and each of you for creating this circle of seeking. It has been our true pleasure to share the beauty of your vibrations and your meditations at this time. Again, we ask each of you to guard your thoughts. We are not perfect and we have no desire to be an authority among you. But we are most happy to share our humble opinions.

We are those known to you as the principle of Q'uo. We leave you in the love and in the light of the one infinite Creator. Adonai. Adonai. ❖

YEAR 2006

JANUARY 1, 2006 TO APRIL 1, 2006

L/L Research is a subsidiary of
Rock Creek Research &
Development Laboratories, Inc.

P.O. Box 5195
Louisville, KY 40255-0195

L/L RESEARCH

www.llresearch.org

Rock Creek is a non-profit
corporation dedicated to
discovering and sharing
information which may aid in
the spiritual evolution of
humankind.

SUNDAY MEDITATION
JANUARY 1, 2006

Group question: The question today, Q'uo, has to do with information that you gave some time ago concerning the end of third density and the beginning of fourth density. We're wondering if there is any reason for us to be afraid of anything that's going to occur then. Everything that we know is going to come to an end, as we know it, in third density. An entirely new fourth-density vibration is coming in, entirely new ways of looking at things, of doing and being. Is there any reason for fear?

(Carla channeling)

We are those of the principle known to you as Q'uo. Greetings in the love and in the light of the one infinite Creator. We come in the Creator's service to share our thoughts with you, humble as they are, on the subject of fear. It is our pleasure to join your circle and our privilege to share our thoughts.

As always, we would ask that you guard your thoughts carefully. Listen with some skepticism and a weary ear to what we have to say. If the thoughts seem helpful to you, then by all means work with them. That is why we are sharing them. However, if those thoughts do not seem helpful to you then we would ask you please to drop them without a second thought and leave them behind. It is an important consideration to us, for we do not wish to create a stumbling block for your process. Therefore, if you would guard your thoughts carefully, it would enable us to speak freely. We thank you for your consideration in this regard.

It is with some degree of gratitude and thankfulness that we take up this question of whether there is any reason to have fear at this time in your planetary process. There certainly are great changes taking place, and, indeed, some of the processes of change have completed their pattern to a great extent. The outworking of the forces involved in the planetary shift from third to fourth density, in terms of activation and the interpenetration of third by fourth density, has matured nicely.

We have been pleased to see the degree to which your planet's people as a whole are increasing in their level of awareness of the planetary situation. This new level of awareness among what this instrument would call the grass roots of your globe means that there is more surface area, shall we say, for the light to shine through, which in turn helps the rest of the planetary population if it wishes to join the numbers of those who are awakening, making their choice, and creating for themselves the opportunity to graduate in service to others.

We are pleased, indeed, that groups such as yours all over the planet have enabled the third-density structure they do now enjoy as they have. It is extremely likely at this point that your population shall be able to enjoy uninterrupted and comfortable incarnations at the end of which lies the opportunity to choose the next classroom which you feel that you would best enjoy working in.

It is a very exciting time for your planet and for those of us who have watched your people through a great deal of difficult learning. We see better rates of awakening, shall we say, than the probability vortices of, say, thirty years in the past would have suggested. And we are humbly grateful to be a small part of that energy that has pressed towards the light, has called to the light, and has anchored that light in relatively undistorted form. We thank each heart that beats, "love, love, love." Thank you for the unimaginable effort that it takes each of you to keep your mind, your thoughts, and your heart on the beam, as this instrument would say. It is easy to be distracted by very many things and we find ourselves applauding the efforts of each of you to stay awake and stay on task.

We can say unequivocally that there is no reason to have fear [while] phasing out the stunning changes that are taking place on your planet at this time.

One reason there is no need to fear these changes is that these changes are largely non-physical. As the questioner expressed the question, it was clear that the questioner was aware that they take place in the unseen realms, the inner planes. Therefore, while these changes are absolutely radical and revolutionary, they are not changes that will affect life as you know it on planet Earth. Consensus reality shall reflect only shadows of these changes.

In terms of your living out your natural life, there is no physical catastrophe that is necessary in order to express the changes that the planet is going through. Humankind is another story in terms of the possibility of planetary disaster. The planet itself does not need to extinguish itself in order for fourth density to emerge. However, there is a troubling tendency within humankind to use violence and the expressions of violence of which your people are capable at this time. The only reason for fear that we would see in the picture that we look at this time is that tendency among your people to feel that it is possible to create a better situation than the one that is currently had by destroying people, buildings and the environments with your weapons of mass destruction. Enough of those weapons of mass destruction going off at one time could indeed remove life from the planet entirely.

We are without concern as to whether this happens because of our being [unable] to do anything about it. We hope that each of you can take into your prayer life, your meditations, and your interactions with others the awareness of that shadow side which lies within the heart and the makeup of each human being on planet Earth. Where in your energy do you see the desire to destroy rather than communicate, to blow something up rather than take the long and sometimes messy route of discussion and heartfelt reaction that results in creating light where there was darkness, love where there was bitterness, and so forth?

These are matters with which only you who dwell in the flesh on planet Earth have the right and responsibility to deal. We have the right to rescue entities that may have been blown up in a nuclear explosion. We do not have the right to interfere with such an explosion. As you in your heart live, so does the human tribe as a whole live. And so we put this concern to you: if you have fear, let it be fear of your own human tendency to destroy. And see what you can do to create within yourself a heart that is genuinely, deeply committed to building up rather than destroying.

In terms of what is happening to the planet, the third-density planet Earth on which you live is gradually exhausting its capacity to offer an environment in which third-density entities can incarnate. The energies have been strengthened, especially in the last ten years or so, as we said, by many groups such as yours who gather for reasons larger than themselves, and you have in common a great love for the Creator and a great desire to serve the Creator.

This whole-hearted stretching and reaching for the light and this growing desire to learn the truth among so many of your people have greatly aided the situation as regards the strength of the field of third density at this time. It is very likely—and we are looking only at probability vortices, not actual predictions—that your people will not only be able to live out their current incarnations here but that there will be enough energy within third density to maintain third-density bodies and the energies of evolution, in terms of the spirit, for some of your time, perhaps as many as a hundred or a hundred and fifty of your years. It is difficult but not impossible to predict with any accuracy what shall occur with your people. However, the time of third density for doing third-density work is virtually over.

Those not in incarnation at this time will not have another shot at living on planet Earth, taking flesh, and becoming choice-making, ethical, biological units, as this entity likes to call human beings, from the work of the one known as Dewey. It is not, however, a cause for fear that this is occurring. This is perfectly in order.

And, indeed, that which remains to be done by entities living in third-density bodies on planet Earth is, for the most part, not personal but rather has to do with the energy of so many among your people, which has a kind of group karma to it. This energy is that which those among your people who have destroyed parts of their planet or their entire planet in previous attempts at third-density evolution have carried with them to this point. There is a lot of healing that various entities for various reasons wish to accomplish. In many cases they do not even really know how to accomplish this healing process. More and more entities, we feel, will find a connection between their own health, in terms of their spiritual health, and the health of the planet on which they live.

The key error among your peoples has been to forget that all things are one. It is a very simple truth. There are many, many ways to say this truth. But you are part of the entity sitting next to you, the entity on the other side of the world, the ground that lies closest to your feet at this time, and the ground of the entire planet. All of these energies coalesce within your energy system. You are the Earth, just as you are the creation. The kind of healing that has this karmic tang to it is that healing into the realization that is heart-deep: that you are part of all that there is and that you are able to interact as a steward with the Earth around you.

The term, Earth, is not necessarily literal—for you may not live on earth. You may live in a high-rise or in a place that for some reason has no actual earth to it. Nevertheless, your feet touch, your hands touch, and your eyes see a physical world. Even if your environment is only one room, you can make that one room a room in which there are green and growing things, there is cleanliness and order, there is a sense of peace, there is an atmosphere of thankfulness, and there is a deep note of joy. You can make a home, not only for yourself but for all of the energies that interpenetrate third-density, consensus reality.

And this kind of opening up of the self to the awareness of the environment around you is that about which we are encouraging you to think. It is a simple thing to turn the mind to more of an awareness of what is around you. And once you become aware of what is around you, it becomes more obvious how exciting, how stunningly beautiful and how entirely original each day is, what a gift it is, and what an adventure it is to experience it.

Eventually, your planet will no longer be able to sustain the evolutionary energy necessary to live a third-density life. Once this has occurred and there are no longer any third-density entities dwelling on the planet, fourth density will indeed become able not only to interpenetrate third density but to appear. At this point in its development, all of fourth density chooses not to appear. It chooses to remain as an unseen energy in order to allow the third-density entities to complete their patterns.

We cannot say that there is no reason to have fear. We can only say that there is no reason that we see to have fear. We see a good deal of fear among your people. We ourselves do not share the point of view that produces that fear. To those such as this instrument, who have experienced physical death, there is less likelihood of a thought concerning the ending of the life creating fear. This instrument is not afraid to pass through the gates of larger life. Having done so, she is aware that there is nothing of which to be afraid. Indeed, there is a great deal to which to look forward.

Therefore, her life is not cluttered with the fearful anticipation of her own death. She is aware that, as she was born, so she will die. She is content to let the Creator take her when her time comes. Whenever that is, her hope is to have completed the patterns that she came here to fulfill. That is indeed her only concern and in passing we would say to this instrument that even that is not something to fear. What is done is what is perfect to have been done. That is a way to look at a life's work. Otherwise you can indeed create concerns for yourself where there is truly no concern.

We would indeed encourage each to take hold of life as the gift that it is, realizing that death is part of life, an outworking and a final stitch in a good pattern that you began in your mother's womb. We do not see this event as being one that needs to be feared at all. We see it as part of a benign and healthy pattern. We hope that any time that we speak of the changes that are occurring in answer to your question, you are able to receive the information simply as information. It is, in all of its complexity, not that which need cause any fear whatsoever. Certainly, when the time nears midnight, entities will become more focused on that moment when today becomes tomorrow and a new beginning proceeds. We encourage you to enjoy the dawning of this new day.

You cannot become a fourth-density entity within third density. However you would be surprised how deep a change that you can make in the life of your body, as well as your mind and your spirit, by disciplining your thoughts. This instrument has talked many times about trying to live with fourth-density values, seeing what you can do, when you become aware of the thoughts that you are thinking, to examine them for what they may have to offer you. It is very helpful to see what you are thinking about and then to ask yourself if you could perhaps tune that instrument that you are to clearer and more productive thoughts.

There is a fine balance between this kind of work which is helpful and too much of this kind of work which creates a situation in which you really don't know who you are because you're too busy trying to control your thoughts to be a certain way. We do not encourage that.

What we encourage is a living, plastic, yeasty kind of process in which you are able to become aware of your thoughts and to sit with them and let them show you what your inner environment is. In sitting with that environment, you may ask for guidance and help in seeing with more clarity and in being able to have a broader point of view that enables you to see a larger picture.

We hope that this sort of energy will be that to which you turn if you do feel fearful because that over which you have control remains stubbornly inferior to yourself. The kingdom does lie within and the resources and tools for administering your kingdom lie handy to your use. It is a matter of how you choose to think, to act, and to be.

We would at this time ask if there is a follow up to this query or if you have another question at this time?

P: My question came up in the last session. It was surrounding Maldek and Mars. Why does it seem like such a current theme for planets to be destroying themselves? Not planets but peoples of the planets, destroying themselves, their cultures! Is it central to this solar system or is it a common theme in third density?

We are those of Q'uo, and are aware of your query, my brother. The pattern, my brother, we would agree is well advanced and is indeed endemic to this region of space controlled by the Logos, or shall we say, sub-Logos that is your sun. The creation that was designed by this entity used a great deal of free will and a heavy veiling so that it takes actual effort for most people to retrieve their memory of the larger picture that moves beyond one incarnation into the grand design of the creation itself and you as citizens of eternity.

We are not saying that the Creator has not gained a rich harvest of new information about Itself from this particular design of creation. However it does seem that the combination of advanced free will and advanced veiling of the actual metaphysical situation have created conditions that are unusually likely to produce the thought pattern of aggression in order to get one's way. Since it is so difficult to see that we are all one in your third-density experience, since the veiling is so complete, it becomes possible for entities to contemplate ending another's life with less discomfort than if they were contemplating ending their own life. This has made it possible for entities to become habituated to the destruction of other selves.

And, indeed, the mental processes of entities who have, in lifetime after lifetime after lifetime, been involved in killing have become infected. It is as if you had taken up smoking: you can see that smoking is a bad idea; you can see the statistics that a certain number of people will get emphysema or lung cancer and will be removed from incarnation because of that habit. However, the smoking becomes a habit and it seems very difficult to change the habit once it has set in.

In just the same way, your tribe on planet Earth is made up of entities who have become habituated to violence. There is a great yearning in the heart of all of those who have so become habituated to lose the habit, to stop the violence that lies within the self.

However, in order to change a habit, one must see a viable alternative to the habit.

How can you teach peace? How can you help a planet heal from its easy acceptance of violent acts? We leave this question with you. It is in your hands.

May we answer you further, my brother?

P: That's good for now.

We are those of Q'uo. Is there a further query at this time?

T: Can you offer any suggestions for a process to help make a seemingly important life decision?

We are those of Q'uo, and are aware of your query, my brother. We wonder for this instrument's sake if you could repeat the question, putting it a slightly different way so that she may see into the question?

T: Yes. The question centers around how one can think through and come to a decision about an important life path, of one option or another. Does that help?

We are those of Q'uo, and yes, my brother, that did help this instrument. We are able to respond to your query this time better because you put it a slightly different way and we thank you for that.

There are a couple of things we would share with you, my brother, about making choices. Firstly, we would ask you to be more than usually aware of your guidance and to ask it for help in a very specific way. In other words, my brother, when you pray or converse with your guidance system, rather than saying, "I have some things coming up that I'm concerned about and I would like for your help," we would suggest that you be very specific and try to describe to your guidance system precisely what it is with which you want help. As you describe the specifics of your choice to your guidance system in this inner conversation, you will be opening channels of inspiration and information that will begin to flow instantly.

Secondly, we would suggest to you the virtue of exaggeration. When you are attempting to make a choice it is helpful sometimes to exaggerate the choice, to imagine into how it would be if it went one way and emphasize and exaggerate that projection into one possible future. And then do the same thing with that other path, exaggerating it and imagining into it and seeing how it felt one year down the road, two years down the road, as you project how your life will change because you've made this choice.

(Side one of tape ends.)

(Carla channeling)

We might suggest, for instance, that you could take a period of your time, for instance a week, and for seven days focus entirely on wanting, looking into, imagining and projecting into the future, having made the choice one way. Then take the next week and do the same thing for the other side. There is a point in this process where you will begin to get a resonance on one way of choosing that you do not get on the other way of choosing. This is one way of sharpening your focus as you let yourself drift and dream and imagine what it would be like to live out the implications inherent in making the choice one way or the other.

Thirdly, we would suggest that you be careful to include in each day a time where there is no thought taken about this choice. We do not even want to describe how you would structure this time. But let it be a time that is yours and let your choice for that time be that which opens your heart.

It might be as simple as walking outside in beautiful settings, especially those with trees. It might be any situation in which you choose how you wish to enter the silence. But let this time be free from worldly concerns of any kind. Let this be your gift to yourself. This is important for the balancing of all that is occurring to you at this time.

You might even think of it as a time of invitation and acceptance; an invitation of beauty, truth, justice and peace. Invite them to flow through you as they will, restoring and healing you, for they rest as entities within your energy system and can be called forth and evoked, if you will. And rest, resting from all labor, all thought, all concern; resting into the silence, leaning back into the strength and the power inherent in the ongoing pulse of the Creator's heart.

May we answer you further, my brother?

T: No, thank you, Q'uo, that was lovely.

We are those of Q'uo, and we thank you, my brother. Is there another query?

B: Yes, I have one. You made reference to the third-density pattern which must be completed. Could you describe what the pattern is?

We are those of Q'uo, and are aware of your query, my brother. We have difficulty using this instrument to answer that particular question and therefore we shall attempt to be somewhat creative, for there are many things this instrument simply does not know in terms of scientific patterns.

The pattern of third density, to use your own discussion of densities with this instrument, is oranges. There is an orange-ness that must be completed and that is a complex thing. It has to do with that particular fruit, shall we say. It has a certain smell, it has a certain texture and firmness, and is of certain size and so forth. Third density has a field and it is full of a certain kind of pattern. When the pattern is completed, then there will be no more need for oranges.

We are sorry but this is the best we can do through this instrument. Can we try to answer you further, my brother?

B: Are there specific attributes I could look for in the field?

We are those of Q'uo, and yes, my brother, there are specific attributes. We do not believe we can, at this time, express to you what to look for. We are sorry but we cannot offer you information through this instrument at this time on this question except that we can, through this instrument, affirm that there are indeed characteristics that are available to your observation.

B: Where might I find such information? Anything locally in books or print or other features?

We are those of Q'uo, and would suggest through this instrument simply that you follow research concerning the nature of light. You will find hints and inklings along the way in working with this information, although, of course, my brother, there are as many false leads as there are good ones in such research.

B: This I know. One more question. How is the fourth-density energy impinging on Earth now affecting the people? Is that increasing the amount of violence, being misinterpreted?

We are the Q'uo, and are aware of your query, my brother. We find this a misleading question in that it

is not the interpenetration of fourth density in third that is creating more violence but rather it is that separation of entities into those who are moving forward and those who are caught in fear. Neither those who are graduating service to self nor those who are graduating service to others are caught in fear. The entities that are caught in fear are those who have not yet chosen how to polarize; that are simply, shall we say, resting in the cultural milieu.

If they have not made that first discovery of the true situation, then they perhaps have a very blunted ability to choose at all. Information such as this group offers and many, many other groups offer can awaken certain people who are ready to awaken to the situation. And when entities get the situation well in mind, they are riveted. They are activated and they realize the gravity of this need to choose.

If entities are not yet at that point where it is necessary for them to wake up, necessary for them to get a grasp of the situation and necessary for them, then, to make the choice, they are simply not ready to leave third density and, therefore, they dwell in a sinkhole of indifference that is like a gravity well. They simply cannot get off the bottom of the swing of, say, the pendulum that they represent by not having chosen.

Those who have not made the choice are those, say, that would be hanging straight down into the gravity well. Just as when one swings on a swing, one has to rock back and forth to get a good start. Then once one is swinging, one is able to swing very high. One has developed power. A person that is simply hanging at the bottom of this gravity well of indifference has no power.

So, you are basically looking at entities who are powerless. They sense that they are powerless without having knowledge of how to claim the very substantial power that they indeed do have but do not know how to get to.

May we answer you further, my brother?

B: This is actually describing a pattern. Is this part of a second-density pattern they are trying to complete to move on through the third density? Basically, the great ape motif. Is that what's holding them back and causing the violent reactions?

We are those of Q'uo, and are aware of your query, my brother. We believe that you are reversing cause and effect here and putting the cart before the horse.

The repetitive experiences of entities who have experienced destruction have created a group of entities on your planet who are simply resistant to awakening.

They have successfully avoided [awakening] for a long enough period of time and a significant enough amount of incarnational experiences that there is a continuing resistance to awakening that is expressed very well in some of the outer forms of your culture at this time, with its ways of distracting and amusing entities' thoughts and occupying their thoughts to an extent that keeps them asleep in terms of thinking ethically or morally about who they are or why they are here.

The situation with such entities is simply that they shall need to go through another third-density cycle elsewhere. It was hoped, naturally, by those who created this planetary experience that this would be the best possible environment to take entities that had this pattern and to give them the maximum opportunity for healing and for growth. But there is no guarantee when such a pattern is made that it will succeed. However, each time a new cycle begins, the sub-Logos responsible for that cycle does its very, very best to create that maximally efficient structure for evolution, and if they did not succeed in clearing third-density lessons this time, they shall receive another chance and another opportunity with perhaps an even better creation to play in.

May we answer you further, my brother?

B: Yes. Would there be one particular thing this planetary experience went wrong on that managed to get all these people stuck having to repeat third density?

We are those of Q'uo, and are aware of your query, my brother. There is indeed one thing that entities become stuck on, in general, and that is that illusion that all are not one. It is the saving awareness of all entities who undertake spiritual evolution to realize, in the way that is meaningful to you, that the picture is indeed larger than one person, one nuclear family, and one lifetime, and that, in that picture, everyone belongs. All is one. The lack of awareness of oneness is the key to the clinging to patterns of violence.

It is important to realize, though, my brother, that simply because a group of entities did not make graduation at this time does not mean that there has been a failure. There is no concept of success or failure as such in the outworking of the pattern for a planetary density. Those who are able to be harvested are harvested. Those who are not able to be harvested are given further opportunities to work through the lessons that they were unable to learn so far. There is no reason to be concerned. It is simply a point of information that the particular planet on which you now enjoy living is soon to become unavailable for third-density work. Therefore, [those of] third density shall need to take up their studies elsewhere.

We find that this instrument's energy is waning and we would at this time leave this group, this instrument, and the environment that you have created by the beauty of your vibrations, leaving you in the love and in the light of the infinite Creator. We are known to you as the principle of Q'uo, and we thank you for the privilege of being with you this day.

Group: Thank you.

Adonai. Adonai. ☙

L/L RESEARCH

L/L Research is a subsidiary of
Rock Creek Research &
Development Laboratories, Inc.

P.O. Box 5195
Louisville, KY 40255-0195

www.llresearch.org

Rock Creek is a non-profit
corporation dedicated to
discovering and sharing
information which may aid in
the spiritual evolution of
humankind.

SPECIAL MEDITATION, PALM SPRINGS, CALIFORNIA
JANUARY 9, 2006

Group question: We've been gathering here this weekend to get information and inspiration to help the harvest on this planet. Specifically we would like to know how this group can be most helpful to direct the harvest and to increase the harvest as much as possible. Could you get some information to us on that topic?

(Carla channeling)

We are those known to you as the principle of Q'uo. Greetings in the love and in the light of the one infinite Creator, in Whose service we come to you this day. May we say what a pleasure and a privilege it is to be called to this group. We thank you. The beauty of your vibrations, individually and also commingled, is a source of emotion for us. We are stunned by your courage and your desire to serve.

We consider the experience that you go through in third density at this time as a harsh one and we want to thank each of you for the incredible amount of work that it has taken you to get to this point. Each of you has a different story. Each story is honorable, valuable and worthy. Thank you for this opportunity to share our humble thoughts with you.

As always, my friends, we would ask for you to take full responsibility for discriminating between the thoughts that you will work with and the thoughts that you will leave behind, in terms of what we have to say. We are error-prone just as are you. Some of the things that we share may really help you to work

and if so we are thrilled. Many times, however, we may miss the mark for you and it may not be your truth. If you do not feel resonance with our thoughts, please cast them aside without a second thought, for we would not be a stumbling block before any. If you will take responsibility for guarding your own temple, then we will feel free to share our opinions. We thank you for this consideration.

Your free will is paramount. It is far more important to us that you maintain the freedom of your own thoughts than that we be here or that we say anything in particular. We are here to support you and we know that each of you has guidance not only from entities such as we but from your own guidance system. Please lean into that and depend upon it and do not take the authority of anyone else as being something to which you must bend your will. Retain your orneriness, my friends. Retain your maverick nature.

Be independent of any outside authority, for you are the person who creates your universe. For each of you it is truly your world. That which you forgive is forgiven. That which you do not forgive is not forgiven. This power of which you are becoming more and more aware in your daily lives is that power which is part of the makeup of all of those upon planet Earth at this time. We encourage you to become more and more aware of the truth and power of your being and to look for ways to use that power well.

You asked this day what you as a group could do to help to anchor and further the harvest that is now taking place upon planet Earth. We realize that each of you has more of a tendency to think about what to do than to focus in on being. And yet we would say to each of you that the heart and the seed of each of your service at this time as part of this group is the work that you do in seeking the truth of your own nature and becoming more and more deeply aware of who you are, why you are here, and what you are doing.

There are many, many layers to this question. The conversation earlier ran into the discussion of an onion at one point, and we use this humble and yet wonderful little vegetable that this instrument is so fond of using in her cooking as an example. Take a look, my friends, at the nature that each of you exhibits, for you have many layers to yourself and each layer is distinct. There is that little onion-skin layer in between each bit of onion as it moves into the center. You are trying to move through the resistance, shall we say, or the meniscus that that onion skin represents in our image.

And each time you break through into a more interior portion of your onion-ness, you discover a lot of new information about yourself. You meet those synchronicities that you have called forth by creating a realization, a moment of epiphany. And then you work again to move through to another layer and do the work again, to break through into a more inner awareness.

The analogy falls apart when we come to the center of the onion, because the center of each of you is nothing that has ever taken flesh. It is your very spirit, your very soul. That is your heart, my friends, that experience of feeling the presence of the Creator within is often difficult to come to at first. For you desire to know yourself and at the same time the desire to know the truth always creates a climate that encourages change and, as you know, change can be very uncomfortable.

So we ask you simply to look at, as J has said, each thought and each impulse, and begin to see into the patterns of your being. Who you are is not obvious. The package, as this instrument would say, that you are as a soul contained within is made up of a suitcase full of gifts and limitations, things you are

good at, and things that you are bad at. It is what this instrument would call a personality shell.

It seems, perhaps, at times to be overwhelmingly real, integrated and whole. And this is, of course, the goal of psychology and psychiatry: to reintegrate and bring together the scattered portions of self. But we would go further than that. We would ask you to realize that your personality shell is indeed a collection of things that you have packed in your suitcase to go on this trip, this incarnational trip on Earth. As you spin around the sun and as the galaxy spins around, there is this precious time of opportunity for you, cut off from all possible means of proof, moving towards the situation of embracing the faith that all is well, that all is one, that you are in perfect harmony and accord with your guidance.

In essence, this is the truth of each of you. However, within the veil of forgetting it is not at all simple, usually, to see the pattern except by hindsight. And that developing pattern is, with the yeast of spirit, beginning to create its own thought, its own energies, and its own patterns.

So we would say that the first work that each of you has to do, as part of this group and at this moment of focusing on things to do, is to be yourself and to work daily on the ongoing construction project that this instrument likes to visualize herself as being. Each entity is indeed the Creator. This instrument responded to someone saying that she was part of the Creator earlier today by saying that she acknowledged her godliness but noted that she was a very young god.

We would say that this is a good way to balance your realization. Know who you are but also realize that when you are moving from creatorship, as part of the creative principle, you truly do have the power of a god. See what you can do, my friends, to use that power well, lovingly, compassionately and wisely. Be persistent in your search for who you are beneath the personality shell, beneath the layers, at the interior of the heart which is the precinct of the Creator.

There is a hymn that this instrument often sings. it starts out, "Oh Jesus, thou art standing outside the fast-closed door."[85] It is a hymn about our reluctance

---

[85] Carla: This song was written by W. W. Howe in 1867. The message of the song can be taken better by people who do not enjoy working with the concept of a person named Jesus if they substitute "unconditional love" for "Jesus" and "lightworkers" for "Christians." I also apologize for the 19th-century,

to open the door to the deepest truth of ourselves. We would turn this figure around, my friends, and suggest to you that the Christ is within your heart, at the very center of the holy of holies and waiting for you to knock.

Enter your own inner sanctum daily, if possible. Work with that muscular strength of silence. Allow all of those things at which you have not wanted to look, that rise up when you are silent, to arise. Gaze at them with affection and yet detachment, seeing them, noting them, sitting with them and allowing them to fall away.

This process may seem to be very unlike the ideal of that entity who goes into a deep meditative state and truly transcends thought. When that happens to you, my friends, it is a wonderful gift. But do not sneer or look down upon your efforts when they seem to have failed, when you seem to be full of junk thoughts that keep going and going like a broken record. When you are silent, your subconscious brings you gifts much like the kitty cats that bring unwanted rodents that they have killed to your feet and say, "Didn't I do well? Pet me now for I have killed this for you."

Such is the experience of many who enter the silence and they wonder why they are not experiencing that wonderful peace that work in silence supposedly brings one. For some entities, that is the experience. If it is not yet your experience, than please be patient with yourself and simply enter that silence daily without judging how well you are doing. We find that this instrument considers herself a terribly poor meditator and yet she also considers the work done in meditation to be the linchpin of her process.

How is it possible that the silence can work with such imperfect entities? My friends, it was intended that you be imperfect. You and your guidance system, before incarnation, selected not only your gifts and talents but your limitations and perceived faults. You wanted this opportunity to come and serve and yet also you wanted to do work in

consciousness in the fiery furnace of planet Earth and consensus reality. You risked so much to come to planet Earth as an incarnated being because all that you knew before incarnation had a gentle but firm cover laid over it.

The one known as W was saying earlier that perhaps it is not always a good idea to look too deeply or too far past the incarnation at hand, and we would agree with this entity. Information about other places and other times, other lives and other work, is very interesting but as your knowledge base about what you have physically been through in other incarnations grows, we ask that you continue to identify yourself not with the stream of experiences that lead you here but with the present moment and all that that moment offers.

Secondly, we look through this instrument's mind to find the concept that will help you see what you are as a group entity. Firstly, the power of your own awareness of yourself as a spiritual entity and a spark of the godhead principle makes it possible for you to begin to be a powerful person, metaphysically speaking. Our encouragement to you to begin any process with work on yourself goes back to the simple truth, that you have heard in so many different ways and from so many different sources, that you are all one being. You as a group are a hall of mirrors. You will see within this group, as within any group that attempts to move below the surface of polite conversation, projections coming to you, telling you about yourself. For each entity in the group, that mirroring effect will be very personal and intimate and we would not wish to interfere with your process. We would simply say that it is well to be aware, when you have so many kind, compassionate, honest and loving mirrors about you, of the gifts that you are given by those about you in this group as you interact.

Whatever your experiences in interacting, ponder them in your heart. See what they have to say to you and do that rebalancing that you came here to do bit by bit. Perhaps at the end of the day you might even sit down and take thought for the day. What were you thinking? What were the themes and the patterns of your process this day? What totem spoke to you? What messenger came your way? Use the guidance that your seeking for the truth has brought to you and know that the instant that you ask for help, help is being given.

politically incorrect use of "brothers," where clearly the plea goes out to brethren and sisteren both! This is the first verse:

O Jesus, thou art standing outside the fast-closed door,
In lowly patience waiting to pass the threshold o'er.
Shame on us, Christian brothers, his name and sign who bear,
O shame, thrice shame, upon us who keep him standing there.

It is not our part to make suggestions as to how you shall create projects or environments that will help to awaken the planet of which you are a part. It is only known that this is your time, your moment, and your opportunity. Be aware, in the times to come, when you are attempting to manifest what you have begun in these two days, that each entity within this group wishes to be part of your physical support system. Communicate with each other as you find it possible to do so, moving always deeper, as the one known as J would say, coming to more simplicity and clarity.

This instrument was speaking earlier of unseen help and we would encourage you to lean into that unseen help, for each of you has attracted to yourself not only the entities that each soul has, not only the entity of the higher self or the holy spirit, as this instrument calls it, but also the wanderers among this group have an extended family from their home planet that also have, if they can lean into it and believe it, the support and the encouragement even of those wanderers who are still asleep. For you are connected in other densities.

Can you wake them up? It is your not your place. Can you offer seeds? It is your place. Offering seeds does not infringe upon free will. You may scatter the seeds of thought freely without being concerned that you are infringing upon free will. The essence of sowing the seed is to cast it to the wind, not being concerned at all about where it lands or how it grows.

Realize that, as you lean into this unseen help and as each within this circle does the same thing, there will be activated a tremendous amount of consciousness in the unseen realms. This help is powerful to [have.] Indeed, as this instrument was saying earlier, you are already living on borrowed time and doing so very effectively. Each of you has done much to anchor light. Each of you is a light worker. And that energy that each of you has put out in simple and unconditional love and support for the planet and its people has enabled the energies of fourth density to interpenetrate third density without kicking off the polar shift that at some point is inevitable.

Instead, the shift has been occurring little by little by little, because of your love, because of your work.

Please realize that it is rather like matching funds, if you will, when you donate and your company also donates and so forth. When you work, when you

give, when you stop the analyzing and the worrying and rest in knowing that all is well and that you are alive and present at this moment, you are helping not only yourself but the global community. Unknown [to each other,] groups such as yours are forming all over the globe at this time. So lean into that as well, identifying yourself not as the saviors of Earth but as those who have been touched with the flame of the spirit.

Each of you has had a different tongue of fire touch their heads and bring them alive and awake to spirit. Each of you has a different story to tell and each of your stories is valuable and will open up the consciousness of those to whom you tell your story. Know that about yourself and if entities ask you, bear witness, not to a dogma or an "ism" or even your favorite philosophical *Law of One*, as this instrument calls it. But simply wait for entities to ask you. And when they ask you, share that which it comes to you to share, knowing that the right words will come to you in that moment.

We would at this time ask if there are follow-up questions. We are those of Q'uo. Is there a query at this time?

J: [You seem] reluctant to give us any specific guidance as to the various possibilities that we've been looking at. The one that comes most prominently to mind are the rights to the writings that are currently mired with the Schiffer Publishing Company. Can you speak to that at all, as to the steps that might be taken if necessary for that to be reacquired by L/L Research?

We are those of Q'uo, and are aware of your query, my brother. We cannot speak directly to that query as it is a portion of the active process of several within this room at this time. There are ethical considerations here which far outweigh our desire to share information. We very much feel that part of this group's story is the opportunity to craft a creation that speaks to each of you or to craft creations that together make a pattern that satisfies the larger needs of the group. We would not interfere with your free will choices in this. We have the ability to look at probability/possibility vortices. We can predict, to some extent, what may happen in the future. But it does not interest us to do so on this point. We wish greatly to preserve entirely the range of your free will as individuals and also as a group working within third density.

We ask [you] to realize what you are basically attempting to do. As a spiritually-oriented group, and one whose dedication to the polarity of service to others is absolute, as a group you are a crystal. And when a crystal is composite and made up of more than one element, it becomes a very interesting structure. See yourself individually as a lighthouse or that which radiates light, but as well see the group of which you are a part this day as a composite crystal that accumulates power and allows it [to] shine forth as it will.

It is very difficult to walk that razor's edge between using your will from the yellow-ray position and making things happen, and allowing the energy to move up into the heart and from that heart into the blue-ray chakra and so forth. For you are attempting to work with blue, green and indigo in your chakra system in bringing forth and manifesting spiritually oriented information without significant distortion.

We would simply suggest that you have confidence in yourselves. Know that everything that has gone into bringing you here today is going to be useful. It is not clear yet, obviously, how entities shall combine for the larger good and yet we feel that your attempt to do this creates for you a vortex of fourth-density energy that is substantial. You are attempting to live and to move by higher principles. This, as this instrument said earlier, is protected work.

Resting in that protection, then, fearless as far as what you shall do next, you have only to relax into the conversation and the ideas, always working for a focus that simplifies and simplifies again that which the one known as B called a mission statement. Be aware that it is very powerful to create an intention.

Also, we would suggest to you a concept that is somewhat difficult to grasp but is perhaps helpful to consider. There is, globally speaking, among your people at this time, the rising of a concept that is a new paradigm. It cannot be developed by one group. It must be developed by groups of groups such as this one. Do not push it or pull it! But know that it is growing and see what you can do to tune into the melody not yet heard, the poem not yet written.

May we answer you further, my brother?

J: I would ask that you be with each of us, to assist us in the process of self-discovery. Redouble your

presence in our lives so that each of us can increase the level of perception from which we view.

We are those of Q'uo, and are aware of your request, my brother. May we say what a privilege it is to be asked to do so! We are most happy to be with any of you if you will ask for us mentally as you go into meditation. We have found ourselves to be fairly good at being an undertone that helps to stabilize your own meditative state. We do not attempt to communicate with you individually, usually, for we do not want to break into that personality shell of yours with our somewhat powerful energy. But undergirding your own efforts is something that we can do without any fear of infringement upon free will and it is our delight and our privilege to be with each of you if you call upon us.

Indeed, if you call upon guidance in general, you will be surprised what a number of witnesses form around you to support you, lift you up, and bring you to clarity. We thank you, my brother, for that request and would be happy to do so.

Is there another query at this time?

D1: Is it appropriate to use the traditional media of television and radio and internet to achieve our goals of broadcasting the information, of planting the seeds, as you said earlier?

We are those of Q'uo, my brother, and believe we understand your query. It seems to us a fair and lovely thing for each of you to use the tools which you know to craft that which is your very best effort at sharing the light and the awareness that lie within you. We find all that this group has discussed this day to be appropriate. We do not have any desire to limit you in how you wish to present the information. We would only say to you that to balance the intensive dedication of each of you to manifesting, it is a good idea to spend a significant amount of your time becoming aware of the present moment, relaxing all tension or worry, and simply spending time knowing that all is well and that all will be well. Lighten up and find the light touch, the laughter, the bliss, and the joy that are only available when you are focusing on the present moment. Have fun with this, my friends, just as we are having the time of our lives working with you.

May we answer you further, my brother?

D1: Is there any way that we can help you?

We are those of Q'uo, and we thank you, my brother, for that query. You are already helping us tremendously. We offer our service at this time, speaking through instruments such as this, or simply being with those who are awakening if they ask for our presence, if their asking for guidance is coming in on an energy which is compatible with our own. Consequently, moments such as this when we are able to share our thoughts with you are precisely what we hope to be able to do. So you are giving us our hearts' desire in helping us to serve the Creator. And for this we deeply thank you and honor you.

Is there a final query at this time?

D2: Is there anything else that we can do to increase our awareness and focus?

We are those of Q'uo, and are aware of your query, my sister. There is an endless supply of things that you can do to purify and refine your consciousness.

For each of you there is unique path. There are some key things you have in common. Silence is one of them. The structure of the human organism is such that you are basically dealing with a hybrid, in terms of mental activity. There is a portion of your mental makeup that is the great-ape bio-computer which comes with your body. It came from the factory that way, shall we say. You have a perfectly good decision-making brain and it follows instinctual pathways that are as clear as the pathways of deer or other large mammals as they walk to water and have their routines for finding food.

See what you can do to become more and more aware of your own patterns, your own territories, and your own geography within. It really boils down to becoming more and more aware of who you are. The truth lies within you already, undistorted, whole and perfect. This instrument, because of her mystical nature, has spent a good bit of time in states in which she is completely aware of the perfection of the pattern. She has often expressed that it is almost irritating to have those time of absolute clarity because, like all mountaintop experiences, they cannot be brought back as a gift to those who live in the valley. Just like speaking in tongues, the experience of alternate states is, while a wonderful gift, not that which you can manifest for others' use.

But when those times come for you, when you have moments of clarity, find the discipline and remember to dwell in thankfulness for the gifts that you have received. As you dwell in gratitude and thankfulness, you create an atmosphere or an environment within your electrical body, within your chakra system, as this instrument would say, that encourages further awareness. And just like your Earth, you are an ever-expanding organism. However, you are expanding into the metaphysical realm, rather than into the physical realm.

As your life moves towards its appropriate and condign end, [as] you continue working and creating more awareness within yourself, you are tending your garden. You are nurturing your own seeds so that you can pick an apple out of your own tree of shared experience and storytelling. Eat it with relish and drop the seeds as you go.

(Side one of tape ends.)

J: If I may ask one more question: it would seem to me that in addition to the information that you share with us, there is an unspoken invitation, almost as if it was an induction, inviting us to rise to the vibration, to the point, from which you view so that we may feel and see what you feel and see. Could you speak to that?

We are those of Q'uo, and are aware of your query, my brother. You offer an interesting question, my brother, because, in order to balance our response, we must say two things that are self-contradictory. We ourselves are not afraid of paradox, for we find that paradox is the natural environment of spiritual growth.

It is very well for you to enter into our state of mind and we share it with you freely, wholly and entirely, although not by words as much as simply by our presence, and we believe that was what you had in mind. That which you feel, as this group pulls in the energy of our social memory complexes, is that which can be taken away, examined, and contemplated. You are most welcome to do so.

At the same time, as this instrument was saying earlier, especially for wanderers, it is very important that each entity come down into the planetary miasma and plant the feet firmly on the soil and the earth of Earth.

Take the outer looks of the political, economic and social systems of your culture lightly when doing this grounding work. For you did not come necessarily to change the outer picture. You came to assist with the harvest of planet Earth. That harvest is moving merrily along on its own and, as you do whatever you do to serve with a clarity of intention and a passionate engagement, you are moving ahead with your own program and your own process.

Thusly, be, as this instrument remembers from her Bible studies, innocent and wise.[86] We believe that the combination is not foreign to your nature, my brother. Nor is it foreign to the nature of any here. Be the dove and at the same time use your wisdom.

We are going to leave this instrument at this time for we perceive that there may well be more queries later and we would preserve her somewhat fragile balance of health, which is at this time excellent. Therefore, with many thanks and humblest gratitude to each of you, we would leave you, as we found you, in the love and in the light of the one infinite Creator. Adonai, my friends. Adonai. ✤

---

[86] *Holy Bible*, Gospel of Matthew 10:16: "Behold, I send you out as sheep in the midst of wolves; so be wise as serpents and innocent as doves."

L/L RESEARCH

L/L Research is a subsidiary of
Rock Creek Research &
Development Laboratories, Inc.

P.O. Box 5195
Louisville, KY 40255-0195

www.llresearch.org

Rock Creek is a non-profit
corporation dedicated to
discovering and sharing
information which may aid in
the spiritual evolution of
humankind.

SUNDAY MEDITATION
JANUARY 15, 2006

Group question: The question today, Q'uo, has to do with letting go. Most of the folks talking around the circle today seem to be in a rather harmonious place on their journey. Things are relatively solid and moving forward in a positive manner. But we know that change is always on the horizon. The spiritual seeker can depend upon change. And what we have learned over the years is that letting go is the way for change to happen most easily within us. We've discovered a couple of ways of letting go. If we're a little hesitant of letting go, if we hold on for a while, we finally come to the point where we have to let go. "Let go or die!" That works but it is hard to do it that way. It seems to be much more easily accomplished if we can let go in a conscious fashion and do it at our own pace. We were wondering if you could talk to us about these two types of letting go as a part of the spiritual seeker's journey. Is one more helpful or efficient than the other?

(Carla channeling)

We are those known to you as the principle of Q'uo. Greetings in the love and in the light of the one infinite Creator, in Whose service we come to you this day. We want to thank each of you for creating the time and space in the midst of your busy lives to form this circle of seeking. We realize that there are many times that we say this to you and you must feel that we are repeating ourselves, those of you who have made a practice of coming to these meditations. We assure you that there is no degree whatsoever of repetition to our observations. We are always stunned at the beauty of each of you and encouraged beyond words by your stubbornness and your dedication to seeking the truth as you know it. With energies that are so impossible to extinguish amongst each of your fragile lives and processes, how can we fail to have hope for your planet and its tribe? It is greatly encouraging for us to be amongst such a circle of souls and we thank you for calling us to you.

We would request that you guard your thoughts and your reactions to what we have to say with exquisite care. We would not be a stumbling block in your process. So please, before you pick up and use any of our ideas, run it past your own discrimination and make sure that it is your truth. Make sure that it feels very resonant and lively to you, as if it were something that wanted to grow, something that you remembered rather than having learned it for the first time, something you want to look at more closely. These are the signs of its being that which may be a helpful resource for you. If it does not act like this, if it just sits there and is a thought for you that doesn't resonate, then please let it go. It is not for you at this time.

Your question this day is an interesting one, for it moves into the whole question of process. That is what you are truly asking about when you ask about how to let go as a part of growing and changing. For us to respond adequately to this question, we need to take a step back and try to seat our comments in an environment of thoughts and ideas that form a structure in which this process is seen for that which it is. Our challenge is to find the appropriate starting place.

We would simply move back to that starting place that is our beginning and our ending, that with which we greet you and that with which we say goodbye. We greet you in the love and in the light of the one infinite Creator. The love of which we speak is that unconditional love that is the Logos. We greet you in the Thought that created all that there is and we greet you in light. That light is that which the idea of unconditional love used to impress upon that light the distortions necessary to create the illusions that you see as all the densities, your creation, all your planetary bodies, and all of you—shafts of the sunlight of the infinite Creator, sparkles in the Creator's eye, and holographic portions of the creative principle.

We greet you as creators. We realize that you are very young creators and that you have many distortions and colors in the way you see things. Indeed, the whole point of sending forth each of you from the creative whole at the moment of a new creation was so that you could accumulate experiences and develop these distortions and colors. Each of you has within you the experiences of many lifetimes. Within you, you have your reactions and responses to things of unimaginable joy and things of the most intense and unrelieved suffering, and everything in between. And you have had this panoply of experiences and created, worked through, and finished patterns of learning and service not just once but many, many times have you gone through this creative and energetic process of casting yourself forth into the sea of experience that an incarnation represents, finding your directions by looking at the [stars.]

And once you have set your intention and set your goal, [you] find the rudder and the steering mechanism and start to take control of your boat, that tiny person-sized craft that you navigate through the infinite waters of the unknown and mysterious seas of a lifetime.

What is the correct way to find your stars, to set your intention, to learn your boat and how it works so that you can steer it and set your course? These are questions for you to answer, not for us. But we

can share thoughts with you about this process and this we are glad to do.

We realize that your life has not come clear to you and then retained its clarity. Indeed, we would be somewhat distressed were we to discover that the people of your planet were experiencing no confusion, doubt or distress, for incarnations are created specifically to offer you these gifts. It may not seem like a gift to be confused or to be suffering. Yet this is the dearest of gifts in the sense that you, before incarnation, designed into the specifications of your life ample opportunities to discover within yourself those imbalances which you hoped before incarnation you would notice.

You hoped that you would not only notice them but that you would want to work on them. You provided yourself with difficult people, unfair situations, and repeated cycles of inner storm where you were unclear to yourself. And in all of these gifts to yourself you were not thinking about your comfort but about your growth. You were hoping that your response to confusion would be not only to express the pain of that confusion but also to enter into it, to embrace confusion, to live with it, speak with it, and accept confusion without attempting to make confusion wrong or to get yourself out of confusion as that being your only goal.

When things are in confusion, it does not mean that you have become mistaken in your way. It means that you have entered a pattern within your process whose end you cannot see. In some cases, the pattern is other than it seems. These are usually cases where the confusion is local, or localized and small. Yet, the way you are looking at it, the angle from which you are viewing it, is casting shadows that are not helpful. Consequently, there are some times when confusion is a signal for you simply to rotate your point of view, stepping back if you can to a larger point of view, or simply rotating that point of view so that other ways of understanding the situation might come into view.

There are other points of confusion which bespeak having come into a larger pattern, a pattern that is incarnational rather than local. Indeed, it could be a pattern that moves entirely beyond the limitations of incarnation. It could be, for instance, that you are creating a better balance within yourself as part of the work of wanderers within a social-memory-complex group.

The wanderers themselves do not know about the other wanderers upon the planet that are doing this work, but as each of you wakes up and begins to study the patterns of confusion that you experience, you are helping many unseen friends who do not know that they are being helped by you, any more than you know that you are helping them. Yet, as part of this unseen, and for the most part, undiscovered group, as you do the work on yourself you do the work for the group as well so that your achievements in finding bits of clarity amidst the confusion redound to the understanding of the entire group.

And in a larger and more general sense, all of you are part of the tribe of planet Earth. Therefore, each time that you achieve more clarity for yourself you achieve it also for the tribe of the peoples of Earth. Realize, then, that your process, your confusion, your changes, your choices, and your decisions are not simply for you. As you do the work that opens up your incarnation to receive more and more light from the Creator, you are receiving more and more light not only for yourself [but also] for planet Earth. As you do the work to lay aside those stumbling blocks that would keep you from service, you are laying aside stumbling blocks that lie before each and every soul of your tribe. You do not have to say a word or share any concepts in order to do this work. You have simply to do the work.

The collection agency, shall we say, for the gifts that your clarity offers lies completely beyond your control and is part of the natural and instinctual action of the outworking of the pattern of third density upon your planet at this time. You do not have to be concerned about anything except moving into your process with faith in yourself and in the process.

Your query was about how to let go. There are, indeed, many times in the recurring and cyclical patterns of your spiraling process where you shall, indeed, as the one known as J said, find that there is undergrowth, brush, brambles and fallen limbs that have come down so that you are unable to walk where you had walked before. You must let go of the old route. You must find a new one. These points within your process seem fairly simple and yet the underbrush on a moor or heath[87] can come from many different sources. It might come because of an elemental storm; it might come because an animal has destroyed a tree in its efforts to get to the food that it holds; it might come because there is another third-density entity with whom you are interacting that has seemingly created this impenetrable underbrush where you can no longer find your path.

It could come from that which calls you from beyond, from the realms of love, from the realms of wisdom, or from the realms of unity. There are ideas that, once found, become the center of your life and these ideas can call you forward, as we said, beyond the veil of third density.

If you are excited and passionately energized by devotion to the one Creator and wish to sacrifice yourself and serve to the exclusion of all else, you are probably being called by love itself, that energy that this instrument knows as Jesus the Christ. There is much to learn from that energy of pure and unconditional love and, indeed, it is that central theme that calls everyone forward who wishes to graduate in service to others from third density to fourth density.

If you are passionately and actively involved in justice and fairness issues, it is likely that you are being called from the density of wisdom and being asked to examine the balance of these energies of wisdom within your own life. This energy is most positive, and yet, upon third-density Earth, the energies of fairness, equality and justice have been trammeled and mired in those lacks within entities to be able to see their own issues of unfairness and injustice.

If you are being called to examine the balance between love and wisdom, you are probably being called from sixth-density ideals.

It is not necessarily that you are a wanderer from fourth, fifth or sixth density, depending upon what excites you and makes you passionate. It is much more likely that there are energies within your plan for incarnation that are calling to you to focus on either pure love, pure wisdom, or achieving a better

---

[87] moor: a broad area of open land, often high but poorly drained, with patches of heath and peat bogs. And heath: an extensive tract of uncultivated open land covered with herbage and low shrubs; a moor.

balance between love and wisdom in your decision-making.

It sometimes helps, in terms of seeing into your incarnational pattern and the lessons that you have set for yourself, to identify where your ruling passions lie. You gave yourself these passions and these concerns as a gift. They will tend to drive your experience. But also be aware, my friends, that if you have a love pattern, a wisdom pattern, or a unity pattern, you will have distortions which are offshoots of this basic bias in your studies and in your learning.

Another part of the process that is, very much, something that you offered to yourself as a gift is the very challenging question of how to serve, given your gifts and your passions as well as your limitations. This is where you begin receiving contradictory and paradoxical impulses because of the various portions of your pattern not being, shall we say, in synch with each other. Sometimes, when a passion is too dearly or closely held, it can pull to you experiences for which you are not ready.

Much of what we have said to this group in times past about moving into meditation daily is based on our realization of your blindness in this regard. With the veil of forgetting laid carefully upon you, you have no way of seeing into your own subconscious thoughts. You have a limited ability to communicate with your subconscious through the medium of dreams and occasionally you may well get a waking vision, an image, or a quick sequence of visualized events that speaks to you with the authority that you can feel when deeper portions of yourself surface. And those pieces of information are very helpful. But for the most part you must move through this water dance that you do, and we use that term advisedly, without full knowledge of what the patterns with which you are working are. Consequently, we cannot say to you that such and such a time is the time to let go. We can only say to you that, indeed, it is part of the art of seeing into your process to trust your hunches and to follow them.

Say that you are coming to a time of cusp. There are many ways to discover this time of cusp. The easiest way is to allow it to come fully to cusp and then to decide spontaneously what to do next. This is a tried and true method of going through life and it works

well. It is not, however, the most skillful way to approach a time of cusp.

Now, we use this term, "time of cusp," because this instrument understands that there are times in the astrological year when any given spirit, having been born at a certain time, comes into various cusps. This is a technical term which she does not understand. We are using this term in the general sense which this instrument understands rather than in the specialized astrological sense.[88] However, for those who work with this material, who grasp by what is meant by this term, astrologically, it may actually be helpful for you to think in terms of the astrological cusps into which you enter.

When you are coming to an internally felt time of cusp, various characteristics emerge. You become focused on one particular portion of your experience at the expense of other portions of your experience. You become engaged and have an internal dialogue about this time of choice. You are aware of the intensification of the energies around you and it is often characteristic of such a time that you feel a sense of urgency.

When you experience the concatenation[89] of these various characteristics, you know that something is afoot. As we have said to the one known as T before, it is important to be sensitive to these times, to recognize them, to acknowledge them and to thank the Creator for giving you this time of choice. It is a time when it is well to invoke gratitude. Be thankful that such a time has come to you, for there are many, many times when you simply must wait. When a time of choice begins to crystallize in your spiral dance, this is actually a time of rejoicing. Much that you have done is now coming to fruition.

Indeed, much that others have done that you have harvested in your experience you now have the

---

[88] cusp: This definition matches the instrument's understanding of the term: the point formed by two intersecting arcs (as from the intrados of a Gothic arch). The astrological use of this word: a transitional point or time, as between two astrological signs.

[89] concatenation: the state of being linked together as in a chain; union in a linked series 2: the linking together of a consecutive series of symbols or events or ideas etc; "it was caused by an improbable concatenation of circumstances" 3: a series of things depending on each other as if linked together; "the chain of command"; "a complicated concatenation of circumstances" [syn: chain] 4: the act of linking together as in a series or chain.

opportunity to recreate as the gift that you give to those who come after you. Such is the nature of spiritual decision making. As you choose, as you polarize, as you seek and find the very best and highest path that you know, you are creating seeds of light that others shall be able to see by the roadside, help to bloom, and harvest the fruit of, in their turn.

Again, we pull you back from the intensely personal nature of times of choice to the realization that you are always doing impersonal work. Because a portion—and hopefully a growing portion—of who you are is the impersonal "I" that is the one infinite Creator's love and light flowing through you, not from you. The true letting go is the realization that it is not your choice entirely. It is the choice of the Creator and you are the Creator, choosing your universe and your creation. Allow that impersonal "I" to have its voice within you.

The one known as R was speaking earlier of experiencing a moment when she was at a retreat weekend which was designed to help entities meet the Christ, meet unconditional love, fully. She remembered something that this instrument had said, and, indeed, it was in actuality the quotation of part of a verse of a hymn that this instrument is very fond of singing. The words are those words which challenge entities to meet the Christ. They are, "Oh Jesus, thou art standing outside the fast closed door in lowly silence, waiting to cross the threshold o'er."

The song challenges people to open the door to their hearts. As we have said before, we say it again: we turn that image around and say to you that the Christ, unconditional love Itself, is waiting for you in the heart of your heart, in the holy of holies that is your inner sanctum. It is you who are knocking at the door. The Christ will always open that door to you. Knock, and you shall enter.

This is the basic letting go that we would recommend to you this day. Release the thought of fear for making a wrong decision. For your choices will follow you. You may make a decision that in hindsight you simply say was not a decision of the most service to you. However, it does not stop your forward progress to make what you might consider later to be an incorrect choice. It simply moves you into a pattern which is novel to you.

That is another thing to let go of: that judgment of self that would condemn you for making a wrong choice. Please realize, my friends, that when you are working in the dark, it is very, very easy to mis-see. It is standard operating procedure for entities within incarnation to make choices based on less than a full amount of information and therefore to move out of the most efficient pattern, shall we say, into a pattern that has more detail to it, more color, and certainly, to some extent, less clarity. If you are in one of those many-colored stained glass life situations, relax and cease all judgment of yourself.

You have created this pattern because there were things about it that appealed to you for one reason or another. Do not judge yourself in any way for having made those choices but rather start with the assumption that you have done a perfect job and that that which looks like a great big mess is actually a pattern that is too big for you to see at this time. Resolve to continue to gather information and meanwhile lean heavily into your knowledge that you have done a perfect job and that all is well. Your guidance is right there with you, waiting to be asked for help. But first rest in the unconditional love of your own heart. Become healed. Allow love to be you and you will find that you are ever more healed and ever more balanced.

Then, when you have rested and feel that energy within you, that energy that comes through you, springing forth and you know that you have the strength to examine ideas and to do analysis of the situation, use your mind and your intuition. Analyze your situation as many different ways as you can and begin to get a real resonance and an honest, authentic feeling or intuition about the deeper nature of your situation. Avail yourself of the guidance that is with you. And when you do see that it is good to release something from you, from your patterns of habit and usage, by all means do so.

What we think that you will find is that, for the most part, you will notice what you have let go of in hindsight because you are no longer grabbing for whatever it was that has now fallen away from you.

This instrument, for instance, was at one time extremely fond of chocolate and sweets in general and, indeed, had eaten so many sweets for so much of her life that her entire body chemistry was oriented to using sugar for carbohydrates. She was not doing her body any favors by eating in this manner. And at one point in her life she discovered herself putting into effect many changes in diet.

She missed her sweets up until one day when she noticed that she was not craving them any more. She was not looking at the menu in restaurants to see what desserts that they had first. She was actually looking at the food, the entrees, the salads: items which never appealed to her in her younger years when there were so many difficulties with eating because her body [failed to accept many foods.]

(Side one of tape ends.)

(Carla channeling)

Had she taken thought to give up sweets, she would have found herself in a terrible struggle. Instead she allowed the natural force of her body's reaction to the changes that she was making comfortably to carry her over some completely unseen precipice and into an entirely new area of her experience where she simply did not crave sweets.

Perhaps that is the thought with which we would leave you as we end this time of musing and pondering that we have shared with you. Perhaps it is not as necessary as you may think to make grand gestures, large decisions, and abstract choices. Perhaps it is well to be aware of times of crux, to be aware of the point of the cusp, and yet to allow the maximum amount of guidance to surround you in that environment of choice so that the choice almost makes itself in an organic and living way.

We realize that we have but scratched the surface of this question and we apologize for not finding ways to move deeper within the time limits of this instrument's energy. She is telling us at this time that we need to move into further questions that you might have at this time. Is there a query at this time? We are those of Q'uo.

J: I would like to ask Q'uo is it helpful to consider that positive thought, positive thinking, is a choice that helps to clear a path to the sort of purity of emotion that assists one in serving deeply and truly in a way that is harmonious with one's own truth of beingness as well as the truth of beingness with others, in a way that is non-invasive of others?

We are those of Q'uo, and are aware of your query, my sister. We would agree with you that the habit of positive thinking is a tremendous resource to the spiritual seeker and, indeed, a resource that shines not only, as the one known as J has said, on the self but on all whom that self touches.

What is it to choose positive thinking? Literally, it is to choose to think only positive thoughts. However, the choice goes beyond the surface, for to ask the mind to think only positive thoughts is to ask the mind to play itself false. For the mind creates many thoughts, some of which are positive and some of which are negative.

We are not suggesting that you edit out [those of] your thoughts which you consider less than positive. The one known as J was suggesting and we are suggesting something else entirely. We are suggesting that there are strains of truth that are deeper than circumstance. These strains of truth involve dynamics which—we correct this instrument—each of which are choices. The prayer of Saint Francis says it so clearly, that we will use this instrument's version of that prayer to demonstrate that which we mean.

The prayer goes like this,

> Lord, make me an instrument of your peace.
> Where there is hatred, let me sow love;
> Where there is injury, pardon;
> Where there is discord, union;
> Where there is doubt, faith;
> Where there is despair, hope;
> Where there is darkness, light;
> Where there is sadness, joy.
> Oh divine master, teach us to seek not so much to be loved as to love;
> To be understood as to understand;
> To be consoled as to console;
> For it is in pardoning that we are pardoned,
> It is in giving that we receive,
> And it is in dying that we rise to eternal life. [90]

Each of you knows what it is to be distressed but you also know what it is to be an instrument of peace, for you have done so. And you have done so by choice. All of you have had the experience of receiving disharmony from others and you have made that choice to give back love for discord.

All of you have taken sacrificial choices to give instead of ask, to love instead of seeking to be loved, and so forth.

You know from personal experience what it is like to invoke positive qualities that lie deep within your character. The one known as J is simply saying, and

---

[90] There are many variations of this prayer. This is the one which the instrument uses.

we would agree with her, that there is always within you an awareness, in any difficult situation, of some positive aspects on which you could call if you remembered to call.

You can, for instance, choose to take a difficult situation head on and simply offer thanks for receiving the situation. Thanksgiving and gratitude are like an inhalant to someone who has asthma. If you can breath in gratitude, your lungs begin to hold more air, more love, more light, more energy and more life.

Remembering to give thanksgiving for the breath that you take and the room that you take up on the planetary surface is most helpful in reorienting your thoughts.

What the process is all about is bringing yourself into a situation in which you have more control over the mechanisms of your being. If left to yourself, your personality shell, which is more or less integrated, will go off on a clumsy gallop, taking you and the cart and everything that you want to learn and have to offer in service with it. A great part of the spiritual process is becoming slowly more and more aware of the lightness and the looseness of the situation. It is not a heavy, crushing situation, even though it may seem so. Metaphysically speaking, it is very plastic, pliable situation with which you can work quite a bit, not in terms of how things are playing out in the physical illusion but in terms of how you are processing them and using them in your mind, in your emotions, and in your heart.

It is possible for an unexamined, confused situation to crush you so that you have almost no hope, no power to go on, and so forth. It is also possible with that same situation to do what little you can in your mind at any given time to remember who you are and take back your power from that which is crushing you. It does not matter when you are taking back your power whether or not you have the ability to affect the physical situation at that moment. Taking back your power as a soul or spirit is involved in remembering that you are not limited by life and death: you are a citizen of eternity. You are a creator and you have a creation that you can populate with the ideals and the beauties that you love. You can forgive the people or the situations that are crushing you.

The power to forgive is tremendous. You have the power to declare that a situation is as you see it and not as the world sees it. And by serenely sticking to your story you can save your mind, your emotions, and your heart of undergoing the crushing action of physical circumstance. This is not something that the world can understand easily. It is something for you to take within yourself and with [which you can] experiment.

We would ask you to experiment with taking your power back whenever you feel helpless and hopeless. Remember who you are and why you're here. Take courage and feel the dignity of your reality. You did not come here for casual purposes. You came here as a sacred journey and you are doing very well with it. Take pride in yourself. Have faith in your process. And know that your guidance is closer than your hands and feet and nearer to you than your next breath.

Is there a further query at this time, my sister?

J: No, thank you. Thank you, Q'uo.

We thank you, my sister. Is there another query at this time?

(Pause)

We find that we have used up your questioning for this time of seeking and so we shall leave this instrument and this group, thanking you all for the experience and for being able to serve. It has been a pleasure and a privilege. We leave you in the love and in the light of the one infinite Creator. We are known to you as the principle of Q'uo. Adonai, my friends. Adonai. ♣

L/L RESEARCH

L/L Research is a subsidiary of Rock Creek Research & Development Laboratories, Inc.

P.O. Box 5195
Louisville, KY 40255-0195

www.llresearch.org

Rock Creek is a non-profit corporation dedicated to discovering and sharing information which may aid in the spiritual evolution of humankind.

SPECIAL MEDITATION
JANUARY 16, 2006

Question from K: I would like to thank you for your presence and assistance. I would appreciate it if you would comment on the intentions my soul chose in coming into this incarnation. At this point in my life I wonder what I'm doing here. I feel I may be a sixth-density wanderer, but whether I am or not, I would appreciate any comments you might have, looking at my situation and offering me any information that might be right or helpful to me.

(Carla channeling)

We are those known to you as the principle of Q'uo. Greetings in the love and in the light of the one infinite Creator, in Whose service we come to you this day.

(Pause)

We are again with this instrument, having paused while this instrument pushed the buttons that create more volume in her speaker-phone. We hope that this change has enabled the one known as K to hear better.

We are with this instrument. We are those known to you as Q'uo. My sister, it is a great privilege and pleasure to be asked to join your circle of seeking at this time, and as well, we thank the ones known as Jim and Carla for being part of this beautiful, blended, sacred space of intention and energy. It is very good to share energy with you at this time and to join with you as we attempt to weave some

thoughts that may respond in a helpful way to your query.

Parenthetically, we would like to thank the one known as Carla for attempting to word questions in such a way that we are most effectively able to respond in a way that is perceived by the questioner to be helpful and to create a good resource for further exploration and study.[91] We are indeed very sensitive, as this instrument has said, to the wording of questions as well as to the energy behind that wording. Because of our sincere and deeply rooted interest in preserving the integrity of your own process, my sister, we are careful not to respond to active questions in such a way as to remove their activity within your process.

The one known as Carla had received a statement from the one known as K that she felt that she may be a sixth-density wanderer. The one known as Carla had written back to the one known as K that it might be better to state, "I am a sixth density wanderer. Can you confirm this?"

We would like to take the opportunity to express our appreciation of these differences in the wording. The one known as Carla is indeed correct, that we would have been unable to confirm a question about being a wanderer in which there was any lack of certainty

---

[91] Carla had worked carefully with K to get the best possible wording of her main question. The final version was accepted fairly close to the start of the session.

of that status expressed or inferred. However, we find that the solution that the one known as Carla and the one known as K reached is far better than either of the first two statements. For the one known as K has taken the opportunity to release that question from the stricture of depending upon her wanderer status. Therefore, we are free to respond in the fullest way possible, given the contents of the particular area of concern for the one known as K.

We hope that this excursion into parenthetical information such as this is helpful not only to the one known as K but to others who are attempting to form questions for the discernment of a channeling source such as ours. Little things are indeed important and every word needs to be considered before you place a question into the consciousness of one such as we who is not overly familiar with words and therefore must be very literal and [use] every caution when it comes to interpreting questions.

In gazing at the agenda, shall we say, of your higher self and your soul, as you, together, prepared for your insertion into incarnation upon planet Earth, we find that you and your guidance system created an exquisitely balanced and effectual plan for your incarnation.

It is often the case, when an entity asks us concerning the progress of an incarnational plan, that there is a certain amount of expectation, on the part of the soul asking the question, that there will be a fairly steady rhythm of activity throughout the incarnation, which has a fairly single, simple, unitary direction.

When a period of significant length occurs within an incarnation where there is no perceived activity or forward motion, we find that it is quite normal and quite understandable, in fact, for the entity to question whether the incarnational plan is still on track.

We can confirm to the one known as K that her energies, her agenda, and the structure that she has prepared for herself for what she and those present would call your future are on task, on target, and resting in the loving and compassionate hands that hold you, together with your guidance system, in an embrace of creative love, light and thought.

The challenges of the first portion of the lifetime have been addressed. There is ongoing to this entity a series of excursions exploring avenues of learning as well as avenues of further service to the one infinite Creator as well as [to the] entities which surround the one known as K.

There are times in any entity's incarnation when there is perceived to be a time of waiting. We find in this instrument's mind that her opinion is that waiting times are the hardest times of all. Even when one is fighting for one's life, if one is active, one does not have the concern and the worry which is present when one is unable to do anything. The culture of which you are a part is most fond of doing things. It is used to activity. When there is energy being expended in the doing, it is easier for entities such as this instrument to rest in the knowledge that all that can be done is being done. This is very comforting to this instrument.

Conversely, when there does not seem to be anything to do in a certain situation and it seems as if the only reasonable response is simply to wait for further information or inspiration, time hangs heavy. It is easy to begin to doubt the self and to wonder whether one is still pursuing with all possible speed and urgency the good work that [one] has been given during the incarnation to do.

We would ask the one known as K to look beneath the surface of times of waiting such as the one through which she is now going. Encourage within yourself, my sister, the faith that you are on target and on task. Fortifying your own self-confidence and faith within yourself will create a freedom within you that releases you from concern and worry. We believe this shift in your frame of mind will, in and of itself, be very helpful in recreating the atmosphere and environment in which you live and move, in terms of your mental and emotional processes, and make it far more easy for you to rest, spiritually and metaphysically speaking, within the structure of safety and guidance that your open and loving heart offers to you.

Become more aware, as you are given the light to do so, of the several different energies moving into and through your life at this time. There are threads of thought that you may helpfully pursue in terms of your own spiritual evolution. As well, there are energies within your life that are concluding the bulk of their relevance to your service at this time. And, as is to be expected, at the same time there are threads of thoughts and ideas concerning possible directions which are new to you or somewhat novel to you, in terms of service to others, that are opening and coming into your life at this time for you to consider as possible ways for you to create and re-create your own unique and special brand of love and service to the Creator and to the people around you.

Please be aware, my sister, that it is misleading, when thinking of your planetary agenda, to overemphasize the work of that agenda. To put it another way, some of the activities of your agenda are not activities involved in doing. They are activities increasingly involved, as you mature spiritually within incarnation, in being.

There are qualities to the essence of your nature that are clear, clarion and of the utmost beauty. You have, as one of your goals within incarnation, hoped increasingly to refine that beauty. Your criticism of yourself has been that you have too highly colored your soul nature through subtle biases which are extremely attractive and aesthetically lovely. However, your own suggestion to yourself before incarnation involved reexamining the coloration of some of these beautiful energies which you possess.

You wished to find within yourself the very heart and center of these beautiful aspects, cleansing from them excessive coloration and instead welcoming into these aspects of yourself an increasing amount of transparency that is able to carry the full energy of the love and the light of the one infinite Creator. You were, in other words, hoping to refine your signal and to increase its power.

We are speaking of you as if you were a radio station or some sort of signal attempting to beam out into the surrounding space. This is, in fact, the case except that you are working in time/space, or the metaphysical universe, as you work with the qualities of your being. Therefore, we would suggest not that you reject or criticize any part of yourself but that you look at and evaluate each aspect of yourself in an ongoing and fairly light-hearted matter, gathering information, observing patterns in your thinking and slowly becoming aware at an ever deeper level of the overarching and undergirding aspects of self that reflect up into your everyday expression but have their roots in soul and spirit energies that redound into the invisible realms which shake off space and time and dwell, rather, in eternity.

In sum, we would simply ask you to have full faith in yourself. You are exactly correct in saying that whether or not you are a wanderer you still request the same information. And that is something that we would share with all who are aware of their wanderer nature. Please be aware that there are very special aspects of your being that you carry because of your previous experience in higher densities. However, please also be aware that in accepting the challenge of incarnation on planet Earth in third density at this time, you have localized and grounded your soul energies into a very specific place, time and structure. You now are part of the tribe of planet Earth. Its destiny is your own. Its lessons are yours to express.

You may well have an enhanced ability to understand, mentally and abstractly, the gist of the challenge of choice that is the work of all who are in third density at this time. No matter what your prior status, however, you now have the common task of responding to the challenge of choice. What shall your choice be: the radiance of service to others or the magnetism of service to self?

We know that the one known as K has chosen, and chosen with a great purity of dedication. Therefore, it only remains to awaken each day with the realization that this is the day for expressing that choice. This is the opportunity to live the love and the light of the one infinite Creator in every breath, thought and action that shall never come again.

Coming into the present moment and remembering who you are and why you are here are the two key concepts that we feel we may leave with you at this time. They are simple. They are not new. And yet to come into the present moment and to know who you are are two keys of remembering and affirming that ground you into reality. That is the best possible environment for your spiritual growth.

Is there another query at this time?

K: Q'uo, you often comment that a major lesson for many wanderers who are incarnated right now in third density is to balance love and wisdom. You have often referred to Jehoshua, the Christ, as demonstrating the highest expression of love but perhaps not [of] wisdom. Is there any example of someone known to us in third density who has balanced love and wisdom?

We are those known to you as the principle of Q'uo, and are aware of your query, my sister. You will pardon us if we spend some time working with this instrument's breath and swallowing as she is dealing with a sinus infection at this time and we must take pains to clear her air passages at times.

(Pause)

Sorting through this instrument's mind to see the characters on the world stage of whom she is aware, we would choose two entities about whom to speak with you this day. The first is the [one known as] Lao-Tzu. In terms of personal details, this entity is lost in the fabric of pre-history, having been a part of an ancient culture at a time when that culture was far closer to its heyday. The writings of this teacher were cryptic and brief and yet we would recommend them to one who wishes to look for the twin strains of love and wisdom appearing in a balanced manner.[92] The characteristic of such energy reflected into third density is that characteristic known as paradox or self-contradiction. You may fruitfully see those characteristics played out in this entity's writing.

In the balance between love and wisdom, there is always the quality of paradox. The key to understanding such writings within third density is to focus on the common ground that is held by both self-contradictory ways of thinking that are the dynamics of a particular bit of writing. When you look for the commonality in such dynamics, you can begin to see the direction of thinking which is the special province of one who is working with the concept of the unifying principle undergirding both love and wisdom.

The other character whose name we would mention at this time is that of Mahatma Gandhi.[93] This entity was an entity which came into incarnation to work upon that balance between love and wisdom as a sixth-density wanderer. This entity worked substantially in his early life in areas of fairness and justice. At a later point in this entity's life he founded a spiritual community. And in the third phase of this entity's life he worked to ground an entire nation of diverse people in that sweet spot or common area that is indwelt both by love and wisdom.

He found ways to encourage fairness and justice while never releasing concerns for love itself. In the writings and actions of this entity also lie valuable lessons in the keys to combining love and wisdom in creative and sustainable ways.

Is there another query at this time?

K: In our last session, you gave very detailed information on how to contact my guidance system and I do thank you. However, these instructions rely heavily on the capacity to visualize and this is an ability that is very difficult for me. I most frequently cannot accomplish it. Could you please comment on whether you perceive any difficulty or malfunction in my capacity to visualize? And could you please offer any guidance on how to increase this ability? I've tried over many years to cultivate this ability because intuition and higher psychic ability seem to rely heavily on visualization skills. I feel very frustrated in this quest and I feel this lack of skill really impedes my growth.

We are those known to you as the principle of Q'uo, and are aware of your query, my sister. Our first concern is to assure you that you are not impeded in your growth because of a perceived difficulty in visualization ability. If that were so, my sister, this instrument would have joined you as she herself has almost no native ability to visualize.

We realize that this statement may seem less than clear to you since it is this instrument's experience in visualizing her working place that we used in speaking to you about creating your own place of working. However, it is true that this instrument does not have a native capacity to achieve a three-dimensional visualization. If she attempts to visualize, for instance, a map of how to get somewhere, she is almost certain to be 90 degrees wrong. Not completely [i.e. 180 degrees] wrong but more confusedly than that, only 90 degrees wrong. She has demonstrated this again and again in her driving skills.

Similarly, she is not able to visualize, mentally, a three-dimensional structure such as a cube or circle and then rotate or work with it visually as do those who work with solid geometry. As well, she is not able, when shown the blueprint of a machine or of a house, to be able to use that information. There is, in fact, a block that she set in place before incarnation concerning doing these things. She has never questioned the block because she works

---

[92] Two web sites that seem useful are these. For information about Lao-Tzu, use this site, www.yakrider.com/Tao/laotzu.htm. When you are ready to dip into the text, use this site, www.nokama.com/tao/.

[93] Two web sites on Gandhi that seem good to me (Carla) are www.mkgandhi.org/ and www.mahatma.org.in/index.jsp.

around it. It has not seemed to her to be worthy of question. Indeed, we would agree with her. On the level at which she is working, there is no need for her to understand anything about why she would have placed these limitations within her mind.

We do not suggest that you begin a search for why this is true of you as well. We would rather suggest that you, like this instrument, find ways to work around the limitations of your mental abilities.

Now, how does one work around the inability to visualize in any linear or literal way? What we have suggested to this instrument before and what we suggest to you now is that you retain confidence in yourself when you receive a very small piece of information. When, for instance, you are attempting to visualize your favorite place, it is not necessary for you to make up a place, it is only necessary for you to choose your favorite place and then to accept that place as you know it and as you can see it, as an acceptable version or vision of that about which you are working.

When you are attempting to see your guidance system, you may take a very small impression or hunch about the nature of your guidance system. Trust that much and speak it out to yourself, either mentally or by writing the information down. Say you have simply received the impression that this is a male entity. Given that you were asking to see the male aspect of your guidance system, this may not seem to be a very important piece of information. But it is what has been able to come through the veil to your consciousness. It is a gift. Accept it. You have a male. You can sketch in your mind the clothing and appearance of a male of uncertain age. You have that much.

Use that much, not asking for more but being open to more. Each time that you invoke that male portion of your guidance system, you shall perhaps receive just a bit more of an impression. Whatever you receive, ground it by repeating it, writing it, or otherwise becoming familiar with it. Trust it, accept it, and act on it. By repetition you will gradually be awakening and sharpening your ability to see in ways that you have not seen before.

This instrument almost never receives a clear, inner, visual picture of what she is doing or to whom she is talking. She accepts the impressions that she is given, and as we have said, by repetition she has begun to become able to accept the basic images that are a

part of her visualization process as given and then to make note of anything new that she may see in the visualization process. And, indeed, we use the term "see" in a non-literal sense.

For instance, this instrument had the impression [during tuning for the session today,] when she called forth her male and female guidance—those aspects of the Holy Spirit, in other words, that have to do with love and with wisdom—that both the male and the female figures were wearing white. And, indeed, they were not wearing dresses and pants, they were both wearing robes. This instrument did not question this impression but spoke to herself, saying that she felt that this probably indicated that the entity that was connected with the channeling—that is, the one known as K—was in essence a priest or a spiritually mature, magical being that was calling for information on the level of a priest or a ceremonial magician. This created a feeling of great comfort and sympathy within this instrument because she herself is of a priestly and magical nature although she is not a practicing priest nor does she practice ceremonial magic. Her basic nature, however, is one which is comfortable with the specifically spiritual or monastic in energy, in service, and in learning.

It is this kind of patient, slow working, depending heavily on repetition, that we believe will open up to you the skill and the art of interior impressions and how to record them within your conscious mind. You might perhaps be helped in this regard by an experience this instrument has had recently with Rudolph Steiner's Eurhythmic Dance.[94] Part of the system of dance that is called Eurhythmy is a practice of moving rhythmically across a large space, going forward, focusing on making certain motions and sounds. At the end of doing that particular exercise, the end of that exercise is involved in moving backwards without looking over one's shoulder. One walks backward to the place from which one began, which is a chair, and one then sits without looking for that chair. The first time this instrument did this, she sat down rather abruptly on the floor. The second time this instrument did this, she knew enough to feel with her legs when she got to the place where she thought the chair was for where the chair was.

---

[94] A good web site for becoming familiar with Rudolph Steiner's Eurhythmy is www.rsarchive.org/Eurhythmy/.

Indeed, it turned out that this instrument has a tendency to sway off to the left of a chair when she is moving backwards. This instrument realized that, having two stress fractures in her right foot, she was limping a bit and therefore moving away from a straight line backwards.

(Side one of tape ends.)

(Carla channeling)

Telling herself please to compensate for this out-of-balance condition of the physical body, she was able on her third try to touch the edge of the chair with the back of her knees and was able therefore to sit down safely to begin the next part of this dancing exercise. Through repetition this instrument has begun to feel as though she can see the chair that is behind her. It is as though this aspect of the Steiner exercises has awakened the vision in her back.

Logically, linearly speaking, there is no vision in the back of the head or in the back. Nevertheless, the Steiner exercise is slowly working to increase her ability and the ability of her very human body to be aware of the environment about it.

We hope that this discussion has provided the one known as K with sufficient inklings and ideas that she may follow through with that so that she is able to become more comfortable and to make more progress with this way of seeing. It is indeed a kind of seeing that your culture does not recognize at all. There is nothing in the life experience of your culture that would help you to awaken the visualization ability. The things within your culture that are more able than others to awaken the ability to visualize are the reading of stories and the imagination that creates the seeing of those stories coming alive in one's head. Telling oneself one's own stories is a very helpful exercise in awakening the visualizing ability.

Most of all, it is well simply to trust the self and to trust the impressions of information which are given by the self to the self when in a focused state.

May we ask if there are any follow-up queries at this time? We are those of Q'uo.

K: Thank you again, as always. And no, I don't have any follow ups. You have been very helpful.

We are those of Q'uo, and are aware that you were speaking, my sister, but this instrument's ears were not able to pick up that which you said. May we ask

if you could repeat that which you said before? We are those of Q'uo.

K: Yes, of course. I was saying, thank you, the answers that you gave were very helpful and complete and I appreciate your service very much. And everybody else who is present, especially Carla and Jim. And no, I have no further follow-ups at this time.

We are those of Q'uo, and are aware that you do not have any follow-up queries at this time. In that case, my sister, may we let our hearts overflow with our thanks to you. It has been such a pleasure to be with you, to share the energies of this group, and to rest in your sacred space that you have created together in this circle of seeking.

Thank you for allowing us to share our humble opinions with you. As always, we would ask that you guard your own thoughts carefully and not listen to any of our thoughts if they do not seem to you very resonant, lively and useful. If you will guard your own perceptions and discriminate carefully between thoughts that are helpful and those which need to be left behind, we cannot express our appreciation enough, for that clears us of our concern that we might infringe upon your free will.

We leave you in the love and in the light of the one infinite Creator. We are known to you as the principle of Q'uo. Adonai. Adonai. ☙

L/L RESEARCH

L/L Research is a subsidiary of
Rock Creek Research &
Development Laboratories, Inc.

P.O. Box 5195
Louisville, KY 40255-0195

www.llresearch.org

Rock Creek is a non-profit
corporation dedicated to
discovering and sharing
information which may aid in
the spiritual evolution of
humankind.

SPECIAL MEDITATION
JANUARY 20, 2006

Question chosen by PLW poll:[95] Q'uo, so much of the new age rhetoric that I've been hearing on the internet the past few months is very similar to dialog we shared ten years ago on our on-line spiritual study groups. They talk of ascension, dimensional shifts, earth awakening, the arrival of the Aquarian Age, and so forth. There is clearly a cycle to all this and different waves of people appear to be initiated into the ideas annually. I can remember a decade when spiritual brothers and sisters were "ascending" and leaving our study groups to go back into the world and take on new tasks. Please talk about the different waves of ascension and the why and how of the way it affects us all so differently. I am fascinated at the different time-lines to this. I have a sense that ascension of some kind has been taking place since the beginning of time. Please offer any comments that you might have about this.

(Carla channeling)

We are those known to you as the principle of Q'uo. Greetings in the love and the light of the one infinite Creator, in Whose service we come to you this day. We thank the ones known as S1, S2 and Carla for forming this circle of seeking today. It is a great privilege to be asked to join your circle and to speak with you about these buzzwords of the New Age: ascension, dimensional shift, and the Aquarian Age. We are most happy to do so.

We ask, as always, that each use their discrimination in listening to our thoughts. If the thoughts seem good to you, please use them. If they do not, please drop them and move on without looking back. We would not wish to create a stumbling block in your own experience. If you will guard your discrimination carefully then we will feel free to share our opinions without being concerned that we might infringe upon your free will. We thank you for this consideration.

It is an interesting thing to speak concerning this topic, because the surface aspect of the topic is indeed full of clichés and buzzwords. If one moves beneath the surface of this topic, however, one finds an authentic thread of information that is part of what this instrument would call the eternal wisdom.

There are indeed cycles upon your sphere, within your solar system, and within your galaxy that are impinging upon your Earth at this time. It is an amazing time of the collection of the old and its eventual disposal and the dawning of a new heaven and a new earth. It is, indeed, that time that has been predicted and discussed for many of your centuries and even millennia. It has been a part of the indigenous culture of several of your religious and cultural systems.

Depending upon the source who is studying these systems, they are [classified as] either religious or mythical. However, the basic concept, of there being cycles of time that cover thousands of your years and

---

[95] Planet Lightworker Magazine (www.planetlightworker.com).

that have to do with the perception of the stars and their courses, is a part of the very fabric of all of the cultures of your planet. There are very few of your peoples that do not have, in one way or another, the stories of large portions of time within which entities proceed until they come to the end of the perceived time of things being as they are. There is at that time a sea change. One tide goes out and another comes in. And there is a new way of experiencing time and space, as we have discussed with this particular group.

The cycle that is now ending is marked as ending approximately at the end of the year 2012. It is indeed, among other things, a cycle that is astrological in nature, where there is a shift in the energy that is at the heart or the womb of the space/time continuum, as this instrument would call it. The energy has shifted almost entirely as we now speak.

The departing energy is an energy that has the nature of water, which is the nature of your body and the nature of so much of your planet. It is shifting over to an energy that has to do with air and fire, and these energies are interpenetrating the basic third-density energy, shall we say, of water. This is causing tremendous changes in your planet and in your body systems as that very watery medium, that is the interior of your body, experiences the tremendous interpenetration of the new energies.

This is, in general, the larger cycle about which we would talk at this time. It is, as we said, an authentic change of the way the core of your experience comes to you. You are one of the last generations of those who experience third density in a third-density activated body. There are upon your planet at this time many entities that have a dual activated body, their energy bodies being activated in third density and fourth density.

And this brings us to the discussion of a whole different set of cyclic patterns that the questioner has observed, quite accurately we feel. Let us talk about some of these cycles of those who are approaching the information for the first time. This instrument, being in her sixties, is one of the early type of wanderers that no longer are coming among you. This instrument and many, indeed, millions of those who were called to the travail of your planet, came among you as pioneers of a kind. They choose to incarnate in third-density bodies, but they also chose to come into third density with a certain degree of awareness of their home densities, which were mostly of those of fifth-density and sixth-density social memory complexes.

There are a few fourth-density positively-oriented wanderers among you at this time, but, for the most part, if you are a wanderer you are probably from the density of wisdom or from the density of unity, that density in which wisdom and love are balanced.

Indeed, the majority of those who are among you at this time as positively-oriented wanderers are those from the sixth density. And your interest in coming to the Earth at this time was to improve the balance of love and wisdom in your active, conscious personality.

The reason this was so attractive to you is that within the boot camp atmosphere of third density you can get a lot done in a short time if you have the dedication of your will to a chosen and carefully manicured or articulated goal. The key is continually to review your goal and dedication so that you maintain a focus over time.

The great difficulty with wanderers of this type is that they may fail to wake up to who they are. Many of those among your wanderer population on this planet have indeed not awakened. However, under the pressure of the increasing dynamic between the new fourth-density energy and the old third-density energy, the polarity that is native to each of your systems is being tweaked and prodded by the dynamic energies so that it becomes more and more obvious to entities that there is something going on to which they need to wake up. That is one large generation of those to whom this information is especially important and attractive.

The next wave of entities which came upon your planet is of those which arrived in births during the 60s and 70s. These were an intermediate type of wanderer whose goals were not so much oriented to work in consciousness within their own personalities. These were personalities who were still hearing the travail of planet Earth as the planet itself became more and more reactive to the energies of hostility and aggression that have been increasing among your global population in response to the increasing dynamic betwixt the light and the dark, that is which is to come and that which is ending.

These entities were less concerned with their own studies in learning and more concerned, in a more urgent fashion or more of a feeling of urgency to wake up and create a shift in consciousness among the tribes of Earth. Among these wanderers, there is a tendency to be overly concerned with the urgency of the situation. In so many cases the problem is not waking them up but rather moving them to a more balanced and calm point of view where their very real skills can be used more fully. And so, to this very large bunch of wanderers, we find the challenges of awakening being very slight but the challenges of spiritual maturity to be much larger.

The third generation of those who have moved into the energies of planet Earth at this time from other places in space and time are those pioneers of fourth density who have wandered here with the firm intention of helping not only the planet's people, but the planet itself. These entities are equipped with the ability to withstand a tremendous amount of disharmony and chaos. They do not do this with a great deal of native joy, but their makeup is such that they are capable of independent action and have little use for the traditional kind of authority which expresses itself in your established religions and those cultural icons such as the classical philosophies and so forth. To these entities, the Earth itself is speaking.

These entities are often called the Indigo Children or the Crystal Children. There are many words that try to describe the difference betwixt this generation of wanderers and previous ones. The hallmark of this breed is an insensitivity to traditional modes of expressing religious dedication while maintaining a great sensitivity and an authentic feeling for the most intensive kind of work in consciousness that is chosen by the self for the self and created as an individual expression rather than there being a great desire to become a part of an already established religion.

Nevertheless, in this last generation of wanderers there remains a feeling for the group. So you will find entities in all three generations whose interest includes the desire to reconnect with their families.

This group of large groups constitutes the wanderer population of planet Earth.

We naturally encourage all wanderers to awaken and to be aware that entities that they meet may well be entities [of] their larger group, since there are millions of wanderers upon Earth. They have in common a tremendous love for the planet, for its people and for the Creator and a serene and undisturbed belief and faith, in an unconscious and carefully protected part of the personality shell, that they are in the Creator's service and part of the godhead principle.

There is a small group of entities who are native to the planet Earth. These entities have won through, in some cases, to graduation and have indeed graduated but have decided to move back into third-density incarnation to see what they can do to bring the rest of the people of the planet along with them in embracing the light.

Then there are people who come from many different places, who have entered your planetary system as souls from other third-density planets that have failed to complete their third density. These include entities from the planet you know as Mars, where they were unable to finish out third density because of creating conditions that made their third-density planet uninhabitable. These entities have in common with the Indigo wanderers a great desire to be stewards of planet Earth, to stop the destruction of the planet that your people have thoughtlessly promulgated over the last 200 or so of your years and to restore and constitute a healthy third density to leave behind as third-density [as] planet Earth closes itself out.

This will not occur suddenly in terms of there being a necessity for a sudden change of third to fourth density. Rather, there will be a time of between one and three hundred of your years, from the probability/possibility vortices at which we now look, where your peoples will be able to continue to incarnate in third density to continue to heal the planet and to harvest those entities who are ready now to choose light over darkness, love over fear, and the lessons of the compassionate heart over the lessons of self interest. These are the cycles that we see at this time.

The great cycle is that cycle of almost 76,000 years that coincides with your astrological periods. During this 76,000-year period, your Earth has had three harvests, what this instrument would call three minor cycles. Third density is made up of three of these minor cycles. Your third cycle has now matured. Its patterns are being seamlessly finished. Each of your entities is choosing, at a soul level, their choice of polarity, their choice of service, and their choice of learning.

We are here to speak with those who have chosen at this time to polarize to service to others, to attempt to find out how [to] open the heart and to seek the truth of that heart. We are here to help you in any way that we can with that task. It is a formidable one. It has been a pleasure to work with groups such as this one for some of your years now.

We have seen a tremendous dawn break upon your planet. We realize that the outer picture remains grim. We ask you to look beyond the surface. Those who are in power upon your planet have a great tendency to be oriented to service to self. It is natural for this to be so at this time, as the dynamic between service to others and service to self becomes more and more obvious. However, this does not have much to do with life as lived by the majority of those upon your planet.

In general we see the peoples of your planet awakening in record numbers all over the globe. It is very exciting to see and feel the energies of the people stir and to become aware of the fact that there is something happening of which they can be a part, that it is truly positive, and that it will truly change the face of the Earth. It is a dim awareness but there is a stirring that cannot now be put back to bed.

And those among your people who are indeed service to self are most troubled to feel the muscularity and the power of the awakening of the tribes of Earth. It is occurring. Groups small and large have begun banding together for positive purposes, not to gain power or to maintain power, but to share power with those who are powerless. That time is now arriving when the last shall be first, the hungry shall be fed, and the rich shall be sent empty away.[96]

It is a time of rejoicing, for it is the herald of a new day. There is a great deal of difficulty that is inherent in the changing of the guard. Your planet will continue to go through difficulties. The weather will

be disturbed as the natural processes of your planetary change are pursued in an inevitable and appropriate manner. Do not be dismayed.

This is a time that may try you physically. You may be caught in difficult weather or in times of trouble where people are without [electrical] power and have to respond to the trauma through which the planet itself is going as it releases a good deal of what this instrument would describe as hot air.

There is a tremendous amount of heat that has been stored in the planet through its natural process of cooling. As the planet expands, there are bands of points of heating that must come up through the crust of the planet and express the extraneous heat, so that the planet itself does not break apart. This has changed your weather patterns.

The tendencies of your more developed cultures to misuse high technology and create further difficulties with the air, the water, and the earth in terms of its organic balance have accentuated these natural processes of planetary change.

So for you who are in incarnation at this time, these cycles have created an interesting and challenging environment in which you can guarantee that things will not stay the same. There is a feeling of planetary change in the climate as well as in the climate of the emotions of the heart of the people.

We would encourage you at this time to realize that you are here, not to be concerned with these changes, not to react in fear of them but rather to lend to this environment, which could be distressing for many, the comfort of your faith. Many are listening and looking for some indication that there is hope and a positive expectation possible for those upon planet Earth at this time. And so we would say to you that if you are awake and if you wish to serve, you are in an excellent position to do so, simply by being who you are.

Please see yourself as magical, powerful parts of the godhead principle. You are spiritual entities who have chosen to take flesh for very laudable purposes at this time, and we do praise you for having the courage to come into incarnation at a time that is very challenging to the senses.

For whose who would wish to remain safe and unchallenged, this is a difficult time. We ask you to respond to these waves of intense energy that you are feeling not with fear but with faith. Take this

---

[96] This is a rough quote from part of Mary's words when her angel told her she was to give birth. These words were made into a song, the *Magnificat*, so named because in Latin, the quote begins "My soul doth magnify the Lord." The precise quote, as found in the Episcopalian Hymnal, is: "He hath filled the hungry with good things and the rich he hath sent empty away."

opportunity to stand on your own two feet and remember who you are and why you are here. As you breathe in and as you breathe out you are little lighthouses, able to take that breath and that energy of life and bless it with your firm intention to serve. The glow and the radiance of your beings shall be a beacon for many. You do not have to explain, or discuss, or *do* anything to be light workers at this time. You have only to be yourselves and to know yourselves. So we would ask you to investigate and explore who you are and why you are here. We thank you for this question and at this time we would ask if there are any questions with which you would [wish] to follow up. We are those of Q'uo.

(Pause)

We find that there are no more questions at this time. We thank you for calling this circle. It has been our pleasure to be a part of your meditation and we have greatly enjoyed the beauty of your vibrations. We are known to you as the principle of Q'uo. We leave you in the love and the light of the one infinite Creator. Adonai. Adonai. ❦

L/L RESEARCH

L/L Research is a subsidiary of Rock Creek Research & Development Laboratories, Inc.

P.O. Box 5195
Louisville, KY 40255-0195

www.llresearch.org

Rock Creek is a non-profit corporation dedicated to discovering and sharing information which may aid in the spiritual evolution of humankind.

© 2009 L/L RESEARCH

SPECIAL MEDITATION
JANUARY 23, 2006

Question from P: Q'uo, I continually live with the feeling that I'm missing something critical in the understanding of what my purpose is for having incarnated on Earth. Because of this unease, my life is one of constant questioning, searching for answers and explanations, and an overall lack of peace and wellbeing. Because I don't have a sense of purpose or even feel that I belong here—alive, living on Earth—I feel I've not learned key lessons properly in regards to right activity, right companionship, right home, knowing my true identity, and loving myself. I feel I am a woman-child, locked in my own world with myself and by myself. I sense that I'm not dealing with or conscious of how to scatter the ashes of the past and walk through the threshold of the future joyfully in order for the maturation and harvest to unfold. Please offer guidance and assistance as you look at my situation and offer thoughts and spiritual principles you feel will help me on my individual path to self-realization. Thank you.

(Carla channeling)

We are those known to you as the principle of Q'uo. Greetings in the love and in the light of the one infinite Creator, in Whose service we come to you this day. Thank you for the privilege of asking us to be a part of this circle of seeking. We, however, ask you a favor and that is that you use your discrimination very carefully in listening to our thoughts. Sometimes our thoughts are helpful and we certainly hope that our thoughts will be helpful

to you but we do not always hit the nail on the head, shall we say, and we want you to realize that we may not speak words that mean a lot to you. If they do not resonate to you, please leave them behind and do not try to work with them. If you will use your discrimination in this way we will feel far more free to speak with you without being concerned that we will infringe upon your free will or be a stumbling block in your process. We thank you for this consideration.

My sister, our first consideration upon receiving your query is to reassure you that you have not lost your way. You have not wasted time. There are ways in which perhaps we may be able to offer you resources and we are glad to do so. But our first concern is simple encouragement and reassurance.

We are aware that you feel isolated, indeed, to an extreme, where you are not only isolated from the normal companionship that so many entities upon planet Earth find very easy and almost unnoticeable to achieve but also that feeling of isolation even from parts of yourself. There is a hunger within you to integrate all of those elements of self that exist within your skin and to find some comfortable arrangement which makes you feel whole, complete and, as this instrument would say, comfortable in your own skin.

This isolation is a natural and normal part of the personality shell experienced by an entity who has awakened within the dream of Earth to the knowledge that there is a great deal more in heaven and Earth than has been dreamt of by most peoples' philosophies. Some of those who have these feelings are called wanderers. Their isolation comes from the experience of coming from higher densities where the situation as regards being aware of the inner thoughts and feelings of the self and other selves is extremely open compared with the guarded and veiled realizations and expressions of unity available to those upon planet Earth in third density.

Others, being Earth natives and not being from higher densities, nevertheless having awakened, feel similarly isolated.

Whether or not you have a past that is involved with relationships with those in higher densities, your experience at this time is typical of what this instrument has often called, "the wanderer's blues." Once having awakened, one cannot go back to sleep. Once one has realized that one is on a journey that cannot be circumscribed by life and death, one cannot go home again. Such is the experience of the wanderer.

The good news for such entities is that they are not permanently locked in such isolation, nor are they alone. The key to the door behind which you find yourself isolated is a cluster of realizations which we will attempt to discuss with you. We welcome your queries at the end of our discussion to further particularize that which you wish to know.

We find that your experience at this time is that which occurs when an entity who is attempting to accelerate her rate of evolution of mind, body and spirit reaches a critical point in her journey. Indeed, my sister, you have been at this critical point for some time but you have not known how to move forward because of a very understandable linkage of spiritual understanding with cultural understanding.

The culture of which you are a part identifies moving forward with action. In order to progress, there needs to be some marker that indicates that action has been taken and has been taken successfully.

However, you are not attempting to work in the world of space/time. You are not attempting to change anything in the physical world. Your prey lies in the land of the metaphysical and is part of what this instrument would call the time/space continuum. You are attempting to work in the inner worlds where instead of the illusion of matter you are dealing directly with energy and instead of physical things, you are working with thoughts. This is the realm of mystery, paradox and spirituality. And it is a world that you know very well.

However, the nature of movement forward in this particular world is other than you have suspected. And we would attempt at this time to share a few thoughts with you that are intended to help you to see what our thinking is here.

We would start our discussion with the red-ray energy center. There are blockages within any entity's system starting with the red ray and moving upward. And in your case, my sister, we find that you have an over-activation and a blockage in combination within the red-ray energy center created by your feeling, on an unconscious level, that you have erred and made mistakes. This has contracted your survival mechanisms and has created for you a situation in which you are frequently and instinctively in the position of feeling the emotions and physical sensations involved with the fight or flight mechanism. It is a signal that has gone wrong within your energy system.

We would like to note at this point that we would not condemn [you] or express the feeling that you have made a mistake in creating this blockage. We would wish to point out to you that the dedication, the love, and the courage that you have shown in being persistently and determinedly concerned to fulfill your mission and your purpose within this incarnation is quite commendable. That it has inadvertently placed you in a situation where your energy system is somewhat off-balance is simply part of that which you are taking in as catalyst and that which you will work out in time and with love as part of your spiritual journey upon planet Earth during this incarnation.

Since you are very well aware of blockages that you have experienced both in the orange-ray chakra of personal relationships and the yellow-ray chakra of legal relationships such as marriage, we will simply note that we would agree with you that there have been imbalances in these energy centers which have produced for you an untold bounty of suffering and have given you much information and learning which you have used to a great extent with a dispassionate and objective intention of harvesting every bit of learning and service that you could from each experience. Again we commend you, my sister.

The crux that faces you at this time lies within the green-ray or heart chakra. There would seem to be, to the untutored eye, a unified and holistic heart that awaits the one who approaches the gateway to the open heart. However, in point of fact, the heart chakra has two distinct levels. We would call them the outer courtyard of the heart and the inner sanctum of the heart.

You come into the outer courtyard of your own heart when you are ready at last to face your shadow self. Whatever you have not yet recognized or developed within your full personality, meets you in the courtyard of the open heart. It is here that you will find your shadow self. In order to enter the inner sanctum of your own heart, you must do the work of greeting, understanding, accepting, feeling compassion for, and eventually redeeming every bit of undeveloped light that is a part of yourself.

It is our belief that each entity is the Creator. Just as a holographic image can be seen by any part of that image and reflect the whole, so are you a holographic spark of the one infinite Creator. Therefore, as you move into the inner sanctum of your heart, you need to carry your entire self with you.

This is the crux that you now face. The part of yourself which you must now redeem we would characterize to you only very vaguely by saying that you have high expectations of yourself, and this has created for you a distortion in the way you experience yourself.

You have been a judge instead of a redeemer to yourself. This is acceptable. Again, this is not a mistake. However, your faculty of judgment, honed brilliantly as it is, is not that all-compassionate and all-loving faculty that waits for you in the open heart. Therefore, judgment itself, as a part of your personality, needs to be called into that outer courtyard of the open heart. Perhaps you may create for yourself a conversation with this judge that is a portion of your personality.

What is there about this faculty of judgment that is important? What could the faculty of judgment be omitting as it attempts to assess the situation of a soul dwelling in the midst of the illusions of planet Earth?

There are times when a love of detail and the desire to find the bottom line and solve every problem do not serve you well. When you are attempting to love, forgive and come into a deeper understanding of yourself, such rationalization may well be a very blunt instrument to use in comparison to your faculties of faith and intuition.

Thusly, we would encourage you to suspend all judgment of yourself and to gaze—blessed only by your native intuition—at this beautiful "women-child" that you have described yourself as being. Can you see the absolute fidelity to doing the very best that you can? Can you see the purity of your intentions and the beauty of the colors of your character, your wit, your sense of humor, and all of those things that make you unique?

Look now for the judgment. Can you see in this judgment the very human desire to come into a position of control? That is not actually a portion of the heart. This is a subtle point and we would allow you to ponder it.

We would take a step back from gazing specifically at you, my sister, and simply talk about the way it feels to experience unconditional love. Visualize, if you will, approaching the door to your heart, to that inner sanctum in which is safety, acceptance and compassion.

There is a portion of yourself that is already there. It has been there since before your birth. It will be there until the moment when your consciousness shifts through the gateway into larger life. That portion of you is the part that you are attempting to meet once again. It is a portion of yourself for which you are starved, and it does indeed lie waiting for you—as it always has.

It is that portion of yourself that is the Creator. To this instrument, who is a mystical Christian, the face of this entity is the face of the Christ. This makes it very easy for her to visualize what is awaiting her in the open heart, for she has a visual image already created in her mind's eye of this entity. We would suggest that you find a face for unconditional love as it awaits you in your own heart. This image is a portion of your own self, and yet at the same time it is a portion of the Godhead principle.

It may help you to relate to it intimately if you can find a face for that image. There are many mythological, philosophical, religious and cultural figures from which to draw. We have suggested to some whose feelings ran along lines of thought that took in the Oriental world, the face of Quan Yin, Buddha, Mohammed or that unnamed God of Yod-He-Vau-Heh. There are many images from which to draw. Personalizing that loving presence that awaits you with open arms and a full heart is often helpful in creating the environment for you to move forward through this period or place of resistance that is like a meniscus[97].

There is a resistance to breaking through into the open heart. That judgment does not want to let go and simply say, "Well, perhaps judgment is not appropriate here. Perhaps there is an end to the decimation and the evaluation of a critical mind." Again, this is a subtle point and we welcome you to ponder it as long as you wish.

However, what has been backing up for you and creating pressure in this situation is the hunger that you have to work with your higher energy chakras. You are oriented very much to working with the blue ray of open communication and to do the work in conscious[ness] of the indigo ray. In your desire to move ahead with this higher-chakra work, you have unknowingly placed a good deal of pressure on yourself. The end result of this has been a kind of locking up of the energy body.

The way to relax it and to allow it to move as it will to find a more natural balance is to open yourself up to a new level of belief in yourself and a new level of faith that all is well.

My sister, it is almost impossible to soothe a seeker's doubts or to create an effective reassurance from the level of concerns. We cannot give you specific information on repairing or improving your energy body, your relationships or any of the other points you mentioned having to do with the outworking of the details of a physically lived life. From our standpoint, the repair must come from taking a higher point of view and then looking with that improved, broadened, and deepened point of view back at the situation.

From that higher point of view that is ours, we would suggest to you in a humble way, realizing that you may not agree with us, that you already have accomplished that which you wish to accomplish but that you have not yet given yourself permission to enjoy it.

We would suggest that all is truly well.

Now, as we gaze at the thoughts within this instrument's mind at this time and within your mind at this time, we find ourselves drawn to speak concerning this intense feeling of being alone and the accompanying feelings that you have deficiency in your ability to create sound and loving relationships, either with yourself or with others.

We would agree with you that you have created a protected space about yourself that is unconsciously but efficiently designed to offer to the outside world a challenging persona that is not designed to be easy to become close to. We would suggest to you that this defense mechanism was put in place by you at a time in your life when you were young and unable to defend yourself against the thoughtlessness and insensitivity of those who were important to you. It was done at an early enough age that the mechanism is buried and the pain that caused the mechanism to occur buried with it.

You may find it helpful to move through early childhood memories with a therapist who is not only fond of you but also trained to guide you through discussion of situations that may be difficult for you to face. This is an issue that is entirely for you to consider. We are not encouraging you to do this. We are saying that you might find complete closure with some of this early childhood material to be helpful in freeing you from some of the strictures within your energy body that you are now experiencing.

We believe the only thought that you need, to bring you at last into a comfortable growth environment within your own inner sanctum, is trust and faith in yourself. As you seek to know more and more who you are, you are going to find that you are discovering the sacred nature of your true self. More and more you are going to be finding reasons to be able to forgive yourself.

We heard in your query that you had considered that perhaps confused and chaotic transactions between you and other people in previous lifetimes may have placed you in this rocky and uncomfortable situation. And to this we would

---

[97] meniscus: "the curved upper surface of a nonturbulent liquid in a container that is concave if the liquid wets the walls and convex if it does not." Surface tension creates a thickness of surface in the shape of the meniscus. (www.dictionary.com)

respond to you by saying to think in terms of this lifetime alone.

The veil over other incarnations was drawn for good reasons in third density. Please know that after each incarnation you go through a process of healing and balancing. That period of healing heals that incarnation so that, characteristically, entities do not go forward into an incarnation carrying a heavy karmic load. Characteristically, entities, at this point in third density—this point being the very latter portion of third density—come into an incarnation with balanced karma, and this, my sister, was your situation.

The energies with which you are working in this incarnation are as you have said: those energies within yourself. There is not work to do with other entities in this incarnation in order for you to become whole, integrated and able to move forward with your process of evolution. What is necessary, rather, is that you catch up with yourself. And to do that you shall have to give yourself some time to seat the considerable knowledge that you have gained and to open yourself to the possibilities that lie before you in the present moment.

Therefore, we would simply ask you to release all fear. You do not have to worry about being unsuccessful. You are already successful. You have done much in this lifetime. Your concern now needs to be simply, "What shall you have me to do with this day, with this moment, with this present time of unlimited possibility?"

Release the fear that you are not capable of opening yourself to another entity. Focus instead on opening yourself to yourself. We believe that you will find in each area of your life that if you can forgive yourself, love yourself, support yourself, and encourage yourself, you will be creating for yourself a healthy, sound atmosphere in which you become relaxed and begin to have what this instrument would call "fun."

It is well for this to occur, not because we encourage frivolity, but because we encourage balance. A lifetime of spiritual seeking is a very long journey. It takes stamina and persistence.

(Side one of tape ends.)

(Carla channeling)

The best friends that a seeker can have are a sense of proportion and a sense of humor.

We salute you, my sister, as a warrior of love and light. We affirm that you are on track, on course. And we hope that we can help you. When you enter into meditation, if you will mentally ask us to be with you, we can help to deepen and stabilize the silence that lies within you. We would strongly suggest to you that you enter that silence each day. Do it in your own way. Find your own inspirational words to read, your own songs to sing, or your own silences to keep. But, if you can, my sister, make the practice a daily one.

May we ask if there is another query at this time?

P: There's one more question, Q'uo. What is impeding my ability to have a sincere, enriching and intimate relationship with a man and to move forward joyfully with my life, using my talents and abilities to their fullest? I seem to want to live in a vacuum, pushing everyone away for fear they'll get too close to me.

We are those of Q'uo, and are aware of your query, my sister. We would suggest to you, my sister, that the entity that you are pushing away at this time is yourself. The time will come when you will be able to look into your own eyes and love yourself dearly, unquestioningly and honestly.

You will not love yourself because you have become perfect within third density and within incarnation; you will not become perfect. You will love yourself because you finally see yourself as you truly are, as a child of the one infinite Creator who is often confused, often mistaken, and often wildly off-kilter but who always and ever is perfect.

You are as a star or a tree or the north wind or the butterfly that flies from the cocoon to give its patterns and its color to the spring air. You are you. What you are doing within incarnation is rediscovering who you are and examining that world in which you live. This, my sister, you have done very well. You have examined and examined and reexamined. Continue that process, my sister, but seat the examination in love, thanksgiving and appreciation.

In your query you spoke of moving forward in joy. You may free yourself to move forward in joy by beginning to notice the present moment. When one is powerful in the mind and in the personality as you are, my sister, and as this instrument is as well, it is easy to become confined within the power of your own thoughts. It is well, then, occasionally to break out of those thoughts completely, to let them all fly away and to look at the world as if it were new this moment. What is in your world this moment? What vision comes to you? What is there out the window?

When you are involved with a transaction with a stranger in a store, my sister, stop just a moment and look at that person with new eyes. Here is the Creator. Here is the Creator. Where is the love in this transaction? If you do not feel it from the other entity, then you shall need to be the author of what love there is in the situation.

When you are driving in the car or walking upon the sidewalk in the country, stop and look. What life do you see around you? It is the outworking and expression of the infinite Creator. Contact it with your eyes, with your fingers, with your ears, and with your consciousness.

Become engaged in the world around you; not as a visitor, not as one who questions her purpose but as one who chose to come to planet Earth and who has become a native of that planet by being born into the bone and the blood of the body that is part of planet Earth. You belong here. You have a right to be here. You earned the right to be here. You were chosen for an incarnational experience because you had a great deal of desire to come here, to be of service here, and to work on a very delicate balance between love and wisdom.

Perhaps you have suspected that you have overbalanced into wisdom and now wish to see-saw back and forth until you find that exquisite sweet spot where love and wisdom flow through you as one thing so that you are your highest and best self and you have all of those gifts which you brought into incarnation available for offering to the Creator and to the global tribe of planet Earth.

May we ask if there is a follow up query at this time? We are those of Q'uo.

(No further queries.)

As there is no follow-up query at this time, my sister, we leave you with all of the love in our heart, leaving you in the love and the light of the one infinite Creator. We are those known to you as the principle of Q'uo. Adonai. Adonai. ✿

L/L RESEARCH

L/L Research is a subsidiary of
Rock Creek Research &
Development Laboratories, Inc.

P.O. Box 5195
Louisville, KY 40255-0195

www.llresearch.org

Rock Creek is a non-profit
corporation dedicated to
discovering and sharing
information which may aid in
the spiritual evolution of
humankind.

SPECIAL MEDITATION
FEBRUARY 6 2006

Question from E: *(Jim reading E's question.)* "Carl Jung's book, *Personality Types*, which was published in 1929, and Kathryn Briggs and Isabel Briggs Myers' subsequent development of the Myers-Briggs Type Indicator® personality preferences of Extraversion or Introversion, Sensing or iNtuition,[98] Thinking or Feeling, and Judging or Perceiving are used to describe sixteen different personality types. I believe that the sixteen MBTI personality types are indicative of the personality shells referred to by Q'uo in prior meditations. Can you confirm this? Would you offer any comments that you feel might be helpful in this issue?"

(Carla channeling)

We are those of the principle known to you as Q'uo. Greetings in the love and the light of the one infinite Creator, in Whose service we come to you this day.

We thank the one known as E for calling this circle of seeking together. It is a privilege to join the circle. We thank you for the beauty of your beings and for the energy and will that it takes to create this kind of moment where a circle of seeking may be called. It is our privilege to speak with you. We will attempt to share our opinions with you as we can.

Please be aware, as always, that we very much hope that you will use the utmost discrimination in listening to what we have to say. Work with any thoughts that may appeal to you but if there is any question in your mind as to the opinion that we offer, then we would suggest that you put it aside without a second thought. For you are not well-advised to follow the authority of anyone. Rather, you are well-advised to follow the resonance of your own discrimination, to pick up those things which seem good to you and to leave behind those things which do not. We thank you for this consideration. It will enable us to speak freely without being concerned that we will infringe upon your free will or interfere with your process.

The phrase, "personality shell," is one which we have encouraged this instrument to use without ever having, to our knowledge, made a careful attempt at defining precisely in what a personality shell may consist. We gather that your request is aimed at discovering more about this term, personality shell, especially as it may resemble the sixteen types of the personality traits in combination that the Myers-Briggs test offers as its sixteen ways of describing various personality types.

We may say that there is a rough correspondence between the phrase, personality shell, and the general concept of the MBTI test. Indeed, any of your tests designed to differentiate between different types of ways that entities process information and come to

---

[98] The N in iNtuition is capitalized on purpose by the authors. That N is used instead of the I that starts that word in order to differentiate it from Introversion, which uses up the I in their abbreviation system.

decisions fulfills the rough designation of an examination of the personality shell. However, there is no more than a rough correspondence for the reason that a personality shell is the entire structure of an entity, whereas tests test certain aspects of a personality that seem to be helpful to measure.

When we use the phrase, [personality shell,] the attempt to measure the personality is not present in our use of that word. To us, the term, personality shell, is indicative of a loose collection of items that have been selected from the 360 degrees of your infinite or eternal soul or spirit.

You have experienced many things through many incarnations. You have gained in life experiences and in the long list of deeds well-done and those deeds which upon reflection after incarnation you have decided to revisit in future incarnations. [These] make up the whole of what we have before called that suitcase full of gifts and limitations which you have chosen as your garments, shall we say, for the dressing of your personality in this incarnation.

The ways that the Myers-Briggs test looks at characteristics of a personality can be seen to be extremely helpful, as the one known as E has said, for determining in a short amount of time a substantive and sturdy bit of information that offers keys to the entity who has taken such a test.

It is not the view that we see when we gaze at the personality shell of an entity because, as we said, we do not measure in the same way. We see into each entity's surface mind and down into that mind to the extent that we are allowed and that we are able. Those are two separate qualifications. In the first place, some entities have extremely closely-controlled minds and they have spent a certain amount of time defending their territory or energy field, which the consciousness or the thinking of that being has created.

Most entities among your peoples are not well-defended in terms of their thoughts and the structure of their personality and therefore they are fairly transparent to those such as we who see or sense into the qualities of the various combinations of energies that make up your energy pattern. You might see this in terms of colors and shapes. We certainly do.

We do not have to analyze or think about what we see because we are used to viewing energies in this

way as pure vibration, and, therefore, it is second nature to us to see you in this way, whereas it is more difficult for us to enter into your language and to find specific information within your minds.

We gaze at this question for those items on which we may speak further to you that might be a resource in considering this question of what the personality shell is. We believe that we have expressed the concept that the personality shell, as we use that term, is not only a selection of personality traits such as preferences and ways to acquire information and process information but also includes items that are difficult to categorize to a mind such as we find this instrument to have. She does not grasp how you would characterize or categorize limitations, certain placements of limitation, and so forth. The placement of limitation has a special niche in the personality shell.

Many of those among your peoples in incarnation at this time have placed certain stoppages or limitations that will keep them from moving too far along an extreme towards an end that is not desired by the soul or spirit. An example of this is this instrument's lifelong dynamic of frail and fragile health. This instrument carefully placed in its personality shell before incarnation a limitation that would come forward whenever this instrument chose, of her own free will, to move into a physical activity to the extent that she was unable to pursue a daily, inner, meditative and contemplative side. When this instrument has in the past developed such an aggressive and ambitious program of physical activity that it has found itself unable to feed its deeper needs in terms of contemplation and meditation, the physical body has simply broken down.

There are entities who have not placed this stoppage in their personality shell because they do not have the personality setup that this instrument created for herself before incarnation. For each entity, there will be a completely different dynamic, undoubtedly a different incarnational balance that needs to be followed and therefore a completely unique way of limiting unwanted activity within the spiritual process.

This is the kind of hidden material that a test such as the one known as E has been studying cannot cover and could not be expected ever to cover because of the fact that the means of instrumentation for recording such preferences [does not exist,] since they are unknown in any conscious way to the entity within incarnation. It would be impossible to gather this information.

Further, the personality shell, as it is brought in at the beginning of incarnation, is organized not in terms of characteristics but in terms of energy center originations. There are some energies that are especially adapted to red ray, some that are adapted to orange ray, some to yellow ray, and so forth, through all of the colors of the various energy centers.[99]

In many cases, what seems on the surface to be one characteristic is in actuality an entire octave[100] of characteristics because of the fact that that characteristic coming from red ray is of one coloration, coming from orange ray is of another coloration, and so forth.

May we ask if there is a follow-up query before we move on to your next question, my brother? We are those of the Q'uo.

E: No, thank you, Q'uo, I understand your words.

Jim: *(Reading from E's questions.)* "Second question: I believe that the various paths of spiritual growth identified by Sandra Krebs Hirsh and Jane Kise's book, *Looking at Type and Spirituality*, are indicative of the various paths to spiritual growth and possibility evolution for our personality shells. Can you confirm this?"

(Carla channeling)

We are those of the principle known to you as Q'uo, and are aware of your query, my brother. Because this study is a portion of your active process at this time, we are not able to infringe upon your own judgment by making a judgment of our own.

We would simply say that we feel that all of the study that you have engaged yourself in doing has been helpful in your process and we would

encourage you to continue searching and seeking for the truth within the folds of the illusions which reveal and yet conceal so much of the infinity of the human whole in potentiation.

May we ask if there is another query at this time?

E: I can understand how this would be helpful to me to continue the study, but would it be helpful to others?

(Carla channeling)

We are those of Q'uo, and are aware of your query, my brother. We believe that, in general, a careful and thoughtful consideration of the nature of the self is always healthful and helpful in the outworking of a spiritual process within incarnation.

We find that, depending upon the nature of the central core of the personality, shall we say, and, further, the nature of the training of the mind of that entity in terms of intellectual training, the information involved in the study of psychological types is very variable in its helpfulness.

To one kind of person, looking at the self in genuine pondering, musing and questioning, such information is powerful material and conducive to helpful reflection. We find that in other cases, there is almost no interest in this kind of information because the entity who is working through the study of his or herself is looking at the self from a non-materialistic way.

In general, those who work analytically and mentally will find the study of psychology and psychological types to be far more helpful than those who are what this instrument would call mystics or spiritual students of the kind that this instrument would call chelas, under the guidance of a guru or teacher.[101]

For those who are focused on a guru or a beloved teacher of some kind, the only truly helpful information involving personality is that information given by the very being or presence of the teacher. Caught within the unspoken wholeness of this entity's presence lies the entire whole of the information that is interesting to that type of personality.

To move to the extreme of this type of personality, there is an entity such as this instrument which does

---

[99] The colors to which the Q'uo are referring are the "Roy G Biv" rainbow colors of red, orange, yellow, green, blue, indigo and violet. The chakras are assigned to the body along the spine, starting at the spine's base for red ray, with orange ray in the abdomen, yellow ray at the solar plexus, green ray at the heart, blue ray at the throat, indigo ray at the center of the forehead, and the violet ray at the top of the head.

[100] The Q'uo seem to be suggesting that within each chakra or energy center there is a complete sub-octave of associations, red through indigo ray, presumably with the crown chakra, just above the head and white in coloration, as the octave chakra.

[101] In Hinduism, a disciple is called a chela, or as it exists in ancient Hebrew, selah.

not accept any guru or teacher except the Creator Itself, in the guise of the Christ, which this instrument has come to know not only from its culture and its religious training but from personal experience.

Whether an entity is of the type, such as this instrument, who puts a face on the Creator or whether an entity which is of the mystical type is of that type of personality which does not require any personal information in order to be devoted to the infinite Creator, the Creator Itself is the image, the icon, and the entire information database, shall we say, that such a mystical person needs in order to investigate the self.

On the one hand, an analytical entity is moving into pondering itself as a self, possibly a Creator. On the other hand, a mystical entity of a non-analytical type is moving into the self from the energy of the Creator, moving or reaching up into that area which is called the gateway to intelligent infinity, which in terms of the physical body is placed at the top of the head and is generally called the eighth chakra or the crown chakra.

The call, then, is from the Creator downward and the entity is pulling into the self that knowing that moves beyond all analysis. It is to this type of entity that information will come in a conceptual form rather than in an analyzable form.

The beauty of this kind of personality in terms of receiving information of a helpful, spiritual nature is that it is received in relatively intact form. The limitation of this kind of information is that it is difficult to translate into words, and therefore it is difficult in some cases to analyze in such a way that one may see the composite parts of the structure of thought that are involved in the concept.

Similarly, the value of analysis and measurement is that it is very clear and offers substantive information that can be picked up and used in third density. It fits language and it works in the space/time continuum, in consensus reality. The limitation of moving from analysis, study and research into a knowledge of the self is that it will forever escape the reach of analysis to comprehend or "feel" into the texture and the sense of self that comes from an acceptance of the self as part of the Creator, and, therefore, an acceptance of the whole of the self without understanding the way that that whole can be analyzed or divided up in the most skillful or intelligent manner.

May we answer you further, my brother?

E: No, Q'uo, I appreciate the examples of the various processes of the seekers. It has helped me understand better.

Jim: (Reading from E's questions.) "I believe that I am a wanderer and that my son, H, and daughter, M, are wanderers. Can you confirm this? Please offer any comments you feel may be helpful to me to ponder in dealing with this facet of my personal history and those of my family on Earth."

(Carla channeling)

We are those of the Q'uo, and are aware of your query, my brother. We may indeed confirm that each of those whom you have mentioned is a wanderer. As always, when we offer this kind of information, we do wish to seat it in our understanding of what it means at this time to be a wanderer upon planet Earth.

Many are the wanderers who have not awakened as they hoped to awaken within the dream of incarnation upon your planet. For those who have not awakened, it means nothing to be a wanderer on the planet Earth. Without the awakening into a realization that there is a larger perspective than the one offered by the culture in which you all are embedded, the usefulness of the knowledge of being a wanderer has not yet taken effect.

Once a wanderer has awakened within that dream of consensus reality and has become aware that he is a child of eternity and that he has come into limitation and finitude for carefully worked-out reasons, then it is helpful to realize that one is a wanderer. It is extremely helpful in that it enables one to deal in a sensible and rational fashion with certain feelings of isolation, abandonment and distaste that are often the concomitant experiences of wanderers who have moved into third density in order to serve and to learn.

It is very helpful for entities to realize why they feel out of place on planet Earth. They feel out of place because they have come from elsewhere, and this is in some cases a new experience. In other cases [it is] not a brand new experience but certainly an experience that does not match those memories of times long past when the vibrations were of a higher density and the conditions of living were more attractive in some ways.

Once an entity becomes aware of the reasons for feelings of alienation and loss it is far easier for that entity to review that which he knows about his estate and to attempt to recover the essence of his determination to make the choice to enter incarnation upon planet Earth.

In all cases, this spot of coming into a body on planet Earth at this time was very difficult to obtain. Each entity who wished to serve and learn at this crucial time in your planet's progress offered itself, its being, its plan of incarnation, and its hope both to learn and to serve. You were given a spot because you were exceptionally well-geared to come into incarnation, to wake up, and to recall your program, and therefore to be able to be a co-creator for the rest of your incarnation in manifesting that which you worked so hard to achieve the opportunity to express.

We would say two things to those who have awakened within incarnation and are now aware of their wanderer nature.

Firstly, we would ask you to humble yourself fully, and to realize that you are not from a higher density now. Now, you are natives of planet Earth. You have earned that right by taking a grave risk. You have jumped into third density, shall we say, at the deep end of the pool. There is no guarantee that you will remember, and if you remember there is no guarantee that you can manage to come fully into incarnation. That is the first thing that we encourage wanderers to do. It is very easy to miss higher density experience, and yet that is not why you came. If you wished higher density experience, you would never have left.

You very much yearned to serve at this time. Therefore, we ask you to fully incarnate, to the best of your will and zeal to do so. See the beauty of this environment. See the Creator within your fellow beings, as confused as they are. See the Creator within your own confusion, and forgive yourself for taking a long time, in some cases, to awaken fully.

Once you have fully brought yourself down to the earth of Earth, once you have grounded yourself as an Earth native, then the second thing that we would encourage you to do is to rest daily in an open-ended willingness to see into your pattern and your purpose.

The full shape of any entity's life is hidden in that which surrounds the appearance of an incarnational life. There is much of your consciousness that does not move into the light of day but rather continues its work during subconscious and unconscious processes. However, it is given to those who ask to find answers. And if you do not ask, if you do not avail yourself of your guidance, you shall not be able to be visited by those blessed ones who await your requests for guidance and help.

May we answer you further, my brother?

E: No, Q'uo, thank you for the beauty and perception of your comments. I feel especially moved and ready to implement them.

(Carla channeling)

We are those of Q'uo, and greatly appreciate your comments, my brother. It is a blessing to us to know that some of our comments may have helped in your seeking. That is far more than we could hope and we are extremely grateful that this has occurred.

Is there another query, my brother, before we leave this instrument?

E: No, thank you.

(Carla channeling)

In that case, we will leave this instrument and this group, glorying in the peace and power of the one infinite Creator and resting in Its love and Its light. We are known to you as those of Q'uo. Adonai, my friends. Adonai. ☙

L/L RESEARCH

L/L Research is a subsidiary of
Rock Creek Research &
Development Laboratories, Inc.

P.O. Box 5195
Louisville, KY 40255-0195

www.llresearch.org

Rock Creek is a non-profit
corporation dedicated to
discovering and sharing
information which may aid in
the spiritual evolution of
humankind.

SPECIAL MEDITATION
FEBRUARY 7, 2006

Question from E: *(Jim reading E's question.)* "Edgar Cayce said that most modern astrologers use the wrong zodiac and should be using one based on the "Persian calendar." The use of the sidereal zodiac, which accounts for precession of the stars as espoused by Cyril Fagan and Donald Bradley, results in rotating the planets about 24 degrees clockwise in the horoscope chart or eight-tenths of a sign backwards when compared to the use of the tropical zodiac. For example, my Sun sign is Pisces in the tropical zodiac, yet falls back into the sign of Aquarius in a horoscope based on the sidereal zodiac. I believe that my Sun sign is Aquarius. I also believe that the use of the Fagan/Bradley sidereal zodiac is more accurate than that of the tropical zodiac to determine the placement of the "planets," which also include our Sun and Moon, in the signs and houses of a natal horoscope. Can you confirm this?"

(Carla channeling)

We are known to you as the principle of the Q'uo. Greetings in the love and in the light of the one infinite Creator, in Whose service we visit with you today. Thank you so much for inviting us to join your circle of seeking at this time. Thank you for the gift of your calling and the beauty of your vibrations. It is a great pleasure to respond to your queries at this time.

We would ask of each present and each who may read these words, please, to value greatly and honor your own powers of discrimination. Be careful in discriminating between those ideas that seem resonant to you and those which do not. Select only those ideas with which it seems resonant to you to work. We are then far more able to relax and offer our thoughts without being concerned that we might infringe upon your free will. We thank you for this consideration.

With regard to the query asked by the one known as E concerning the use of the sidereal astrology as opposed to the tropical astrology, we cannot confirm the choice of one type of reading over another, and we would make a few comments about our inability to confirm this preference.

It is our understanding—and we offer it humbly since we feel that it is only a rough approximation of the truth rather than the precise truth—that the use of both sidereal and tropical astrological charts is appropriate when studying the influences which make up the geography of an entity's interior landscape.

There are two aspects to a density. One aspect is relatively fixed; one aspect is relatively unfixed. The masculine side of the study of astrology is that of the tropical astrological chart. It represents that which is fixed into the Earth by the occasion of your birth into third-density existence.

There is another aspect which influences the use of astrology and this is the feminine aspect of the density. In this focus of astrology, the information is considerably helpful, but it does differ from the tropical chart in that it embraces more of the unfixed or soul-driven, if you will, aspects of personality.

Therefore, if an entity is actively investigating his own soul aspects, it is quite likely that he will find sidereal astrology more helpful in describing the environment in which he finds himself in his inner work than if he uses the tropical astrological chart.

Gazing at the differences between a sidereal and a tropical chart will give to an entity an interesting view of the various aspects of his own character. The sidereal aspects describe more the soul aspects of the entity, whereas the tropical chart describes more the personality or applied incarnational aspects of a personality.

Looking at the difference between the two gives to the student of his own personality an idea of the dynamics of the earthly self with respect to that self which entered incarnation and that self which shall remain after incarnation.

Neither aspect is higher than the other aspect. We wish to make that clear. The two aspects are, as it were, the vertical aspect and the horizontal aspect of that cruciform nature of personality. There is that vertical aspect that touches down into the earth and holds into incarnation certain aspects of the personality, and there is that floating or horizontal aspect to the personality that is never completely nailed down by incarnation, but rests within the energy body as the deeper aspects that the soul has brought forward into incarnation at this time.

May we answer this query in any fuller way, my brother, before we move on? We are those of the Q'uo.

E: No, Q'uo, that's fascinating information to learn about, and I'm still mulling it over at this time.

Jim: *(Reading from E's questions.)* The second question is: "I believe that the planets in the signs of our natal horoscope are representative of the energies of our inner or hidden soul pattern. Can you confirm this? I also believe that the natal planets in the signs in a sidereal horoscope are comparable to the potentiators identified by Ra in Book IV. I believe that the planetary aspects with small, close orbs in our natal, sidereal horoscope represent our lessons to be learned in this incarnation and I believe the transiting planets, which aspect our natal planets, identify the functional energies that Ra called catalysts of our experiences and significators of our choice. Can you confirm my beliefs in the astrological relationships? Please offer any comments you feel may be helpful."

(Carla channeling)

We are those of the Q'uo, and are aware of your query, my brother. We find that we cannot confirm the correspondences that you so carefully have put forward. We find them provocative and interesting. There is fruitful subject matter within these assumptions for much thought, and we encourage you [to] go forward with your observations and your attempts to find correspondences.

We would, however, suggest that the attempt to wed astrological information and functions or aspects of the archetypes is doomed to failure if the attempt is made to bring correspondences forward on a one-to-one basis.

The reason for this is that each entity is an unique expression of the infinite Creator. Each relationship that an entity makes to an archetype is made often unconsciously and almost always without any firm intention of addressing an archetype. The situations that an entity enters are full of possibilities, and when an entity's response to those possibilities moves along a line that identifies feeling or emotion and allows that feeling or emotion to be filled with the information of love and light, by whatever means such an entity chooses to use, that entry into the archetype becomes a thing in itself, or as this instrument calls it, a *ding an sich*.[102]

It is not dependent upon the personality or the situation of an entity, but rather it is dependent upon the choices and the attitudes of a moment. For an entity to move as often as possible into archetypal work, it is well for that entity to observe carefully thoughts and their attendant emotions and feelings.

When thoughts contain passion, will, emotion or feeling—and we are vague about this carriage of energy because the color of thought is a very complex subject—then it becomes a candidate for helping a spirit who is seeking to move deeper in knowing itself to do so. Without this carrying of color, feeling or emotion, the thought remains interesting and valuable on an intellectual level, but

---

[102] ding an sich: German phrase meaning "thing in itself." Carla studied in college German philosophers, such as Kant, who used this phrase. (See the *Philosophical Dictionary*, www.philosophypages.com.)

it does not become fixed into a vehicle that will move the entire seeking spirit deeper into its own experience of itself.

Consequently, although there is much interest and much potential within this question and the pursuit of it by the one known as E, we would suggest that the initial correspondences suggested are simplistic.

We would also suggest in this regard, that if the one known as E expands the kinds of information that he moves into this correspondence list, he may find interest in several different avenues of expression. The one that we would suggest that this entity examine further is that seemingly disparate correspondence set of organs of the body and the various planets.

It may well be that as more details are compounded in this correspondence list, there will come to the one known as E a subtle and interesting pattern that creates for this entity a more satisfying overall set of correspondences than this entity has yet discovered.

Is there any further query on this topic before we move on, my brother? We are those of Q'uo.

E: No, Q'uo, I see I have my work cut out for me. Thank you for the suggestion of the comparison of organs of the body and planets. I'll pursue that.

Jim: *(Reading from E's questions.)* The third question is: "I believe that the positions of the moon's north and south nodes in a sidereal natal chart identify the energies that express the dharma and karma, respectively, that are to be experienced and possibly balanced in our lives. Can you confirm this? Please offer any other comments that you feel may be helpful."

(Carla channeling)

We are those of Q'uo, and are again, my brother, aware of your query and at the same time unable to confirm your initial conjecture. Again, we would suggest that you be very patient with gazing at and sensing into the kinds of correspondences that you may find.

The road that you are on in this query, we may say, is encouraging and we believe that you will find quicker bounty in working with this correspondence than you will find in your previous query. However, because of the complexity of the soul involved, it is impossible to identify the sidereal aspects as the only aspects that move into helpful information or

resources [with regard to] what you have called the dharma and karma.

We would further suggest that once you have uncovered and identified that which is your settled opinion, it is helpful to release such information and conjecture from becoming completely literal. It is helpful at all times to remember that astrology is partly science and partly art. It is partly an examination of mathematical relationships and the structure that those mathematical relationships build when one decides that the center of the universe is the self.

May we ask if the one known as E has any follow-up queries on this question before we go forward?

E: No, Q'uo, not at this time.

Jim: *(Reading from E's questions.)* The fourth question is: "I am preparing an Archetypes in Astrology presentation that I believe may be comparable to the use of the Tarot's major arcana cards for archetypical study as outlined in *Book IV* of *The Law of One*. How may I improve the presentation to reach others interested in studying techniques for spiritual growth and evolution using astrological archetypes?"

(Carla channeling)

We are those of Q'uo, and are aware of your query, my brother. We respond to your query indirectly, in a certain sense, in saying that we do not wish to discuss with you any of your concepts. However, you asked how you may improve your presentation and we find that you are in a good position to increase the efficacy of your presentation because of the fact that you are very visual, as you have told this instrument, in the way that you see things and in your ability to create visual aids.

We would suggest that in a presentation of this kind your greatest challenge is familiarizing entities who come from many different places in their own knowledge and understanding with the basic icons or images used in the discussion not only of the archetypes but also of the astrological signs.

Create, then, clear-cut and recognizable and somewhat simplified images and use them repetitively so that, by approximately halfway through your presentation the participants in the discussion that you are facilitating have become aware of your images. Then, each time that they are seen again, the repetition will help to seat the information that you are offering.

We find that entities are also aided by the objective, or what this instrument would call the hard-copy, representation of that which you have to offer. Therefore, it would also improve the entity's ability to follow your presentation if you give out fact sheets. The first of these fact sheets, then, would be the simple or simplified images that you are using in your presentation. Backing these up would be information sheets on each of the images which an entity would be able to read at a later time when the entity was reviewing the information in attempting to seat it.

Is there a follow-up query to this question before we ask for further questions, my brother? We are those of the Q'uo.

E: No, thank you, Q'uo, that's good advice.

Jim: *(Reading from E's questions.)* Question 5 is: "I believe that there are correspondences in the energies of the planets and our chakras. For example, Saturn's energies correspond to the first chakra; Mars, the second; the Sun, third; Venus, the fourth; Mercury, fifth; Moon, sixth; and Jupiter, the seventh chakra. Can you confirm this? Please offer any comments you feel would be helpful."

(Carla channeling)

We are those of Q'uo, and are aware of your query, my brother. Again, we cannot confirm these correspondences. We would instead suggest that it may be helpful for you to examine each chakra in the sense of identifying the octave of energies that are available to that chakra. That is, in the red-ray chakra, for instance, there is the red ray's relationship with itself. There is the red ray in its foreshadowing of orange. There is the red ray in its relationship to the yellow ray, the green ray, the blue ray, and the indigo ray.

For each of those chakras, one through six, there is an entire octave of correspondences that may be used to consider the more subtle aspects of work within any one chakra. Any of those chakras mentioned— that is, the first six chakras, not counting the seventh chakra—may have over-activation, under-activation or blockage. And that blockage may be simple or complex. It may involve one chakra or it may have connections into two or three chakras.

For the most simple work, it is enough to think of a chakra and its basic attributes or the material with which it is associated. For more subtle work, when the initial blockages and so forth have been examined and yet the entity still feels that there is more examination that would be helpful because of some set of feelings, analyses or reasoning in the process of attempting to see the self and to help the self evolve, then it may well be helpful to do the more subtle work and see what some of these more subtle relationships feel like.

Sometimes there is a situation where two chakras at once are caught in a dynamic that is hard to see, and it is very helpful if you will take the time, perhaps at the end of each day, to sit down with the self and move through the thoughts and feelings of the day. When you can identify a particular feeling that you wish to investigate, ask yourself if it reminds you of more than one center of activity.

Perhaps it is a relationship between a question of survival and a question of ethics that moves into either personal dynamics between the self and another self or legal or family dynamics in the relationship with a family member. This is a simple example.

The ways that an entity can become caught in a dynamic between two chakras or even three are almost infinite, and no two entities can do work the same way, not only because each entity is different, but because the experiences that impinge upon each entity are unique.

Our final comment to you, my brother, is not to be discouraged by our many negative responses to your questions on correspondences. You are on a good track of research and a better track in terms of the metaphysical attempt to enter into an understanding of dynamics both in astrology and in the study of the archetypes that escape the bounds of reason, and are found half, as we said, in the science of the subject and half in the art.

When you consider mythology with its many stories and when you consider the story-telling nature of almost all representative art, music and literature, you may easily see that the stories and their influence, in terms of being parables or containing pointed morals or lessons, is quite rich. You may find such considerations interesting and helpful.

May we respond in any further way to this query before we ask for any more questions, my brother? We are those of the Q'uo.

E: No, thank you.

(Carla channeling)

We are those of the Q'uo. In that case, my brother, is there a query that you would like to ask at this time before we leave this instrument?

E: Yes, Q'uo, one final question. Am I correct in believing that the energies or vibrations of the Sun, the Moon, or planets do, indeed, affect a being on Earth? Could you comment on the energies that permeate the atmosphere?

(Carla channeling)

We are those of the Q'uo, and are happy to comment on this query, my brother. The energies of planets are very powerful in their drawing of certain geographies that are like a street map or a road map of a person's inner landscape. The influences, both fixed and non-fixed, that affect an entity at the time of his birth, and certainly before the birth in terms of the unfixed energies, create the structure of ways which an entity may move to get from here to there.

Now, if this instrument wished to go from Louisville to Chicago, she would look at the map and discover that there was a big interstate that connected those two towns. She might decide to go up Interstate 65 north from Louisville to Chicago. If she decided to go that way, the situation as regards repairs to the road and problems that were experienced on that road at the time that you were traveling to Chicago would impinge upon that journey.

If this instrument decided that she did not wish to go directly to Chicago, she would find that her map extended all the way around the planet. She could choose to go to Europe and then to Asia and then to move around to Siberia and Russia and Alaska, coming over into Canada and down into North America to reach Chicago. That is also a route, and it is interesting to look at an entity's information, as regards astrology and so forth, to make an educated guess as to whether an entity shall choose an interstate and a very direct route to a certain lesson, or whether an entity will choose a roundabout or an outrageously roundabout route that still, eventually, has the capacity to deliver one to the supposed location of one's desire.

Perhaps it may be seen by this example that a great part of the use of astrology is in gazing at one's desires and looking at the use of one's will. What is the most efficacious and skillful way to set about choosing one's goals? And, once those goals and ambitions have been set by the self and acknowledged as that about which the self feels passionately and which it wishes to pursue with all of its heart, all of its soul, all of its mind, and all of its strength, then it is interesting to ask, in the light of these pieces of information about the self, what are the most skillful ways to pursue such a goal?

We would emphasize that the influences upon the self from the stars, planets and other aspects of astrological charts are both clear and offered without the necessity to give up one's free will. One retains one's free will to a complete extent. One may choose to disregard one's planetary influences.

In our humble opinion, it is well to cooperate with one's planetary influences.

The choice that each entity entering incarnation made as to the moment of that birth, as well as the moment of conception and the moment of the entity's entrance into the fetus and/or the infant, are interesting points to consider.

They do not mean that your free will is limited. They indicate the strengths, weaknesses and general topography of the inner landscape. It is always helpful to have a reasonably good idea of what one's strengths and limitations may be as an entity as one gazes at the self, its goals and aims in life, and its heart, its desires, and its will.

In this regard, it is well to know that built into astrology, built into archeology, built into study of the archetypes, indeed, built into almost every way that one can examine the self, there is that combination of science and art, fact and myth, reason and inspiration. Allow these dynamics to play as your mind considers these relationships.

We thank you, my brother, for all of these questions. They are most interesting to consider and we have greatly enjoyed this conversation.

We wish that we could share more positively pointed information with you but we hope that in clearing out some of these first suppositions, we clear the way for you to consider afresh the subject matter before you, which is indeed most ambitious.

We wish you good fortune and good hunting, for you truly are one who puts together the puzzle.

E: Thank you, Q'uo.

We thank you, my brother. We would at this time leave this instrument and this group, as we found you, in the love and in the light, the thought and the manifestation of the one infinite Creator. We are known to you as Q'uo. Adonai. Adonai. ✤

L/L RESEARCH

www.llresearch.org

SPECIAL MEDITATION
FEBRUARY 12, 2006

The Archetype Gathering

Group question: How does working with the archetypes to become them help us in the development of the magical personality?

(Carla channeling)

We are those known to you as the principle of Q'uo. Greetings in the love and in the light of the one infinite Creator, in Whose service we come to you this day to join in your circle of seeking. Thank you, my friends, for inviting us to be a part of your circle.

We are most happy to respond to your question concerning the use of the archetypes in the pursuit of adepthood. However, as always, we would caution you strictly to use your very adequate and competent powers of discrimination to discern what of that which we have to say is helpful to you and what is not resonant to you. If there is no resonance in anything we say, no matter how intellectually interesting it might be, we ask you to leave it alone.

Follow and use the information that does resonate to you, my friends, and in that way we may be assured that we are not infringing on your free will but rather are enjoying a conversation with equals. We would not be an authority over you and we cannot be considered as that and have peace in our minds about that which we offer you this day. Therefore we greatly thank you for your kind indulgence in this manner.

Your query this day revolves around the use of the archetypical mind and its study within the process which you have called evolving the magical personality or becoming a priest or an adept. We realize that the one known as T has been concerned about the issue of adepthood and priesthood and therefore we would like to address this concern as our first topic of discussion, for we feel that it bears much of import.

Not only the one known as T but this instrument [as well] is cautious when faced with the possibility that one might, by asking a certain question or following a certain line of inquiry, be committing oneself to the full requirements of a lifelong, intensive study of the magical personality, the Tree of Life,[103] and the inferred duties and responsibilities accruing to a member of the white magical priesthood, that surprisingly large and largely unknown group of entities who, for millennia of your time upon your planet have maintained stewardship of the Earth, of those energies beneath the Earth, and of those energies within, what this instrument calls, inner or unseen planes, thus working ceaselessly and without any regard for personal fame or renown to balance your island home on its keel as it sojourns about your sun and as your sun sojourns about the edge of the galaxy.

---

[103] The Tree of Life glyph is the central figure of the Kabbalistic study of the magical personality. You can see a representation of it on this site: www.ucalgary.ca/~elsegal/Sefirot/Sefirot.html.

By identifying with their native mountains, plains and oceans, by calling down the highest of the high, and by dealing fearlessly and constantly with that which this instrument calls the shadow or the unknown side of self, this priesthood has served ceaselessly.

And there is that energy within many of those in this group that resonates to the idea of a life lived in service and a life lived in priesthood. We are aware of the concern within this instrument and the one known as T that there might be any hint or shadow of ethical commitment that would be beyond that which entities living as you live, in the lives that you live, could complete. We wish to assure each that those mental reservations create, in the metaphysical world, a contract not to be such a priest.

There is a limit that you have set upon yourself. You wish to relate to the world directly. You do not wish to go into retreat from the world. You wish to engage in the world. This is acceptable within the limits of a more generalized conceptualization of the commitment to living life as a priest or an adept.

There is a general sense in which every entity is a priest. It is said in your holy work that you are a nation of priests and a holy people.[104] We believe this to be precisely correct and, as several of you have noted during this weekend's rich conversation which we have greatly enjoyed being a part of through this instrument's mind, the priestly aspect of your incarnations is becoming and more and more clear to you. You are becoming more and more aware that you carry within you the consciousness of what this instrument calls the Christ or unconditional love.

That which you are pursuing so relentlessly—that being the one infinite Creator, or alternately, the truth about yourself—lies waiting for you not outside your awareness but rather at the very heart of it. You seek for that which is within your heart of hearts.

In that way, adepthood or priesthood can be seen as the movement into the outer courtyard of the heart and into that inner door to the *sanctum sanctorum*, your heart of hearts, and the throne of the one infinite Creator.

Or is it instead, my friends, a manger? And does the Creator await you as a child or an infant lying in the straw, waiting for you to swaddle it with your recognition of the Christ within?

Do you seek an authority figure in your heart? Do you seek a white-haired, ancient Lord of Lords, that Old Testament figure that judges as well as loves?

What figure do you have in your mind that partially reveals and partially hides the truth of creatorship? What do you seek? Do you seek an image? Do you seek an icon? Or do you seek that mystery which lies beyond all words but bears the name of unconditional love?

Therefore, on this point, we would say to you that if you genuinely, sincerely and honestly seek the truth of your own being and if you are willing to commit ineluctably and simply to living your life in the pursuit of that seeking, you are worthy to be called a priest and an adept.

You may not be able, because of your lifestyle, to commit hours out of each day to the ritual involved in priesthood as it is seen in holy orders. You may not be able to invoke and evoke specific energies at specific times in a ritualistic manner, for that would indeed take a great deal of subtle work in visualization that would require you to maintain a level of focus given only to what this instrument would generally term madmen, saints and fanatics. Such is the nature of priesthood.

We expect and understand that this is not the level of your commitment and we specifically express our understanding that this is ethically acceptable in terms of the metaphysical balance not only of your individual life but also the life of your group as you experience yourselves during this gathering and that group which is the tribe of humankind upon planet Earth.

Your service is acceptable as it is, just as it is, and without improvement. You are already upon what we would term a sound and good path. And we thank you for being on that path, for calling us to your group, and for being ethically conscious and concerned enough to have cautionary feelings concerning these questions.

We turn now to gaze at the magical personality. The definition which this instrument has learned from

---

[104] *Holy Bible*, Isaiah 62:12: "And they shall be called the holy people, the redeemed of the LORD." There are several other references to this concept in the Old Testament.

the works of the one known as William[105] is simple enough. A magician is one with the ability to effect changes in consciousness at will.

You have been a magician each time that you have faced a situation in life and made a conscious choice to respond to catalyst that is offered you in a way which was not automatic in your responsive system. When you have chosen a higher path, when you have chosen a soft word instead of a harsh one, a kind action instead of a rude one, or an honest if hard answer instead of a hypocritical though easy one, you have acted in a magical way, choosing to lift your consciousness to a higher path.

This instrument calls a good deal of this kind of work that she does, "tuning", and we would agree that there is something to be said for seeing the tuning of your consciousness in this figure of speech.

What is it to create changes in your consciousness by an act of will? There are three basic factors weighing on this matter.

The first is yourself as an actor and a chooser.

Second is your will, its recognition as a factor, and its discipline by your daily work.

The third is that which you effect as an act of will, that choice that lies before you that is entirely subjective. No two people shall see catalyst in precisely the same way. Therefore, no two people as magical entities shall create the same change in consciousness.

It is the right use of will that becomes the key to the working of the puzzle that lies before you when you face a choice in how to respond to a situation that you perceive.

It is in the state of your mind as you approach the present moment that the use of the archetypes lies. The archetypical mind, as has been iterated often during this gathering, is a resource of the deep mind. It is a plat,[106] if you will, of energy paths that are possible within the system of illusions that constitutes space/time and time/space within third density upon your planet. It is a finite, delimited resource created for use by third-density entities within incarnation upon planet Earth.

It is a comprehensive encyclopedia of what this instrument has several times called the road maps available for getting from here to there within the inner geography of that infrastructure of roads, byroad, lanes and little tiny paths that constitutes ways in which you may turn and make choices when you are investigating how to respond to that which you see coming into your view in the present moment.

Most often you use the archetypes inadvertently. You become one of them by moving through a situation with a certain degree of purity. We cannot be more specific that this, for within each situation there is a wide range of ways in which you may be pure, depending on how you are assessing the situation that you see before you and from what standpoint you are assessing it.

There are many levels from which you may view consensus reality and from each level there are many choices that you make, before you make the choice of how to look at a given situation, which bring you to the point of choice biased or distorted in a certain set of parameters, all of which are useful.

We have often said through this instrument that there are no mistakes and in this wise we would say it with a special emphasis. When you are working with that which is quite nebulous to the conscious mind, you must not restrict yourself to the concept of being right or correct but rather offer yourself permission to explore resonant paths of seeking.

When you feel that you may perhaps have evoked or become part of the archetypal part of the human experience, that does not mean that you have moved from humanhood to an archetype. It means that you have hollowed yourself with enough clarity, honesty and purity that you have made room within the dedication of your seeking for your experience to be filled with the resonance that moves from finity to infinity, from specificity or locality to universality or non-locality.

Becoming an archetype is a kind of knowing that does not depend on fact, detail or learning. Touching into the archetypal is touching into the entirety available within specificity. It is certainly not available consciously or by the application of learning or analysis. Archetypal truth is essential, and

---

[105] The Q'uo is referring to William E. Butler, whose works include *Apprenticed to Magic* and *Magic, Its Ritual, Power and Purpose*. You can look for other books by W. E. Butler on www.amazon.com.

[106] plat: A map showing actual or planned features, such as streets and building lots. (www.dictionary.com)

as several have suggested throughout this weekend, that which is archetypal remains forever mysterious, so that it is by your being that you explicate and bear witness to that which is pure or purified within you.

This instrument would call this purified substance feeling or emotion, and we would agree that these are the words closest to describing those rivers of energy that water the land of archetypes, that rich, mountainous treasure trove in which one range leads to another and to another and to another in an unending set of discoveries and realizations.

That which is magical within you awaits your choice. Let us look then at the nature of the choice before you and the resources with which you meet it.

In each moment your choice is to accept yourself as the self that your culture and your environment suggest that you are or to accept yourself as something far more articulated. It may seem grandiose to those who like the idea of being powerless and without responsibility in any ethical sense. To those who are thirsty for the one infinite Creator, it seems a positive blessing to be pulled forward by the desire to seek. Those who wish to become more than they know are those who would choose to become co-creators with the forces placed into motion at the time of birth.

When you choose to accelerate the pace of your spiritual evolution, you are activating a magical portion of yourself. That is the nature of your choice. It is perfectly all right to choose to rest and refrain from the practice of the recognition of the power of your own being. When you have gathered your strength and wish to step forward upon your journey, you are indeed the fool. Whether or not you feel that you need baggage, you pick up your self, your energies and your intentions and you leave the familiar safe and sheltered valley of your past understanding.

Thus, all entities conceiving of themselves as working on their magical personalities may also conceive of themselves [as being] upon a journey in common with many, many others. This is a pilgrimage in which you are never alone. Certainly each entity is solitary within the confines of its own choices and its own processes. However, other shards and splinters of the sunshine of the Creator are walking beside you, praying for guidance from the same Creator, being shined upon by that great and

unending source of light and love, gaining inspiration from the same guidance.

So although in some ways you are endlessly alone, if you can open your awareness to the larger vision of your situation you may see that you walk with many in a space made sacred by each footstep, each tear, each sigh, each moment of rejoicing, each time of wonder, amazement and awe, and each midnight of suffering and woe. These are all most sacred.

That which surrounds you upon this journey is a many-storied, almost infinite world. As you move the focus of your perception you will choose to focus upon certain portions of the 360 degrees of investigation possible to one who is fully able to turn and gaze in any direction. Each time that you change the focus of your seeking, something will be illuminated and many other things will be cast into the darkest shadow.

You will always be working in what seems to you to be poor light. You've gazed at the many indications in the tarot cards images of the sun, the moon, and the tendency within spirit of the moon to overshadow and hide the sun. That is the environment of your seeking.

You may never become able to invoke archetypes or allow them to come into your being and fill you with the skill and the art of the true magical adept. You may have to content yourself with what you yourself consider to be imperfect attempts to invoke or become the archetype. We assure you that, in the process of forming the intention, at each moment that you form such an intention to seek and to serve the one infinite Creator, to heighten your devotion to the one infinite Creator, or to increase your passion for developing your will in order to maximize your service to the Creator, you have done work that, in a magical sense, is highly polarizing regardless of the actual outcome of your intention.

Make the shift within your mind of the doingness of consensus reality to the beingness of time/space or metaphysical reality. Realize that those things which in the physical are mere shadows—that is, your thoughts—become living, breathing objects, essences and creatures in the metaphysical world.

Your intentions are very real, metaphysically speaking, and your subsequent actions, metaphysically speaking, are as the shadows of those intentions. That which may seem glorious in consensus reality may have almost no weight in the metaphysical world and that which seems only a shadow in the physical world may have tremendous weight in the metaphysical world, thereby turning logic on its ear and all of your ambitions to dust.

Please allow that to happen forthwith if there is any materialistic implication having to do with actions that are real in space/time. Release them, my friends, and know that your work is the work of the crystal that wishes to tune itself.

For each of you is a Creator. And you are a Creator in a certain way. You are an instrument. You have certain characteristics, much as any crystal does. You are set up with regularity within the logic of your own structure, metaphysically speaking. Your energy system is balanced in its imbalance in a certain way that works and that is your perfection at this time. It is a stable setting.

The one who wishes to adjust the setting of the crystal is one who wishes to do magical work. You are working with the structure of your own consciousness in order to improve your tuning or your setting as an energy field that is receptive, much like a crystal radio is receptive.

This instrument has before used the analogy of herself as that which can receive a radio station. When she attempts to tune for channeling, she is tuning for the highest and best source of information that she can receive as a stable, conscious entity. She's tuning the crystal of her instrument. When she's done that to the best of her ability she consciously sets and crystallizes that setting and then she carefully chooses the recipient or source of the contact that she is going to channel.

In a less formalized and much more everyday way, everyone at all times is receiving the love and the light of the one infinite Creator and is transducing it to a certain extent as it moves through the energy system of the chakras.

(Side one of tape ends.)

By the time that it leaves your energy system at the violet ray, moving through into the octave ray of the crown chakra, it has undergone the adjustments necessary to move through your energy system. If you are resting on your default setting and not attempting to tune your instrument, then your signal, shall we say, shall be correspondingly unfocused and weak. Depending upon the work that

you have done in the present moment, meeting those situations that you see in your present moment, your output may well be much different than your default setting. You may have chosen to work with the energy of the one infinite Creator in several different ways, sharpening it in this way, defusing it in that way, and so forth.

If you, as a crystal being, have come to a point within your incarnation where you are relatively restful and content within yourself, then you are probably allowing a good deal of the light of the one infinite Creator to pour through your system undistorted.

Discontent and worry is the one perturbation that will most effectively destroy the energy of light. Consequently, as you work to be more and more comfortable within your own skin, you are not being selfish. You are not taking too much time for yourself. You are, rather, working in service to the Creator and to others by clearing your own energy system. It is not selfish to do this work but rather of service to others.

It is a very difficult tangle within the mind to many service-to-others oriented entities to be able to set aside the time and the attention for oneself that is indeed needed for you to keep clear and useful and an instrument for spirit. Nevertheless, you may have to take that time, five minutes at a time, around the edges of the busy day. But we assure that if you choose those five minutes carefully and if you pour yourself into those five minutes, you shall create magic aplenty. You shall not run out of time, for you can do much in a small space, magically speaking.

You are attempting to take that which your culture has taught you is worthless: your thoughts, your feelings, your hunches, and your intuition and to glean from them the information that your culture has not respected or honored. In doing so, you are bereft of the tools comfortable to one who deals with the mind. For in doing magical work or in attempting to create one's focus for being increasingly magical you are moving constantly to move from head to heart and from thinking to knowing.

What is the faculty of knowing? The one known as S was speaking this weekend of the difference between that energy that comes through the soles of the feet and up through the base chakra or the red-ray chakra and pours upwards and out through the top of the head and that energy that is called forth by seeking, that energy which is pulled down through the gateway to intelligent infinity [at the crown chakra] by the force, the focus, and the purity of your desire.

The one known as S noted that the place where those two energies met was that point at which the tremendous energy of what you have called the kundalini lies, the object of the kundalini movement being to create that evolution of spirit that is symbolized by the trope or figure of kundalini. That place where the kundalini rests within you is that place from which you may most stably and faithfully work.

Attempt, then, in preparing yourself to do magical work to, as this instrument has said, become truly humble and empty. Examine your chakra system each day, looking for distortion, either over-activation or under-activation. When you find it, sit with it, gaze at it, invite it, and seek to understand what is triggering your attention on this particular issue. If you can find distortion within yourself from which this fountain of triggering affect stems, move to the origin of that trigger and see what you can do to unearth this buried treasure of it. By removing the gift from its surrounding ore, create the appreciation of the diamond that you have made from your suffering. See the beauty of its purity and know from experience the tremendous pressure of suffering in the fiery furnace of the catalyst of an incarnation. What it has cost you to produce this beauty, this truth, and this treasure!

Spend time, if you can, in the silence each day. We do not concern ourselves with your mode of entering the silence or what you do during that time. You may do nothing. You may have a practice of prayer, visualization or other regularized or ritualized method of structuring such time or you may simply go on a solitary ramble, listening to the calls of the birds and gazing at the beauty of the trees, bushes and the meadows.

However you structure this time, we encourage you to commit yourself to a daily practice of the presence of the one infinite Creator Whose voice is only heard in silence.

Lastly we encourage you to practice the recognition of the Creator. Know it when you see it, whether it is within yourself, within nature, within others, or simply within the moment itself.

We thank you for this question. As always, we have barely scraped the surface of this fascinating and deep topic but we thank you for the opportunity to share our thoughts with you. Before we leave this instrument and this group we ask if there are one or two follow-up queries at this time. We are those of Q'uo.

S: It seems to me that a prerequisite for … *(inaudible).*

(The question has to do with what archetype(s) would it help to invoke as one goes about beginning and spiritualizing a mated relationship or a spiritual companionship.)

We are those of Q'uo, and are aware of your query, my brother. Rather than suggesting a single archetype in terms of addressing your query about how to approach adjusting one's very personal and intimate practices to the exigencies of a relationship with a significant other, as this instrument calls that general relationship of the mated pair, we would say that a characteristic that has been discussed during this gathering repeatedly may be focused upon as helpful. That characteristic is the characteristic of the courting or wooing male which courts the Potentiator or the reaching for that which awaits the reaching.

Whenever an entity, whether male or female, is considering how to approach negotiating something as personal as a prayer life or a practice or rule of life with a mate, that entity may see itself as that figure which goes forth to court or to woo rather than to control or to manipulate.

The mate has a dynamic with the self within which there are areas of commonality. The magic of such a situation, then, is in finding that area of commonality and staying within it with the utmost of fastidiousness, creating a spiritual practice that is satisfying to both entities in spite of their many differences.

It is a challenging and a subtle negotiation. And negotiation it is, for there is no quick way to move from the standpoint of beginning such a discussion to the outworking or a manifestation of a happy result.

Working against such a happy result is not only the difference between you and the other self but also the variation between your true self and that part of yourself which you know and are able to share without distortion. The better you know yourself and the more of yourself you can see, including those parts which this instrument would call less developed or more of the shadow side, the more successful you shall be in finding your area of commonality and make the most of it without significant distortion.

May we answer you further, my brother?

S: No, that was wonderful. Thank you.

Is there another query at this time? We are those of Q'uo.

J: Q'uo, I have a question that has to do with the spirit as articulated in the archetypes. Can you comment on the home of the spirit from your point of view and what differentiates it from the body and the mind and the mechanics thereof?

We are those of Q'uo, and are aware of your query, my brother. And we have a very tricky situation, looking at your question, because of the fact that in several of those entities within this room at this time this forms an active portion of their process. Consequently, we must be guarded in our discussion and we apologize for this but it is necessary in order to maintain the freedom of will.

That which we may say without infringing upon free will is this: the spirit is that which allows travel between the inner and outer planes of third density. In terms of its function within the archetypal mind it is difficult to explicate how the shuttle of spirit functions because of the fact that it functions in what the one known as Don[107] called the 90 degree phase shift, taking one from space/time to time/space.

There is an extra-dimensional change in location or even order of magnitude in a sense between space/time and time/space. You move from a very microcosmic and ordered chaos, shall we say, in terms of space/time, to a much less obviously ordered but far less chaotic and very vast situation in time/space. And you do that within the body, without leaving incarnation. You do it safely and you do it consistently, working within the archetypal mind. It is that which is used to create the creatures of vision and dreams.

And as you touch the edges of archetypal imaging, those messengers come back to you, called through the shuttle of spirit into manifestation, be they from first density such as elementals, or second density such as the messengers of your totems, or be they those entities from the inner planes from many densities that may well be called to your seeking self by the radiancy of your vibrations and the focus of your desire.

May we answer you further, my brother?

J: No, thank you.

Is there a final query at this time? We are those known to you as Q'uo.

S: Thank you, Q'uo.

We are those of Q'uo, and we thank you as well. We thank each. We often have commented on the beauty of a group of people but we have never seen a more beautiful rainbow than the very complex living dance of your joined and harmonized beings. It is a blessed work that you have accomplished in blending your energies, in loving each other without reserve and in seeking together. We assure you that you shall carry with you that blessing, that added stability, and that fellowship as you go forth rejoicing. And so shall we. It has been a very special time.

We leave you in the love and in the light of the one infinite Creator. We are known to you as the principle of Q'uo. Adonai. Adonai. ☙

---

[107] Don Elkins began L/L Research with Carla in 1970 and his research inspired all of the eventual archive of channeling and other work on www.llresearch.org and www.bring4th.org.

L/L Research is a subsidiary of
Rock Creek Research &
Development Laboratories, Inc.

P.O. Box 5195
Louisville, KY 40255-0195

L/L RESEARCH

www.llresearch.org

Rock Creek is a non-profit
corporation dedicated to
discovering and sharing
information which may aid in
the spiritual evolution of
humankind.

SPECIAL MEDITATION
FEBRUARY 26, 2006

Question chosen by PLW poll:[108] Many, many people speak often of Atlantis and Lemuria as the supreme ancient advanced civilizations that existed on Earth. I believe that there was a world that existed before them as well. Can you give us any insight to the tribes that existed on Earth before Atlantis and Lemuria?

(Carla channeling)

We are the principle known to you as Q'uo. We greet you through this instrument in the love and the light of the one infinite Creator. It is in this Creator's service that we come to you this day. We thank you for the privilege of being called to your circle of seeking. We are most glad to share our thoughts with you on the subject of the tribes of Earth.

Before we begin, we would ask a favor of you. Please listen carefully to what we have to say, using you powers of discrimination in order to decide what is for you and what is not. If something resonates to you, please, by all means use it. If that which we have to say does not seem helpful to you, we ask you to leave it and move on.

Be very careful about what you accept into the web of your thinking, feeling and actions. You create your own universe by what you pay attention to and use. Create the universe that is dear to your heart, that inspires your soul and that lifts you until you

are soaring, for that is your nature. You need to become passionately engaged and enthusiastic about the creation of which you are a part. And you can do that by the choice of that to which you pay attention. We thank you for this great kindness in listening to us, for it will allow us to speak our thoughts freely.

How precious each of you is to us as we rest with you in the circle of your vibrations and how precious as well is every member of the tribe of humankind on planet Earth! We thank you for asking us about the tribes of Earth.

In truth, your query is not one about which we have a great deal of information to share. We can affirm that there were indeed tribes of late second-density entities here before that point at which the Earth itself, as a planet, became able to support the kind of vibratory energy field that would be a good environment for a self-aware being such as you are. Therefore, if we go back before Lemuria and Atlantis on planet Earth, we are talking about late second-density beings which were striving for third-density graduation.

They were doing so very successfully at the very end of a long second-density period that had moved through geological ages such as your ice age and back beyond that quite a ways in your planetary history. These were entities of what this entity would call the great ape family. These entities were striving towards self-awareness.

[108] Planet Lightworker Magazine (www.planetlightworker.com).

If you are a person who is owned by a cat or dog, you are aware of the many childlike and humanlike qualities that are encouraged within a pet's disposition and character as he or she goes through a life of being noticed, listened to, fed and offered affection. It changes that second-density entity and creates a more obvious likelihood that when such an entity reincarnates, he may have earned the right to choose to incarnate in a third-density physical vehicle.

Such was the case with theses entities of various species of the great ape genus. The animals, if you would call them that, which were of the second-density nature certainly had bestial natures. They were not conversing as you would with your friends.

However, they were developing means of communication with each other, starting with their second-density ability to sense into the truth of what is. That is the unique advantage of being a second-density entity rather than a third-density entity. Second-density entities such as the great apes had, and continue to have, a greatly enhanced ability to know the truth. That is, there is not a veil of forgetting between the conscious mind and the reaches of the racial mind, the planetary mind, the archetypical mind, and the Creator's mind.

All of these noumenal, unknowable reaches of mind that are sought so eagerly by third-density entities were available without effort to the tribes of Earth before third density began to unroll its scroll of history.

These entities attempted to deal with each other and did so in the way of second-density entities, by creating territories which were theirs and common territories between tribal territories where they could all hunt. Therefore, there were the rudiments of communication, government and society.

There was the attempt to use tools, and the attempt to create beautiful things. Above all there was an overarching and underlying knowledge, we shall not call it faith, we shall call it knowledge, of the oneness of all things, and the sacredness of life. There was no question in these entities' minds that they were children of the one Creator.

Therefore there was, in the late second-density being that was a member of the tribes of planet Earth in prehistory, every potential for the flowering of the spirit, and every ground laid for the third-density planetary experience that was to come.

We as a group did not approach such entities, in that there was no call and we are those who move by the rules of free will. The call from entities such as you asked for information concerning did not feel the need to call outside of the web of being that surrounded them all, which was instinctually known to be sacred.

Therefore, rather than calling for entities such as we, the call was immediate and moved into the earth, sky, the water and the fire, the plants and the animals which shared its environment and the Creator herself. In late second density, the Creator was seen to be a feminine character as females [give] birth [to] everything that exists.

Our experience with the tribes of Earth, indeed, does begin with Lemuria and Atlantis. Consequently, this is the sum of that about which we can speak concerning those tribes that danced the dance of late second density upon planet Earth and prepared the ground for the density of choice that was to come.

Is there a follow-up query at this time, my friends? We are those of Q'uo.

J: Did these second-density entities become third-density entities that again formed in tribes and behaved as mind/body/spirit complexes?

We are those of Q'uo, and are aware of your query, my brother. In essence, you are correct. The story, however, is a bit more tangled than it would appear.

As third-density conditions become prevalent on planet Earth, beings with this body type of the great ape continued to incarnate and live lives that were of a nature of a tribe or clan, seemingly unchanged from second density.

However, the light of third density is that light which supports and encourages the development of the spirit complex. The probable course of development of these Earth-native entities that were now ensouled as they came into incarnation but dwelling in these particular bodies is unknown, for that evolutionary line was interrupted by those who felt it would be helpful to offer the third-density entities of planet Earth a much improved physical vehicle, one in which the jaw was manipulated in order that speech was more possible more easily, and one in which an upright posture was more possible.

To the adjustments to the body were added adjustments made to the mind complex in order to sharpen mental acuity. This experiment, shall we say, interrupted the normal course of evolution.

In a way it accelerated that evolution by making it far more possible for the body types of what you now are aware of as your human form to do the work of third-density entities. They were more able to make tools. They were able to think about the tools they made and to make changes to make them better.

However, the natural course of the development of the great ape into third density is one in which peaceful means of resolving disputes is valued almost to the exclusion [of] open hostility. There is a knowledge, shall we say, that is the carry-over from the awareness of late second-density of how things are. This territory is for group A, this territory is for group B and so on. There is a natural tendency in entities with this genetic heritage to find peaceful means of resolving differences of opinion.

As the advantages mounted, in the newfangled genetically adjusted human being, this [type of] being began to feel not at all humble, but rather begin to be filled with the arrogance of that concept that is almost unknown within tribal societies, the feeling of arrogance; that feeling that not only do you have a place in nature, but that you may take whatever place you can defend and make it your own.

The changes wrought by entities which were truly innocent of intention to do evil or to wreak negative consequences became that which was judged by the so-called Council of Nine as a disaster. There have been attempts made, ever since these genetic adjustments were offered to the tribe of planet Earth's humans, to make amends, to rebalance that which was done without awareness of the quite substantially difficult consequences of these changes.

May we answer you further, my brother?

J: *(Inaudible).*

We are those of Q'uo, and fear that this instrument's ears did not catch your question. Could you please restate your question. We are those of Q'uo.

J: At some point, this second-density tribal group of entities, Earth's first third-density group, was joined by populations from other third-density planets that failed to make harvest to fourth [density]. Ra mentioned that sixteen other planets had given their populations to Earth when they had their harvest to fourth density and the populations did not make it to fourth density. So they came to Earth to repeat the cycle. Was this second-density tribal group able to keep its identity throughout the third-density cycle of Earth, to live together and evolve together? I'm wondering if the second-density group of entities that you spoke about was able to evolve, on Earth, in the third density, as a group, or were they assimilated into other groups?

We are those of Q'uo, and are aware of your query, my brother. The second-density great ape bodies, when compared with the second-density genetically altered bodies that were available for use, in the natural flow of the reproductive cycle, were seen by those entities who were coming into third-density Earth and taking form to complete their third-density cycle, to be the model [which was] more highly developed and easier to use, to the extent that the second-density bodies did not receive ensouled beings and simply reverted to [being] second-density animals carrying second-density souls, or rather mind/body complexes, as this instrument would call them, to differentiate them from mind/body/spirit complexes, which are the ensouled third-density type.

May we answer you further, my brother?

J: No, thank you.

We thank you, my brother. Is there a final query before we leave this instrument?

S: There was, I've read, one civilization called Ur that was highly evolved before the Atlantean and Lemurian times. Do you have any insights or information on this civilization?

We are those of Q'uo, and are aware of your query, my brother. We find that our only awareness of the civilization which you call Ur is that in this instrument's mind. In this instrument's mind there is the information that this was an entity or tribe of people in the Middle East. This, however, to the best of our understanding, was a third-density civilization and society that pre-dated the height of, say, the Egyptians with which this instrument is familiar, that being the Egypt of Akhenaton, Tutankhamen and Amenhotep. It did not pre-date the third density.

If there was an advanced civilization on Earth before third density, we are not aware of it and we simply cannot share any information on that subject. We are sorry, my brother, for our lack of information.

We thank this group and this instrument for the blessing of companionship and the privilege of sharing the beauty of your beings. It has been a pleasure. We are those of Q'uo, and we leave you in the love and in the light of the one infinite Creator. May the oneness of all that is penetrate your isolation within the illusion. May you know, as the early tribes knew, and as you shall know in fourth density once again, by faith alone, that all is one, and that you are a perfect part of the perfect dance that will unfold every mystery to you as you move through the steps that lead to infinity and eternity.

Adonai. Adonai. We are those of Q'uo. ❦

L/L Research

L/L Research is a subsidiary of Rock Creek Research & Development Laboratories, Inc.

P.O. Box 5195
Louisville, KY 40255-0195

www.llresearch.org

Rock Creek is a non-profit corporation dedicated to discovering and sharing information which may aid in the spiritual evolution of humankind.

SPECIAL MEDITATION
FEBRUARY 26, 2006

Group question: Q'uo, today we would like to focus on some experiences that B has had recently. He's had some very meaningful metaphysical experiences like seeing a city of light in the sky that really does seem to exist, having a contact with Titans and entities from the past that he has relationships to, and feeling his heart open in ways it has never opened before. Now he's wondering how he can communicate this, how he can get access to this in a way that he can understand, in a way that is not intellectual, which was his previous way of understanding. We need to get some information about how to get a language of the heart that is understandable to B and that allows him to share what he's feeling with himself and with others.

(Carla channeling)

We are those known to you as Q'uo. We greet you in the love and in the light of the one infinite Creator, in Whose service we are privileged to come to you this day. Thank you for calling us to your circle of seeking. As always, we request that you listen to our words using your powers of discrimination. If our words resonate to you, that is a wonderful thing. We encourage you to use the information to continue to investigate your creation. If the words do not resonate, we ask you to leave them behind. If you will take responsibility for your thoughts, that will enable us to speak our thoughts freely without being concerned that we will infringe upon your free will or interfere with the very

appropriate process through which you are going at this time. We thank you for this consideration, my friends.

The instrument was somewhat startled to discover that those of Hatonn were going to speak rather than those of Latwii this day. For it has been many years since those of Hatonn have been that entity of the three that was most appropriate to speak. However, this query concerns the heart in a special and unique way that calls forth the energies appropriate for the one known as Hatonn to intercept. Therefore, this instrument was forgetful in squeezing the hand of the one known as Jim and we apologize for startling this instrument and disturbing the beginning of the session.[109]

We would pause at this time for we wish simply to share the love of the infinite One that flows through us with you.

(Pause of approximately one minute.)

Ah, my brothers and my sister, this love transcends all the words that we can find to use. This love of the one infinite Creator is that which creates and destroys, that which causes changes.

---

[109] Carla was so distracted because of realizing that Hatonn was speaking for the Q'uo group that she forgot to squeeze Jim's hand, which is his signal to start the tape recorders. Therefore, the session had to be restarted in order to pick up the initial greeting. Usually the Hatonn group and the Ra group are silent and the Latwii group speaks for the triad of energies which make up the principle of Q'uo.

Each change, each aspect of the one infinite Creator, is beautiful and worthy of love and we share with you only that which we are given a hundred-fold, a thousand-fold, and a million-fold. Rest always in the knowledge that you are loved completely. There is no part of you that is not loved infinitely. You are cherished as the children of the Creator. You are the treasure of great price that the Creator has tossed forth, with total trust in the outworking of the present moment, into the field of the creation.

Through eons of time, encompassing vast numbers of individual experiences, you have come to love the planet called Earth. You have chosen it. Again and again you have given yourself to it.

And it has given itself to you. And you have partnered together and dreamed together. And together you have created the illusions that mask the truth that you now experience and with which you now dance.

When the world as you know it was very young, each of you was a being full of potential who moved into choices of environments. It placed each one of you on a certain track. Each in this room has a unique track. May we say, humbly and with knowledge that it is only our opinion, that it does not matter whence you came, any more than it matters whither you shall go when you leave the precincts of Earth.

You have met at this day of Sabbath and rest to seek the truth and your paths have met. There is a feeling of blessing as each within the group rests within the affection and regard of those who have affection and regard for each other, not only because you have met before in this world, in this incarnation, in this place, but also because you have done work for the light together before. You have soldiered together in faith and fearlessness. You have encouraged each other in deep times. You have rested upon the bosom of each other in other lifetimes and you have been comforted.

And so this gathering is a kind of family, a kind of nest. We have observed through many years of working with the group that no matter what group gathers, we find a tremendous amount of interrelationship. Whether entities come from far or near they are responding to subtle suggestions from deep within themselves that cause them to flock into groups of people of like mind.

Those whom you see in this particular circle of seeking represent three separate lineages of family in terms of inner-planes and outer-planes connections. And this is an aspect which enriches and deepens the connections and empowers this group. Again this is true not only of this particular group but of each group that gathers to seek the truth and to offer honor, love and praise to the one infinite Creator.

Such families of lineage have an energy and a field that is outside of space and time as you know it. It is a portion of that which this instrument calls time/space or the metaphysical continuum. It is in that space that information and energy is collected from all times and all spaces, as if in a circle, everything moving and tending towards the central sun of self to be collected in your heart.

We take the time to draw a picture of your environment because we wish to speak concerning the process of opening the heart. There are entities such as this instrument who are born with a heart that is open and that has no way to close. Were this instrument not possessed of a powerful intellect, this instrument would be greatly overbalanced. As it is, this instrument is able to maintain a good balance in her life experience in terms of the consensus reality portion of it and to maintain a stable and responsible lifestyle despite the constant waves of feeling and emotion that flow through her heart.

Because this instrument was born with this gift, she herself does not have a clue as to how one actually works to open the heart. She is much more conversant and familiar with how to use the powers of the intellect to create means of registration for the feelings or the emotions of her heart.

Working from the intellect to the heart is a completely different matter. And we would express our sympathy in understanding of the plight of those who are attempting to move from the head and the powers of the intellect to the heart and the powers of the intuition. Perhaps it may help to realize that the heart is ready to accept the entity that is lost in the mud in all of its confusion.

To put it another way, an entity which is attempting to process incoming catalyst through use of the intellect is an entity that is working with the connection between the intellectual mind of the second-density body and consciousness itself, which is that portion of yourself which thinks from the heart.

That part of awareness, while not at all intellectual, is extremely intelligent. In fact, rather than thinking, its power is a power of knowing. This instrument was attempting to express this shade of difference between thinking and knowing to the one known as Jim just the other day, without achieving a very successful result in communication because it is a difficult concept to grasp. But the faculty of the heart is knowing.

When information stems from the heart and its powers of intuition and direct perception, it is a knowing that is functionally stable and solid as long as the intellect does not begin to take it apart. Gnosis[110], or knowing, has a validity that is not vulnerable to methods of investigation in proof.

From the point of view of the heart, the workings of the intellect seem young, untrained and immature. However, it is our feeling that it is helpful not to scorn the use of the intellect completely but to do as this instrument does, and depending primarily upon the knowing aspect of the heart, move into the use of the intellect, directing the intellect rather than being directed by the intellect, in the perfectly just and reasonable attempt to look into what might be happening, as the one known as B said, in terms of geometry or densities or however one can think about the experiences that have been so powerful and so plentiful for the one known as B in these last few weeks. It is not necessary to scorn and lay aside the intellect. It is only necessary to remove it from the driver's seat and to ask it to take up its rightful place as a servant.

Let us refocus and look at a word that may be of help in reorganizing the way that you may think about what is occurring in incarnational experience. That word is will. Each entity possessed of a soul and spirit that is incarnate upon planet Earth at this time has the potential of being a magical and powerful entity.

The power of an entity resides in its ability to focus its consciousness at a steady state on a single-pointed desire.

An entity becomes magical when it chooses to allow itself to become powerful. Entities within your density become powerful when they choose their manner of being and serving. They have a choice to make. This choice is well known to those to whom I speak. It is the choice of service to self or service to others.

Once that choice is made, the remainder of the incarnation may be profitably spent in remaking that same choice with absolute tenacity. Over and over again, you will be offered choices. And each time that you choose consciously to serve others, you will intensify the energy of your field of being.

Perhaps you have had the experience, as this instrument has, of having those moments of realization when the choice becomes completely effortless and you rest in realms of builded light. Perhaps you have yet to have that experience. Perhaps you have had other experiences which indicate to you that there are many levels of awareness of which you are capable of at this particular time and place.

As you use your will to choose to open yourself to the light and the love that is in each moment, in each situation, and in each relationship, you will find that love itself will teach you what love is. It may feel awkward for quite awhile, off and on, to experience the rush and the roar of emotion. We encourage the one known as B to realize that these experiences are safe for him because they are being experienced in the nest and family of a group whose energy is able to help move energy aside in certain cases within the energy body where there have been blockages so that the love and the light of the infinite Creator can flow through in an uninterrupted and balanced manner where previously there was a shortage of that infinite energy coming from the Earth. It was moving into the body but it was being blocked at the red-ray energy center.

There has been an adjustment by the healer of which the one known as B is aware. This is an adjustment that can hold for a certain amount of your time and it can be renewed by this entity at will. Yet the hope in an experience such as the one known as B is experiencing—which is held by not only the healer known as R but also those vast families of unseen friends that have been brought into combination by those groups coming together—create the

---

[110] gnosis: intuitive apprehension of spiritual truths, an esoteric form of knowledge sought by the Gnostics. (www.dictionary.com) The word has its roots in the Greek, in which language the word means "knowledge." To look into the Gnostic belief system further, a good site is this one: www.webcom.com/gnosis/gnintro.htm.

opportunity for the one known as B to choose to do that good work which lies before him.

The ability to speak of things that are too precious and too dear for words will not come easily, not only to the one known as B but to anyone who attempts to share the astounding richness of the experience of life itself. For there is an infinite flow of riches, beauty, truth, strength, peace and joy that flows throughout creation at all times. Tuning into that is like opening a door in the summer. There is never any need to feel alone, abandoned, neglected or discouraged in a universe so replete with loving energies of every imaginable nature that cluster and gather around each soul that is attempting to seek the infinite Creator.

We encourage any who choose to open the heart to make use of the gifts that are so close and so easy to use. The main gift is that of silence. The ability to choose silence, to enter into the silence, and to listen to the silence, is an ability that will stand any seeker in good stead. Waiting in silence is the whole undistorted essence of unconditional love, that Thought, that Logos that created you and the creation in which you exist. That Thought is your deepest and most primal self. You are love.

As you seek to understand love, know that you already are love. So you need to engineer from that truth the ways in which your intellect can come to grips with a universe in which the foundational truths are gnosis rather than empirical investigation and the results of that ongoing experiment.

We would mention in passing the advantage of remembering resources such as humor, persistence and the ability to visualize. It is not everyone who can use this ability but to those whom this gift has been given, the ability to visualize sharpens and helps to discipline the magical personality. You may visualize certain shapes, fields of color, or icons subjectively meaningful to yourself.

In the attempt to move into an understanding of the open heart, it is helpful to begin to feel the focused power of yourself as a magician or a shaman or a priest. Taking yourself seriously as a priest creates within the seeker a certain attitude and engenders a desire to live a sacred life. This is a line of heart-logic that coincides with a line of mind-logic and therefore we would offer that to you as a key thought.

Each entity within incarnation is love, a sacred being whose essence has come into flesh. Why did you come to this place at this time? Why have you taken flesh? With what shall your heart and your mind focus and choose to love or express love? As the eagle flies, as the deer runs, as the wind blows, as the grass grows, and as the sun shines upon all, you dance the mystery dance. Take it all as lightly as you can. Laugh and enjoy yourself, for you are doing the most serious work of your life and the laughter is needed for balance.

Again, as we end this portion of our discussion, we would pause, for always the words end but the love flows on, ever-powerful beyond description and more real than anything else.

(Approximately one minute of silent pause.)

We are those of Q'uo, and would ask if there are any queries at this time.

B: Yes. The part where you're discussing the relation of the magician with the heart, and, I assume, the scientist with the mind, and the connection of energy that flows between. I didn't quite understand that. Could you extrapolate?

We are those of Q'uo, and are aware of your query, my brother. We shall do our best to focus on this aspect once more.

The heart and the knowledge of the heart is the higher knowledge when compared with the knowledge of the mind. We do not wish to denigrate the knowledge of the mind or the process of investigation of that incoming information which is precisely what the mind and the intellect were created to process. Indeed, we encourage the natural functions of the mind and would only suggest that the mind be honest with itself and not indulge in sophistry and shallow thought but go deeper and penetrate, to the best of your intellectual ability, the tendency towards shallow analysis as opposed to a deeper and broader point of view that shall bring you more information at a level that shall be helpful to you.

Rather, we were suggesting that it is helpful, when attempting to move from head to heart, to start with the knowledge that the higher faculty is heart and the lesser of the two is mind. Therefore, you have that powerful ally of the heart to ask for help when you are attempting to invite the mind to rest within the mystery of that which is unknown and which must forever, within third density, remain essentially unknown and mysterious. There are guards upon the knowledge that is the gnosis or knowing. It can only be approached through the faculty of faith.

(Side one of tape ends.)

(Carla channeling)

The experiences that you have had recently have numbed your mental faculties and awakened your faith. You have been rebalanced in order that you might take in this content which now is amazing you and making you wonder if you shall ever be able to master the experience or control it in any way.

We do not believe that it is possible to master or control the knowing of the heart. What needs the mastery and the control is the use of the mind. When the mind has been given greater honor and respect than it deserves, when it has been enshrined, there is born an inherent imbalance in the construct of thought within that entity's mental, physical and spiritual nexus. The experience that the one known as B has had recently has removed the glamour of the intellect and so the entity has awakened to the deeper knowing of the heart.

As the one known as B said earlier, if he does not find a way to encompass this new kind of knowing, he will lose it. That which is not understood and has no place to rest is lost. Therefore, this entity is seeking to find a way to seat this heart-knowledge.

We have talked to you of the will and how you may will to do this simply by having a firm intent and by backing up this intention with the daily seeking, not the seeking of an arrogant person who knows what it is that he wants but the seeking of a humble person with an empty mind, ready to be filled with new things.

There will be a good deal of shuffling and reorganization if the one known as B has the courage and faith to continue in this wise with this seeking. There will be moments of great clarity and many more moments of confusion. But all through that experience, if it is remembered that you may start with the heart and you may rest in the heart, in all your confusion, then you have a place to rest, you have a nest, even if you are by yourself in any particular moment or in any crisis or situation.

You may go to your own heart and you will be let in. And you will be in a place of tremendous

unconditional love. You will be back to the true roots of your being. It is from there that you will be able to rest and to know that you are calling the rest of yourself into balance.

It is difficult to talk to an entity about faith. It cannot be proven. It is a fool's choice. Yet it is the archetypal choice of third density. Shall you, by faith alone, acknowledge the love and the light that is your essence and therefore become more and more deeply who you are? Or shall you wander from place to place attempting to put together the puzzle that never can be completely placed in a finished frame by intellect alone?

Those things that have occurred to you have shown you that there is reason to have faith even though it is unreasonable to do so. This is the paradox you now face. Your mind and your heart seem to be paradoxical also, but we ask you to look at the figure of the mandorla, that figure where two circles intersect with a fish-shaped section of commonality. What do your mind and your heart have in common? You. They are two faculties of one being. The way you allow them to be integrated defines your experience.

We grasp that you greatly wish to allow this area of commonality to enlarge and we assure you that you are fully capable of doing this as a part of your group, as a part of the experience that never explains but always brings to you that which you need, day by day.

You shall continue to dwell in a great deal of chaos and confusion in terms of that which you have been used to, for you are in the process of transformation.

B: So, basically I have to have faith that all this will pass and I will grow?

We are those of Q'uo, and, my brother, basically that is correct. Yet, by the faculty of will you may choose, again and again in matters small and great, to enlarge your faith, to square it and cube it by the choices that you make.

May we answer you further, my brother?

B: I think that about covers it. I had a few moments of clarity there while you were talking, I'm not sure that I grasp it all. It's going to take me a while. I assume these things I've been seeing, cities of lights and dragons and whatnot, are there to challenge [the] intellect because my intellect is saying, "You're crazy," while my heart is saying, "You know you saw them." And it seems to be a bit of a conflict at this time. But I am assuming that common area in the center where the circles intersect will eventually work out how to deal with it.

Is there anything you can tell me, a clue on what the commonality area is? I'm basically looking how to express the heart to the intellect. I understand the heart is based in love but maybe I just don't understand what the consciousness is. I'm having trouble talking between the two. One wants to repress the other. I don't want to get into that fight. If that question makes any sense at all, any advice would be appreciated.

We are those of Q'uo, and are aware of your query, my brother. Let us see what we may do to offer you resources that will be helpful to you in this wise. Consciousness is a very good word for you to think more about, for in the time/space continuum, although you are a person, an individual—and will be for many densities to come in this octave and experience—you are also a very impersonal energy. In time/space you are aware that you are but a drop of water in the ocean of life. And although you can feel your drop-ness and your uniqueness, there is no fear in blending and melting into the ocean. That same drop that is "you" shall separate out as naturally as it dissolved into the surrounding sea of creator-ness that is all of those whom you meet and everything that your eyes fall upon, in addition to many unseen realms that your eyes never fall upon.

All of these things are in that drop of consciousness that you brought into your flesh and bone, your muscle and your heart. [Consciousness] rests within your mind and your heart, easily, comfortably, given a good safe birth by the natural processes of ensouling during the beginning of an incarnation.

You are a living blend of mind and spirit. The knowing of the heart is connected with consciousness, an element of the mind is connected to the mental faculties. Both are a part of you and both are good parts of you within incarnation. You need the balance to go on.

However, the truth is that you exist within a very rich and dynamic environment in terms of consciousness. You have access [through] the consciousness to the planetary mind, the racial mind, the archetypical mind, and the mind of the

Creator. All of these depths within are available to consciousness.

Naturally, as the door is cracked between the deeper mind and the conscious mind—and we carefully differentiate between the words "conscious mind" and the term consciousness—the door is cracked just a bit and light comes through, but it is not much light and so you get the dream or the vision or the seeing into other realms without enough context to allow you to understand what is going on. If you have a certain frame of mind that is curious and wants to know more about the unseen realms, then we would encourage you to investigate them for yourself.

Every time that you have a vision, write it down. When you have the gift of moving into unseen realms, do not dishonor or disrespect what you see. Do not allow the intellect to paw at it. Write it down. It is the journal of mystery. It is not that which is to be solved. It is that which is to be felt, treasured and accepted as that which is being learned in a classroom whose true construct you at this point do not clearly see.

We cannot say too much about the faculties of psychic sight that have been given you at this time by your mentor. We can only suggest that the experiences that you have are not crazy. They are simply psychic. You are being given glimpses into the larger picture. What you do with those glimpses is a matter of choice.

We encourage you to continue the road upon which you are now set, and as you do so, to give thanks and allow yourself to feel that uplifting of joy that creates a softness to the harshest experience. May you go forth on wings of love, my brother.

We find that, although this instrument is not aware of it, the energies of her body are fading and so we would choose at this time to end this time of fellowship and seeking. We thank each of you for the pleasure of joining your meditations and for the beauty of your beings. We are those known to you as Q'uo. We leave you in the love and in the light of the one infinite Creator, Whose name is love. Adonai. Adonai. ⚜

L/L Research is a subsidiary of
Rock Creek Research &
Development Laboratories, Inc.

P.O. Box 5195
Louisville, KY 40255-0195

L/L RESEARCH

www.llresearch.org

Rock Creek is a non-profit
corporation dedicated to
discovering and sharing
information which may aid in
the spiritual evolution of
humankind.

SUNDAY MEDITATION
MARCH 5, 2006

Group question: The question today, Q'uo, concerns the transition that we call death from the third density, either to the next density or to the afterlife. We are wondering if you could tell us something about how this affects the people around the one who are going through the death transition. They are the most affected here in our world. Could you tell us how this affects the people that are left behind, the friends and the family? How can people be inspired to support each other and the person who is going through the death transition? And then, for the person going through the death transition, tell us something about how that works. How does this person look back—or does this person look back—at the world that is being left behind? [Does the person] look forward to the world to come? Could you relate this in terms of both space/time and time/space, in terms of what the person going through the death transition experiences?

(Carla channeling)

We are those known to you as the principle of Q'uo. Greetings in the love and in the light of the one infinite Creator. We come to you in His service, answering the call from your circle of seeking for information and thoughts concerning the process of death looked at from several different viewpoints. We are most happy to be called and thank you for the honor and privilege of being allowed to share our thoughts with you.

As always, we would ask for you to be responsible for discriminating between those thoughts of ours that help you and seem resonant to you and those thoughts that do nothing for you. If a thought of ours does not seem resonant to you, we ask you to let it go. We are not an authority over you. Rather, we are your fellow seekers. If you will take responsibility for filtering the thoughts that really help you from the ones that do not, then we shall feel much more free to share our thoughts without being concerned about the issue of your free will or our infringing upon your sacred process of evolution. We thank you for this consideration with all our hearts.

We make this instrument smile quite often and we can feel her smiling as we express the thought that we are surprised to a certain extent that you have asked about death. We have found among your people that that subject is not one which is often something that pulls at peoples' interest. Whatever curiosity they may have about death seems to be buried in the overlay of cultural taboo. It is not a subject with which your people feel comfortable in general. Consequently, we are very pleased to be able to share our thoughts on this subject and we thank you for the opportunity.

This instrument was recently part of the [group of] friends and family [around] two [of their] close friends who had lost their mother. These entities, a brother and sister, have been involved with L/L

...arch and with this instrument since the early ...s. Therefore, the friendship and companionship between the ones known as M and B1 and this instrument and the one known as Jim is very close and very deep.

Consequently, this instrument and the one known as Jim spent perhaps six hours over the period of two days walking the steps of your culture's way of finding solace, comfort and closure to the life, the goodness, the virtue, and the beauty of that entity, their mother, who had passed through the gates into larger life.

(Pause while the telephone rings and is then is hung up.)

We are those of Q'uo, and are again with this instrument. There was, in the experience of this process of ritual and communion, every bit of comfort that those who loved this soul could pack into the ritualized remembrance of the viewing and the funeral. There was almost no awareness within the group that gathered of the closeness and the intimacy of the presence of that entity whose body lay in its casket on display for the mourning family and friends. There was no awareness that this entity was alive and part of the proceedings. It might not even have been comfortable as an awareness, had the truth been known.

The pastor who offered his sentiments at the burial imagined that the one known as E, the mother of the ones known as M and B1, was out of pain and with her Lord Jesus the Christ. These things were comforting and yet, in terms of the actual situation, were not accurate.

Certainly the one known as E has experienced being greeted by that beloved Savior whom she expected to see. Yet, in time/space, things happen in a non-local manner. And the one known as E was a part of the funeral, curious as always, wanting to see what everyone was wearing, how everyone was speaking, what they were saying, and in general, enjoying the gathering and experiencing a great deal of love, affection and gratitude that so many good people had taken the time and effort to come together.

We find that your culture does not have the kind of relationship with death that allows the comfort factor to increase beyond a certain point. Entities feel that, to some extent, they need to be solemn and serious, even if the entity has been very ill and full of years and ready, in many different ways and on several different levels, to move on. There is a knee-jerk reaction of feeling that it is a sad and negative occurrence; that somehow it would have been better had the person been able to live on.

Again, from a standpoint of time/space, this is an awkward and even primitive attitude, shall we say, not taking into consideration the marvelous experience that it is, especially when one has been limited, as was the one known as E, unable to speak because of strokes and so forth. It is still considered a sad thing because this woman was able to move on into the next experience.

That is what your experience of death looks like to us as we observe, through the mind of this instrument, the obloquies offered for the one known as E so recently.

We salute the tremendous love that went into these rituals for the one known as E. And yet we simply comment that, were the culture to be more comfortable with the concept of the physical death and to be able to separate this event from any thought of an ending of any kind for that soul, the obloquies would become festivities and sorrow would contain a great deal more of joy among your peoples.

The entry into incarnation is often somewhat traumatic, not only for the mother who is birthing the child but for the child. There is a frightening and hurried journey from warm, rich darkness into cold, sanitary glare. There is the necessity to begin breathing, which is traumatic in itself. And there is the indignity of being worked with and patted and poked and even slapped as the doctors and nurses make sure that the new child is breathing properly, cleaned up, and so forth.

When that process has reached its conclusion, when an incarnation's patterns have been completed and the Creator has called that entity out of incarnation, the process is again sometimes traumatic on the Earthly side of the gateway to larger life, as this instrument is used to calling death.

There may be a protracted illness. There is often a perceived difficulty as an entity is dying. We salute the wisdom and compassion of what this instrument calls the hospice movement.[111] As these [hospice

_____

[111] A good supply of information about hospice is found on this web site: www.hospicecare.com. Searching the web for

worker] entities are trained to see death as part of a process, not an ending but also a beginning as well, this attitude has helped many families to cope far more sensibly and practically with the mystery of death.

Caught up in the sadness of losing a beloved friend or a relative, it is easy to lose sight of the fact that death is not an ending of any kind but rather is an end point for those who remain dwelling on the terrestrial orb of Earth. For the entity who has died, there is a very smooth transition, unless there is some difficulty with the death in the sense that it may be sudden or unexpected. For an entity who is ill and is aware that life is slipping away, the senses are growing dim and the life force is ebbing, death is effortless and welcome.

It is experienced by the entity who is dying in various ways depending upon how clear the energies of that entity are. When this instrument died at the age of 13 for a brief time, there was no effort whatsoever, as this instrument had been at the point of death for two weeks before the actual death occurred and was fully aware that it was a great blessing to be out of pain and to be moving ahead onto a new adventure.[112]

This instrument was informed before she got too far into the [after-death] experience that she really could not stay. She really needed either to enter incarnation again using the body that she had left or to start the incarnational process again and come back into incarnation as a baby in the normal way, for she had work to accomplish and lessons to learn. This instrument decided to move back into the physical vehicle that she had left and she is indeed still using that physical vehicle with great joy and gratitude. This instrument, therefore, has absolutely no cultural bias and is fearless when it comes to the physical death.

However, for the most part your peoples remain constrained by fears that they shall cease to exist. There is a lack of true faith in the culture, for all of the fine words and the gaudy rituals that it embraces. We may simply say on this point that each of you existed before time began to unroll its scroll in space/time. And you shall exist long after not only your physical body but the Earth itself is dust.

We look now at the patterns involved in entities' being able to move through their grief process when there is the loss of a loved entity. It is not that there is a true loss, for energies connected with the dynamic between the self and the one who has passed through the gates of death continue to live in the mind, the heart, and the emotions of those who are left behind.

One of the most difficult things to deal with or to grasp, if you are a grieving person, is that there is no true loss. There is no ending to the relationship that has matured throughout the time shared by the self and the one who has died. What was true and authentic about that relationship endures.

And, indeed, it is truly said that a beloved entity becomes an angel on your shoulder. This is often very true, especially for parents and children. Where there has been devotion on the part of the parents, there will reliably be an energy that is left behind with the beloved child. If that child can remember to ask for the feeling of that beloved being, great comfort can come into the conscious mind.

This is a very subjective suggestion and we do not expect all to be able to deal with this. Nevertheless, it is so, as far as we know. Certainly this instrument is aware of several entities that nestle inside of her heart because of the devotion that they have had for her and the devotion that she has had for them. Her mother, her father, and the one known as Don, especially, rest comfortably and intimately in her very heart of hearts, a part of her strength, a part of her roots, and a part of what makes her who she is. There is a dynamic there that strengthens her for work.

And we would encourage everyone who has had losses to touch into the relationship that remains, if you possibly can, where there is strength there. Those entities believed in you; they supported and encouraged you; and they are still leaving that nurturing, compassionate understanding with you. Take advantage of that. Do not force away memories of beloved people. Rather, appreciate each of your ancestors, not just with memory, but perhaps even with conversation.

It is often helpful to have an imagined conversation, that is perhaps not so imaginary, when things are on

---

"hospice" will bring up many more good sources of information as well.

[112] Carla died after her kidneys failed when she was 13. She was revived approximately two minutes later by hospital personnel.

your mind and you have found someone who has passed through that gate of death helpful. Talk to them now. You may have to imagine what they say or it may come to you that this is a real conversation.

In a sense, you are able to do this with anyone who has lived at any time and touched your life. When you have once connected with someone, that connection exists eternally. You may trust it and you may rest in it. There is no loss through death except loss of the company of the physical body of the entity with whom you were used to being.

This does not make it easy to say goodbye to a beloved person. And certainly, as the one known as B2 was saying earlier, in the case of someone like the one known as V, where a twin has been lost, there is a physical, although difficult to measure, loss as well as a metaphysical loss. For that entity was V in the sense of the DNA being united. And it is particularly dislocating to experience such a death when one is an identical twin. Even a fraternal twin, which in this case was the relationship, has a unique link with its twin and consequently the loss of a twin is especially difficult. It is as if something were torn from you and there is a wound that bleeds. Rather than blood in the physical sense, there is the heart's blood, which is the emotion. These emotions have been wounded and there is raw and painful discomfort from the shock of the loss.

The Creator does not leave any of Its beloved children without comfort. This source of comfort starts with the guidance system that is part of your being. Your higher self is waiting to be asked for help. This instrument calls that higher self the Holy Spirit. We suggest that, whatever you call your guidance system, when you are dealing with death, you need, in a very central way, to access your guidance and to remember to keep asking it for news.

For you are moving very quickly if you are grieving. You are taking a journey very fast, faster than you normally like to go. It is a journey everyone takes when there is a change of any kind, good or bad in terms of your value system.

That entity who has left has changed everything because those energies are now taken out of your personal equation. When it is someone very close to you especially, this leaves a tremendous hole. No one else can replace the companionship or the affection

that that entity had for you, for each two people relate in a unique way.

Therefore, when you are attempting to help someone who has had a loss, you can certainly distract them by your presence and comfort them with your kindness, your affection, and your good words. These are substantive gifts to offer an entity who has had a loss. However, you cannot replace that entity who has gone on. Only the processes of time will allow the grieving entity to catch up with the tremendous changes that it has experienced.

We see from this instrument's memories that when her mother died it was very sudden. Death was immediate and painless. And this instrument knew that her mother had hoped to leave the incarnation before the processes of old age brought her illness and loss of faculties.

This instrument was the person responsible for creating the service to honor the instrument's mom and was the executrix of this entity's will. And so, as soon as the event occurred, this instrument was locked into several days of creating the memorial service, gathering family, and moving through the processes of closure that ended with the memorial service's conclusion. It was then, at that time, the instrument's job to straighten out a terribly complex and troubled financial situation and gradually and gently begin to straighten out its mother's earthly affairs.

In the process of all of these things, this instrument did not grieve. It was so aware of the mother's desire to move on into larger life while it was yet well, that the only emotion the instrument could feel was happiness and being pleased for her mom.

It was months later, when this instrument was in the hospital undergoing surgery, that this instrument finally was able to miss her mother's presence and to grieve and to begin that healing process that had so long been in abeyance because events moved too quickly for her emotions to respond.

One thing that entities who wish to help a grieving person can do is to allow that person the timing and the expression that are appropriate for that person, in working through the process of grieving and closure. Some entities can do this within several of your months. Other entities are not capable of coming through the process in less than a matter of years. And each timing, each choice of a way to move through the process is correct for that entity.

Consequently, you may comfort someone who is grieving simply by listening, affirming and understanding. Even if you feel that perhaps this person is taking it too hard or perhaps you wish that there was something you could do to make it easier, we encourage you to allow entities to have a hard time. That may be their best way of going through the process.

It is not necessary for this process to be comfortable. It is helpful, in the midst of whatever discomfort the grieving person is, for that person to know and to feel that you are with them, that you hold them in prayer, and that your heart thinks of them and sends messengers of love and light.

And those small times, those tiny seconds of remembrance that come to those who love, [are helpful.] Certainly, now that this instrument is aware of the one know as V and her loss, there will be a constant stream of thoughts going her way, for this instrument is one who has a cycle of remembrance that turns itself over perhaps three of four times in a day.

Use that part of yourself that remembers and send those thoughts out without mentioning it to anyone or even taking it so seriously as to mention it to yourself. Whenever that beloved friend who has had a loss is thought of, send a prayer her way.

And the same is true if you have a loss and you wish to pray to be with the entity who has died. In prayer, all happens at one time. As you think the prayer, it is being offered to that one who is in the inner planes, moving through the processes of death and transformation. There is no loss of time. There is no lag. When you pray, that thought has reached its goal and help is immediate. Know that the help is immediate, whenever you pray about anything.

Trust that, for the response is one that is protected within your own system of mind, body and spirit. You have comfort with you, as close as this instrument's hand upon her bosom. As she touches the skin above her heart, that prayer is already answered. In the time it takes you to form your thought, help is on its way.

Knock and it shall be answered; seek and you shall find; ask and you shall be answered. These are metaphysical facts. Count on them. They will comfort you.

You cannot prove them. You can only "know" them. And the one known as B2 will know exactly what we mean.[113] Know them. Take them to the bank. They will stand you in good stead.

What you see as difficult emotion is that which needs to occur for that entity who is grieving to move through that condign process. Therefore, see what you can do to make it all right for that entity to be uncomfortable, disconsolate and sad. Rest in the acceptance of what is. As you are not disturbed or distraught because of this grieving entity's emotions, that acceptance will register with the one who grieves. Beyond that it is simply a matter of allowing that person to move through the process in her own way, on her own terms, at her own timing.

(Side one of tape ends.)

(Carla channeling)

You asked concerning what the process looks like from the vantage point of time/space. We are glad to give you some information on this. We do have to pick and choose a bit for we do not wish to infringe on free will in any way.

From time/space's point of view, an entity outside of incarnation chooses to move into incarnation and then chooses to leave the incarnation at pretty much the same space.[114] So it is as if there was a bubble of incarnation that was created by the higher self and the self, agreeing on that which the incarnation would accomplish in terms of service and in terms of learning, what karma would be balanced, and what relationships would be called forth to create the appropriate suffering for the incarnation.

---

[113] In the transcript dated February 26, 2006, Jim asked the following question of the Q'uo on B2's behalf: "We need to get some information about how to get a language of the heart that is understandable to B2 and that allows him to share what he's feeling with himself and with others." Talking about "that portion of yourself which thinks with the heart," the Q'uo said, "That part of awareness, while not at all intellectual, is extremely intelligent. In fact, rather than thinking, its power is a power of knowing." B2 was part of the circle of seeking for today's session as well.

[114] Carla: This wording puzzled me. However, on reflection it occurred to me that if time/space is reciprocal to space/time as Larson posits, then theoretically their space is a river that flows one way only, just as our time is, while their time is a field, just as our space is.

From the vantage point of time/space, then, when an entity returns to the larger self or the soul stream, as this instrument has called the larger self, there is that sense of never having been gone that you have when you visit old friends who have been apart for years. Somehow they pick up right where they left off, if the relationship is a good one. And to your soul stream, the you that comes back to that soul stream is not at all a prodigal son but rather a returning hero.

Each of you has a great deal of courage and you have showed that by taking incarnation at all. It is a risk of a high caliber. You may forget to wake up. You may forget to perform your mission. You may pass on [working upon] the lessons that you wanted to learn.

When you return from an incarnation and look at the pattern that you have created, you may find that you have missed some opportunities that on hindsight you are sorry that you missed. Nevertheless, every incarnation is perfect. There are no mistakes.

And when you return home from this illusionary experience of life on Earth, there is a fullness to your experience that was not there before. You have added to the self in ways that you know not while in incarnation. And you have given a harvest of new information to the one infinite Creator. It is a joyful time. And it is as though you had never been gone.

There is, in the process of death, a final thing that we would say and that is that there is a crossover right in the gateway to intelligent infinity or larger life, as this instrument has called it, where the death has taken place and the will of the entity who has just died is still connected with the belief system of the lifetime. Therefore, entities will tend to see whatever they hoped to see or expected to see when they died. For entities who are Christian, that sight may include the one known as Jesus, the one known as Mary, the mother of Jesus, or other saints or entities within that Christian story that have been meaningful and to which prayers have been offered on a continuing basis throughout the life.

For those who do not tend to focus on personalities, there may not be any visions or sights at all. There may simply be the switching of environments as if you are walking out of one room and into another without a loss of time or consciousness of any kind.

The point of death seems like an instant within space/time, within the terrestrial reality. However, from the standpoint of time/space, that moment of death, so-called, might well take a while, might take up some space within time/space while the various threads and aspects of the self are gathered together in a relaxed, comfortable, easy and unhurried way.

Once the self has been collected and all psychic ties have been completed and closure has been found there, that part of the self that wishes to stay with beloved entities left behind does so, and the entity itself rejoins the soul stream.

Again, communing with the guidance system, the self determines what healing is needed. Some incarnations leave one a bit tattered, psychically speaking, and there is energy healing that is done.

Unlike Earth healing, this is a matter of allowing things to come into balance rather than proactively or energetically doing anything. There is an allowing of help to come in and, again, this may take a reasonably substantial amount of space—what you would call time—to accomplish.

Once this healing process has been completed, there is a time to contemplate that which the Creator is calling forth most deeply from within that soul stream. How shall you serve now? How shall you point the lessons that will continue to bring you into a more and more clarified and balanced situation within your energy system? Then it is time to think about what shall occur next.

Naturally at this time among your peoples, it is quite likely that those who die will be able to graduate and therefore their choices of what to do next are dramatically enlarged.

We believe that this is a good place to pause and ask if there are any follow-up questions or if there are any other questions that you may have at this time.

B2: How does the process of harvest differ from the process of death? You just spoke of graduation and more options, so whether one makes the changes from physical form to metaphysical form via death or from physical form to whatever is resulting from the fourth-density body, I don't see what the difference is there.

We are those of Q'uo, and are aware of your query, my brother. The process of graduation differs from the process of death and rebirth because, as we said, when one has graduated, one has quite a bit more free range in terms of the options available.

If one is dying and is not ready for graduation yet, that is, if one is in the middle of the cycle and graduation is not called forth by the energies of the being at the time of death, then the options involved are to remain in the inner planes or to move into incarnation within third density on planet Earth once again.

If one is able to call forth the energies of graduation by one's state of mind, shall we say, or state of heart, at the time of death, one goes through the normal moment-of-death experience and the healing experience and, when all of that has occurred, the higher self and the self may decide together that it is time to walk the steps of light and see if one may graduate.

Now, these steps of light are a figure [of speech] that was devised by the part of this principle known as the Ra group to try to describe a very fastidious operation, guarded carefully by unseen friends, in which an entity is given a construct of the different gradations of light up to the very highest level of third density and beginning with the very lowest level of fourth density.

The gradations are all shown equally so there is not a sense of, "Oh, I am approaching fourth density now. I'm going to have to push through." There is simply an invitation to walk in the light until the light feels too strong. Then, it is suggested that you take one step back and stop and see if that is the best possible light for you, giving you the best comfort and the best sense of joy.

In a way, [the graduation process] is looking for the place that you belong, if you would accept that construct.

Once you have decided that this is the place that you are most comfortable, you are then offered the information concerning whether or not you have graduated into fourth density. If you have graduated into fourth density—and this is where we must be somewhat vague about the process—[you are] offered the view for the first time of this new density and your place in it. You are still yourself, having dropped away those bits of personality that you carried into incarnation because they would be handy in incarnation. Nevertheless, you are essentially and unmistakably you.

And you discover that in fourth density, entities are easy to read. You know everybody. Even before you take fourth-density incarnation, you become aware of a dramatically changed environment. You are still between incarnations at this point but you have now moved into the fourth density and you have space to become comfortable there before you choose that which you wish to do.

From the fourth-density position, your options are greater than in third density. In fourth density, you are able to choose what group of entities with which you wish to work. You may choose to be a wanderer and to come immediately back into third density, as the one known as B2 did at a time when he graduated from the third density of this planet with a few friends only to find that his concern for his beloved tribe of humankind would not let him rest until he had done his best to call as many people to follow him to a larger life, wider vistas, and increased opportunities for service and learning as he could.

You have the opportunity to stay in fourth density and do your studying. You have the opportunity to move into the unseen realms, as this instrument calls them, or the inner planes of fourth density which are much more subtle and filled with much more of an interesting mix of entities from which to learn than is the inner-planes environment of third density because of the different nature of the light in that density and the possibilities for information being so much more rich in that density.

May we answer you further, my brother?

B2: For being vague, that was pretty good. One other thing: a lot of people in a near-death experience have visions of a crystal city of light. I've actually seen that myself but not in a near-death experience. It's being seen more and more frequently. Could you tell me what that is?

We are those of Q'uo, and are aware of your query, my brother. Again we shall have to remain vague. However we can say a bit about this construct.

The construct is precisely that. It is the awareness of fourth density in the minds of many, many, many people, too many people to have it stay a private vision. It is not fourth density itself. It is not the planet Earth itself. But it is information which is coded in a certain way that is characteristic of crystals. It is being built up day by day, in terms of your space/time experience, because of people that have begun to graduate and have begun to have a fourth-density existence. This existence and this fourth-density Earth are unseen by [their] choice so that there will be no disturbance for the third-density entities that are still using the third density of planet Earth.

There will not be made obvious or overt the existence of the fourth-density entities until the third-density patterns have been completed on planet Earth. Nonetheless, this energy, these essences and this new Earth are very real.

Since it is impossible for the human mind to conceive of two Earths interpenetrating each other and not bothering the existence of each other in any way, the construct occurs. It is a mass-consciousness construct, much like your UFOs and it expresses a reality that is beyond the conscious grasp of the human mind but not beyond the unconscious awareness of the tribe of humankind as a whole.

Imagine how powerful fourth density is, interpenetrating third density at this time. It is at least as real as the third density that seems to be the sum of reality to those with physical eyes. Therefore, it needs to be expressed.

And for those who have contact at all with their deeper mind, there will be some version of this vision that may pop up. And this will increase in terms of the number of people that are able to see it and even, as the one known as B2 said, able to go there and to work with the information.

B2: That's good. You're running very long. How's the instrument doing?

We are those of Q'uo, and we are glad you asked that question, my brother. It is undoubtedly time to relinquish control of this instrument and to say goodbye to this instrument and this group.

We thank each of you for the clarity and the sweetness of your natures, for the beauty of your vibrations, and for asking us to join your meditation. We thank you for being able to share our poor words with you. Again we ask you to take them lightly, use them if you can, and leave them behind if they bother you at all.

Thank you for this session of seeking. It has been a pleasure. We are known to you as the principle of Q'uo. We leave you in the love, the light, the power, and the peace of the one infinite Creator. Adonai, my friends. We are Q'uo. ❖

L/L RESEARCH

L/L Research is a subsidiary of
Rock Creek Research &
Development Laboratories, Inc.

P.O. Box 5195
Louisville, KY 40255-0195

www.llresearch.org

Rock Creek is a non-profit
corporation dedicated to
discovering and sharing
information which may aid in
the spiritual evolution of
humankind.

SPECIAL MEDITATION
MARCH 18, 2006

Question from A and R: *(Read by Jim.)* The first question is: A experiences visitations by a person who is not visible but whose footsteps he can hear. Can you please offer any comments and thoughts you feel might be helpful to learn more about this experience?

(Carla channeling)

We are those known to you as the principle of Q'uo. Greetings in the love and in the light of the one infinite Creator. We come to you this day as part of our service to the Creator. Thank you for requesting our presence at your circle of seeking. It is a great blessing and privilege to be so called. It has been a pleasure already to rest in the beauty and dedication and we thank you for setting aside this time for seeking the truth.

As always, we would ask that you use your discrimination in listening to our thoughts. Be careful to ignore and lay aside any thoughts of ours that do not seem resonant to you. That way, we can offer our opinion without being concerned that we will infringe upon your free will or the sacredness of your evolutionary process.

(Pause)

You ask this day concerning the entities involved in creating the effect of presence for the one known as A, and you wish to know how to deal with this somewhat unsettling phenomenon. Gazing at your situation we see that it falls under the general category of unknown visitors. It is more common than one would think for people living on planet Earth within incarnation to be visited by presences that they cannot explain or see.

The inner planes are crowded with entities of all kinds, polarities, orientation and description. There are points of opportunity where various types of entities can interact with incarnate beings that happen to be sensitive to finer vibrations, shall we say. And this is occurring with the one who is known as A.

We would observe that, in general, there are three categories of visitation. And we do not divide these into three in terms of the particular kind of visitor, but rather the orientation of whatever visitor is being experienced.

The first orientation is positive or service-to-others oriented. There are many service-to-others oriented entities that flock around one throughout the incarnation, and as loving hearts are opened and choices are made to increase the polarity of a seeking individual, the crowd of those entities who wish to associate themselves with such a source of light and love becomes larger.

There is a large category of non-polarized contacts. These involve mischievous spirits, passers-by who are basically in the position of kibitzing, looking over your shoulder as you play the game of life and other entities who desire neither to help you nor to harm you, but simply to be witness to that which is occurring with a particular entity.

The third category of visitation is that which could be described as negative or service-to-self oriented. The marks of the service-to-self visitor are those energies of discomfort, alienation, discouragement and irritation. When there is no communication from a service-to-self visitor that is audible or received according to the perceptive way of the individual involved, then the negativity of the contact may be inferred from the discomfort which accompanies such contact.

It is to be remembered that the self is inviolable. There have been in your culture many frightening stories of possession of an incarnate being by those of the inner planes. Ninety-nine percent or more of the stories are heavily skewed.

Because of your cultural tendency, when anything is not able to be explained by empirical data there is created in the mind of your particular culture an inborn bias against the validity of such information. Therefore, any visitation that cannot be explained by clearly observable facts will be suspect and even considered perhaps not to be happening at all.

This is acceptable to us if those among your people wish to turn your backs upon felt experience. However, we would suggest that it is a more skillful response to such feelings of being accompanied to assume that in some way, shape or form you are indeed being accompanied. The question of why then becomes interesting.

Further than this we cannot go without infringing upon the free will of the ones known as A and R. And so we shall at this time ask for the second question. We are those of Q'uo.

Jim: A senses that this being or source is somewhat unfriendly. Please offer spiritual principles and thoughts you feel might be helpful in his determining whether he should try to communicate with this source.

We are those of Q'uo, and are aware of your query, my brothers. As this instrument is well aware, it is a delicate procedure to come into a mutually helpful contact with an unseen entity. Entities from the unseen or inner realms of your planet are many and their interactions with those who are incarnate on your planet are numerous.

A large category of the interaction between spirit and flesh is the interaction of the self with the guidance system of that self. Your guidance system is, in the words of this instrument, the Holy Spirit, and in the words of the social memory complex known as Ra, the higher self. It is helpful to think in terms of the latter configuration of words in terms of determining who your guidance system really is, for your guidance system is not an entity other than yourself; rather, it is an access point into your larger self.

You are part of a soul stream that is not tied to any particular space or time. In the metaphysical world, time/space, all things occur in a circular ubiquity, happening all at once and tending towards being harvested, in terms of any experience that one has towards the middle or the source of your incarnation, so that things that you learn in all incarnations are being harvested into the soul stream's center.

When the march that you experience now through the densities is complete, all of that harvest will be offered to the one infinite Creator. And the Creator will then have learned more about Itself than It knew before. Such is your gift to the one infinite Creator in every moment of your life as you accrete interesting information and gradually digest and understand more and more of that which you see.

However, communication with your higher self is a uniquely protected activity. It is, in fact, the only case in which we would feel quite comfortable recommending that the one known as A or the one known as R pursue the conversation that is possible with one's guidance system. Such a conversion is occurring completely within one's own protected heart. There is no outside interference that is possible in this communication.

Opening such a communication can be somewhat difficult for those who are not entirely used to moving on instinct, intuition or insight. Avenues of direct perception are almost entirely blocked and denigrated by the values of your culture. Consequently, even those with very sensitive natures, who are aware of much more than they can explain, do not tend to feel confident about opening such a communication. Nevertheless, it is relatively easy to open such communication. It simply requires patience and persistence, once the goal of opening communications with your guidance system has been decided upon.

When an energy feels inimical or uncomfortable, the marks of one's guidance system are not present. And in such a case we would in no way advise the attempt to create a communication with such a source or entity. The reason for this is the relatively unformed nature of any entity's personality with regard to metaphysical work.

There is a very specific discipline which must be approached, grasped, invoked and pursued before an entity is ready to begin thinking about communicating with any spirit that is perceived. The nature of the human personality is such that unless care is taken, any attempt to open communication will be difficult, faulty or even harmful to the integrated personality shell of the being attempting the opening of the communication.

The need, then, before opening communication of any kind, is to go through a lengthy process wherein an entity discovers himself, defines his nature, and explores thoroughly those principles and central themes for which he is living and for which he would die. When an entity knows himself so well that he knows the ground upon which he stands, he has then become an entity in the metaphysical world of time/space. For the first time he has achieved the discipline of a personality. He has examined the self. He is aware of what he believes; what he loves; that for which he feels most passionate; that for which he lives and that for which he would gladly lose his life if it were necessary.

When an entity has come to that extreme of knowledge of self, he is then ready to have conversations with other spirits. He is then able to challenge them and to say, "If you come in the name of that for which I live and that for which I will die, then I will speak with you. If you do not, then you must go away." And that entity will perforce need to go away if he cannot meet your challenge.

To be able to make that challenge, knowing the self thoroughly, is the work of years. And if the one known as A wishes to communicate with this entity, that work lies before him yet to do. And this in no case a thing to be taken lightly or to be done as a lark or because it might be interesting. This instrument has watched personalities disintegrate under the bludgeoning power of a careless, uncaring inner-planes entity whose delight in breaking through to the physical world was such that that entity did not care what damage it did to the

personality of the being whose energies it took over. We would encourage the one known as A to be very careful and thoughtful if it is decided that communication with such an entity as the one he describes would be desirable for him.

May we ask if there is another query at this time? We are those of Q'uo.

Jim: Please offer any thoughts you feel might be helpful to A and R as to how they can be a helpful part of their young nephews' spiritual growth.

We are those of Q'uo, and are aware of your query, my brother. To be a part of the good in a child's life is a very precious gift and we salute and applaud those entities known as A and R for wishing to be a part of the spiritual development of those children with whom they are associated.

Being a part of the good in a child's life begins with that which the ones known as R and A are already doing, which is simply to love the children involved with all of their hearts and to wish them well. The atmosphere of unconditional love is a tremendously powerful influence on a young child. In a world in which seldom does anything go unchallenged in terms of the life of a schoolchild and a child in general learning how to be a part of society, such beings as doting uncles are definitely appreciated. Be assured that those whom you love are aware of your energy and feel the sunlight of that love as warmth and healing.

When entities around children are living their lives in a spiritually oriented manner, this has a strong effect upon the children. For the children are able to see that spirituality is a normal part of a daily, everyday life, not something special for Sundays or for holidays but rather part of the routine of living.

Entities who are children at this time period in your planet's evolution are very special entities. They have come for very specific reasons into the Earth's plane at this time. And for them to bump into those concepts of spending time in the silence each day and dedicating one's life to service to others is a very helpful experience.

It is not necessary to preach or even to say anything about the things that one is doing. It is only necessary so to live the life that the whole life is seen as sacred. Then when entities such as your nephews come into contact with you, they experience that aura of sacredness to the light.

In a way, it is as subtle and simple as taking oneself seriously, metaphysically speaking, and creating a daily life that reflects the priorities given to the spiritual process. When an entity young in years sees a mature individual spending his free time completely on self-indulgence—food, drink, games and so forth—an entity begins to assume that that is the sum and substance of Earthly life.

However, when a young child experiences life with [one who seeks the silence daily,] its vistas and its options open up. And it finds that it has a good array of things from which to choose in spending its time. It is not trapped in the world of materiality as it might be trapped if it did not know people who have refused to live their lives in the material universe entirely.

As you live your life sacredly, so shall that energy shine forth for entities such as your nephews to observe. You do not have to preach, as we said before. Indeed, we would encourage you not to say anything more than just a thought here and a thought there. Entities young in years are wise in terms of observational powers. And their interests will be sparked in an organic way as things come up and as they happen to be attentive.

And notice what certain particular time [there might be] that is just the right time for you to offer them a seed thought. Do not feel that you must lecture or teach but rather be yourself. Keep your heart open and allow the natural radiation of love and the light of the one infinite Creator to radiate through you. It is a matter of continuing to be aware of the present moment as you go through your day. Bring yourself back to the awareness of that love. Allow that love and light to remain in your day even when it becomes a matter of routine, of fulfilling the [duties of the day.] Keep moving back into that space of remembrance where you connect with the core of your being which is wholly involved in the business of sacred living.

For you truly open your life up to the full potential that you have as the spark of the one infinite Creator as a part of the principle of that Creator. You are co-creator in this universe of Earth, sea, sky and stars. You can choose a good deal of that which occurs in your experience by focusing with sincerity and dedication on those things that you feel are worthy of remembrance.

It is this dedication to right living, shall we say, that will inform your life and crystallize and clarify your energy, so that the children with whom you come in contact know that they are touching into a strong and powerfully positive energy. The natural curiosity of childhood will open up that entity's mind to wonder what you have and the relationship will bloom from there in a completely organic manner.

We thank you for the love which informs this question and wish you every opportunity to offer love and light to those about you.

Is there another query at this time? We are those of Q'uo.

Jim: The fourth question: R's ex-partner has moved on and their relationship has ended. However, he remains grateful for the learning received from this relationship. He would like to know any way he can be of a metaphysical help to his ex-partner without infringing on his present life or his free will.

We are those known to you as Q'uo, and are aware of your query, my brothers. We appreciate the fastidiousness of the one known as R in asking this question. For it does not often occur to entities that those prayers and wishes for good health and good fortune that entities may offer to each other could have any possibility of being an infringement. There are indeed ways in which free will can be infringed upon by one who is supposedly simply praying and we will attempt to describe those conditions.

When an entity has been unable to release the energetic dynamic that informed a relationship that has ended, it is indeed possible to infringe upon the other entity's free will in the process of prayer because the entity's connection with the other entity has not been appropriately broken.

If there is any doubt in the mind of the one known as R that this energetic dynamic has not been fully severed, then we would suggest to the one known as R either that he alone or he and his previous partner together create a ceremony which states an effective and final closure to the relationship.

If this is done with the ex-partner, that energetic exercise will be the complete closure.

If, on the other hand, this exercise is undertaken by the self and not with the ex-partner then we would suggest that the ritual of closure be written down, be expressed out loud by the one known as R and when the ritual that has created full closure has then ended, that he take the piece of paper on which the ritual was written and either burn it to ashes, or bury it in the earth.

If there was a difficulty in the separation, it is better to burn the paper to ashes and then blow the ashes away.

If there was no difficulty in the separation, but rather it was agreed upon by both that it was time for the separation so that there are no hard feelings or unhappy endings involved, then it is better simply to give that relationship back to the earth. And that would be the situation in which we would suggest burying the piece of paper on which the ritual of closure was written.

In either case, it is well to be absolutely sure that there is energetic closure before one begins an intentional and conscious program of prayers or good wishes [for] a beloved entity.

Again we salute the loving heart of the one known as R in asking this question. It is very well indeed to realize that all entities with whom one has come into contact in a meaningful and a deep way in an incarnation are those entities who have come there as the one known as Ray says, perhaps in this case or that case, there was pain because of such a relationship. This is often the case with any two entities that spend deep time together.

The process of change involves discomfort. And the dynamic of two souls who are attempting to learn together creates many opportunities for growth. Consequently, it is very common in relationships for two entities growing together to experience a good deal of discomfort. This is not because there is incompatibility but rather because of the inevitable effect of spiritual beings learning together. The effect of two such powerful beings, striving together to learn, is that effect which causes each entity to become a mirror for the other entity, so that all of those things which you did not wish to see in yourself, your partner has kindly offered you a mirror so that you may see better.

This is seemingly a difficulty, looked at from the spiritual point of view. For in order to enter the open heart, every part of the self that has not yet been loved, accepted and blessed by the self must be brought before the self so that you can do the work of loving your entire self, including that part of your shadow side which does not [seem so attractive.]

Once the work has been done to sever any lingering energetic dynamic between two people, it is perfectly acceptable to offer prayers at any time for an entity. You are offering prayers to the higher self of that entity rather than to that entity. And that higher self, the spirit, will direct that loving energy where it needs to go or will lovingly shunt it aside if it is inappropriate. As long as there is not an adhesion of energy between two people this is the spiritual rule that manifests.

We find that we have time and this instrument has energy enough for one more query.

Is there another query? We are those of Q'uo.

(No further queries.)

We are those of Q'uo, and as we hear through this instrument's ears that there are no questions, we believe that we have exhausted the questions for this session. May we say what a pleasure it has been. Again we ask that you be careful. Think about that which we say. If there is a false note anywhere, please disregard this information, for we would not wish to be a stumbling block in your way.

We are those of Q'uo. We leave you in the love and in the light of the one infinite Creator. Adonai. ✤

L/L RESEARCH

L/L Research is a subsidiary of
Rock Creek Research &
Development Laboratories, Inc.

P.O. Box 5195
Louisville, KY 40255-0195

www.llresearch.org

Rock Creek is a non-profit
corporation dedicated to
discovering and sharing
information which may aid in
the spiritual evolution of
humankind.

SUNDAY MEDITATION
MARCH 19, 2006

Group question: The question today has to do with the general idea of "ascension," or transitioning into fourth density and we're wondering what role the Holy Spirit plays. Is it something that comes into us and inspirits us and helps us along on this transition? Is it the same thing as the higher self? Is this transition something into which we're moving or is it moving towards us? Just how does this work? We're wondering what Q'uo could tell us that would give us a little more clarity on this whole concept of moving from third density to fourth density, how it happens, who helps, and how it works.

(Carla channeling)

We are those known to you as the principle of Q'uo. We greet you in the love and the light of the one infinite Creator, in Whose service we come to you this day. We thank each of you for laying aside this precious time to seek the truth and we are most honored and privileged to be called to your circle of seeking. As we gaze upon you, we, as always, are moved by the beauty of your vibrations and the harmony of your interrelating auras.

You have truly created a special chapel that takes in many entities in many places and it is a very special moment for us to experience the internet's addition to the group, for we are able to see you as a group in the non-local precincts of time/space and you truly have a builded structure of light from the combined and collaborative efforts of all of you to join into the unity of a seeking circle. We thank you for this privilege and for the beauty that lies before us in each of you.

As always, we would ask a favor of you, please. Be very careful to discriminate as you listen to or read those words which we offer through this instrument. Words are fragile things and in a sense that which we intend may not be conveyed. Therefore, we need you to discriminate between those thoughts that are helpful to you and those thoughts that do nothing for you. If a thought is not resonant to you, please let it go and use only those thoughts that you recognize, almost as though you had thought it but had forgotten that you knew. That is the hallmark of material that it is time for you to use. If you will make that distinction in working with our words then we will feel much more free to be open in our communication with you and not be worried about infringing upon your free will. We thank you for this consideration, my friends.

In speaking about the ascension process and the Holy Spirit's part in it, which is the way we understand your query to be centered, we take on, as this instrument said earlier, a good bit of terminology that is loaded with distortions because of the heavy use of both these words, [in] the portions of the religion that you call Christianity, in which much focus is placed upon ascension and the second coming of Jesus the Christ.

The problem with using religious terminology, in general, is that it is distorted in the way that anything will be distorted while gazing at it through a corrective lens. The perceived job of religions, as seen by the religion itself, is to create a distorted lens so that entities with bad eyesight can see their vision of the one infinite Creator. Therefore, they set up terminology, structures of thought and words which create a correction to the innocent vision of the faithful, offering to them the corrections of points of dogma in a certain pattern which, when received in faith, shall create that correction to the sight that will give them the heavenly vision of the new Jerusalem.

The problem with any dogmatic source, of course, is that the Creator Itself is not dogmatic nor is it subject to being described by the humans who are attempting to honor and worship that Creator or that great creative force or Thought. Therefore, the terms used—that is, the term "ascension" and the term "Holy Spirit"—alike are weighed down with an inadvertently heavy burden of inference and assumption. When what this instrument would call fundamentalist, inerrantist Christians use these terms, they are using them in a very narrow sense, specific to the New Testament and even more specifically to the Book of Revelation.

We would like to start there and work our way back to, may we say, a less distorted valuing of those words, and then we would like to lift away from the burden of the terminology and talk a bit about the underlying picture that this terminology is attempting to depict.

This instrument has a long and intimate relationship with the Holy Spirit as it is understood by her. She calls this entity, "Holly." She talks to this entity many times each day. She begins each day by calling upon Holly and asking for her help. She does not know what the day will bring but she has learned that it will bring something. And so before she arises from her bed in the morning, she calls upon Holly. She asks for her to be with the one known as Carla during the day and to speak in her ear, to shed her wisdom, her love, and her compassion upon the situations that meet this instrument's eye.

This is the general sense in which we would use the term, "Holy Spirit." That is that being which comforts a certain entity with all of that entity's distortions in place. The spirit that belongs to an

entity is not a judge but a witness, an advisor, and an enspiriter.

The nature of the Holy Spirit is well summed up by a prayer that this instrument uses each time she tunes for working with us in a session or for giving a speech or offering an interview on the radio or television. The prayer is one that we would repeat at this time in order that each may see the intended function and nature of this powerful part of the principle of the one infinite Creator. This is her prayer. It is one that she learned in 1983 when she was a part of the Episcopal Cursillo movement, taking a weekend out of her life to examine that life, create a rule of life, and dedicate her life even more intimately and firmly to the following of the teacher that she calls Jesus, the Christ.

> Come Holy Spirit. Fill the heart of your faithful and kindle in her the fire of your love. Send forth your spirit and she shall be created and you shall renew the face of the Earth. Oh God, who by the light of the Holy Spirit did instruct the hearts of the faithful, grant that by the same Holy Spirit I may be truly wise and ever enjoy its consolation. Through Jesus Christ our Lord. Amen.

Looking at the structure of this prayer, you may see that this instrument perceives the spirit as coming down, being pulled into her by her calling and her yearning for the divine, yet also being called forward by her emptiness and her willingness to be filled with new inspiration, new thoughts, and new ideas.

The Holy Spirit is not a comfortable comforter. It can create in the seeking soul a divine discomfort. It can help to sharpen and hone your particular vision of what it is to be yourself, what it is to be a part of the one infinite Creator, and what it is to face the world and look at that world, not for solace or for riches but for the opportunity to serve the light.

The one known as R was asking if the Holy Spirit could be considered an inner-planes or an outer-planes entity. We may say to the one known as R that you may consider this energy source to be both. In its function as guidance it is inner-planes. The calling is within the inner planes of your planet and in the inner bodies of your self. The connection is from the unseen realms directly into the heart, coming through the crown chakra, the gateway to intelligent infinity, down through indigo and blue, to rest in the heart itself.

When you have prayed to the Holy Spirit for a long period of time, you have created the connection that is instantaneous and strongly comforting, a never-failing source of wisdom, compassion and good advice.

The outer-planes portion of the Holy Spirit is that portion that has nothing to do with planet Earth or with your perceived notions of who you are or what the Creator is, for the Creator Itself is transcendent to Its creation. It is not an actor caught within the play of creation. It is uncreated, inorganic, infinite and eternal.

This Creator has a nature. That nature is absolute, unconditional love. And we use that word reluctantly, for love is a feeble, flaccid, effete word, badly used, abused and drawn through the mud of a dozen different usages of that word to mask impure intents, imperfect emotions, and confusion betwixt the desires of the body, the desires of the mind, and the desires of the spirit.

Indeed, those languages which contain many terms for the word love would be a blessing to us. However, this instrument speaks English and in your language love stands alone to indicate everything from lust to that unconditional love which causes a mother to give her life for her child or a soldier in combat to give his life to save his comrades.

We speak of a love that is beyond all of the boundaries and limits of human feeling. We speak of love that creates and destroys. We speak of love that changes things. If you can imagine a Thought that has the power to create the universe, then in your imagination you have seen love in its full meaning. To call the Creator love, however, is to limit that entity, for the creative principle is a mystery beyond the plumbing of any, including ourselves.

We would content ourselves then with describing this enlivening, invigorating, enspiriting energy and essence as the Holy Spirit.

Before we leave this particular term we would simply say that the term "higher self," as used in Confederation teachings such as those of the Ra group, is a concept which describes the Holy Spirit but from a point of view that is quite different from the religion-driven concept of the Holy Spirit.

Like the concept of the Holy Spirit in Christianity, the concept of the higher self is of an essence or an entity which is called down from the resting place of the higher self, which is mid-sixth density, to the self by prayer and supplication.

Unlike the term Holy Spirit, the term higher self indicates and specifies that the self, the higher self, and the Creator are all part of one thing. There is not another self, independent and apart from the self, that is being called down from some heavenly place into the heart. Rather, in the concept of the higher self, the self, the higher self, and the Creator Itself are all part of one entity.

The self is the self caught within the world of illusion by choice, veiled from awareness of the larger experience, and enjoying life within incarnation. The higher self is that same entity within sixth density. The explanation offered by those of Ra was that the self within sixth density pauses at a moment when it realizes that it is being ineluctably drawn forward into seventh density and will soon turn its back upon creation as known in the past in order that it may open its arms to the process of the increasing spiritual gravity of its nature and be drawn ever more quickly back into the heart of the one infinite Creator.

That resource of the self speaking to the self, then, is the self at is wisest and most loving. The concept, unlike the concept of the Holy Spirit, creates an atmosphere in which the self is seen specifically as sacred and no less of a Creator than the Creator itself but rather seen as a young Creator in need of advice.

We feel that both concepts are helpful and we leave it to each seeker to play with those terms and to find for the self what each entity feels is the proper terminology for the guidance system which is a part of each person's web of resources and tools for living.

The term "ascension" is similarly trammeled with a heavy overlay of religiosity. Ascension is a term which is used in what this instrument calls the Holy Bible, in the New Testament. It is a process which is heavily laden with fear in the minds of those faithful people who attempt to understand the workings of ascension from the Christian viewpoint.

In the Christian viewpoint, the picture of the end of the Earth upon which you now enjoy life is harsh. The end comes suddenly. The world dissolves into the one known as Jesus coming down from heaven and all of the graves being opened so that all of the entities that who have died can then spring forth, take on a new and spiritual body, and if you are lucky enough to be one of the chosen, you ascend into an entirely new creation, that Utopian heaven in which you have a mansion prepared for you and are free to spend the rest of eternity praising the one infinite Creator.

As a bit of religious fiction or myth, shall we say, it is unsophisticated and simplistic and we would not know what to do with a question about this concept. We would not know where to start in order to untangle the love from the fear, the joy from the sorrow, and the good from the seemingly difficult and negative.

In terms of our understanding of spirituality, there is an ascension process that we see going on all the time. It is a natural rising of entities through the mists of confusion and ignorance into a gradually more and more light and airy place where heaviness falls away, fear falls away, and what is left in the human breast is gratitude, joy and devotion.

My friends, this is your true nature. This is who you are. You are not a person seeking enlightenment. You are a person seeking yourself. To put it another way, you stand within flesh looking out [of] your physical eyes and hearing through physical ears and consequently you feel that you are a person of flesh and blood, limited by the senses that you experience as part of your physical body.

We would say to you that our perception of you is entirely different. In our perception you are extremely powerful and magical beings. Even within flesh, you have within you the ability to access the divine. This is because your very nature is love. Therefore, as you call out for your guidance, it is love calling to love. Certainly you are love that is confused at times, troubled and distorted in your perceptions, often fearing, often trembling, often discouraged and tempted greatly to be cynical and smart.

It is very likely that entities who seek find themselves fairly often in times of deep darkness, when the soul is hungry. The oasis that you seek at such times lies within you. The question is how to create good access to that self that lies within the illusion of your personality, your physical body, and your culture. How many different sources that you respect have said in essence, "You must know yourself. An unexamined life is not worth living. I think, therefore I am"?

The question of guidance and how it will affect entry into fourth density is a powerful question and one which we cannot even begin to answer in this session. But it begins with clearing out and cleaning out your perceptions of ascension and of your guidance system, or the Holy Spirit, so that you are not caught on the various thorns of religiosity and instead can focus on the reality of your divinity and your way of creating a powerful and strong access to an enhanced awareness of yourself.

What you are attempting to do when you pray to this Holy Spirit is to become enspirited. You are asking the higher, better, wiser and more loving part of yourself or of the creative principle to come upon you, to fill you, to reveal to you your true nature, which is love, and to give you those marching orders that make love itself into a plan for the day. It is not that love will tell you what to do. It is that love will tell you how to do it with love.

As you do ordinary, everyday things with this intense, overshadowing love, something magical occurs. As you seek to pull that enhanced vision of a life lived in love into yourself from the regions of the divine, you activate powers within you that are incredibly strong. And you begin emitting light. It is not coming from you but rather it is coming through you. You've turned the switch by turning your mind to love.

You've gotten the power upped by your prayers and supplications to be enlivened and enspirited by that which is clearer, purer and higher than you, in your perceptive web of everyday five senses, can remember how to do by yourself without often having trouble.

But help is available. That help is the Holy Spirit. And when the life is given over to that higher and better self that is love, when your consciousness has become that which carries the energy of the divine, then you have only to radiate, as you naturally will, as you move through your day and you shall make a difference in that day.

Whether you are alone or in the midst of many, many people, you shall make a radiation by your focus that is precious to the Creator, for it is by your free will that you have chosen to access that enlivening spirit and to give your life, your day, and your moment over to the intentions, hopes and dreams of the sacred within you and within the creative principle.

You asked concerning the transition from third to fourth density. My friends, this in itself is a topic that would take a great deal of time to examine with any degree of care. And so we shall touch on this subject as best we can in the time and energy that remain within this instrument's physical body and emotional body and within the limitations of time for all of those within this circle.

You are all familiar with the concept of channels on your television set or stations on your radio. If you would like to think of it in a way that is a little bit more comfortable than the phrase of "interpenetration of third and fourth density," you may think of third density as vibrating or radiating as a vibration or energy at a certain point on the dial and fourth density as radiating in a discrete and separate point on that same dial. You can tune into one station or you can tune into the other.

Each of you was set up, in order to come into third density, with third-density parameters being met. You cannot become fourth-density entities. You would not be useful to the planet and to the approach of fourth density if you attempted to live in fourth density. Rather, your glory is that you have earned the right to an incarnation at a time when you are capable of helping to shift the consciousness of the planet you call Earth in such a way that it calls forth from entities the desire to awaken and remember who they are so that they, too, may be part of the graduation from third to fourth density.

In a way, all of you are engaged in one mission together. You are attempting to awaken humankind. Focus that attempt upon yourself. As you awaken, the world awakens. Do not feel that you must go forth and teach in order to do this job. As you work on yourself, you are working for all of humankind. Be content, therefore, to seek ever more deeply within yourself for your true nature.

Oh, my friends, if you could only know for sure who you are, your hearts would soar. For you are love. You are a consciousness to whom the worlds are open. You can create and you can destroy, and, my friends, you do this each and every day.

For your thoughts are powerful things, and as you gain in power as a being you are ever more capable

of creating metaphysical hurt or healing by the thoughts that you think. Therefore, we ask you to be aware of your thoughts, to patrol them with love and compassion, and when you find yourself being cynical, petty, judgmental or foolish—and we will allow that word to be what it means to each of you—we ask you to remember that one of the things you came here to do was vigorously and relentlessly to go after consciousness itself and find ever more fully that joy that comes from knowing who you are and why you are here.

The planet itself is going through its own transformation. The energies that are hospitable to third-density life are waning and because of the actions of your peoples in their thoughtlessness …

(Side one of tape ends.)

(Carla channeling)

… with regard to their planetary resources, that time that is hospitable to third-density life has been shortened to a certain extent. It is normal, at a time of shift, for there to be as much as a thousand years after the shift while third density clears the planet of all energies that have been unfriendly or inhospitable. Unfortunately for planet Earth, the entities upon your planet have not come to the end of third density ready to embrace love, peace, freedom and justice. They do not see the beauty of harmony.

There has been within your culture a stubborn and persistent love of aggression and violence, where entities are moved by fear and therefore seek to protect and defend those things and people which are dear to them while rejecting the oneness of the planet as a whole. It is only in this atmosphere of separation that it is possible to consider slaughtering one's fellow beings as your peoples do each and every day.

Therefore, the end of your third density is not going particularly well from the standpoint of comfort and it will be uncomfortable for some time to come. You knew this when you took incarnation. You were eager to come here and to make a difference.

You do not have to rescue planet Earth! However, there is a karmic energy within many of your peoples which comes from actions in other lifetimes which resulted in making third-density environments uninhabitable. Therefore, the karma is involved in restitution and stewardship of planet Earth. And there are many people among your tribes all over the globe who feel a tremendous love for the planet itself and a desire to heal it. We would encourage this line of thinking, for truly all is one and your planet is a part of you.

As you move into the future, realize that part of your job has to do with radiating the love and light of the infinite Creator. And another part of it may well have to do with working with whatever energies that are about you in your natural, everyday environment, to attempt to become better stewards of that which is around you. What is your environment? How can you interact with it lovingly? How can you create islands of peace and joy so that when you enter the door to your home you are entering a sacred place? If you perceive of the Earth as a sacred place, what shall you do to clear the moneylenders out of the temple? We leave this to your consideration.

Fourth density already exists. It is a very sound and healthy child. It is a new heaven and a new Earth. And it is being filled more and more each day with those who have ascended, in the natural way of things, from planet Earth through the gateway of death. It is the great hope of many energies and essences of your inner planes, such as your angels and your guardians, that each of you may enjoy a leisurely, organic and natural ascension through that gateway to larger life that is the physical death.

From the standpoint of planet Earth, that is perfectly acceptable. Gaia herself does not at this time need to shake you off like fleas. However, as we have said before, we caution you, for there are entities all around your globe whose vision of ascension includes a self-created apocalypse. There is almost a hunger within that part of the planetary consciousness that is invested in power for the dark pleasure of blowing everything up once again.

See what you can do, my friends, to elect officials who are not caught in that "glorious Gotterdammerung" vision. See what you can do to elect officials whose hearts are stayed on love itself and whose vision is one which includes all entities in any plans that it may make, not just those who are wealthy or powerful.

We encourage you to wake up to this life, to embrace third density and to orient yourself as to who you are and why you are here. That is where the Holy Spirit can be so very helpful. Whether you see

that energy as a Christed energy as in Christianity or whether you see that energy as coming directly from a larger vision of the Creator which includes all of the galaxies, all of known space and time, and all of the inner and unseen realms as well, whichever vision helps you the most, we encourage you to take that vision.

There is nothing wrong with the Christian vision. It is a distorted vision, but so is any structure that is pulled into logic and mentality and intellect from the realms of spirit. The heart does not deal in quantities, it deals in qualities. When you attempt to define the Holy Spirit, you are attempting to quantize it. It cannot be done. So the best we can do is to give you ways to think about these terms that may help you.

To respond, finally, to the question of the one known as T, it is indeed so that the transformation of the self by calling on the spirit is an essential part of ascension, however one describes or configures this relationship.

It is by the guidance that penetrates into our heart of hearts that we finally learn to let our lives go and to open them to the unfathomable and mysterious presence of the divine. It is a release that is miraculous, just letting the boundaries of the intellect go. We do not encourage moving without regard to the intellect in everyday life but rather we encourage the opening up of your point of view to encompass a self that is both physical and spiritual, not separately but all together in one glorious confusion, as the one known as M said earlier.

Our wish for you would be that you were in this moment to determine to be ready to listen, to say, as this instrument does, "Come Holy Spirit!" And we say to you that you are asking for a lot when you ask for the spirit. You are not simply asking for a nice or a pretty or a beautiful experience. You are asking for the truth. Be ready, when you ask, for whatever may happen, for a sincere request to the spirit shall never be unheard. You shall be answered, my friends, and your lives shall change.

We realize that our time is up and we believe that it is best, examining this instrument's energy levels, that we ask for only one or two brief questions before we leave this instrument. Is there another query at this time? We are those of Q'uo.

B: I have one. You mentioned we are beings of love and beings of consciousness. What's the difference between love and consciousness?

We are those of Q'uo, and are aware of your query, my brother. Love is an essence. It is not necessarily tied to a point of focus. It is rather that focus that creates all that is and, as such, its nature transcends consciousness, as we use the term to indicate that portion of a human being which is not caught in space and time.

May we answer you further, my brother?

B: I understood.

Is there another query at this time? We are those of the Q'uo.

B: Let me check on the internet.

(Pause)

B: I think P has one. Hold on.

(Pause)

P: *(Speaking through the internet from Nevada.)* I was wondering if you could clarify how love is destructive.

We are those of Q'uo, and are aware of your query, my brother. And may we say what a pleasure it is to embrace the energy and the spirit of the one known as P as well as all of those whom we have not experienced as part of this group for a time. It is a great pleasure to us to say hello.

That which is the Creator is that which equally creates and destroys. To the Creator, the two are part of one process. There is a dynamic between light and dark, creation and destruction, love and fear, and so forth. It is one of the powerful dynamics that are a part of the illusion which you now enjoy.

It is perhaps easier to see this destructive and creative aspect when one examines, say, the life of a sun or the life cycle of an animal within your second density. There are portions of that cycle in which the animal involved is growing. There are portions in that cycle in which the animal is food for another animal. Yet the entirety of the creation is harmonious.

And rather than feeling that there is a wickedness involved in nature, "red in tooth and claw,"[115] as the

one known as Alfred said, it is to be seen that this is all a perfectly acceptable part of the dance of life in which entities eat food and are food in their turn. As your body dies it shall be food for worms. And the Creator has provided natural ways in which the seemingly destructive process of various creatures, like worms and other bugs eating the body, makes it a part of the Earth once again and the cycle of that particular body is complete: dust to dust, ashes to ashes. That is the sense in which we meant the destructive nature of love. It, in being creative, must also complete the cycle and be destructive as well in the natural and organic whole of a 360 degree world.

May we answer you further, my brother?

P: That sounded pretty good, although I'm interested on your point on a 360 degree world. Are there levels below that?

We are those of Q'uo, and are aware of your query, my brother. This instrument's use of the term "360 degrees" is meant simply to indicate there is no such thing as an arc that is uncompleted in the creation. All energies have their dynamics and form perfect circles or spheres, to be more accurate.

We find that this instrument's energies are waning and so we would take this opportunity to thank each of you for this opportunity to be a part of your circle of seeking. We would leave you at this time with great joy and thankfulness in the love and in the light of the one infinite Creator. We are known to you as the principle of Q'uo. Adonai. Adonai. ⚶

---

[115] Alfred Tennyson, "In Memoriam":

Who trusted God was love indeed
And love Creation's final law—
Tho' Nature, red in tooth and claw
With ravine, shriek'd against his creed—

L/L RESEARCH

L/L Research is a subsidiary of
Rock Creek Research &
Development Laboratories, Inc.

P.O. Box 5195
Louisville, KY 40255-0195

www.llresearch.org

Rock Creek is a non-profit
corporation dedicated to
discovering and sharing
information which may aid in
the spiritual evolution of
humankind.

SPECIAL MEDITATION
MARCH 21, 2006

Question chosen by PLW[116] poll: In a previous meditation, there was mention of souls from Mars who were unable to finish their third-density cycle there because of the destruction of their environment and who are now acting as stewards of this planet. Could you tell us about how many there are, when did they come here, and what are the majority of them doing today?

(Carla channeling)

We are those known to you as the principle of Q'uo. Greetings in the love and the light of the one infinite Creator, in Whose service we come to you this evening. It is a privilege and a pleasure to be called to your circle of seeking and we are honored to share our thoughts on your query this day, which has to do with those entities who came to Earth from the Red Planet, Mars.

We would, however, as always, ask of each who listens to or reads this material that each take responsibility for discriminating between those thoughts we share that have a meaning to you and seem resonant and those thoughts that we share that do not seem to hit the mark for you at all. If there is no resonance in the thoughts we share this day, please leave them behind. If you will agree to do that, we will feel to speak with you without being concerned overly much for infringing upon your free will or interfering with the process of your evolution.

We are happy to share information with you about those entities which came from the planet which you call Mars. We would, however, precede this information with a few words about our understanding concerning the importance of this information.

We are those who greatly enjoy speaking concerning spiritual principles that may be of service to you in your seeking. Information concerning where the various populations of your planet come from is fairly dry and mechanical information which we cannot infuse with a great deal of spiritual meaning except by the indirect references to what has occurred with those of the Red Planet and to some extent as to why things might have fallen out the way they did. Therefore, we would ask you to seek this information concerning the what and the when of the immigration from the Red Planet in the knowledge that our voice is a voice of love.

The details are never as important as the source of all the details, which is the one infinite Creator. The love that created the planets and their courses and all the mysteries in the universe has also created each of you, regardless of whence you come or whither you shall go in the worlds of illusion which abound in creation.

Therefore, no matter how interesting the details, we ask you to reserve a part of [your thoughts] for love Itself, that great Creator that has brought into manifestation all that is, including each of you,

---

[116] Planet Lightworker Magazine (www.planetlightworker.com).

whether or not you might have at one time been a part of third density upon the Red Planet.

We shall tell you a story about a series of populations that arrives at Earth for the purpose of joining in the experience of sharing third density with those few people who actually graduated as natives from second-density Earth to the third density Earth.

The first and the largest of these populations was that of Mars. The entities of Mars had made some decisions in the practice of governments upon their planet which resulted in the nature of the surface of their planet changing from a planet which was relatively hospitable to third-density physical vehicles to a planet which was not at all hospitable to third-density vehicles. They were not able to finish the cycle of the Density of Choice in third density upon Mars.

The Guardians of this planet went before the Council of Saturn and asked for permission to move that population to Earth. The second-density vehicles available for physical use upon planet Earth at that time were late second-density great-ape bodies, which the guardians felt might be improved upon by articulating facial features a bit more carefully, by altering the set of the body so it would be able to stand upright, and by improving the dexterity of the physical vehicle, especially in the hands. And by creating a larger capacity within the mind that came with that biological species. In essence they created a new and improved great-ape body which looked a good deal like the one you are now enjoying.

The Guardians at that time found, within the space of several hundreds of your years, that they had made what they considered an error in creating the new and improved version of the great ape body used by the denizens from Mars and thereafter used by entering souls from planet Earth or from elsewhere, simply because it was indeed a new and improved physical vehicle that looked like it would be handier to use to the entering souls and their guidance systems.

The Guardians' mistake was in creating better physical vehicle with the attitude that these physical vehicles were better and that the people that inhabited those physical vehicles were special. Naturally, the Guardians were very fond of the incoming population and felt great love for them, as they were placing them carefully and gently upon planet Earth to take up again their search for love.

What they did not anticipate was that the people themselves would feel that they were special. They were aware that their intellect [was more powerful] than other great-ape species that inhabited the Earth at that time. They felt privileged and special. And they created within themselves an attitude of "better than."

The energy of the beings from the Red Planet was naturally somewhat progressive and fiery. They had demonstrated this aggression, this ability to wage war on their home planet and had succeeded in destroying the surface of it as an acceptable environment for third-density life. They carried these biases with them into third density upon this planet.

The very beginning of your cycle of third density upon planet Earth was nearly 76,000 of your years ago, by your counting. The [Martian population] incarnated in what you would call the Middle East and parts of Africa first, their thickest area of population in that area of the planet. Gradually they become the populations that you now know of as the Moslems, the Jewish people, the Palestinians, and others of Middle Eastern heritage.

As the population settled in and began their cycles of reincarnation to gain experience and learn the lessons of love, they spread out, becoming the populations that you now know as the Russian and Eastern Orthodox churches, the Christian church, and the Christian Protestant church as opposed to the Christian Roman Catholic church. All of these populations are heavily "larded" with those originally from planet Mars.

You will note that these entities comprise the bulk of those who believe in one God. The up-side in the belief in one Creator is that it is closer to that mystery of the Creator than the solution which posits many gods. It is our understanding that all things are one, and the infinite Creator is as single as Its universe and creation.

The down-side in believing in one God is that belief that only if you believe in that one God—and believe in a certain way—shall your soul reach heaven. This creates a bias within the religious, and oftentimes the political mind of those [who so believe] that there is their way or the highway, as this instrument would put it.

You will note that in the Moslem church, the Christian church, and in the church of the Jews that there is a strong tendency to exclude certain of their members who do not believe specifically in the points of dogma in which they hold to be true. The tendency of this energy of belief in one God, then, has its challenging aspects when it comes to using that religion as a springboard for the lessons of love.

If you will examine the writings that are at the heart of any of those three religions, you will find a mystical understanding of unity that is very similar between those three churches. However, for the entity that is living an everyday life, the tendency with dogmatic churches is to be very exclusionary and judgmental, so that an entity is told basically, "Either you believe the way we believe or you are consigned to one of the circles of Hell after you are dead." They then feel that it is permissible and even desirable to proselytize and attempt to create that bias within those whom they meet.

This nest or web of actions is basically the end result of the Guardians, 75,000 years ago, making too many improvements on physical vehicles and creating pride and arrogance as a birthright of the new and improved human species. You may still see those energies playing themselves out in your Earth world at this time.

What are those of Mars doing these days? As the one known as J said jokingly earlier, they are running your countries, parking your cars, taking care of your children, and doing every other human thing you can think of. For there are millions and millions of those who came from Mars. They are, as are all of those within third density at this time, striving to learn the lessons of love.

Many of those who come from the Red Planet have earned the right to graduate into fourth density. They have achieved that shift in consciousness from fear to love, from war to peace, from doubt to faith, and from despair to hope. There is no stigma in being from Mars, anymore than there is a stigma to anyone for being born of a certain genetic heritage.

It is not that the physical vehicle that you inhabit is unimportant. It should be honored, respected and loved, for it has given its life so that you and your consciousness may walk the planet and learn the lesson that you came to learn. It is that body whose hands reach out to do the service you would do for your fellow human being. It is that voice that sings the praises of the one infinite Creator. Without your body you would be unable to have incarnation.

At the same time, it is not well to identify entirely with the body that carries you about. For the body that is carelessly [used] and not justly appreciated will tend to wish to rule over the mind and spirit. It has strong instincts, not because of genetic changes but because of the inherent second-density heritage. It wishes instinctually to mate, to form a clan for family, to gather resources so that the clan may live, and to protect those resources, and, if necessary, defend them to the death.

We may note that in our humble opinion some of the actions of your governments at this time fall solidly under the influences of those instincts. You are at the end of your third density, moving into that time of graduation. Those who do not choose to graduate will necessarily fall back to the instincts to late second density as they prepare to start another third-density cycle elsewhere.

We would ask each of you with a resonance with the history of those of Mars, "Do you wish to take a leap forward, to wake up from the dream of hostility?"

If so, then you have every necessary capacity and have probably already made the choice to turn your back on violence and negativity and to choose love as your expression, your being, and your goal. We encourage you to trust yourself and to give all that you have into making this shift. It is not too late. The decision to choose love is a matter of a heartbeat. Each decision to choose love is a matter of a heartbeat.

We would ask if there is a follow up question at this time. We are those of Q'uo.

(No further queries.)

We are those of Q'uo. The silence that we hear expresses to us that you have exhausted your questions for this evening. In that case we wish only to express our gratitude for being [asked to join your circle of seeking.] We are those of Q'uo. We leave you in the love and the light, the peace and the power of the one infinite Creator. Adonai. Adonai, my friends. ❧

L/L Research is a subsidiary of
Rock Creek Research &
Development Laboratories, Inc.

P.O. Box 5195
Louisville, KY 40255-0195

L/L RESEARCH

www.llresearch.org

Rock Creek is a non-profit
corporation dedicated to
discovering and sharing
information which may aid in
the spiritual evolution of
humankind.

SPECIAL MEDITATION
MARCH 28, 2006

Question from T: Q'uo, there is an increasingly popular global trend happening right now. Young people are tending to spend their time playing online games with one another. Some or most of these children may even have the dual-activated bodies of which Ra spoke in the *Law of One* material. Thus, it seems to me that most of the online gaming is a distraction and a waste of time for children of that nature or any individual, really. My first question is this: What is the influence of online games to this world, especially to young people?

(Carla channeling)

We are those known to you as the principle of Q'uo. Greetings in the love and in the light of the one infinite Creator, in Whose service we join your group this evening. Thank you for the privilege and the pleasure of being called to your circle of seeking. It is a great blessing to us to be asked to share our thoughts with you and we thank you for the opportunity.

As always, we would ask that you be very careful in discriminating between those thoughts of ours which seem good to you and those which do not. Please discard any thoughts that do not seem accurate or excellent to you. We would not be a stumbling block before you.

Thank you for this consideration, as it will allow us to feel quite free to speak with you without being concerned that we would infringe upon your sacred spiritual process.

Your question this day concerns the joining of many among your people, especially among your young people, with the online games that are so popular in your cultures at this time. There are a wide variety of these games of which this instrument is somewhat aware and we see this phenomenon through her eyes and through the ramifications of your query.

To us it would appear that there are several different energies in motion at this time which influence the popularity of such means of recreation. And so we would discuss various aspects of this question.

Firstly, let us look at the status or the estate of young people, spiritually speaking. Entities within your cultures at this time that are young are, as the one known as T mentioned, possessed of bodies in which the fourth-density energies are in potentiation. The double activation creates an atmosphere in which the mind of the person is sensitive to unspoken thoughts and unexpressed emotion. For the most part, these entities have found it somewhat difficult to achieve a sense of peace dwelling within third-density conditions.

In this atmosphere of internal turmoil, it is natural for entities to seek means of soothing and calming their troubled natures. The online game which this instrument plays is of a type that has the tendency to entrain those troubled thoughts and allow them a means of relaxation and drifting away. This is the simplest type of game. It is not played with other people and its purpose is simply to relax the mind and loosen the bonds of tension and stress that have been built up because of the attempt to do intellectual work for a long period of time.

Indeed, for entities of this type, the repetition of the play of the cards or whatever game is being played is as effective as some of your prescriptions which would similarly affect the mind, reducing tension, lowering the blood pressure, and so forth. This type of gaming is, when a part of a lifestyle that is enjoyable to the entity, an acceptable and spiritually neutral part of the coping mechanism of entities such as this instrument.

The next aspect of gaming at which we would look is that aspect which expresses hostility. Many of your computer games, whether played by the self or played with others, involve a great deal of dramatic action in which the online characters are embattled. There is a good deal of destruction and mayhem that is a part of the game. It is necessary, in order to play the game, to move through the patterns of aggression, warfare and the concept of winning over one's enemies.

Games such as this have a mixed polarity in terms of their effect upon the people who play them. In one sense, there is something to be said for a person who is aware that, within the heart, she has many hostile and aggressive feelings which she cannot, in good conscience, express in the normal course of everyday life. Such a seeker may consciously choose to play such an aggressive game in order to express the shadow side of the self in terms of negative emotions like anger, impatience, judgment and resentment in a way that does not infringe on anyone's free will. [When] played in a conscious way, where the time is dedicated to expressing such feelings in a non-harmful manner, such an entity may experience a psychological release from the opportunity which has been taken to unload the harmful and toxic emotions and remove [them] from the interior emotional system of the self.

However, it is far more often the case, when entities enter into such games, that quite another psychological structure is being expressed. Rather than there being a conscious awareness of love and a desire to maintain that love by bleeding off negative emotion, the intention of the majority of entities who choose to play such aggressive games is to enjoy

the process of being powerful and able to defend the self successfully. This motivation is fear based.

There is, in many entities, a very accurate perception that the culture of which they are a part is one in which they do not feel comfortable. Certainly within this instrument's feelings and thoughts there is often a reaction to the choices and decisions made by those in power. She wonders what is happening to her world. She is puzzled, and more than puzzled, she is disturbed. These emotions are mild compared to the kind of fear that is generated by eyes that look upon what seems to be a hostile world that is unresponsive to the gentle and sensitive portions of human nature. Fear builds up within such an entity and there is a desire to find an environment in which, even in a game, there is the illusion of being in control.

In the last aspect of which we would speak concerning the online gaming, there is another level of expression which has to do with expression in groups. For many entities there is a feeling of being isolated and apart from any comfort. The outer environment, not just for young people but for people of all ages within your culture, can often seem to be bleak.

When the eye gazes upon the outer scene, there seems to be no way to create the atmosphere that is yearned for, the atmosphere which would encourage feelings of relaxation, enjoyment, friendship, companionship and the desire to come together socially in a positive way. Instead of such a general feeling of trust in social rightness, there is, in many entities, a profound dislocation and distrust of the outer world.

However, in an online game there is the joining of a group under rigid rules of play in which there are adventures to be had in a controlled atmosphere. These virtual dramas are absorbing, complicated and self-expressive. There is the opportunity to create the self and [then] recreate the self anew in another game. There are opportunities for companionship of a certain kind. It is a substitute for the innocent and everyday interactions of people in real life in real situations coming together in groups to play a game of baseball or do homework together or other such social opportunities.

We would pull back the vision now and take a look at the society in which these online games are taking place. Certainly, many entities do not dwell in urban situations. However, a large percentage of your people do dwell in groups, in towns, cities and large groups of cities that form corridors of great density of population. Ironically, the denser the population becomes, the more isolated the people within such populations feel.

This instrument was recently speaking with a couple who had lived in the Orient for the past few years. The one known as L was saying to this instrument that when she first arrived in the crowded cities of China and other countries in the Orient, she was struck by the physical closeness of entities. She could not walk on the street without being repeatedly bumped because there was so many people on the streets that there was no room to have one's own space.

She found, after a certain number of months had gone by, that she had learned how to ignore those souls around her which were passing her on the street. It was necessary for her own sanity and peace of mind that she downplay the presence of other souls within her aura and protect herself against even acknowledging their existence. This is the atmosphere which breeds people who turn within for their recreation and their companionship.

The general effect of the online gaming is part and parcel of the general effect of the way your culture works. That effect is to deaden the sense of focus and awareness within an entity. This tendency of the culture to deaden or numb the emotions and the thought processes of entities is, from the standpoint of spiritual seeking, unfortunate. You have placed yourself in an environment which is heavily overlaid with cultural encouragement to stay asleep. Whether it gaming or any other aspect of the pop culture, the phenomenon involves a great many people aware of a few names, games, events or social circumstances, and focusing on those few icons to the exclusion of becoming interested in the exploration of the self.

We find that this is the extent to which we are able to offer thoughts upon this subject. The spiritual principles involved are slight and therefore we find that our commentary is limited.

Is there another query at this time?

T: Do these games bring more positive or negative polarity to this world in general?

We are those of Q'uo, and are aware of your query, my brother. There is very little net gain or loss of polarity because of gaming. Certainly, in some entities who are already negatively polarized, some of the more aggressive and hostile games help them to hone the edge of their anger and rage. But for the most part the net result of these games is distraction and sleep, along the lines of your television, your movies, and your other entertainment.

Is there another query at this time?

T: Does online gaming play any part in the creation and development of a social memory complex?

We are those of Q'uo, and are aware of your query, my brother. The gaming itself does not have the characteristic of building a social memory complex.

We would find it interesting to see what entities who are interested in games could do to create a game [which has] the stated purpose of working with metaphysical principles in order to examine the life, the society, and the age-old questions of, "What is truth? What is beauty? What is goodness? What is justice?" and so forth.

The phenomenon of the [world-wide web on the] internet in general has the characteristic of creating far more of a global awareness for all of the people who are looking for information on the internet and forming a global group. This is, as this instrument has said, a kind of training-wheels exercise, getting people ready to think of all of the tribe of humankind as one tribe. When one is on the internet and bouncing around from site to site, one bounces all over the planet, depending upon the links which one is following. One quickly begins to grasp oneself as a member of the global community.

Further, it seems to be a very friendly, interactive and lively community. Thusly, we would look at the internet itself as an experience with what a social complex feels like rather than confining that to the gaming.

Certainly, any large group of entities all getting together to experience one event has that feeling of a global group. However, the events for which entities gather as a global group are fleeting and therefore there is not the continuous experience of the self as part of a global group when watching, say, the Superbowl or the final playoffs of any of your sports such as soccer or hockey.

Is there another query at this time?

T: Since free will is utmost as a principle for us to respect, what is our proper attitude to [take when we] talk about online games with kids?

We are those of Q'uo, and are aware of your query, my brother. When dealing with other selves of any age, it is well to meet them where they are.

There is a certain amount of time available to your people; a certain number of heartbeats between birth and death. If an entity takes the self too seriously, an entity can attempt to use every minute of every day for the entire lifetime in a positive, constructive, useful way. This attitude, while commendable, results in an incarnation that is dry and arid, emotionally.

Other entities may choose to spend an incarnation doing nothing useful whatsoever. The balance, in our humble opinion, is that unique point where an entity has integrated the desire for play, the desire for good work to do and the desire for learning with the underlying desire to serve the Creator and to serve humankind. Play, distraction and recreation are very valid and positive parts of a useful working life. Therefore, we would encourage you to react to a child who wished to do gaming by playing the gaming with him, being a part of his environment, and sharing his recreation.

In general, we would suggest that the key to dealing with entities who look up to you, as children often do, is to relate to what they are saying, to listen to their concerns, and to enter into their life, not as one who must always be teaching but as one who is listening and learning. See yourself as a partner with this entity, regardless of the difference in your age. You are partners in exploring the dynamics between you. If you are older, naturally, part of the dynamic of your relationship will be the desire to protect, care for and support that entity.

As you deal with children, then, relate with them where they are, remembering always that it is who you are within yourself that the child really "gets" rather than that image of yourself which you may feel that you are putting forward.

In the end, we simply encourage honesty. You may not be completely accurate or correct in your opinions, but your opinions are your gift to a child with whom you are in relationship. Indeed, this is true of relationships of any age but your query is about children.

And when you are an adult dealing with children there is a special element of the desire to lead them in the right way. Be honest in your opinions. If you find that a game or anything else that a child is interested in has negative or troublesome aspects, discuss them with the child. Be frank and open and share your heart. That way the relationship is clean and clear and the love of the one infinite Creator will find ways to enter into the conversation.

Your goal is to be with that child. The direction of the conversation is unimportant. It is the heart listening to another heart, the thoughts interested in another's thoughts, and the atmosphere created of love, encouragement and support that are important.

We thank the one known as T especially for asking this question, for in it he expresses his heart.

May we ask if there is another query at this time?

T: Since we're going to enter the fourth density soon and all artificial or man-made things will be gone, as Ra told us, what kind of games do souls play in the fourth density? I assume they need to have fun too, right?

We are those of Q'uo, and are aware of your query, my brother. We do not find that this question is one we can answer. We apologize for our inability to respond in a way that is helpful.

We may offer some general concepts on the topic of what is fun in higher densities. My brother, when the veil is lifted which hangs so heavily over your eyes and your senses in third density and you behold the creation with the eyes that are unveiled …

(Side one of tape ends.)

(Carla channeling)

…you will find that it is literally bursting with the most extravagant excitement, passion and joy. The inner workings of your mind are exteriorized. Imagination becomes palpable. What would you do if you could create a shape, a picture, or a story so that others could see it? Would you lack for fun?

Again, we are apologetic that we cannot be more specific. However, there are issues of free will involved in this query that are subtle. Yet they stop us as substantively as if it were a brick wall.

Is there another query before we leave this instrument? We are those of Q'uo.

Jim: *(Responding on behalf of T.)* I believe that's it, Q'uo.

In that case, we shall leave this instrument and this group, thanking each for dedicating the time to seek the truth. We thank the one known as T also for initiating this session and we thank each of you for the beauty of your vibrations. We are known to you as the principle of Q'uo, and we leave you in the love and in the light of the one infinite Creator. Adonai. Adonai. ❧

L/L Research is a subsidiary of
Rock Creek Research &
Development Laboratories, Inc.

P.O. Box 5195
Louisville, KY 40255-0195

L/L RESEARCH

www.llresearch.org

Rock Creek is a non-profit
corporation dedicated to
discovering and sharing
information which may aid in
the spiritual evolution of
humankind.

ABOUT THE CONTENTS OF THIS TRANSCRIPT: This telepathic channeling has been taken from transcriptions of the weekly study and meditation meetings of the Rock Creek Research & Development Laboratories and L/L Research. It is offered in the hope that it may be useful to you. As the Confederation entities always make a point of saying, please use your discrimination and judgment in assessing this material. If something rings true to you, fine. If something does not resonate, please leave it behind, for neither we nor those of the Confederation would wish to be a stumbling block for any.

SPECIAL MEDITATION
APRIL 1, 2006

Jim: Our first question today has as its focus the role of the spirit guides in the ascension process. We would like for Q'uo to tell us what this role is.

(Carla channeling)

We are those known to you as the principle of Q'uo. Greeting in the love and the light of the one infinite Creator. We come to you in the Creator's service this day. Thank you for asking us to join your circle of seeking. It is both a privilege and a great blessing to be with you, to marvel at the beauty of your vibrations, and the intensity of your seeking for the truth. As always, we would ask each to use discrimination in considering the ideas that we offer. If they have resonance for you please feel free to work with them. But if they do not, please leave them behind; we would not be a stumbling block to any. We thank you for this consideration, my friends.

You have asked this day concerning the role of spirit guides in the ascension process. We find this somewhat humorous because this instrument has been working for the past several days upon a manuscript of channelings from the Holy Spirit, which is this instrument's spirit guide. Consequently, this instrument is steeped in that companionship and comfort which is the role of the guidance system of each entity.

Your guidance system, whether you characterize it as this instrument does in the Christian term of Holy Spirit or whether you characterize it in other ways,

is, nevertheless, a part of the interwoven consciousness of Creator and created. You are never without your guidance system.

A key concept to remember when thinking of your guidance is not what form or shape it takes, but what its essence is. The essence of that spirit that companions you throughout and incarnation is unconditional love, absolute support, unending compassion, and a clarity of understanding that takes in the full sweep of the octave of densities within which you now enjoy consciousness.

It is not an event that occurs in a moment to ascend. Ascension is rather a process. Think of third density, if you will, as a spiritual distillery. You know of how a distiller creates spirits from the fruit of the vine or grain using various substances such as yeast, hops, raisins and many other choices of ways to create a chemical reaction which will distill the raw ingredients into the finished wine that is full of the delicious taste of all of its ingredients and due to the chemical processing has transformed its nature. Such is your process in enjoying incarnation upon planet Earth.

We have observed that the dogma-driven thinking of your religions, especially the one known as Christianity, has skewed the thinking about the ascension process and has created of it not a joyful celebratory event, but a fear-driven, doom-filled event. It is not the intention of the Creator that the process of ascension be narrowed down to an event of any kind. However, were a very narrow view to be taken of ascension so that one could see it as an event, it would be an event that was as full of positive emotions as one's birthday, ones wedding day, or any other celebration or party to which one looked forward greatly. The whole concept of ascension as a terrifying moment when the world ends and suddenly you are standing before a righteous judge, is far from the Creator's mind, as far as we understand the Creator's mind and we note here that our understanding is faulty; we offer only our humble opinion at all times.

Your life is a process of gradual ascension. You start with raw ingredients. Throughout your life, each choice that you make advances the distilling process. At the moment of death, the gateway to larger life opens and you yourself are able to see with the enhanced vision of time/space where you are in your ascension process. You are the judge that you have so feared. Your spirit guide, guidance system, or higher self, is there with you as a resource to you.

From our point of view, we see the term spirit guide as somewhat lacking in specificity. We would rather discuss the higher self for in terms of the structure of this resource of the self, the higher self comes from a place in the circle of your personality stream, shall we say, or your soul stream, that is far in advance of your consciousness within incarnation at this time. The higher self is your self at a point within sixth density where the lessons of unity have been so far advanced that you as an entity have become aware in sixth density that you are moving away from close contact with that which has been laid within your memory as the occurrences of all of the densities up through sixth.

They are falling away from you at this point and your mind, heart and will are turning ever more toward the face of the Creator. You are acquiring enough spiritual gravity that you are aware that this is your goodbye to the self of this creation. You are not any longer interested in your personality shell. You are ready to be absorbed into the godhead principle once again.

And so you turn in the midst of sixth density in this very precious and pivotal point in the distillation of your soul and you leave a resource behind as a gift to yourself. It is available in third density, fourth density, fifth density, and, if needed, in the beginning of sixth density for that soul and spirit that you are. *(Inaudible)* inextricably bound into your consciousness. It must be asked in order to be heard. The spirit, or higher self, will not speak unless it is asked; it can not intrude upon free will. It must wait for your interest, your desire, your questions, your cries, your groanings, your rejoicings, and any other conversation that you wish to have. It waits patiently, full of love, knowing you because it is you but you at your highest and best. So there is color to the spirit. There is energy and liveness, [but] there is not is physicality. The spirit is uncreated. It is a resource, an essence if you will.

Therefore, at the moment of death your higher self is with you, part of you, supporting and encouraging you as you walk into the light of larger life.

Is there a follow-up query to this question before we move on?

B: Q'uo, are there other selves that act as spirit guides, like angels or other forms?

We are those of Q'uo, and are aware of your query, my brother. There are indeed other entities that help to guide. This is why we were attempting to be more specific about the term that we were using, for the term spirit guide can mean any of a dozen things or more.

There are so many sources of guidance that are around you that to discuss them in depth is impossible, but we can simply name them. They include, as you said, angels—and there are many varieties of angels—pixies, elves, fairies, nature divas and spirits of all kind, the essences of elements, their spirits such as undeens, sylphs, niads, dryads, and all of the totem with which you have been associated in past lives. As well, there are many entities in the inner realms who are drawn to you when you are conspicuously loving, patient or intent upon the truth. Passion for goodness, for fairness, for love, or for devotion to the one infinite Creator all draw to you entities that dwell within the inner realms in one capacity or another. And so you may have about you literally dozens of helpful, loving sources of inspiration and guidance. Each is in harmony with the other sources of guidance that are about you and they constitute your family in the unseen realms. Also to be considered are those entities which are associated with you in other densities, especially for those of you who are wanderers.

When you have incarnated as many times as each of you has incarnated, the web of connections becomes truly amazing, expanding infinitely and including virtually everyone on the planet. Consequently, the concept of one spirit guide or two spirit guides or a limited number of them is not accurate in our opinion, for if you are sufficiently motivated to focus your will to that laser-like quality that it can achieve when your emotions and your desires are coherent, you call a very large percentage of the unseen realms to aid you and support you. Thus it is that we encourage entities to find their passion and follow it.

May we answer you further, my brother?

B: No thank you. Jim?

Jim: Our next question: "Q'uo, could you tell us what the role of the guardians is in the graduation, in the ascension?"

We are those of Q'uo are aware of your query, my brother. The guardians of your planet are a group, some of whom are inner planes entities and some of whom are Confederation entities. There is a rotation of those who are responsible for planet Earth at any one time but a constant number of those who guard and keep stewardship of the planet, its people, and its resources, and by that we do not mean the kind of natural resources of which your peoples general think when they say the word "resources," but rather we speak of the metaphysical resources of the planet as it moves through its own ascension process, shall we say.

The role of the guardians is to care for and be a steward to the people and the planet. During the ascension process, the guardians stand by the steps of light which are walked by those who are moving ascension or graduation. They look carefully to be sure that the gradations of light are precise, steady and stable. They look to be sure no one stumbles or is confused, for they wish each to walk comfortably into the light until they have chosen their most comfortable place. So they guard the sanctity of this process. It is by this process that each decides or chooses the nature of its next experience. If walking into the light and stopping one has stopped at a place that is yet in third density, then that entity shall next incarnate in another third density planet elsewhere. For the planet you call Earth has begun its fourth density positive incarnation and is even at this time accepting new entities as they graduate through the natural processes of death.

May we answer you further, my brother?

B: Is there another process besides death to make the transition?

We are those of Q'uo, and believe we understanding your query, my brother. There is not in the duties of the guardian any process other than that which occurs at the death, as you know this walk through the gateway to larger life. We are aware that there has been discussion among your peoples of that which this instrument calls the rapture and indeed this instrument is aware of the teachings of the one known as Jesus who said that when the time came there would [be] two people in the field—one would be taken and one would be left. It is our understanding of this teaching—and again we offer it humbly—that this was as were almost all of the things that the one known as Jesus taught, like a parable in nature.

The literal meaning of the stories that the one known as Jesus told was not intended but rather the stories were those stories in which the parable pointed out metaphysical truths rather than physical ones. Therefore, it is indeed so, in terms of the functionality of the graduation process, that in the moment of choice on the steps of light, an entity either chooses third density or fourth density and therefore moves into life in third or life in fourth density. We do not believe it was intended that there would be this adventurous drama suggested of a sudden and fell rapture in which life as you know it stopped suddenly and [completely] and entities were either tossed into the pits of hell or lifted up to heaven.

We believe that the reality is less dramatic but much more understandable. We believe that the reality is that you, each of you, will choose the manner of your being. You will choose it not because you judge yourself but because you realize that there is a sweet spot in the light for you. Walking those steps of light, you are not looking to push past your abilities, you are looking to find that place where you belong, and when you have found just the right place, it does not matter if it is third density or fourth density, it is the place that you have earned, it is the gift of your long and adventurous life and all that has brought you to that point at which you were vibrating in a certain way when you passed into larger life. That vibration is your being. You want your being to be comfortable. You want that being that you are to be placed where it belongs. This as we understand it is the process of graduation or ascension.

May we answer you further, my brother?

B: No, thank you.

Jim: Our third question is [about] ensoulment. When and how does a spirit enter the body in third density to take part in the third-density incarnation?

We are those of Q'uo, and believe we grasp your query, my brother. The body which you inhabit during third density has its own anima. It is not precisely a soul; it is of the nature of second-density entities, inhabiting a great-ape-with-very-little-hair gene pool, if you will. When the physical body that you are using, that serves you so well now, dies, it, as opposed to your consciousness, will sink back into that pool of naked apes that constitutes the human race as a second-density species.

Therefore, it is independent of the need for a soul or a spirit. It can live, enjoy its nature, and pass from life all without the need for a third-density spirit inhabiting the body.

When a woman becomes impregnated, the arrangements, shall we say, for the birth of a certain entity to that woman are already fairly well advanced. There is a great demand for opportunities for incarnation. Entities must wait for an opportunity to inhabit a particular physical vehicle. An entity and its higher self, or its guide, will have pondered the idea of an incarnation for some time, as you would call it, and you will have created a plan or an agenda for the creation that involves being born to a certain woman, living in the family of a certain family, and meeting various key people throughout the life experience. When you and your higher self plan an incarnation, you are redundant in your planning. You have not one or two or three possibilities, but virtually endless possibilities lined up so that if one straight road to Rome does not avail, the next straightest road—with a little kink in it and a little curve there—comes up. And if you stray off of that road, another comes up. They all lead to Rome.

When a woman actually becomes pregnant, this seals the opportunity. There is to some extent an unconscious agreement betwixt the soul of the entity who is the mother and the soul of the entity who is going to be her child.

The time of the entry of a soul or spirit into a physical vehicle with its anima varies widely. In some cases, within three months of the woman becoming pregnant the soul will already have begun inhabiting the physical vehicle that is the fetus within the womb. In other cases, as the other extreme, an entity may not inhabit that body until after the birth. There is a target of opportunity from conception to about three months after birth for the entry of the soul into the body. The choice of when this connection is made has a good deal to do with the relationship of the child to its mother in terms of how that relationship will function as catalyst in the lifetime to come.

May we answer you further, my brother?

B: I have a question from D, Missouri who wants to know, "Can a physical body exist without a soul?"

We are those of Q'uo, and are aware of your query, my sister. That is affirmative. The physical body is capable of living without being ensouled. It is, however, very seldom that this situation occurs. When the consciousness of an entity is withdrawn from a physical vehicle, that physical vehicle is without a rudder, shall we say. It is not geared to functioning as a natural second-density entity but, rather, it has given its life over to carrying consciousness. Generally, when the silvery cord—as this instrument calls the connection between spirit and body—is severed, the anima of the second-density physical vehicle, or animal, is not strong enough to maintain the health or life of that physical vehicle and it perishes because of the lack of the soul which it was designed to carry.

Is there another query at this time?

B: I've got one from L in England. She would like to know what happens to the chemical complex at the time of fourth-density transition.

We are those of Q'uo, and are aware of your query, my sister. The term ashes to ashes and dust [to dust] is familiar to all and would be the burden of our response if we understand your question accurately. Therefore, we assume that we do not understand your query.

May we ask if you could phrase it in another way, my sister? We are those of Q'uo.

B: It may take a moment to type her response.

(Pause)

B: Jim, why don't we go on to the next question and we can touch the last later.

Jim: Our fourth question has to do with how social memory complexes talk, how they relate each to the other, and to other social memory complexes.

We are those of Q'uo, and are aware of your query, my brother. This instrument can feel us laughing for the challenge of this question is such that we doubt our abilities to express, in any way that is useful, the response that would make sense.

Imagine that the entire creation is dancing. Imagine that it is dancing in a way that is unified and harmonized so that every speck and mote and iota of the one infinite Creation of the Father is dancing in perfect harmony and in full awareness of the vast and infinite reaches of that dance.

We who are not of third density incarnation, whether we are dwelling between incarnations or are essences that were uncreated and therefore have not incarnated at all, are part of this dance. It is the dance of the heavens and the Earth, the elements and the essences of creation. In infinite variety and color, the patterns of the dance swirl in sacred geometry, in joy, in thanksgiving, and in grace and symmetry that create a beauty that is never ending, ever flowing, and an expression of unconditional love in its every facet and coloration.

Communication betwixt social memory complexes is that kind of communication that you may have experienced at times with those to whom you were very close. Perhaps you have known what someone else was going to say. Perhaps you have felt that there was someone else in the room with you and you turned around and there someone was. You felt the palpable energy of their presence. So it is when coherent energies wish to speak with each other; the wish creates a connection, it is instantaneous.

May we answer you further?

B: I have one clarification request on what does it mean, "essences that were uncreated"?

We are those of Q'uo, and are aware of your query, my brother. To begin with, the Creator is uncreated. The angels that you know of in your Christian mythology are uncreated beings. Nature spirits are uncreated beings, they have never had incarnation. They express the spirit …

(Side one of tape ends.)

(Carla channeling)

…which lives in elements such as earth, air, wind, and fire, and second density-creatures such as your plants and animals. And even in the stories that entities tell over long periods of time in which entities which never lived become real and have lives within the inner planes of your planetary sphere.

May we answer you further, my brother?

B: Going back to ensoulment, a couple of quick questions. E would like to know, "Does the self or higher self attempt to choose a father as well as a mother?"

We are those of Q'uo, and are aware of your query, my brother. And may we say that it is a wonderful thing to respond to each of you. The energy of each of you is a blessing to us and we thank each of you for taking this time to tabernacle with us.

The father, the siblings, the authority figures, the mate, and the friends of an entity are all considered, indeed, in creating the opportunity for an incarnation. However, in terms of choosing when to be born and in what circumstances, it is the relationship with the mother that is the most pivotal. The relationship with the father is one step removed in that the woman who is a mother carries not only her consciousness as guardian and guide to her unborn child, but also she carries the ocean of infinity and eternity within the springs of her womb. Consequently, it is her energy that is most intimately connected with the one infinite Creator in the process of sacred birth.

May we answer you further, my brother?

B: T in New York would like to know, "Does abortion incur the need for karmic reparations for the mother or father?"

We are those of Q'uo, and are aware of your query, my brother. There is no one answer to this query, my brother. And we are aware that it is a very tender subject, certainly in this instrument's heart as well as many others. However, each entity creates an agreement with the mother. If the mother is considering abortion, then it is well for that mother to sit in mediation until it feels beyond a shadow of a doubt, subjectively speaking, that it has made contact with that being that is knocking at the door for the opportunity to incarnate.

Some entities are perfectly willing to move on and find another opportunity. Other entities have a great desire to be born to this one person and be placed into incarnation in just this way. Therefore, each case must be decided on its own merits by the woman involved and by no other source. Only that woman can make contact with that soul that is asking for incarnation and ask for permission to pass up this opportunity.

An entity who is attempting to incarnate does not want to cause its mother difficulty. Therefore, if a mother can take the time to commune with that child that is to be, it is entirely possible that there is no karma necessary to experience as a result of choosing to abort when circumstances are not opportune. The child understands as well as the mother.

However, it is well to go through this period of inquiry and communion with the child and to have a very deep and profound discussion as to whether or not that child is happy to have another opportunity with the same parent but at a later time, or with another family altogether.

May we answer you further, my brother?

B: We have one more from P who would like to know, "When does the seed of thought begin?"

We are those of Q'uo, and would like to say that this shall be the final query of this session. We thank the one known as P for this question, it is an interesting one.

The seed of any thought is thought itself. The Logos is the original Thought. All thoughts spring form the Logos. Unconditional love is the essence of the Logos. Therefore the seed of every thought is love.

May we answer you further, my brother?

B: I think we're all set! He said he should have thought of that.

We are those of Q'uo, and we thank all who have gathered for this most adventurous and exciting type of meeting. It is an unusual occasion and one we celebrate. Thank you to each.

We offer our seeds of thought to you with a humble heart but a happy heart indeed. May each of you thrive and enjoy the adventure of incarnation. May you realize the stunning excitement of the possibilities that await you this day. Within you lies the power to reshape your world according to the way you think, the way you hope, and the dreams that you dare to dream.

This instrument and the one known as Jim have been reading a book called *Handbook for the New Paradigm*. And in it there is discussion of how a few people dreaming together can re-imagine the Earth. That is the function of the spirit as well, that guide that is ever at your side. It also hopes that you shall reach up to the one infinite Creator and to all of the guidance that you have and ask each and every day, "What is your will for me this day? How shall I serve? What shall I learn? And in what shall I rejoice?"

We leave each of you in the power and the peace of this adventure. We are those known to you as the principle of Q'uo. We leave you in the love and in the light of the one infinite Creator. Adonai. Adonai. ❧